MONTVALE PUBLIC LIBRARY, NJ

3 9125 05008804 6

Y0-CJH-891

MONTVALE PUBLIC LIBRARY

ON LINE

974.923   59582
HAR   Harvey, Cornelius
        Genealogical
        history of Hudson
        & Bergen counties

DEMCO

GENEALOGICAL HISTORY

OF

Hudson and Bergen Counties

NEW JERSEY

CORNELIUS BURNHAM HARVEY
EDITOR

The New Jersey Genealogical Publishing
Company, 114 Fifth Avenue, New York
1900

THE WINTHROP PRESS
NEW YORK

Hail to posterity !
* * *
Let the young generations yet to be
Look kindly upon this.
Think how your fathers left their native land.
—*Pastorius.*

What he was and what he is
They who ask may haply find.
—*Whittier.*

HUDSON AND BERGEN COUNTIES

THE FIRST SETTLERS AND THEIR ORIGIN

UP TO the close of the Civil War family origin and lineage received but a small measure of attention in the United States. Here and there, along the line of the centuries, persons possessed of wealth and leisure had caught up and reunited the broken threads of kinship; but the great mass of the common people considered time thus spent as time squandered. In accounting for this it should be remembered that the early settlers of the country never expected to set foot again on European soil. Having deliberately severed all the ties that connected them with the past, they lived to remember only—and that with hatred—the tyranny, despotism, hardships, and persecutions of a church and state which had forced them from the land of their birth. Again, these pioneers of a new civilization had little time to think of remote family ties. With them "self preservation was the first law of nature." Boundless forests must be felled; lands must be cleared and tilled; crops must be reared, harvested, and protected; the savages must be watched, fought, and exterminated; civil government must be organized and maintained; highways, canals, churches, schools, court houses, and jails must be constructed and paid for; villages, towns, cities, counties, states, even a nation, must be built up; and, when, after long years of untold hardships, all these things had been accomplished, then came the great revolt from, and struggle with, the mother country for freedom and national independence.

After the republic, the War of 1812, then the war with Mexico, and, lastly, the Civil War, the great and final struggle for national life and perpetuity. This "building of the nation," and the wars incident thereto, did not stimulate genealogical research. The American Revolution arrayed the descendants of the early settlers against the descendants of their European oppressors, and the American Civil War arrayed father against father and brother against brother. Both of these conflicts tended to keep alive in the breasts of Americans the animosities kindled by wrongs committed on European soil several generations before.

But the surrender at Appomattox soon changed all this. The new nation had emerged triumphant from her great crucial struggle, freed from the curse of human slavery. Moreover, and quite as important, she had shown that she could and would maintain the integrity of the

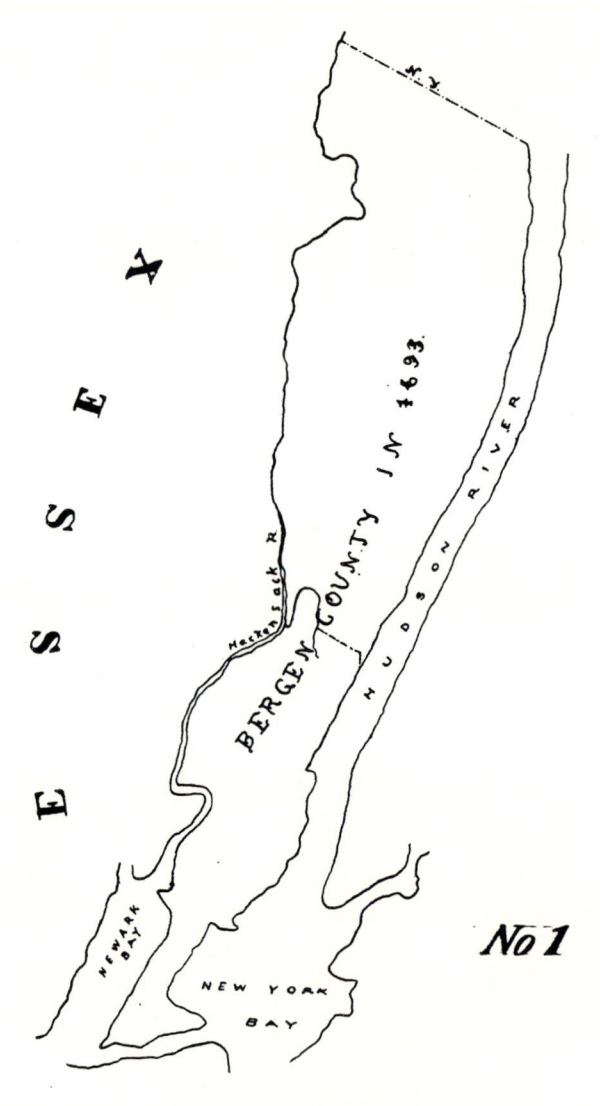

Union. She immediately took a commanding position among the nations of the earth, a position which has grown stronger and more commanding as time has rolled on, until at last the respect of Europe has been won. Equality breeds sociability. And now the descendants of the early emigrants to America hobnob with Europeans with as much freedom as if they were members of the same household.

All this has aroused a deep and abiding interest in family lineage, and this interest has been greatly intensified in the last decade by the organization of the Holland Society, the Huguenot Society, the

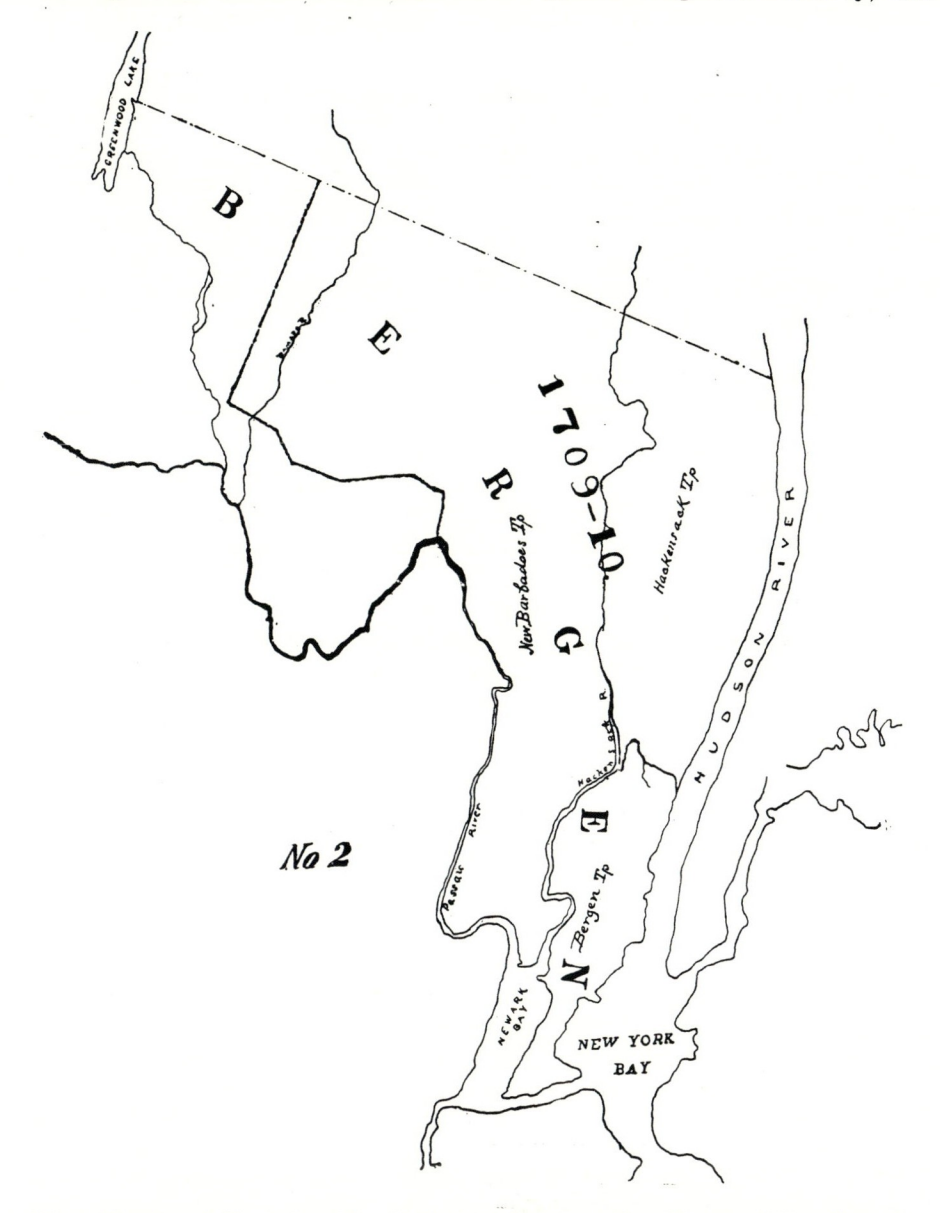

New England Society, the Colonial Dames, the Sons of the Revolution, the Daughters of the Revolution, and numerous societies of a similar character. The desire among all classes of the people to know something of their ancestry has been still further stimulated by

the numerous genealogical societies now established throughout the Union.

It is a source of deep regret that the early records of Northern New Jersey are so widely scattered—more so, perhaps, than those of any other section of the country. The historian and genealogist must find them at Albany, New York, Goshen, Richmond, and New City in New York State, and at Trenton, Perth Amboy, Newark, Jersey City, Paterson, and Hackensack in the State of New Jersey. Then, again, the chirography of the early records of this section is peculiar, and many of the documents and records are in a foreign language. Thousands of grants, deeds, wills, and other documents relative to Bergen County, all of the greatest importance to the searcher for knowledge, were never recorded and never even deposited in any public record office, owing to the bitter controversy between the Colonies of New York and New Jersey over the location of the boundary line between them,—a controversy which lasted more than a century from the time the country began to be settled by Europeans. I am forced to the conclusion that he who would make a successful plotting of the early grants of land in Northern New Jersey would need to spend at least five years in a house-to-house hunt for the necessary data, in trunks and chests of the old pioneers, now hidden away and forgotten, in the garrets of their descendants. I have prepared this article from such data as I have been able to find, but for the reasons above stated the matter it contains must necessarily be replete with errors and important omissions. Nevertheless, I am not without strong hope that it may be of some assistance to the thousands of descendants of the sturdy men and women who settled the Counties of Bergen and Hudson. I have prepared and inserted four maps: No. 1, showing Bergen County as erected in 1693; No. 2, showing the greater part of the same county as re-erected in 1709-10; No. 3, showing Hudson County at the present time; and No. 4, showing the greater part of Bergen County as erected in 1709-10, and, as far as possible, the locations of the original land patents. In the text these are called and on map No. 4 are numbered " Sections." The outlines of these " sections " are, of course, only approximately correct, but they will be found useful to the reader in locating any particular settler. I have also set forth the counties into townships, boroughs, and other municipalities, and, lastly, I have given in tabulated form the surname of each of the principal settlers, his nationality, and, as far as possible, the name and domicile of his European ancestor.

FORMATION OF BERGEN AND HUDSON COUNTIES

The first municipality within the limits of New Jersey was erected by order of Director General Stuyvesant and his council on September 5, 1661, and christened "The Village of Bergen." The origin of the name "Bergen" rests in some doubt. Some writers confidently claim it to have been derived from "Bergen," the capital of Norway,

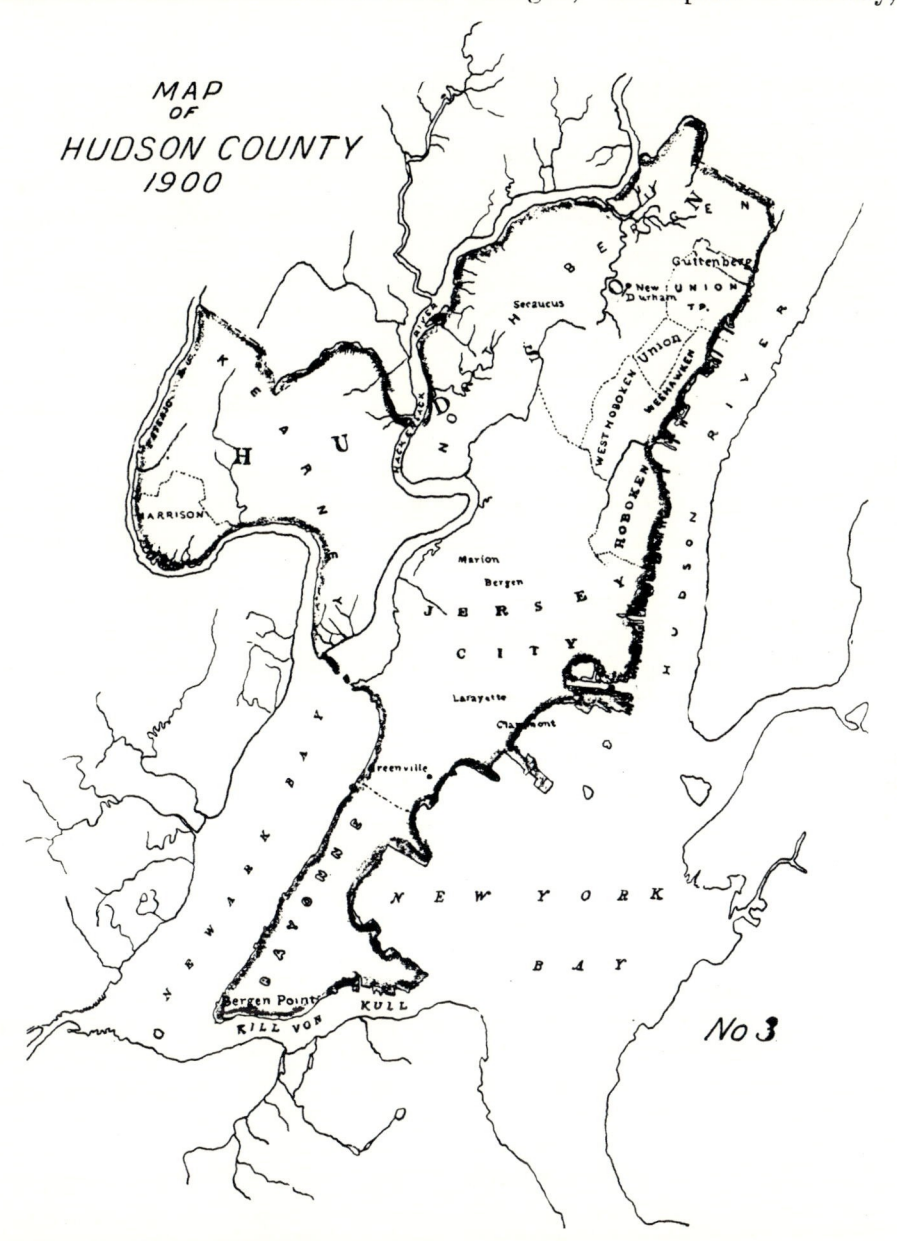

MAP OF HUDSON COUNTY 1900

No 3

while others as confidently assert it to have been derived from *Bergen op Zoom*, an important town on the River Scheldt, in Holland, eighteen miles north of Antwerp. Without expressing an opinion,

I may say that, so far as my investigations have extended, the evidence seems to favor those who claim the name to have been derived from the Holland town. During the seven years following the christening new settlers rapidly purchased and located on lands outside of the "Village" limits. These, with a view to more effectually protecting themselves from the savages, asked that they might be annexed to the main settlement. Accordingly, on the 7th of April, 1668, Governor Philip Carteret and his council, of East New Jersey, granted to the settlers of Bergen (then comprising some forty families) a charter under the corporate name of "The Towne and Corporation of Bergen." This new "Towne" comprised the present County of Hudson as far west as the Hackensack River. The line on the north, as described in the charter, started "at Mordavis meadow, lying upon the west side of Hudson's River; from thence to run upon a N. W. lyne by a Three rail fence that is now standing to a place called Espatin [The Hill] and from thence to a little creek [Bellman's Creek] surrounding N. N. W. till it comes unto the river Hackensack [Indian name for "Lowland"], containing in breadth, from the top of the Hill, 1½ miles or 120 chains." During the next sixteen years new settlements sprang up north of Bergen, but in matters of government these were termed "out lands" or "precincts," without any corporate power whatever, and subject to the jurisdiction of the authorities of the "Towne."

As time went on and population increased, courts became necessary; and as all the colonial officials were Englishmen, and many English immigrants had settled in the colony, it was but natural that they should desire the adoption of the English system of county government. On the 7th of March, 1682, the provincial legislature passed, and Deputy Governor Rudyard approved, an act under which New Jersey was divided into four counties: Bergen, Essex, Middlesex, and Monmouth. Bergen County, as then defined, contained "all the settlements between Hudson's River and the Hackensack River, beginning at Constable's Hook and so to extend to the uppermost bounds of the Province, northward between the said rivers with the seat of government at the town of Bergen." (See Map No. 1.) Essex County comprised "all the settlements between the west side of the Hackensack River and the parting line between Woodbridge and Elizabethtown, and northward to the utmost bounds of the Province." By this division the greater part of the present County of Bergen fell within the limits of Essex County, where it remained until 1709-10.

This division into counties caused great dissatisfaction among the people, particularly in Northern New Jersey. They complained that the counties were too large, that the distance between their homes and the county seat was too long, and that traveling such long distances, over the worst of roads, in all sorts of weather, interfered with their pursuits and subjected them to great expense and bodily discomfort. Sheriffs found it difficult to summon and compel the attendance of jurymen and witnesses. The administration of justice and the transaction of all other public business were seriously retarded. From every part of the province petitions came pouring into the colonial assembly, sometimes accompanied by delegations of indignant citizens. For several years the assembly stood out against these numerous complaints and petitions, but in the end it was obliged to yield, and on the 2d of January, 1709-10, an act was passed and approved directing a redivision. By the terms of this act the boundaries of Bergen County were fixed as follows:

"Beginning at Constable's Hook, so up along the bay to Hudson's River, to the partition point between New Jersey and the Province of New York; thence along the line and the line between East and West New Jersey to the Pequannock and Passaic Rivers; thence down the Pequannock and Passaic Rivers to the sound; and so following the sound to Constable's Hook where it begins." (See Map No. 2.)

In the northwestern part of the county, as above described, was included the County of Passaic, and on the 22d of February, 1840, all that part of it lying south of the original north bounds of the "Town and Corporation of Bergen," together with a considerable area of territory west of the Hackensack River known as New Barbadoes Neck, were, by legislative enactment, erected into the County of Hudson. A part of this was annexed to Bergen County in 1852, leaving the boundaries of Bergen and Hudson Counties as they are to-day. (See Map No. 3.)

INTRODUCTION OF TOWNSHIP GOVERNMENTS

The first division of the counties into townships was made pursuant to two acts of the colonial assembly, one approved in September, 1692, and the other in October, 1693. The reasons for this division were set forth in the preamble to the second of the above mentioned acts, as follows:

"WHEREAS, several things is to be done by the inhabitants of towns, hamlets, tribes, or divisions within each county, as chusing of deputies, constables &c., taxing and collecting of several rates for publick uses and the making orders amongst themselves respectively about swine, fences &c.

"WHEREAS, a great many settlements are not reckoned within any such town or division, nor the bounds of the reputed towns ascertained, by means thereof the respective constables know not their districts, and many other inconveniences arising from them, and forasmuch as the act made in Sept 1692, for dividing the several counties and townships, the time for the returns of the said divisions, being too short and the method of dividing by county meetings inconvenient. Therefore be it enacted," etc.

Under the above acts Bergen County (then including the present Bergen and Hudson Counties) was divided into three townships: *Hackensack, New Barbadoes,* and *Bergen.* Of these, Hackensack comprised " all the land betwixt the Hackensack River and Hudson's

BLOCK'S "FIGURATIVE MAP," LAID BEFORE THE STATES-GENERAL IN 1614.

River, that extends from the corporation town bounds of Bergen to the partition line of the Province." New Barbadoes comprised " all the land on Passaic River, above the third river, and from the mouth of the said third river northwest to the partition line of the Province, including also all the land in New Barbadoes neck, betwixt Hackensack and Passaic rivers, and thence to the partition line of the Province." Bergen comprised what is now that part of Hudson County east of the Hackensack River. (See Map 2.)

THE FIRST SETTLERS

The following table shows the names of the several townships erected in Bergen County to date, the dates of their erection, and the names of the townships or municipalities from which they were erected:

NO.	NAME OF TOWNSHIP.	DATE OF ERECTION.	NAMES OF TOWNSHIPS FROM WHICH TAKEN.
1.	Hackensack.	October, 1693.	Original.
2.	New Barbadoes.	October, 1693.	Original.
3.	Saddle River.	1737.	New Barbadoes.
4.	Franklin.	1767.	New Barbadoes.
5.	Harrington.	June 22, 1775.	Hackensack and New Barbadoes.
6.	Pompton.	February 8, 1797.	Saddle River and Franklin.
7.	Lodi.	December 1, 1825.	New Barbadoes.
8.	Washington.	January 30, 1840.	Harrington.
9.	Hohokus.	February 5, 1849.	Franklin.
10.	Union.	February 19, 1852.	Harrison in Hudson County.
11.	Midland.	March 7, 1871.	New Barbadoes.
12.	Palisades.	March 22, 1871.	Hackensack.
13.	Englewood.	March 22, 1871.	Hackensack.
14.	Ridgefield.	March 22, 1871.	Hackensack.
15.	Ridgewood.	March 30, 1876.	Franklin.
16.	Boiling Springs.	April 17, 1879.	Union.
17.	Orvil.	April 20, 1885.	Hohokus and Washington.
18.	Bergen.	February 22, 1893.	Lodi.
19.	Teaneck.	February 19, 1895.	Englewood and Ridgefield.
20.	Overpeck.	March 23, 1897.	Ridgefield.
21.	Hillsdale.	March 25, 1898.	Washington.

There is no record of the erection of Saddle River and Franklin. They are first mentioned as townships in deeds and other recorded instruments in 1737 and 1767 respectively. Prior to that they are called "Precincts." Franklin is first mentioned in the county freeholders' book May 17, 1772.

The following table shows the names of the several townships and municipalities erected in Hudson County to date, the dates of their erection, and the names of the townships and other municipalities from which they were erected:

NO.	NAME OF TOWNSHIP.	DATE OF ERECTION.	NAMES OF TOWNSHIPS FROM WHICH TAKEN.
1.	Bergen (Tp.).	October, 1693.	Original.
2.	Jersey (City).	January 28, 1820.	Bergen.
3.	Harrison (Tp.).	February 22, 1840.	Lodi, Bergen County.
4.	Van Vorst (Tp.).	March 11, 1841.	Bergen.
5.	North Bergen (Tp.).	February 10, 1843.	Bergen.
6.	Hoboken (Tp.).	March 1, 1841.	North Bergen.
7.	Hudson (Tp.).	March 4, 1852.	Bergen.
8.	Hoboken (City).	March 28, 1855.	North Bergen.
9.	Weehawken (Tp.).	March 15, 1859.	Hoboken.
10.	Bayonne (Tp.).	February 16, 1861.	Bergen.
11.	Union (Tp.).	February 28, 1861.	Bergen.
12.	West Hoboken (Town).	February 28, 1861.	Bergen.
13.	Greenville (Tp.).	March 18, 1863.	Bergen.

NO.	NAME OF TOWNSHIP.	DATE OF ERECTION.	NAME OF TOWNSHIPS FROM WHICH TAKEN.
14.	Town of Union.	March 29, 1864.	Union.
15.	Kearney (Town).	March 14, 1867.	Harrison.
16.	Bayonne (City).	March 10, 1869.	Bayonne.
17.	Guttenberg (Tp.).	April 1, 1878.	Union.
18.	West New York (Town).	March 21, 1898.	Union.
19.	East Newark (Town).	———, 1898.	Harrison.
20.	Secaucus (Bor.).	March 12, 1900.	North Bergen.

Of the above, all of Pompton and a large part of Franklin and Saddle River in Bergen County became part of Passaic County by act of February 7, 1837. (See Map 4.) Union in Bergen County was taken from Harrison in Hudson County, February 19, 1852, and Harrison in Hudson was taken from Lodi in Bergen County, February 22, 1840. Part of Lodi in Bergen was annexed to New Barbadoes in 1896. Van Vorst, Hoboken, Greenville, Hudson, and Bayonne Townships in Hudson County have been absorbed by the remaining municipalities in the county. Kearney was made a "Town" March 23, 1898. West New York absorbed the whole of Union.

BOROUGH GOVERNMENTS

The borough system of government for small communities was first introduced into New Jersey March 28, 1789, by an act incorporating the "Borough of Elizabeth." During the next ninety years a number of similar municipalities were erected in various parts of the State, each of which was the creation of a special act of the legislature. No general law on the subject was enacted until April 5, 1878, when what has since been known as "The General Borough Act" became a law. It provided that the inhabitants of any township, or part of a township, embracing an area not to exceed four square miles, and containing a population not exceeding five thousand, might become a body politic and corporate in fact and in law whenever, at a special election to be called for that purpose, it might be decided by a majority of votes of the electors of the proposed borough qualified to vote at elections for State and township officers.

For a period of sixteen years following the passage of this act very few boroughs were organized in the State, only three of them being in Bergen County. In the spring of 1894 an act was passed establishing an entirely new system of public instruction. By this act the old school districts were blotted out and each township erected into a separate and distinct district. All the taxpayers of each township were thenceforth required to assume and pay, pro rata, the debts already incurred by the several old districts, as well as all future debts of the township for school purposes. The people complained against the injustice of such a law, and sought a way to escape its operation. By the terms of the law it was inoperative in all incorporated boroughs, towns, villages, and cities, and accordingly a rush was made to form boroughs, particularly in Bergen County, and had not the legislature hastened to check this rush by amending the school law the whole county would have been carved into boroughs in less than two years. As it was, twenty-six boroughs were created in the county from January 23, 1894, to December 18, of the same year. The amendment which the legislature made to the school act provided that no borough might maintain a school separate from the township unless there should be four hundred children within its limits. This so effectually checked the borough movement that only five have since been formed.

The following table shows the names of the boroughs organized in Bergen County to date, the dates of their organization, and the townships from which they were respectively taken:

NO.	NAME.	DATE OF ORGANIZATION.	FROM WHICH TOWNSHIPS TAKEN.
1.	Rutherford	September 21, 1881. Enlarged June 10, '90	Union.
2.	Ridgefield.	May 25, 1892.	Ridgefield.
3.	Ridgefield Park.	May 25, 1892.	Ridgefield.
4.	Tenafly.	June 23, 1894.	Palisades.
5.	East Rutherford.	March 29, 1894.	Boiling Springs.
6.	Delford.	May 7, 1894.	Midland.
7.	Creskill.	May 8, 1894.	Palisades.
8.	Westwood.	May 8, 1894.	Washington.
9.	Park Ridge.	May 14, 1894.	Washington.
10.	Bergenfields.	June 2, 1894.	Palisades and Englewood.
11.	Carlstadt.	June 27, 1894.	Bergen.
12.	Maywood.	June 29, 1894.	Midland.
13.	Riverside.	June 29, 1894.	Midland.
14.	Schraalenburgh.[1]	July 19, 1894.	Midland.
15.	Hasbrouck Heights.	July 21, 1894.	Lodi.
16.	Woodcliff.	August 25, 1894.	Washington and Orvil.
17.	Montvale.	August 30, 1894.	Washington and Orvil.
18.	Glenrock.	September 12, 1894.	Saddle River and Ridgewood.
19.	Little Ferry.	September 18, 1894.	Lodi and New Barbadoes.
20.	Old Tappan.	October 16, 1894.	Harrington.
21.	Allendale.	November 8, 1894.	Orvil, Hohokus, and Franklin.
22.	Bogota.	November 14, 1894.	Ridgefield.
23.	Woodridge.	November 15, 1894.	Bergen.
24.	Saddle River.	November 19, 1894.	Orvil.
25.	Upper Saddle River.	November 20, 1894.	Orvil and Hohokus.
26.	Leonia.	December 5, 1894.	Ridgefield.
27.	Undercliff.	December 5, 1894.	Ridgefield.
28.	Fairview.	December 18, 1894.	Ridgefield.
29.	Wallington.	December 31, 1894.	Saddle River.
30.	Cliffside Park.	January 15, 1895.	Ridgefield.
31.	Englewood Cliffs.	May 19, 1895.	Englewood and Palisades.
32.	North Arlington.	March 9, 1896.	Union.
33.	Eastwood.	March 26, 1896.	Washington.
34.	Garfield.	March 15, 1898.	Wallington Borough.
35.	Palisades Park.	March 22, 1899.	Ridgefield.

[1] The name of Schraalenburgh Borough was changed to Dumont in 1899.

EARLY SETTLERS OF HUDSON COUNTY

A great majority of the pioneer settlers of Bergen and Hudson Counties were emigrants from Holland, or descendants of persons who had emigrated from that country and settled on Manhattan Island or Long Island. The rest were English, French, Germans, and Scandinavians. What brought these to the shores of America? What led them to settle in New Jersey? Who were they? The limits of this article will permit of only a brief reference to the two principal causes which impelled them to leave their native land,—overcrowding of population in Holland and the desire to better their condition.

More than a century had elapsed since the Augustinian monk,

AMSTERDAM, HOLLAND.

Luther, had nailed his ninety-five theses on the church door at Wittenberg. That act had, at last, wakened into activity all the dormant forces of christendom. During the Middle Ages all learning and religion had been controlled by the Roman hierarchy. All that time the papacy had been a confederacy for the conservation of learning, against the barbarism and ignorance of the times; and so long as the pontiff retained the character of chief clerk of such a confederacy his power remained irresistible. But as soon as he abandoned the rôle of chief clerk in spiritual affairs, and assumed that of secular prince, the great revolution began. His former friends became his enemies. The British schoolmen led the way in the revolt, followed by Wickliff, Huss, Jerome, and others. The breach kept widening, until all the countries of Western Europe started like giants out of their sleep at the first blast of Luther's trumpet. In Northern

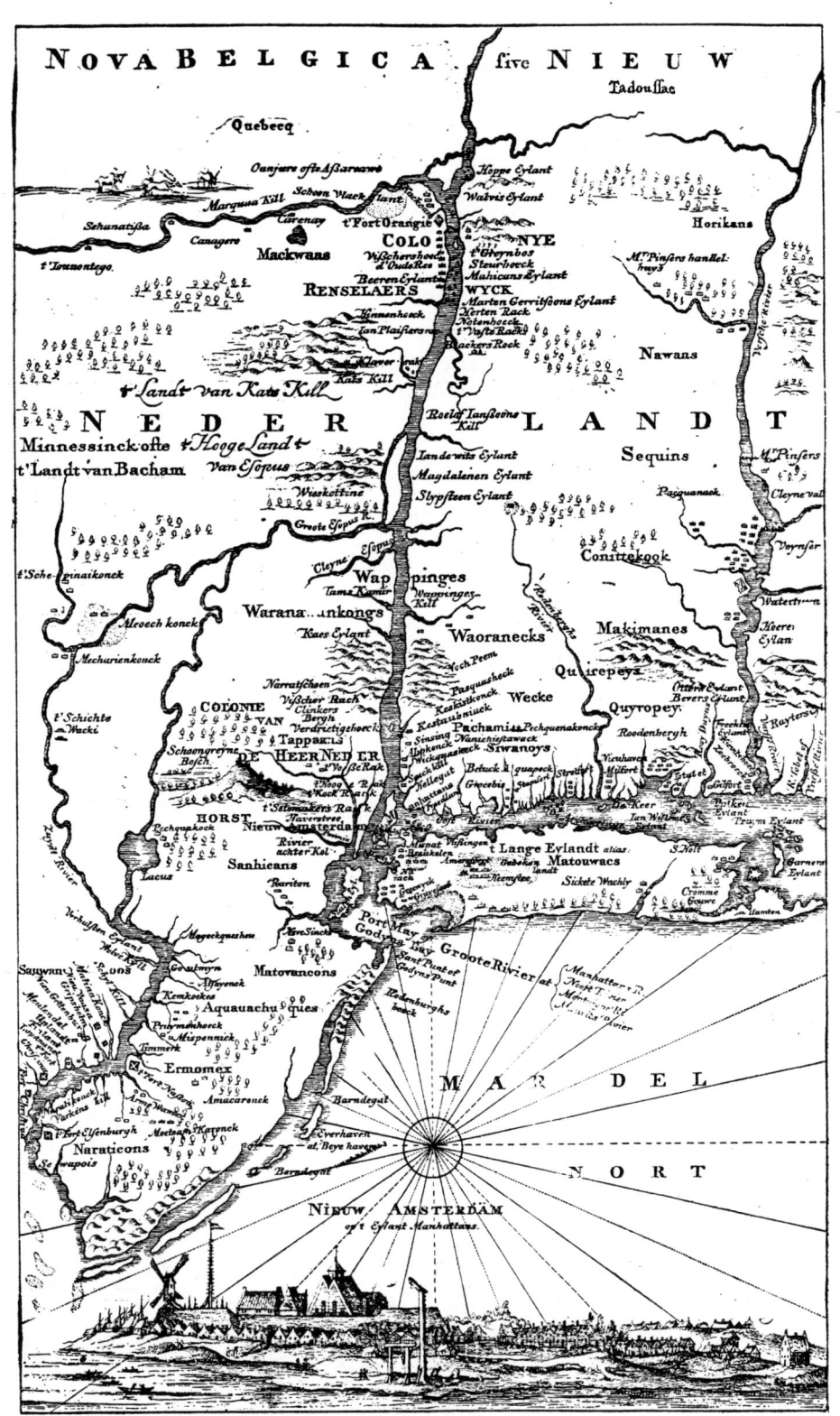

ADRIAEN VAN DER DONCK'S MAP, 1656.

Europe the best half of the people embraced the Reformation. The spark which the monk had kindled lighted the torch of civilization, which was to illuminate the forests of the Hudson in America.

At no time since this terrible contest began had the Catholic monarchs of Europe been more persistently active and relentlessly cruel toward the believers in the new religion than at the beginning of emigration to New Netherland. The bloody conflict known as "The Thirty Years' War" was then raging with all its attendant horrors. Nevertheless, Holland, of all the circle of nations, had guaranteed safety to people of every religious belief, and enforced, within her own borders at least, respect for civil liberty. As a result she had become the harbor of refuge and the temporary home of thousands of the persecuted of almost every country; the Brownists from England, the Waldenses from Italy, the Labadists and Picards from France, the Walloons from Germany and Flanders, and many other Protestant sects, all flocked into Holland. Across her borders flowed a continual stream of refugees and outcasts. This influx of foreigners, augmented by the natural increase of her own people, caused Holland to suffer seriously from overcrowding, particularly in her large cities. A learned Hollander, writing at that time, said of the situation: "Inasmuch as the multitude of people, not only natives but foreigners, who are seeking a livelihood here, is very great, so that, where one stiver is to be earned, there are ten hands ready to seize it. Many are obliged, on this account, to go in search of other lands and residences, where they can obtain a living."

THE "NEW NETHERLAND."

In the few years preceding 1621 several voyages of discovery and adventure had been made by the Dutch to New Netherland, but no colonies had been founded. Letters from these voyagers declared that New Netherland was a veritable paradise—a land "flowing with milk and honey," traversed by numerous great and beautiful rivers, plentifully stocked with fish; great valleys and plains, covered with luxuriant verdure; extensive forests, teeming with fruits, game, and wild animals; and an exceedingly fertile and prolific soil. These and many similar letters aroused and stimulated many of the discontented and unemployed of Holland to emigrate to New Netherland with their families in the hope of being able to earn a handsome livelihood, strongly fancying that they could live in the New World in luxury and ease, while in the Old they would still have to earn their bread by the sweat of their brows.

In 1621 the "States-General" took steps looking toward relief from the situation, the gravity of which they now fully comprehended. On June 3 they granted a charter to "The Dutch West India Com-

THE FIRST VIEW OF NEW AMSTERDAM, IN 1635.

pany" to organize and govern a colony in New Netherland; and in June, 1623-4, an expedition under Captain Cornelius Jacobsen Mey, of Amsterdam, carrying thirty families, most of whom were religious refugees, came over to New Amsterdam and began a settlement on the lower end of Manhattan Island. Mey, not liking the job of being director of the new colony, soon returned to Holland, leaving matters for a time in charge of William Verhulst, who was succeeded by Peter Minuit in 1626. This first colony was not a success. The colonists were "on the make." Aside from building a few rude bark huts and a fort, they busied themselves dickering with the savages for skins and furs. They tilled no ground, and for three years were non-supporting. On the 7th of June, 1629, the "States-General" granted a bill of "Freedoms and Exemptions" to all such private persons as would plant any colonies in any part of New Netherland (except the Island of Manhattan), granting to them the fee simple in any land they might be able to successfully improve. Special privileges were also granted to members of the West India Company. Whoever of its members should plant a colony of fifty persons should be a feudal lord, or "Patroon," of a tract "sixteen miles in length, fronting on a navigable river and reaching eight miles back."

As yet only exploring parties bent on trade with the savages had traversed Bergen and Hudson Counties. No one had ventured to "take up" any lands there. But now, under the stimulus of the bill of "Freedoms and Exemptions," one Michael Pauw, then burgomaster of Amsterdam, was impelled, for speculative purposes no doubt, to obtain from the Director General of New Netherland, in 1630, grants of two large tracts, one called "Hoboken Hacking" (land of the tobacco pipe) and the other "Ahasimus." Both of these tracts were parts of what is now Jersey City. These grants bore date, respectively, July 13 and November 22, 1630. The grantee gave one place the name of "Pavonia." Pauw failed to comply with the conditions set forth in his deeds and was obliged, after three years of controversy with the West India Company, to convey his "plantations" back to that company. Michael Paulesen, an official of the company, was placed in charge of them as superintendent. It is said he built and occupied a hut at Paulus Hook early in 1633. If so, it was the first building of any kind erected in either Bergen or Hudson County. Later in the same year the company built two more houses: one at Communipaw, afterward purchased by Jan Evertse Bout, the other at Ahasimus (now Jersey City, east of the Hill), afterward purchased by Cornelius Van Vorst. Jan Evertse Bout succeeded Michael Paulesen as superintendent of the Pauw plantation, June 17, 1634, with headquarters at Communipaw, then the capital of Pavonia Colony. He was succeeded in June, 1636, by Cornelius Van Vorst, with headquarters at Ahasimus, where he kept "open house" and entertained the New Amsterdam officials in great style.

FLAG OF HOLLAND.

In 1641 one Myndert Myndertse, of Amsterdam, (bearing the ponderous title of "Van der Heer Nedderhorst,") obtained a grant of all the country behind (west of) Achter Kull (Newark Bay), and from thence north to Tappan, including part of what is now Bergen and Hudson Counties. Accompanied by a number of soldiers, Myndertse occupied his purchase, established a camp, and proceeded to civilize the Indians by military methods. It is needless to say that he failed.

THE FIRST SETTLERS

He soon abandoned the perilous undertaking of founding a colony, returned to Holland, and the title to this grant was forfeited. Early in 1638 William Kieft became Director General of New Netherland, and on the first day of May following granted to Abraham Isaacsen Planck (Verplanck) a patent for Paulus Hook (now lower Jersey City).

There were now two " plantations " at Bergen, those of Planck and Van Vorst. Parts of these, however, had been leased to, and were then occupied by, Claes Jansen Van Purmerend, Dirck Straatmaker, Barent Jansen, Jan Cornelissen Buys, Jan Evertsen Carsbon, Michael Jansen, Jacob Stoffelsen, Aert Teunisen Van Putten, Egbert Woutersen, Garret Dirckse Blauw, and Cornelius Ariessen. Van Putten had also leased and located on a farm at Hoboken. All these, with their families and servants, constituted a thriving settlement. The existence of the settlement of Bergen was now imperiled by the acts of Governor Kieft, whose idea of government was based mainly upon the principle that the governor should get all he could out of the governed. His treatment of the Indians soon incited their distrust and hatred of the whites. The savages, for the first time, began to show symptoms of open hostility. Captain Jan Petersen de Vries, a distinguished navigator, who was then engaged in the difficult task of trying to found a colony at Tappan, sought every means in his power to conciliate the Indians, and to persuade Kieft that his treatment of them would result in bloodshed.

The crafty and selfish governor turned a deaf ear to all warnings and advice and continued to goad the Indians by cruel treatment and harsh methods of taxation. In 1643 an Indian—no doubt under stress of great provocation—shot and killed a member of the Van Vorst family. This first act of murder furnished a pretext for the whites and precipitated what is called " The Massacre of Pavonia," on the night of February 25, 1643, when Kieft, with a sergeant and eighty soldiers, armed and equipped for slaughter, crossed the Hudson, landed at Communipaw, attacked the Indians while they were asleep in their camp, and, without regard to age or sex, deliberately, and in the most horrible manner, butchered nearly a hundred of them. Stung by this outrage upon their neighbors and kinsmen, the northern tribes at once took the war path, attacked the settlement, burned the buildings, murdered the settlers, wiped the villages out of existence, and laid waste the country round about. Those of the settlers who were not killed outright fled across the river to New Amsterdam. Nor was peace restored between the savages and the whites until August, 1645, when the remaining owners and tenants of farms returned to the site of the old village, rebuilt their homes, and started anew.

Kieft having been driven from office, Petrus Stuyvesant was made

18   HUDSON AND BERGEN COUNTIES

Director General, July 28, 1646. Under his administration the settlement at Bergen was revived, grew rapidly, and prospered. Between his arrival and the year 1669 the following named persons purchased or leased lands, though all of them did not become actual residents:

POPPLE'S PLAN OF NEW YORK AND ITS ENVIRONS, 1733.

Michael Pauw, Michael Paulesen, Jan Evertse Bout, Cornelius Van Vorst, Myndert Myndertsen Van der Heer Nedderhorst, Abraham Isaacsen Planck (Verplanck), Claes Jansen Van Purmerend (Cooper), Dirk Straatmaker, Barent Jansen, Jan Cornelissen Buys, John Evertsen Carsbon, Michael Jansen (Vreeland), Jacob Stoffelsen, Aert Teunisen Van Putten, Egbert Woutersen, Garret Dircksen Blauw, Cornelius Ariesen, Jacob Jacobsen Roy, Francisco Van Angola (negro), Guilliaem Corneliesen, Dirk Sycan, Claes Carsten Norman, Jacob Wallengen (Van Winkel), James Luby, Lubbert Gerritsen, Gysbert Lubbertsen, John Garretsen Van Immen, Thomas Davison, Garret Pietersen, Jan Cornelissen Schoenmaker, Jan Cornelissen Crynnen, Casper Stimets, Peter Jansen, Hendrick Jans Van Schalckwyck, Nicholas Bayard, Nicholas Varlet, Herman Smeeman, Tielman Van Vleeck, Douwe Harmansen (Tallman), Claes Jansen Backer, Egbert Steenhuysen, Harmen Edwards Paulus Pietersen, Allerd Anthony, John Vigne, Paulus Leendertsen, John Verbruggen, Balthazar Bayard, Samuel Edsall, and Aerent Laurens.

All these persons received their deeds, or such titles as they had, from the Dutch, through the different Director Generals.

The English captured New Netherland from the Dutch in 1664, and, thereupon, Philip Carteret, by an appointment of the "Lords-Proprietors" of the Province of East New Jersey, became its first governor. The titles of the settlers of Bergen were confirmed by Carteret and his council in 1668. In 1669, following his appointment as governor, Carteret also granted other portions of the lands in Hudson County to the following named persons: Maryn Adrianse, Peter Stuyvesant, Claes Petersen Cors, Severn Laurens, Hendrick Jansen Spier, Peter Jansen Slott, Barent Christianse, Mark Noble, Samuel Moore, Adrian Post, Guert Coerten, Frederick Phillipse, Thomas Frederick de Kuyper, Guert Geretsen (Van Wagenen), Peter Jacobsen, John Berry, Ide Cornelius Van Vorst, Hans Diedrick, Hendrick Van Ostum, Cornelius Ruyven.

SEAL OF NEW NETHERLAND.

"The town and corporation of Bergen," as appears by Carteret's charter, had an area of 11,500 acres. Up to the end of 1669 scarce one-third of this area had been patented to settlers. The balance, more than 8,000 acres, was used in common by the patentees, their heirs, devisees, and grantees, for nearly a century before it was finally divided and set off to those entitled to it. As is ever the case under similar circumstances, many of the patentees and their descendants and grantees encroached upon these common lands. "Tom, Dick, and Harry" pastured their cattle on them, made lavish use of the timber, and in various other ways committed waste with impunity. Many patentees caused surveys to be made, presumed to "take up," and used divers parts of the public domain "without any warrant, power, or authority for so doing, without the consent of the majority of the other patent owners," so that in the course of time it could not be known how much of these common lands had been taken up and appropriated. This state of things caused great confusion and numerous violent disputes between the settlers, who, in January, 1714, petitioned Governor Hunter for a new charter empowering them, in their corporate capacity, to convey or lease their common lands, in fee, for one, two, or three lives or for years.

Governor Hunter, in response to this petition, procured a new charter for the town and corporation, known as "The Queen Anne Charter." The power given by this charter had little or no effect in putting a stop to encroachments upon, and disputes between, the settlers about the common lands. Thus matters continued until 1643, when another effort was made by the settlers to protect their rights in the common lands. An agreement was made, dated June the 16th, of that year, providing for a survey of the common lands and a determination of how much of the same had been lawfully taken up, used, or claimed, and by whom. For some reason this agreement was not carried out, and matters continued to grow worse until December 7, 1763, when the settlers appealed to the legislature for relief. That body passed a bill, which was approved by Governor Franklin, appointing commissioners to survey, map, and divide the common lands of Bergen among the persons entitled thereto. These commissioners, seven in number, made the survey and division and filed their report and maps on the 2d day of March, 1765, in the secretary's office at Perth Amboy, copies of which report and maps are also filed in the offices of the clerks of both Hudson and Bergen Counties.

In the division made by the commissioners the common lands were apportioned among the patentees, hereinbefore named, and their descendants, as well as among the following named persons: Michael de Mott, George de Mott, Gerebrand Claesen, Joseph Waldron, Dirk Van Vechten, James Collerd, Thomas Brown, Andries Seagaerd, Dirk Cadmus, Zackariah Sickels, Job Smith, Daniel Smith, Joseph Hawkins, John Halmeghs, Philip French, Ide Cornelius Sip, Herman Beeder, Nicholas Preyer, Sir Peter Warren, Anthony White, Michael Abraham Van Tuyl, Walter Clendenny, John Cummings, David Latourette, John Van Dolsen.

Several other families, namely, those of Day, de Grauw, de Groot, Hessels, Hopper, Banta, Huysman, Van Giesen, Earle, Franzen, Morris, and Swaen, had become residents of the county without having lands granted them. It may therefore be safely said that the families above named constituted nearly all of the original settlers of Hudson County east of the Hackensack River. The westerly portion

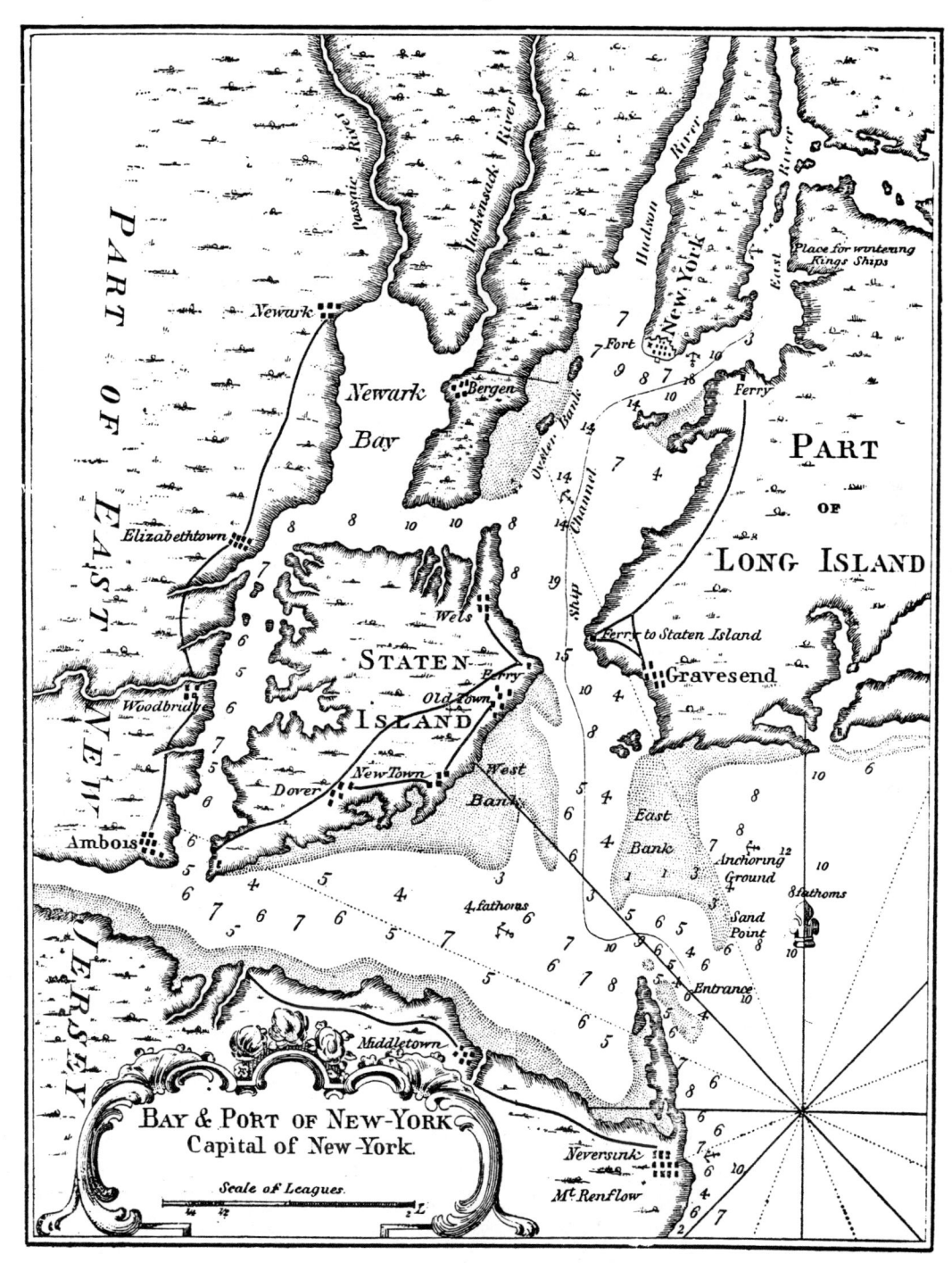

S. BELLIN'S RARE MAP, 1764.

of the county was included in the purchase by Captain William Sandford from the Parish of St. Mary's in the Island of Barbadoes. Governor Carteret and council granted this tract to Sandford, July 4, 1668. It contained within its boundaries an area of 15,308 acres, extending from the point of union of the Hackensack and Passaic Rivers about seven miles northward along said rivers, to a spring now known as the Boiling Springs, or Sandford Spring, near Rutherford. This purchase was made by Sandford for himself and Major Nathaniel Kingsland, also from the Island of Barbadoes, and the same was subsequently divided between Sandford and Kingsland. Kingsland, who became the owner of the northern part (including part of the present Bergen County), resided at what is now known as "Kingsland Manor," south of Rutherford, in Bergen County, while Sandford, who became the owner of the southerly part, resided at what is now East Newark, in Hudson County. Much of this large section of territory remained vested in the respective descendants of Sandford and Kingsland for many years after their deaths.

EARLY SETTLERS OF BERGEN COUNTY

Some of the original settlers of what is now Bergen County were descendants of those who have been mentioned as having settled Hudson County. Others came from Manhattan Island, Long Island, New Harlem, Yonkers, Albany, Esopus, Kingston, and other already established settlements, while still others came direct from Europe. The grant of section 1 to William Sandford, in 1668, as before stated, extended north as far as Boiling Springs near Rutherford.[1] The northern half of this was released to Kingsland. In 1702 Elias Boudinot, a French Huguenot, purchased a large tract from the Kingslands, described as butting on the Passaic River, in Bergen County. John and William Stagg, Bartholemew Feurst, Daniel Rutan, Jacob Van Ostrand, Cornelius Vanderhoff, Herpert Gerrebrants, John Varrick, David Provost, John Van Emburgh, Jacob Wallings (Van Winkle), and Henry Harding acquired title to portions of the tract in Bergen County, but the bulk of Kingsland's estate, at his death, passed by his will to his near relatives, who settled on it and retained it for many years. In 1668 Captain (afterward Major) John Berry received from Governor Carteret a patent for section 2, being all the lands between the Hackensack and Saddle Rivers, for a distance of six miles north from Sandford's purchase, or nearly as far as Cherry Hill, on the New Jersey and New York Railroad. Berry settled and built his home mansion on the southerly part of this tract, and on his death, most of it passed to the ownership of his

---
[1] For sections, refer to Map No. 4.

THE FIRST SETTLERS 23

heirs. The northerly part he had conveyed in parcels at various times to his son, Richard Berry, his daughter, Hannah Noel, and Garret Van Dien, Laurence Laurensen Ackerman, Rev. Guilliaem Bertholf, David Thomas, Thomas Nicholson, Albert Albertsen (Terhune), Arie Albertsen (Terhune), Claes Jansen Romeyn, Dr. John Van Emburgh, Hendrick Hopper, Ryck Lydecker, Juriaen Lubbertsen (Westervelt), Herman Brass, Abraham Huysman, Isaac Vreeland, Nicholas Devoe, Walling Jacobsen (Van Winkle), Elinor Mellinot, Folkert Hansen (Van Nostrand), Thomas Staag, Alexander Alliare, Peter France, Nicholas Kipp, Corneliese Christiansen, John Christiansen, Charles Maclean, and Anthony Anthonys (a negro), each of whom

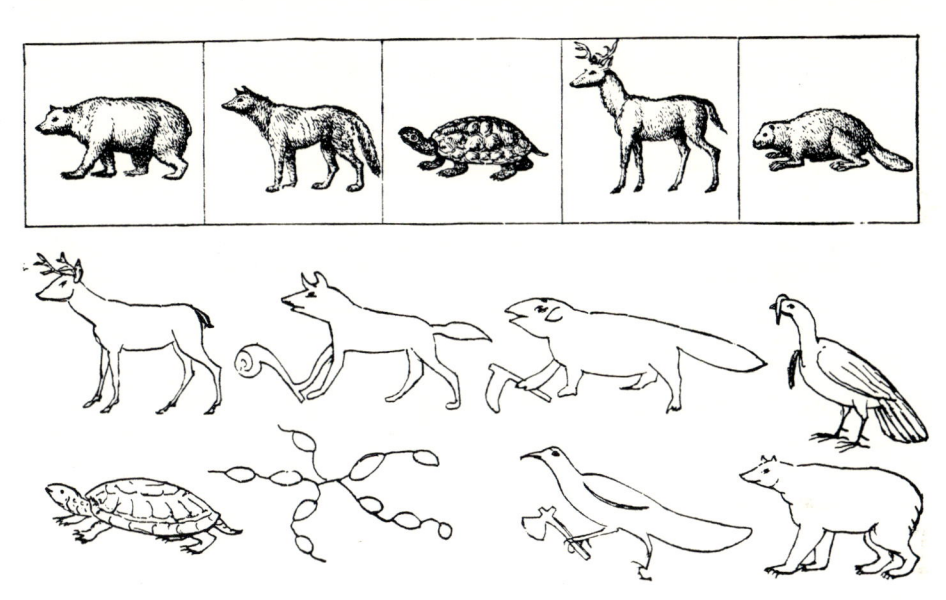

INDIAN TOTEMS AND TOTEMIC SIGNATURES.

settled on the portions purchased by them. The "Moonachie" section he sold to Rutt Van Horn, Nicasie Kipp, and Thomas France. The Zabriskies, Voorheeses, Brinkerhoffs, Demarests, Coopers, Van Reipens, and Powlesses acquired interests in the tract at an early date. In 1668 Samuel Edsall and Nicholas Varlet bought from the native Indians section 3, comprising 1,872 acres of "waste land and meadow," bounded east by the Hudson River, west by the Hackensack River and Overpeck Creek, and south by the "Town and Corporation of Bergen." The extent of this tract was two and a half miles from north to south, and the north boundary, beginning at Aquepuck Creek below Fort Lee, on the Hudson, ran northwest to the Overpeck Creek near Leonia. Subsequently Carteret gave Edsall and Varlet a patent of this tract. Nicholas Varlet soon after sold his interest in it to Edsall, who, in 1671, conveyed the northerly part of it to Michael Smith (a son-in-law of Major John Berry). Smith, at his death, left it to his son and heir-at-law, Johannes Smith, who, in 1706, conveyed it to John Edsall, son and heir-at-law of Samuel Edsall, deceased, who settled on it and devised it to his children.

In 1676 Samuel Edsall, by deed of gift, transferred the westerly part of the remainder of the original tract to his sons-in-law, Benjamin Blagge, of London, and William Laurence, of Newtown, L. I., who divided it between them, Blagge taking the northerly part and Laurence the southerly part. On Blagge's death his widow and devisee conveyed it to Wessel Peterson, who, in 1690, conveyed it to David Danielsen, who settled on it. Laurence's part of it passed to his son, Thomas Laurence. He sold half of it, said to contain 550 acres, in 1730, to Matthew Brown, who, in 1737, sold it to Cornelius Brinkerhoff. Joseph Morris and Adriaen Hoagland must have got the balance of Laurence's half, as they were living on it in 1730, and they and the Brinkerhoffs were the first actual settlers. Brinkerhoff's purchase included the present Borough of Ridgefield. The easterly part of the remainder of the original tract, which fronted on the Hudson River, was, on March 12, 1686, conveyed by Samuel Edsall to Jacob Milburn, who, with Jacob Leisler, then Governor of New York, was attainted of and executed for high treason, in 1691. Milburn's estate (which by his will, executed just before his death, he devised to his wife Mary), was, by operation of the attainder, forfeited; but parliament, by special act, restored the estate to his widow and sole devisee. The widow (who at the time of her death was the wife of Abraham Governeur) left a will empowering her daughter Jacoba, as executrix, to sell her lands on the Hudson. The executrix conveyed the lands in separate parcels to Hendrick Banta, Arie de Groot, Peter de Groot, Michael Vreeland, William Day, John Day, Mary Edsall (alias Mary Banks), John Edsall, and John Christiansen, who mutually released each other and settled on the same. The tract between the high rocks and the Hudson River was claimed by John Christeen, of Newark, under a grant from Berkley and Carteret, prior to that of Edsall and Varlet. This land Christeen sold in 1760 to his daughter Naomi, wife of John Day, and it seems to have become

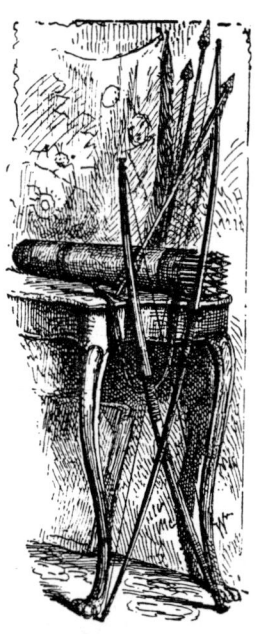

BOWS AND ARROWS.

THE FIRST SETTLERS

vested eventually in the same persons to whom Mrs. Governeur's executrix conveyed it.

On June 10, 1669, Governor Carteret patented to Major John Berry section 4, comprising a tract of 1,500 acres, lying between the Hudson River and Overpeck Creek, extending one and one-half miles north from the Edsall and Varlet patent. Berry sold the north half of this tract to George Duncan, an English merchant in New York. James Duncan inherited it from his father. Richard Backer, John, Samuel, and Matthew Benson, Jacob Day, Michael Vreeland, Hendrick Banta, and Jacob Cowenhoven subsequently acquired and settled on portions of it. The south half of it Berry conveyed to his son-in-law, Thomas Noel, who, at his death, devised it to his son, Monteith Noel, and to his wife's son, Richard Hall. Monteith Noel died intestate and without issue. By the terms of his father's will the lands passed to Elizabeth Patterson and James Martin, the two infant children and only heirs of Richard Hall, then deceased. By order of the court it was sold to Robert and Ann Drummond in trust for the two Hall children. On April 4, 1726, the trustees sold it to John Stevens and William Williamson, who soon after sold it to Samuel Moore, an Englishman from the Island of Barbadoes. William Laurence, Cornelius Brinkerhoff, Walter Briggs, Thomas de Kay, and others eventually bought parts of it.

Sections 5, 6, and 8, containing 6,770 acres of wildland, were, in 1661, granted in one parcel, by Carteret and his council, to Philip Carteret. It was described as being seven miles in length, north and south, and three

FORT LEE, 1776.

miles in width from the Hudson River to Overpeck Creek. It adjoined Berry on the south and Bedlow on the north. Carteret failed to settle within the prescribed time and it was again granted, in 1669, to Robert Vanquillan, of Caen, France; James Bollen, an Englishman (then a resident of Ridley, Pennsylvania); and Claude Vallot, of Champagne, France. Vanquillan sold his interest to Carteret in 1670. These gentlemen, failing to make any settlement within six years, lost their titles by forfeiture and the tract remained a wilderness without an owner until 1698, when it was granted to Mary, widow of Jacob Milburn, who also failed to settle it. On December 10, 1702, the southerly portion of section 5, forty chains wide and said to contain 500 acres, was granted by the proprietors to Michael Hawdon, a native of Ireland, but then a resident of New York and engaged in land speculation. On July 16, 1676, Hawdon conveyed to George Willocks, of Kenay, Scotland, and the heirs of Andrew Johnston, deceased, of Leith, Scotland.

John Johnston, Andrew's heir-at-law, released to Willocks and Willocks sold to George Leslie, of Barbadoes, W. I., a strip on the south, next to the Berry tract, half a mile in width. Leslie, on November 5, 1733, sold the southerly half, this being a quarter of a mile in width and containing 330 acres, to Mattias Demott, of Bergen, who, it is said, settled on it. Garret Lydecker, then a resident of New York, acquired the title to the remainder of the Willocks and Johnston purchase and to the remainder of section 5, one mile in width, and containing 1,000 acres. This made Lydecker's farm one and one-quarter miles in width on the Hudson River and the same width on Overpeck Creek. It extended northward as far as Englewood. On his death, in 1754, Lydecker's lands, comprising section 5, passed by his will to his four sons, Ryck, Abraham, Cornelius, and Garret Lydecker, whose descendants still occupy portions of it.

John Lodts, or Loots, a native of Norwich, England, came to this country in 1694, and in the fall of 1695 married Hilletje Powless, widow of Lubbert Lubbertsen Westervelt, Jr., of Bergen (now Jersey City). He removed to Bergen County and purchased a large portion of section 6, adjoining Lydecker on the south, on which he settled. Upon his death his lands were inherited by his sons, John and Paulus Loots; his daughters, Tryntie, wife of Henry Wierts Banta, and Gessie, wife of Daniel Commegar. Roeloff Lubberts Westervelt, a brother of the first husband of Loots's wife, purchased a strip north of Loots in section 6, as did also Cornelius, Hendrick, Dirk, and Seba Banta, the sons of Epke Jacobs. The purchases were all made in 1695. The combined purchases of Loots, Westervelt, and the Bantas, according to references in old deeds, must have included all of section 6, which extended north nearly as far as Tenafly. Descendants of the de Motts, Demarests, and Romaines subsequently acquired parts of section 6.

The triangular lot, section 7, lying between the east and west branches of Overpeck Creek, was first patented by the East New Jersey proprietors, in 1688, to Samuel Emmett, of Boston. Without settling it, Emmett conveyed it, September 17, 1695, to Roloff Lubbertsen Westervelt. The Indians disputed Westervelt's title in 1705, and he was obliged to procure from them a release. This tract extended from the junction of the two branches of the Overpeck, at

Englewood, northward to the head of the Tiena Kill Brook, a little south of Tenafly. The acquisition of section 7 by Westervelt gave him one of the largest farms on the Hudson. He settled on it and his descendants still occupy parts of it.

Section 8, containing 2,120 acres, extending from the Hudson River to the Tiena Kill, and one mile in width, was granted, April 27, 1688, to Colonel Jacobus Van Cortlandt, of New York, who, on April 10, 1738, conveyed it to Abram de Peyster, Margaret, his wife, John Chambers, Anna, his wife, and Peter Jay and Mary, his wife, all of New York City. The wives of these three men were the daughters of Van Cortlandt. They divided the tract, Mrs. Chambers taking the northerly third, Mrs. Jay the next third south, and Mrs. de Peyster the most southerly third. Mrs. de Peyster's third included the present village of Tenafly. Mrs. Chambers devised her share to her nephew, Sir James Jay, who, by his father's will, also got the latter's third. Sir James devised the north third to his son, Peter Jay, and the other third to his daughter, Mary O'Kill. The north or Chambers third was sold by the sheriff in 1820 to William Van Hook. Van Hook sold it in 1821 to Moses Field, who sold it to David O. Bell, in 1829. The three farms were then divided into lots and mapped, being known respectively as the Bell, O'Kill, and de Peyster tracts. This section was settled by the Van Buskirks, Bantas, Baldwins, Powlesses, Demarests, Westervelts, and other of the families already mentioned.

SEAL OF EAST JERSEY.

Section 9, adjoining No. 8 on the south, was patented by Carteret and his council to Isaac Bedlow, a Swede, June 20, 1669. It was also one mile in width, and extended westerly from the Hudson River to the Tiena Kill Brook. Its extent northward was to a point near Demarest, N. J., and it contained 2,120 acres. Bedlow had an Indian deed for this tract as early as 1661. He held it until 1728, when he sold it to Colonel Jacobus Van Cortlandt, of New York. Captain John Huyler, Johannes Rolofse Westervelt, Samuel Peters Demarest, Barent Jacobs Cole, and Peter Mathews Bogert became the owners and settlers on this section, and their descendants still occupy it.

Another section, No. 10, one mile wide, adjoining and extending north from the Bedlow tract, was granted by Carteret, July 30, 1669, to Balthazer de Hart. De Hart's heirs sold it March 5, 1701, to Bernardus Vervalen, Gideon Vervalen, and Rynier Vervalen. Under a grant from the Colony of New York it was claimed by Captain Lancaster Symes, of London, who, prior to 1711, had sold parts of it to Casparus Mabie, Jacob Hertie, and others. Eventually, however, Bernardus Vervalen, by a grant from Queen Anne in 1709, and a release from Symes and his grantees in 1717, acquired the title to the whole tract and conveyed portions of it to Matthew M. Bogert, Peter M. Bogert, Cornelius Harmensen Tallman, Dowa Harmensen Tallman, Isaac Johns Meyer, Martin Powless, and Walter Parsells, who settled it. The remainder of the tract descended or was conveyed to Bernardus Vervalen's heirs, who also became settlers. Vervalen's sons were Isaac, Daniel, John, Frederick, Abraham, Jacobus, Bernardus, Gideon, and Cornelius. His daughters Alida, Cornelia, and Hester married, respectively, Hubartus Gerretsen Blawvelt, Peter Van Schuyven, and Jacob Cole.

Until 1772 the Colony of New York claimed that this tract was within its boundaries and so treated it.

The "L" shaped section, No. 11, adjoining this last tract on the north, contained 1,300 acres, and was also claimed to be within Symes's patent from the New York Colony. It remained wild and unoccupied until April 28, 1710, when Symes and his wife conveyed it to two brothers, Barent and Resolvert Naugle. It was an irregular shaped tract, extending, on the north side, from Hudson's River to the Tiena Kill. On the west it was narrow, but on the east end it extended from the de Hart tract northerly beyond the present south boundary of New York. The Naugle brothers divided it between them in June, 1748, Barent taking the north half and Resolvert the south half. The sons of Barent and Resolvert Naugle and their sons-in-law, Nicholas Demarest, Arie Auryansen, Teunis Van Houten, Roloff Van Houten, John W. Ferdon, and Roloff Stevens, together with William Ferdon, Daniel de Clark, John Parcells, and Peter Quidore, settled this tract.

GOVERNOR THOMAS DONGAN.

The section No. 12, the next tract north of the Naugle tract, containing 3,410 acres, extended northerly into the Colony of New York, and was granted by Governor Dongan, of New York, in 1687, to Dr. George Lockhart, a London physician. The title passed from Dr. Lockhart to his half-brother, Colonel William Merritt, whose heirs sold it to John Corbett, an English sea captain, in 1703, who, at his death, devised it to his only child, Mary, wife of Henry Ludlow, of New York. The Ludlows sold it to the following persons, who settled it: Wilhelmus and John W. Ferdon, Hendrick Geisener (Gisner), his sons John and Nicholas Gisner, Matthias Concklin, Jacob Concklin, John Reyken (Riker), Abram Abrams Haring, Teunis Van Houten, Johannes Hyberts Blawvelt, John J. Naugle, John Sneden, Cornelius Smith, Jonathan Lawrence, Nicholas Ackerman, William Campbell, and Jacob Van Weart, who settled that part lying within the present County of Bergen.

The "Tappan patent," section 13, consisting of several thousand acres lying west of the Lockhart patent, was purchased from the Indians

HOBOKEN IN 1769.

in 1681, and in 1687 patented by Governor Dongan, of New York, to Daniel de Clark, Peter Jansen Haring, Cosine Haring, Garret Steinmets, John de Vries (Van Dolsen), Jr., Claes Manuel, John Straatmaker, Staats de Groot, Lambert Arianse (Smith), Arianse Lamberts (Smith), Cornelius Lamberts (Smith), Hyberts Gerrits (Blawvelt), Johannes Gerrits (Blawvelt), and Ide Cornelius Van Vorst, the Indian purchasers. In 1704 it was surveyed and mapped and a part of it partitioned between the last named persons and their heirs and assigns. A final division was made of the balance in 1720. The persons named in the two divisions, in addition to the above sixteen original purchasers, were Manuel Claesen, Lewis Claeson, Elizabeth Claeson (children of Claes Manuel, deceased), Barbara de Groot (widow of Staats de Groot, deceased), Garret Hyberts Blawvelt, Maritie Hyberts Blawvelt, and Dirke Hyberts Blawvelt (children of

Huyberts Gerretse Blawvelt, deceased), Abram Johns Haring, Jacob Mattyce Flearboom, Cornelius Jansen Haring, Antje Meyer, John Harmensen Tallman, Henry Van Campen, Isaac Gerrets Blawvelt, Jacobus John de Vries (Van Dolsen), Abram Jansen Haring, Ryniere Ryserick, Laurence Reed, Daniel Blawvelt, Joseph Blawvelt, Jacob Blawvelt, Tunis, Roeloff, and Nicholas Van Houten, John Van Dolsen, John and Cornelius Eckerson, Jurie (Aaron) Tomassen, Gysbert Bogert, William de Graw, John Ward, Jacob Cole, Jacobus de Clark, Jr., Jeremiah Borroughs, Abram and France Van Salee, Jacob King, Conrad Hertie, and Myndert Myndertsen Hogencamp. Of these, all except the Claesens, Reed, Ward, Borroughs, and King became settlers on portions of it.

Early in 1669 Oratani, the great chief of the Indian tribes of the Hackensack Valley, in consideration of her services as interpreter between his people and the whites, presented to Mrs. Sarah Kierstead, of New York, a deed of the southerly part of section 14, containing 2,260 acres, described as "A neck of land between Hackensack River and Overpeck Creek, beginning at the north line thereof of Hackensack River at a swale brook that runs about twenty rods into the woods, thence to cross over upon a direct east and west line to Overpeck Creek." The tract extended north as far as Nordhoff on the Overpeck, and to a point above Bogota on the Hackensack. Mrs. Kierstead was the eldest daughter of the celebrated Anneke Jans and the wife of Dr. Hans Kierstead, at that time New York's leading physician, with a residence on the corner of Pearl and Whitehall Streets. Dr. Kierstead died in 1660, leaving Sarah, his widow, and eight children. She afterward married Captain Elbert Elbertson (Stoothoff), of Flatlands, L. I., one of the purchasers of section 29. Upon his death she married for her third husband Cornelius Van Borsum, whom she also survived. She died in 1693. On June 24, 1669, Governor Carteret issued a patent to Mrs. Kierstead containing a condition that the grantee should settle it within three years.

On January 6, 1676, Tantaqua, Carquetiem, Wechlampaepeau, Hamougham, Hanagious, Anesaschere, and Poughquickquaise, sachems representing the Hackensack tribes, with the consent of Governor Philip Carteret, deeded to Laurense Andriesen Van Buskirk and company "a parcel of land commonly called by the name of New Hackensack, bounded on Old Hackensack, and from thence to a small kill adjoining to the great Indian field, called 'the Indian Castle' northward forward." Old Hackensack was the name given to the Demarest patents, which are mentioned later on, and the "Indian castle" was a little south of Palisades Park, opposite the mouth of Overpeck Creek. The description given in the grant covers, or was intended to cover, sections 14, 15, and 16, and indicates that Mrs.

Kierstead either lost her title by failing to comply with the condition in her deed or conveyed her interest in section 14 to Laurence Andriesen and company.

During the year 1669 Governor Carteret patented sections 15, 16, 17, 18, and 19, each containing 2,000 acres, as follows: section 15, to Robert Van Quillian; section 16, to James Bollen; section 17, to Matthias Nichols; section 18, to William Pardon; and section 19, to Major John Berry. Each of these five patents contained a condition that the patentee should settle on his patent a certain number of families within six years. The grantees failed to comply with the conditions, and the patents were declared forfeited. Sections 14, 15, and 16 were afterward, in 1676, granted by the Indians to Laurence Andriesen (Van Buskirk) and company, the "company" consisting of John Corneliesen (Bogert), Martin Powlesen (Powles), Hendrick Joursen (Brinkerhoff), Roloff Lubbertsen Westerfield (Westervelt), and John Loots, or Lodts. The patents (two or more) of Governor Carteret for the last mentioned sections designated them as "parts of New Hackensack." The lands described extended south from the Demarest patents at a point between Highwood and Tenafly and were bounded west by Hackensack River and east by Overpeck Creek. Lady Elizabeth Carteret confirmed the patents on April 10, 1682. A large part of these patented lands was allotted to the patentees. Other portions of them were sold to Nicholas Lozier, Peter Vandelinda, and John, Peter, and Lawrence, the sons of Lawrence Andriesen (Van Buskirk), the latter of whom had the largest interest in them. The balance was sold or released by the patentees November 20, 1686, to Rolof Vandelinda, Albert Zabriskie, Dirk Epke (Banta), Lawrence Lawrencen (Van Buskirk), Cornelius Christianse, and Gerret Gellis Mandeville, who subsequently made a division between them. The subsequent owners and settlers in section 14 seem to have been John Zabriskie, Joost Zabriskie, Jacobus Hendricks Brinkerhoff, Jacob Van Wagoner, Samuel Demarest, Wiert Epke Banta, Hendrick Epke Banta, Garret Diedricks, Jacob Banta, Johannes Terhune, and Christiaen Zabriskie, as appears by a release which they executed June

FROM AN OLD PRINT.

19, 1763, of a tract which is declared to be a part of the Sarah Kierstead patent.

After the forfeiture of the titles to sections 17, 18, and 19, James Bollen claimed them under an alleged patent procured by him in 1672. Berry also claimed section 18, and the subsequent patentees of these three tracts were finally compelled to procure releases from both Bollen and Berry.

David Demarest, Sr., purchased from the Indians, June 8, 1677, (by estimation,) about 5,000 acres, including sections 17, 18, 19, and 20, and lands north of them, but received patents for only sections 18 and 19. Upon his death, in 1693, his lands were divided between his sons John, Samuel, and David, Jr., his nephew, John Durie, and his numerous grandchildren. His granddaughters married, respectively, Jacobus Slott (Slote), Peter Slott (Slote), Abram Canon, Thomas Heyer, John Stewart, Abram Brower, James Christie, Peter Lubbertsen (Westervelt), Andries Jans Van Orden, Wiert Epke (Banta), Andries Lawrencen (Van Buskirk), Rynier Van Houten, Stephen Albertsen Terhune, Cornelius Epke Banta, Samuel Helms, Cornelius Van Horn, Jr., Peter Durie, Christian Debaun, Johannes Juriansen Westervelt, Jacobus Peack, and Benjamin Van Buskirk. All these, except Canon, Heyer, and Stewart, settled on portions of the original grant. Demarest's land was sometimes known as "Schraalenburgh" and sometimes as "Old Hackensack." Section No. 20 was settled by Samuel Demarest (son of David Demarest, Sr.), Jacobus Peack, Adolph Brower, Carel Debaun, John Van Schuyven, John Durie, Cornelius Jansen Haring, Cornelius Cornelissen Van Horn, John Hertie, and Abram Davids Demarest. Some of the grants were made by Governor Gawen Laurie and some by Peter Sonmans, representing the East New Jersey proprietors. The intermediate owners were Jurie Maris (Morris) and Ruloff and Hendrick Vandelinda, who, however, did not locate on any of the section, which was known as the "North West Hook."

The first attempt to settle lands west of the Saddle River was made in 1681, when a patent was issued by Governor Carteret and his council to Jacob Cortelyou, Hendrick Smock, Rutgert Joosten, and others, for 3,525 acres of section 29, adjoining the Saddle River on the east and south, partly on the Passaic River and partly on a brook, on the west. This patent was declared forfeited for non-settlement. The second attempt was made seven years later (March 25, 1687), when section 18, containing 5,320 acres, described as lying between the Passaic and Saddle Rivers,—"beginning at the meeting of the said rivers and running northerly along the Passaic River, its several turns, reduced to a straight line, four miles and thirty-six chains to a white oak tree marked on four sides at the Bound Brook, thence from the Bound Brook north east by a great Rock of Stone, eighty four chains, thence north east along the line of the Indian purchase, one hundred and eight chains, thence along Saddle River southwesterly to the place where it began. Being in length, reduced to a straight line, six miles and a half,"—was patented by the proprietors to nine persons, to wit: Colonel Richard Townley, of Elizabethtown, N. J.; Captain Elbert Elbertsen (Stoothoff), of Flatlands, L. I.; Jaques (James) Cortelyou, of New Utrecht, L. I.; Richard Stillwell, of Staten Island, N. Y.; William Nicholls, of the City of New York; Catharine Hoagland, of Flatlands, L. I.; Peter Jacobus Marius (Morris), of the City of New York; and Roloff Joosten (Van Brunt) and Hendrick Matthiesen, of New Utrecht, L. I. The survivors of these persons, and the heirs of those deceased, partitioned the tract, May 16, 1692, and thereafter sold it to settlers as follows: Joshua Bos (Bush), Thomas Jurianse (Van Reipen), John Van Horn, John Post, Halmagh Van Houten, Garret Jurianse (Van Reipen), Garret Garretson (Van Wagoner), Garret Garretson (Van Wagoner), Jr., John Garretson (Van Wagoner), Peter Garretson (Van Wagoner), Dirck Barentsen, Thomas Fredericksen, Warner Burger, Abram Van Varrick, Laurence Toers, Peter Jacobsen Morris, David Laurencen Ackerman, Dirk Van Zyle, Hendrick Vandelinda, Jacob Marinus, Thomas F. and Andries F. Cadmus, and John Billfield. This section is sometimes called in deeds "Acquackannock" and sometimes "Slotterdam," and comprised the greater part of the present Township of Saddle River. The "Rock" referred to is supposed to have been what is now Glen Rock.

A portion of section 22 (adjoining Major Berry) was patented by Lady Elizabeth Carteret, in 1682, to Jaques (James) Laroux and Anthony Hendricksen. The same year Lady Carteret patented to Cornelius Mattys 420 acres adjoining Laroux on the north and 424 acres to Albert Zabriskie, adjoining Mattys on the north. Zabriskie seems to have acquired the title to the Mattys and Laroux purchases, and all the land west of himself, Laroux, and Mattys, as far as Sprout Brook.

North of Zabriskie, in section 22, lay lands patented to Claes Jansen Romeyn, fronting east on the Hackensack and extending to Sprout Brook. Romeyn conveyed parts of these to his sons, John, Albert, Daniel, and Claes Romeyn, and to David Ackerman, John Zabriskie, Peter Laroe, and Henry Van Giesen, husbands of his daughters Gerrebrecht, Elizabeth, Lydia, and Sarah, respectively. Jurian Westervelt, Isaac Van Giesen, Paulus Vanderbeck, and John Berdan each purchased farms from Romeyn, in this section, all bounding east on the Hackensack. Section 24 comprised the Kinderkamack patents, granted by Governor Gawen Laurie to David Demarest, Sr., his son John, his son-in-law John Durie, and Peter Franconier. The latter sold his portion to John Demarest, who a few years later conveyed it to Cornelius Claes Cooper. The Demarests, Duries, Coopers, and Van Wagoners were the principal settlers in this section. The Indian sachems who signed the grants in this vicinity were Mamche, Sackamaker, Coorang, Rawatones, and Towackhack.

Section 21, known as the Paramus patent, containing 11,067 acres, was bought by Albert Zabriskie in 1662. Zabriskie's title to this tract was not confirmed by grants from the proprietors during his lifetime, but his son Jacob procured a release from Peter Sonmans, agent of the proprietors, May 13, 1731. In 1675 the sachems of the tribes of Northern New Jersey became indebted to Albert Zabriskie for a considerable sum, to secure the payment of which they verbally promised to convey to Zabriskie a large tract in Rockland County known as "Narranshawe." The promise to convey was not, however, followed by the execution of a deed from the Indians, and in due course of time a new set of sachems sold and conveyed the "Narranshawe" tract to other persons. These sachems were probably ignorant of the promises which their predecessors had made to Zabriskie. The latter demanded a fulfillment of the Indian promise and a deed from the sachems of lands in Bergen County N. J., equal in area and value to the "Narranshawe" tract. On June 1, 1772, Orachanap, Metachenak, Coorang, and Memerisconqua, then sachems of the tribes of Northern New Jersey, executed to Zabriskie a deed for 2,100 acres of land in Bergen County, described as "bounded West by the Saddle River, North and East by Claes Jansen Romeyn, and South by Albert Zabriskie." This large tract, constituting parts of 21 and 23, was known as the New Paramus patent, but is frequently referred to as "Wieremus," and sometimes as "Paramus Highlands." Zabriskie procured grants from the proprietors of this last tract, which, added to his previous grant, made him one of the largest landholders among the original settlers. One-half of the tract last mentioned Zabriskie conveyed March 20, 1708, to

HAMILTON-BURR DUELING GROUND, WEEHAWKEN.

Thomas Van Buskirk, of New Hackensack, who settled on it, and whose descendants still occupy portions of it. John George Achenbach, a German emigrant, together with persons named Baldwin, Ackerman, and Conklin, settled on parts of it. Zabriekie's children and grandchildren settled in this section as well as in section 23. His sons were Jacob, John, Joost, Christian, and Henry.

Section 23, besides Zabriskie's 2,100-acre grant, included several patents granted at various times to Claes Jansen Romeyn and Jacob Zabriskie, son of Albert, who cut it up into farms and parceled it out to their children. Romeyn's children have already been named. Jacob Zabriskie's sons were Albert, Peter, Stephen, and Jacob, and his sons-in-law were Anthony Lozier, Peter Lozier, John Ackerman, and Sylvester Earle. These with families named Duersen, Stagg, Hopper, Bogert, Terhune, Meyer, Van Gelder, Trapgagen, Verway, Tibout, Conklin, Volker, Banta, Vanderbeck, Van Blarcom, and Laroe settled in these several Paramus tracts.

Section 25, known as the "Old Hook Tract," consisting of 1,300 acres, was purchased from the Indians, April 24, 1702, by Jaques (James) La Roux and John Alyea. This tract was part of the share of Peter Sonmans, one of the proprietors of East New Jersey. On December 1, 1727, Nicholas Le Sieur (Lozier) purchased a one-third interest in it. The three owners then made a division of the tract between them, and on June 23, of the same year, Sonmans was induced to confirm the Indian grant by a deed in which the grantees named are Jaques (James) La Roux, Peter Alyea (son of John Alyea), Nicholas Lozier, Hendrick La Roux, and Samuel La Roux (sons of Jaques (James) Laroux). The tract was settled by the last named persons and their numerous sons and sons-in-law. Peter Van Buskirk, Andrew Hopper, Peter Debaun, Jacob Debaun, Richard Cooper, Daniel Duryea, and Jacob Cough purchased parts of it. Families named Bogert, Blawvelt, Vandelinda, Ackerman, Rutan, Demarest, Perry, and Quackenbush also became settlers on parts of the tract.

The southwest part of section 28 was called "Wierimus" and fell within a patent granted to Samuel Bayard, in 1703. The title passed from Bayard's heirs, by purchase, to Roloff Vandelinda, who died in New York in 1708. By his will he devised these lands to his son, Hendrick Vandelinda. The area of land devised to Hendrick is not given, but it was large, and by several deeds from Peter Sonmans, as agent of the proprietors, he afterward acquired several other tracts in the vicinity. His lands were, as the deeds state, bounded on the south partly by Zabriskie and Romeyn and partly by the Musquampsont Brook, a branch of the Pascack River. He sold it in parcels to Rolof Vandelinda, Rev. Benjamin Vandelinda (pastor of Paramus

Church), Frederick Wortendyke (the first settler at Pascack), Cornelius Haring, John and Albert Van Orden, Jacob Zabriskie, John Bogert, Rev. Bernard Van Duersen, Jacob Arents, John Durye, Daniel Haring, Carel Debaun, Abraham Post, David Hopper, Abram La Roux, Abraham Van Horne, and Rev. Samuel Verbryck (pastor of Tappan Church). The two "dominies" conveyed parts of their purchases to Garret and David Eckerson, John Forshee (Fiseur), Garret Haring, William Holdrum, Frederick Van Reiper, and Michael and John Ryer. West and north of the above Cornelius Mattys, William Sandford Van Emburgh, John Guest, Peter and Andrew Van Buskirk, Cornelius Epke Banta, James Johnston, and John Stagg secured patents from the proprietors. The locality of Arent's, Mattys's, and Van Emburgh's purchases was called "Awashawaughs's" plantation.

Nearly all of the above purchases and settlements were made between 1728 and 1732.

The lands comprising section 26, between the Hackensack River and the Pascack River, were within that part of the Honan and Hawdon patent which was purchased by John McEvers and Lancaster Symes, and at the division between McEvers and Symes it fell to McEvers. About 1,800 acres of this he sold to Dirk Cadmus, Garret Hybertsen Blawvelt, Jacob Flierboom, John Blawvelt, Abram Blawvelt, John Berry, Carel Debaun, Thomas Clark, Jonathan Rose, and Colonel Cooper. Owing to the long dispute between the Colonies of New York and New Jersey over the location of the boundary line between them but very few of the conveyances of lands in sections 26, 27, and 28 were ever recorded, and it is therefore next to impossible to locate all of the original settlers of these sections. It is known, however, from old gravestones and other sources that, besides those above mentioned, families named Demarest, Post, Merseles, Meyers, Storms, Mabie, Haring, Bogert, Banta, Holdrum, Cooper, Eckerson, Van Houten, Peack, Van Reiper, Westervelt, Hopper, Campbell, Zabriskie, Van Emburgh, and Peterson were among the earliest settlers of section 24.

Section 30 appears to have first been settled by the Ackermans. Garret Ackerman bought of the proprietors 478 acres butting on the Saddle River as early as 1712. David Ackerman and Andries Hopper purchased large tracts adjoining Garret on the south, while on the north of them were the purchases of Peter Van Buskirk and John Verway, in 1724, and William Sandford Van Emburgh and John Guest, in 1729.

On December 10, 1709, Peter Sonmans, styling himself "Sole Agent, Superintendent, General Attorney, and Recorder General" of the rest of the proprietors, conveyed to seven persons, to wit: John Auboineau (3-24), Elias Boudinot (3-24), Peter Franconier (7-24), Lu-

MILITARY MAP, 1776.

cas Kierstead (2-24), John Barberie (3-24), Thomas Bayaux (2-24), Andrew Fresneau (2-24), and Peter Board (2-24), a tract between the Saddle and Ramapo Rivers, afterward known as the Ramapo patent. Auboineau, Boudinot, Barberie, Franconier, and Bayaux were Frenchmen. Kierstead was a Dutchman and Board was an Englishman. This tract contained 42,500 acres and was eight and nine-tenths miles in length from the head of Saddle River southerly to the junction of the Hohokus Brook with the Saddle River, from which point its boundary ran N. 67° W. 150 chains to a great rock or stone called Pamackapuka (now Glen Rock), thence N. 63° W. seven and twenty-nine-fortieths miles to the Ramapo River, thence N. 13° W. 77 chains to the top of the Ramapo mountains, thence along the top of the said mountains about nine and a half miles, and thence southeasterly to the beginning. This included all of the present Township of Ridgewood, nearly all of Franklin and Hohokus Townships, and part of Orvil. William Bond surveyed and mapped it in 1709. The map is filed in the clerk's office at Hackensack.

On February 4, 1742, Franconier conveyed his interest to Theodore Valleau and David Stout, who, on August 10, 1752, conveyed to Madalene Valleau, daughter of William Franconier. In the same year the proprietors discovered, or affected to discover, that Sonmans's conveyance of December 10, 1709, to Auboineau and company was invalid, and forthwith took steps to regain the title. On March 29, 1753, John and William Burnett and Cortlandt Skinner, pursuant to a warrant of the proprietors, induced Madalene Valleau to execute a release to the proprietors of all her interest in the original 42,000 acres, upon receipt of a deed from the proprietors to her of 900 acres at Campgaw. This 900 acres, located in section 30, Mrs. Valleau afterward sold in parcels to Dirk and John Tiesbots (Tiebout), John Pullisfelt (Pullis), John Billfield, Isaac Bogert, William Winter, Barent Van Horn, and Harman Nax, who settled on it. Between 1699 and 1753 several grants had been made of portions of this 42,000 acres—some by the proprietors or their representatives, and some by the grantees of Sonmans, under the deed of December 10, 1709. Thomas Hart, of Enfield, Middlesex County, England, procured a patent for several thousand acres in the locality called Preakness, then in Bergen County, but now in Passaic County. By his will in 1704 he devised an undivided part of this tract to his sister, Patience Ashfield, and the other part to one Mercy Benthall.

Patience Ashfield's will, made in 1708, made Joseph Heale executor with power to sell. Thereupon Heale with Mercy Benthall and Richard Ashfield, heir of Patience Ashfield, sold their patented lands in parcels, the earliest purchasers being Anthony Beem, Conrad Lyn, Abram Lyn, Derrick Day, Peter Post, Cornelius and John Blinkerhoff,

THE FIRST SETTLERS

Jacob Arents, Philip Schuyler, George Ryerson, Rip Van Dam, John de Reimer, John Berdan, and Cornelius Jans Doremus, who, with the exception of Van Dam, were the principal settlers in that locality. The lands were in section 31.

Andrew Johnston, Edward Vaughn, William Skinner, and George Leslie, all Scotchmen, received a patent for about 1,000 acres in the same locality, which was sold, among others, to John Berdan, John Bogert, Gysbert Van Blarcom, and Abram Garretsen (Van Wagoner).

In 1699 George Willocks and Andrew Johnston procured a patent for several thousand acres, consisting of tracts in various localities, west of Saddle River at Preakness, The Ponds, Paramus, etc. These lands were mostly in section 31, and were sold, among others, to John Laurence Ackerman, Jacobus Laurence Ackerman, Jacobus Kipp, John Romaine, Jacob Kipp, Teunis Hennion, David Hennion, Edo Merseles, Martin Ryerson, John Bogert, Jacob Outwater, Nicholas Slingerland, John Le Toere, John Berdan, Samuel Van Saun, Ruloff Romaine, George Vreeland, Stephen Camp, and Zekiel Harris.

What was, and is still, known as the Totowa section was purchased by Anthony Brockholst and company. On Brockholst's death it passed to his son Henry, who sold it, among others, to David Marinus, Gerrebrecht Van Houten, Halmagh Van Houten, Bastian Van Giesen, Abram Godwin, and Martin Ryerson, in 1768. These lands were in section 31.

George F. Ryerson procured a patent for a considerable tract in 1748, adjoining north and east on the Preakness patent, which he sold to persons having similar names to Urie Westervelt, John Stagg, John Romaine (Romeyn), and others. These were in section 31.

Peter Franconier and others had sold several parcels, in the meantime, on the west side of Saddle River, in section 30. Garret Van Dien, Peter Johns Van Blarcom, and Dr. John Van Emburgh had procured from them the land between the Saddle River and Hohokus Brook, for some distance northward, and Major Isaac Kingsland, Peter Johns Van Blarcom, Hendrick Hopper, and Garret Van Dyke owned extensive tracts west of Hohokus Brook. John and William Van Voorhys, John Rutan, and John Berdan had procured grants and were located at what is now Wyckoff, where later families named Van Horn, Halstead, Ackerman, Winter, Van Blarcom, Stur, Folly, and others located.

By reason of these many prior titles the proprietors, after they had acquired the release from Magdalene Valleau, in 1753, found themselves face to face with the exceedingly difficult task of dealing with numbers of settlers who had supposed their land titles were without flaw. The proprietors undertook this task, getting some settlers to take leases,—thereby admitting the title of the proprietors,—purchasing from some, and compromising with others. Many of the settlers would make no settlement, the courts were appealed to, and a bitter controversy ensued, which was not entirely settled until 1790. In 1767 the whole 42,000 acre tract was surveyed and mapped by George Ryerson, Jonathan Hampton, and Benjamin Morgan. The original map, a piece of sheepskin four feet square, is in the surveyor general's office at Perth Amboy, N. J. It is badly worn, and much of the writing is obliterated therefrom by time and use. After the map was filed the lots were, from time to time, leased or sold to actual settlers.

In 1789 John Stevens, James Parker, and Walter Rutherford obtained a grant of 5,000 acres of the Ramapo patent, made up of many tracts located in different places. The following persons purchased from Stevens and company and from the proprietors and became settlers on the Ramapo patent or on lands south of it: Albert H. Zabriskie, John Fell, Albert A. Terhune, Baron Steuben, Cornelius Haring, Jacob de Baun, Abraham Van Voorhis, John D. Ackerman, John Doremus, Nicholas Hopper, David Bertholf, Henry Van Allen (the latter at The Ponds), Abraham Laroe, John Christie, Benjamin Westervelt, James Traphagen, Andrew Hopper, John Stevens, Andrew Van Orden (the last two at New Foundland), Matthias Stuart, Garret Hopper, John Moore, James Crouter, John Ramsey, Jacobus Van Buskirk, John Zabriskie, Conrad Wannamaker, Derrick Wannamaker, Henry Smith (the last named at New Foundland), Peter Haring, Abram Stevens, Rolof Westervelt, Ryer Ryerson (The Ponds), Gerret Garretson, Teunis Van Zyle, Andrew Van Allen, Edward Jeffers, Cornelius de Graw, Richard de Graw, John Neafie, Derrick Tise, Isaac Conklin, David Simons, Daniel Rutan, Christiaen, Henry, and Peter Wannamaker, Douglas Caines, Adolph Sivert, Solomon Peterson, Conrad Massinger, William Jenkins, John Meyer, John Winter, John Straat, Joseph Wood, and Peter Sturr, and also families named Fitch, Chappel, Oldis, Courter, Camp, Fountain, Folly, Fox, Osborn, Parker, Bamper, Dater, Frederick, Youmans, Mowerson, Packer, Quackenbush, Bush, Vanderhoff, Van Dine, Van Houten, Terhune, Bogert, John Arie Ackerman, and John Labagh.

On November 11, 1695, the proprietors granted to Anthony Brockholst, Arent Schuyler, and Colonel Nicholas Bayard section 32, 4,000 acres of land, on the east side of Pequannock and Passaic Rivers, one and a half miles wide, and running northerly from near Little Falls, up the Passaic River, along the Pompton River four and a half miles. This was then in Bergen County, now in Passaic. Both Schuyler and Brockholst located on the tract on the east bank of the Pompton River a little south of Pompton Lake. The purchase was made for mining purposes, but the grantees conveyed the greatest part of it December 17, 1701, to George Ryerson, John Meet, Samuel Berry,

THE FIRST SETTLERS

David Mandeville, and Hendrick Mandeville. They settled on portions of it and sold other portions to Elias Smith, Michael Vanderbeck, Thomas Juriansen (Van Reiper), Peter Van Zyle, Gerebrecht Gerrebrants, John Westervelt, Michael Hearty (Hartie), Casparus Schuyler, Dirk Van Reiper, Steven Bogert, Cornelius Van Horn, Garret Bertholf, Michael Demott, and Rolof Jacobs.

In 1764 Oliver Delancy, Henry Cuyper, Jr., and Walter Rutherford, representing the proprietors, sold to Peter Hasenclaver what are known as the Ringwood and Long Pond tracts, in the northwest part of Bergen County, containing about 12,000 acres. This is now in Passaic County. The lands were first patented to and occupied by Cornelius Board, James Board, Joseph Board, John Ogden, David Ogden, Sr., David Ogden, Jr., Uzal Ogden, Samuel Governeur, Thomas Ward, John Morris, David Stevens, and Andrew Bell.

It would require too much space to give the names of all those who purchased or settled on the Ramapo, Pequannock, Totowa, Preakness, and other patents of lands west of the Saddle River. The reader will note that nearly all the surnames given of settlers west of the Saddle River are the same as of those settling east of that river, thus indicating that the Ramapo patent and the lands south of it were settled principally by the descendants of those who settled the older parts of Bergen and Hudson Counties. It would therefore be a repetition of names to describe in detail the numerous sub-divisions of the Ramapo and other tracts.

LANDOWNERS AND SETTLERS

For the information of the reader and those who may become interested in genealogical research a list of the earliest and most prominent landowners and settlers of Bergen and Hudson Counties is hereto appended.

SURNAME OF SETTLER.	LINEAGE.	NAME AND DESCENT OF EUROPEAN ANCESTOR.		
ACKERMAN	Dutch	David Ackerman	Berlikum	Holland
ACKERSON	Dutch	Johannes Tomassen	Oostenvelt	Holland
ADRIANSE	Dutch	Maryn Adrianse	Veere	Holland
AERISON	Dutch	Cornelius Ariesen	N. Brabant	Holland
ALLEN (1)	Dutch	Pieter Van Hallen	Utrecht	Holland
ALLEN (2)	Flemish	Lorens Van Hallen	Limbourg	Flanders
ALYEA	French	John Alyea	Artois	France
ANDERSON	Scotch	John Anderson	Inverness	Scotland
ANTHONY	Dutch	Allerd Anthony	Amsterdam	Holland
ARENTS	Dutch	Johannes Arents	Vanderbilt	Holland
AURYANSE (1)	Dutch	Jan Auryanse	New York	United States
AURYANSE (2)	Dutch	Lambert Arianse	Gelderland	Holland
BACKER (1)	Dutch	Claes Jansen Backer	Hertogenbosh	Holland
BACKER (2)	English	Richard Backer	Barbadoes	West Indies
BACKER (3)	Dutch	Jacobus Backer	Amsterdam	Holland

SURNAME OF SETTLER.	LINEAGE.	NAME AND DESCENT OF EUROPEAN ANCESTOR.		
BANTA	Dutch	Epke Jacobse	Harlengen	Holland
BARENTSEN	Dutch	Dirk Barents	Amsterdam	Holland
BASTIENSEN	Dutch	Johannes Bastiansen	Aernheim	Holland
BAYARD (1)	French	Balthazar Bayard	Daupheney	France
BAYARD (2)	French	Nicholas Bayard	Alphen	France
BEDLOW	Swedish	Isaac Bedlow	Stockholm	Sweden
BEEDER	Dutch	Herman Beder	Amsterdam	Holland
BEEM	German	Anthony Beem	Flammersvelt	Germany
BELL (1)	German	Hermann Bell	Darmstadt	Germany
BELL (2)	English	William Bell	New York	United States
BENSON	Swedish	Dirck Bensingh	Gronengen	Holland
BERDAN	Dutch	Jan Baerdan	Amsterdam	Holland
BERRY	English	John Berry	Barbadoes	West Indies
BERTHOLF	Flemish	Guillian Bertholf	Sluys	Flanders
BILFIELD	English	John Bilfield	Enfield	England
BLACKLEDGE	English	Philip Blackleach	London	England
BLAGGE	English	Benjamin Blagge	London	England
BLANCH	English	Richard Blanch	Bristol	England
BLAWVELT	Dutch	Gerret Hendericksen	Deventer	Holland
BLAUW (1)	Dutch	Gerret Dircks Blauw	Drenthe	Holland
BLAUW (2)	Dutch	Herman Jansen Blauw	Gronengen	Holland
BOARD	English	Cornelius Board	London	England
BOGERT (1)	Dutch	Cornelius Jansen	Schoendewoert	Holland
BOGERT (2)	Dutch	John Louwe	Schoendewoert	Holland
BOGERT (3)	Dutch	Tunis Gysbertsen	Heykoop	Holland
BOUT	Dutch	Jan Evertsen Bout	Barnevelt	Holland
BRAECKE	Dutch	Dirk Claesen Braecke	Amsterdam	Holland
BRIGGS	English	Walter Briggs	Providence	Rhode Island
BRINKERHOFF	Dutch	Joris Dircksen	Drenthe	Holland
BROCKHOLST	Dutch	Anthony Brockholst	Amsterdam	Holland
BROSS	Dutch	Hendrick Brass	Albany	New York
BROWER (1)	Dutch	Peter Clementsen	Hoorn	Holland
BROWER (2)	Dutch	Adam Brower	Cologne	France
BROWER (3)	Danish	Jacob Eldertsan Brower	Holstein	Denmark
BROWN	English	Thomas Brown	London	England
BURGER	Dutch	Burger Joris	Hersburg	Silesia
BUSH	Dutch	Hendrick Bosh	Leyden	Holland
BUYS	Dutch	Jan Cornelisen Buys	Beest	Holland
CADMUS	Dutch	Dirck Fredricksen	Friesland	Holland
CAMPBELL (1)	English	Alexander Campbell	North Britain	England
CAMPBELL (2)	Scotch	James Campbell	Aberdeen	Scotland
CAMPBELL (3)	English	William Campbell	Isle of Man	England
CAMPBELL (4)	Irish	William Campbell		Ireland
CARSTENS	Norwegian	Claes Carstiaens	Sant	Norway
CHAMBERS	Scotch	John Chambers	New York	United States
CARSBOON	Dutch	Jan Elbertsen Carsboon	Gelderland	Holland
CHRISTIANSE (1)	Danish	Christiaen Pietersen	Holstein	Denmark
CHRISTIANSE (2)	Danish	Barent Christianse	Holstein	Denmark
CHRISTIE (1)	Scotch	James Christyn	Edinburgh	Scotland
CHRISTIE (2)	Dutch	John Christianse	Amsterdam	Holland
CLAESEN	Dutch	Gerbrand Claesen	Hoorn	Holland
CLARK	Irish	Robert Clark	Caven Co.	Ireland
CLENDENNY	Scotch	Walter Clendenny		Scotland
COLE	Dutch	Barent Jacobsen Kool	Amsterdam	Holland
COLLERD	English	Jacobus Collerd	London	England
COMMEGAR	Dutch	Hendrick Jans Commegar	Amsterdam	Holland
COOPER (1)	Dutch	Claes Jansen	Purmerend	Holland

THE FIRST SETTLERS

SURNAME OF SETTLER.	LINEAGE.	NAME AND DESCENT OF EUROPEAN ANCESTOR.		
COOPER (2)	Danish	Teunis Fredericks	Oldenburg	Denmark
CONKLIN (1)	English	Mattys Conkelin	Philipsburg	New York
CONKLIN (2)	English	John Conklyne	Not'ghamshire	England
CONOVER	Dutch	Jacob Wolfortsen	Amsterdam	Holland
CORBETT	English	John Corbett	London	England
CORNELISEN	Swedish	Cornelius Mattys	Stockholm	Sweden
CORNELL	French	William Cornelise	Kalbrist	France
CORS	Dutch	Claes Petersen Cors	Amsterdam	Holland
CORTELYOU	French	Jacques Cortelyou	Utrecht	Holland
COX	German	Michael Cox	Hanover	Germany
CUMMINGS	English	John C. Cummings		Scotland
DANIELSON	Dutch	James & Jacob Danielsen	Amsterdam	Holland
DAVIDSON	Dutch	John Davidsen	Liveden	Holland
DAVISON	English	Thomas Davison	London	England
DAVISON (2)	Irish	William Davison	Dublin	Ireland
DAY (1)	Dutch	Tunis Dey	Amsterdam	Holland
DAY (2)	English	William Day	New York	United States
De BAUN	Flemish	Joost de Baen	Amsterdam	Holland
DEBOW	Dutch	Hendrick De Boog	Amsterdam	Holland
De CLARK	Dutch	Daniel de Clerq	Amsterdam	Holland
De GRAW	Dutch	Albert Leendertsen	Amsterdam	Holland
De GROOT (1)	Dutch	Dirk Jansen de Groot	Rylevelt	Holland
De GROOT (2)	Dutch	Staats Jansen de Groot	Tricht	Holland
De GROOT (3)	Dutch	Wm. Petersen de Groot	Haarlem	Holland
De HART	Dutch	Balthazar de Haert	Utrecht	Holland
De KAY	Dutch	Theunes de Kay	Amsterdam	Holland
De KLYN	Dutch	Hugh Barents de Klyn	Buren	Holland
De KUYPER	Danish	Thomas Fred. de Kuyper	Oldenburg	Denmark
DELAMATER	French	Claude de la Maister	Riechburg	France
De La MONTAGNE	French	Jean de la Montagne	Saintong	France
DEMAREST	French	David des Marets	Beauchamp	France
DEMEYR	German	Nicholas de Meyr	Hamburg	Germany
De MONT	German	Frederick Temont	Darmstadt	Germany
De MOTT	Dutch	Mattys de Mott	Kingston	New York
De REIMER	French	Petrus de Reimer	Amsterdam	Holland
De RONDE	Dutch	Jacob de Ronde	Cortl'd Manor	New York
De VOE (1)	French	Frederick de Voe	Rochelle	France
De VOE (2)	French	Nicholse de Voe	Walslandt	France
De VRIES (1)	Dutch	Jan Jacobs de Vries	Vries	Holland
De VRIES (2)	Dutch	Jan Garretsen de Vries	Workum	Holland
De VRIES (3)	French	Jan Petersen de Vries	Amsterdam	Holland
De WITT	Dutch	Dirk Claesen de Witt	Zunderland	Holland
DIEDRICKS	Dutch	Hans Diedricks	Isleven	Holland
DOREMUS	Dutch	Johannes Doremus	Middleburgh	Holland
DOUGLAS	Scotch	William Douglas	Leith	Scotland
DOW	Dutch	Douwe Jans	Harlengen	Holland
DOUW	Dutch	Volkert Jansen	Lenwarden	Holland
DUNCAN	English	George Duncan	Bristol	England
DURIE	French	Jan Durje	Manheim	Germany
EARLE	English	Edward Earle, Jr.	Maryland	United States
ECKERSON	Dutch	Jan Tomassen	Oostenvelt	Holland
EDSALL	English	Samuel Edsall	Reading	England
EDWARDS	Welsh	Harman Edwards	New York City	New York
ELBERTSEN	Dutch	Elbert Elbertsen	Nieukerk	Holland
ELY	English	Nathaniel Ely	Hartford	Connecticut
EVERTSEN	Dutch	John Everts Bout	Barnevelt	Holland
FELL	French	Symon Fell	Dieppe	France

SURNAME OF SETTLER.	LINEAGE.	NAME AND DESCENT OF EUROPEAN ANCESTOR.		
FELTER	German	William Velta	Hamburg	Germany
FERDON	French	Thomas Verdon	Amsterdam	Holland
FEURST	Flemish	Bartholmew Feurst	Bruges	Flanders
FLIERBOOM	Dutch	Mattys Flierboom	Albany	New York
FRANCE	Dutch	Frans Jacobsen	Beest	Holland
FREDERICKSEN	Dutch	Dirk Fredericksen	Friesland	Holland
FRENCH	English	Phillip French	London	England
FOUNTAIN	French	Charel Fonteyn	Brooklyn	Long Island
GARRABRANTS	Dutch	Gerebrand Claesen	Hoorn	Holland
GARRISON	Dutch	Gerret Gerretsen	Wageningen	Holland
GARRETSON (1)	Dutch	Gerret Gerretsen	Wageningen	Holland
GARRETSON (2)	Dutch	Wouter Garretsen	Workum	Holland
GILBERTS	Dutch	Gysbert Lubberts	Hilversam	Holland
GISNER	German	Hendrick Geisener	Westchester	New York
GROOME	English	Samuel Groome	Stepney } London }	England
GUEST	Dutch	John Guest	Pennsylvania	United States
HALMAGHS	Dutch	Peter Roloefsen	Utrecht	Holland
HARDING	Swiss	Hans Jacobsen Harding	Berne	Switzerland
HARING	Dutch	Jan Pietersen	Hoorn	Holland
HARRIS	English	Ezekiel Harris	New England	United States
HART	English	Thomas Hart	Enfield	England
HAWKINS	English	Richard Hawkins	London	England
HELMS	Dutch	Hendrick Teunis Hellinck	Leyden	Holland
HENNION	Dutch	Nath'l Pietersen Henyon	New York	United States
HERTIE	Swiss	Hans Jacob Hertie	Berne	Switzerland
HESSELS	Dutch	Peter Hessels	New Utrecht	Long Island
HOLDRUM	Dutch	William Holdrum	Amsterdam	Holland
HOOGLAND (1)	Dutch	Dirk Jansen	Maarsendeen	Holland
HOOGLAND (2)	Dutch	Cornelius Adriance	Amsterdam	Holland
HOPPER	Dutch	Andries Hoppe	Amsterdam	Holland
HOUSMAN	Dutch	Guert Cornelius Huysman	Amsterdam	Holland
HUYLER	Dutch	Capt. John Huyler	New York	United States
JACOBS	Dutch	Peter Jacobs	Beest	Holland
JACOBUS	Dutch	Roloff Jacobus	Amsterdam	Holland
JANSEN (1)	Norwegian	Peter and Roloff Jansen	Sant	Norway
JANSEN (2)	French	Mattice Jansen	Cologne	France
JANSEN (3)	Swedish	Barant Jansen	Stockholm	Sweden
JAY	French	Peter Jay	London	England
JEROLEMON	Dutch	John Hans Jerolemon	Albany	New York
JOOSTEN	Dutch	Rutgert Joosten	Amsterdam	Holland
JURIANCE	Dutch	Andries Juriance	Bergen op Zoom	Holland
KIERSTED	German	Kier Wolters	Magdeburg	Germany
KINGSLAND	English	Nath'l & Isaac Kingsland	Barbadoes	West Indies
KIPP	Dutch	Hendrick de Kype	Amsterdam	Holland
KUYPER	Dutch	Claes Jansen	Purmerend	Holland
LAMATER	French	Claude de Lamaister	Riechbourg	France
LAROE	French	Jaques Laroe		France
LAURENCE (1)	English	William Laurence	St. Albans	England
LAURENCE (2)	Dutch	Arent Laurens	Ysselstein	Holland
LAURENCE (3)	Danish	Serven Lorens	Holstein	Denmark
LAURENCE (4)	Danish	Laurens Andriesen	Holstein	Denmark
LEENDERTS	Dutch	Paulus Leenderts	Amsterdam	Holland
LOCKHART	English	George Lockhart	London	England
LOOTS	English	John Loots	Norwich	England
LOZIER	French	Francoix Luseur	Colmenil	France

SURNAME OF SETTLER.	LINEAGE.	NAME AND DESCENT OF EUROPEAN ANCESTOR.		
LUBY	Dutch	Jacob Luby	Amsterdam	Holland
LUDLOW	English	Gabriel Ludlow	London	England
LYDECKER	Dutch	Ryck & Gerrit Lydecker	Amsterdam	Holland
LYN	German	Courad and Abram Lyn	Darmstadt	Germany
MABIE	Dutch	Casparus Meebjë	Amsterdam	Holland
MACLEAN	Scotch	Charles Maclean	Leith	Scotland
MANDEVILLE	Dutch	Gillis Jansen de Mandeville	Garderen	Holland
MARINUS	Flemish	Cornelius Jansen Marinus	Oostberg	Flanders
MARTIN	English	James Martin	New York	United States
MERSELIS	Dutch	Peter Merselles	Beest	Holland
MATTYS	Swedish	Cornelius Mattice	Stockholm	Sweden
MEET (1)	English	Adam Meet	Essex	England
MEET (2)	Dutch	Pieter Jans Meet	Amersfort	Holland
MELLINOT	Italian	Michael Mellinot	Savoy	Italy
MERRITT	English	William Merritt	London	England
MEYER (1)	German	Adolph Meyer	Ulsen	Germany
MEYER (2)	German	Nicholas Meyer	Hamburg	Germany
MEYER (3)	German	Harmanus Meyer	Bremen	Germany
MILBURN	English	Jacob Milburn	London	England
MOORE (1)	English	Francis Moore	Boston	Massachusetts
MOORE (2)	English	Samuel Moore	Barbadoes	West Indies
MORGAN	Welsh	Carl Morgan	Hamburg	Germany
MORRIS (1)	English	Robert Morris	Liverpool	England
MORRIS (2)	English	Richard Morris	London	England
MORRIS (3)	English	Anthony Morris	London	England
MORRIS (4)	English	Jury Maris		
NAUGLE	Dutch	Barnt Naugle	Gronengen	Holland
NEWKIRK	Dutch	Gerbrand Claesen	Amsterdam	Holland
NOBLE	English	Mark Noble	New England	United States
ONDERDONK	Dutch	Adrian Vanderdonk	Breda	Holland
OUTWATER	Dutch	Frans Jacobs Outwater	Oudewater	Holland
PARCELLS	French	Thomas Parcells	Huntington	England
PAUW	Dutch	Michael Pauw	Amsterdam	Holland
PEACK	English	Johannes Peack	Amsterdam	Holland
PERRY	French	Jan Perie	Pont-le-feekes	France
PETERSEN (1)	Dutch	Gerret Petersen	Friesland	Holland
PETERSEN (2)	Dutch	Peter Rolofsen	Utrecht	Holland
PHILLIPS	Dutch	Frederick Phillipse	Bolswaert	Holland
PINHORNE	English	William Pinhorne	London	England
PLANCK	Dutch	Abram Isaacsen Planck	Amsterdam	Holland
POST (1)	Dutch	Jan Jansen Postmail	Harlingen	Holland
POST (2)	Dutch	Capt. Adrian Post	Harlingen	Holland
POWLESS	Dutch	Powles Pietersen	Merven	Holland
POWLESSEN	Dutch	Powles Pietersen	Merven	Holland
POWLESSEN (2)	Dutch	Michael Powles	Veendoren	Holland
PRIOR	Dutch	Casparus Cornelissen	Amsterdam	Holland
PROVOST	Dutch	David Provost	Connecticut	United States
PULIS	German	John Pulisfelt	Darmstadt	Germany
QUACKENBUSH	Dutch	Petrus Quackenbos	Oostergeest	Holland
QUIDORE	French	Petrus Quidore	Havre	France
RAMSAY	English	Samuel Ramsay		Scotland
REYSERICK	Dutch	Rynier Reyserick	Amsterdam	Holland
RIKER	Dutch	Abram Reyken	Amsterdam	Holland
ROMAINE	Dutch	Claes Jansen Romeyn	Amsterdam	Holland
ROY	Dutch	Jacob Jacobsen Roy	Amsterdam	Holland
RUTAN	Dutch	Daniel Rutan	Esopus	New York

SURNAME OF SETTLER.	LINEAGE.	NAME AND DESCENT OF EUROPEAN ANCESTOR.		
RYERSON	Dutch	Adrian & Martin Ryerson	Amsterdam	Holland
RUYVEN	Dutch	Cornelius Ruyven	Ruyven	Holland
SANDFORD	English	William Sandford	St Marys Barbadoes	West Indies
SAUNIER	French	Paul Saunier	Normandy	France
SCHOONMAKER	German	Cornelius Jans Schoomaker	Hamburg	Germany
SCHUYLER	Dutch	David Pietersen and Philip Petersen	Amsterdam	Holland
SEGER	Swedish	Andries Seagard	New Albany	New York
SCHOENMAKER	Dutch	Jan Cornelius Crynnen	Aernheim	Holland
SHUART	German	James Shureg	Darmstadt	Germany
SICKLES	Austrian	Zacharias Sickels	Vienna	Austria
SIP	Dutch	Jan Adrianse Syp	Amsterdam	Holland
SIMMONS	English	George Simmons	Philadelphia	Pennsylvania
SIVERT	German	Adolph Sivert	Pruynes	Germany
SLINGERLAND	Dutch	Albert Slingerland	Albany	New York
SLOTE	Danish	Jan Pietersen Slott	Holstein	Denmark
SMEEMAN	Dutch	Herman Smeeman	The Marsh	Holland
SMITH (1)	Irish	Morgan Smith	Co. Cavan	Ireland
SMITH (2)	English	Matthew Smith	London	England
SMITH (3)	English	Michael and John Smith	London	England
SMITH (4)	Dutch	Lambert Arianse	Gelderland	Holland
SMOCK	Dutch	Hendrick Mattice Smock	Friesland	Holland
SNEDEN	Dutch	Johannes Sneden	Amsterdam	Holland
SNYDER	German	Abram Snyder		Germany
SOMERINDYKE	Dutch	Necaseus de Stille	Aernheim	Holland
SONMANS	Scotch	Pieter Sonmans	Wallingford	Scotland
SPIER	German	Dirck Jansen Spier	Bremen	Germany
STAGG	Dutch	John and William Stagg	Amsterdam	Holland
STEENHUYSEN	Dutch	Egbert Steenhusen	Soest	Holland
STEVENSEN	Dutch	Oloff Stevensen		Holland
STEWART	Scotch	John Stewart	Stirling	Scotland
STILLWELL (1)	Dutch	Alex. Stillwell	Dunkirk	Holland
STILLWELL (2)	English	Nicholas Stilwell	Staten Island	New York
STIMETS	Dutch	Caspar Stimets	Zeeland	Holland
STOFFELSEN	Dutch	Jacob Stoffelsen	Zirrickzee	Holland
STOOTHOFF	Dutch	Elbert Elbertsen	Newkerk	Holland
STORMS	Dutch	Dirk Storms	Utrecht	Holland
STRAATMAKER	German	Dirk Straatmaker	Bremen	Germany
STRAUT	German	Dirk Straatmaker	Bremen	Germany
STUYVESANT	Dutch	Petrus Stuyvesant	Friesland	Holland
SUFFERN	Irish	John Suffern	Antrim Co.	Ireland
SWAEN	Swedish	John Swaen	Stockholm	Sweden
SYCAN	Danish	Dirk Sycan	Holstein	Denmark
TALLMAN	Dutch	Douwe Harmensen	Friesland	Holland
TER BOSH	German	John Terbosh	Delmanhorst	Westphalia
TERHUNE	French	Albert Albertsen Terhune	Hunen	Holland
TIBOUT	French	Michael Jan Tibout	Bruges	France
TISE	Dutch	Dirk Tysen	Gelderland	Holland
TITSORT	Dutch	John Titsort	Amsterdam	Holland
VANDELINDA	Flemish	Joost Vanderlynden	Belle	Flanders
VANDERBEEK	German	Paulus Vanderbeek	Hamburgh	Germany
VANDERHOFF	Dutch	Cornelius Vandehoff	Gelderland	Holland
VANDERPOOL	Dutch	Myndert Gerritsen	Amsterdam	Holland
VARLET	French	Nicholas Varlet	Amsterdam	Holland
VARRICK	Dutch	Rudolphus Van Varrick	Gelderland	Holland

THE FIRST SETTLERS

SURNAME OF SETTLER.	LINEAGE.	NAME AND DESCENT OF EUROPEAN ANCESTOR.		
VAN ALLEN (1)	Flemish	Lorens Van Halen	Limbourgh	Flanders
VAN ALLEN (2)	Dutch	Petrus Van Halen	Utrecht	Holland
VAN BLARCOM	Dutch	Johannus Van Blarcom	Blarcom	Holland
VAN BUSKIRK	Danish	Lourens Andriesen	Holstein	Denmark
VAN BUSSUM	Dutch	Cornelius and Gerret Van Borsem	Emden	Holland
VAN CAMPEN	Dutch	Garret Jansen	Campen	Holland
VAN CORTLANDT	Dutch	Oloff Stevens Van Cortlandt	Wyck te dunnerstede	Holland
VAN DAM	Dutch	Rip Van Dam	Albany	New York
VAN DINE (1)	Dutch	Gerrret Cornelisse Van Dyne	Niewkirk	Holland
VAN DINE (2)	Dutch	Dirk Garretsen	Tricht	Holland
VAN DOLSEN (1)	Dutch	Jan Garretsen Vries	Workum	Holland
VAN DOLSEN (2)	Dutch	Dirk Jan Van Dolsen	Haarlem	Holland
VAN DUSER	Dutch	Abram Pietersen	Dursen	Holland
VAN DYKE	Dutch	Jan Tomasse Van Dyke	Amsterdam	Holland
VAN EMBURG	Dutch	Gysbert Gysberts Van Imbrooch	Amsterdam	Holland
VAN ETTEN	Flemish	Jacob Jansen Van Etten	Brabant	Flanders
VAN GELDER	Dutch	Jacobus Evertse Van Gelder	Gelderland	Holland
VAN GIESEN	Dutch	Rynier Bastianse	Giesen	Holland
VAN HORN	Dutch	Claes Jansen	Hoorn	Holland
VAN HOUTEN	Dutch	Peter Roelfsen	Utrecht	Holland
VAN IMMEN	Dutch	Dirk Garretsen Van Immin	Bextel	Holland
VAN NESS	Dutch	Hendrick Garretsen Van Ness	Emberlandt	Holland
VAN NOSTRAND	Dutch	Hans Hansen	Zeeland	Holland
VAN ORDEN (1)	Dutch	Claes Jansen	Naerden	Holland
VAN ORDEN (2)	Dutch	Dirk Jansen	Naerden	Holland
VAN OSTUM	Dutch	Hendrick Van Ostum	Amsterdam	Holland
VAN PUTTEN	Dutch	Aerent Teunesen	Putten	Holland
VAN REIPEN	Danish	Juriaen Tomassen	Reipen	Denmark
VAN SALLE	Dutch	Anthony Franzen	Saale	Holland
VAN SAUN	Dutch	Jacob Van Saun	Zauwen	Holland
VAN SCHALCKWYCK	Dutch	Henry Jans Van Schalckwyck	Schalckwyck	Holland
VAN SCIVER	Dutch	Petrus Van Schuyven	Schuyven	Holland
VAN TUYL	Dutch	Michael Abrams Van Tuyl	Tuyl	Holland
VAN VALEN	Dutch	Johannes Vervielle	Amsterdam	Holland
VAN VECHTEN	Dutch	Tunis Dircksen Van Vechten	Noeg	Holland
VAN VLECK	German	Tielman Van Vleck	Bremen	Germany
VAN VOORHIS	Dutch	Coert Albertsen	Voorhuysen	Holland
VAN VORST	Dutch	Cornelius Van Vorst	Gelderland	Holland
VAN WAGENEN	Dutch	Guert Gerretsen	Wageningen	Holland
VAN WART (1)	Dutch	Mattice Van Waert	Utrecht	Holland
VAN WART (2)	Dutch	Tunis Jacobsen Van Woert	Schoendewoert	Holland
VAN WINKLE	Dutch	Walling, Jacob and Simon Jacobsen	Middleburg	Holland
VEDDER	Dutch	Harman Albertsen Vedder	Gronengen	Holland
VERBRUGGEN	Dutch	John Verbruggen	Amsterdam	Holland

SURNAME OF SETTLER.	LINEAGE.	NAME AND DESCENT OF EUROPEAN ANCESTOR.		
VERBRYCK	Dutch	Jansen Verbryck	Isveren	Holland
VERWAY	Dutch	Cornelius Verway	Amsterdam	Holland
VINGE	Flemish	John Vinge	Bruges	Flanders
VREELAND	Flemish	Michael Jansen	Brockhuysen	Flanders
WALDRON	Dutch	Resolved Waldron	Amsterdam	Holland
WANNAMAKER	German	Peter Wannamaker	Darmstadt	Germany
WARREN	English	Peter Warren	London	England
WESTERVELT	Dutch	Lubbert Lubbertsen	Meppel	Holland
WHITE	English	Anthony White	Boston	Massachusetts
WILSON	Scotch	Peter Wilsey	Leith	Scotland
WINANS	Dutch	Cornelius Wynhard	Gronengen	Holland
WINNE	Flemish	Peter Winne	Ghent	Flanders
WORTENDYKE	Dutch	Nicaseus de Stille	Aernheim	Holland
WOUTERSON	Dutch	Egbert Wouterson	Ysselstine	Holland
YEREANSE	Dutch	Andries Jurianse	Bergen op Zoom	Holland
ZABRISKIE	Polish	Albrecht Sobeiski	Zolkieu	Poland

DUTCH WIND MILL.

GENEALOGICAL

ABRAHAM OOTHOUT ZABRISKIE belonged to one of the most numerous and eminently conspicuous families of Bergen County. In Poland the name was "Sobieska," and Albrecht Sobieska was the first of the family in America.

It has been claimed by many of his descendants that royal blood coursed in Albrecht's veins, because he was a brother of John III., the last king of Poland. The facts do not sustain such a claim. Albrecht Sobieska was not a brother of the last king of Poland. James Sobieska (the king's father) and his wife, Theophila, had but three children: Mark, John (the king), and a daughter. Mark was killed in the battle of Batog, leaving behind no issue; John, the king, had two sons, James and Alexander, both of whom died childless, as did also the king's sister.

Albrecht Sobieska (who in America was known as Albert Zabriskie) was a cousin of the king of Poland. That fact, however, did not make royal blood flow in his veins, for the crown of Poland when attained by King John was not inheritable. That quality had long since been forcibly taken from it. None of John's ancestors had ever worn it, and John was elected to wear it. Hence, there was no more inheritable quality in it than in the Presidency of the United States. There was, however, *noble* blood in Albert's veins. His ancestors for two centuries had been Palatine nobles of Poland—famous generals who had fought long and bravely in the cause of their country, distinguished for their virtues in peace and for their courage in war. Albert's cousin John, upon his merits alone, not only became king by the voice of the people of his native country, but he had also become one of the greatest warriors of the sixteenth century. Albert's father was a soldier, but the son had no taste for the favorite calling of a long line of noble and warlike ancestors. Born at Zolkiew in Poland, in 1638, he grew up in the shadow of the church and school, receiving a fair education. His turn of mind was such that his father had early hopes of seeing his son in the pulpit preaching the Reformation. To that end he sent Albert to a Protestant school in Holland. The strict rules and Puritan tenets of the institution were not, however, relished by Albert, and he soon ran away. While roaming about from one city to another, without occupation or funds, he was seized by the government authorities of Prussia and pressed into the army. Watching his opportunity he escaped to Amsterdam, early in 1662, from which port he sailed to America in the ship "Fox," reaching New York in August of that year. For ten years he seems to have wandered among the settlements about New York without any settled purpose in life; but in 1676 we find him at Bergen (Jersey City), where he met, and on December 17 of that year married, Miss Machtelt (Matilda) Van der Linden, daughter of Yost Van der Linden, a young lady then twenty years of age and a native of the City of Brussels, Belgium, whose brother, Roloff Van der Linden, was destined later to become, like her husband, one of the largest landowners in Bergen County. The marriage ceremony was solemnized in the Dutch Reformed Church at Bergen, near what is now "the Five Corners."

In the year of his marriage (1676) Albert made his first purchase from the Hackensack and Tappan Indians—a tract of 1,067 acres—abutting south on Captain John Berry's purchase, extending north one and five-eighth miles, and from the Saddle River east to what is known as Sprout Brook. This tract was known as "Paramus" or "The Point." On this he built his family mansion, and spent his life in agricultural pursuits. Much of it is still occupied by his descendants, who have become numerous in Bergen, Hudson, and Passaic Counties. It has been said that the Indians captured his eldest son, Jacob, and refused to give him up to his father until he should be taught the Indian language; that the father acquiesced; that the boy mastered the language, and the chief of the tribe then gave the father title to his lands. This is probably only tradition. At any rate, the deed recites the consideration to have been wampum (white and black), peltries, clothing, rum, and implements of husbandry. In 1682 Albert obtained from Lady Carteret grants of several tracts of land adjoining his first purchase, principally one of 420 acres on the east and extending to the Hackensack River. In 1679 the Indians in some way (not stated) became indebted to Albert, and to liquidate such indebtedness the sachems verbally agreed to convey to him 2,000 acres in Rockland County, N. Y. This agreement was not performed until 1702, when Albert agreed to take lands in New Jersey instead of Rockland County lands. Accordingly, the sachems of the tribes deeded him 2,100 acres in Bergen County, north of his first purchase, and fronting west on the Saddle River. Albert's patents are known as the "Paramus" and "New Paramus" patents. Altogether Albert must have owned more than 4,000 acres in Bergen County. Much of this was afterward claimed by Peter Sonmans, whose claims to it were not released until 1731-35, long after the death of Albert. In his day he was considered a very wealthy man. He was highly respected, not only for his great liberality, but for his integrity, and above all for his fair dealings with the savages, who esteemed him highly. He understood their language and frequently acted as their interpreter. In 1686 he helped to organize the "Church on the Green" at Hackensack, of which he was one of the first members. He took an active part in civil affairs and was the first Justice of the Peace for Upper Bergen County, to which office he was commissioned by Governor Hamilton in 1682. He died September 11, 1711, having been one of the most active and enterprising of the pioneer settlers of his county, and his descendants are noted for the same qualities. His wife survived him, dying in 1725.

His children (of the second generation) were (1) Jacob A., born about April 12, 1679 (married Ann Alberts Terhune), and had ten children; (2) John A.; (3) Joost A., born in 1687 (married November 12, 1712, Christina Casparus Mabie), and had eight children; (4) Christian A., born July 3, 1696 (married May 28, 1714, Lea Hendricks Hopper), and had five children; and (5) Henry, born in 1696 (married Gertrude Hendricks Hopper), and had four children.

John A. Zabriskie, of the second generation, was born at Hackensack about 1682. He married (1) September 20, 1706, Elizabeth Claes Romeyn, who was born in 1683 at Graves End, L. I., and died near Hackensack,

GENEALOGICAL 51

N. J., in 1712. He (2) married again December 6, 1712, Margaretta Johns Durie. He succeeded to the ownership of part of his father's lands. In 1720 he bought of Samuel Des Marest (2) a large farm at what is now Hawroth, N. J., some of which, until very recently, was owned by the descendants of his eldest son Albert. It extended from the Schraalenburgh road west to the Hackensack River. Some of his lands were claimed by Peter Sonmans, but were released to Zabriskie about 1751, by Hans Spier, agent of Sonmans.

John Zabriskie (2) was a farmer, but was active in township and church

ABRAHAM O. ZABRISKIE.

matters. He died in 1766. His second wife survived him. His children of the third generation were four by his first wife and nine by his second wife, to wit: Albert, Matilda, Nicholas, Christina, Elizabeth, John, Jacob, Elizabeth, Peter, Joost, Rachel, Cornelius, and Christian.

Of the above named thirteen children Jacob J. Zabriskie, of the third generation, born near Hackensack, July 27, 1718, married, in 1743, Sarah Varrick, a descendant of an old aristocratic family of New York. Their issue of the fourth generation was a son, John L. Zabriskie, baptized February 27, 1752. He died April 24, 1782. He married December 7, 1775,

Lena Lansing, of Albany, N. Y., where she was born October 5, 1750. She died April 26, 1826.

John L. Zabriskie's widow, after his death, married (2) November 14, 1786, General Abraham Oothout. John L. Zabriskie (4) had issue one son, John Lansing Zabriskie (5), who married Sarah Barrea. He was a prominent clergyman at Greenbush, N. Y., and had issue two children of the sixth generation: John Barrea Zabriskie (a prominent physician at Flatbush, L. I.) and Abraham Oothout Zabriskie (the subject of this sketch).

Abraham Oothout Zabriskie, LL.D., of Hackensack and Jersey City, was born in Greenbush, N. Y., June 10, 1807, and when four years old went with his parents to Millstone, N. J. He received an academic education and matriculated at Nassau Hall, Princeton, in 1823, becoming a member of the junior class when only sixteen. He was graduated from that institution in 1825, read law with James S. Green, of Princeton, and was admitted as an attorney in November, 1828, and as a counselor in 1831. He practiced in Newark two years and in Hackensack nineteen years, and in 1838 was appointed Surrogate of Bergen County and was re-appointed in 1843, serving in all ten years. He not only learned how to frame statements of execution and administration, but acquired a full knowledge of ecclesiastical law as pertaining to estates of descendants, and also evinced a method and accuracy that distinguished his life.

In 1842 he was appointed Prosecutor of the Pleas of Bergen County and became master of the principles of criminal law. Later he often acted as counsel in criminal and civil cases, and in cases involving land titles. He became familiar with the duties of a practical surveyor and also with the proprietary history of New Jersey, and understood every patent in the old "Field Book of Bergen County," and the common lands assigned to each patent. He was regarded as a formidable adversary in all cases involving title to land, and was for several years Supreme Court Reporter to 1855. In 1844 he removed to Jersey City, and in 1850 he was elected State Senator and served three years.

He was a member of the committee of citizens which framed the charter of Jersey City, passed March 18, 1851; was the author of the "Long Dock Charter" of 1856; and from 1856 to 1866 was a Director of the New Jersey Railroad and Transportation Company. In 1859 he was appointed by Governor Newell Chancellor of New Jersey, but the Senate refused to confirm him, and the State, during that memorable struggle, was without a Chancellor for a year. In 1866 he was nominated by Governor Ward and confirmed by the Senate as Chancellor, and began his official duties May 1, 1866. He performed the duties of that office with a promptness and ability that have never been surpassed by any of his successors. He took a prominent part in the great railroad war as opposed to the monopoly, and for an expression used in a public speech earned the sobriquet of "Captain of the Pick-axe Guard." He was an eminent jurist, an able and learned lawyer, a sagacious business man, and officially connected with several corporate enterprises. He traveled extensively, and while on a trip to the Pacific slope died at Truckee, California, June 27, 1873.

He married (1) April 7, 1836, Sarah Augusta Pell, born September 9, 1810, died April 3, 1845. He married (2) January 2, 1848, Julia M. Halsey. His children of the seventh generation were Abraham, Lansing, Sarah A., and Augustus. Of these, Abraham (8) was commissioned Adjutant of the Ninth New Jersey Volunteers, October 18, 1861, promoted to Major February 10, 1862, to Lieutenant-Colonel December, 1862, and subsequently to

Colonel. He died May 24, 1864, of wounds received in the battle of Drury's Bluff, Va. Sarah A. (8) is the wife of Franz Ernst de Bille, a native of Denmark, who is at present Danish Minister to England.

Lansing Zabriskie (8), now deceased, was a prominent lawyer in Jersey City, as is also his brother Augustus, at the present time. Augustus and Sarah have children of the ninth generation.

JOHN N. ACKERMAN is a descendant in the direct line from David Ackerman, the first American ancestor of the family. Southeast of Rotterdam, in Dutch Brabant, twenty-four miles from Breda, is the City of Bois-Le-Duc, called by the natives Hertogenbosch. It is now the chief town of North Brabant, and was built and strongly fortified in the eleventh century, though it was a place of some note much earlier, being near the Maas River and the great highway built by the Romans in their later conquests in Northern Europe. In the seventeenth century there was much heath land to the south and west of it which has since been reclaimed. Agriculture and manufacturing were then, as now, the main employments of the people, Tilbury, the nearest city, being noted for its extensive cloth manufactories. The city contains the chapel and church of St. John, built in 1260 and rebuilt in 1312,—one of the oldest and best preserved edifices in Northern Europe. From the city a road leads almost direct to the renowned battlefield of Waterloo. Near Bois-Le-Duc, in about 1620, was born David Ackerman, the son of a farmer and the progenitor of the Ackerman family in Hudson and Bergen Counties. Growing to manhood, he married in 1644, and engaged in tilling the soil until the stampede to the New World, caused by religious persecution and the threatened war with Spain and England drew him into its vortex. Being an ardent Protestant, he could not brook the fanatical domination of Romanism, and when in August, 1662, the power of the state could no longer protect him in the exercise of his religious liberty, he, with many of his neighbors, including the Storms, Terbosches, and others, whose descendants have since become a numerous host in Bergen County, embarked with their families on board the Dutch West India ship "Fox" (Captain Jacob Huys), and on September 2, following, landed at New Amsterdam. David had with him his wife and six children—the latter aged respectively twenty, eighteen, sixteen, twelve, eight, and six years. It has been said "it may be doubted whether he survived the voyage"; but there is little reason for such doubt. It is true that the emigrant list published is a list of those who sailed *from* Holland ports, not of those who actually *arrived* at New Amsterdam. It is likewise true that the records make no further mention of either David or his wife. But these facts furnish no ground to doubt their arrival on our shores. The first family abode was in the *Markvelt Stegg*. In 1668 the family nucleus was at New Harlem. Whether David or his wife were living at the time of the removal to Harlem, whether Elizabeth on her marriage and removal to Harlem took her brothers with her, are at best subjects of conjecture. David may have died at the Markvelt Stegg residence, or he may have removed to Harlem and died there. However this may be, as no public records of deaths were kept, the date of his death and that of his wife, as well as her name, are facts which are likely never to be ascertained, except by accident. Of the children, Ann was the first to break the family circle by her marriage in 1664, and subsequent removal up the Hudson. Elizabeth followed her example in 1668, uniting in marriage with the somewhat renowned Kier

Walters (ancestor of the Kiersens), who, however, died two years later. Lawrence was a youth of untiring energy and persevered in everything he undertook. In 1669, being then only nineteen, he hired a portion of what was then called the Archer farm at Harlem. In 1679 he married Greetje Egberts and remained at Harlem until 1685, during which time two daughters were born to him. David, the eldest son, went to New York, where, in 1680, he married Hellegorid Ver Planck, and remained there until 1686, during which time several children were born to him. Lodowyck, who seems, at first, to have been rather a wild boy, went to Kingston, N. Y., where, in 1681, he wooed and wedded Miss Jenneke Blaeck, by whom he had at least two children. After his removal to Bergen County his wife died and he married Hillegorid Bosch, by whom he had two children.

Abraham, the youngest of the children, married, in 1683, at New York, Aeltje Van Lear, by whom he had six children before his removal to New Jersey, and four more in New Jersey. Lawrence and David were the first of the family to remove to Bergen County in 1686. Lodowyck and Abraham followed in 1694. They all settled on large tracts of land between the Hackensack and Saddle Rivers, and also west of the Saddle River. The family became very numerous both in Bergen and in what is now called Passaic County. Numerous members of the family have been the most active and influential in the county, and have been honored with town, county, and State offices. Others have been important factors in religious work, and have attained eminence in various branches of learning.

Lawrence Ackerman was buried at Wyckoff or Oakland. His children were John and James.

John Ackerman, son of Lawrence, married Catherine Romaine. Both are buried at Wyckoff or Oakland. Their children were Lawrence, Nicholas, and James.

Nicholas Ackerman, son of John, was born January 24, 1795, died June 1, 1869, married Polly or Maria Snyder, who was born in 1801, died March 24, 1877. Their children were John N., born January 28, 1818; Abraham, born August 27, 1830; and George.

John N. Ackerman, whose name heads this sketch, was born in Franklin Township, Bergen County, N. J., January 28, 1818, and is now one of the oldest residents of Hackensack. He is the eldest son of Nicholas Ackerman and Polly or Maria Snyder, a grandson of John Ackerman and Catharine Romeyn, and a great-grandson of Lawrence Ackerman. He was educated in the public schools of Franklin Township. He left home at the age of fifteen, and for two years worked at the trade of carriage making. Since then he has earned his own livelihood. When seventeen he went to New York City and learned the carpenter's trade, mastering every branch. In 1837 he returned to Hackensack, N. J., married Rachel R. Vanderbeek, and engaged in business as a manufacturer of sash, doors, and blinds, which he followed with marked success until 1896, a period of fifty-nine years. He then retired to enjoy in private life the fruits of a long and honorable career. Mr. Ackerman has resided in Hackensack since he established himself in business there in 1837, and from the first has taken an active interest in the growth and development of the town, and all those public matters which appeal to the progressive spirit of a patriotic, energetic citizen. Though never aspiring to office, and as a rule avoiding political life, he was for ten years a Justice of the Peace, and in this and other minor capacities has displayed great ability, sound judgment, and commendable enterprise.

Mr. Ackerman was married, June 14, 1837, in Hackensack, to Rachel Ryerson Vanderbeek, born February 7, 1806, died June 26, 1891, a descendant, like himself, of one of the old Holland Dutch families of Bergen County. Their children are George J. Ackerman, born March 27, 1839, and Mary R. Ackerman, born September 27, 1845.

George J. Ackerman, oldest child of John N. and Rachel R. Ackerman, married Julia A. Groesbeck, December 24, 1863. She was born November 27, 1842, and died April 11, 1886. They had one child, George Groesbeck Ackerman, born November 6, 1867, who married, September 27, 1893, Emeline Inglehart, of Watertown, N. Y., who was born December 3, 1869. They have one child, Alison Groesbeck Ackerman, born October 13, 1896.

AARON E. ACKERMAN, of Hackensack, is of the seventh generation from David Ackerman, the first of the family in America (see sketch on page 53). He was born at Saddle River, Bergen County, September 6, 1836, and is a son of Peter Ackerman and Eliza Eckerson, and a grandson of Albert Ackerman and Eliza, his wife. This Albert served as a soldier in the War of 1812. Aaron Ackerman's maternal grandparents were Aaron Eckerson and Matilda Westervelt. As will be seen, Mr. Ackerman is of Dutch extraction on both sides of the family tree.

He was educated in the public schools of Bergen County, remaining on his father's farm until he reached the age of seventeen. He then entered the employ of Conklin & Post, of Schraalenburgh, as a carpenter, and continued with that well known firm for about twenty-three years. On the death of Mr. Post he became a partner with Peter L. Conklin, the senior member of the old firm. The new firm of Conklin & Ackerman continued in business eight years, or until 1882, when Mr. Conklin retired after an active life of forty years. Mr. Ackerman succeeded to the business, which he still conducts, and which is one of the oldest of the kind in East Jersey, having been in continuous existence for nearly sixty years. And under his able and energetic management it has not only retained but greatly increased its old-time prestige and usefulness. The buildings and other carpenter work which he has erected in Hackensack and vicinity would, if enumerated, make a list that would fill a good sized volume.

Mr. Ackerman is a man of acknowledged ability and integrity, and both in business and social relations has always enjoyed the respect and confidence of his fellowmen. Enterprising, patriotic, and public spirited, he has taken from the first a deep interest in municipal affairs, and liberally encourages every worthy project. He served three years and one month in the War of the Rebellion, becoming a second sergeant, and is a prominent member of the Second Reformed Church of Hackensack.

He married Miss Abigail Wygant, and they have two daughters: Nellie, born in 1863, and Fannie, born in 1871.

ALEXANDER TAGGART McGILL, A.M., LL.D., for thirteen years Chancellor of the State of New Jersey, was born October 20, 1845, in Allegheny City, Pa., where his father, Rev. Alexander T. McGill, D.D., LL.D., was a professor in the Western Theological Seminary. His great-grandfather was an Indian fighter of note in Pennsylvania, and served as a Lieutenant-Colonel in the Continental Army under Washington at Trenton and Princeton. The Chancellor's father was for some years a lawyer in Georgia, but later studied theology and became professor in the Western Theological Seminary. When the Chancellor was nine years old, in 1854, his father accepted a professorship in Princeton Theological Seminary and the family moved to New Jersey. His father held that position until his death in 1889.

Chancellor McGill thus spent his early life in the midst of the best educational and social advantages, which he imbibed with an eagerness characteristic of his race. While a youth he exhibited scholarly tastes, and rapidly acquired a high standing as a thorough and painstaking student. His chief aim was to master every problem, no matter how difficult, that came to his attention. He was a keen observer, possessed of

ALEXANDER T. McGILL.

analytical powers of a high order, and won the praise and respect of both teachers and associates. Entering Princeton College, he pursued the regular course and received the degree of A.B. in 1864 and that of A.M. in 1867, and afterward his alma mater and Rutgers College of New Jersey each conferred upon him the honorary degre of LL.D. In June, 1866, he was graduated from the Columbia Law School, and thereafter continued his legal studies with the late Hon. Edward W. Scudder, of Trenton. He came to the bar in New Jersey as an attorney at the November term, 1867, and as a counselor in November, 1870.

For a few months he remained in Trenton as an associate of his preceptor, Judge Scudder, and then, in 1868, moved to Jersey City, where he afterward resided. Chancellor McGill soon achieved prominence as an able, industrious, and conscientious lawyer. From 1870 to 1876 he was the law partner of the late Attorney General Robert Gilchrist. In 1874 and 1875 he was counsel for the City of Bayonne and also member of Assembly from the then First District of Hudson County. He was active and influential in the Legislature, and served on the leading committees. In April, 1878, Governor McClellan appointed him Prosecutor of the Pleas for the County of Hudson, and in April, 1883, he was appointed Law Judge of that county by Governor Ludlow.

On March 29, 1887, he was appointed by Governor Green as Chancellor of the State of New Jersey, and the appointment was unanimously confirmed by the Senate on the 31st of the same month. His first term expired May 1, 1894, and he was re-appointed to the office by Governor Werts, and at once unanimously confirmed by the Senate without reference.

It was during his term as Chancellor that the famous coal combine bill was passed by the Legislature. When Governor Abbett refused to sign the bill the railroad companies in the combination contended that they were protected by existing laws, and proceeded to act accordingly. The attorney general brought suit against the Coal Trust in the Court of Chancery. The Chancellor rendered a decision which not only laid down the relations of corporations to the State with a clearness and fairness that placed his ruling beyond attack, but dealt a blow to all the monopoly combinations of the Coal Trust class.

In the fall of 1895 the Democratic party nominated the Chancellor for Governor. In the campaign that followed he took no part, but continued to discharge the duties of the office of Chancellor. The election resulted in his defeat by John W. Griggs, now United States Attorney General, by a plurality of 26,900.

Chancellor McGill died April 21, 1900, at his home in Jersey City. His friends declare that he died a martyr to duty. His office killed him. He was a scrupulously conscientious man, and thought of duty above everything else. He would never shirk a responsibility, however much he might suffer in fulfilling it. His learning, dignity, good judgment, and ability long adorned the highest equity bench in the State. He was one of the most popular jurists that ever presided over the Courts of Errors and Appeals and Chancery. As a citizen, lawyer, and judge he was universally respected and esteemed.

Chancellor McGill married Miss Olmstead, a relative of the Stevens family, of Hoboken, who survives. He had no children. He is also survived by a brother, Dr. John D. McGill, Surgeon-General of New Jersey.

MATTHEW J. BOGERT.—The Bougaerdts were a numerous and influential family in Holland, where they filled many important military and civic positions, and attained lasting fame in the arts, sciences, and literature centuries before the advent of any of them in America. Guilliaem Bougaert was Schout of the City of Dordrecht in 1423. His son Adam became first Professor of Music and Rector of the Academy at Leyden, where he died in 1482. He is buried in St. Peter's Church in Leyden, beneath a stone surmounted with a copper plate on which is an inscription setting forth his fame. This church was built in 1315 as a monument to Boerhave, the great physician, and contains the remains of the most distinguished worthies of Holland. Adam's son Jacob became first physician to the City of Antwerp and afterward was Profesor of Medicine and Surgery at Leyden for more than twenty years. Like his father he also attained the rectorship of the academy. He was a fluent writer on medical science, on which he published a treatise in five parts, the manuscript of which is now in the public library at Antwerp. Harman Myndertse Bougaert came to New Amsterdam in 1629, and was probably the first of the name to locate in America. He was a medical man of long experience and was appointed official physician to the infant metropolis. In 1634 Rev. Everard Bogardus, a son of William Bougaert, and who wrote his name in Latin Everardus Bougardus, came over to New Amsterdam in company with Governor-General Wouter Von Twiller. Bogardus was the first regular preacher on Manhattan Island, where he married, in 1637, Ann, widow of Roelof Jansen, of Maeslandt, Holland, the lady about whom, and whose estate and Trinity Church, so much has been written and said during the last thirty years. Dominie Bogardus rented a tobacco plantation on the island and spent much time and labor upon it, tobacco being at that time the principal currency of the country. In time he quarreled with Governor Kieft because of the latter's cruelty to the New Jersey Indians. Kieft brought charges of immorality against him, the investigation of which was cut short by the superseding of Kieft, who was drowned off the coast of Wales.

Joost (Justus) Bougaert, in 1641, was appointed by Queen Christina, of Sweden, commander of a colony on the east side of the Delaware River below Philadelphia. He held that position some time on an annual salary of 500 florins.

In 1652 Teunis Gysbert Bougaert emigrated to New Amsterdam from Hey Koop, a little hamlet northeast of Leyden. Two years later he settled at Brooklyn, when he married Sarah Rapelje, a daughter of one of Brooklyn's earliest settlers. He was Mayor of Brooklyn for three years. His farm fronted on the Walabocht (Wallabout). His descendants scattered over Long Island and along the Raritan River in New Jersey.

Matthew J. Bogert is descended from Jan Louwe Bougaerdt, a cousin of Gysbert, above named. Jan was cradled and grew to man's estate at Schoondewoerdt (a word meaning finer words), a small fortified village noted for its salmon fisheries, on a branch of the Maas River twenty miles above Rotterdam and about two miles from Hey Koop, the former home of his uncle Gysbert. Jan was reared a farmer, but early in life struck out for himself. Reaching manhood, he married Cornelia Evertse, the daughter of a well-to-do neighbor, and settled down to farming in his native town. In common with thousands of Hollanders he seems to have caught the prevalent emigration fever, for, on April 16, 1663, we find him and his family with many of his neighbors embarking at Amsterdam on the Dutch West India ship "Spotted Cow," bound for the shores of America. A month later the stanch craft touched the wharf at New Amsterdam, where some of the cargo of emigrants remained and others went to Brooklyn, Staten Island, and Albany. Jan, no doubt, desiring to be near his uncle, repaired to the vicinity of Bedford, L. I., where he bought a farm, and remained there until 1672. He must have been possessed of some means, as in the spring of that year he had an opportunity, of which he availed himself, to take charge of the farm of Dr. John de la Montagne near Harlem. On the 1st of May, 1671, he removed thither from Bedford, and thenceforward for a period of twenty years was an active participant in the civil and religious affairs of Harlem. That he prospered is evidenced by the fact that in 1679, 1691, and 1701 he bought lands at Hoorns Hook, Spuyten Duyvil, and on Hellegat Sound. He was chosen magistrate of Harlem in 1675 and 1676, but failed afterward in the realization of his political aspirations, which seem to have been strong. In 1695 he sold his lands at Bedford and in 1706 his farm lands at Harlem. The following spring, stricken in years, he and his wife removed to New Amsterdam (joining the Dutch Church there May 27, 1707), where they died soon after at a ripe old age.

Jan Louwe Bougaerdt was a man of firmness and decision of character; born to command, rather than to follow; hasty in his temper, but prone to justice when cool; a man of his word, who demanded of his neighbor the exercise of the same quality; shrewd in protecting his own interests, but honest in his dealings with his neighbor; a man of sound judgment, keen intelligence, and possessing a large fund of general information; a stern but affectionate and dutiful husband and father, and a devoted Christian,— all qualities which, under the trying circumstances in which he was placed, fitted him for the trials of a frontier life. They had nine children of the second generation, to wit: Peter Jansen, Margaretta, Gysbert, Nicholas, Elizabeth, Catharine, Cornelia, Janneke, and John.

Peter Jansen Bogert (2d gen.), born at Schoondewoerdt, Holland, in 1656, married in New York, September 29, 1686, Sophia, a daughter of Judge Matthias Flierboom, of Albany. He, with his sister Margaretta, and his brother Gysbert, removed to Tappan, then a part of Orange County, N. Y. Gysbert and Margaretta's husband purchased large tracts of land at Tappan, on which they settled. Peter Jansen died in New York, but his children remained at Tappan. These were of the third generation, to wit: Cornelia, Maria, Elizabeth, Catalyntie, John P., Matthew P., Peter P., and Willemina.

Matthew P. Bogert (3d gen.), baptized at Hackensack in 1702, married, in 1735, Margaretta Tunisens Talman, and in January, 1740, bought of Bernardus Van Valen 250 acres of woodland south of Closter and extending from the Hudson River to the Tiena Kill Brook. The westerly part of this was soon cleared and stocked and a family mansion erected on the east side of the old road leading to Piermont. Matthew P. Bogert followed agricultural pursuits until his death in 1784. His children of the fourth generation were Peter M., Sophia, Cornelius, Maria, Matthew M., Maria, and Dowe.

Matthew M. Bogert (4th gen.) by will obtained and resided on part of the homestead of his father at Closter until his death. He married, in 1777, Sarah Bogert, a relative of his, who survived him. He served as a private in the New Jersey militia in 1776. He was a farmer and left children of the fifth generation, to wit: Margaretta, Sarah, Maria, Matthew M., Albert M., and Sophia.

Matthew M. Bogert (5th gen.), born November 6, 1779, died March 30, 1871, married May 9, 1801, Willempie Haring, born March 28, 1783, died July 25, 1859. Matthew M. (5) was also a farmer and resided on the homestead occupied by his ancestors at Closter. His children of the sixth generation were Sally, Jane, Margaret, Maria, and Jacob M.

Jacob M. Bogert (6th gen.), born at Closter, N. J., May 15, 1819, died March 18, 1874, married, November 30, 1842, Maria Haring, born in 1823. She survives him and resides in Hackensack. He was a farmer by occupation. Their children of the seventh generation were Henry Ver Valen (deceased), Matthew J., Cornelia, Sarah Jane, Leah, and Huyler.

Matthew J. Bogert (7th gen.), the subject of this sketch, born at Closter, N. J., May 1, 1846, was educated in the public schools at Closter and worked on his father's farm until 1864, when he became a clerk in the wholesale store of Pangborn & Bronner in New York City. Later he became a bookkeeper in the hardware house of H. Carter & Son. May 22, 1873, he married Miss Mary A. Hopper, daughter of James G. Hopper, of Etna, N. J. In 1874 he embarked in the business of wood-turning in Pearl Street, New York. This he made a success, and with his partner, Abraham J. Hopper, now conducts an extensive business in William Street, New York, with mills at Kingsfield, Me. Mr. Bogert is an active, energetic, and thoroughly practical business man. Though an active Republican, with the exception of being Postmaster at Demarest, N. J., since 1892, he has never held any really political office. He has for several years been a member of the School Board of Harrington Township, and for twelve years has been a Director and Treasurer of the Harrington Building and Loan Association, which he helped to organize. He is prominent and active in religious work. He is now an Elder and has during several years held other offices in the Reformed Church at Closter, and for thirteen years has been Superintendent of the Sunday School of that church. His living children of the eighth generation are Jessie (married in 1900 Frederick W. Mattocks, a New York lawyer), Virgil (now associated with his father in business), and Clarence, who has just entered Princeton University.

JOHN M. BOGERT is descended from the same common ancestor as Matthew J. Bogert, whose genealogy has been given. Peter M. Bogert, of the fourth generation from Jan Louwe Bougaerdt and son of Matthew P. Bogert (3d gen.), was born at Closter, April 12, 1736, died there 1809, married November 22, 1759, Rachel Banta, born 1740. He was a plain farmer and resided near Closter on part of the lands which his father had bought. He also purchased other lands adjoining them. His children of the fifth generation were Margaret, Mary Ann, Matthew P., Seba, Sophia, Samuel, and Margaret. His uncle, Peter Bogert, resided and was one of the earliest settlers west of the Hackensack in Washington Township. He was born in 1705 and died in 1786. He was a man of wealth, a Judge of the Bergen County Common Pleas, and held many other offices.

Seba Bogert (5th gen.), born at Closter, March 25, 1774, died April 27, 1846, married Sarah Blackledge, born May 20, 1776, died December 20, 1811. Seba was a farmer and resided all his days at Closter. His children of the sixth generation were Peter S., Benjamin S., Matthew S., Samuel S., Henry S., Jacob S., Peter S., and Rachel.

Matthew S. Bogert (6th gen.), born at Closter, April 9, 1799, died October 23, 1874, married January 31, 1824, Maria Kipp, who died March 2, 1833. He married (2) November 13, 1833, Margaret Christie, widow, born October 27, 1794, died September 18, 1874. Matthew S. Bogert was a farmer, but was active in township affairs. His children of the seventh generation were Seba M. (now a Wall Street broker), Eliza, Sally, Catharine, David (a soldier in the Union army who died in the service), John M., and Samuel M., who served as a Union soldier and died April 5, 1871.

John M. Bogert (7), the subject of this sketch, was born at Closter, N. J., August 6, 1839. He was reared on his father's farm, where he imbibed a great liking for horses, which he still entertains. His business is farming and training horses for speed. He married, June 5, 1858, Jane Bogert, a daughter of John J. Bogert, born August 26, 1839. Upon his father's death he succeeded to the ownership of the old homestead at Closter, where he now resides. They have had seven children of the eight generation, to wit: Margaret (died), David, Clark, Morton, Emma (died), Mabel (died), and Elmer.

David Bogert (8th gen.) married in 1885 and has issue four children of the ninth generation, and Morton has one child.

GARRET A. HARING.—The City of Hoorn is located on a small arm of the Zuyder Zee in Holland. It is now a place of little importance, but from the beginning of the fifteenth to the seventeenth century it was a city of considerable magnitude and trade. During the Spanish wars it was sufficiently so to be fortified and stubbornly defended by the Spanish under Admiral De Bossu. It glories in being the birthplace of William Schouten, who in 1616 first doubled the southmost cape of South America, which he named after his birthplace, Cape Horn. Abel Jansen Tasman, who discovered Van Dieman's Land and New Zeeland, was also a native of Hoorn. Back from the city the land is low but fertile, adapted to grazing and dairy purposes. Manufacturing and shipbuilding were, two centuries ago, extensively carried on there. It was at Hoorn that the great fleet of Admiral De Ruyter was built. But the most extensive of its varied interests were its herring fisheries, which were numerous and of great value, employing large numbers of men.

Among the families residing at Hoorn were the Harings. The name is mentioned on the pages of history as far back as 1573, and when the Dutch were defeated at the battle of Diemark, in that year, it is related of one John Haring, of Hoorn, that he stood with sword and helmet, on a narrow part of the dyke, and singly by miracles of valor kept back a thousand Spaniards, until his comrades had made their retreat. Then plunging into the sea, he escaped unhurt. Not long afterward, in a sea fight, he climbed on board the great Spanish ship "The Inquisitor" and hauled down her flaunting colors and was fatally pierced by a bullet. Among his descendants Pieter Jansen Haring (1) is said to have been a native of Newenhuysen in Holland, where he was born in 1610, and from whence he removed to Hoorn. His third son, Jan Pietersen Haring (2), one of a large family, was born at Hoorn, December 26, 1633. He emigrated to America in 1660, and on Whitsuntide in 1662 became the second husband of a young widow named Margaretta Cozine, born in Haarlem, Holland, in 1634. This was the first marriage in the Dutch Church, on the farm called the Bowery, which church was situated where now stands St. Mark's Church, corner of East Eleventh Street and Second Avenue, in New York.

John Pietersen Haring purchased and resided until his death (December 7, 1683) on a farm of 100 acres, which extended from the Bowery Lane westward to and beyond Bedford Street, including both sides of Broadway, from Waverly Place to Bleecker Street. His descendants continued for more than a century to own portions of it. John Pietersen Haring (2) had children of the third generation Peter, Cozine, Cornelius, Abraham, Brechie, Vroutie, and Maretie. All of these with their mother, Margaretta Cozine, removed to Tappan in 1686. The widow had previously (February 2, 1685) taken a third husband in the person of Daniel de Clark, by whom she left no issue. John Pietersen Haring's children all married and settled at or near Tappan on the Tappan patent, of which two of the sons were joint purchasers with de Clark, the Blawvelts, Smiths, and others, in 1686. They all reared large families. Peter, Cozine, Cornelius, and Abraham settled within the limits of Harrington Township in Bergen County, N. J., where their descendants are very numerous. The township received its name from the family in 1775. Garret A. Haring, the subject of this sketch, is descended in the seventh generation from John Pietersen Haring, the first American ancestor. The line of descent is as follows: (1) John Pietersen Haring and Margaretta Cozine, (2) Cozine Johns Haring and Margaretta Garrets Blawvelt, (3) John Cosines Haring and Aeltje Van Dolsen, (4) Garret Johns Haring and Cornelia Lent, (5) Abram Garrets Haring and Elizabeth Blawvelt, (6) Garret Abrams Haring and Maria Smith, (7) Abram Garrets Haring and Charity Johnson, and (8) Garret Abrams Haring and Lavina Van Houten.

Rev. Garret Abram Haring, for many years the beloved pastor of the True Reformed Church of Schraalenburgh, Bergen County, is one of the oldest and best known clergymen in Eastern New Jersey. His great-grandfather, Abram G. Haring, born May 18, 1755, settled in Tappan, N. J., and followed agricultural pursuits. By his wife, Elizabeth Blawvelt, also of Holland descent, he had a son, Garret A. Haring, who was born March 22, 1781, and who was the grandfather of the subject of this sketch. This Garret A. Haring settled in Ramapo, Rockland County, N. Y., and spent his active life as a farmer and miller, dying December 12, 1869. He married Maria Smith and had two children: Abram G. and Hetty (Mrs. Albert J. Terhune). Abram G. Haring was born on the homestead in Rockland County on the 16th of July, 1803, and was also a farmer, succeeding his father in the management and ownership of the family estate. He married Charity Johnson, of Ramapo, and had two sons: Rev. Garret A. and John J. Mr. Haring died March 12, 1864, after a career which equaled in usefulness and prominence that of his honored father, who survived him nearly six years.

Rev. Garret A. Haring, eldest son of Abram G. and Charity (Johnson) Haring, was born on the family homestead in Ramapo, Rockland County, N. Y., on the 18th of November, 1829. There he also spent his early life, acquiring in the district schools the rudiments of an education and following various business pursuits. But he was not destined for a mercantile nor an agricultural life. His tastes were scholarly; his inclinations were for a profession. And with this end in view he took up the study of theology. Having thoroughly fitted himself for the ministry, Mr. Haring received a call and was duly ordained pastor of the True Reformed Church of Schraalenburgh, Bergen County, and in that capacity has labored ever since. Under his pastorate, which covers a generation, the church has grown and prospered until now it is one of the largest in that locality.

Mr. Haring is a man of broad scholarly attainments, of noble and generous impulses, and universally esteemed and respected, not only for his learning and culture, but also for those affectionate and sympathetic qualities which make him so popular among all denominations. He has always interested himself in the affairs of the community, and is an ardent advocate of every movement and project which has the welfare of the people at heart. He is a Democrat in politics, a friend of education, and a benevolent, patriotic, public spirited citizen.

January 1, 1851, Mr. Haring married Miss Lavina Van Houten. They have three daughters: Melissa, Ellen H., and Anna Naomi.

ALBERT ZABRISKIE HARING is a lineal descendant of Jan Pietersen Haring, the first emigrant of the name (see sketch on page 61). Cornelius Jansen Haring (2) (the third of the children of Jan Pietersen Haring (1) and Margaretta Cozine), born in New York in 1672, married, in 1693, Catalyntie, daughter of Judge Matthew Flearboom, of Albany, N. Y. Cornelius removed to Tappan, N. Y., with other members of the family, in 1686, and in 1721, when the Tappan patented lands were divided, he received as his portion a large tract in Harrington Township, on both sides of the Tappan road and extending east of that road as far as what is now Northvale. He subsequently bought of Samuel Des Marest (2) a farm of several hundred acres near what is now Haworth, N. J., on which he erected his family mansion and resided until his death. Much of this farm remained in the ownership of his descendants up to twenty years ago. His seven children of the third generation were John C., Margaret, Sophia, Vroutie, Daniel C., Cornelius C., and Jacob C.

Of these seven children, Cornelius C. Haring (3) married, in 1710, Rensie Blawvelt, and dying left eight children of the fourth generation: Caroline, Abraham J., Cornelius C., Margaret, Maria, Elizabeth, John C., and Sophia.

Abraham Johns Haring (4) married Elizabeth Mabie. He bought and settled on a large farm just north of what is now called West Norwood, in Bergen County. This farm had formerly belonged to his grandfather, Cornelius Haring (2). He left three children: John A., born in March, 1751 (died); Peter A.; and John A. (2), born April 9, 1762. Of these Peter A. resided on his father's farm until his death.

Peter Abrams Haring (5), born at Norwood, N. J., April 16, 1754, married Maria Blawvelt, by whom he had two children of the sixth generation: Elizabeth, born January 20, 1773 (married Abraham A. Blawvelt), and David P.

David Peters Haring (6), born May 27, 1775, married Lydia Zabriskie, and lived all his lifetime on a portion of his grandfather's farm near West Norwood. His children of the seventh generation were Margaret (died), Lavina (married John Tallman), and Peter D.

Peter D. Haring (7) married Betsey Bogert, and had issue of the eighth generation David P. (married Catharine Bross), Samuel B. (married Letty Blawvelt), Albert Z., Newton (died), Ann Maria (married Isaac Onderdonk), and James (married Jane Van Houten).

Albert Zabriskie Haring, the subject of this sketch, was born near Norwood, N. J., December 21, 1846. He attended the common schools of Bergen County until fourteen years of age, and then became a clerk in the grocery business, which occupation he followed for a number of years. In 1871 he entered as a clerk the Hudson County National Bank of Jersey City, then under the management of John Armstrong, John Van Vorst, and Hon. A. A. Hardenburgh. He has been in the bank for twenty-nine years, has occupied various positions in it, and for the past twelve years has been its Paying Teller.

He married in 1866 Jemima, the daughter of the late Senator Ralph S. Demarest, and has two children of the ninth generation: Chauncey and Minnie C. The latter is married and has issue of the tenth generation, Clarisse, born in 1900. He has a summer residence at Demarest, N. J.

ELMER WILSON DEMAREST is a direct descendant of Jean des Marest (1), a prominent citizen and resident of Beauchamp in the Province of Picardy, France. There, about 1620, was born his son, David des Marest (2), who, upon reaching manhood, espoused the Protestant faith and fled to Holland to escape persecution, locating at Middleburgh on the Island of Walcheron in Zeeland. Here, on July 24, 1643, David married Maria, a daughter of François Sohier, of Nieppe, a town in Hainault. The couple resided at Middleburgh until 1651, when they removed to Manheim on the Rhine River, in the lower Palatinate, then under the protection of the Elector Charles Lewis. At Manheim, the Protestants were already being threatened by the Catholic princes, and David des Marest, with others of a like religious faith, determined to go to America for safety. Accordingly, early in the spring of 1663 they journeyed down the Rhine to Amsterdam, where they embarked for New Amsterdam on the ship "Spotted Cow," reaching the latter port on April 16, 1663. Des Marest first went with his wife and three sons to Staten Island, where they joined the Huguenot settlement, recently started. The following year he was elected to represent the settlement in the provincial assembly. The savages proving troublesome, Demarest bought and located on lands at New Harlem, then a name applied to the upper end of Manhattan Island. Here he prospered, acquired several town lots, and became prominent in town affairs. In 1677, a tax having been levied on him for the support of the Dutch Church at Harlem, he refused to pay it, claiming immunity therefrom because he was neither an attendant nor a communicant of the Dutch Church. The "powers that be" sued him for the tax, procured judgment, and proceeded by execution and levy to collect it. This angered Demarest and he determined to leave Harlem. On the 8th of June, 1677, he purchased from the Hack-

ELMER W. DEMAREST.

ensack and Tappan Indians a large tract (estimated at about 6,000 acres) of land on the east bank of the Hackensack River, extending northward from New Bridge. By subsequent purchase he added an extensive tract west of the Hackensack, on which he built two mills. He built his family residence at what is now Old Bridge and erected a French Church on the east side of the river, a little west of the Schraalenburgh road. The lands he purchased were claimed by several white persons and by the savages. Some of these claims were not extinguished until after his death. He died in New York City in 1693, leaving a will by which he devised all his lands to his two surviving sons, John and Samuel, and to his very numerous grandchildren.

David des Marest, Jr. (3), the second of the emigrant's sons, died in 1691, before the decease of his father. At the time of his death he was residing east of the Hackensack on part of his father's original patent near Schraalenburgh. He was born at Manheim in the lower Palatinate in 1652, and married, April 4, 1675, Rachel, daughter of Pierre Crasson, a French refugee. His occupation was that of a farmer. He had twelve children: David, Peter, Susanna, Rachel, Jacobus D., Samuel, Mary, Daniel, Benjamin, Jacomina, Lea, and Lydia.

Jacobus Davids des Marest (4), the fifth of these, baptized at New York October 3, 1681, married (1) Lea De Groot and (2) Margaretta Cozine Haring. Farming was his principal occupation and he held several township offices. He resided in the Schraalenburgh district and left at his death twelve children, of whom Garret Jacobse Demarest (5), born at Schraalenburgh, June 30, 1725, died there December 17, 1798, married, in 1747, Jacomina (Tunis) Helms. They resided at Schraalenburgh, where Garret pursued the calling of a farmer. His issue were fifteen children, of whom Abraham Garrets Demarest (6) was born at Schraalenburgh March 15, 1767, and died there March 18, 1860. He married Margaret Demarest, a relative, born December 3, 1761, died May 16, 1832. Abraham was a farmer and left three children: Garret A., John A., and James A.

John A. Demarest (7), born April 11, 1798, died May 23, 1864, married, in 1818, Jane, daughter of Peter Merseles, born March 3, 1803, died September 22, 1888. He purchased and resided, at the time of his death, on lands at what is now Eastwood, N. J., where, on his death, he left two children: Margaretta J., wife of Albert Z. Ackerman, and Abraham J. Demarest. He was a cattle dealer, purchasing cattle in the west and selling them in New York, under the firm name of Demarest & Grant. He also conducted an importing house of willowware, etc., in New York, and a country grocery store on the farm at Eastwood.

Abraham J. Demarest (8), born at Eastwood, N. J., April 30, 1840, married, May 18, 1859, Eliza W., daughter of Jacob G. H. Lozier, of Teaneck, now Englewood. She was a descendant of Peter Wilson, a Scotchman, who held the degree of Doctor of Laws, and was for some time a member of the faculty of Columbia College, New York. Abraham J. followed farming until his father's death, when he removed to Closter, N. J., where he conducted a meat market until 1892, when he retired from business and is now residing at Bayonne, N. J. He has had three children: Nettie Marcelia, married Horace Roberson, a lawyer, at Bayonne; Edwin S., died; and Elmer Wilson, the subject of this sketch.

Elmer Wilson Demarest (9) was born at Eastwood, N. J., May 15, 1870. He was educated in the public schools of Closter, N. J., the Rutgers Preparatory School, Rutgers College, and Columbia Law College, graduating from the last named institution as a Bachelor of Laws in 1892. He was admitted to the New Jersey bar as an attorney in February, 1892, and as a counselor in June, 1895, and to practice in the United States Courts in January, 1897. Since his admission he has practiced law in Bayonne and Jersey City, and has been successful in litigations, having conducted a number of important cases. He is counsel for a number of corporations.

He not only stands high in his profession, but is also prominent as a Republican leader, having always affiliated with the Republican party. He has shown great activity in this connection. In 1892 he was a member of the Bergen County Republican Executive Committee. He has been a member and Vice-President of the Hudson County Republican Committee from 1893 to the present time. He is also a Trustee and a member of the Executive Committee of that organization. In 1897 he was elected to the New Jersey House of Assembly, was prominently connected with the equal taxation measure of that year, and conducted the fight in the House for the Voorhees Judiciary Constitutional amendments. He is a member of the New Jersey Athletic Club of Bayonne, of the Newark Bay Boat Club of Bayonne, and of the Palma Club of Jersey City.

On September 9, 1896, Mr. Demarest married Miss Blanche Adeline Bristow, of Bayonne, and they have one child, Kenneth E. Demarest (10), born August 14, 1897.

GARRET I. DEMAREST is descended from the same common ancestor as is Elmer Wilson Demarest (see sketch on page 64). David des Marest, the first American emigrant of the name, had a great-grandson, Garret Jacobus des Marest (5), who married Jacomyntie Tunis Helms, and had fifteen children. One of these, John G. Demarest (6), was born at Schraalenburgh, January 23, 1771, and died there November 6, 1834. He married Catharine Blawvelt, who died May 4, 1849, aged seventy-one years eleven months. John G. was a farmer and had issue ten children, of whom John J. Demarest (7), born at Schraalenburgh, N. J., November 1, 1824, married Elizabeth, a daughter of Weirt Banta and Margaret Demarest. John G. Demarest was a farmer and resided near the North Church at Schraalenburgh. He left two children, Garret I. and Margaret.

Garret I. Demarest (8), the subject of this sketch, was born at Schraalenburgh May 25, 1828. He is a prominent farmer and resides in the Borough of Dumont on part of the farm originally owned by his French ancestor. All of his long line of ancestors, both paternal and maternal, have been honored citizens of Bergen County, active and influential in local affairs of both church and State.

Mr. Demarest was educated in the public schools of Schraalenburgh, which he attended until he reached the age of sixteen. Since that time he has devoted his energies to the conduct of the old family homestead. He succeeded his father on the farm, and through his integrity, industry, and sound judgment has achieved marked success. Having been born and reared on the place he has always occupied and now owns, he has imbibed the associations and traditions which have descended to him from an honorable ancestry, and from the first has improved and beautified the home so dear to him and his family by reason of these ancestral connections. His patriotism is attested by his service of nine months in the Civil War as a sergeant in the Twenty-second Regiment New Jersey Volunteers. He was for one year a member of the Town Council, is a member of the North

Reformed Church of Schraalenburgh, and enjoys the confidence and respect of his fellowmen.

Mr. Demarest married Miss Catherine Demarest, a member of another branch of the Bergen County Demarests. They have had three daughters of the ninth generation from their original French ancestor.

DAVID DEMAREST is another of the lineal descendants of David des Marest and his wife, Maria Sohier, who came to America in 1662 (see sketch on page 64). The emigrant had a great-grandson, David Demarest, who resided at Schraalenburgh more than a hundred years ago. This last named David had several children, one of whom was James D. Demarest (6), born at Schraalenburgh March 2, 1763, died there April 28, 1830. His wife Rachel, born July 28, 1768, died April 26, 1828. James D. was a farmer residing at Schraalenburgh. One of his several children was Abraham J. Demarest (7), who married Rachel Blawvelt, daughter of David Blawvelt. They lived at Schraalenburgh. Both of them have been dead several years. Among their children was David Demarest.

David Demarest (8), the subject of this sketch, was born at Schraalenburgh (now Dumont) February 1, 1832. He owns and resides on part of the farm which his French ancestor owned two hundred and twenty-three years ago. This tract has passed from father to son in an unbroken line for more than two centuries. In a barn on the premises is a beam which was first used in a barn on the same farm in 1721. Mr. Demarest was educated in the public schools of the county. At the age of seventeen he ceased studying books and took charge of the old family homestead, which he has ever since conducted. During the War of the Rebellion he served nine months as a private in the Twenty-second Regiment New Jersey Volunteers, being honorably discharged at the end of his term of enlistment. Mr. Demarest is regarded as one of the best and most substantial farmers in Bergen County, where he has spent his entire life. He is deeply interested in public affairs, active and prompt in the support of all worthy objects, prominently identified with the welfare of the community, and thoroughly alive to the needs of his fellow citizens. As a member of the North Reformed Church of Schraalenburgh he has been influential in promoting various moral and intellectual movements which have contributed materially to the general welfare.

In early life Mr. Demarest married Christina de Baun, who died May 11, 1895. They were the parents of five children—four daughters and a son—of the ninth generation.

EDMUND W. KINGSLAND, President of the Provident Institution for Savings of Jersey City and one of the ablest and best known financiers in Eastern New Jersey, was born in Jersey City on the 15th of December, 1839, his parents being Edmund W. and Sarah A. Kingsland. He is a direct descendant in the sixth generation from Isaac Kingsland, an Englishman from the Parish of Christ Church, on the Island of Barbadoes, W. I., and a nephew of Major Nathaniel Kingsland, of the same place. On July 4, 1668, one Captain William Sandford, also of Barbadoes, W. I., purchased of the Hackensack Indians a tract of land between the Hackensack and Passaic Rivers, extending "northward about seven miles." This purchase was made in the interest of Major Kingsland. On June 1, 1671, the Major conveyed the south half of this to Sandford and kept the north half after extinguishing the Indian title. By the Major's will, dated March 14, 1685, he gave one-third of his New Jersey lands—about 3,402 acres—to his nephew Isaac. Isaac's residence was at Kingsland Manor near Rutherford in Bergen County. His descendants are still numerous in both Bergen and Hudson Counties. The name of his wife does not appear.

Edmund W. Kingsland received his early educational training under the tutorship of the late William Leverett Dickenson, and subsequently attended the New York Polytechnical School, from which he was graduated with honor in the class of 1856. After completing his studies, which were designed to fit him for the practical affairs of life, he accepted a clerkship in the wholesale notion house of Lyman Cook & Co., of New York City, and remained with them until 1863, gaining a broad and accurate knowledge of business matters as well as the entire confidence and respect of his employers.

In 1863 Mr. Kingsland resigned his position as clerk for Lyman Cook & Co. and was made general clerk of the Provident Institution for Savings in Jersey City. There he soon gained recognition for those abilities which have ever since characterized his business life and which have long made him a powerful factor in local financial circles. He gradually rose by promotion and in 1888 was elected Secretary and Treasurer, which positions he filled with great energy and satisfaction until July 20, 1896, when he was elected President. In this capacity he has maintained and in a large measure increased the prestige and substantial character of the Provident Institution for Savings, making it one of the soundest and best known fiduciary concerns in Eastern New Jersey.

Mr. Kingsland is one of the leading citizens of Jersey City, where he has spent his entire life. He is public spirited, progressive, and enterprising, thoroughly identified with every project which promises advancement to the community, and generously encourages those movements that have the welfare of the place at heart. He is a member of the Union League Club of Jersey City, a man of broad and accurate learning, and universally respected and esteemed. In 1877 he married Miss Justine Bayard Blackwell, of New York City, and of their five children two are living.

DAVID D. BLAWVELT.—After the Demarests and Harings, the Blawvelts are the most numerous of the families that settled the northern part of Bergen County. On the east bank of the River Yssel, in the Province of Overyssel, in Holland, nestles the by no means sleepy town of Deventer—the birthplace of the great Gronovios and the still greater Groote,—a town of iron foundries and carpet manufactories, famous for its "honeycakes,"—a species of gingerbread, tons of which are annually shipped to different parts of the kingdom. The Valley of the Yssel, traversed as it is by numerous tributaries to the river, is exceedingly fertile, and the lands about Deventer are among the most productive of any in Holland. Near Deventer, in 1623, was born of well-to-do Dutch parents one Garret Hendricksen, who, as a youth, is said to have been possessed of a restless spirit. In 1644 he tired of agricultural pursuits, left the paternal fold, and found his way to America, landing, as all emigrants in those days did, at New Amsterdam. Two years later he married Mary, the eldest daughter of Lambert Moll, a native of Berne, who had emigrated to America a few years earlier and was then domiciled at Bushwick, L. I. Garret Hendricksen and his wife, Mary Moll, lived and died in New Amsterdam, having had thirteen children, most of whom adopted the surname of Blawvelt (Blue-Field), in memory, it is said, of the blue hills about Deventer. Of Garret Hendricksen's sons, Hybert, John, Abraham, and Isaac Blawvelt were destined to transplant the name in Bergen County, principally in Harrington and Washington Townships. Hybert and John (2) joined in the purchase of the Tappan patent, in 1686, and in 1689, with others of the family, became members of the Tappan settlement. Hybert married, April 15, 1679, Wellempie Ariense, a sister of one of his co-patentees, and located in Harrington Township on the Tappan road, just north of what was once known as the "Old Jug" tavern. His brother Abraham (2) settled on the west side of the road leading along the run north of the mill, late of Peter A. Demarest. Isaac and another brother settled on a large tract on which are now the residences of John R. Herring and others. Like the Demarests and Harings, though not to such an extent, the Blawvelts had much to do with the administration of civil, military, and religious affairs of Bergen County.

David D. Blawvelt is of the sixth generation in direct line from Garret Hendricksen, the emigrant. He was born at Tappan, Bergen County, November 17, 1819, and is a son of David C. Blawvelt (who was born February 10, 1773, died January 30, 1835, married Maria Demarest, born April 12, 1770, died May 13, 1843), a grandson of Cornelius Blawvelt (born January 9, 1744, died January 11, 1832), who also married a Demarest. His father had six children—four sons and two daughters: one daughter died in 1824, aged nineteen; the other July 6, 1887, aged eighty-eight; James D. Blawvelt died in 1891, at the age of ninety; Cornelius D. died aged eighty-two; and John D. is still living at the age of eighty-four. Educated in the public schools of his native county and reared amid scenes of ancestral associations and agricultural activity, Mr. Blawvelt started, at the early age of sixteen, to learn the trade of cabinet making, which he followed successfully for fourteen years, gaining in the business a wide and honorable reputation. But this was not to be his life work. The influences and surroundings of his youth drew him back to rural pursuits, and since 1853 he has been actively engaged in farming in Schraalenburgh. When the War of the Rebellion broke out Mr. Blawvelt enlisted in the Union cause, becoming first sergeant of Company C, Twenty-second Regiment New Jersey Volunteers. He served nine months, returned with an honorable discharge, and resumed his labors on the farm.

In public life Mr. Blawvelt has rendered valuable service to his town and fellow citizens. He was surveyor of township roads for a number of years, one of the Township Committee for three years, a member of the Bergen County Board of Chosen Freeholders for four years, Town Assessor for six years, and a member of the Town Council for three years. In each of these capacities he displayed eminent ability, sound judgment, and great sagacity. He has been a consistent member of the Dutch Reformed Church since April, 1860.

Mr. Blawvelt has been married fifty-eight years, his wife's maiden name being Elizabeth Quackenbush. They have had eight children, seven of whom—four sons and four daughters—are living. They also have thirty-four grandchildren and four great-grandchildren. Mr. Blawvelt inherited and early developed the sturdy characteristics of his race, and, emulating his ancestors' worthy lives, has instilled into the minds of his descendants those qualities of head and heart which have served him so well, and which have won for him the confidence and respect of the entire community.

GILBERT COLLINS, a Justice of the Supreme Court of New Jersey, was born in Stonington, New London County, Conn., August 26, 1846, and is a descendant of an old English family which originally came from Kent, England. His great-great-grandparents were Daniel Collins and Alice Pell. His great-grandfather, Daniel Collins (1732-1819), of Stonington, served in the Revolutionary War, and according to existing records was First Lieutenant in the First Regiment Connecticut line, formation of 1777, and it is also known that he was in service from 1775. He married Anne Potter. His son Gilbert (1789-1865), grandfather of the present Gilbert Collins, served several terms in the Connecticut Legislature. His wife was Prudence Frink. Judge Collins's father, Daniel Prentice Collins (born in 1813, died in 1862), was a manufacturer in Stonington throughout his life; he also had business relations in Jersey City, and on this account his son eventually made choice of that city as his field of labor and his home. His mother, Sarah R., was a descendant of the Wells family, of Connecticut.

GILBERT COLLINS.

Judge Collins was prepared for Yale College, but the death of his father and the involved state in which his financial affairs were left rendered the completion of his course there impracticable. The family, which consisted of his mother and one sister, removed to Jersey City, N. J., in 1863, and in 1865 he there entered the law office of Jonathan Dixon, now a Justice of the Supreme Court of New Jersey. He was admitted to the bar as an attorney in February, 1869, and as a counselor in February, 1872. On January 1, 1870, he became a partner of Mr. Dixon and continued in that relationship until that gentleman was elevated to the bench in April, 1875. He afterward formed a partnership with Charles L. Corbin. In 1881 William H. Corbin was admitted as a member of the firm, which continued under the style of Collins & Corbin till March 8, 1897, when Mr. Collins was appointed a Justice of the Supreme Court of New Jersey, which position he still holds, having recently been assigned to the Hudson circuit.

His jury practice was the largest in his county, and probably was not exceeded by that of any one in the State. He was counsel for the Hudson County National Bank, of which he was a Director; counsel for the New Jersey Title Guarantee and Trust Company, of which he was one of the founders and active promoters; and local counsel for the Lehigh Valley Railroad Company.

Judge Collins is, in politics, a Republican; he has been nominated by his party for State Senator (1880) once and for Congress twice (1882 and 1888). For two years, from May, 1884, to May, 1886, he served as Mayor of Jersey City, having been elected by a combination of an independent organization of citizens with the Republicans. For five years previous to 1893 he served as Chairman of the Republican County Committee, when he declined a re-election.

June 2, 1870, he was married to Harriet Kingsbury Bush. Of their six children, a son and two daughters survive. Their son, Walter Collins, was graduated with honors from Williams College, and is now practicing law in Jersey City. Judge Collins is a member of the Union League and Palma Clubs of Jersey City, and one of the Board of Managers of the New Jersey Society of the Sons of the Revolution.

JACOB H. HOPPER.—The Hopper family, it is said, started in France. They spelled the name Hoppe, and finally changed it to Hopper. Some of them went to Holland during times of religious persecution. It is known that Andries (Andrew) Hopper came to America from Amsterdam, Holland, with a wife (and, perhaps, two or three children), as early as 1653, and located in the City of New Amsterdam. The name of his wife does not appear in the New Jersey records. After their arrival the couple had three children born to them: William in 1654, Hendrick in 1656, and Matthew in 1658.

Of the three last named children William (2) married Mynen Paulus and had issue three children: Christina, Gertrude, and Belitie (Bridget), all born in New Amsterdam. William's two brothers, Hendrick (2) and Matthew (2), went to Bergen (Jersey City) in 1680. There, on March 14, of the same year, Hendrick (2) married Mary Johns Van Blarkum, a daughter of the American emigrant of that name, and April 15, 1683, Matthew (2) married Ann Peterse, afterward called Antje Jorckse. It does not appear that Hendrick and Matthew purchased lands in Bergen. They probably lived on leased lands while there. William (2) went to Hackensack in 1686, where he joined the Dutch Church in March of that year. His brothers Hendrick (2) and Matthew (2) went to Hackensack the following year. William (2) had a child, Andrew, baptized at Hackensack in March, 1686, shortly after his arrival. Nothing more is said of William (2), and the inference is that he died soon after. Hendrick (2) and Matthew (2), soon after their arrival, each purchased from Captain John Berry a farm of between two and three hundred acres at Hackensack (partly in the present village), and extending from the Hackensack River to the Saddle River. Each of them settled and built on his farm, where they remained until their deaths. Both were farmers, but took an active part in town and church matters. Matthew was a deacon of the "Church on the Green" in 1705.

Matthew's children (of the third generation) were Andrew, born in 1684, at Jersey City, married Elizabeth Bross; Christina, born in 1686 (married John Huysman); Lea, born in 1695 (married John Vanderhoff, of Albany); Rachel, born in 1703 (twice married); and John, born in 1705 (married

Elizabeth Kipp). All except Andrew were born at Hackensack. Hendrick's children of the third generation were Andrew, born in 1681 (married Abigail Ackerman); John, born in 1682 (married Rachel Terhune); William, born in 1684; Catharine, born in 1685 (married Peter Garretse Van Allen, of Rotterdam, Holland); Garret, born in 1696; Gertrude, born in 1699 (married Hendrick Alberts Zabriskie); and Lea (married Christian Alberts Zabriskie).

Many of these, with their children, removed to Paramus and scattered through Saddle River, Ridgewood, and Midland Townships, where their descendants are to-day numerous. Members of the family have represented Bergen County in both houses of the Legislature; others have worn the judicial ermine with dignity and respectability; still others have held from time to time county and township offices, and have become famous as physicians, clergymen, lawyers, mayors of cities, publicists, mechanics, sailors, soldiers, and agriculturists.

Jacob H. Hopper, the subject of this sketch, is a lineal descendant of Andrew Hopper, the first emigrant of the name. He is a son of John Hopper and Elizabeth (Goetchius) Hopper, and was born at Saddle River, in Bergen County, August 6, 1823. Having received a fair common school education in the schools of his native county, he acquired while quite young the trade of harness-making, which he followed successfully at Hackensack until 1880, when he was made superintendent of the cemetery in that village. He still holds this position, having filled it with great ability and fidelity during the last twenty years. Mr. Hopper has also been a prominent figure in public affairs. He was Town Collector of Hackensack for three years and a Justice of the Peace for ten years, and has served as a member of the Town Committee. For forty-nine years he has been a leading member and one of the chief supporters of the Hackensack Christian Reformed Church. The ability, faithfulness, and integrity with which he has discharged every trust, and the active interest he has taken in the progress and welfare of his town and county, have won for him great respect and the confidence of all who enjoy his acquaintance. He is public spirited, enterprising, and patriotic, and a liberal, progressive citizen, whose energies have been directed toward useful and charitable ends.

He married Lydia Bogert, a descendant of one of the old Bergen County families, and their children are Ann Elizabeth, John Henry, and Martha Amelia Hopper.

JOHN H. POST.—Captain Adriaen Post first came to America from Harlengen, Holland, about 1653, as agent or manager of Baron Van der Cappellan's colony on Staten Island. Upon the destruction of that colony by the savages early in 1655, Mr. Post fled to Bergen (Jersey City), whence, in September following, he, with his wife, five children, two servants, and one girl, were taken prisoners by the savages at what is known as the second massacre at Pavonia. The family escaped by the payment of a heavy ransom, and Post was thereupon dispatched by the Bergen colonists to treat with the sachems of the Hackensack tribes for a release of other prisoners. After his return from a successful performance of this duty he settled at Bergen and eventually became one of the most active and influential members of the struggling colony. Having had some military experience in Holland, the Bergen colonists appointed him Ensign of the militia September 6, 1665. On May 12, 1668, he bought from Governor Philip Carteret lots Nos. 35, 55, 117, 100, and 164, of the Bergen common

C B Harney

lands, containing in all about 165 acres. He built and resided on lot 164, containing fifty-five acres. On June 10, 1673, he was elected to represent the Town of Bergen in the provincial assembly, where he acquitted himself with distinction. On July 19, 1672, he was appointed Prison Keeper for East Jersey, and was the first person to hold that position. "Captain Post," by which official title he always went, died at Bergen in February, 1677. His wife's name is not mentioned. He left a large family. He was the ancestor of all the Posts in Bergen and Hudson Counties. He resided in the town on lot No. 164. His children were Adriaen, William, Elias, Margaretta, Francis, and Gertrude. Adriaen (2) became one of the patentees of the Aquackanonck patent. The latter's two sons, Adriaen and Abraham (3), came to Bergen County in 1735, and married respectively Hendricke Ackerman and Rachel Hertie. Abraham located on the upper Saddle River, purchasing lands of Hendrick Vandelinda.

John H. Post, the subject of this sketch, is descended in the seventh generation from Captain Adriaen Post. His paternal grandfather, Henry Post, a farmer, was born in the western part of the county, but died in Secaucus, where his son, Adriaen Post, the father of John H., was born in 1818. Adriaen Post was a farmer in New Durham and Secaucus, and died in the latter place March 15, 1896, in his seventy-eighth year. His wife, Mary Van Giesen, daughter of Garret Van Giesen, died December, 31, 1891, aged seventy-two. Her family was also a very early one in Hudson County, and like the Posts was of Holland Dutch descent. Mr. and Mrs. Adrian Post had five children, namely: Henry, Leah Ann, John H., Adrian, Jr., and one who died in infancy.

John H. Post was born in New Durham, Hudson County, October 7, 1844, but has spent most of his life on a part of the old family homestead on the Paterson plank road in Secaucus. He received a thorough education, attending the public schools of Secaucus, Union Hill, and Bergen Point, and a boarding school at Deckertown, N. J., and since completing his studies has devoted himself to agricultural pursuits. Mr. Post is one of the best farmers in Hudson County, and has been eminently successful. He has always taken a deep interest in public affairs, and, though never aspiring to office, has served three years as a school trustee and three years as district clerk. With these exceptions he has declined political or public preferment. In politics he is a consistent Republican, and in a quiet way has rendered efficient service to his party. He is a progressive, patriotic citizen, honored and respected, and enjoys the confidence of the entire community.

Mr. Post was married April 6, 1868, to Fredericka Huber, daughter of Frederick Huber, of Secaucus. They have four children: Adrian, Christina, William H., and Walter.

CORNELIUS BURNHAM HARVEY.—The surname Harvey is corrupted from Hervey, and is from an ancient Norman name, Herve or Hervie. M. de Greville in his *Mem. Soc. Ant. Norm.*, 1644, observes: " We sometimes call it Hervot le Hervurie. As a family designation it appears in the twelfth century." Didot, however, in his *Nouvelle Biog. Universale*, shows the name to have been adopted much earlier, when he speaks of Hervie, Archbishop of Rheims, who, he says, died A.D. 922, and Polydore Virgil, in his *Chronicle*, says " Harvey and Hervey " was Hervicus. " One of the family," he adds, " came over to England from the Flemish coast in the time of King Hardicanute and participated in subduing the British."

Lower (*English Sur-names*) maintains that in the time of the Conquest Harvey was Hervie, and that in Brittany and France Hervieu retains its primitive termination Herve. The same writer in his *Patronimica Britannica* remarks: "Osbert de Hervey is styled in the Register of St. Edmundsbury the son of Hervey. From Hervic spring the Herveys ennobled in England and Ireland and also (in all probability, from the resemblance of the arms) the Herves and Hervies of Aberdeenshire and other parts of Scotland."

Both Stubbs (*Registrum Sacrum Anglicanum*) and the author of *Le Neues Faste Ecclesia Anglicana* make mention of Herve le Breton, Bishop of Bangor, in 1092, and Ely in 1109, who died A. D. 1131. Didot, in his *Biographie Universale*, mentions a Hervie who was a noted monk in the eleventh century, and also of a Hervie who was abbot of St. Ghildas de Rhins in Brittany in 1125, and of Hervie, a monk famous as a religious teacher, who died A. D. 1145. This writer also praises the skill of a celebrated French writer named Hervie Freerabras, who flourished A. D. 1550; of one Francois Cucq de Hervie, a poet and Knight of St. John of Jerusalem in the sixteenth century; of William Harvey, the discoverer of the circulation of the blood; of Daniel Hervie, a great French Theologian, who died in 1694; and of Gideon Harvey, a great English physician, born A. D. 1625, and died A. D. 1700. Michaud in his *Biographie Universale* mentions a monk named Hervie as having acquired great oratorical fame, and he tells something of Noel Hervey, or Hervie, who was general of the Order of Preachers and Philosophers and died A. D. 1323. The *Rotuli Hundredorum* (of Edward I.) names Herves as having become the holders of lands in England A. D. 1272, and by *Domes Day Book* Hervies are domiciled in Helts, Suffolk, and Bucks. Oridge, in his *Citizens and Rulers of London*, makes honorable mention of Sir Walter Harvey, High Sheriff of London A. D. 1268 and Lord Mayor of that city A. D. 1272; of Sir James Harvey, High Sheriff of London A. D. 1573 and Lord Mayor of the same city A. D. 1581; and of Sir Sebastian Harvey, Sheriff of London A. D. 1609 and Lord Mayor A. D. 1616. Cooper in his *Athenae Cantabrigiensis* makes note of William Harvey, a famous divine in London in 1525, and of one Robert Harvey, another equally noted preacher there in 1570.

Camden comments on several prominent Herveys and Hervies, to wit: "The great gate of the church-yard of St. Edmonds was constructed by Hervey the Socrist in the time of Anselm 7th, Abbott of St. Edmonds in the eleventh century." Again he says: "William de Hervie was king's attorney in June, 1179, and pleaded a celebrated land case in London in that year." He extols the bravery of Sir Nicholas Harvey and other nobles in the battle of Tewkesberry in 1471. He briefly alludes to John Harvey, the boatman at Calais, France, in 1347; and further says: "Some of the Harveys were merchant adventurers at Lyme, England, in Queen Elizabeth's time. Richard Harvey gave the pulpit at Lyme Church in 1613 with an inscription on it 'Faith is by hearing.'" Rose in his *Biographical Dictionary* states that Richard Harvey was famous as a writer, astrologer, and antiquarian in the sixteenth century, and that another almost equally noted astrologer in London was John Harvey in the seventeenth century. Watts in his *Bibliothea Britannica* mentions one Henry Harvey as an eminent preacher and master in chancery and John Harvey as a great writer, who died A. D. 1592. Chalmers in his *General Biographical Dictionary* notes Gabriel Harvey, a great English lawyer and poet, born A. D. 1546, died A. D. 1630, and Lord John Harvey, of Icksworth, a political writer and versifier A. D. 1696; while Foss in his *Judges of England* highly commends the wisdom and justice of Sir Francis Harvey. From *Collection Top. Gen.* it appears that a Hervie was abbot of Hingham County, Salop, A. D. 1236-37; that one Thomas de Harvye was clerk of St. Nicholas Priory at Exeter in the third year of Edward III.; that Goldstan Harvey was a truant at Beauchamps A. D. 1222; that Walter Harvey and his son were tenants at Drayton in 1222; and there were one Godeman Hervie and one Ulrica Hervie at Thorp at the same time. At St. Leonard's Parish, Aston Clinton, Bucks County, England, is the will of one Sylvester Baldwin wherein the testator leaves all his property to Henry and Sylvester Harvye and to the six children of Freamor Harvye A. D. 1564. Freamor Harvye married Baldwin's daughter Avelyne. This marriage license was made at the registry of the Bishop of London. She died in 1585 and Harvey married (2) and died June 15, 1621. Walker in his *Independency* says Adam Harvey, a silk merchant, was made a Colonel by Cromwell, and got the Bishop of London's house and Manor of "Fulham." Clarendon in his *Rebellion* says this man was "a decayed silk man," and Buckle in his *History of Civilization* refers to the same person.

The Harveys, two centuries after the Norman Conquest, had become numerous in Bedfordshire, Lincolnshire, Kent, Suffolk, Middlesex, Hertfordshire, and Norfolkshire; at Beachamwell in Norfolkshire were John Harvey, his son Robert, and his grandson Robert; at Northwald Thomas Harvey; and at Norwich John Harvey, twice Lord Mayor of that city.

Robert Harvey, a descendant of one of these Norfolkshire Harveys, had a son Robert, who was a man of note, possessing a considerable fortune, which his eldest son, under the laws of primogeniture, inherited to the exclusion of his brothers and sisters. This eldest son had two brothers, Samuel and Robert Harvey, who emigrated to America about 1750, and located in New York City, whence, after a brief stay, they went to Shrewsbury, Monmouth County, N. J. In May, 1763, they purchased a tract of 170 acres in what was then Shrewsbury Township in Monmouth County. This tract lay south of what is now Ocean Grove. Robert's first wife, who came over from England with him, died in 1762 and in January, 1764, he married Hannah White, who survived him. He was a farmer and iron smelter. His children of the second generation were Jacob, Stephen, Thomas, Peter, and Samuel, besides daughters.

Of these, Thomas Harvey (2), born in Monmouth County, N. J., November 17, 1755, married there, January 10, 1775, Elizabeth Sutton, born there December 10, 1758. Thomas was a farmer and resided there on a farm of 115 acres, near what is now Belmar. He died December 11, 1811, and his wife survived until April 6, 1836. Their children of the third generation were Lydia, Abigail, Nathan, Asher, Reuben, John, Elizabeth, Charity, Jesse, and Sarah.

Of these eleven children Reuben Harvey (3) was born at Shrewsbury, N. J., May 12, 1782, died at Enfield, N. Y., June 23, 1866, married, in 1806, Lydia Bennett, born in Monmouth County, N. J., January 9, 1784, died at Enfield, N. Y., May 23, 1862.

In 1806 the "Genesee Country" began to open up and emigrants, particularly from New Jersey, began to pour into the "Empire State." All of Thomas Harvey's sons caught the emigration fever, and loading their families and their household effects upon canvas-covered wagons or carts, drawn by ox teams, they made a journey of more than 300 miles, occupying several weeks. Their route lay much of the way through an unbroken wilderness, through which roads had to be cut as they went. They subsisted on what they could find en route, and slept in their wagons. In time they reached a point half way between the Cayuga and Seneca Lakes in Tompkins County, where they located on various tracts of wildland. These tracts, which they purchased from the original grantees of the State, were densely wooded, but exceedingly fertile. Reuben Harvey, with his wife Lydia, was in this "caravan." He settled on a "half section" of rich and heavily timbered land near what is now Enfield Center, about eight miles west of Ithaca, and with the aid of his sons cleared and fenced a large farm. His nearest neighbor was then about five miles, and the surrounding forests rang with the howls of wild beasts. Bears and wolves played havoc with the pigs, poultry, and lambs. In the course of time his farm was cleared and became one of the finest in the county. After his boys grew up he, for several years, followed droving, buying up sheep and cattle, principally in Ohio and Pennsylvania, and driving them to New York City to a ready market. He accumulated wealth and was greatly respected by his neighbors, who always gave him the prefix of "Uncle." His children of the fourth generation were Seneca, Charlotte, Charles, Joel B., Eleazer B., Asher, Cornelia, Mary A., Elizabeth, and Reuben.

Of these Joel B. (4) was born at Enfield Center, N. Y., November 21, 1813, died at Howell, N. J., August 11, 1880, married (1) Lydia A. Wood; (2) Susan Arzilla Buck; and (3) Elizabeth B. Hagerman. Joel B. engaged in farming at Enfield, N. Y., until the winter of 1856, when he removed to Howell, Monmouth County, N. J., where he continued agricultural pursuits until his death. He was a respected citizen and a member of the Methodist Episcopal Church at Jerseyville, N. J., which he helped to organize. His children of the fifth generation were Cornelius Burnham, Lucretia M., Huldah B., Samuel H., Mary E., Charles W., Winfield S., Euphemia H., Joseph H. and Joel B. (twins), and Ida S.

Cornelius Burnham Harvey (5), the subject of this sketch, is the eldest of these. He was born in Enfield Center, Tompkins County, N. Y., October 20, 1839, and married, March 4, 1873, Mary F., daughter of Peter J. and Sarah (Zabriskie) White, of Closter, Bergen County. He received the characteristic discipline of hard work on the farm throughout the summer, with attendance at the district schools in the winter. He was ambitious, and between 1855 and 1859 every moment of leisure was devoted to study and reading. Having passed the requisite examination, in 1859 he received a license to teach school from the School Board of Monmouth County. After teaching for two terms in that county he attended school for some time in New York City.

Moved by a war sermon preached by Henry Ward Beecher in Brooklyn, early in the summer of 1862 he enlisted as a private in Company D, Fourteenth New Jersey Volunteers, and was in camp on the Monmouth battleground at Freehold, N. J. Having been mustered into service in August, 1862, the regiment was sent to Monocacy, Md., and did its first campaigning in West Virginia and Maryland. After the battle of Gettysburg it was attached to the Third Corps of the Army of the Potomac, under the command of General Sickles, and subsequently was attached to the Sixth Corps, under the command of General Sedgwick and later of General H. G. Wright. Mr. Harvey served for three years, until the close of the war. He became one of the non-commissioned officers on the regimental staff, becoming Chief Musician of the regiment.

At the close of the war he resumed teaching, in Bergen County, following this profession for three years. In the fall of 1868 he began the study of law in the office in Jersey City of the late Hon. Robert Gilchrist, then Attorney-General of New Jersey, and was admitted to practice in 1873, and as counselor in 1876, and for a time was associated with Mr. Gilchrist in professional practice.

He thus became employed in the arduous historico-legal work of preparing the case for New Jersey in the famous jurisdiction and boundary suit between the State of Delaware and the State of New Jersey, begun in 1872, and not yet settled. It was essential in this case to locate and identify the original land-grants in certain sections of New Jersey, and in this work Mr. Harvey and others were engaged. The results of this research can be seen by anyone fortunate enough to examine the large octavo volume privately printed at Trenton in 1873 for the lawyers in the case, and entitled "The State of the Question of Jurisdiction and Boundary between New Jersey and Delaware, A. D. 1873." To achieve accuracy in this, every conceivable source of information was drawn upon, including the State records at Trenton, the records of the early Proprietors at Perth Amboy, those at Albany, together with local records and original deeds, and whatever of use could be found in the State libraries of New Jersey, Delaware, New York, and Pennsylvania.

While engaged in researches in this case Mr. Harvey began to take notes with reference to the original land-grants of Bergen County, N. J. This labor of love—for such it necessarily is—has been prosecuted to the present time. He has had the record offices of New Jersey and other States ransacked for every scrap of information ascertainable respecting the early land-grants and transfers in Bergen County, has unearthed numerous deeds that were never recorded, and has engaged in the arduous labor of identifying boundaries and preparing maps. The use, in the original surveys, of the old mariner's compass, which was not perfectly accurate, renders this work of identification one of the most delicate tasks imaginable. Mr. Harvey has also collected and arranged in alphabetical arrangement all the marriage records for Bergen County known to be in record offices. In another series of manuscript volumes he has, in alphabetical order, the inscriptions from the tombstones in all the graveyards in Bergen County, N. J., and Rockland County, N. Y., with the single exception of that at Nyack. The labor and expense involved in acquiring these collections would be quite incredible to one unfamiliar with the requirements of such work. He also has a set of large manuscript volumes containing miscellaneous historical and genealogical collections, never before used in historical works, and which would fill many printed volumes. From these collections, together with all the more ordinary sources of historical information, he is preparing a work upon the original families and land-grants in Bergen County, which will be more exhaustive and accurate, probably, than anything of the kind ever attempted for a similar section of territory by historical workers in this country. He has also compiled, and in 1889 published, a genealogical volume on the *Origin, History, and Genealogy of the Buck Family*, and has compiled the *Origin and Genealogy of the Harvey Family*, not yet published.

On his mother's side Mr. Harvey is descended from Emanuel Buck, who came from England in 1634, and settled at Wethersfield, Conn. His great-grandmother was Elizabeth Sherman, wife of James Buck, a Revolutionary soldier, and a sister of Roger Sherman, a Signer of the Declaration of Independence. His paternal grandmother was a descendant of Wilhelmus Burnett, who emigrated to New York from Holland in 1660. Mrs. Harvey was a student at Swarthmore College, Pa. On the paternal side she is descended from Jonas White, who emigrated to America from Avon, Somersetshire, England, in 1814, and became a farmer at "The Flatts" in Bergen County. On her maternal side she is descended from Albert Zabriskie, the Polander, whose family has been traced in these pages.

Mr. Harvey's children are Augustus Hardenburgh Harvey, born in 1880, now an accountant with the Mutual Life Insurance Company in New York, and Arzilla B., born in 1886, now at school.

Mr. Harvey is a member of the New Jersey Historical Society, of the Englewood Council, Royal Arcanum, of Guilliam Van Houten Post, No. 3, Grand Army of the Republic, of Jersey City, and of several other organizations.

ISAAC ROMAINE, of Jersey City, is a lineal descendant of (1) Klaas Jansen Romeyn, who came from Holland to America in 1653 and eventually settled in Hackensack, N. J., where his son (2) Albert was born in 1680, and where the latter's son (3) Nicholaas was born in December, 1711. The next in descent, (4) Albert Romein, son of Nicholaas, was born in Schraalenburgh, N. J., February 11, 1752, and had a son (5) Roelef A., whose birth occurred July 24, 1774. John R. Romine (6), son of Roelef A. Romein, was born in Bergen County, N. J., May 18, 1806, and married Ann, daughter of John Zabriskie, of old Bergen (now Hudson) County. They were the parents of Isaac Romaine, the subject of this sketch, who was born in Bergen Township, Hudson County, N. J., on the 4th of May, 1840. These worthy ancestors not only took a lively interest in public and business affairs, but transmitted to their numerous descendants in general and Mr. Romaine in particular their sturdy Dutch characteristics and habits of thrift, and left behind them careers which illumine the pages of history and grace the annals of their respective communities.

Mr. Romaine attended the Columbia District School until 1852, prepared for college at a private school in the Township of Bergen, Hudson County, and was graduated from Rutgers College in 1859. Having studied law with Hon. A. O. Zabriskie, subsequently Chancellor of the State of New Jersey, he was admitted to the bar as an attorney in November, 1862, and as a counselor in November, 1865, and since the spring of 1863 has practiced in Jersey City. He was Corporation Counsel of the City of Bergen from 1865 to 1867, and, becoming an Alderman in May, 1869, was President of the Board of Alderman in 1869 and 1870, immediately preceding the consolidation of Bergen and Jersey City. From 1880 to 1885 he was a member of the Board of Education of Jersey City. In 1883 he was appointed a member of the Board of Finance and Taxation, but was not seated on account of legal complications until 1885. In 1884 he was elected to the New Jersey Assembly, in which body he served on the Committees on Claims and Revolutionary Pensions and Stationery, as well as on the Joint Committee on Passed Bills.

Throughout his career Mr. Romaine has been a stanch and active Republican. He is a master and examiner and a special master in chancery for New Jersey. Prior to the expiration of that office by legal limitation, July 1, 1897, he was a Commissioner of the Circuit Court of the United States for the District of New Jersey. At the present time he is a Commissioner of the District Court of the United States for the District of New Jersey. He has been President of the Star Mutual Building and Loan Association of Jersey City since 1886, having been one of its founders and its first Vice-President in 1885. He is a member of the Holland Society of New York City and was its Vice-President from Hudson County, N. J., in 1897 and 1898. He is also a member of the Jersey City, Carteret, and Union League Clubs of Jersey City, and of other important organizations.

December 29, 1863, he was married to Miss Annie A., daughter of John W. Morton, of Jersey City. She died February 1, 1895.

WHEELOCK HENDEE PARMLY, D.D., for forty years the beloved pastor of the First Baptist Church of Jersey City, N. J., was born in Braintree, Vt., July 27, 1816, his parents being Randolph Parmly and Elizabeth B. Murray, the former of English and the latter of Scotch descent. He came of good New England stock. His father was the first male child born in the village of Randolph, Vt., the date of his birth being January 15, 1783, and at the request of the selectmen his parents, Jahial Parmly and Eunice Hendee, named him Randolph, after the town. His mother, a niece of Eleazer Wheelock, the founder and first President of Dartmouth College, was born in Chester, N. H., May 19, 1782, and was the daughter of Robert Murray and Jane Ramsey. In 1795 her parents moved into the State of Vermont, and there both families became prominent in all public and private affairs.

When four years of age Wheelock H. Parmly removed with the family to Hancock and three years later to Middlebury, Vt., whence they came, seven years afterward, to New Jersey, locating at Shrewsbury, Monmouth County. In 1838, after a residence of eight years in that town, they moved to New York City.

Dr. Parmly's parents did all in their power to give him a good early training, but their means were limited and he was dependent in a great measure upon his own efforts for his education. While residing in Shrewsbury he prepared himself for college by teaching and performing various other kinds of work, and at a very early age became a great Bible reader, a trait which characterized his entire life. His parents, though not members of any church, attended with their children the Episcopal services, but young Parmly, convinced of the truth of the Baptist principles, adopted the faith and practice of that denomination, and amid considerable opposition, from both his family and the Episcopalian clergy, was baptized August 3, 1834, in the Shrewsbury River. And connecting himself with the Baptist Church at Middletown, N. J.,—the nearest society of that faith to his home,—he was faithful in his attendance on worship, active in all departments of church work, and influential among both old and young.

In 1838 Dr. Parmly entered Columbia College in New York City and was graduated from that institution in 1842, standing high in his class and receiving many tokens of excellence in scholarship during his collegiate course. About the time he entered college he united with the old Amity Street Baptist Church in New York, of which Rev. Dr. William R. Williams was pastor. He also formed a close friendship with Rev. Dr. Spencer H. Cone, of New York City, which, with that of Dr. Williams, lasted until his death. It was undoubtedly from these eminent clergymen and great teachers that he learned many of the principles which made him so successful during his career of half a century in the ministry.

On leaving college Dr. Parmly was confronted with the problem of determining his vocation in life—a problem which all young men must solve. He had been urged to enter the ministry by many friends who thought him peculiarly fitted for that profession; others assured him of success in a mercantile career, while others still tempted him with flattering offers in various branches of business; but the guiding voice of nature bade him preach the gospel, a labor to which his "mind rather inclines." On August 10, 1842, at the request of Dr. Williams, he preached to the people of the Amity Street Church, and immediately afterward made this entry in his diary: "The subject of the ministry has occupied my mind for a long time. It is now settled, and I hope for good."

Dr. Parmly was unanimously voted a "license to preach the gospel" by the Amity Street Church on the 16th of July, 1844, and in the following month (August) was graduated from Madison Theological Seminary, where he had pursued a thorough course of study. On August 6, 1867, Madison University conferred upon him the honorary title of Doctor of Divinity.

Soon after graduation he received a call to the pastorate of the Harlem Baptist Church of New York City, which he was obliged to refuse on account of impaired health and a serious affliction of the eyes that had developed during his course in the seminary. A three weeks' sea voyage brought him to New Orleans, where he began to preach, and while there he accepted the assistant pastorate of the Baptist Church at Clinton, La., which he filled most acceptably for two years, declining during that period three calls to become pastor of churches in the North. He developed a strong friendship for the negro, frequently visited them in their cabins, took a fearless stand on the slavery question as an advocate of human rights, and afterward sheltered many a fugitive slave. During his residence in the South he also acquired that habit of great hospitality which always characterized his home.

WHEELOCK H. PARMLY, D.D.

The illness of his mother, however, compelled him to return at the end of two years to New York City, and on November 15, 1847, he accepted a call to the Baptist Church at Shelburne Falls, Mass., where he remained two years, and resigned, the winter climate of the Berkshire hills being too hard for his constitution. Shortly after he accepted this pastorate he married Katharine Dunbar, daughter of Rev. Duncan Dunbar, of the Macdougal Street Baptist Church, New York City, and a lady "lovely in character, strong in faith, wise in judgment, remarkable for patience, prayerful, and zealous in every good work." Upon her death on July 10, 1877, he wrote in his diary: "The brightest light of my home has gone out," while another expressed these words and sentiments: "She added to the sum of human joy, and were everyone to whom she performed some loving service to bring a blossom to her grave, she would sleep to-night beneath a wilderness of flowers."

Dr. Parmly assumed the duties of pastor of the Baptist Church at Burlington, N. J., in May, 1850, and remained there nearly five years, during which time the "church grew mightily."

On the 1st of September, 1854, at the age of thirty-eight, he entered upon his labors as pastor of the First Baptist Church of Jersey City, and ably, honorably, and satisfactorily filled that pastorate until his death, August 1, 1894,—a period of forty years, lacking one month. When he came to Jersey City there was but one church of the Baptist faith in the place, and that was made up of the scattered membership of churches which had been formed and which had proved too weak to continue their organizations. The church was then known as the Union Baptist Church and had 206 members. Three other vigorous Baptist churches now exist in the city, the beginnings of which came largely from the old church during Dr. Parmly's pastorate. The mother church changed its name on the establishment of the other churches to the First Baptist Church of Jersey City, and now has a membership of nearly four hundred.

Dr. Parmly labored hard with great success, baptizing in the winter of 1865 alone over one hundred converts. In that year he spent four months in Europe, and, returning with new energy, entered into his work with redoubled force, giving also a vast amount of his time to the general interests of the city, the State, and the Nation. He was especially active in the establishment of the denominational school now known as Peddie Institute at Hightstown, N. J., contributing years of labor and large sums of money for that purpose.

As a pastor Dr. Parmly certainly excelled. His people were strongly attached to him, and under no circumstances would they allow him to go in response to the successive calls which he received from other societies. He was recognized as the man for the place. Once each year he endeavored to visit personally every family in his congregation, and his calls upon those who were sick were frequent. Believing in this method as he did, it certainly added largely to his success in pastoral relations. He preached, while in Jersey City, five thousand sermons, made addresses on public occasions to an equal number, attended 844 funerals, performed 1,425 marriages, raised nearly $300,000 for the church and $50,000 for benevolent purposes, received into the church over 1,000 members, and baptized more than 1,300 others.

He remained as the faithful servant of that church until September, 1887, when, at the age of seventy-one, he was unable to bear longer the burden of the pastorate alone, and at his request the church called to his aid an assistant pastor. Two years later he again asked to be relieved, and by unanimous vote of the church was made its Pastor Emeritus, a position he held until his death, which occurred August 1, 1894. He was survived by four children: Duncan D. Parmly, Mrs. Elizabeth P. Thompson, Randolph Parmly, and Christine D. Parmly. One son, Walter, died in his youth.

His only installation as pastor of the church in Jersey City was the singing by the congregation of Montgomery's beautiful hymn, of which the following is a part:

" We bid thee welcome in the name
  Of Jesus, our Exalted Head;
Come as a servant, so He came,
  And we receive thee in His stead.

" Come as a messenger of peace,
  Filled with His spirit, fired with love!
Live to behold our large increase,
  And die to meet us all above."

Dr. Parmly was especially interested in the cause of Christian education, and gave himself unreservedly to the upbuilding of Peddie Institute and the New Jersey Baptist Education Society, becoming a member of the latter in 1852, serving it for more than forty years as a member of its Board of Managers, for seven years as President, and then being elected its Honorary President, an office specially created for him. From almost the first he was also a member of the Board of Trustees of Peddie Institute and for many years one of its Education Committee. In every capacity he was a good man, a true Christian, a benefactor, anchored in the Baptist faith by an intense study of the Scriptures, and loyal to all the trusts confided to his care. No man had a more honored leadership in his church in the State, and none was more beloved or more universally esteemed.

DUNCAN DUNBAR PARMLY, the oldest son of Rev. Wheelock H. Parmly, was born in Shelburne Falls, Mass., May 25, 1849, and until recently resided in Jersey City. He was graduated from Mount Washington Collegiate Institute of New York City and at an early age entered the office of Henry G. Marquand, banker, of New York City. Later he was connected with the St. Louis, Iron Mountain and Southern Railroad—now a part of the Missouri Pacific System,—and was one of the founders and for many years the senior partner in the firm of Marquand & Parmly, bankers, of New York. Owing to ill health he was compelled to give up his active business and in 1893 became the President of the Phenix National Bank of New York City, and has since acted as the head of that financial institution. For the past eight years he has been a resident of the State of New Jersey with his home at Middletown in Monmouth County.

RANDOLPH PARMLY, of New York and Jersey City, was born April 2, 1854, at Burlington, N. J., and is the son of Rev. Wheelock H. Parmly and Katharine (Dunbar) Parmly. He was educated at Hasbrouck Institute in Jersey City and at the University of the City of New York, from which he was graduated in 1875. Afterward he continued his course of study in the Columbia Law School.

Mr. Parmly was admitted to the bar of the State of New Jersey in June, 1878, and has continuously practiced from that time to the present. He is also a member of the New York bar. Having made a specialty of corporation law, he has spent a good portion of his time with certain corporations for whom he is counsel in the City of New York. He is a member of the Association of the Bar of Jersey City and of New York, and of the Lawyers' Club and the University Club of New York City.

JOHN J. VOORHEES.—Steven Coerts (or Koerts, as he wrote it), the common ancestor of the Voorhees family in Bergen and Hudson Counties, emigrated to this country in April, 1660, coming over on the ship "Spotted Cow," with his wife and seven children. They came from Ruinen, in the Province of Drenthe, Holland, and from in front of the little hamlet of Hees, near that locality. Hence the name was at first Van Voorhees, "Van" meaning "from," "Voor," meaning "near," and "Hees" (the hamlet name) "from near" or, "over from Hees." Steven was not the first of the family to emigrate. In February, 1659, Harman Koerts had preceded him on the ship "Faith," with his wife and five children. Steven settled at Flatlands, L. I., where many other Dutch emigrants had already located. He must have been born about 1600. Who his first wife was does not appear, but she died in about 1675, and he married (2), in 1677, Wellempie Roeloffse Leubering. He died about February, 1684. He bought, November 29, 1660, of Cornelis Dircksen Hoogland, eighteen acres of corn land, fourteen acres of woodland, twenty acres of plainland, and ten acres of salt meadow—in all sixty-two acres—for $3,000; and also the house and lot lying in the village of Amersfoort, with the brewery and all the brewing apparatus, kettle-house, and casks, with the appurtenances, which shows that he must have been a brewer as well as a farmer. He was assessed at Flatlands in 1675, and was manager of taxes there in 1683. His name appears as one of the patentees there in 1664 and 1667. He died about February 16, 1684. His children were Hendricke, Mergen, Coert, Lucas, John, Albert, Aeltje, Jannetje, Hendricke (2), and Abraham. His son, Albert Stevens Voorhees, and his wife, Jelletie Rynieres Wisselpennick, went to Hackensack in 1686, joined the Dutch church there, and bought an extensive tract of land from Major John Berry between the Hackensack and Saddle Rivers.

John J. Voorhees is a lineal descendant of the sixth generation of Steven Coerts Van Voorhees, the emigrant. His father, Peter Voorhees, was born on the old farm at Flatlands, L. I., where Steven first settled in 1660.

Mr. Voorhees was educated in the public schools of New Utrecht, L. I., and in 1863 accepted a clerkship in a country store, where he remained five years. After filling similar positions he obtained a position as assistant bookkeeper for the New Jersey Car Spring and Rubber Company, and at the end of one year was promoted to head bookkeeper. Not long afterward he was made Secretary of the company and held that position until 1885, when he was elected Treasurer of the corporation. In 1888 he was made General Manager, and at the present time is President of the Voorhees Rubber Manufacturing Company, of Jersey City, which is one of the largest and most successful concerns of the kind in the country, having an extensive business and employing a large number of hands.

In 1885 Mr. Voorhees was appointed a member of the Board of Education of Jersey City and served for three terms, during five successive years of which he was President of the board, being annually re-elected without opposition. As a member of the Condemnation Commission on the County Roads in 1892 he rendered most efficient services to the community at large, and displayed that eminent ability and superior judgment which have characterized his entire business career. He is a member of the Board of Directors and a member of the Jersey City Board of Trade, of which he was President in 1892. He is also a member of the Board of Directors of the Commercial Trust Company of New Jersey, of the Board of Trustees of the Free Public Library of Jersey City, and of the Palma Club, the Carteret Club, and the Holland Society of New York City.

Mr. Voorhees was married October 14, 1874, to Annie M. Collier, of Brooklyn, N. Y. They have had three children, and reside at 57 Duncan Avenue, Jersey City.

CHARLES E. VOORHIS is a descendant in the eighth generation from Steven Coerts Van Voorhees, the first American ancestor of the family in America, whose pedigree has been written in the sketch on page 83. One of Steven's children, Albert Stevens Voorhees (2), emigrated with his father to America in 1660, and located with the rest of his family at Flatlands, L. I., where he married (1) Barentie Williamse, (2) Tjelletje Wizzelpenning, and (3) Elina Vander Scheur. He was living at Flatlands as late as 1683, as the assessment roll then shows. He removed with his family, in 1686, to Hackensack, where he purchased from Captain John Berry a large farm extending from the Hackensack to the Saddle River. He joined the church in 1686, and subsequently became an officer in it. His children of the third generation were Cornelia, Stephen, Stephen, Jannetje, Margrietie, Lucas, Rachel, Feumietje, Albert, William, Peter, Isaac, Willempie, John, and James.

Of these Lucas Alberts Voorhis (3) married, September, 2, 1726, Ann Kipp. They resided at Hackensack. Their children of the fourth generation were Ann, Henry, Lena, Elizabeth, Margrietie, Nicholas, Catharine, Isaac, and Jacob. Of these, Nicholas (4) married Jannetje Ackerman and had issue Albert N., Ann, Lucas, Henry, and Jannetje.

Albert N. Voorhis (5) was born in 1767. He was a farmer and resided at Schraalenburgh. He married, December 10, 1791, Grietie Demarest, who died in 1854, leaving several children of the sixth generation.

Of these children of the sixth generation Henry A. L. Voorhis (6), who was born September 26, 1792, married Levina Blawvelt, born September 14, 1792, and died July 15, 1872. He was a farmer and resided near Demarest, N. J., on part of the farm formerly belonging to John Peack. Among his children of the seventh generation were Elizabeth, Maria, Margaret, Henry D., David H., Nicholas H., and John.

Nicholas H. Voorhis (7) married Caroline, daughter of Peter B. Westervelt, of Cresskill, N. J. He resided at Cresskill until his death.

Charles E. Voorhis (8), son of Nicholas H. and the subject of this sketch, was born at Cresskill, Bergen County, N. J., September 11, 1856, and was educated in the public schools of his native town. He left school when seventeen years of age and began his business career in the grocery trade, in which he remained for ten years. At the end of that time he engaged with the firm of Peter Henderson & Company, the famous New York City firm of seedsmen and florists. He has continued with this house to the present time. He is a member of the Dutch Reformed Church.

Mr. Voorhis married Ruth Richardson and has four children: Edward, aged thirteen; Henry, aged eleven; Raymond, aged nine; and Clarence, aged seven.

JOHN ALBERT BLAIR, Judge of the Court of Common Pleas, General Quarter Sessions, and Orphans' Court of the County of Hudson, was born near Blairstown, N. J., on the 8th of July, 1842, his parents being John

H. Blair and Mary (Angle) Blair. He is the grandson of William and Rachel (Brands) Blair, of Knowlton Township, Warren County, N. J., and descends from one of the most distinguished families in the State. His ancestors sprung from the noted Blair family of Blair-Athol, Perthshire, Scotland, whence they came to this country in 1720, settling in Pennsylvania and New Jersey. Among them were two brothers, Samuel and John Blair, both of whom were educated at the Log College on the Neshaminy under the celebrated William Tennant. They became distinguished ministers of the Presbyterian Church. The Rev. Samuel Blair was called to Fagg's Manor in Chester County, Pa., in 1739, where, in conjunction with his pastoral work, he conducted a school that was among the most noteworthy of the early Presbyterian academies. His son, also the Rev. Samuel Blair, was pastor of the Old South Church in Boston before the Revolution. He became Chaplain of the Pennsylvania Battalion of Riflemen that participated in the siege of Boston. The Rev. Samuel Blair, the second, was offered the presidency of the College of New Jersey (Princeton), but declined in favor of Dr. Witherspoon. The Rev. John Blair was ordained pastor of Big Spring, Middle Spring, and Rocky Spring in the Cumberland Valley in 1742, but resigned in consequence of the frequent Indian incursions on the frontier (1755-57) and succeeded his brother at Fagg's Manor. In 1767 he became Professor of Divinity and Moral Philosophy at Princeton, and was acting President of the college until the accession of Dr. Witherspoon in 1769. He died at Wallkill, in the New York Highlands, in 1771.

JOHN ALBERT BLAIR.

While one branch of the family was devoting its energies to the work of the ministry and the dissemination of knowledge, another was molding the commerce which has since become one of the mainstays of the State of New Jersey. In the latter part of the eighteenth century another Samuel

Blair was sent by a Philadelphia firm to take charge of the iron industry at Oxford Furnace, in Warren County, N. J. This Samuel Blair was the great-great-grandfather of Judge John A. Blair and the great-grandfather of the late John Insley Blair, who died December 2, 1899, at the age of ninety-seven, after one of the most eventful careers in the history of New Jersey.

Judge John A. Blair's rudimentary education was obtained in the public schools of his native place, and later on he prepared for college at the Blairstown Presbyterian Academy. He entered the College of New Jersey at Princeton and was graduated from that institution in 1866. At the close of the college term he began the study of law in the office of the Hon. J. G. Shipman, at Belvidere, N. J. He was admitted to the bar as an attorney at the June term, 1869, and as a counselor at the June term, 1872. In January, 1870, he came to Jersey City, where he has ever since resided and been engaged in his profession.

On the passage of the law creating district courts in Jersey City Hon. Bennington F. Randolph and Mr. Blair were appointed the first judges thereof by the Hon. Joseph D. Bedle, who was at that time Governor of the State. In May, 1885, Mr. Blair was appointed Corporation Counsel of Jersey City, which office he held until his resignation in 1889. He was re-appointed in 1894 and served in that capacity until April 1, 1898, when he resigned to accept the appointment of Judge of the Court of Common Pleas, General Quarter Sessions, and Orphans' Court of the County of Hudson, to which he had been appointed by Governor Griggs just before the latter became Attorney-General in President McKinley's Cabinet.

Judge Blair is a sound lawyer, an attractive and eloquent speaker, a man of fine classical acquirements, and the possessor of a large and choice library. He is a prominent and active Republican in politics. Although never seeking office, his name has been frequently mentioned in connection with some of the most prominent positions in the State. He is a regular attendant of the First Presbyterian Church of Jersey City. He is a member of the Palma Club, was one of the organizers of the Union League Club, and was President of the latter organization for several years.

ALBERT V. HUYLER.—Johannes (John) Huyler came to America from Holland about 1741, and went to Bergen County, where he married, in 1742, Eva, daughter of Cornelius Banta. He purchased of the heirs of Colonel Jacobus Van Cortlandt a large tract of land (several hundred acres) between Cresskill and Tenafly, extending from the Hudson River to the Tiena Kill, where he resided until his death. His children were Cornelia, married John Banta; Joris (George), married Maria Symonson; John, married (1) Effie Westervalt and (2) Anntje Banta; Jannetje (dead); and Wilhelmus, married Christina Cole.

John Huyler (2) known as "Captain John," born in 1748, resided on his father's farm above Tenafly and was in the Revolutionary War. By his wife he had children John, Peter, and George.

Peter Huyler (3), born April 8, 1781, married Catharine Benson, and had children Barney, Garret, Henry, John, and George, the latter of whom obtained title to the old homestead.

Henry Huyler (4) married Margaret Voorhis and by her had three children: Peter E., Harry, and Albert V., the latter of whom is the subject of this sketch.

Albert V. Huyler (5) was born at Tenafly, N. J., and there received his education in the public schools. At the age of nineteen he left school and engaged in the watch and diamond business at No. 21 Maiden Lane, New York City, in which he has continued for the past fifteen years, doing business under the style of N. H. White & Co. He is a public spirited and progressive citizen, and thoroughly identified with the affairs of the community.

Mr. Huyler married Miss Virginia Connor, and they have two children: Cleveland C. and Washington E. Huyler.

ALBERT IRVING DRAYTON, President and General Manager of the New Jersey Title and Abstract Company and one of the leaders of the younger bar of Jersey City, is the son of Henry S. Drayton, M.D., and Almira E. Guernsey, and a grandson of William R. and Mary M. (Shipman) Drayton and of Dr. Henry and Martha J. (Halsey) Guernsey. His paternal great-grandparents were Henry and Mary (Rood) Drayton and Jacob and Mary (Mulford) Shipman, while those on his mother's side were William and Elizabeth Nancy (Scofield) Guernsey and Rensselaer and Jane Halsey. These names represent some of the oldest families in New Jersey, many of whose members have been prominent in the history of the colony and State, and distinguished in both civil and military life. William Henry Drayton, one of Mr. Drayton's ancestors, was Chief Justice and Governor of South Carolina in 1776-77 and a member of the Continental Congress in 1778-79, and another member of the family was Captain Percival Drayton, an eminent naval commander.

Albert I. Drayton was born in Jersey City on the 14th of August, 1869. He received his preparatory education in the various public and private grammar schools of that city and at the Jersey City High School, and subsequently entered the New York University, from which he was graduated with the class of 1888. Determining upon the law as his profession, he was a law student from 1888 to 1891, and in the meantime took a course of lectures at the Columbia Law School. He was admitted to the bar of New Jersey as attorney in November, 1891, and as a counselor February, 1895, and ever since his admission as an attorney has been actively and successfully engaged in the practice of law in his native city. In the many cases in which he has been identified in all the courts of the State he has displayed marked ability, sound judgment, and broad and accurate learning, and, although a young man, he has gained a leading position at the Hudson County bar. His legal connections with important real estate matters led him finally into a close study of that subject, and as President and General Manager of the New Jersey Title and Abstract Company of Jersey City he is widely known and an acknowledged authority on land titles.

He is also an officer in various other corporations, being President of the Jersey City Golf Club, first Vice-President of the Alumni Association of Gamma Chapter of Delta Phi, a member of the Delta Phi fraternity, and a member of the Cosmos Club, of the Jersey City Chess Club, of the New Jersey State Bar Association, of the Hudson County Bar Association, of the Nyack Country Club, of the Deal Golf Club, of the New York University Alumni Association, and of St. John's Episcopal Church of Jersey City.

Mr. Drayton was married on the 14th of October, 1896, to Sarah Conselyea Traphagen, a descendant of one of the oldest families of New Jersey. Their children are William Rood and Grace Traphagen Drayton.

HENRY D. WINTON, for thirty years editor and proprietor of the *Bergen County Democrat*, of Hackensack, N. J., is the son of Eben Winton, and was born on the 14th of February, 1848. He received a common school education, and in 1863, at the early age of fifteen, entered the office of the *Democrat*, where by assiduous attention to his duties he soon became a thorough practical printer. In 1870, when but twenty-two years old, he became proprietor and assumed the editorial control of the *Bergen County Democrat*, which under his judicious management has steadily grown in influence and popularity, and which now ranks among the leading newspapers of New Jersey.

Mr. Winton is an able editor and business man —a fact which is abundantly shown by the success and development of his paper. He is one of Hackensack's most public spirited citizens, deeply interested in local affairs, and thoroughly identified with everything affecting the community. In politics an active and influential Democrat, he represented his Congressional district as a delegate to the Democratic National Convention at Cincinnati in 1880 and at the convention in Chicago in 1896, and in various other important capacities has rendered efficient service to his party and town. He was elected Senator from Bergen County in 1889 and served two terms, and has the record of being the only Senator from Bergen County who has served six years in the Senate of New Jersey.

HENRY D. WINTON.

ABRAM QUICK GARRETSON, for nine years prosecuting attorney of the most populous county of the State, during five years more Law or President Judge of the Court of Common Pleas of Hudson County, and now an Associate Justice of the Supreme Court of New Jersey, is descended from the old Holland stock which contributed so largely in early colonial days to the stability and prosperity of the States of New York and New Jersey. The names of his ancestors appear in the old Dutch records of New Jersey, the first of them having come over from Holland soon after the first planting of New Amsterdam. The Garretsons were among the number who originally settled in the present territory of New Jersey, in the vicinity of New York City. Later branches of the family pushed into the western counties with the first pioneers. Judge Garretson's direct ancestors were among the earliest settlers of Somerset County. He is the son of Martin Schenck Garretson and Ann Beekman Quick and a great-grandson of Abraham Quick, a colonel of New Jersey militia in the Revolutionary War.

Judge Garretson was born in Franklin Township, Somerset County, on the 11th of March, 1842. He was sent to school in Trenton at the age of thirteen, and entered Rutgers College in the fall of 1859. His preparation had been such that he was enabled to enter the sophomore class in the classical course at the age of seventeen, graduating with honors three years later, in 1862, and standing first in his class. In 1865 he received the degree of A.M. in course. He chose the legal profession as promising the best opportunities for a career. He also determined to select the largest city of his State as his field of operation. Accordingly, we find him, almost immediately after graduation, entering as a student the law office of the well known Chancellor A. O. Zabriskie, of Jersey City. After spending two years in the Chancellor's office, he rounded out his legal studies by a year at the Harvard Law School. In November, 1865, he was admitted to practice at the bar of New Jersey as an attorney, and at the end of three years, in 1868, and as soon as the law of the State permitted, he was admitted as a counselor, giving him the right to practice in the highest courts of the State. He was afterward admitted to practice before the United States Supreme Court at Washington.

The young lawyer's success was not only immediate, but quite phenomenal, as was shown by his appointment in February, 1869, only one year after his admission as a counselor and only four after his first practice, to the responsible position of Prosecutor of Pleas for Hudson County, an office identical in every respect except its name with that of the ordinary district attorney of other States. He was appointed for a term of five years by Governor Randolph, and filled the position so ably and with such general satisfaction that at the end of the time he was re-appointed for a second term by Governor Parker. He served four years of this second term, making a continuous service of nine years, and then resigned to accept in 1878 the appointment by Governor McClellan as Law or "President" Judge of the Court of Common Pleas of Hudson County. He served in this capacity for five years.

The ability and integrity displayed by Judge Garretson upon the bench only served to greatly increase the esteem and respect of his fellow-citizens. But notwithstanding all this, he desired to return to private practice, and this he eventually did in 1883, when his term as judge expired, he having announced that he was not a candidate for re-appointment previous to the expiration of his term.

In the same year he formed a legal partnership with James B. Vredenburgh in Jersey City. In 1900 he was appointed an Associate Justice of the Supreme Court of New Jersey.

While Judge Garretson has always been a consistent Democrat in politics, in local affairs his sympathies are fully enlisted in the welfare of the community. He has served as one of the Commissioners for the Adjustment of Tax Arrearages for Jersey City since 1887, when that commission was organized. In Jersey City an immense amount of property has been snowed under a great burden of tax arrears which it was utterly impossible for its owners to meet, while if they abandoned their property the city treasury was unable to realize upon it, and it has been the delicate and difficult task of the commission to readjust such old claims of the city and fix a sum which the property owners could pay and thus put such property on a tax-paying basis, and at the same time lift a burden which could not fail to depress values and impede municipal growth and development. Claims aggregating millions of dollars have been thus readjusted, while the commission is now beginning to see the prospective end of its labors.

Judge Garretson was a founder in 1888 and is President of the New Jersey Title and Guarantee Trust Company, the only one of its kind in Jersey City, and is a Director in the Third National Bank. He is also similarly interested in other directions. His name must ever be linked with the progressive development of his adopted city, where he has resided since 1865.

November 12, 1879, he married Josephine, daughter of Joseph and Mary (Davis) Boker, of Philadelphia. Their children are Leland Beekman, Josephine Boker, and Eleanor Helen.

JAMES CHIDESTER EGBERT, D.D., for forty-two years the beloved pastor of the First Presbyterian Church of West Hoboken, N. J., and now pastor emeritus of that society, is a lineal descendant of James Egbert, who was born in 1695. His paternal ancestors were Germans, coming from Saxony or Hanover to this country several generations ago. Lewis Egbert, a member of his branch, served in the Revolutionary War. Dr. Egbert's father, James Egbert, was the son of Enos Egbert and Sarah Lyon, both natives of New Jersey, and was born at Elizabeth, in this State, in 1801. He learned the trade of printer in the office of the *Palladium of Liberty* at Morristown, N. J., and, moving to New York, became a partner of Mahlon Day, one of the earliest printers in that city and for many years the publisher of the weekly *Bank Note List*. Mr. Day, with his wife and daughter, was lost at sea on the ill-fated ship *Arctic*. James Egbert succeeded to the firm's business, and for nearly fifty years conducted a large and successful printing establishment in New York on Pearl Street, opposite Frankfort. He finally retired, and died in West Hoboken, N. J., November 17, 1881, having settled there about 1867. His father, Enos, was a blacksmith and iron founder, and also a native of Elizabeth. James Egbert married Joanna Jones Chidester, daughter of James and Peninah (Guerin) Chidester, all of whom were born in New Jersey. She died in 1866.

Dr. Egbert was born in New York City on the 17th of October, 1826, and there received his education. He attended one of the public grammar schools and then taught for four years in the same institution. Afterward he continued his studies and also taught in the private school of Professor John Jason Owen, of New York, and in 1848, having received a thorough preparatory training there, entered New York University, then under the presidency of Theodore Frelinghuysen. He was graduated with honors in 1852, receiving the degree of B.A., and on March 4, 1889, the university conferred upon him the honorary degree of Doctor of Divinity in recognition of his eminence as a minister and of his learning and standing as a scholar. In 1852 Dr. Egbert began the study of theology at the Union

Theological Seminary in New York. He was graduated from that institution in April, 1855, and licensed to preach by the Third Presbytery of New York on the 11th of the same month.

On June 13, 1855, he was ordained pastor of the First Presbyterian Church of West Hoboken, N. J., and continued in that capacity for forty-two consecutive years, resigning June 13, 1897. Soon afterward he was made pastor emeritus of the congregation. This church was organized June 12, 1850, with eight members, and the church edifice was dedicated June 25, 1851. For four years Rev. Charles Parker supplied the pulpit, and through his efforts, and with the aid of Rev. William Bradford, then editor of the New York *Evangelist*, the church building was erected. Dr. Egbert was their first settled pastor, and faithfully and diligently discharged the duties of the trust, gaining not only the love but the confidence and affection of the entire community as well as of his own parishioners. From a very small congregation he built it up to a membership of over 435 and the Sunday school to 500 scholars, with a chapel in Jersey City of about 250 members. The society made a strong effort to retain him as their active pastor, but advancing years and the evident need of rest impelled him to resign, and the pastorate has since been under Rev. Charles Alexander Evans, a graduate of Princeton, class of 1884. As pastor emeritus, however, Dr. Egbert continues to exercise a broad and wholesome influence in the church.

He has twice been Moderator of the Presbytery of Jersey City, is a member of the Associate Alumni and of the Alumni Club of the Union Theological Seminary, and is known throughout the State and in other Presbyteries as a man of broad culture, of great learning, and of fine intellectual attainments. His sermons, many of which have been published, bear evidence of high literary skill as well as sound logic and doctrinal knowledge.

Dr. Egbert was married, August 1, 1855, to Harriet Louise Drew, daughter of George and Philinda Drew, of New York City. Their children are Annie Lake Egbert, a teacher in the New York public schools; James C. Egbert, Jr., professor of Latin in Columbia College, New York; Rev. George Drew Egbert, pastor of the Presbyterian Church at Cornwall, N. Y.; and Marion Dupuy Egbert, also a teacher in the New York public schools. Two other children died in infancy.

RAYMOND P. WORTENDYKE is descended from Cornelius Jacobse, alias Stille (or The Silent), a farmer, who, with his brother John, came to New Amsterdam from Amsterdam, Holland, in 1639. Shortly after their arrival they assumed the surname of Somerendyke. Cornelius, after remaining a short time in New Amsterdam, bought and located on a plantation at Bushwick, L. I. From thence he removed to what is now the Williamsburgh district of Brooklyn. In 1664 he took the oath of allegiance to the British king, at which time he was residing on a farm of one hundred acres in what was formerly the Greenwich district of New York City. He married (1) August 24, 1692, Classie Teunis, and (2) July 28, 1695, Tryntie Wallings Van Winkle, of Amsterdam, Holland. He died in New York in 1679, having had nine children of the second generation, the eldest of whom was Jacob Corneliesen, born in 1644, who married, March 11, 1671, Aeltje Fredericks, an estimable Brazilian lady. Their children were four of the third generation, to wit: Jacob, Nicholas, Frederick J., and Cornelius. Frederick (3d gen.), known as Frederick Jacobsen Somerendyke, located on the upper west side of Manhattan Island. He and his descendants adopted the surname of Wortendyke, while those of his brothers retained that of Somerendyke. The old Somerendyke mansion house, built of stone, stood, a few years ago, on the Bloomingdale road near West Seventy-fifth Street. Frederick (3d gen.) married, June 10, 1707, Divertie Rynearsen Quackenbush, a granddaughter of Peter Quackenbush, of Oostergeest, Holland. About 1722 Frederick removed to Bergen County, N. J., where he purchased several tracts of land, the principal one of which was nearly five hundred acres in area at what is now Park Ridge, formerly Pascack. On this tract, lying on both sides of Pascack Brook, he built his residence and two or more mills. He was the founder of Pascack settlement and left a large landed estate. After his death his will became the subject of a long litigation. His children of the fourth generation were Aeltie, Rynier, Elizabeth, Frederick F., and Classie.

Frederick F. Wortendyke (4th gen.), born in New York City, April 10, 1720, married April 3, 1748, Sara Peters Durie, of Pascack. By the will of his father he obtained half of the homestead at Pascack on which he resided, besides lands at Tappan and on the Palisades. He died about 1770, leaving issue of the fifth generation Frederick, Jannetje, Jacobus, Marya, Elizabeth, Judith, Peter F., Sara, Susanna, Divertie, Mensie, and John. Of these, Frederick was taken by the British in 1776 and confined for some time a prisoner in the old Sugar House in New York.

Peter F. Wortendyke (5th gen.), baptized August 29, 1754, married Martha Demarest. He resided at Pascack, where he was a farmer and miller. His children of the sixth generation were Frederick P., Augenitie, Peter P., and Jacobus.

Peter P., of the sixth generation, born June 15, 1797, died at Pascack, January 31, 1885. He was a farmer and married, January 6, 1816, Maria Banta, by whom he left issue of the seventh generation Peter P., Maria, Frederick P., Cornelius P., Martha, Laney, and John.

Peter P. Wortendyke, of the seventh generation, born June 14, 1816, died April 12, 1900. He married Harriet Cummings, a native of Spring Valley, N. Y. He resided at Pascack and spent most of his life as a tanner. His children of the eighth generation were Maria, Raymond P., John H., and Charles P., the second of whom is the subject of this sketch.

Raymond P. Wortendyke (8th gen.), one of the prominent members of the bar of Jersey City, was born at Pascack, Bergen County, N. J., December 30, 1845. He is the youngest son of Peter P. and Harriet (Cummings) Wortendyke, and inherits from a long line of ancestors on both sides the sturdy characteristics of his race. He attended the public schools at Pascack and Hackensack, Bergen County, and was graduated from the New Jersey State Normal School at Trenton, June 15, 1862. Subsequently he taught school for upward of seven years, during the last three of which he was connected with Hasbrouck Institute in Jersey City. In the meantime he studied law in Jersey City three and one-half years in the office of Hon. Jacob R. Wortendyke, member of Congress, and for six months with Hon. William Brinckerhoff, State Senator. He was admitted to the bar at Trenton as an attorney June 3, 1869, and as counselor June 6, 1872, and for over thirty years has been actively and successfully engaged in the general practice of his profession, his present office being in Jersey City.

Mr. Wortendyke resides in Englewood, Bergen County, where he has served as a public school trustee for twenty years and as counselor of the old Public Road Board for ten years. He has been counsel for the Township of Englewood for many years, and is now City Attorney for the City of Englewood. During his career at the bar he has been connected with a number of important cases in which he has displayed marked ability, sound judgment, untiring industry, and great force of character. He is public spirited, progressive, and patriotic, thoroughly identified with the best interests of the community, and holds a prominent place at the bar.

Mr. Wortendyke has been twice married, first on December 30, 1869, to Caroline, daughter of Levi and Wilhelmina (Ackerman) Gurnee, of Pascack, N. J., who died February 11, 1895. On September 29, 1897, he married Mrs. Ann E. H. (Demarest) Gurnee, of Hackensack, daughter of David A. Demarest, of Tenafly, Bergen County.

DAVID A. DEMAREST was without doubt in his day one of the most widely known and highly respected men in Bergen County. He was of the sixth generation from David des Marest, the French Huguenot emigrant, concerning whom see page 64. The line of descent was as follows: David des Marest (1), the emigrant, and his wife, Maria Sohier, had four children, one of whom was David Demarest, Jr. (2), who married Rachel Cresson and had twelve children, one of whom was Jacobus (3), who married Lea de Groot and Margrietie Cozines Haring, and had fifteen children, one of whom (by the second wife) was Abraham D. Demarest (4), born at Old Bridge, Bergen County, September 25, 1738, died near Closter, N. J., July 9, 1824, married, in 1763, Margaretta Garrets Demarest, born at Schraalenburgh, December 2, 1744, died June 13, 1834. Abraham D. Demarest (4) resided at Old Bridge for many years, when he removed to Hackensack and kept the Mansion House. About 1781 he purchased a large farm on the west side of the Schraalenburgh and Tappan road, lying on both sides of the road to Old Hook. There until his death he kept a general store of groceries, hardware, and such wares as farmers require. He also kept (until 1809) a tavern where the elections were held and other public business transacted. In April, 1787, he added to his farm on the south by purchases from the Harings and Van Horns. Abraham was a man of some note. His store and tavern were known and patronized by the people for miles around. From 1781 until 1799 he held many town offices, including those of Commissioner of Appeals, Townsman, Road Master, and Justice of the Peace. He was one of the most active members and workers in the North Church at Schraalenburgh, in which he several times held the offices of Deacon and Elder. His issue were David A.; Rachel, 1768; Margaret, 1773; John, 1775 (died); and Christina, 1783.

Of these David Abraham Demarest (5), the subject of this sketch, was born at Old Bridge, August 28, 1764, and died at Nyack, N. Y., February 1, 1860, aged ninety-five years, five months, and three days. He married, in 1787, Charity Haring, daughter of Cornelius Haring, of Pascack, where she was born July 24, 1769. She died at Schraalenburgh, January, 29, 1849, aged about eighty years. She was a lady of sound judgment, with a kind and cheerful disposition, who was her husband's faithful helpmeet and companion for more than sixty years. The issue of this union was only one child, a daughter, Margaret Demarest, born at Schraalenburgh, N. J., September 5, 1789.

David A. Demarest (5) was an unusually bright and active boy. Realizing this, his father sent him to the best school in the village of Hackensack, where he acquired a fair education, including a knowledge of penmanship and composition. Clerking in and purchasing stock for his father's store, as well as attending to the wants of the tavern guests, threw him in contact with all kinds and conditions of people from whom he obtained a large fund of information which, in later years, he turned to good account. When the Revolutionary struggle broke out he was a lad twelve years old, yet the father had difficulty in restraining the patriotism of his son sufficiently to prevent him from offering his services as a drummer boy to the Continental forces.

That struggle over, and having married and settled down to business,

DAVID A. DEMAREST.

he gave his attention not only to the store but to agricultural pursuits, which were then profitable. Products of the farm were sent by sloop from Old Bridge, or Closter Dock, to New York. A considerable trade in pig iron was carried on with the iron works at Ramapo. Groceries were exchanged for pig iron and the iron shipped to New York and sold at a profit. In October, 1794, he was one of the militia force from New Jersey, Virginia, and Pennsylvania sent by President Washington to Pittsburg to suppress what in American history is known as the "Whisky Insurrection." In 1796 he began to mingle in and wield influence in town affairs. From that time to 1843 he held numerous town offices, including that of Justice of the Peace. In 1809 he superintended the construction of his father's new stone dwelling (still standing). The tavern business was abandoned with the demolition of the old family mansion.

His daughter Margaret married, in 1810, John Perry, a member of one of the oldest and most prominent families in Rockland County, N. Y., by whom she had issue two daughters, Catharine (1811) and Charity (1822). In 1812 the quota of Bergen County drafted troops for the war with Great Britain rendezvoused at Jersey City for three months. Captain Samuel G. Demarest (of what is now Westwood, N. J.), who raised a company of men for that war, recruited part of his force at the store of Abraham D. Demarest. It has been said that David A. Demarest served in the War of 1812, but if so his name does not appear upon the muster rolls of the companies that went from his vicinity, commanded by Major Van Saun.

At his death in 1824 Abraham D. Demarest gave all his lands to his son, David A. Demarest. The latter soon after purchased several adjoining tracts, until the whole area of his homestead farm was over 300 acres. He also owned a large farm west of the Hackensack River and a tract at Ramapo. Henceforth and until his death he was considered a wealthy man. But he was one of those men whom wealth makes neither proud nor avaricious—a most genial and hospitable man, noted for his liberality. Nearly all his life he had been a member and liberal supporter of the North Church at Schraalenburgh, which he helped to organize and to which he liberally gave. His commodious mansion was always open to the ministers of that and sister churches. They came and went at their pleasure, sometimes staying with their families for weeks at a time. Their host's hospitality was of the good old-fashioned variety, spontaneous and hearty. Everybody was welcome beneath his roof. He had great influence over his neighbors and a happy way of settling disputes. As a Justice of the Peace for many years his practice was to avoid trials, if possible, and usually he would bring the parties to an agreement to settle before the trial day came on. He was a gentleman of "ye olden time"—a sort of "Cadi" in the community to whom the people went for advice in time of trouble and did not go in vain. He was a lover of music, and in 1801 organized a band in which he played second clarinet. The minutes of this band in his handwriting show that it prospered for some time. He was an entertaining conversationalist and story-teller who never lacked for listeners. Physically he was remarkably robust, and was never severely ill. He was found dead in bed one morning at the home of his daughter, at Nyack, N. Y., whom he was visiting. He lay as though he had quietly dropped into a peaceful sleep. He was of the type of man rarely to be met with in these days. He saw the Revolutionary War, the War of 1812, and the Mexican War, and had he lived another year he would have seen the beginning of the Civil War. The year before his death the Northern Railroad was completed. The company gave him a pass, but he never used it, and died without having experienced the sensations of riding on a moving railroad train.

Catharine and Charity Perry, has granddaughters, married, respectively, Isaac and Tunis Smith, of Nyack, N. Y., who, for many years, owned and operated a steamboat line between New York and Nyack. Isaac and Tunis Smith were descendants of Lambert Ariaense, a native of Gilderland, Holland, who came to America when a young man and settled at New Amsterdam, where, on April 9, 1682, he married Margaretta Garrets Blawvelt, a daughter of Garret Hendricksen Blawvelt, of Deventer, Holland. In 1686

Lambert and his brothers-in-law, the Blawvelts, and others purchased the Tappan patent. Lambert settled on part of it at the "Green Bush," in Rockland County. His descendants soon became so numerous that it was necessary to distinguish one from the other, and as Lambert was a smith by profession it became convenient to designate him as Lambert Ariaense Smidt. Most of the family eventually dropped the Ariaense and called themselves Smith. Lambert Smith and Margaretta Garrets Blawvelt had issue, among other children, a son, Garret Smith (2), who married Brechie (Bridget) Peters Haring, of Tappan, and had issue, among other children, a son, Peter G. Smith (3), who married Annetie (Hannah) Blawvelt, and had issue, besides other children, a son, Isaac (4), who married Rachel Smith, and had issue several children, among whom was Peter Smith (5), who married Christina Demarest (a sister of David A. Demarest, above mentioned). Old patrons of the steamer "Chrystenah" will remember her portrait at the head of the stairway to the upper deck. They had issue of the sixth generation: Isaac, Abraham, Tunis, and David.

Isaac married Catharine Perry, and Tunis married Charity Perry, as above stated. The issue of Catharine Perry and Captain Isaac Smith were John, James, and Margaret Ann, all now deceased. The issue of Charity Perry and Tunis Smith were six children, all now deceased except David and Sidney.

JAMES KIPP is of the tenth generation in lineal descent from Roeloff (Ralph) de Kype, who, as the prefix "de" unmistakably indicates, was of French origin, but who resided at Amsterdam, Holland, whither he had fled from France. His life-long calling was that of a soldier, wherein he exhibited bravery, energy, and capacity of the highest order. He attained prominence as a military leader in 1555, during the long and bloody struggle between the Catholics and Protestants, in which the latter finally triumphed. It has been said that in 1559 he returned to France and fought against the Protestants under the banner of the Duke of Anjou. Whether he did or not is at this late date a matter of little importance. It is known that his sons espoused the Protestant cause. One of them is said to have been a stockholder in the Dutch East India Company and an active promoter of the voyage of Hendrick Hudson to New York in 1609. His son, Hendrick de Kype (3d gen.), born at Amsterdam in 1578, came to America accompanied by his son Hendrick (4th gen.). They were the first of the name in the New World. Hendrick (3d gen.), owing to ill-health, soon returned to Holland, but his son Hendrick (4th gen.), who seems to have been the first to drop the "de" from the name and who was usually known as "Hendrick Hendricksen Kype," married and became one of the first permanent settlers on Manhattan Island. Being a tailor by occupation, he was sometimes dubbed "Schneider Kype." On April 28, 1643, he purchased a lot 30 x 110 east of "The Fort" (now Bridge Street, near Whitehall), on which he built his family residence and shop. There, for years, he was the principal tailor of the town. He married Ann de Sille, a daughter of Nicholas de Sille, of Wyck, Holland. About this time Kieft was Governor of New Amsterdam. Kype despised the governor and publicly denounced him as "a butcher" for permitting the massacre of the Hackensack Indians at Pavonia. Kieft summoned him to appear and answer for his insolence, but Kype replied by messenger that he would not appear before "a man of blood." Mrs. Kype likewise denounced Kieft as a false judge. Upon the succession of Stuyvesant to the governorship

Kype was made a Councilor. Later he was chosen to be one of the nine Selectmen, because, as is said, he was one of "the most notable, reasonable, honest, and respectable citizens of the city." Two years later he was made a Burgher, but becoming dissatisfied with the management of town affairs he soon after sold out and removed to Amstel, in Delaware, where he embarked extensively in the brewing business on the west bank of the Delaware River. The governor of Delaware soon made him a member of the Council, and later, in 1660, appointed him Commissioner of Amstel. About 1694 he seems to have returned to New Amsterdam and about the same time purchased from Captain John Berry a tract of two hundred acres of land south of Hackensack, from the Hackensack River to the Saddle River, and including in it the present village of Lodi. He died in New Amsterdam about 1703, leaving children of the fifth generation Cornelia, Catharine, Peter, and Nicasie (Nicholas).

Nicholas (5th gen.), born at Amstel, Del., in 1668, went to Hackensack in 1694, and married Ann Breyant, of old Bergen. The same year the couple joined the Dutch Church at Hackensack. In 1698 Nicholas, with Thomas Fraunce and Rutgert Van Horn, of Bergen, purchased from Captain Berry a large tract at Moonachie. Nicholas made other purchases in due time—one of two hundred acres from Garret Lydecker extending from the Hackensack to the Saddle River, and another large area of "meadow land" for which, as his deed recites, he gave a "fatted calf." Upon his death he inherited a large portion of his father's lands, and passed as one of the most extensive landholders in that section. He resided on the Polifly road, was active in town and church affairs, and held several responsible official positions. His eleven children of the sixth generation were Henry, Peter, Isaac, Cornelius, Jacob, Ann, Catherine, Elizabeth, Garret, Nicholas, and John.

Nicholas (6th gen.), born at Moonachie in 1720, married in 1749 Lea Vreeland, of Bergen. He was a farmer by occupation and resided for thirty-five years in Lodi Township. In 1755 he removed with his family to Schraalenburgh, where he bought a large farm lying on both sides of the Schraalenburgh road near the present North Church. The same year he and his wife joined the Schraalenburgh South Church, of which Nicholas was made a Deacon in 1766. He was a man of means and greatly respected by his neighbors. His children of the seventh generation were Sophia, Isaac, Catharine, Peter, John, Maria, Ann, and Jemima.

Isaac Kipp (7th gen.) was born at Schraalenburgh, May 14, 1756, and died there March 10, 1813. He joined the South Church in 1785, and became one of the principal and, in fact, the most influential man in Schraalenburgh. He owned and managed a large farm on both sides of the road near the North Church. Though wealthy, both he and his father Nicholas fervently espoused the cause of the colonists. For this the British and Tories raided the Kipp farms and buildings, drove off the live stock, and committed other acts of spoliation. Isaac joined the local militia, known as the "train bands," and served against the British during the last years of the Revolutionary struggle. At its close he became active in the organization and drilling of the State militia, in which he was at first a Major and later a Colonel. He was one of the principals in the organization of the North Church Congregation, and one of the seven men chosen by resolution of the Consistory in 1800 to build the present church edifice, receiving for that service six shillings per day. He died in March, 1813, and was buried near the church in which he was so long prominent. His children of the eighth generation were Nicholas, David, Henry (who became a prominent physician), Ann, Leah, Maria, Christina, Isaac, and James.

David Kipp (8th gen.) was born at Schraalenburgh, January 24, 1783, and died May 18, 1864. He was reared on his father's farm, and in 1806 married Elizabeth, daughter of William de Graw, of Old Tappan. David resided and for many years kept a general store at what is now Bergenfield, on the corner of the road leading from Schraalenburgh road to the South Church. His children of the ninth generation were Maria (married Matthew S. Bogert), William, and Fanny (married Cornelius L. Blawvelt).

William Kipp (9th gen.) was born at Schraalenburgh, August 19, 1812, and died in 1871. He married, November 24, 1831, Elizabeth Banta, born in 1813. William resided for many years at Old Tappan, now Harrington Park. Although reared a farmer, he was a born politician, and for many years was the Democratic leader in Harrington Township. Late in life he removed to Closter. At his death he left living issue David, John B., Isaac, Levina, James, and William de Graw, the last two named being the subjects of this and the following sketch.

James Kipp (10th gen.) was born at Old Tappan, N. J., October 15, 1844, and received his schooling in the public schools at Tappan. At the age of fifteen he left home to become a clerk in the grocery store of his brother David, at Sparkill, N. Y. He was called home in the fall of 1862 to take the place of his brothers John B. and Isaac, who had joined the Union Army in Virginia. Upon the return of his brothers James sought and obtained a clerkship in the grocery house of Elbert Bailey, then at 518 Sixth Avenue, New York. After four years' service with Mr. Bailey he entered the office of the Lorillard Insurance Company, but remained there only three months. A more lucrative position was offered him with the New York Rubber Clothing Company at 347 Broadway, which he accepted. In July, 1867, this company combined with the Goodyear Rubber Company. Mr. Kipp acquired an interest in the business and was given the responsible position of manager, a position which he still holds at Nos. 787-789 Broadway, New York. To manage a concern doing the great volume of business which the Goodyear Rubber Company is doing demands business tact and judgment of the highest order. These qualities Mr. Kipp possesses in a marked degree, and his untiring energy, activity, thorough knowledge of the business, and close attention to its details have marked him for the early future as one of the great army of successful mercantile men in the great city. He is thoroughly domestic in his habits and tastes, and spends his spare time with his family. He belongs to no city clubs, does not dabble in politics, has never held political office. He " leans toward " the Dutch Reformed Church and the Republican party.

He married, February 21, 1872, Rachel, a daughter of John J. and Hannah M. Naugle. Mrs. Kipp was born at Closter, N. J., March 25, 1850. They have three daughters: Ada (married in 1895 to Edward Livingston Gilbert, a New York stock broker), Eva, and Florence, the last two both unmarried. Florence is a recent graduate of the Comstock School of New York City, and her sisters are graduates of the New York City public schools. Ada has a daughter, Margery (11th gen.), born in 1897.

WILLIAM DE GRAW KIPP (10th gen.), brother of the above, was born at Old Tappan, N. J., February 25, 1848, and like his brother obtained his education in the public schools of his native township. He left home in 1866 to take a position as clerk in the grocery store of Ward Carpenter,

No. 520 Sixth Avenue, New York. Here he remained for a year and then entered the employ of E. C. Hazard & Co., where he filled the position of salesman for nine years, after which he embarked in the grocery business on his own account at Closter, N. J. This venture being unprofitable, he became a salesman in the house of Wright Gillies & Brother, New York. He left them in 1880 to take charge of the city sales department of the well known house of E. R. Durkee & Co., of New York, and still fills that position. Their factory and office are at 534 Washington Street. As a salesman his knowledge of general merchandise and his long experience on the road and behind the counter have made him one of the most expert and valuable men in his line of business. At home he is public spirited and enterprising, favoring public-education, local improvements, and athletics, and opposing the liquor traffic and dishonesty in public office. He is an independent Democrat in politics, but has never held political office. He served a term in the Board of Trustees of the public school at Closter. He was a Trustee and Treasurer of the Congregational Church for a number of years, and was also the prime factor in placing the railroad station at Closter in its present location.

He married in 1874 Sarah Elizabeth, a daughter of John J. and Hannah M. Naugle. Sarah E. Naugle was born at Closter, N. J., March 25, 1853. They have four daughters living: Edna, born October 31, 1875 (married in 1899 William C. Bouton, an employee of the Union Trust Company, of New York); Lizzie, born in 1878; Ethel, born in 1882; and Grace, born in 1884. Three others—two daughters and a son—died in infancy.

THE WESTERVELTS (or Von Westervelts, as they once called themselves) are another of the very prolific families of Bergen and Hudson Counties. Should the traveler happen to journey through the Province of Overyssel in Holland, about a mile east of the coast of the Zuyder Zee, on the highroad from Deventer to Groningen, he will pass through a considerable town called Meppel. In the middle of the seventeenth century this town was a mere hamlet. Three miles east was the town of Zwolle, where Thomas à Kempis for half a century resided, where he wrote his famous book, *In Imitation of Christ*, and where he died about 1471. East of Meppel the country for miles was then a desert waste of lowland. To-day this has been bought up by humanitarian societies to secure from beggary able bodied laborers and their families by locating them on these lands and employing them in bringing the lands to productiveness. South and west of Meppel were rich, green pasture lands. Near Meppel lived William and Lubbert Lubbertsen, two sturdy brothers, tillers of the soil, and raisers of cattle.

In April, 1662, these two brothers joined the throng of emigrants which was then heading from Amsterdam to America to better their condition in life. William, with a wife and four children, and Lubbert, with a wife and six children, reached New Amsterdam about the first of May, 1662, in the Dutch West India ship "Faith." William repaired to New Utrecht, L. I., and Lubbert, with his wife, Gessie Roelofs Van Houten, and family, went to Flatbush, where a considerable Dutch settlement had been collected. At Flatbush, Lubbert bought a house and lot December 15, following his arrival, and went to farming, assisted by his boys. He soon became an extensive and prosperous farmer, bought much land, and owned a number of slaves. Upon his death, near the close of the century, his sons Lubbert, Jr., Roeloff, John, and Juriaen went to Bergen County, N. J., and settled. Lubbert, Jr., who married Hilletje Pouwless, resided for a time in what is now Jersey City, and then removed to the vicinity of what is now Highwood, N. J., where he died and his wife remarried. Roeloff and John (who married respectively Ursolena Stimets and Magdalena Van Blarcom) bought lands south of Highwood and in the vicinity of Cresskill, N. J. The Indians disputed their titles, but subsequently the sachems signed releases. Juriaen, who married (1) Gessie Bogert, (2) Antjie Banta, and (3) Cornelia Van Voorhis, bought and settled on lands on the Hackensack and Saddle Rivers. Lubbert's two daughters, Margretie and Mary, married and settled at New Hackensack. The descendants of these four sons and two daughters of Lubbert Lubbertsen, intermarrying with the Demarests, Naugles, Harings, Blawvelts, and others, became a mighty host, and are scattered throughout Bergen, Hudson, and Passaic Counties, N. J., and Rockland County, N. Y.

SAMUEL WESTERVELT is of the seventh generation from Lubbert Lubbertsen, the first emigrant, and was born at Tenafly, Bergen County, N. J., on the 16th of August, 1853, being the son of David I. Westervelt and Sophia Parsels, and a grandson of John R. Westervelt and Samuel Parsels. He received his education in the Bergen County public schools, and at the age of seventeen associated himself with the well-known firm of Lord & Taylor, of New York City, with which he has remained for twenty-eight years, and where he now holds a responsible position. This house is widely known as one of the leading dry goods establishments in the East, and has few equals in the quality or kind of its business. As an attaché of this great establishment Mr. Westervelt has displayed the highest business abilities, great executive energy, and superior judgment. He is a public spirited, patriotic, and progressive citizen, and as a resident of Tenafly, Bergen County, has taken an active interest in local public affairs. He has served two years as President of the Board of Education and still holds that office, and is also Trustee and Treasurer, as well as a member, of the Presbyterian Church of Tenafly.

Mr. Westervelt married Miss Charlotte E. Bolden, and they have four children: Florence E., born in 1880; Ralph E., born in 1884; James B., born in 1887; and Martha B., born in 1891.

THE BERRY FAMILY.—One of the earliest emigrants at Bergen was John Berry, an Englishman who came from Christ Church Parish in the Island of Barbadoes, presumably with Kingsland, Sandford, Moore, and one or two others. He was, perhaps, one of the most active and energetic of all the emigrants, and certainly the most liberal. In 1668 he bought all the lands between the Hackensack and Saddle Rivers, extending from the Sandford patent as far north as Cherry Hill in Bergen County. The same year he bought three other tracts: one of 1,500 acres on the Hudson River adjoining Edsall, another of 2,000 acres at Schraalenburgh, and another of nearly that number of acres on the upper Saddle River. He came to be one of the most wealthy of the Bergen settlers, and in a sense "ran the towne." He was a member of the Governor's Council several years, at one time acting Governor, member of the Colonial Assembly, a Justice for Bergen County, a Captain and Major in the militia, and Commander of the "Bergen Rangers" or train bands. In 1670 he bought land at Bergen, where he made his home. He gave lands for various purposes, especially the land at Hackensack on which stands the "Church on the Green." He died in New York, leaving a large family of children, among whom were John, Mary, Samuel, Richard, Francis, and Francina. Most of these remained in Bergen County, where their descendants are still numerous.

HENRY H. BRINKERHOFF, Jr., M.D., member of the Board of Health and one of the leading physicians of Jersey City, was born at Rocky Hill, Somerset County, N. J., on the 23d of May, 1865. His ancestors were among the earliest settlers of the State, coming originally from Holland. "Joris Dircksen Brinckerhoef, the founder of the American branch of this family, came from the County of Drent, or Drenthe, in the United Provinces, and having lived some time at Flushing, a seaport in Zealand, arrived in this country in 1638. He settled on Staten Island, and entered into a contract with Cornelius Melyn, the owner of the island, to reside there; but owing to the murder of some neighboring planters by the Indians, in 1641, he obtained a release from the contract, August 15, 1641. Then he went to Long Island and settled in Brooklyn. He married Susannah Dubbels, who died January 16, 1661." The family settled in Bergen County at a very early day, and is one of the oldest and best known in the eastern part of New Jersey. In 1677 Hendrick Brinckerhoef, son of Joris Dircksen Brinckerhoef, purchased land on Bergen Hill, Jersey City, and was the ancestor of the family in Hudson and Bergen Counties, while another son of the original emigrant, Abraham Brinckerhoef, is the founder of the Long Island branch.

HENRY H. BRINKERHOFF.

Dr. Brinkerhoff's parents were Henry H. Brinkerhoff and Elizabeth Vreeland, daughter of Michael Vreeland, granddaughter of Michael Vreeland, Sr., and a great-granddaughter of Johannis Vreeland, who was the son of Michael Vreeland, who was the son of Cornelius Vreeland, who was the son of Michael Jansen. The Vreeland family arrived in this country in 1636 from Holland. On his father's side Dr. Brinkerhoff is a grandson of John V. W. Brinkerhoff, a great-grandson of Hartman Brinkerhoff, a great-great-grandson of Hendrick Brinkerhoff, and a great-great-great-grandson of Hartman Brinkerhoff, whose father, Cornelius Brinckerhoff, was the son of Hendrick, the founder of the New Jersey branch of the family.

Dr. Brinkerhoff was educated in the public schools, graduating from the High School of Jersey City in 1883. Subsequently he spent half a dozen years in mercantile pursuits, and then, having decided upon medicine as his life work, entered Bellevue Hospital Medical College, and after graduating began a private practice which he has since continued, and in which he has achieved eminent success.

He is one of the best known physicians in Jersey City. He is City Physician, member of the Jersey City Board of Health, Visiting Physician and Associate Surgeon of St. Francis Hospital, Treasurer of the Hudson County Medical Society, and prominently identified with the Home for the Homeless and the Hospital for Contagious Diseases in Jersey City. He enlisted as a private in Company A, Fourth Regiment, N. G. N. J., November 9, 1886, was promoted Corporal December 13, 1887, became Sergeant of his company April 3, 1888, and was commissioned Second Lieutenant of Company C January 15, 1894, Captain July 2, 1894, and Major of the Fourth Regiment in 1899, which latter position he still holds.

He is a member of Woodland Lodge, Knights of Pythias, of the Holland Society of New York, of the Hudson County Medical Society, of the New Jersey State Medical Society, and of the American Medical Association, and is thoroughly identified with the affairs of the city and active and influential in promoting every worthy object. He is especially generous in the encouragement of those movements which have the welfare of the community at heart.

Dr. Brinkerhoff was married on the 28th of April, 1897, to Ella Adelaide Hayes, of Newark, N. J.

RYNIER J. WORTENDYKE is descended from the same ancestor as is Raymond P. Wortendyke (see sketch of latter on page 91). His great-great-grandfather, Rynier F. Wortendyke (son of Frederick Wortendyke and Divertie Quackenbush), baptized in New York March 14, 1714, married (1) December 10, 1746, Jannetye Peters Durie, and (2) March 2, 1752, Jannetje Smith. With his brother Frederick, the ancestor of Raymond P., he obtained part of the homestead farm at Pascack. Rynier spent his days in farming and running a mill. His children of the fifth generation were Frederick, Peter, Jannetje, Cornelius (1), Divertie, Cornelius (2), Rynier, John, Jacob R., Mary, Albert, and Aeltje.

Jacob R. Wortendyke, of the fifth generation, born May 5, 1764, died December 18, 1858, married December 7, 1792, Elizabeth Campbell, born October 26, 1773, died March 20, 1862. He was a farmer and resided at Pascack. Their children of the sixth generation were Lutische, Rynier J., and Elizabeth. Of these, Rynier J. (6th gen.), born August 16, 1793, died December 3, 1884, married, January 10, 1818, Cornelia Haring, who died August 12, 1891. They resided at Pascack. Their children of the seventh generation were Jacob R., Peter R., Garret, and Elizabeth.

Jacob R. Wortendyke (7th gen.) was born at Pascack, N. J., November 27, 1818, and died at Jersey City, November 2, 1868. He married, June 2, 1853, Susan J. Doremus, born August 9, 1826, who now resides in Jersey City. Jacob R. Wortendyke was graduated from Rutgers College in 1839, after which he read law in the office and became a partner of Chancellor A. O. Zabriskie. After his admission to the bar he was successful in his practice and held numerous official positions in Hudson County. He organized the Jersey City Water Board and served as a member of the Riparian

Commission. In 1857 he was elected to Congress from the Hudson district and served two terms in that body. In 1868 he was a delegate to the Democratic National Convention. His children of the eighth generation were Nicholas D., Cornelia E., Rynier J., Jacob (died), and Jacob R.

Rynier J. Wortendyke (8th gen.), the subject of this sketch, was born in Jersey City, N. J., August 24, 1860, and has always resided there. Having received a thorough preparatory education, he entered Rutgers College and was graduated from that institution with honors in the class of 1882. He then took up the study of law with James B. Vredenburgh at Jersey City, and after the usual course was admitted to the New Jersey bar as an attorney in June, 1885, and as a counselor in June, 1888. He has been actively and successfully engaged in the general practice of his profession in his native city. He is a prominent member of the Presbyterian Church, a public spirited and patriotic citizen, a man of broad and accurate learning, and a leading factor in the affairs of the city in which he was born, and in which he has spent his life.

Mr. Wortendyke married Miss Carolyn M. Cooley, October 11, 1893, and their children of the ninth generation are Rynier J. Wortendyke, Jr., and Howard B. Wortendyke. Mrs. Wortendyke died September 22, 1900.

JAMES B. VREDENBURGH is of Holland descent, the respectability of which has been strengthened by intermarriage with the Coles, Schuremans, Van Dorns, Brinckerhoffs, and other of the most prominent Holland families.

Isaac Van Vredenburgh (1), a well-to-do citizen, resident, and burgher of the City of Hague, in Holland, had a son who bore the somewhat elongated name of William Isaacsen Van Vredenburgh (2), who, while yet a very young man, enlisted as a soldier in the service of the Dutch West India Company and came to America in May, 1658, on board the good ship "Gilded Beaver." He seems to have done military duty in and about New Amsterdam for several years, during which time, on October 19, 1664, he married Apollonia Barents, a daughter of Barent Jacobsen Cole (Kool), a prominent officer of the West India Company, of Amsterdam, Holland. He continued in the military service after his marriage, being stationed and residing with his family, part of the time, at Fort William Hendrick, and part of the time in the new fortification at New Orange. In 1677 he must have left the military service, as he then, and as late as 1680, was living with his family at Esopus, N. Y. His children were eight in number, the eldest of whom was Isaac Van Vredenburgh (3), baptized in New York, October 4, 1665, and who married March 7, 1694, Janneken Joosten, a daughter of Joost Carelszen, by whom he had six children. William (4), the second of these six, baptized in New York, October 4, 1696, died February 4, 1773, married April 22, 1717, Catharina, daughter of Patrick Schott or Scott, of Kingston, N. Y. William's children were nine, the fourth of whom, Petrus Benedict Vredenburgh (5), born July 30, 1721, died July 26, 1810, married (1) Margarita, daughter of Jacobus Schureman, and (2) Elizabeth Fisher. His children by his two wives were eleven in number. He removed to New Brunswick, N. J., in 1742. One of his sons, Petrus (6), baptized in New Brunswick, N. J., August 4, 1745, died August 24, 1823, married December 17, 1772, Margarita, daughter of John Schureman. This Peter was for many years a prominent merchant at New Brunswick, where he became one of the most influential men in Middlesex County. He was County Collector of that county for forty-one years (from

1782 to 1823) and a member of the New Jersey Assembly from 1790 to 1795. He also held many local offices, including that of Justice of the Peace. Of his two children Petrus (7), born in New Brunswick, October 5, 1778, removed to Somerville, N. J., where he became one of the most prominent physicians of the State, and where he died September 15, 1848. He married December 20, 1804, Maria, daughter of Joseph and Sarah (Vanderbilt) Van Dorn, who was born April 7, 1783, and died April 2, 1855. Petrus (7) left a large family of children, one of whom, Peter Vredenburgh, Jr. (8), born at Somerville, N. J., October 31, 1805, entered Rutgers College and was graduated therefrom in 1821. He read law at Somerville and was admitted to the New Jersey bar in 1829. Soon afterward he removed to Freehold, N. J., where he commenced the practice of his profession. In due time he was appointed Prosecutor of the Pleas for Monmouth County, and soon after was elected to the State Legislature as a member of the Council. Subsequently he was made an Associate Justice of the Supreme Court of New Jersey, which position he held for fourteen years from 1854. Many of the opinions which he rendered were beautifully expressed and are continually quoted as precedents. He married April 19, 1836, Eleanor, daughter of Abraham and Catharine (Remsen) Brinckerhoff, born July 1, 1815, died March 29, 1884. Judge Vredenburgh died at Freehold, N. J., March 24, 1873. His children were Peter, William H., and James B. (9). Of these the eldest was Major of the Fourteenth Regiment of New Jersey Volunteers in the War of the Rebellion. He served as Inspector-General of the Third Army Corps, on the staff of General William H. French, and was present and took part in all the battles in which his regiment was engaged. At the battle of Oppequan Creek, near Winchester, on September 19, 1864, while in command of his regiment, he was killed while bravely leading it in a charge.

On his mother's side James B. Vredenburgh is descended from an old New Jersey family, the founder of whom was Joris Dircksen Brinckerhoff, who came to America from Drenthe in the United Provinces in 1638, settling on Staten Island and subsequently in what is now Brooklyn. His sons subsequently settled in Bergen and Hudson Counties.

James B. Vredenburgh, the subject of this sketch, is of the seventh generation from William Isaacsen Van Vredenburgh, and was born at Freehold, N. J., October 1, 1844. He received his early education in Freehold, was graduated from Princeton University in 1863, read law with Aaron R. Throckmorton, of Freehold, and was admitted to the bar of New Jersey as an attorney in June, 1866, and as a counselor in June, 1869. Upon his admission he located in Jersey City and soon came into prominence as a lawyer of ability, industry, and perseverance. In 1872, when the late Isaac W. Scudder was elected to Congress, Mr. Vredenburgh formed a partnership with that eminent man and thus acquired an equal share in an extensive and lucrative practice. This partnership continued until the death of Hon. Isaac W. Scudder in 1881. In 1883 Mr. Vredenburgh associated himself with Judge Abram Q. Garretson, and the two have ever since carried on a large and successful business, practicing in all the State and United States courts, the firm name being Vredenburgh & Garretson. Mr. Vredenburgh succeeded his former partner, Judge Scudder, as counsel for the Pennsylvania Railroad Company and still holds that position. He has appeared in all the important cases affecting the interests of that company and in many others of note. He served on the staff of Governor Joseph D. Bedle with the rank of Colonel, has always taken an active interest in public affairs, and is a member of the American Bar Association.

He has never sought political preferment, yet he has discharged the duties of the citizen with characteristic energy and is widely known as a man of commanding influence. He has maintained the high reputation, not only of his father, but of his ancestors, and has displayed those sterling attributes and high legal qualifications which have distinguished the family for generations.

Mr. Vredenburgh married Miss Emily H. Van Vorst, a descendant of the well known Van Vorst family, the founder of which was Cornelis Van Voorst, who came to this country from Holland as early as 1636. Their children are Peter, James, John, William, Eugene, and Eleanor.

CORNELIUS BRINKERHOFF, of Secaucus, is the son of James D. and Jane (Alcorn) Brinkerhoff and a grandson of John Brinkerhoff and Kate Bogert, and was born in West Hoboken, N. J., October 31, 1859. He is descended in the ninth generation from Joris Dircksen Brinckerhoef, of the Province of Drenthe, in Holland, who left Holland and lived for a time in Flushing, a seaport in New Zealand, whence he came to this country in 1638. Settling on Staten Island, N. Y., he contracted with Cornelius Melyn, the owner, to reside there; but on account of the murder of some of the planters by the Indians, in 1641, he secured a release from the contract and moved to Brooklyn, Long Island. He married Susannah Dubbels, and died January 16, 1661. Of their four children the second, Hendrick Brinckerhoef, married Claesie, daughter of Cornelius Boomgaert, and settled near English Neighborhood in New Jersey. In 1677 he purchased land on Bergen Hill, and became the founder of a numerous family in Hudson and Bergen Counties, his children being Geertje, Margrietje, Cornelius, Joris, Derrick, and Jacobus. Most of these as well as their parents united with the Hackensack church. James D. Brinkerhoff still resides in West Hoboken, his wife having died in December, 1893.

Mr. Brinkerhoff was educated in the public schools of his native town and spent much of his early life on the farm. Afterward he was employed by his uncle, C. H. Brinkerhoff, on a tugboat in New York harbor, and here developed that mechanical and professional genius which he has since displayed with so much credit and honor. Becoming an engineer by trade, he has filled various responsible positions, and at the present time is superintendent of the New Jersey Trap Rock Company at Snake Hill, N. J. He is also Chief Engineer of the Fire Department of North Bergen Township, having been appointed to that office in August, 1898, and having been a leading member of the department for about eight years. He is also a member of the Royal Society of Good Fellows. Mr. Brinkerhoff inherits the sturdy mental and physical qualities of his race—a race famous for its attributes of thrift, industry, integrity, and uprightness of character. He has always taken a deep interest in public affairs, has contributed materially to the growth and advancement of his county, where his ancestors have resided for more than two centuries, and is active in the support of all worthy projects. His attention, however, has been given chiefly to the duties of the different engineering positions which he has held, and in which he has achieved marked success. He resides in Secaucus.

September 9, 1882, Mr. Brinkerhoff married Mary Margaret Leahy, daughter of Thomas and Mary Leahy, of County Tipperary, Ireland. They have one daughter, Lillian May, born November 15, 1883, in New York City.

CORNELIUS CHRISTIE belongs to one of the most numerous and influential families in Bergen County, members thereof having held numerous and important positions of trust and responsibility, civil and religious, during the past two hundred years. His first American ancestor was James Christie, who emigrated to this country from Aberdeen, Scotland, it is said about 1685, but the probability is that it was much later, unless he was a boy at the time of his emigration. He went to Hackensack in 1703, and from thence, the same year, to Schraalenburgh, where, on the 8th of September, he married Magdalena, daughter of John Demarest (2), and became the owner, by purchase, or in right of his wife, from the Demarests, of a large farm (about 300 acres) just north of the North Church, and extending from the Tiena Kill Brook westward to the Schraalenburgh road. His residence was on the site recently occupied by John H. Anderson. On this farm some of his descendants have ever since resided. He died in 1768, at the advanced age of ninety-six or ninety-eight years. His children were Jacob, Jacomina, Anetje, Lae, John, Maritie, Elizabeth, James, David, and William.

CORNELIUS CHRISTIE.

William Christie (2), the last named, baptized at Schraalenburgh August 28, 1720, died September 28, 1809, married September 20, 1743, Catharine Demarest. He was a farmer, resided at Schraalenburgh, and left ten children: James, Margrietie, Magdalena, Maria, Peter, John, Cornelius, Jacomina, David, and Sophia.

James Christie (3), known as "Captain James," was born at Schraalenburgh, August 20, 1744, died July 3, 1817. He married Maria Banta, born

August 4, 1754, died September 13, 1815. "Captain James" was a farmer by occupation, but patriotic and public spirited. He volunteered his services to the Continental cause in 1777, was commissioned Captain, and raised a company of sixty-five men, with whom he served gallantly. His children were William, John, Magdalena, Maria, David, Peter, Henry, and Jacomina.

David Christie (4), born December 1, 1789, died April 8, 1848, married March 12, 1814, Anna Brinkerhoff.

Cornelius Christie (5), one of their children and the subject of this sketch, was born in English Neighborhood (now Leonia), N. J., December 6, 1835. He was graduated from Yale University in the class of 1855. After reading law one year in the Harvard Law School he studied in the offices of Mercer Beasley, at Trenton, N. J., and of Abraham O. Zabriskie, at Jersey City. He was admitted to the New Jersey bar in February, 1860, and his practice since has been largely an office practice and in consultation. For many years he has served as counsel for his own township and for the boards of adjoining municipalities. In 1867 he was elected to the House of Assembly in the New Jersey Legislature, from the County of Bergen, and was re-elected in 1868. From 1870 to 1876 he was editor and proprietor of the *New Jersey Citizen*, a local weekly journal, independently Democratic, published by him at Hackensack. He has been from time to time interested in various real estate enterprises and in developing and carrying them forward to successful issues. Among others he has devoted himself to the development of Leonia, the place of his lifelong residence, and was prominent in effecting its incorporation as a borough in December, 1894. He was elected the first Mayor of the borough, and has since held that office. By the insertion of explicit provisions in his own deeds and influencing others to follow his example he has been instrumental in keeping the borough exceptionally free from nuisances and vicious influences, and in bringing to it a peculiarly desirable population.

THE ALLEN FAMILY of Bergen County is descended from Peter Garrets Van Halen. The name is probably derived from Haelen or Haalen, a town in Belgian Limbourg, from which place the family originally hailed. The name has gone through several forms: Haelen, Halen, Aelen, Alen, and Allen. Peter Van Halen was the son of Gerret Van Halen, of the City of Rotterdam, in Holland, where Peter was born about 1687. He came to America in 1706 and settled in the Paramus section of Bergen County, where, on the 11th of August of that year, he married, at Hackensack, Tryntie Hendricks Hopper. He purchased lands on the west side of the Saddle River, where he resided and reared a large family of children, whose names were Henry, 1707; Garret, 1709; William, 1710; Andrew, 1712; Maritie, 1714; Willempie, 1716; Lea, 1718; Rachel, 1723; Andrew, 1725; and John, 1727, all baptized at Hackensack. The descendants of these by the name of Allen and Van Allen are very numerous in the western part of Bergen County.

THE BERTHOLFS, who are very numerous in Bergen County, particularly in the western part, are descended from Guilliam Bertholf, who was born at Sluys in Flanders, and with his wife, Martina Hendricks Verwey, came to America in 1684 and first located at Bergen in New Jersey, where they joined the church, October 6, 1684, and where their son Henry was baptized April 6, 1686. Guilliam had studied theology at Middleburgh,

Holland, and had come to America in the capacity of catechiser voorleser and schoolmaster. In these capacities he labored at Bergen until 1690, when he removed to Hackensack, where the people so esteemed him that in 1693 they sent him to Holland to be licensed as a minister of the Dutch Church. The Classis of Middleburgh, Holland, ordained and licensed him, and on his return in 1694 he accepted the pastorate of the "Church on the Green," at Hackensack, where he preached until his death. For the first fifteen years of his ministry he is said to have been the only Dutch preacher in New Jersey. During his pastorate he had the control of all the surrounding churches, preaching at Tappan, Tarrytown, Staten Island, Raritan, Pompton, Belleville, and The Ponds. He was a well-read and eloquent man, indefatigable in his work, and organized many churches. His issue were Sarah, Maria, and Elizabeth (all born at Sluys in Flanders), and Henry, Corynus, Jacobus, Martha, and Anna, all of whom joined the Hackensack church. Sarah married David D. Demarest, Maria married John Bogert, Elizabeth married John Terhune and Rolof Bogert, Henry married Mary Terhune, Corynus married Anna Ryerson, Martha married Albert Bogert, Jacobus married Elizabeth Van Emburgh, Anna married Abraham Varrick. Rev. Guilliam Bertholf purchased from John Berry a farm at Hackensack, extending from the Hackensack to the Saddle River, on which the village of Hackensack is now partly located, and there he died, universally respected, in 1724. All his children remained in Bergen County, over which their descendants are thickly scattered.

JAMES SHREWSBURY ERWIN, one of the leaders of the Hudson bar and Prosecutor of the Pleas for the County of Hudson, was born in Jersey City, September 5, 1857. He is the son of Matthew Erwin and Caroline A. (Gore) Erwin and a grandson of John Erwin, a native of Ireland, who came, at an early date, to New York City, where Matthew was born. On his mother's side Mr. Erwin is a grandson of William Gore, of Deal, Kent, England, the birthplace of both William Gore and his daughter, Caroline A. One of Mr. Erwin's maternal uncles, William Shrewsbury, was a missionary to Africa in 1835, while another, James Shrewsbury, for whom he was named, was a prominent English barrister in London. John Erwin, his paternal grandfather, was in the War of 1812, being a member of a New York company called "McQueen's Men."

Judge Erwin received his preliminary education in Public Schools Nos. 1 and 3 in Jersey City. He also attended Cooper Institute, New York, and finished his studies under private tutors. Having received a thorough training, he took up the study of law in the office of Washington B. Williams, and, in February, 1881, was admitted to practice as an attorney in his native State. In February, 1884, he became a counselor. Mr. Erwin has been actively and successfully engaged in the general practice of his profession in Jersey City since his admission in 1881, and in a large number of important cases with which he has been identified he has displayed high legal qualifications, a broad and accurate knowledge of the law, and great skill and ability. He has established a reputation as a lawyer and advocate.

In 1890 Mr. Erwin represented his district in the General Assembly of New Jersey, and there magnified an already high reputation. He served as District Court Judge from January 26, 1897, to February 27, 1898, when he resigned on his acceptance of the office of Prosecutor of the Pleas of Hudson County. His term expires in 1903. Judge Erwin is a prominent, progressive, and public spirited citizen, a man of broad attainments, and a member of the Union League of Jersey City, of the Minkakwa Club, of the Royal Arcanum, of the Loyal Additional Royal Arcanum, of Bayview Lodge, No. 146, Free and Accepted Masons, of Jersey City, and of Amity Chapter, No. 31, Royal Arch Masons, of Bayonne, N. J.

November 22, 1882, Judge Erwin married Martha J. Robinson, and their children are Margaret J., Martha, James R., and Hobart G. Erwin.

WARNER W. WESTERVELT, a prominent member of the New York bar and a leading citizen of Woodcliff, Bergen County, N. J., is of the seventh generation from Lubbert Lubbertsen, the emigrant (see sketch on page 99), and was born in Spring Valley, Rockland County, N. Y., on the 13th of July, 1847. He is descended from a long line of worthy and distinguished Holland ancestors, his parents being Sylvester Westervelt and Margaret Blauvelt, his grandparents James and Hanna (Ten Eyck) Westervelt and Joseph C. and Rebecca (Remsen) Blauvelt, and his great-grandparents Albert Westervelt and Cornelius and Bridget (Talman) Blauvelt. James Westervelt, his grandfather, was a private in the War of 1812. These names represent some of the oldest and most prominent families in Rockland County, New York, those who have borne them having been conspicuous in civil, military, professional, and business life.

Mr. Westervelt acquired his educational training at the New York State Normal School in Albany, from which he was graduated in July, 1867. At the age of twenty he began teaching, first in the Union Academy at Belleville, N. Y., later at Union Hall Academy in Jamaica, L. I., and then at the Polytechnic Institute in Brooklyn, N. Y. Subsequently he taught in the Ashland Public School at East Orange, N. J., and finally in the schools at Plainfield, N. J. These various positions gave him a broad and valuable experience as well as a high reputation for scholarship and ability as a teacher.

WARNER W. WESTERVELT.

But teaching was not to be his life work, though he had been eminently successful. His tastes, his ambition, and his efforts were for the law as a profession. Having pursued the regular course of legal study, he was admitted to the New York bar in May, 1880, and since then has practiced in New York City with marked success. He has built up a large and successful clientage, and as a lawyer and advocate has gained a wide reputation.

Mr. Westervelt is a prominent citizen and a member of the Reformed Church of Pascack at Park Ridge, Bergen County, near where he resides. He is thoroughly identified with the affairs of the community. His attention, however, has been devoted to his professional labors to the exclusion of public trusts and responsibilities, which have often been urged upon him. He married Miss Mary A. Beach, of Orange, N. J., and they have six children: Jennie E., born in 1870; Burton B., born in 1872; Mary A., born in 1876; Margaret, born in 1878; Warner W., Jr., born in 1883; and Stuart C., born in 1891.

ABRAHAM GARRISON DEMAREST is descended in the seventh generation from David des Marest, the French emigrant and first American ancestor of the Demarests (see p. 64). Samuel Demarest was born in Bergen County in 1778 and removed to "The Ponds" (in Franklin Township) while a young man, where he settled and married Miss Maria Garretson, a descendant of Gerret Gerrets, the Dutch emigrant and first American progenitor of the Garretson, Garrison, and Van Wagenen families. Samuel Demarest, who was a farmer, died in 1837, and his wife in 1850. They left several children, one of whom, Abraham Demarest, the father of Colonel Abraham G., married Margaret Garrison, and resided at Oakland, where their son, Colonel Abraham G., was born on the 16th of November, 1830. While the latter was still quite young he moved with his parents to New York City, where he early became imbued with the military spirit, and at the age of twenty-two recruited a company for the now celebrated Seventy-first Regiment, of the City of New York, then known as the American Rifles. Organized during the "Know Nothing" movement, this regiment was composed exclusively of American citizens.

Colonel Demarest received his first commission from Governor Horatio Seymour in 1853. In 1855 he was again commissioned, by Governor Myron H. Clark, while in 1857 he was commissioned by Governor John A. King. In 1860 he removed to Cresskill, N. J. When the Civil War broke out he recruited a company at Closter, N. J., for the Independent Battalion of the Bergen County Brigade, and in 1862 was commissioned its Captain by Governor Charles S. Olden. One hundred and fifty men rendezvoused at Trenton under his command, becoming a part of the Twenty-second New Jersey Volunteer Infantry. When field officers were appointed Captain Demarest became Major. He held this rank until January, 1863, when he was commissioned Colonel. The regiment left Trenton for Washington, September 22, 1862, joined the Army of the Potomac, and thereafter participated in all the campaigns and hard-fought battles of that army.

Colonel Demarest is a prominent member of the Military Order of the Loyal Legion, the Grand Army of the Republic, and the Society of the Army of the Potomac. After his return to civil life he removed from Cresskill to Tenafly, N. J., where he has since engaged successfully in mercantile pursuits.

Colonel Demarest's first wife was Charity Ferdon, daughter of Henry

Ferdon and Frances Tallman. She died in October, 1872. He married (2) Ellen Van Giesen, of Paterson, N. J. His issue by the first wife were Margaretta, Maria Louise, and Edwin, and by the second wife Clifford, Amy E., Marion L., and H. Le Roy.

WALTER CHRISTIE is descended from the same American ancestor as Cornelius Christie (see sketch on page 106), James Christie, of Aberdeen, Scotland, the emigrant, who had ten children or more of the second generation, one of whom, William (2), married Catharine Demarest and by her had ten or twelve children. One of these was "Captain James," and another was Peter W. Christie (3), who married Belitie Westervelt, by whom he had several children, one of whom was Ralph P. Christie (4), born at Schraalenburgh, October 12, 1783, died June 15, 1873, married Catharine Westervelt, born October 7, 1787, died April 26, 1848. They resided at Schraalenburgh and had three sons: Cornelius R. and Doweh, who were apprenticed to the harnessmaking trade, and Peter, who was apprenticed to the trade of mason. Cornelius R. Christie (5) married Annie Christie. One of their children was Walter Christie, the subject of this sketch.

Walter Christie (6) was born at Schraalenburgh, near the South Church, November 16, 1863, and still resides on the old homestead of his paternal grandfather, Ralph Christie, purchased by the latter March 31, 1808, from Wiert Banta. The locality is now known as the Borough of Bergenfield, of which Walter Christie is now the Mayor. For many years after his purchase from Banta, Ralph Christie conducted a tannery on the farm, and when his sons, Cornelius and Doweh, reached the age of sixteen he apprenticed them to the harnessmaking trade, which they successfully followed until the breaking out of the Civil War.

WALTER CHRISTIE.

Walter Christie attended the public schools of his district, and succeeded his father as a farmer, having inherited the homestead. He still conducts the farm, and has, in addition, built up a thrifty real estate and insurance business. He has also managed with great success a number of large and important estates, for several of which he has acted as executor. In all these connections Mr. Christie has gained an honorable standing as a man of ability, integrity, and enterprise.

He has also been prominent and influential in public affairs, having served for eight consecutive years as Collector of Taxes for the old Township of Palisade, which embraced the territory lying between the Hudson

River on the east and the Hackensack River on the west, in Bergen County. In March, 1897, he was elected Mayor of the Borough of Bergenfield, and served two years, declining a renomination in 1899, and was succeeded by Mr. Van Valkenburgh, the present Mayor. On the 15th of March, 1900, he was elected a member of the Board of Chosen Freeholders of Bergen County by the largest majority ever given any candidate for any office in Palisade Township. Mr. Christie has discharged every duty with satisfaction and credit, not only to himself, but to all his constituents, and is widely respected and esteemed for those qualities which mark the successful man, and for that public spirit, methodical devotion, and genial good nature which have characterized his life. He is a member of Lodge No. 3,638, Knights of Honor, of Tenafly, N. J., and a regular attendant at the Christian Reformed Church.

Mr. Christie married Maria Van Wagoner, daughter of John Van Wagoner, Jr., of Kinderkamack, now Etna, N. J.

JOHN W. HECK, who has been actively and successfully engaged in the practice of law in Jersey City since 1876, was born in Trenton, N. J., July 27, 1855, and when three years old (1859) came with his parents to Jersey City, where his father took charge of the oil works of I. & C. Moore, located at the foot of Morris Street. His father died in 1865. On the 1st of April, 1867, young Heck entered the office of the late Stephen Billings Ransom, with whom he later began the study of law. He became a clerk and student at law in the office of L. & A. Zabriskie on September 28, 1874, and at the November term of the New Jersey Supreme Court in 1876 he was admitted to the bar.

After the dissolution of this firm Mr. Heck remained with Lansing Zabriskie, the senior member, until 1884, when Mr. Zabriskie retired from practice. Mr. Heck then assumed charge of the business as Mr. Zabriskie's attorney, and upon the latter's death on March 29, 1892, continued as the attorney for estates for which Mr. Zabriskie had been trustee. Mr. Heck's practice has been largely in that field of legal work.

In 1884 Mr. Heck was elected a member of the New Jersey Assembly from the Sixth Hudson District, and during his term introduced the famous citizens' charter, which was defeated by his Republican colleagues from Jersey City. He also introduced and secured the passage of the firemen's tenure of office act, removing the Jersey City Fire Department from politics, and re-introduced the bill providing for a bridge over the "Gap," on Washington Street, which, as in a former attempt to pass this bill, was defeated, owing to the powerful influence brought to bear against it. In 1885 Mr. Heck was renominated for member of Assembly, but was defeated by Hon. R. S. Hudspeth. Two years later, in 1887, a committee of the Hudson County Bar Association, of which Mr. Heck was made a member, was appointed to prepare a bill to provide proper indices in the office of the register of deeds, and in connection with Spencer Weart, a fellow member of the committee, Mr. Heck secured the passage of the law providing for the well-known "block system." The work under this act was performed by the commission appointed by Judge Manning M. Knapp, of which Mr. Heck was clerk, and completed in fourteen months. Hudson County now has the best set of indices to its land records that exist in the State.

Mr. Heck was a charter member of the old Jersey City Athletic Club, and served in official capacities during the first six years of its existence, and in 1884 was its President. He is a member of Amity Lodge, F. and A. M., of Jersey City, and of several social and fraternal orders, and a Trustee, Secretary, and Treasurer of the Bay View Cemetery Association.

He was married October, 1884, to Miss Lillian Benson, of Haverstraw, N. Y. They have had two children.

J. HULL BROWNING, prominent financier and railroad president, was born at Orange, N. J., December 25, 1841, and is the son of John Hazzard Browning and Elizabeth Smith (Hull) Browning, both natives of New London County, Conn. His paternal ancestor, Nathaniel Browning, came to this country from England in 1645 and settled at Warwick, R. I. On the maternal side he descends from Rev. Joseph Hull, born in Somersetshire, England, in 1595, who settled in Weymouth, Plymouth Colony, in 1635, and in 1639 was one of the founders of Barnstable, Cape Cod, Mass. The descendants of Rev. Joseph Hull were conspicuous in the Revolutionary War and in the War of 1812, both in the army and navy. Colonel John Hull, grandfather of J. Hull Browning, commanded a regiment at the battle of Stonington, Conn.

Mr. Browning was brought to New York at the age of two years, was educated in the public schools, and was graduated from the New York Free Academy (now the College of the City of New York). He engaged in the wholesale clothing business in New York City with two brothers until 1883. Upon the death of Charles G. Sisson, his wife's father, he was left as executor of his estate, and one year later (1875) succeeded him as President of the Northern Railroad of New Jersey, a position which he held till July, 1897, when he sold out his interest in that corporation. He was left, also, as executor of his father's estate and succeeded him as Director and later became President of the Richmond County Gas Light Company. He has been prominently and successfully connected with numerous railroad and commercial enterprises. He improved the facilities of the Northern Railroad of New Jersey, and built some of the finest railroad depots in the country to accommodate its business.

Although a prominent and influential Republican, Mr. Browning has always refused offers of nominations for public office, but he has taken a leading part in every movement made to advance the interests of Bergen County and of the Town of Tenafly, where he resides. He was for some time President of the County Republican League and is Vice-President of Christ Hospital in Jersey City, a charity which has profited by his business ability and generous liberality. He was a Presidential Elector on the Republican ticket in 1892 and 1896, but with the exception of these honors, and local responsibilities in the Borough of Tenafly he has held no offices.

In 1871 he married Eva B. Sisson, daughter of Charles G. Sisson, of Jersey City, and they have one son, J. Hull Browning, Jr.

HENRY SIMMONS WHITE was born at Red Bank, Monmouth County, N. J., July 13, 1844, and is of the fifth generation of his family in this country, the founder, Thomas White, coming over from England about two hundred years ago. His father, Isaac Pennington White, a well known lumber merchant, who died January 28, 1876, was the son of Esek White and Ann Besonet, his wife, of French Huguenot extraction; a grandson of Thomas White, Jr.; and a great-grandson of Thomas White, Sr., the immigrant. On the maternal side Mr. White is of English and Irish ancestry, his mother, Adaline Simmons, being a descendant of the old Simmons family of Maryland, from which State her parents, Abraham Simmons and Temperance Jones, removed to Ontario County, N. Y., where she was born.

Mr. White was graduated from the College of Physicians and Surgeons of New York (Medical Department of Columbia University) in 1864, but, being under age, did not receive the degree of M.D. until March, 1866. He was Acting Assistant Surgeon in the United States Army in the War of the Rebellion, enlisting in 1864. From 1865 to 1868 he practiced medicine at Red Bank, N. J. He then read law with Hon. William A. Lewis, of Jersey City, was graduated from Columbia Law School, and in June, 1870, was admitted to the bar of New York. In October, 1872, he was admitted to practice as an attorney at the bar of New Jersey, and in November, 1875, as a counselor. Since 1872 he has successfully practiced his profession in Jersey City. He was Assistant Collector of Customs, Port of New York, from 1878 to 1882, delegate from New Jersey to the Republican National Convention at Chicago in 1888, United States Attorney for the District of New Jersey from 1890 to 1894, and at present is Chairman of the Monmouth County Republican Committee. He is President of the Red Bank Board of Trade, Vice-President of the Navesink National Bank of Red Bank, a Director in the Hudson County National Bank of Jersey City, and was at one time President of the Hudson Tunnel Railroad Company. He is a member of the Union League of Jersey City and the Grand Army of the Republic, of which he was Department Commander in 1895 and 1896.

Mr. White was married, November 19, 1878, at Freehold, N. J., to Annie H., daughter of Judge Amzi C. McLean and a granddaughter on her mother's side of John Hull, a Revolutionary soldier who was captured and held a prisoner by the British. They have one child, Margaretta P.

CHARLES PITMAN BUCKLEY, Mayor of the Borough of Tenafly, Bergen County, and a prominent member of the bar of New York City, was born in West Bloomfield, Essex County, N. J., on the 22d of December, 1834. His father, John Buckley, who became a resident of Bergen County in 1845, was a native of Yorkshire, England, while his mother, Elizabeth Van Gieson, was descended from Rynier Bastienstianse, a native of Giesen, a village in North Brabant, who came to this country in 1660 and taught the first school at Flatbush, L. I., also performing the duties of court master, rung the bell, kept the church in order, and performed the duties of precentor, attended to the burial of the dead, etc., for a salary of 200 florins, exclusive of perquisites. He removed to Bergen, N. J., where he and his sons Garret, Isaac, George, and Rynier bought land and later purchased and settled on lands north and northeast of Hackensack in Bergen County. Isaac died in 1703 and a son, Jacob, died in 1704.

Mr. Buckley received his education in the public schools of New York City and Bergen County, N. J., and subsequently took up the study of law, being admitted to the bar by the Supreme Court in New York City at the October term in 1858. Entering at once upon the active practice of his profession in New York, he was in partnership with William G. Wheelright until 1862, and afterward with Jesse C. Smith and John S. Woodward under the firm names of Smith & Woodward, Smith, Woodward & Buckley, and Woodward & Buckley. Since January 1, 1891, he has been associated with William W. Buckley under the firm name of C. P. & W. W. Buckley. In 1873 he was appointed master in chancery by Chancellor Runyon.

Mr. Buckley has resided in Tenafly since 1865. Upon the formation of Palisade Township in 1870, and thereafter for about ten years, he took an active part in political matters, attending all the State and county conventions, at the same time declining all nominations for office. In March, 1899, however, he became Mayor of the borough. He is a member of the Lawyers' Club and of the New York Athletic Club, of New York City, and of the Long Beach Club, of Barnegat, and the Tenafly Club, of Tenafly, N. J.

Mr. Buckley was married in New York City, in 1857, to Ella Augusta Mix, who died in 1884, leaving four children: William W. Buckley, a graduate of Columbia College, New York City; Thomas J. Buckley, a graduate of Stevens Institute, Hoboken, N. J.; and two daughters.

WILLIAM JAMES TILLEY, pastor of the Protestant Episcopal Church, in Harrison, Hudson County, was born in Bristol, R. I., on the 16th of September, 1845. He is the son of Benjamin Tilley and Susan W. Easterbrooks, a grandson of Benjamin Tilley and Rachel Simmons, a great-grandson of William Tilley and Catherine Sabine, and a great-great-grandson of William Tilley, Jr., and Dorcas, his wife. William Tilley, Jr., was born in Exeter, England, about 1685. He came to Boston, Mass., where he married his wife, Dorcas, in 1736, and subsequently went to Newport, R. I., and established himself in business. From that early colonial period until the present the family has been conspicuous in civil and public affairs, and respected in the communities in which they resided. The name Tilley is first found on the roll of the companions of William the Conqueror in England, in 1066, and since that date it is found in every county in England, France, and Holland, and in 1620 in America. The coat-of-arms of the Tilleys of France is the same as of the family of England to-day. The first of the name in America were Edward and John Tilley, who came over in the "Mayflower," and whose names are on the Plymouth monument.

Mr. Tilley is a brother of Benjamin F. Tilley, Commander in the United States Navy, who was in command of the United States gunboat, "Newport," of the blockading squadron during the late Spanish-American War, and who in that capacity captured numerous prizes and distinguished himself for bravery, patriotism, and loyalty to duty.

Rev. William James Tilley was educated in the schools of his native town and at North Yarmouth Academy, near Portland, Me. He also took a special course of classical study under the direction of Dr. Leonard Bacon, of Yale University, and under Dr. McClintock, and was graduated from Drew Theological Seminary in 1871, receiving the degree of Bachelor of Divinity. In the meantime he had spent three years in the Treasury Department at Washington.

After graduating from Drew Theological Seminary he was successively pastor of charges at Sand Lake, N. Y., Dalton, Mass., Troy, N. Y., and Brandon, Vt., in which State he remained about ten years. In 1880 he took a special course in divinity under the direction of Bishop Bissell, of Vermont, and entered the ministry of the Protestant Episcopal Church, with which he has ever since been actively connected. He was called to Amherst, Mass., in 1888, and remained there about five years, being called from there January 1, 1893, to Newark (Harrison), N. J., where he still resides. He has built the Harrison church up to its present flourishing condition.

Rev. Mr. Tilley has achieved notable distinction in the priesthood, and during his twenty years with the Protestant Episcopal Church has exerted a wholesome influence in advancing its doctrines throughout the communities in which he has held rectorships. Endowed with intellectual ability of the highest order, he is an eloquent speaker, forcible and convincing in his arguments, simple and concise in diction, and beloved and esteemed by all who know him. He has also gained distinction in literature, having contributed a number of important articles to various magazines and periodicals. His poems in the New York *Independent* and other journals

have been favorably received. He was awarded the second prize out of four hundred competitors by judges appointed by *The Great Divide* for a poem on Colorado, and is also the author of a volume entitled *Masters of the Situation*, which has been issued in both trade and subscription editions. Mr. Tilley married Katharine J. Travis, of Cohoes, Albany County, N. Y.

EDWIN MANNERS, A.M., LL.B., is the son of the late Hon. David Stout Manners and Deborah Philips Johnes, and was born in Jersey City, N. J., on the 6th of March, 1855. His father was for several terms Mayor of Jersey City and universally esteemed and respected as one of its best executives and citizens. He is a grandson of David Manners, a great-grandson of John Manners, and a great-great-grandson of John Manners, Sr., of Yorkshire, England, who was born in 1678, emigrated to America about 1700, and married Rebecca Stout, of Middletown, N. J., a granddaughter of Richard and Penelope Van Princess Stout, of interesting memory, and the first in America. John Manners, Sr., settled at Upper Freehold, N. J., but afterward moved to Amwell, Hunterdon County, in this State, where he died in 1770. The American branch is connected with the noble family of Manners in England, which traces its distinguished lineage back to the time of William the Conqueror, and indeed is of Norman origin.

On his mother's side Edwin Manners is a grandson of David Johnes, a great-grandson of David Johnes, Sr., a great-great-grandson of Stephen Johnes, and a great-great-great-grandson of Samuel Johnes, Jr., who was the son of Samuel Johnes, Sr., whose father, Edward Johnes, of Somerset, England, came to Charlestown (Boston), Mass., with Governor Winthrop in 1630; he later was one of the founders of Southampton, Long Island, and died there in 1659. Edward married Anne, daughter of George and Alice Griggs, natives of Dinder. The Johnes family in the United States may be distantly related to that of Dolan Cothi, in Wales, which traces to Godebog, King of Britain, but is directly descended from the Johnes family of County Berks, County Salop, and London and Somerset, England, the branches living in those counties and also in Bristol all proceeding from the same original stock. Sir Francis Johnes was Lord Mayor of London in 1620. Edwin Manners's great-grandfather, John Schenck, was a Captain in the Revolutionary War, took an active part in the principal battles in the State, and by a well-planned ambuscade prevented the British troops from overrunning Hunterdon County. His grandfather, David Manners, who married Captain Schenck's daughter Mary, was an officer in the War of 1812, and won honorable mention in several important engagements. On the maternal side Mr. Manners's great-great-grandfather, Stephen Johnes, married Grace Fitz Randolph, whose brother Nathaniel gave to Princeton the land upon which Nassau Hall is erected, and his great-grandfather, David Johnes, was a Major in the Revolution and rendered efficient service in establishing American independence.

Edwin Manners early displayed unusual intellectual abilities, and in preparatory school and college won prizes for composition and select and original speaking which distinguished him as a scholar. From his earliest school days he exhibited a disposition for the world of letters. While a student at Hasbrouck Institute, Jersey City, he was connected with the *Quill*, a school paper, and while pursuing his studies at Sing Sing-on-the-Hudson was the editor of the *Mount Pleasant Reveille,* the organ of the Mount Pleasant cadets. During his senior year at Princeton University, from which he was graduated Bachelor of Arts in 1877, he was one of the editors of the *Nassau Literary Magazine,* and on class day delivered to the distinguished class of 1877 a characteristic presentation address. Princeton conferred upon him the degree of Master of Arts in 1880.

After leaving college Mr. Manners began the study of law with Collins & Corbin, of Jersey City, and at the same time took a course at the Columbia Law School in New York City, graduating from that institution with the degree of LL.B. in 1879. In November, 1880, he was admitted to the bar, and since then he has been actively and successfully engaged in the practice of his profession in his native city. Although interested in municipal matters and politics, he has declined offers of political preferment. A large portion of his time is taken up with the care and management of his own property and business affairs.

Mr. Manners has ably assisted those who have procured for Jersey City an improved water supply and other public improvements. Greater Jersey City has also claimed Mr. Manners's attention, and received his favorable comment. Many advantages are to be gained in bringing the various municipalities of Hudson County under one name and government. This unity of development in particular is much to be desired. With the extension of rapid transit facilities the last of apparent excuses for delaying consolidation has disappeared, and it would seem a needless expense to keep up separate charters in contiguous towns.

As a landlord Mr. Manners is liked by his tenants, and their praise is in evidence of his liberality and forbearance. He is a member of the Hudson County Bar Association, the University and Palma Clubs of Jersey City, the Princeton Club of New York City, the Sons of the American Revolution, and other societies. Of literary aptitude, he writes occasionally for newspapers and magazines. He is unmarried.

PETER E. MOORE, merchant, Borough Collector, and since 1877 Postmaster of Schraalenburgh, Bergen County, N. J., was born in New York City on the 18th of October, 1842. He is the son of Peter D. and Elizabeth (Voorhis) Moore, his mother being of Holland Dutch descent. Samuel Moore and his wife Naomi emigrated to America from the Island of Barbadoes, W. I., in 1671-72. Barbadoes was then under the control of England, and both Samuel and his wife were English people. They landed and located at Boston, where their son, Francis Moore, was born about 1674. Francis Moore came to New York and from thence in 1690 to Bergen County (English Neighborhood), where he married Jannetje Laurens, daughter of Thomas Laurens, of Newtown, L. I. They eventually settled at English Neighborhood (near Ridgefield), in Bergen County, where some of their descendants have ever since lived. He had several children, the youngest of whom was Samuel, who married Sara (Michaels) Smith, another of the original settlers in Ridgefield Township. From this couple have sprung most of the Moores in Bergen County.

Peter E. Moore was educated in the public schools of Bergen County, whither his parents removed from New York City when he was a mere boy. He left school at about the age of seventeen and went to work on his father's farm, and in the active and healthful duties of an agriculturist continued until he was thirty. This period was one of constant usefulness. He laid the foundation of a sturdy physique, acquired habits which insured success, and gained a reputation for industry, enterprise, and integrity. But farming was not destined to be his life work. In 1873 he engaged in the grocery business in Schraalenburgh, which he has ever since followed, building up a large and successful trade. He has been for many years one of the principal merchants in that village. In 1877 he was appointed Postmaster of Schraalenburgh, and by successive re-appointments has continued to hold that important position. Mr. Moore is also Collector of the borough, having held that office since 1895. He is a regular attendant at the Dutch Reformed Church of Schraalenburgh, and in every capacity has distinguished himself for ability, sound common sense, enterprise, and public spirit.

Mr. Moore married Miss Charlotte Christie, and has had five children—three sons and two daughters.

ABRAM I. AURYANSEN, of Hackensack, whose career as a locomotive engineer dates from 1852, is the son of John and Elizabeth (Auryansen) Auryansen, and was born in Closter, Bergen County, N. J., April 5, 1822. His first American ancestor was Lambert Arianse, who came from Holland to America in 1682, and became one of the original patentees of the Tappan patent. Most of his descendants adopted the name of Smith and are scattered principally throughout Rockland County, N. Y. Lambert Arianse (or Auryansen) married in New York, in April, 1682, Margaretta Gerrets Blauvelt, a daughter of another of the Tappan patentees, and resided in Rockland County. Two of his sons, John and Arie (Aaron), who married respectively Margaretta Meyers and Cornelia Naugle, settled near Closter, Bergen County, N. J. The subject of this sketch is descended from Arie (Aaron) Auryansen and Cornelia Naugle, who had children John, Resolvent, Vroutie, Garret, Ann, and Maria. Mr. Auryansen's paternal grandparents were Daniel and Tiny (Cole) Auryansen, Daniel being a son of John Auryansen. His maternal grandparents were Garrett and Elleanor (Van Valen) Auryansen and his great-great-grandfather Aaron Auryansen, above mentioned.

Mr. Auryansen received his educational training in the public schools of Harrington Township in Bergen County, and in hard work and study developed those traits which have marked his long and honorable career. As a boy he exhibited unusual mechanical genius and a strong inclination for that line of industry, and leaving school at the age of seventeen began to learn the trade of blacksmith. In 1843 he engaged in this business for himself and followed it with great success for eight years, leaving it in 1851 to accept a position as fireman on the Erie Railroad. In 1852 he was promoted to locomotive engineer, and in this capacity has ever since been in active service. He is one of the oldest and best known engineers on the Erie system, his career on that road covering a period of forty-eight years. His profession has always been of a nature which precluded his entrance into public and political life, yet he has from the first taken a deep interest in local matters, and in Hackensack, where he has so long resided, he has exerted no small influence upon the general welfare. As a member of the Dutch Reformed Church he has been active in the support of those movements which benefit a town and its people. He is a loyal, public spirited citizen, a firm friend, and a man of unswerving integrity.

Mr. Auryansen married Cornelia Haring, whose ancestors were also early residents of Bergen County. They have four children: John, Maria, Ellen, and Eliza.

ROBERT LINN LAWRENCE, one of the prominent members of the bar of Jersey City, was born in Sparta, Sussex County, N. J., October 4, 1851. He is the son of Thomas and Margaret Rembert (Taylor) Lawrence and a great-grandson of Thomas Lawrence, of "Morrisvale," Sussex County, who was appointed Judge of the Sussex County Court of Common Pleas in February, 1801. His great-great-grandfather, Lewis Morris, was one of the Signers of the Declaration of Independence and Judge of the Court of Admiralty from 1760 to 1876, and the son of Lewis Morris, Sr., who was Judge of the Court of Admiralty in 1738, having jurisdiction in the Provinces of New York, New Jersey, and Connecticut. Lewis Morris, the father of Judge Lewis Morris, Sr., last named, was Governor of New Jersey, Judge of the Court of Common Pleas in 1692, and Chief Justice of the Supreme Court of New York from 1715 to 1733.

Robert L. Lawrence thus numbers among his ancestors some of the most distinguished men in the professional history of New Jersey and New York, and at an early age developed those sterling qualities which characterize his race. He was graduated from Princeton College in the class of 1873, with honors, and afterward read law with Thomas Anderson, of Newton, N. J., being admitted to the bar of the State as an attorney in November, 1876, and as a counselor in June, 1885. Since 1876 Mr. Lawrence has been actively and successfully engaged in the practice of his profession in Jersey City, where he steadily rose to prominence among the members of the Hudson County bar. Endowed with broad intellectual qualifications, with superior judgment and great energy, he has through his own efforts achieved distinction as an able, industrious, and painstaking lawyer, and is highly esteemed and respected by all who know him. He was associated with Stewart Rapalje in conducting the *Criminal Law Magazine* from the commencement of the work until 1883 and in the preparation of that valuable and well known work entitled *Rapalje and Lawrence's Law Dictionary*. These enterprises as well as a number of other important achievements in the field of legal literature have gained for him a wide reputation in both legal and literary circles.

Mr. Lawrence was married on the 18th of December, 1893, to Lillian M. Fisher, daughter of the late John H. Fisher and Jeannette P. (Walters) Fisher, of Jersey City, N. J., where they reside.

JOSEPH CHILD, Street Commissioner of the Town of Kearny, N. J., is the son of George and Bridget (Noon) Child, and was born in Bradford, Yorkshire, England, on the 26th of September, 1849. The family is an old one in both England and America, and is descended from three brothers who figure conspicuously in the early shipbuilding interests of the English nation, and who received titles for their activity in both industrial and public affairs. Mr. Child's parents were both born and married in England, and spent their active lives in that country. There he received an excellent private school education, and after completing his studies he engaged in the business of brick contracting, which he followed successfully until 1873, when he came to America. Locating first in New York City, he soon mastered and for some time followed the trade of iron moulder. In 1884 he removed to Kearny, Hudson County, N. J., where he still resides. Here he resumed his trade for a few years and then engaged in the meat business for himself. He followed that line with marked success until he was obliged to abandon it in order to devote all his energies to the public positions which his fellow-citizens conferred upon him.

As a stanch and consistent Republican Mr. Child has taken an active interest in the affairs of his adopted town, and for several years has wielded an important influence in party councils and municipal matters. He has served as Water Purveyor and Street Commissioner of the Borough of Kearny with great satisfaction and still holds those positions. He is an active member of the Exempt Fire Department of Kearny and has held the positions of Foreman and Assistant Foreman. He is a member of the

Methodist Episcopal Church, a prominent member of Victory Lodge, Knights and Ladies of the Golden Star, of Arlington, public spirited, patriotic, and enterprising, thoroughly interested in the affairs of the community, and highly respected as a liberal and energetic citizen. His integrity of character, his faithfulness in all business relations, and the close attention which he has given to public duties have brought him into more than local prominence, and stamp him as a man of the highest attributes. Though born and reared in England, he is descended from ancestors who came to America during the early history of the colonies and fought with distinction in the Revolutionary War.

Mr. Child was married first to Martha Ann Berry, daughter of William and Sarah (Greaves) Berry, of Oldham, England. She died leaving two children, William and Matthew. He married for his second wife, Eva Gilbert (*nee* Revere), daughter of Judge Revere, of Harrison, N. J. She died January 23, 1899. For his third wife he married Mrs. Annie Eastwood, of Kearny, N. J., where they reside.

PETER BENTLEY, Sr., was one of the most illustrious members of the bar of the State of New Jersey, and was peculiarly identified with Jersey City as one of two or three lawyers who first practiced in that municipality. Mr. Bentley was the son of Christopher and Eleanor (Althouse) Bentley, of English descent upon his father's side. His mother's family was one of the ancient Holland stocks of New Amsterdam. Their son was born in 1805 upon a farm in the village of Half Moon, Saratoga County, N. Y.

Young Bentley's services were required upon the farm during the summer season, and he enjoyed only such educational facilities as the crude district schools of that pioneer country afforded. The very excellent education, classical as well as English, which he enjoyed during life was wholly the result of his own application in reading and study. In 1825, after twenty years spent upon the farm, he came to Jersey City and entered the employ of Yates & McIntyre, who conducted a species of printing business. He remained with them for five years, and during this time determined to adopt the more ambitious profession of a lawyer, which had been his desire from early boyhood. Thus early in 1830 he entered the law office of Samuel Cassedy, whose practice extended throughout the old County of Bergen, from Rockland County in New York to Kill von Kull.

Mr. Bentley read law assiduously, and was soon practicing with unusual success in the justices' courts. He gained the confidence of the old Dutch farmers of Bergen County, and became in a special sense their lawyer. He was admitted to the bar of New Jersey at the May term of the Supreme Court in 1834, and in the September term of 1839 was admitted as a counselor, with the full privilege of practice in all the higher courts of the State. But in 1833, a year previous to his admission even to ordinary practice, we find him holding the office of City Clerk, or "Clerk of the Board of Select Men of Jersey City," as the title reads, in the rising young municipality which he had chosen as the scene of his life's work. Nothing could bear more striking testimony than this fact to the universal confidence and esteem which he inspired. Later on, as a full-fledged lawyer, he became the attorney of the selectmen of Jersey City, and represented them in 1842 in the celebrated case of the selectmen against Dummer, in which he triumphantly established the doctrine of dedication by maps.

In 1843 Mr. Bentley was elected to the office of Mayor of Jersey City, which, as has been well said, " was not so much a matter of party success as an expression of confidence and good will among neighbors." During this same year (1843) was inaugurated the famous case in which Mr. Bentley maintained the right of Mrs. Bell to lands under water, on the western shore of the Hudson River, which had descended to her by will and been re-affirmed by an act of the New Jersey Legislature. This controversy was carried from court to court, and contested in all the higher courts in the State during the greater part of a quarter of a century, when Mr. Bentley finally triumphed, to the great surprise of those who had prophesied failure.

Peter Bentley

This case well illustrates the persistence which was so characteristic a feature and such an important element of his success in all his cases throughout his life.

Mr. Bentley also contributed largely toward the commercial upbuilding of Jersey City. Finding the banking facilities wholly inadequate to the needs of the growing city, and having the full confidence of capitalists, in 1853 he organized the Mechanics' and Traders' Bank and became its President. In this position he manifested remarkable business abilities, and to his personal efforts the institution is principally indebted for its prosperity.

He also became a prominent Trustee of the Provident Institution for Savings in Jersey City, and continued as its legal adviser until his death. Similarly, he was Vice-President of the Savings Bank of Jersey City, a Director and at one time Treasurer of the Gas Company, and Treasurer of the Jersey City and Bergen Plank Road Company. Beginning with an extensive purchase of land in 1854, he was also a pioneer in the development of real estate interests on the western slope of Bergen Hill. Here he built the elegant mansion which still remains the home of his wife. The activity he manifested outside the strict lines of his profession, as shown in these various enterprises, gives us good evidence not only of his unusual business abilities, but of the great confidence which was reposed in him by shrewd business men on every hand.

"Peter Bentley," says Jacob Weart, Esq., of Jersey City, "was one of the active men who laid the foundations and who helped to plan our municipal corporations, and draft our laws and charters, upon which the institutions of this great county have been reared." Mr. Bentley also interested himself in the cause of his fellow-citizens to prevent municipal extravagance and unjust and wasteful tax extortion. Finding that the accumulations of unpaid taxes of many years had imposed burdens upon millions of dollars worth of property which were absolutely unjust and unendurable to the property holders, he conceived the idea of a commission composed of leading citizens which should readjust these burdens upon an equitable basis, advantageous to the suffering citizens and the city treasury alike. Accordingly, in 1873, he brought his plan before the consideration of the Legislature, and had the pleasure of seeing it enacted into law. Under its provisions a commission was appointed with Judge Haines, an ex-Governor and ex-Justice of the Supreme Court, at its head. The work accomplished by this commission has been simply invaluable to Jersey City, and has satisfactorily solved the most formidable problem which ever threatened the welfare of the municipality. The accomplishment of this plan of relief was the last great service which Mr. Bentley rendered to his fellow-citizens ere he passed away, on the 26th of September, 1875.

He was a rare gentleman, peculiarly attached to his wife and children, most gracious and hospitable in his home, sincere and earnest in his religious faith, and so honest and honorable in all the affairs of life that the faintest breath was never raised to question his perfect integrity.

On the 13th of October, 1842, Mr. Bentley was married to Miss Margaret E. Holmes, of Jersey City, the descendant of an ancient English family. Highly cultivated, and of the most kindly disposition, she was the devoted companion of Mr. Bentley, and was a source of strength and inspiration to him until the day of his death. She still survives him, as she does also her son, Peter Bentley, Second, and holds their memory in reverent affection. In addition to this son, a sketch of whose life is also given here, they were blessed with but one other child, a daughter.

PETER BENTLEY, Second, the only son of the subject of the previous sketch and the heir of all his hopes, succeeded his father in the respect and affection of the community, just as he succeeded him in his legal practice and other business affairs. Never was a father more wrapped up in a son, and never did a son respond more perfectly to the high ideal of his father. He was born in Jersey City on the 5th of December, 1845, and received his education entirely at home and in his father's law office. As a boy he manifested a most amiable disposition, and was much given to serious reading—the thorough investigation of historical questions, and peculiarly of everything concerning his father's affairs and important law cases. The Rev. Van Cleck was the boy's tutor, and he grounded him in a most thorough education. When a boy, during his summer vacations and on Saturdays, he used to accompany his father to his office, and there copy

papers and entertain himself with various law authorities. His father encouraged him to think that he was thus of great assistance, and presently, indeed, he was enabled to copy briefs and make citations, etc., with a skill which was of real service.

As his general education was finished, and he began to study law in earnest, a room in his father's office was especially fitted up for his use, and here he mastered the intricacies of legal lore and prepared himself for the examination which must precede his admission to the bar. It has been said that the hopes of the father were completely wrapped up in the son. The desire of the former that the young man should do well in the examinations was so great that, as the ordeal approached, his anxiety quite unnerved him, and he was obliged to absent himself during the examination. In this suspense his relief can be imagined when a neighbor brought him the news of the result, remarking with a laugh, "You need not have felt anxious, Bentley, for your son has carried off the honors, with the highest standing in the entire class of thirty candidates who took the examination." And such indeed was the fact. Immediately upon his son's admission to the bar, the elder Mr. Bentley formally turned over his office to him, placed all his affairs in his hands, and gave him the full revenues of their joint practice. Thus gradually the elder lawyer withdrew from active practice, devoting his energies in other directions, until the full burden of his extensive legal business was fully settled upon his son's shoulders.

Nor was the latter in any way unworthy to take his father's place. He maintained the same relative position in the community as his father, displayed similar abilities and the same unimpeachable integrity, and inspired everywhere the same widespread confidence and respect. He frequently championed the cause of his fellow-citizens, as his father had done. For example, he was the successful counsel in proceedings whereby the unjust water rents on vacant property, and upon property where the water privileges were not used, were set aside and made inoperative, with thus a great saving effected to the taxpayers. Again, at the time of his death, he was the representative of the citizens in proceedings instituted to set aside the whole tax levy on the ground of gross inequality in its assessment. But his practice was most remarkable for his handling of commercial entanglements and the adjustment of the affairs of great corporate enterprises. He manifested great ability in settling disputes, and thus keeping them out of the courts. He was the counsel for the Standard Oil Company, one of the leading counsel of the Lehigh Valley Railroad Company, and counsel for the Barber Asphalt Company, of New York City, and the Provident Institution for Savings and the Consumers Gas Company, of Jersey City. He also rendered important legal services to the Pennsylvania Railroad Company.

Mr. Bentley was a man of remarkable powers of memory. He kept the most minute details of all of his cases in his mind, and could lay his finger on any given fact at any time. After his father's death he, in 1875, formed a legal partnership with Charles H. Hartshorne, under the firm name of Bentley & Hartshorne. This endured until January 1, 1886, when Mr. Hartshorne was obliged to withdraw on account of ill health. From this time until his own death Mr. Bentley practiced alone. This sad event occurred on the 30th of April, 1888, when he was in the prime of life, and it was considered a public calamity by the whole community. He was never strong in constitution, yet did not himself realize this fact, and often worked beyond his strength. He was of a refined, sensitive, and sympathetic nature, benevolent and whole-hearted like his father, and as deeply attached to his own family.

November 30, 1869, Mr. Bentley married Miss Emma Parker, of Jersey City, daughter of Captain Robert Parker, who was the owner of Watts Island, in Chesapeake Bay, where he died and was buried. This island has been the old family patrimony for many generations, since its first occupation in early colonial days. Their children were Eleanor, born July 13,

1871, now the wife of Warren H. Dixon, son of Judge Dixon, of Jersey City; Emily, born December 5, 1872, now Mrs. Joseph M. Rector; Peter Bentley, third, born February 6, 1874; Richard Parker Bentley, born September 25, 1875; John, born June 16, 1879; Eugenie, born December 23, 1881; and Parker, born June 16, 1884.

PETER BENTLEY, Third, eldest son of Peter Bentley, Second, and Emma (Parker) Bentley, was born in Jersey City on the 6th of February, 1874. He pursued his studies at Princeton College for a time and subsequently read law with Warren Dixon. He was admitted to the bar of New Jersey

PETER BENTLEY, 3D.

before the Supreme Court November 27, 1895, and since then has been actively and successfully engaged in the practice of his profession in Jersey City. Mr. Bentley has displayed marked legal qualifications, and though a young man has already gained distinction as a lawyer and advocate. He is prominently identified with public affairs and respected and esteemed by all who know him.

THE BLACKLEDGES of Bergen County are descended from John Blackleach, of Boston, and his second wife, Elizabeth (daughter of Benjamin Herbert). One of their three children, Philip Blackledge, came, it is said, from Wethersfield, Conn., to New York, in 1709, and on November 29, 1710, married Willempie Conwell, born in England in 1680.

Philip Blackledge removed from New York to Elizabethtown, N. J., early in 1723, and there remained until his death in 1761. His will was proved and recorded at Trenton, N. J., July 11, 1761. He was a man of some means and wrote the title "Gentleman" after his name. By his will he gave his children each five shillings and the balance of his estate, lands and money, to his wife absolutely. His issue were eight children, four baptized at New York and four at Elizabethtown, N. J.: Annatie, 1713; Philip, 1716; Zacharias, 1718; Philip, 1720; Catharine, 1730; Jacob, 1735; Sarah, 1740; and Benjamin.

Benjamin Blackledge (2) was born at Elizabethtown, N. J., August 25, 1743. While still a young man he went on foot from Elizabethtown to Closter and taught school there, the first one in the northern part of Bergen County. Here he married, April 20, 1770, Cathelyntie Tallman. He became the most prominent man in the northern part of Bergen County, was the first Town Clerk of Harrington Township in 1775, a Justice of the Peace, a Judge of the County Court of Common Pleas, and filled other township and county offices. He was a splendid penman, of which fact hundreds of old deeds and other documents still extant bear witness. He died at Closter, November 27, 1815, and his wife died October 5, 1836. His issue were Benjamin, 1770; Maria, 1772; Cornelius, 1774; Sarah, 1776; Jacobus, 1779; Peter, 1782; Henry, 1784; Jacob, 1786; and Elizabeth, 1788. These married as follows: Benjamin, Deborah Westervelt and Lea Powless; Maria, Daniel Van Sciver; Cornelius, Rachel Powless; Sarah, Seba P. Bogert; Peter, Elizabeth D. Naugle; Henry, Catharine Manning; and Elizabeth, Cornelius Van Valen. Their descendants are still numerous throughout Bergen County.

THE BLANCHES of Bergen County are descended from Richard Blanch, a native of Bristol, England, where he was born in 1704. He came to America prior to 1732, and settled near Closter in Bergen County. In 1733 he married Classie Van Giesen, of New York. He owned lands in what was then called the "Closter Mountains," on the Palisades of the Hudson. He died September 6, 1767. His issue were Ann, 1734; Isaac, 1736; Thomas; and Cornelia, 1745. Of these Ann married John Blawvelt, of Tappan. Isaac married Geertje Johns Haring. Cornelia married David Smith. All of Richard Blanch's children settled at Tappan and in the upper part of Bergen County. The issue of Isaac Blanch were Isaac, Martina, Richard, Abram, Thomas, John Henry, and Classie.

Thomas Blanch (2) was one of the most prominent men in Bergen County in his day. He was a magistrate and held other township and county offices. He raised and was Captain of a company of volunteers from Bergen County during the Revolutionary struggle. He was born near Closter in 1740, and died June 3, 1825. He married, in 1761, Effie Johns Mabie, of Tappan, who was born in 1741, and died August 28, 1825. Their issue were thirteen children: Elizabeth, 1762; Classie, 1763; Ann, 1765; Richard, 1766; Susanna, 1769; John, 1770; Thomas, 1774; Isaac, 1776; Elizabeth, 1779, and Cornelia, 1779 (twins); Effie, 1783; and Lea, 1786, and Rachel, 1786 (twins). The descendants of these are scattered over Bergen County, particularly the northern part.

MARKHAM E. STAPLES, of Jersey City, President of the New Jersey State Board of Prison Inspectors, was born in New York City on the 10th of December, 1850. He is the son of John Buthune Staples and Elizabeth Douglass Young, daughter of William Young, his paternal grandfather being Seth P. Staples. The family is an old and prominent one in American history and for generations have been influential citizens.

Mr. Staples was educated at Dwight and Holbrook's School in Clinton, N. Y., and at Poughkeepsie (New York) Military Institute. Afterward he spent one year as draughtsman with J. A. Wood, a prominent architect in Poughkeepsie, and three years as draughtsman and rodman in the Croton Aqueduct Department, New York City. For fourteen months he was brakeman and baggagemaster of the Iowa division of the Chicago, Burlington and Quincy Railroad, and for twenty-seven years he has been associated with the Erie Railroad as conductor, yardmaster, station master, superintendent of floating equipment and lighterage, and general agent of the New York terminal, which responsible position he now holds. In all these capacities Mr. Staples has displayed untiring energy and devotion to duty, great executive ability, and all those qualities which win both respect and approval.

MARKHAM E. STAPLES.

In public life he has also achieved distinction. He has been an Inspector of the New Jersey State Prison for eight years and President of the Board of Inspectors for five years, and has four years more to serve. He was appointed to this office by Governor Abbett and was re-appointed by Governors Werts and Voorhees, and has discharged its duties with universal satisfaction and approval. Mr. Staples is a prominent member of St. Mary's Episcopal Church of Jersey City, of the D. McLaughlin and Robert Davis Associations, and of the Carteret Club, all of Jersey City, and of the Commercial and Railroad Clubs of New York City. He is a life member of Jersey City Lodge, 211, B. P. O. E., and Vice-President of the National Board of Steam Navigators.

Mr. Staples was married, in 1880, to Miss Mary Willis, of Jersey City. They have two children, Francis George and Mary W.

EDWARD EVERSON, of West Hoboken, N. J., who has been associated with the Delaware Coal and Canal Company ever since 1863, was born at Homestead, North Bergen, Hudson County, January 14, 1840. His father, Benjamin Everson, was born at Pompton Plains, N. J. His mother's maiden name was Sarah Riker. Mr. Everson is of Holland lineage, being descended from the Evertsens who settled in New York two centuries ago.

He received his education in the public schools of North Bergen, and at the tender age of eleven began working on a farm in Bergen County. Thrown upon his own resources at that age, he has ever since depended upon himself. He followed farming until he had reached the age of seventeen, when he entered upon the trade of gold beating, which he followed for a year and a half. He then entered the employ of Edward Ackerman as an apprentice at the blacksmith trade, continuing in that capacity until 1862. In that year he enlisted in Company E, Eighth New York Volunteer Militia, for three months, and at the expiration of his term of enlistment was honorably discharged. He then entered the service of the Federal Government at the Brooklyn Navy Yard, where he remained for a short time, and in 1863 he associated himself with the Delaware Coal and Canal Company, with which he has ever since remained. During his long and active service of over thirty-three years in the employ of this corporation Mr. Everson has discharged every duty with singular fidelity and great satisfaction, and from the first has enjoyed the respect and confidence of both employers and associates. He is in the fullest sense a self-made man, having depended entirely upon himself since the early age of eleven years.

Mr. Everson is an ardent and consistent Republican, a member of the Reformed Church, and a member of the Independent Order of Odd Fellows. In July, 1863, he married Miss Ellen Gotchuns (deceased), by whom he had three children: Edward, Jr. (deceased), Eliza Ann (deceased), and Maud Alice, who resides with her father.

EGBERT SEYMOUR, Mayor of the City of Bayonne and widely known as a merchant in that part of Hudson County, was born in Ulster County, N. Y., December 15, 1850, the son of James Seymour and Sarah Ann, daughter of David and Elenor Radiker, and grandson of Charles and Eliza Seymour. His boyhood was not unlike those of other country lads. He attended the district schools, spent six months at the academy in Montgomery, Orange County, and another six months at the academy in Newburgh, in the same county, in New York State, and subsequently served as a clerk for twelve years. These advantages, however, afforded him an opportunity to lay the foundation upon which he has built a successful career. From a clerk he became a merchant, and for eighteen years has been actively and successfully engaged in the butter and cheese trade in New York City.

Mr. Seymour is one of the foremost citizens of his adopted city, a man universally esteemed and respected, and prominent and influential in every movement and especially in political affairs. For two years he rendered efficient service as a member of the Board of School Trustees. As Mayor of the City of Bayonne he has served three terms. He has been instrumental in advancing the best interests of the community, in building up the city, and in promoting many important public improvements. When his present term expires on May 1, 1901, he will have filled the office for six consecutive years, and it is safe to say that no man ever discharged its duties with more fidelity and honesty of purpose. Mr. Seymour is respected and esteemed for his ability and integrity of character, and in every capacity has gained the confidence of all who know him. He is a prominent member of the Newark Bay Boat Club, of the Exempt Firemen of Bayonne, of Council No. 695, Royal Arcanum, and of Council No. 434, Benevolent and Protective Order of Elks, of Bayonne. He is also a leading member of the Bayonne City Democratic Club and of the Robert Davis Association of Jersey City.

Mr. Seymour married, October 22, 1873, Marietta H. Neafie, and their children are James H. and Everett E. Seymour.

THE BROWER FAMILY is another very numerous family in Bergen County. They are descended from Adam Brouwer, who emigrated to New Amsterdam from Cologne, France, in 1642. Three years later he married Madalena Jacobs Ferdon, of Long Island. He was a miller, and lived in New Amsterdam until 1647, when he removed to Brooklyn, where he joined the Dutch Church in 1677 and paid taxes from 1675 to 1698. His issue were fifteen children: Peter, Jacobus, Aeltie, Matthew, William, Mary, Magdalena, Adam, Abraham, Sophia, Ann, Sarah, Nicholas, Daniel, and Rachel.

Peter, baptized in 1646, married (1) Pieternella Uldricks, (2) Gertrude Jans, and (3) Anne Jansen. He first resided at Flatlands, L. I., and subsequently removed to Brooklyn, where he died. His issue were Abram, John, Adolph, Magdalena, Ulrick, Adrientie, Vroutie, Cornelia, Jacob, Hanse, and Madeline.

Abraham, John, and Adolph removed to Hackensack about 1700, where Abraham married (1) Lea Johns Demarest and (2) Elizabeth Ackerman. Ulrick married Hester de Vow, and John married Ann Hendricks Mandeville. The descendants of Abraham, Ulrick, John, and Adolph are to-day very numerous and scattered over the Counties of Bergen and Hudson.

THE De CLARKS are still numerous in Bergen County. Daniel de Clerque (de Clark) emigrated to America prior to 1676. The name of his first wife does not appear, but the couple brought two or three children with them and had two baptized in New York (Daniel and Abraham, twins), March 13, 1678. His wife died soon after, and he married (2), March 4, 1685, Geertje Cozines, a widow, by whom he had no issue. Two of his sons, John and Henry, were evidently married when they left Holland, the family having sailed from Amsterdam. Both John and Henry subsequently had children in New York. Another son of Daniel, Jacobus de Clark, was born in Holland. Daniel, in 1686, became one of the Tappan patentees with the Harings, Blawvelts, Smiths, and others, and removed to Tappan, where, in 1702, he was made a Justice of Orange County, and he took the census of Orangetown the same year. He was probably the first Justice ever appointed in the county. At that time there were only a few families huddled at Tappan, and Daniel seems to have been the biggest man of them all. The marriage of his son Jacobus to Antie Van

Houten, September 14, 1706, is one of the earliest in the county. Jacobus had eight children, all of whom reared large families and gravitated southward into Bergen County.

JAMES S. NEWKIRK, Secretary and Treasurer of the Provident Institution for Savings, of Jersey City, was born in Bergen (now Jersey City) September 9, 1852. His family at one time was one of the most numerous in Hudson County, and the name is still very common. More than a century ago some members of the family settled in New York State, in Ulster and Sullivan Counties, where their numerous descendants have spread rapidly and become prominent in the various walks of life.

Mattheus Cornelissen, who is said to have been a native of Nieūwkercke (New Church) in Holland, emigrated to America in about the year 1660, and after landing and staying at New Amsterdam a short time went to Flatbush, L. I., where he bought and located on a "Bouwerie" of about thirty-six acres of land, butting, as his deed declared, on "Corlears Flats." This tract he sold March 10, 1665, to one Arent Evertse, and he removed thence to the "Towne of Bergen," in New Jersey. Here, on December 14, 1670, he married one Anna Luby, daughter of Jacob Luby, who had served as a non-commissioned officer (Sergeant) in the Dutch West India service, but who had for some years been a resident and landholder at Bergen.

JAMES S. NEWKIRK.

Mattheus Cornelissen assumed the surname of Newkirk—in honor of his birthplace, no doubt. He leased lands at Bergen which were afterward conveyed to his children. His occupation seems to have been that of a farmer. His wife, Anna, died December 20, 1685, and he married in 1686 Catharine Pouwless, a daughter of Poulus Pieterse, of Bergen. She died in April, 1764. The children of Matthew Cornelissen Van New Kirk were twelve—five by the first wife and seven by the second wife: Gertrude, Gerritie, Jacomina, Cornelius, Jacob, Jannetje, John, Jannetje, Peter, Gerrit, Poulus, and Cornelius.

Those by the first wife scattered to different parts of the country, while those of the second wife remained in Bergen County, inheriting all their mother's property, which was considerable. The eleventh of these children, Gerrit Newkirk (2d gen.), born at Bergen November 18, 1696, married September 5, 1730, Catrina, daughter of Hendrick Kuyper (Cooper). She died September 12, 1751. He died April 23, 1785. Their children of the third generation were four: Catrina, Janneke, Matthew, and Henry.

Matthew (3d gen.) married Caroline, daughter of Arent Toers. He died July 10, 1811, leaving three children: Garret M., Aaron, and Henry.

Garret M. Newkirk (4th gen.), born at Bergen April 9, 1766, died August 28, 1832, married Polly Ackerman. They had six children: Catharine, Margaret, Sally, Sally, Henry, and Garret.

Garret G. Newkirk (5th gen.), born at Bergen October 17, 1808, married (1) October 25, 1828, Rachel, daughter of Halmigh Van Houten. She died December 1, 1835. He married (2) Jane Fowler, widow of Abram Tice. She died October 6, 1849. He married (3) September 6, 1851, Eliza Ann Beatty, daughter of George E. Beatty, born in 1820. His children by three wives were: two by first wife, ten by second wife, and four by third wife. One of these children is the subject of this sketch.

James S. Newkirk (6th gen.) inherited all the sturdy characteristics of his race and early displayed those intellectual qualities which have since won for him so much distinction in the affairs of life. He was educated in the common schools, at Columbian Academy, and at District School No. 1 in the Town of Bergen. He commenced his business career as clerk in the grocery store of Jacob Van Winkle, of Bergen Square, in 1865. Five years later, or in 1870, he entered the Provident Institution for Savings in Jersey City, with which he has ever since been actively identified, having filled important positions in all the departments up to and including the offices of Secretary and Treasurer, which he now holds.

Mr. Newkirk has not, however, aspired to public or political office, having devoted himself almost exclusively to business affairs. For five years he was a member of the Fourth Regiment, N. G. N. J. He is a member of the Jersey City and Union League Clubs, of the Free and Accepted Masons, of the Independent Order of Odd Fellows, and of the Junior Order United American Mechanics.

Mr. Newkirk's first wife, Mary Elizabeth Terhune, died in 1878. In 1881 he married Annabella Meeker Randall, and they have four children of the seventh generation.

ALBERT Z. BOGERT, of River Edge, Bergen County, is descended from one of the oldest families in New Jersey. His first American ancestor, Cornelis Jansen Bogaerdt, came to America from Holland with his wife, Geesie Williams, a few years prior to 1661. He bought and settled on a village plot in Flatbush, L. I., which he subsequently sold to one Peter Jansen. In 1677 he was one of the patentees of the Flatbush patent. He resided at Flatbush until his death, about 1684. His children were Wyntie, John Cornelise, Classie, Roloff, Maritie, and Peter, all of whom, except Wyntie, eventually removed to Hackensack, N. J. His son Jan Cornelius (2) married Angenitie Strycker, and resided at New Lots, L. I., until 1694, when he sold his farm there and with several others purchased a large tract of land southeast of Hackensack. His numerous descendants have spread over the County of Bergen, and have exerted an important and wholesome influence in shaping the affairs of the county, having been prominent in business, in the professions, and in all the walks of life, honored and respected for those noble virtues which characterize the Dutch, and energetic and enterprising in promoting every worthy object.

Albert Z. Bogert, the subject of this sketch, is of the eighth generation from Cornelis Jansen Bogaerdt, the emigrant above named. His parents were Albert James Bogert and Catherine Aletta Zabriskie. His grandparents were John and Catharine Zabriskie Bogert and Albert G. and Sally Annie (Winters) Zabriskie. Mr. Bogert was born in Spring Valley, Bergen County, N. J., on the 14th of November, 1864. He received his education in the Bergen County schools, which he left at the age of nineteen to assist his father on the farm, where he remained five years. In 1888 he settled permanently in River Edge and bought a half interest with P. V. B. Demarest in a large coal, lumber, and grocery business. A year later Mr. Demarest sold his interest to John H. Banta and the business was continued by Messrs. Bogert and Banta until 1892, when Mr. Banta died. Since that time Mr. Bogert has successfully continued it alone.

Mr. Bogert's activity, enterprise, and influence in the community stamp him as one of the leading citizens, while his success in business has won for him a high reputation. He is a member of the Borough Council of the Borough of Riverside and of the Dutch Reformed Church of Schraalenburgh, and active in various other capacities. In March, 1900, he was elected a member of the Bergen County Board of Chosen Freeholders from Midland Township.

His wife, Anna Van Wagner, who was also descended from an old Holland Dutch family of New Jersey, died in 1892, leaving two children, James Gordon Bogert, born in 1888, and John W. Bogert, born in 1891.

JOHN J. BOGERT, the miller of Harrington Park, is a descendant in the ninth generation from Cornelis Jans Bougaert, the emigrant (see sketch on page 132). Stephen Bogert, of the seventh generation, son of Guilliam Bogert and Maria Banta, was born in 1753, married Sophia Alyea, and left issue a son, Jacobus (James) Bogert, of the eighth generation.

Jacobus Bogert (8) was born January 24, 1788, died March 6, 1871, married Jane Meyers, who was born February 13, 1794, and died May 7, 1873. They had several children of the ninth generation, among whom were John J., James, and Stephen.

Of these John J. (9), the eldest, married Margaret, daughter of John R. Blawvelt and Leah Demarest. Their issue, of the tenth generation were four children: Jane, Leah Ann, Elma, and John J., the latter being the subject of this sketch. John J. Bogert once raised a horse which he sold to Robert Bonner, of New York City, for $10,000.

John J. Bogert (10) was born December 6, 1846, at Harrington Park, N. J., where he still resides. He was educated in the Bergen County schools, which he left at the age of eighteen to engage in the milling business and in farming with his father. Upon his father's death in 1892 he took charge of the entire business and has since conducted it with marked success. During his active life he has wielded an important and wholesome influence in all local affairs.

Mr. Bogert married Hester Jemima Ackerman, and has four children: Eugene, Walter, Clyde A., and Mary L.

EDWIN BERKLEY YOUNG, a leading and successful real estate and insurance man of Union Hill, is descended from a distinguished family of United Empire royalists. The Youngs made the first settlement in Athol, Prince Edward County, Ontario, Canada, at East Lake. Some historians claim they were the first settlers in that county. Certain it is they went there when the country was a forest, unbroken and practically unpenetrated by man, and out of the wilderness carved for themselves and their families a home which still remains in the possession of their descendants. Colonel Henry Young, born in Jamaica, Long Island, in 1737, was

EDWIN B. YOUNG.

the second son of six children of an English gunsmith, who came there from Nottingham at an early age, and who founded a family which has spread over this country and Canada. Some of his posterity still live on Long Island. Henry joined the British army when a young man, served with distinction for six years in the French and Indian wars under Generals Amherst and Abercrombie, and with the English participated in the battle of Bennington and in no less than seventeen other engagements against the continentals. For gallant services at Bennington he received an ensigncy in the "King's Royal." His title of Colonel, by which he was popularly known, was conferred upon him by provincial appointment. At the close of the American Revolution he retired on half pay, and received a grant of 3,000 acres of land for himself and other tracts for various members of his family. His first residence in Canada was at Cataraqui. With a brother officer he set out in a canoe in 1783 and selected a site at East Lake in the Town of Athol. Thither he brought his family in the fall of 1784. He died there in his eighty-fourth year, leaving numerous descendants, many of whom became conspicuous in civil and official affairs. His four daughters, Elizabeth, Mary, Catherine, and Sarah, married East Lake settlers and lived to be over eighty years of age. Of his two sons, Henry and Daniel, the former settled on the homestead, and as a soldier in the English army died at Kingston of cholera during the War of 1812. Richard Young, son of Henry, Sr., was a farmer in Athol, and married Nancy Van Vlackren, now spelled Van Vlack. Their son, William Henry Young, served in the Ontario militia during the Fenian raid, and is now a retired farmer living in Picton, Canada. He is a cousin of the Rev. George Young, D.D., President of the Methodist Episcopal Conference of Ontario. He married Sarah Jane Clark, daughter of Enoch Dorland Clark and Nancy Smith, of Ontario, who, like the Van Vlackrens, were descended from Holland Dutch stock. The family have long taken a leading part in the agricultural and military affairs of Ontario, and have always borne high reputations for honor and integrity.

Edwin B. Young, eldest son of William Henry Young and Sarah Jane Clark, was born in Athol Township, Prince Edward County, Ontario, Canada, January 4, 1860. He attended the public schools and remained on the homestead until he reached the age of twenty-one, when, having received a good education, he came to New York City. His capital consisted of three or four dollars in money, a robust constitution, and indomitable pluck and courage. For a few months he was employed in various capacities. Becoming superintendent of the Grove Church Cemetery at New Durham, Hudson County, N. J., he took up his residence in the Town of Union, and has ever since been identified with its best interests. During the past nine years he has also been extensively interested in real estate in the town, and in 1896 he opened a general real estate and insurance office at 433 Bergenline Avenue, which he still conducts, and to which he devotes his entire attention, having resigned the superintendency of the Grove Church Cemetery in January, 1899. In addition to this he has lately established a mercantile collection agency, the first one of the kind on Union Hill.

Mr. Young has achieved marked success in real estate operations, and by untiring devotion to business has won the confidence and respect of the entire community. He is a genial, companionable, public spirited man, deeply interested in the general welfare, and always ready to respond to the demands of good citizenship. Progressive in all that the word implies, he has been active and influential in the advancement of the town, a liberal contributor to its growth and moral improvements, and ever alert in increasing its useful institutions. He was Secretary of the old Literary Society of the Town of Union, and later became one of the prime movers in organizing the Free Reading Room and Library Association, of which he was for many years Treasurer, and of which he was an original Director.

It may be safely said that he was a founder and the chief organizer of this association, which succeeded the old Literary Society. Later a special act of the Legislature enabled the Town of Union, and other towns in the State, to levy a tax for the support of such institutions, and this association has since been maintained by the public as a free library. In all of these movements Mr. Young was active and influential, and to him is due in a large degree the establishment of this institution. He is an ardent Democrat, a Justice of the Peace, and a prominent member of various fraternal and social organizations, including Mystic Tie Lodge, No. 123, F. and A. M., of New Jersey, of which he was for four years the Worshipful Master. He is also a member of the Scottish Rite bodies, 32°, of New York City, of the Nobles of the Mystic Shrine, Masonic fraternity, and of the Royal Arcanum. In September, 1899, he was elected Most Worthy Grand Patron of the Order of the Eastern Star of New Jersey, and in the spring of 1900 he was one of the organizers of the Past Masters' Association of Hudson County, of which he was elected the first President.

Mr. Young's brother, George Alfred Young, was born May 14, 1869, came to New Jersey when seventeen, and is now head bookkeeper for the Hudson Trust and Savings Institution of West Hoboken. He is a member and Worshipful Master of Mystic Tie Lodge, No. 123, F. and A. M.

Mr. Young was married October 10, 1883, to Henrietta Bell, daughter of Henry and Ellen (Westerfield) Bell, of the Town of Union. Her father was born near Liverpool, England, while her mother was descended from an old Holland Dutch family. They have three sons: Edwin Henry, Ralph Percy, and Herbert Eldred.

ROBERT CAMPBELL DIXON, Jr., one of the leading architects of Union Hill and Eastern New Jersey, is of English and Scotch parentage, being the son of Robert and Margaret (Campbell) Dixon and a grandson of Robert Dixon, Sr., and Hannah Lawson. His maternal grandparents were John and Isabel (Anderson) Campbell. His father was born in Nicholforest, Cumberland, England, and his mother in Perthshire, Scotland. Some of his ancestors were prominently engaged in the East India service, others filled important positions of trust, one branch had a representative in the English Parliament in the person of Sir Wilfred Lawson, and others occupied posts in the Church of England. The Dixon and Lawson families have been for generations conspicuous in civil, military, governmental, and professional affairs, contributing to their respective communities a wholesome influence, and achieving for themselves distinction as men of learning and ability.

Mr. Dixon was born in New York City on the 15th of May, 1857. He attended the public schools of Poughkeepsie, N. Y., until he reached the age of about fourteen, and afterward pursued his studies in private schools, developing a naturally strong and brilliant intellect, and laying the foundation for an honorable career. He completed his literary education at Riverview Military Academy and finished with a business course, graduating from Eastman's Business College at Poughkeepsie. A large part of his early education was intended to fit him for a military career, but he turned his attention to architecture, and in the early part of 1876 entered the office of D. & J. Jardine, architects, of New York City, as a student. He continued with them a little over four years, after which he was for a brief period in the office of J. C. Cady & Co. In 1883, having received important work in competition, Mr. Dixon engaged in business for himself as a practical architect, and has ever since been devoted to his profession, achieving marked success and a notable reputation. He has had an office in New York City for about fourteen years, and many important public and private buildings have been erected from his designs. The town hall, the Palma and Columbia

Club houses, public schools, many church edifices, and numerous other principal buildings in Union Hill, N. J., have been built by him. All of these show great artistic taste and practical skill, and represent some of the finest and choicest work in the country.

In political matters Mr. Dixon has been an active and influential leader since about 1884, serving frequently as delegate to local and State Democratic conventions, and being at the present time a member of the Board of Education of Union Hill, of which he was formerly President. He is a member and at times has served on important committees of the Columbia Club of Hoboken, and has also been a member of the Palma Club of Jersey City for several years. He was one of the organizers of the New Jersey Society of Architects and has held some of its most important offices. He is also an associate member of the American Institute of Architects, a member of the Central Democratic Organization, a warden of Grace Episcopal Church of Union Hill, where he resides, and a member of Columbia Lodge, No. 151, Knights of Pythias. He is a public spirited, enterprising citizen, a man of broad and liberal culture, and is and has been prominently identified with many of the leading charitable organizations.

Mr. Dixon was married September 22, 1886, to Sadie Gardner Morgan, only daughter of James G. Morgan, of Union Hill, N. J.

DAVID DEMAREST ZABRISKIE, Law Judge of the County of Bergen, is a direct descendant in the eighth generation from the Polish emigrant, Albert Zabriskie (see sketch on page 49).

Jacob A. Zabriskie (2), eldest son of the Polish emigrant, born about April 22, 1677, at Pembrepoch, Bergen County, married (1), September 20, 1706, Ann (daughter of Albert Alberts Terhune and Hendricke Voorhis), born in 1678 on Long Island. He resided at Upper Paramus on part of his father's large estate, where he died in 1758, having had issue ten children of the third generation: Hendricke, Sophia, Maritie, Albert A., Peter, Jannetje, Rachel, Matilda, Stephen, and Jacob.

Albert A. (third generation) was baptized February 1, 1708, and married, May 8, 1739, Maritie Hopper. He resided at Paramus, and had at least two children, Ann, born 1749, and Andrew.

Andrew Zabriskie (4), born in 1746, died about 1805, also resided at Paramus, where he married Jannetje Lozier, and had issue of the fifth generation at least three children, John A., Christina, and Andrew.

John A. Zabriskie (5) was born at Paramus, November 11, 1768, and died there. One of his children of the sixth generation was Casper J. Zabriskie (6), born at Paramus, April 27, 1799; died there June 4, 1849. He married Catharine Post, who died in February, 1872. They lived at Paramus and had issue of the seventh generation: Andrew C., Robert, Catharine J., Mary M., Alletta L., Sophia, and John C.

John C. Zabriskie (7), born September 20, 1822, married (1) Maria Hopper, (2) Jane Demarest, and (3) Maria C. Bogert. He resided at Paramus, and was a farmer by occupation. His children of the eighth generation were Andrew J., Maria J., Catharine, Emma, David D., Ida, Simon, John, and Alletta.

David D. Zabriskie (8) was born at Paramus, N. J., November 27, 1856, and received his preparatory education at Erasmus Hall Academy in Flatbush, Long Island. He was graduated with honor from Rutgers College in the class of 1879, and then entered Columbia College Law School, from which he was graduated with the degree of LL.B. in 1881. He was admitted to the New Jersey bar as an attorney at the November term of the Supreme Court, 1882, and at once began active practice. In June, 1889, he was admitted as a counselor. Judge Zabriskie has for many years maintained law offices in both Hackensack and Jersey City. Soon after entering upon his professional career he came into prominence as a lawyer of unusual ability, and steadily won recognition for those eminent legal and judicial qualifications which he has since displayed both at the bar and on the bench. He was uniformly successful, and as an all-round advocate and counselor achieved a high reputation.

His law practice, however, though constantly growing in volume and importance, did not prevent him from taking an active interest in public and political affairs. As a Republican from boyhood he has contributed much to the success of the party as well as to the government of his town and county. In 1894 and 1895 he represented his district in the State Legislature, serving on some of the most important committees, and taking a prominent part in shaping legislation. In 1896 and 1897 he was County Counsel for the County of Bergen, and from 1894 to 1898 he was Chairman of the Republican County Committee of Bergen County. In January, 1898, Governor Griggs appointed him Law Judge of Bergen County for a term of five years, and since April 1 of that year he has served on the bench with conspicuous ability and universal satisfaction.

Judge Zabriskie was married in October, 1883, to Lizzie S. Suydam, of New Brunswick, N. J. They have one daughter, Ethelind S., of the ninth generation, and reside in Ridgewood.

ABRAM DE BAUN.—The common ancestor of all the DeBauns in Bergen and Hudson Counties was Joost de Baen, a native of Brussels in Flanders (Belgium), who came over to New Amsterdam in 1683. The next year he married Elizabeth Drabb and located at Bushwick, L. I., where he was soon afterward made town clerk. In 1686 he removed to New Utrecht, where he was elected town clerk and taught the village school. This was during the controversy over the conduct of Governor Leisler. De Baen entered that contest and took an active part against the Governor, which caused him to lose his clerkship. He, however, continued to teach school and to reside at New Utrecht, where he took the oath of allegiance to the English king in 1687. Early in 1704 he sold his lands, of which he acquired a considerable area, and removed to Bergen County, N. J., where he joined the Kinderkamack settlement. He died in 1718 or 1719. His children of the second generation were Matie (married, in 1705, David Samuels Demarest), Christian (married Judith Samuels Demarest), Mayke, Carrel, Christina, Jacobus, and Maria.

Of these seven children Carrel (Charles) (2) married, in 1714, Jannetie Peters Haring, of Tappan. He first bought a large farm, in 1719, on the north side of Hardenbergh Avenue (now in Harrington Township), extending from the Schraalenburgh road to the Tiena Kill (including part of what is now Demarest), on which for a time he resided. Shortly after 1721 he sold this farm and bought several large tracts between the Hackensack and the Pascack Rivers, on one of which he settled and died. His issue of the third generation were Joost, Margaret, Elizabeth, John, Jacob, Carrel, and Christiaen.

Carrel (3), born in 1728, married (1) Bridget Ackerman (born December 10, 1731, died January 27, 1793) and (2) Lea Van Orden. He was a farmer by occupation, and settled in the upper part of Bergen County. His issue of the fourth generation were Carrel, Margaret, Abram, Jannetie, Andrew, Sarah, David, John, and Isaac.

Isaac de Baun (4) was born December 9, 1779, and died June 18, 1870. He was a farmer and resided nearly all his life at Monsey, N. Y. He married June 13, 1807, Elizabeth Yeury, who died August 24, 1875. Their children of the fifth generation were Abram, Elizabeth, Jacob, Maria, Bridget, Rachel, Jane, and John Y.

John Y. de Baun (5) was born at Monsey, N. Y., August 22, 1827. He was a remarkably precocious child. Although he had but an ordinary common school education he, by dint of an untiring perseverance and constant application to study, qualified himself for the ministry (which under the circumstances was a rare achievement), and on April 17, 1855, was licensed to preach by the Classis of Hackensack of the True Reformed Dutch Church. His first charge included the churches at Hempstead in Rockland County, N. Y., and at Ramseys in Bergen County, N. J., where he preached alternately until 1860, when he took charge of the two churches at Hackensack and English Neighborhood, N. J. Of these two churches he was the pastor for twenty-six years. During this time he resided at Hackensack, where he established and was the editor of the *Banner of Truth*, a monthly magazine, which is still the organ of the True Reformed Dutch Church. He died at Leonia, N. J., in February, 1895. He was twice married: (1) April 8, 1849, to Margaret Iserman, who died about 1893, and (2) to Jane Van Houton, who survives him. He was a thoroughly self-made man, an eloquent preacher, and in every way worthy of his high and noble calling. His issue of the sixth generation were Susan E., Martha A., James D., Abram, Edwin, Anna, John Z., James E., and Isaac C., of whom Abram (6) is the subject of this sketch.

Abram de Baun (6) was born April 2, 1856, at Monsey, N. Y., where he spent his childhood days. When old enough he entered Hackensack Academy, where he had the benefit of a full course of study, and then entered the law office of A. D. Campbell, at Hackensack, as a law student. He was admitted to the New Jersey bar as an attorney in June, 1877, and as a counselor in June, 1880. After his call to the bar he became a business partner of his old tutor, with whom he remained until March, 1894, when he formed a law partnership with Milton Demarest, with whom he is still associated in a lucratice practice.

Mr. De Baun was clerk of the Bergen County Board of Chosen Freeholders from 1878 to 1895 and for three years a member of the Hackensack Improvement Commission, during two years of which he was treasurer. For twelve years he has been counsel for the Hackensack Mutual Building and Loan Association. He is a Director of the Hackensack Old Ladies' Home.

He married (1) in 1878 Mary B. Christie, of Leonia. She died in September, 1881, and he married (2), October 2, 1884, Lydia B. Christie. He has no children.

JAMES A. ROMEYN.—The Romeyns, Romaines, and Romains, of Bergen County, claim to be of Italian lineage, which they trace to one Giacomo de Ferentino, an Italian gentleman who settled at Rongham Manor, Norfolkshire, England, in the early part of the thirteenth century, and married an English lady, Isabella de Rucham, by whom he had issue two sons, one of whom was Peter. This Peter was sent to Rome to be educated, and on his return took the surname of Romaeyn (Peter the Roman). He married a daughter of Thomas de Leicester. Many of Peter's descendants became noted men in England. One of them, Jan Romeyn, went from England to the low countries (Holland) and settled in Amsterdam. He had several children, among whom were Claes Jansen, Simeon Jansen, and Christofer Jansen. Claes and Christofer sailed from Rotterdam, Holland, to Brazil, as members of an expedition to that country commanded by Prince Maurice of Nas-

JAMES VAN CAMPEN ROMEYN.

sau. Soon after arriving in Brazil that country was ceded to Portugal, and thereupon the two Romeyns sailed for America. There is a disagreement as to the date when they arrived, but it was probably about 1661. They settled first at New Amersfoort, L. I. Christofer married, in 1678, Grietie Pieters Wyckoff, and settled in Monmouth County, N. J. Claes married (it is said), May 2, 1680, Styntie Alberts Terhune, and in 1690 went to Hackensack, where he bought four Indian fields between the Saddle River and the Hackensack River, called in his deed Wierimus, Paskack, Gemagkie, and Marroasonek. These four tracts were north of Paramus, on the east side of the Saddle River. He did not locate on these lands, but returned to New York and located in the Greenwich district of the city, where he died. His children, to whom he devised all his lands on his death, divided them into farms and mutually released or sold to actual settlers. Claes

JAMES ROMEYN.

Jansen's children of the second generation were Gerrebrecht, Elizabeth, Lydia, Albert C., John C., Rachel, Sarah, and Daniel.

Jan Claas Romeyn (2) married, in May, 1690, Jannetie Bogert, at Hackensack, and resided on part of his father's lands. He was a member and church master of the "Church on the Green" in 1715. His issue of the third generation were Nicholas, John, Christina, Roelof, Rachel, Isaac, Angenetie, Christina, and Ursula.

Nicholas Romeyn (3), baptized at Hackensack in February, 1699, married, in 1726, Elizabeth Outwater, who died in 1732. He died in 1763. He married (2) Rachel Vreeland, who died in 1761. The issue of Nicholas Romeyn (3) and his two wives of the fourth generation were Rev. Thomas Romeyn and John Romeyn.

Rev. Thomas Romeyn (4), born at Pompton, N. J., March 2, 1729, died October 22, 1794. He was graduated from the College of New Jersey in 1750, studied theology, and after preaching a few times on Long Island

THEODORE B. ROMEYN.

went to Holland, in 1752, for ordination, and was settled at Jamaica, L. I., until 1790. He married (1) June 29, 1756, Margaretta Frelinghuysen, who died at Jamaica, December 13, 1757. He married (2) Susanna Van Camppen. He died at Fonda, N. Y., October 22, 1794, and was buried there under the pulpit of his church. His issue of the fifth generation were seven: Rev. Theodore F., Rev. Thomas, Nicholas, Abraham, Rev. Broadhead, Benjamin, and Rev. James Van Campen.

Rev. James Van Campen Romeyn (5) was born at Minsink, Sussex County, N. J., November 15, 1765, and died at Hackensack, June 27, 1840. He attended Schenectady Academy in 1784, studied theology under Rev. Theodore Romeyn, his uncle, was a Trustee of Rutgers College, and preached at several places, the last in the Reformed Church of Hackensack and Schraalenburgh from 1799 to 1833. He married (1) Susanna Maud Van Vranken,

JAMES A. ROMEYN.

of Schenectady, and (2) Elizabeth Pell, who survived him. His issue of the sixth generation were Susan, Harriet, Anna, Maria, Rev. James, D.D., Anna, Eliza, Caroline, Theodore, and Sarah.

Rev. James Romeyn (6) was born at Blooming Grove, N. J., September 30, 1797, and was graduated from Columbia College in 1816 and from the Theological Seminary at New Brunswick, N. J., in 1819. He declined the Doctor of Divinity degree bestowed on him by Columbia College. He preached at several places, was pastor of the old "Church on the Green" at Hackensack from 1833 to 1836, and was a Trustee of Rutgers College in 1842. He married Joanna Bayard Rodgers, daughter of John R. B. Rodgers, M.D., of Columbia College, New York. His children of the seventh generation were James R. and Theodore B.

Rev. Theodore Bayard Romeyn (7) was born at Nassau, N. Y., October 22, 1827. He attended school at Hackensack and other places, was graduated from Rutgers College in 1846 and from the Theological Seminary in New Brunswick in 1849, and received the degree of D.D. from Rutgers College. He preached at Blawenburgh, N. J., and at Hackensack, and was the author of the History of the Reformed Church of the latter village. He married Amelia A. Letson, who died October 22, 1897. He died at Hackensack, August 29, 1885. His issue of the eighth generation were Mary L. (deceased) and James A., the latter being the subject of this sketch.

James A. Romeyn (8) was born in Blawenburgh, N. J., May 15, 1853, and received his education at Rutgers College. He studied law with Bedle, Muirhead & McGee, of Jersey City, and successfully practiced his profession until 1890. Since then he has been the editor of the *Evening Record* of Hackensack, where he resides.

Mr. Romeyn is a man of acknowledged ability and untiring energy, and has always taken an active part in public affairs. He was for eight years a member of the Hackensack Board of Health, and for seven years (1888-95) served as Treasurer of the Hackensack Hospital. At the bar and in the editorial chair he has won distinction and honor, and as a citizen he is highly respected.

In 1884 Mr. Romeyn married Flora May Cochran, of Lancester, Pa., who died in 1891. By her there were two children: Theodore B. and Katharine. He was married, second, in 1894, to Susie Burgess Conover, of Newark, N. J.

JOHN LANE has achieved distinction in the twofold capacity of marine surveyor and public officer. He is a native of Shrewsbury, N. J., where he obtained his early education in the public schools. Subsequently he pursued a course of study at Cooper Institute, New York.

Reared on his father's farm in Shrewsbury, he developed a strong constitution, and at the same time acquired those habits of thrift and industry which mark the successful man. His studies were designed to enable him to enter professional life, for which he was mentally and physically qualified, and in which he has won an honorable reputation. Entering, as a youth, the shipyard of McCarthy & Brother, of Hoboken, he filled successively the positions of clerk, timekeeper, bookkeeper, and general manager, and gained the respect and confidence of all with whom he came into contact, and especially of his employers. His experience was at once broad and practical, and included a thorough knowledge of every branch of ship building, even to designing, carpentering and joining, calking, and marine draughting. After a period of sixteen years in these different capacities he withdrew to engage in business for himself as a marine surveyor, a profession for which his duties had eminently fitted him, and one in which he has achieved remarkable success. In 1888 he removed from Jersey City to West Hoboken, N. J., where he has built, on Malone Street, a neat and attractive home after his own plans and designs.

Mr. Lane has for many years been an active and influential leader of the Democratic party, especially in the town where he resides, and in various capacities has served both party and town with ability, honor, and satisfaction. In 1891 he was appointed a member of the West Hoboken Board of Health. In 1893 he was elected a member of the Board of School Trustees. Since 1895 he has served as one of the Councilmen of West Hoboken, and in 1898 and 1899 was chairman of the board. He discharged the duties connected with these positions with signal efficiency and fidelity. Public spirited, energetic, and progressive, he has always encouraged and supported every movement calculated to advance the general welfare of the community. He is a prominent member of the Masonic order, of the Royal Arcanum, and of the Foresters of America.

CORNELIUS LYDECKER.—Ryck Lydecker, the common ancestor of the Lydecker family in Bergen County, was from Amsterdam, Holland, but that city was probably not his birthplace. At all events he was a Hollander. The time of his arrival in America does not definitely appear. He first settled permanently at Bushwick, L. I., on a grant of land obtained by him in 1660 or 1661. There he resided several years—perhaps until his death, which is said to have occurred prior to 1696. He was magistrate of Bushwick from 1682 to 1685. On June 24, 1663, he was appointed captain of a company of militia and received orders from Governor Stuyvesant to fortify the town, which he did. The records show that his company contained forty men, including its officers, and that this company was divided into four watches, of whom one-fourth, or ten men, were on duty every night to guard against an expected attack by the savages, who were at the time very troublesome to the settlers. His wife's name was Clara Vooreniere, and his issue of the second generation were Garret, John, Ryck, Cornelius, and Abraham.

Ryck (2) married Maritie Benson and settled at Hackensack, where he bought a large tract of land of Captain John Berry. Garret (2) married Neeltie Cornelis Vandehuyl, of Holland. He purchased a tract of land between Leonia and Englewood, in Bergen County, extending eastward from Overpeck Creek to the Hudson River. This he devised to his four sons after named, who partitioned it between them. It contained more than one thousand acres. His issue of the third generation were Ryck, Elizabeth, Clara, Cornelius, Garret, and Abraham.

Garret (3) married Wintie (Levina) Terhune, and resided near Englewood on his father's homestead. His issue of the fourth generation were Neeltie, 1724; Garret, 1728; Geertie, 1731; Cornelia, 1734; Ann, 1736; Elizabeth, 1738; and Albert, 1740.

Garret (4) married Lydia Demarest. He became a man of note, and commanded a company of Continental troops during the War for Independence. Both he and his wife were prominent members of the Old South Church at Schraalenburgh. His issue of the fifth generation were Garret, 1753; James, 1755; Levina, 1757; Margaret, 1759; Garret, 1761; James and Cornelius (twins), 1764; Lydia, 1766; James, 1769; Elizabeth, 1771; and Maria, 1774.

James (5), last above named, born in 1769, married, September 25, 1790, Maria Day, and had issue Lydia and Garret J. of the sixth generation.

Garret J. (6) was born in 1797 and died in 1880. He occupied a prominent position in the locality then known as English Neighborhood, having large farming interests, and being one whose advice was sought in all leading questions of the day. He married Sarah Ryer and had issue of the seventh generation James, John R., and Cornelius, the last of whom is the subject of this sketch.

Cornelius Lydecker (7) was born at Englewood, N. J., on the place where he now lives, April 6, 1827. He has been prominent in public and private affairs. In 1846 he entered as a clerk the dry goods store of his brother John R. in New York, where he remained two years. In 1849 he caught the gold fever and went to California *via* Cape Horn. Two years in the gold "diggins" was enough for him. He returned home and soon after entered the political field by being elected Surveyor of Highways in his native town. Following this venture up, he became Township Collector in 1862, and later County Collector, which office he held for five years. In 1872 he was elected to the State Senate on the Democratic ticket, and was from year to year returned until 1875, when he became a candidate for State Treasurer and Controller. For seven years thereafter he was a member of the "Third House" in the Legislature. With William B. Dana he built in 1871 the Palisade Mountain House, and then took a rest by traveling for a time, finally returning to embark in the real estate business.

He married in 1852 Miss Catharine S. Van Blarcom, by whom he has had six children of the eighth generation: Mary (wife of Oliver Drake Smith), Sarah Ryer (wife of Stanley P. Parsons), Elizabeth, Garret (now in a banking house at No. 18 Wall Street, New York), Kate, and Cornelius, now at Englewood. Mr. Lydecker is a member of Masonic Lodge No. 114.

CHARLES WESLEY RANDALL, of Jersey City, has been actively and successfully engaged in the practice of architecture in Hudson County since 1880, or during a period of twenty years. He was born in the Hudson City section of Jersey City in 1856 and is the son of George W. Randall and Sarah Hellier, both of whom are of English descent. His family originally settled in old Hudson City in 1837, and has ever since been active and influential in important capacities.

Mr. Randall was educated primarily in Public School No. 1, of Hudson City (now Jersey City), and subsequently took a course at Cooper Institute, New York, graduating therefrom as an architect. In 1880 he entered upon the active practice of his profession in Hudson County, and from that time to the present has built a large number of houses and other buildings, in all of which appear evidences of his genius. He is a man of decided artistic talent, energetic and influential in all the affairs of life, thoroughly identified with the best interests of the community, and one of the best architects and builders in the County of Hudson.

In 1880 Mr. Randall married Eleda Erickson. They have three children: George E., Elizabeth G., and Josephine E. Randall.

JOHN RATHBONE RAMSEY is one of the leading lawyers of Hackensack, Bergen County, N. J., and, in November, 1895, was elected to the office of County Clerk by a majority of 961, being the first Republican ever elected to that position in that county. He is the son of John P. Ramsey, a farmer, and Martha Rathbone, his wife, and a descendant on his father's side of Samuel Ramsey, a native of Scotland, who with his son, John Ramsey, came to America in 1772, and settled at New Scotland, Albany County, N. Y. The son John, born in 1757, married Margaret Connolly, and settled at New Scotland, where he enlisted and served in the Continental Army against the British in the war for independence.

Peter Ramsey, said to have been another son of Samuel, and to have followed his father and brother to America, had two sons, Peter P. and William P. Ramsey, both of whom settled in the Ramapo district of Bergen

County. Peter P. married Jane Reyerson, and William P. married Hannah ———. The inscriptions on their tombstones show the following facts: Peter P. Ramsey, born July 18, 1770, died March 30, 1854; Jane Reyerson, his wife, died January 28, 1825. William P. Ramsey, born December 25, 1774, died July 19, 1863; Hannah, his wife, born January 29, 1775, died August 6, 1849. These were the first of the name in the county, and were undoubtedly the ancestors of all the Ramseys in Bergen County, including the subject of this sketch. On his mother's side John R. Ramsey's ancestors were of English descent.

Mr. Ramsey was born in Wyckoff, Bergen County, N. J., on the 25th of April, 1862, and spent much of his early life—from 1872 to 1879—with his maternal grandfather, John V. Rathbone, in Parkersburg, W. Va., where he received a private school education. In 1879 he returned to New Jersey and entered the law office of the late George H. Coffey, of Hackensack. He subsequently continued his law studies with the firm of Campbell & De Baun, also of Hackensack, and was admitted to the New Jersey bar as an attorney in November, 1883, and as a counselor in February, 1887. For nearly twelve years following his admission he was actively and successfully engaged in the practice of law in Hackensack, displaying marked ability as a counselor and advocate, and gaining an extensive clientage.

Mr. Ramsey has always been an active, ardent, and consistent Republican, and for many years has been a power in the councils of his party. He was the Republican candidate for the office of County Clerk, of Bergen County, in 1890, but was defeated by a very small majority, although he ran ahead of the rest of the Republican ticket by several hundred votes. In November, 1895, he was again the Republican candidate for that office and was elected by a majority of 961, for a term of five years from November 18, 1895, being the first Republican ever elected County Clerk in the County of Bergen. He has discharged the duties of this office with marked ability and satisfaction, and has displayed the same energy which characterized his career at the bar. He is a member of Fidelity Lodge, No. 113, Free and Accepted Masons, of Ridgewood, N. J., of Wortendyke Lodge, No. 175, Independent Order of Odd Fellows, and of various social organizations and clubs.

He was married, January 26, 1898, to Mary Evelyn Thompson, of Clarksburg, W. Va. She died very suddenly April 27, 1898.

CHARLES A. HAMILTON, of Closter, Bergen County, N. J., was born at Canaan Four Corners, Columbia County, N. Y., March 24, 1859. He is the son of Silas B. and Emily J. (Haight) Hamilton, a grandson of James Hamilton and William Haight, and a descendant of a long line of Scotch ancestors.

Mr. Hamilton received his education in his native State. He left school at the age of seventeen and entered a railroad office, where he remained three and a half years. He then accepted a position with the Mutual Life Insurance Company, of New York City, and has since continued with that well known corporation. In this latter capacity he has developed ability in a line which requires accurate knowledge of mathematics and all business forms, and he has discharged his duties with satisfaction and earned for himself the confidence of the officials of the company.

As a resident of Closter, Bergen County, Mr. Hamilton has taken part in the affairs of the community, has served as a member of the School Board, and is a member of the Dutch Reformed Church.

Mr. Hamilton married Carrie L. Preston. They have two sons: Charles H., born in 1883, and Kenneth P., born in 1885.

WILLIAM OUTIS ALLISON, of Englewood, N. J., is descended in the eighth generation from Lawrence Ellison (or Allison), a Puritan, who moved from Watertown, Mass., to Wethersfield, Conn., thence to Stamford, in the same State, and finally to Hempstead, Long Island, with other emigrants who accompanied Rev. Richard Denton in 1644. These emigrants are supposed to have been a part of the colony which came over from England with Robert Winthrop and Sir Richard Saltonstall in 1630. John Ellison, son of Lawrence, became one of the founders of Hempstead in 1644. His son John, a native of Hempstead, was the immediate founder of the family of Allisons which, for several generations, have lived and slept within the limits of Haverstraw, Rockland County, New York. He was one of the company that purchased the north part of the Kakiat patent of land in Orange County, which is now Rockland County, in 1719, and founded the Town of New Hempstead, now Ramapo. He died in 1754, after a life of great usefulness and activity. Of his nine children, Joseph, the third, was born in August, 1721 or 1722, resided in Haverstraw, and died January 2, 1796. He was called Captain Joseph Allison, and became one of the largest landowners and farmers in his section. March 10, 1743, he married Elizabeth, daughter of Matthew Benson, who died December 12, 1767, leaving ten children. His second wife, whom he married May 4, 1769, and who died April 16, 1815, was Elsie Parsells, and she bore him eight children.

Matthew Allison, the eldest of all these eighteen children, was born in Haverstraw, and died before 1795, leaving several children, among them Hendrick Allison, who married Sarah Marks, daughter of George Marks, of the same town. They moved to Manhattan Island, thence to New

WILLIAM O. ALLISON.

Dock, N. J., and finally to Hackensack Township, Bergen County, to a point beneath the Palisades, near what is now Englewood Township. They were the grandparents of the subject of this article. William Henry Allison, son of Hendrick and father of William O., was born in Hackensack Township on the 10th of September, 1820. In 1840 he married Catherine, daughter of David and Elizabeth (Blauvelt) Jordan and granddaughter of Joseph Jordan, a French soldier, who came over with Lafayette and fought for American independence, and who, after the Revolution, married Elsie Parsells, and settled at Closter, on the top of the Palisades, where he died.

The maternal ancestors of William O. Allison were among the original Dutch settlers at Old Tappan, one of the earliest settlements in New Jersey, and have resided in Bergen County for more than two hundred years.

William O. Allison was born in old Hackensack (now Palisade) Township, Bergen County, N. J., March 30, 1849. From his early boyhood he lived much of the time in the family of William B. Dana, a prominent resident of the Palisades, a man of forceful and exemplary character, and a journalist of culture. The accident of this environment had an important part in his career, and he has never failed to fully acknowledge, by word and deed, the benign influence which Mr. Dana's wife, Mrs. Katharine Floyd Dana, exerted upon him. She took a deep interest in the boy, and his intellectual development was guided by her in a manner born of superior intelligence and refinement and by the great strength of character which she possessed. Finding in him the inherent traits for development, she saw them expand into manhood, and broaden and increase in power. Never was a friendship more liberally rewarded. His gratitude was expressed by the devotion which he accorded to her and by his adoption of the name "Outis" in compliment to a fancy of hers that his initials should correspond to those of her *nom de plume*, "Olive A. Wadsworth."

In 1868 Mr. Allison, having received an excellent training at the hands of this childless woman, entered the office of the *Financial Chronicle* and the *Daily Bulletin*, which were owned by Mr. Dana and John G. Floyd, Mrs. Dana's brother. Here he acquired a thorough and general knowledge of the publishing business, and with this and keen business instincts he soon developed into the best commercial reporter ever connected with the New York press. He invented and instituted a system of thoroughness in reports which had previously been unknown, and which few reporters have been able to copy successfully. When he entered Mr. Dana's employ he received $7 per week; inside of three years he had a weekly salary of $40 as a reporter. But this rapid progress did not satisfy his ambition. The confidence which he felt in his system of making a specialty of a few markets and doing them thoroughly led him, on October 21, 1871, to issue the first number of the *Oil, Paint and Drug Reporter*, a small four-page paper of extremely modest appearance when compared with other publications already prominent in the industries to which it was devoted. The *Reporter*, however, contained more of real value to the subscribers than any other sheet, and its growth in circulation was remarkable, while its advertising patronage, in connection with added departments of valuable reading matter, forced numerous successive enlargments.

But it was not until after a hard struggle of several years that Mr. Allison saw the fulfillment of the hope which he had entertained at the beginning of his career. His perseverance, united with great business tact and skill, alone brought him into prominence in a field in which he now has no superiors and few if any equals. As a result of the policy of obtaining and furnishing accurate, comprehensive, and valuable information concerning all the markets which the paper covers and reports, the successful growth of the business is believed to have no parallel in commercial journalism. The *Reporter* soon became one of the most profitable class publications in the country, and exerts an influence in the trades to which it is allied such as no other commercial publication has wielded. In 1874 he established *The Painters Magazine*, with which was subsequently consolidated the *Wall Paper Trade Journal*, and about the same time he purchased *The Druggists Circular*, which was started in 1857. These three publications—the *Oil, Paint and Drug Reporter*, *The Druggists Circular*, and *The Painters Magazine*—not only continue to hold their prestige and influence among the trades which they represent, but enjoy a constantly increasing measure of success and a world-wide popularity and reputation.

These relations have brought Mr. Allison into close personal contact with a large clientage, have made his judgment and opinions much sought after, and have led him into enterprises outside of the publishing business. Inheriting a tendency to operate in real estate, he has acquired from time to time considerable tracts of land on or near the Palisades until he has become one of the largest landowners in that section. And the eminent success which he has achieved as publisher, financier, and real estate operator has won for him the respect, confidence, and admiration of all who know him. His industry and good judgment, his commercial and financial enterprises, and his many successful achievements, together with his unostentatious benefactions, mark him as a man of distinction and honor. He has gained by his own efforts an enviable place among the foremost publishers and financiers of the day, and may well regard with pride the career which he has carved out of surroundings shorn of none of the difficulties and temptations which every one encounters.

Mr. Allison was married October 22, 1884, to Caroline Longstreet Hovey, daughter of Alfred Howard Hovey and Frances Noxon, of Syracuse, N. Y. Her parents dying when she was very young, she was adopted by the late Hon. George F. Comstock and his wife, and took the name of Comstock. Mrs. Comstock was a sister of Mrs. Allison's mother, and Mr. Comstock was at one time Attorney-General of the United States and Chief Justice of the New York Court of Appeals. Mrs. Allison was born in Syracuse on June 12, 1862, received her education at Keble School in that city and at a French school in Neuilly, near Paris, France, and resided in Syracuse until her marriage. She died at Paris on March 31, 1896. Their children were Katharine Floyd Allison, born July 13, 1885; Frances Cornelia Allison, born November 23, 1887; Allis Allison, born September 30, 1888, died April 14, 1889; William Dana Allison, born September 8, 1890, died September 8, 1894; John Blauvelt Allison, born January 13, 1893; and Van Kleeck Allison, born May 23, 1894. All were born in Englewood, N. J. Mr. Allison married, second, Mrs. Caroline A. Comstock, daughter of David Shaw, of Detroit, Mich.

JOHN ENGEL, formerly Postmaster of Hackensack, and one of the most popular hotel proprietors in Bergen County, was born in Prussia, Germany, on the 16th of April, 1845. His parents, Charles Engel and Agustia Kuehn, were both born and married in Prussia.

Major Engel received his education at the military school at Schloss, Annaburg, Province of Saxony, and in 1860 came to this country, arriving in

New York City on the 16th of October. His first business here was as a barber in New York. In 1868 he removed to Hackensack, N. J., where he has since resided, and where he was for some time engaged in the barber business. He became Postmaster of Hackensack in 1888, and served one term. Afterward he engaged in the hotel business in Hackensack, in which he has since continued, becoming one of the most popular and best known hotel keepers in Bergen County.

As a soldier in the Civil War Major Engel made an enviable record. He enlisted, in 1862, in the One Hundred and Sixty-fifth New York Volunteers and served until the close of the war in 1865, receiving an honorable discharge after a long and active service at the front. In 1898 he enlisted for active service in the War with Spain, becoming Major of the Second Battalion, Second Regiment, New Jersey Volunteers, and going into camp with his regiment at Jacksonville, Fla. He was mustered out in November, 1898. He is Past Commander of James B. McPherson Post, No. 52, G. A. R., and also Captain of Major John Engel Command, No. 56, Spanish War Veterans. He served twenty-seven years (1872-1899) in the National Guard of New Jersey, rising from a private to the command of the same battalion in which he enlisted in 1872.

Major Engel is a man of great energy, ability, and enterprise, and during his entire career has maintained the respect and confidence of all who know him. He is one of the most public spirited citizens, deeply interested in the affairs of the community, and thoroughly identified with every movement which has for its object the general welfare. He is a member of Lodge No. 177, Independent Order of Odd Fellows, of Hackensack, of the Improved Order of Red Men, of the Hackensack Wheelmen's Club, and of the Hasbrouck Heights Field Club.

On October 31, 1867, he married Miss M. H. Gehrels, of Charleston, S. C. Their children are Charles W., George S., John A., Augusta, Herbert B., Frank P., Emma T. B., and Daniel C.

ALEXANDER FISHER was born in Buffalo, N. Y., on the 14th of May, 1849, his parents being John Fisher and Margaret Cortelyou. His ancestors came to this country from England. He was educated in the public schools of Buffalo and spent his early life as a traveling salesman. In this capacity he gained a wide practical experience. He is now private secretary to Henry Dalley, of New York City.

In 1892 Mr. Fisher became a resident of Closter, Bergen County, N. J., where he has since remained. As a citizen he is thoroughly identified with public affairs, liberal in promoting every worthy object, and prominent in the community. He is a member of the Protestant Episcopal Church, public spirited and progressive, patriotic and enterprising, and highly esteemed and respected. He married Mrs. H. R. Downs (*nee* Du Bois).

NELSON JAMES HARRISON EDGE was born in Jersey City, N. J., and has long been one of the leading bankers and citizens of Hudson County. He is a member of one of the oldest families, not only of Jersey City, but of the country, his first American ancestor, Robert Edge, embarking with twenty others with their families at London, September 15, 1635, in the ship "Hopewell," Thomas Babb, Master, for New England, where they first settled. Mr. Edge's grandfather, Isaac Edge, left Brooklyn, where he had been residing from about 1797, and came to Jersey City—then Paulus Hook—in the year 1806, when there were but three houses in the place: a tavern, the barracks, and a private residence. The family has resided here ever since. In 1815 this Isaac Edge built a large windmill (the material for which he imported) near what is now the northeast corner of Green and Montgomery Streets, and which at that time was lapped by the waves of the river. The old mill was for many years a prominent landmark and still lives in the memories and traditions of the oldest inhabitants. He married Frances Ogden, of Duffield, England, and died July 7, 1851, leaving surviving him four sons: Isaac Edge, Jr., who died March 10, 1859; Benjamin O. Edge, who died June 11, 1871; George W. Edge, who died January 1, 1880; and Joseph G. Edge, who died

ISAAC EDGE, JR.

May 10, 1883. He also had two daughters: Alice Edge, who died December 11, 1870, and Elizabeth Edge, who died in 1887. George W. and Elizabeth died unmarried; the others, Isaac, Benjamin O., Joseph G., and Alice, married and left families surviving them.

Isaac Edge, Jr., father of Nelson J. H. Edge, at a very early age enlisted in Captain Smith's company, Third Regiment, New Jersey Infantry, and served his country in the army during the War of 1812. He subsequently became one of the pioneer manufacturers of Jersey City and achieved a national reputation as a pyrotechnist. From his establishment for many years went forth all the displays of fireworks which were at one time annually given on the Fourth of July by all the principal cities of the country. He was also the originator of movable pieces, the first being a representation of the battle of Vera Cruz given on Boston Common. He died March 10, 1859, and left surviving him his wife Margaret, who died October 27, 1879; his son, Nelson J. H.; and his daughters, Mary Louisa and Frances Ogden. The latter died January 5, 1885.

Nelson J. H. Edge has been a life-long resident of Jersey City. He first attended old Public School No. 1, afterward studied at Mr. Dickinson's school in the Lyceum, and from there entered St. Francis Xavier College in New York City, where he finished his education. His early training was designed to fit him for an active business life, which he soon entered, and in which he has achieved an honorable reputation. Upon leaving college he entered the Mechanics' and Traders' Bank of Jersey City, now the First National Bank, and from there went to the Merchants' Bank of New York City as cashier's assistant. In 1887 he assisted in the organization of the Bank of New Amsterdam, of New York, and acted as its Cashier until 1896, when he retired from business. He was not long permitted to remain idle, however, for in 1899 he was called to the post of Cashier of the Hudson County National Bank of Jersey City, which he accepted, and which he is now filling with characteristic energy, ability, and satisfaction.

Mr. Edge is one of the foremost bankers of Hudson County. He is a man prompt in the discharge of every obligation, imbued with the highest principles of integrity, and active and influential in promoting business and public interests. Besides discharging his duties as a financier he has taken an active part in local public affairs. He was one of the organizers of the Jersey City Free Public Library, and was appointed one of the original Trustees by Mayor Cleveland in 1889, being re-appointed by Mayor Wanser in 1893 and again by Mayor Hoos in 1898, for terms of five years each. Since his first appointment he has filled the office of Treasurer of the library. In 1896 Mr. Edge was the candidate of the "Gold" Democrats for Presidential Elector on the Palmer and Buckner ticket. He served seven years in Company F, Seventh Regiment, National Guard of the State of New York, enlisting in 1876 and acting as Paymaster the greater part of that period. Mr. Edge is a member and President of the Palma Club of Jersey City, a member of the Carteret and Cosmos Clubs, and a member of the Lincoln Association, of the Jersey City Board of Trade, of the Seventh Regiment Veteran Club, of the Reform Club of New York, and of the Society of the War of 1812. He has never married.

COOK CONKLING, of Rutherford, N. J., is the son of Calvin B. Conkling, a native of Sag Harbor, Long Island, and a descendant of one of two brothers who came from England in Cromwell's time and settled originally in Salem, Mass. This ancestor married Mary Gardiner, daughter of Lyon Gardiner, proprietor of Gardiner's Island, and moved from Salem to Long Island. Calvin B. Conkling's wife was Harriet A. W. King, who was also descended from an old New England family.

Cook Conkling was born in Ledgewood, N. J., on the 4th of November, 1858. He received his preparatory education at Schooley's Mountain Seminary in Morris County, in his native State, and afterward entered Mount Union College in Ohio, where he took an elective course, but did not graduate. After leaving college he taught country school for a time, but soon abandoned that occupation to go "upon the road" as general traveling agent for a machinery house. He filled this position for seven years, in the course of which he visited forty-three States in the Union.

In his younger days Mr. Conkling wrote for the newspapers, and during his travels in America and Canada he constantly wrote for the press. His letters descriptive of the people and their ways and the countries at large encountered in his travels have been reprinted and favorably commented upon. He has probably seen as much of the United States as almost any other citizen of the country, and is well known throughout Northern New Jersey, over which his business connections extend.

Mr. Conkling finally studied law, was admitted to the bar of his native State, and in 1888 began the active practice of his profession with a partner in Rutherford, N. J., where he still resides. This association continued until February, 1893. Afterward he was engaged alone in a general banking and law business in Rutherford until June 1, 1898, when he formed a copartnership with ex-Mayor Luther Shafer, of Rutherford.

Mr. Conkling is a Democrat by inheritance, his ancestral lines on his mother's side—the Phoenixes and Kings of New Jersey—having been prominently identified with that party. He is a public spirited citizen and deeply interested in the affairs of his native State. For many years he has been influential in the growth of Rutherford, and in every capacity has displayed characteristic enterprise.

JOHN T. HARING'S ancestors, for many generations, have resided at Old Tappan. He is descended in the eighth generation from Jan Pietersen Haring, the emigrant from Hoorn, Holland, for an account of whom, and of his children, see page 61. His line of descent as far as the fourth generation is identical with those outlined on pages 61 and 63 of this work.

John Cozine Haring, of the fourth generation, born November 24, 1693, and his wife, Aeltie Van Dolsen, born in April, 1696, had issue of the fifth generation eight children, of whom one was Frederick J. Haring (5).

Frederick Johns Haring (5), born December 7, 1729, died March 6, 1807, married (1), April 30, 1752, Rachel Abrams Haring, born May 13, 1732, died August 27, 1795. He married (2), November 14, 1796, Ann de Clark (widow of Peter Perry), born July 7, 1741, died September 18, 1816. Frederick's children (of the sixth generation) by Rachel Abrams Haring were ten: Aeltie, Abram F., Dirkie, John F., Garret F., Harman, Rachel, Margaretta, Maria, and Abram B.

John Fredericks Haring (6), born June 15, 1760, died August 10, 1836, married, in November, 1781, Jemima, daughter of Tunis Blawvelt, born November 25, 1779, died January 27, 1859. Their issue of the seventh generation were two: Frederick J. and Tunis J.

Tunis J. Haring (7) was born at Tappan, September 17, 1787, died there October 18, 1881, married (1), October 7, 1806, Elizabeth Perry (daughter of Peter Perry), born March 23, 1784, died November 13, 1858. He married (2), November 22, 1859, Lea Demarest (widow of John R. Blawvelt), born February 3, 1785, died August 6, 1872. Tunis (7) by his first wife had issue of the eighth generation Abram B., Jane, Peter T., and John T., the last named of whom is the subject of this sketch.

John T. Haring (8) was born in Harrington Township, Bergen County, May 16, 1822, and received his education in the local schools. He left school at the age of fifteen and went to work on his father's farm, where he has ever since remained, never having engaged in any other business.

He is not only one of the leading farmers of Bergen County, but has also taken an active part in public affairs, and served three years as a Freeholder and three years as Township Collector. He is a member of the Reformed Church, a public spirited citizen, and highly respected and esteemed.

Mr. Haring married Rachel Blawvelt and has three children: Tunis J., of Hackensack; Richard B.; and Elizabeth P., of Sparkill, N. Y. They reside at Old Tappan, Bergen County.

MILTON T. RICHARDSON, a well known publisher of New York City and for two terms President of the Village of Ridgewood, Bergen County, N. J., was born in Westford, Mass., on the 7th of February, 1843. He is the son of Thomas Richardson and Mary Fletcher, a grandson of Abijah and Elizabeth (Livingston) Richardson and of Peletiah and Sally (Woodward) Fletcher, and a great-grandson of Thomas and Hannah (Colburn) Richardson. On his father's side he is descended from Ezekiel Richardson, one of three brothers who came to this country from England in 1630. His mother's family—the Fletchers—are equally old residents of New England, her emigrant ancestor, Robert Fletcher, coming from England also in 1630. Both the Richardsons and the Fletchers as well as their collateral ancestors have long been prominent in the history of New England and other Eastern States, and for generations have contributed materially to the growth and prosperity of the communities in which they resided.

Milton T. Richardson received his education at Westford Academy in Westford, Mass., and at Eastman's Business College in Poughkeepsie, N. Y. In these two institutions he laid the foundation upon which he has built a successful career. Soon after completing his studies he engaged in journalism and in the publishing business, and for a number of years has been successfully connected as publisher of trade and class journals at 27 Park Place, New York City. At the present time he is the publisher of the *Blacksmith and Wheelwright*, the *Amateur Sportsman*, and *Boots and Shoes Weekly*, being President and Treasurer of the corporation styled the M. T. Richardson Company, which publishes these well known periodicals. He is also the publisher of a large number of mechanical and technical books. These publications are known throughout the country, and represent in their respective fields the best interests of the trade and the highest attainments of trade and class publications.

Mr. Richardson has achieved marked success as a publisher, and through his own energy, ability, and superior judgment has brought his periodicals to a high standard of excellence. He has also taken an active part in public life. As a resident of Ridgewood, Bergen County, N. J., he has been called upon to fill important positions of trust and responsibility, being elected, in 1892, a member of the Township Committee and later, upon the incorporation of the village, a member of the Board of Village Trustees, to which he was afterward re-elected and was twice chosen President of the village. In these capacities he rendered most efficient service to the community, bringing to his duties the same energies, ability, and thoroughness which characterize his business affairs. For a time he was a private in Company I, Sixteenth Regiment, Massachusetts Volunteers. He is Vice-President of the Ridgewood Building and Loan Association and President of the Ridgewood Hall and Park Association, a member of the Ridgewood Club, and also a member of the Knights of Honor and of the Royal Arcanum. He is a member of the New York Press Club, of the American

RESIDENCE OF MILTON T. RICHARDSON.

Trade Press Association, and in 1898 was elected President of the latter body. He is also a member of the Masonic order.

In 1870 Mr. Richardson married Annie M. Rochford, by whom he had three daughters: Annie Louise Richardson, Mildred Richardson, and Mrs. H. Dunbar Johnston. He married, second, in 1896, Anna J. Porter, and they have one daughter: Irene Fletcher Richardson.

THE COLE FAMILY.—One of the earliest families to arrive in America was Barent Jacobsen Kool (now written Cole), of Amsterdam, Holland, an officer in the Dutch West India service, who came over to New Amsterdam during the administration of Director-General Peter Minuit, under whom he served for some time with credit to himself and to his country.

His son, Jacob Barentsen Cole, married Maritie Simmons and located at Kingston, N. Y., about 1659. This Jacob had eight children, the youngest of whom was Jacob, baptized at Kingston, N. Y., January 1, 1673, married Barbara Hanse, and in 1695 removed to and settled at Tappan, N. Y., where he died, leaving six children, all of whom married and settled either in Rockland County, N. Y., or in Bergen County, N. J. One of these, Abraham, born in 1707, married Ann Meyer. They were the great-grandparents of Rev. Isaac Cole, who was for many years pastor of the Dutch Church at Tappan, and whose son, Rev. David Cole, of Yonkers, N. Y., has published a History of Rockland County, N. Y., and of the Tappan Church.

Barent, said to be a brother of Abraham, above mentioned, bought a large farm of the Van Valens a little south of Closter, where his descendants are numerous. Other branches of the family started at Hackensack. It may be safely said that many hundreds of the family are scattered over Bergen and Hudson Counties.

THE CONKLIN FAMILY are scattered over Bergen and Hudson Counties, most, if not all, of them being descended from John Conklyne, of Nottinghamshire, England, and his wife, Elizabeth Allseabrook (married in 1625), who came to America in 1638 and settled at Salem, Mass., where he and his brother, Ananias, established the first glass works in America. They moved to Southold, L. I., about 1650. From thence John removed to Huntington, L. I., where he died in 1683, aged about eighty-three years. His brother, Ananias, settled at Easthampton, L. I. His descendants spell the name Conkling, of whom the late Senator Roscoe Conkling was one. John's descendants spell the name Conklin. His grandson, Nicholas became one of the purchasers of the "Kakiate" patent of many thousand acres in Rockland County, N. Y., and settled at Haverstraw in 1711. He left several children, among whom were John, Edmund, Elias, William, and Joshua. Of these, John, born at Eastchester, N. Y., about 1700, married, January 1, 1720, Gertrude, daughter of John de Pew, and settled at Haverstraw. Edmund married Barbara, daughter of John Hogencamp. Joseph Conklin, Rebecca Hyer, his wife, and Samuel Conklin and Jannetie Hyer, his wife, settled at Haverstraw, N. Y., in 1709. Matthias Conklin, probably a brother of Nicholas, above mentioned, left his home at Philips Manor in Westchester County, N. Y., early in 1719, and went to Hackensack, where on the 27th of September of that year he married Sophia Mabie, daughter of Casparus Mabie, the first immigrant of that name. Matthias bought from Henry Ludlow and settled on a large farm on the west side of the Hudson River in Bergen County, N. J., a little south of the present New York State line, bounded south by the Riker farm, north by the Gesner farm, east by the Hudson River, and west by the "Ludlow Ditch." His sons were Jacob, Abraham, and Casparus, of whom Jacob inherited the bulk of his father's lands. He married Hester Lawrence and had issue Delifrens, Barent, Maria, John, Elizabeth, David, and Jacob. Abraham, his brother, married Margaretta, daughter of William Bell, and left a family of nine children, while Casparus, who married Mynote Martling, left six children.

The descendants of the above spread rapidly over Rockland County, N. Y., and Bergen County, N. J.

WILLIAM GALBRAITH, probably the earliest and most noted taxidermist in Hudson County, was born in County Down, Ireland, of Scotch-Irish ancestors, the name being conspicuous in Scotland before the exodus caused by the wars and political disturbances. When a young man he emigrated to America and settled in New York City, but soon went to Long Island, and in April, 1838, removed to West Hoboken, N. J., where he died in October, 1872, in his sixty-seventh year. He was a distinguished taxidermist, and in the constant practice of his profession achieved considerable fame and eminent success. Numerous examples of his work which are still in existence attest his remarkable skill and ability, and stamp him as one of the leading taxidermists of his time. Coming to West Hoboken when the country was new and practically an unbroken forest, he found plenty of birds and animals, many of which exist now only in the specimens which he preserved.

Mr. Galbraith purchased a house and two lots on the corner of Spring and Cortlandt Streets, of Cyrus W. Browning, the founder of the Town of West Hoboken, and during his active life took a prominent part in local affairs, serving as Town Committeeman, etc. He was also a member of the Methodist Episcopal Church. He married, first, Jemima Payne, who bore him four children: Elizabeth Charity (Mrs. Whittemore), of Chicago, Charles S., of West Hoboken, and two who are deceased. His second wife, Eliza Billings, whom he married in New York, died in West Hoboken, leaving two children: William and John, both deceased. He married, third, in New York City, Miss Dorothy Nixon, by whom he had seven children, of whom one is living, namely: Richard E., of West Hoboken.

Charles Stewart Galbraith was born on Long Island, on the 21st of September, 1831, and adopted his father's profession, which he has followed for many years. He has traveled extensively in the interest of his work, and resides in West Hoboken.

RICHARD EDWIN GALBRAITH, eldest surviving son of William and Dorothy (Nixon) Galbraith, was born in West Hoboken, N. J., April 17, 1842. After completing his studies in the public schools of his native town he associated himself with his father, and learned, and for several years practiced, the art of a taxidermist. He was successfully identified in a professional capacity with P. T. Barnum, the Chicago Academy of Sciences, and the Kentucky University at Lexington, and afterward was engaged for nineteen years in the ostrich feather business, in West Hoboken and New York, with E. V. Welch & Co. and their successors, Bene, Creighton & Co. These connections gave him a broad experience and a valuable training in both professional and commercial affairs, and brought him into prominence as a man of unusual ability, of great force of character, and of rare mental and executive attainments.

In 1884 Mr. Galbraith engaged in the real estate and insurance business in West Hoboken, which he still follows with characteristic energy and success. He has been an extensive operator in real property in that section, and through his enterprise and foresight has been instrumental in developing several important tracts.

In politics he is a conservative Democrat. He was four years a member and one year Chairman of the Town Council of West Hoboken, three years

RICHARD E. GALBRAITH.

Chief of Police, two years a member and one year Chairman of the West Hoboken Board of Education, and one of the founders of the Hudson Trust and Savings Institution, of which he is a Director and a member of the Executive Committee. He has been President of the Palisade Building and Loan Association of West Hoboken since its organization in April, 1891. He is a prominent member and for three years was Master of Doric Lodge, No. 86, F. and A. M., of West Hoboken, and is a member of Cyrus Chapter, No. 32, R. A. M., of Pilgrim Commandery, No. 16, K. T., and of the Scottish Rite bodies in the Valley of Jersey City, of Mecca Temple, Nobles of the Mystic Shrine, of New York, and of the

Masonic Veterans' Association, of Brooklyn, and is Past Junior Grand Steward of the Grand Lodge of Masons of New Jersey. He is also a member of Ellsworth Post, No. 14, G. A. R., of the Town of Union, having enlisted in August, 1862, in Company F, Twenty-first New Jersey Volunteer Infantry, and serving in the Third Brigade, Second Division, Sixth Army Corps, of the Army of the Potomac, in the Civil War. This was the first nine-months' regiment from New Jersey in the War of the Rebellion. Mr. Galbraith participated in both battles of Fredericksburg, and at the second battle was captured by the enemy and confined as a prisoner for about ten days. His high standing in the community, the esteem and confidence in which he is held, and his great popularity and wide acquaintance are attested by the several important positions he has filled, the duties of which he has discharged with ability, integrity, sound judgment, and faithfulness. Almost every important movement in West Hoboken, during the last fifteen or twenty years, has felt the impetus of his wholesome and benevolent influence.

Mr. Galbraith was married, June 1, 1865, to Sarah Jane, daughter of William Granger Quigley and Esther, his wife, of New York City and later of West Hoboken.

THE DE BOW FAMILY.—Dirk de Bow, or de Boog, as it appears on the records at Amsterdam, Holland, emigrated from that city to America in 1649, with his four children, and settled at New Amsterdam, where he died. His children were Catharine (married, September 5, 1649, Wilhelmus Beekman), Susanna (married, in 1660, Arent Everson), Frederick (married Elizabeth Fredericks), and Garret (married, September 16, 1663, Hendricke Paden, of San Francisco).

Garret had issue three children: Henry, John, and Isaac. This John was a baker in New York, and had a son, Garret de Bow, born in New York about 1703, died about 1768, at Pompton Plains, N. J., married, May 23, 1727, Maria, daughter of Paulus Vanderbeck and Catharine Ryerson. She was baptized February 21, 1706. Garret settled on the lands of his father-in-law (Vanderbeck) at Pompton, where he spent his days, and left six children: Catalyna, born in 1728 (married Simeon Van Ness); Elizabeth, born in 1729 (married Abraham Gould); Paulus, born in 1731; John, born in 1735; Maria, born in 1737 (married Samuel Berry); and Sarah, born in 1740 (married Philip Schuyler).

The descendants of these children of Garret de Bow have scattered over Passaic County and the west side of Bergen County, were they are quite numerous.

THE COOPER FAMILY is still one of the more numerous families throughout Northern New Jersey, and particularly in Bergen County. Claes Jansen Van Permerend emigrated to America in 1647, from Permerend, a town near the Zuyder Zee, between Amsterdam and Hoorn, Holland. His first stopping place was Brooklyn, where he married Pietartie Brackhoengie, of Gowannus. She died soon after and he removed to Bergen, N. J., where he married (2), November 11, 1656, Ann, a sister of Ide Van Vorst. On January 1, 1662, he obtained a patent for a tract of land near Harsimus, on which he located and remained until his death, which occurred November 20, 1688. His widow survived him until January 12, 1726. Two weather-beaten headstones mark their last resting places in the cemetery of the old Bergen Dutch Church. Claes was an active, energetic man, and attained prominence in town affairs. He was sometimes known as "John Pottagie," and in later days as "Kuyper," it is said, because he was a cooper by trade. His descendants have ever since retained the name Kuyper, anglicized to Cooper. On April 10, 1671, he bought from Governor Carteret 240 acres on the Hudson River, including in it the present Village of Nyack, N. Y. The same year he bought 400 acres adjoining his first purchase on the north, and in 1678 he bought several tracts of meadow adjoining him—in all about 468 acres of meadow. Some of these lands he owned in partnership with the Tallmans. All of them eventually passed to his sons. His issue were Cornelius, John, Claes, Dirk, Henry, Vroutie, Tryntie, Divertie, Pietartie, Janetie, Grietie, Maritie, Hellegond, Judith, and Cornelia—in all fifteen. One or two of these joined in the purchase of the Tappan patent.

Cornelius went from Bergen to Tappan in 1689, but soon sold to Tallman. He then removed to Schraalenburgh, where he bought of John Demarest 256 acres on the Hackensack River, near Old Hook, where he resided. He and his wife, Aeltie Bogert, of Tappan, reared a large family of children, from whom mainly are descended the Bergen County Coopers.

RICHARD B. HARING is descended in the ninth generation from Jan Pietersen Haring, the emigrant from Hoorn, Holland, and the line of descent is the same as that of his father, John T. Haring (see page 154), extending it one generation further, as follows:

John T. Haring (8), born May 16, 1822, married, May 24, 1843, Rachel, daughter of John R. Blawvelt, born August 24, 1822. He resides at Tappan, on part of the farm which his first American ancestor purchased from the Indians. The issue of John T. Haring (8) of the ninth generation are three: Tunis J., Richard B., and Elizabeth P., of whom the second, Richard B. (9), is the subject of this sketch.

Richard B. Haring (9) was born in Harrington Township, Bergen County, January 24, 1856. He acquired his education in the Bergen County schools, which he left at the age of eighteen to go to work on his father's farm. He still remains on the homestead. About 1886 he engaged in the business of general auctioneer. In 1897 he also established himself in the coal business at Tappan, N. Y., and still continues both enterprises.

He was for four years a member of the Township Committee and for four years served as Township Treasurer, discharging the duties of each office with characteristic ability and devotion. For some time he has also served as a member of the Borough Council. He is a member of the American Legion of Honor, of the Independent Order of Odd Fellows, and of the Reformed Church. In every capacity he has maintained a high standard for integrity, honor, and laudable ambition.

Mr. Haring married Mary G. Banta, and has six children of the tenth generation: Lila Ray, Charles B., Abram Demarest, J. Eugene, D. Leroy, and Gertrude.

JOHN JOSEPH NEVIN, Judge of the Criminal Courts of Jersey City, is the son of Patrick Nevin, and was born in Summit, N. J., on the 31st of August, 1870. After attending private schools he entered St. Peter's College of Jersey City and was graduated from that institution in the class of 1889, receiving in July of that year the degree of Bachelor of Arts; a year later he received the degree of Master of Arts. On leaving college he was offered the position of clerk to Mayor Cleveland, which he accepted, and when Mayor Wanser succeeded Mr. Cleveland in office Mr. Nevin was retained on account of his efficiency, industry, and superior qualifications. In these capacities Judge Nevin gained a wide reputation and displayed those broad executive abilities which have since distinguished him in both public and private affairs. He also engaged in journalism, being the Jersey City correspondent of the New York *Morning Advertiser* and also of the New York *Star* and *Daily Continent* during the existence of those papers. He is now Judge of the Criminal Courts of Jersey City, which office he is filling with marked ability and universal satisfaction. In 1899 he was appointed a member for Jersey City of the Hudson County Consolidation

JOHN J. NEVIN.

Commission, and he is now Secretary of that body. Judge Nevin was married April 30, 1895, to Katharine Walsh, of Jersey City, and has two children, Joseph and Edward.

THE DE GROOT FAMILY, still numerous in Bergen and Hudson Counties, are of Holland descent. William Pietersen de Groot came to America in 1662, on board the ship "Hope," with his wife and five children. They were from Amsterdam, Holland. Dirck Jansen de Groot, a native of Ryle-velt, in Holland, came to New Amsterdam as a soldier in the Dutch service, on board the ship "Spotted Cow," April 15, 1660, leaving behind him his wife, Grietie Gerrets, and two children. In April, 1663, Dirck's brother, Staats de Groot, who, the ship's register says, was a resident of Tricht, Holland, came to America on the same ship which had brought over his brother. Staats brought over with him his brother's wife and children. Staats married, in 1664, Barbara Springsteen. Dirck and his first wife, Wybrig Jans, resided in New Amsterdam until 1679, when they removed to Flatbush, L. I., where they remained permanently. From Flatbush several of the children removed to Hackensack in 1695-96. Staats first settled at Brooklyn, where the assessment roll of 1675 showed him to be a taxpayer. He was of a roving disposition. In 1678 he was living in Westchester County, N. Y. He next turned up at Bergen, N. J., where, in June, 1678, his second daughter was baptized. While living at Bergen, where many of his relatives lived, he became in 1686 one of the Tappan patentees. He was at New Amsterdam in 1688, and probably never located on his Tappan lands. He died between 1688 and 1704, having deeded or willed his lands to his wife Barbara, who was a daughter of Casparus Springsteen, of Groningen, Holland. His children were Yoost, Neltje, Mary, and Geesie. Yoost settled at Tappan and his descendants spread into Bergen County. The descendants of Dirck and William Pietersen de Groot spread through Bergen County from Bergen and Hackensack, where they settled.

THE EDSALL FAMILY are still numerous in both Bergen and Hudson Counties. The founder of the family in America was Samuel Edsall, a native of Reading in Berkshire, England, where he was born about 1630. He was a hatter by trade, and came to America early in the spring of 1655 (as is said), settling first at New Amsterdam. There, on May 29, 1655, he married (1) Jannetie Wessels, then a belle of the city, whose mother kept a tavern in Pearl Street, celebrated for burgomasters' dinners. In April, 1657, Edsall was made a small burgher. From New Amsterdam he went to Newtown, L. I. In 1663 he volunteered his services in the Esopus Indian War, and was made a Sergeant. On October 6, 1664, he, with Richard Nichols, bought of Governor Philip Carteret a tract called Nipnichsen on the Kill Von Kull in Hudson County, containing about 400 acres. He sent over four men to Bergen that year to help fortify the "towne." In 1668, with Nicholas Varlet, he bought from the Indians 1,872 acres of land fronting on the Hudson River, bounded west by Overpeck Creek, and extending northward from the town bounds of Bergen to what is now Leonia in Bergen County. After the surrender of the Dutch to the English he took the oath of allegiance to the British king and removed from Newtown to Bergen. There he was a member of Carteret's Council from 1668 to 1672. In 1668 he was appointed a commissioner to assess and collect a tax to resist invasion, and was made treasurer of the fund. He joined James Bollen and John Berry in petitioning the Dutch government that the books and papers of New Jersey be delivered to Secretary Bayard, September 12, 1673, and was one of the commissioners sent by Bergen to the same government. In 1689 he removed to New Amsterdam and became a partisan of Governor Leisler, a member of the Committee of Safety, and of the Court of Exchequer. He was caught in the net with Leisler and put on trial for high treason, of which charge he was honorably acquitted. In 1699 he removed to Queens County, L. I., where he was Justice of the Peace in 1690, and where he died. He married (2) August 27, 1689, at Flatbush, L. I., Janneite Stevens, widow of Cornelius Jansen Beory, of Newtown.

His issue were Ann, 1656; Judith, 1658; John, 1660; Ann; Julia; and Richard. Of these Ann married William Laurence, of New York, and Julia married Benjamin Blagge, of Plymouth, England. John settled north of his father's farm on the Hudson. Blagge and Laurence by the deed of Edsall became the owners of part of his Hudson River farm, and the remainder passed to the ownership of the De Groots, Days, Smiths, and other settlers of Bergen County. Some of Edsall's descendants are still living on portions of the farm bought from the savages by their first common ancestor.

THE FLIERBOOM FAMILY.—The first American ancestor of the Flierboom and Vlierboom families was Mattys Flierboom, a Hollander, who emigrated to America somewhere about 1660 and settled at New Orange (Albany), where he became a man of note, rising to the dignities and honors of a judge of the courts at Albany. There he reared a family of five children: Caroline, Wellempie, Maritie, Servaes, and Jacob, and perhaps others. About 1692 the family removed to New Amsterdam, where Wellempie married in 1693 Cornelius Eckerson. Caroline, in 1693, married Cornelius Jans Haring. Maritie married in 1694 Rynier Reyserick. Servaes, in 1697, married Gertrude Lesting. Jacob married in 1699 Maritie Peters Haring. All these, except Servaes, became residents of Bergen County. Jacob, at the division of the Tappan patent, bought a large farm at what is now Rivervale, in Washington Township. He owned other lands there. His issue were Mary, Matthew, John, Abram, Rynier, Jannetie, James, and Jannetie. All of these except Matthew were baptized at Tappan. Jacob's children (a large family) located west of the Hackensack on lands bought of John McEvers, and their descendants are scattered over Bergen County, some having taken the name of "Freeborn."

THE GARRABRANT FAMILY, the later members of which are numerous in the western part of Bergen and Hudson Counties, claim descent from Gerbrand Claesen, a Dutch emigrant, who, at one time, had much influence over the early affairs of Bergen. Claesen was from Amsterdam, and was at Bergen probably two or three years before he married Maritie, only daughter of Claes Pietersen Cos, which was August 25, 1674. He became a large property owner and held many official positions. In 1689 he obtained permission of Governor Leisler to purchase a tract of land now in Putnam County, N. Y., and, on December 6, 1699, he purchased of George Willocks an extensive tract of land on the Pequanonck River, then in Bergen County.

His issue were nine children: Peter, Claes, Herpert, Cornelia, Metje, Cornelius, Maria, Gerrebrand, and Mindert. Some of these remained at Bergen, where their descendants still live, while others settled on their father's lands on the Pequanonck River, whence their issue spread over Bergen and Passaic Counties.

MOSES E. SPRINGER, the leading undertaker of Englewood, N. J., was born August 5, 1827, in New York City, where he resided until 1857, when he went to Wisconsin, where he remained two years. His education was acquired partly in the public schools, but chiefly through his own exertions and by those means which an ambitious youth finds amid the active employments of life. Thrown at an early age upon his own resources, he manfully paved his way in the world, picked up here and there valuable bits of information, and rapidly acquired a practical experience which has served him well throughout his career.

For about fifteen years, both before and after his residence in Wisconsin, Mr. Springer was successfully engaged in business as a builder and contractor. In 1859 he returned East and settled in Englewood, N. J., where he still resides, and where he has successfully conducted an undertaking

MOSES E. SPRINGER.

business since he retired from contracting. He is now the leading undertaker in that town, and has also been active in public affairs, having served for three years as Tax Assessor. He was one of the founders of Englewood Lodge of Good Templars and was a charter member of Tuscan Lodge, No. 115, F. and A. M., of Englewood, of which he is still a prominent member and Past Master. He is a member of the Methodist Episcopal Church, a public spirited and enterprising citizen, and in all the relations of life has displayed the attributes which mark a successful man. During the past eleven years he has been Secretary of the Englewood Mutual Loan and Building Association, a position which he still holds.

Mr. Springer was married, in 1854, to Mary A. Golding, of New York City. Their children are Hester, Mary E., George W., Charles W., and Josephine Burr Springer.

THE GOETSCHIUS FAMILY is also a numerous family in the western part of Bergen County. They are all descended from John Henry Goetschy, who was born in the Canton of Zurich, in Switzerland, about 1695, where he studied for the ministry in the University of Switzerland. He came to America about 1728, and first preached at Skippach and in the valleys of the Delaware and Susquehanna in Pennsylvania. His son, John Henry Goetschius, born at Liguria, Switzerland, in 1718, studied in the University of Zurich, and came to America with his father in 1728. He was licensed to preach in 1738, and preached on Long Island until 1740, when he came to Hackensack, N. J. There he preached until 1748, when he took charge of the church at Schraalenburgh, which he kept until his death in 1774. He was an able, eloquent, and effective preacher. His son Stephen, also a minister, preached at Saddle River and Pascack from 1814 to 1837. His father, John H. Goetschius, married, August 26, 1749, Rachel Zabriskie. Both John Henry and his son Stephen reared large families, who scattered rapidly over Bergen County.

THE GAUTIER FAMILY, at one time numerous in Hudson County, was a French Huguenot family who came to America after the revocation of the Edict of Nantes by Louis XIV. By intermarriage a considerable landed estate in Bergen, N. J., came into possession of the family. This property, at what is now Greenville, is known as the "Gautier farm," descended through one Captain Thomas Brown. Jasques Gautier, of Saint Blancard, in the Province of Languedoc, France, is said to have been the first American progenitor of the Gautiers. He settled in New Amsterdam, and left issue two sons, Daniel and Francois, besides daughters. Daniel (2) married, at New York, September 6, 1716, Maria Bogert, and had eleven children, one of whom was Andrew (3), who was born in 1720 and married (1) in 1744 an English lady named Elizabeth Crossfield, and (2) in 1774 Elizabeth Hastier. Andrew (3) was a prominent man in New York, and left issue four children, one of whom, Andrew (4), born December 18, 1755, married (1) Mary Brown, of Bergen, and (2) Hannah Turner. Andrew (4) took up his residence at Greenville and left eight children, from whom are descended the Gautiers of Bergen and Hudson Counties.

WILLIAM MINDRED JOHNSON is one of the most prominent lawyers of Bergen County, N. J., and since 1895 has represented that county in the State Senate. He comes from distinguished families, his father being Hon. Whitfield Schaeffer Johnson, Secretary of State of New Jersey from 1861 to 1866, and his mother Ellen, daughter of Enoch Green, granddaughter of John Green, and sister of Hon. Henry Green, Chief Justice of the Supreme Court of Pennsylvania. His paternal grandparents were John Johnson and Maria C. Schaeffer. His paternal great-grandfather was Captain Henry Johnson, a Quartermaster in the Continental Army. Hon. Whitfield Schaeffer Johnson, father of the subject of this article, was eminent in the State of New Jersey, alike as a leading lawyer, a leader of the Republican party, and as a public man. He was born in Newton, Sussex County, No-

W. M. Johnson.

vember 14, 1806, read law in Newark with Chief Justice Joseph C. Hornblower, and came to the New Jersey bar in 1828. For many years he was a successful lawyer in Newton, and for some time served as Prosecutor of the Pleas of Sussex County. In 1861 he was appointed Secretary of State by Governor Olden and served until 1866, and in 1867 he was made register in bankruptcy. He died in Trenton on the 24th of December, 1874; his wife's death occurred there September 16, 1894.

William M. Johnson was born in Newton, Sussex County, N. J., December 2, 1847, and received his preparatory education at the Newton Collegiate Institute and the State Model School at Trenton. He was graduated from Princeton College with honor, receiving the degree of Bachelor of Arts in 1867. Subsequently he also received the degree of Master of Arts from the same institution. Mr. Johnson read law in Trenton with the late Hon. Edward W. Scudder until the latter's appointment to the bench, and afterward in the same city with Garret D. W. Vroom, now and for several

RESIDENCE OF WILLIAM M. JOHNSON.

years State Law Reporter, and was admitted to the bar of New Jersey at Trenton in June, 1870, as an attorney, and in June, 1873, as a counselor. As a member of the firm of Kingman & Johnson he successfully practiced his profession in Trenton from 1870 to December, 1874, when he moved to Hackensack, Bergen County, where he has since resided, becoming one of the recognized leaders of the Bergen County bar. In connection with an extensive legal business, and as a progressive, public spirited, and liberal-minded citizen, he has achieved a wide reputation and an honorable standing throughout the State. He is one of the most conspicuous figures in the public and political life of his section. He has appeared in a large number of very important cases, and is universally regarded as one of the ablest and most talented lawyers of the county, eminent in the profession, and remarkably successful as an advocate and counselor. His sound judgment, his integrity, his broad legal attainments, and his fine sense of honor as a man have won for him the confidence of not only his clients, but of the entire community, in an unusual degree.

He is also one of the influential leaders of the Republican party in the State, having served on the Republican State Committee in 1884, and being a delegate to the Republican National Convention at Chicago in 1888. In the autumn of 1895 he was nominated and elected State Senator from Bergen County for a term of three years, and so ably and satisfactorily did he discharge the duties of that office that in 1898 he was re-elected for a second term of three years. He has been active in proposing and shaping legislation in the interest of the taxpayers of both the State and his district, and has served as Chairman of the Committees on Appropriations, State Library, and the Judiciary and as a member of the Committees on Boroughs and Townships and State Hospitals. In 1898 and 1899 he was the leader of his party on the floor of the Senate. He was the first Republican senator ever elected in Bergen County, and received 6,287 votes in 1895 and 6,999 in 1898; these facts speak volumes for the popularity, the confidence, and the esteem in which he is held by his fellow citizens, while his re-election by an increased vote attests the satisfaction he has rendered in this important trust. In 1900 he was elected President of the New Jersey Senate and became Acting Governor during the absence of Governor Voorhees in Europe in May, 1900, and in August of the same year he was appointed by President McKinley First Assistant Postmaster-General of the United States, *vice* Perry S. Heath resigned.

Senator Johnson has also been prominent in the local affairs and public interests of Hackensack, where he has so long resided. He has held various town offices, has served on the Hackensack Board of Education, and has taken for many years a deep interest in the development of the public school system. "The Johnson Public Library," costing nearly $50,000, was erected in 1900 by Mr. Johnson, at his own expense, and presented by him to the Town of Hackensack. Outside of the lines of his profession he has been eminently successful in the management of a number of business interests. He was one of the original organizers and founders of the Hackensack Bank, and has served upon its directorate continuously from its organization to the present time. He is also President of the Hackensack Trust Company. He is likewise a prominent member and one of the officers of the Second Reformed Church of Hackensack, while he is also a member of the Oritani Field Club, the North Jersey Country Club, the Hamilton Club, the Lawyers' Club, and the Princeton Club of New York. In every capacity and relation in life Senator Johnson has exhibited consummate ability, a broad and liberal knowledge, and a commendable public spirit and enterprise. Privately he is possessed of scholarly attainments, and is universally respected for those virtues which make up the loyal friend and honest man.

He was married October 22, 1872, to Maria E., daughter of William White, of Trenton, N. J. Their eldest son, Walter Whitfield Johnson, died March 16, 1891, aged sixteen. The other two, who are living, are George White Johnson and William Kempton Johnson.

THE MEYER FAMILY.—The first American ancestor of the Meyer family in America was Adolph Meyer (or Mayer), a native of Ulsen, a parish of Bertheim in the German Province of Westphalia, who emigrated to New Amsterdam in 1661. His arrival was followed soon after by the advent of his kinsmen, Andrew and John Meyer, brothers. They must have been on friendly terms with the Van Vorsts at Bergen, for, on November 5, 1671, Andrew's marriage to Miss Vroutie, eldest daughter of Ide Van Vorst, was duly solemnized in the old Dutch Church on the heights, and on June 13, 1677, Miss Ann Van Vorst, Vroutie's sister, was united to John Meyer in the same church. Andrew and John both took their wives to New Amsterdam, where they prospered and reared large families. In 1694 John removed to Tappan and located near the Sparkill Brook. John's wife, then a widow, received her share of the Tappan patent at the division in 1704. Their children, whose descendants spread southward into Bergen County, were Catharine, Ide, John, Judith, Iden, Cornelius, Ann, Elizabeth, and Andrew.

Adolph Meyer removed to near Demarest in Bergen County, where he settled on a large farm purchased by him from the Demarests. His issue spread all over Bergen County and are numerous to-day.

THE OUTWATER FAMILY.—Franz Jacobsen was a native of Oudewater, a small town on the River Yssel, between Leyden and Utrecht, Holland. This town is also the birthplace of Arminius, after whom the "Remonstrants" were called Arminians. A picture in the Stadt-huys, by Dirk Stoop, commemorates the brutal excesses committed there by the Spaniards in 1575. Jacobsen came to America prior to 1657 and located at Albany. One of his sons, Thys Franz Outwater, went from Albany to Tappan, N. Y., in 1686, where he married Geertie Lamberts Moll (widow of John Jacobs Harding). His descendants spread over Rockland County and into New Jersey. One of them, Dr. Thomas Outwater, was a noted surgeon in the Revolutionary Army. Thomas Franz Outwater, another son of Franz Jacobsen, the emigrant, removed to New York, where he married Neetie Peterse. He subsequently removed to and settled in Bergen County, south of Hackensack, where he married (2) in 1730 Jannetie Durie, widow of Cornelius Epke Banta. His children were Jacob, Thomas, John, Peter, Elizabeth, Janneke, and Annatie, all of whom married and settled around Hackensack, where their descendants still reside.

THE LAROE (LA ROUX) FAMILY, still numerous in Bergen County, are descended from Jaques la Roux, who was born in 1657. Mr. Riker in his "History of Harlem" says of him: "From his name and affiliation with the French refugees we conclude he was himself French, though Vander Vin usually carefully writes his surname the first two or three times el Roey, and finally adopts the form of *El Roe*. As he must have had warrant for this, probably Jaques was of mixed blood, Spanish and Walloon. He is always called by Vander Vin 'Jaco,' a juvenile form of his name used by the Walloons. He was at New Harlem as early as 1673, a young man and unmarried. Probably he had then been here but a short time. In 1677 he joined the Dutch Church at New Amsterdam, but early the next year accompanied the Demarest family to their settlement on the upper Hackensack River. At Hackensack he married Hendricke Teunis Helling (Helms), and by her had issue Peter, Henry, Samuel, Samuel, Abraham, and John." On the decline of the French church at New Bridge, "which he must have helped to form," says Riker, he joined the church at Hackensack, April 5, 1696. The same year he, with the emigrant Lozier and others, purchased of the Indians the "Old Hook" patent, containing 1,300 acres on the west side of the Hackensack in Washington Township. The title to this tract was defective and was not made good until April, 1704, after his death. He was known as "Siques La Roux." Upon his death his children inherited his property, married, and reared large families, the descendants of whom spread rapidly over Bergen County. They are still numerous.

HENRY PUSTER is a fine example of the German-American citizen, one of that large class whose industry, economy, intelligence, and sturdy integrity have done so much toward the development of our country, and whose solid qualities and valuable services in all departments of private and public life have been recognized in every portion of the republic. He is a native of Jersey City, N. J., where he was born March 10, 1858, and where he has always resided. His father, Valentine Puster, a native of Bavaria, came to America about the year 1850, and located in Jersey City, where his son enjoyed the advantages of the public as well as the German private schools.

While but a youth he made choice of the jewelry business as his life work; but after a short apprenticeship he became convinced that his tastes, abilities, and natural aptitudes pointed to a very different sphere of action. Hence, with more mature judgment revising his former decision, he resolved to make the law his profession. In the light of subsequent events no one can doubt that this was a most fortunate change. Mr. Puster now entered the law office of Hon. William D. Daly, since State Senator and Congressman. For four years following he received kindly advice and instruction from Mr. Daly, as well as from his partner (at that time), Mr. Wynkoop, who took a lively and warm interest in him, seeing his aptitude and industrious endeavors, and coached him through all the intricacies confronting the law student. Mr. Puster also found a warm friend in the late Hon. Bennington F. Randolph, Judge of the Jersey City District Court, who did much for him while pursuing the rugged course of the law student, and he afterward had the extreme pleasure of succeeding his benefactor and friend on the District Court bench.

At the close of this period Mr. Puster took his examination in company with a number of fellow-students from the same building (Flemming Building), and to-day is the only living and successful lawyer of all those who took the journey to Trenton bent on attaining the same goal. After becoming regularly admitted to the bar of New Jersey, he at once entered

HENRY PUSTER.

upon the practice of his profession in his native city, where his courtesy, ability, and knowledge of the law, his tireless activity, with prompt and thorough attention to business, rapidly added to his circle of friends and steadily built up for him an extensive and valuable practice. He is a man of kind and generous impulses, as is evidenced by the fact that he is known as a friend of the poorer classes, who often receive the benefit of his legal services and advice with little remuneration or quite gratuitously.

So bright and energetic a man could scarcely fail to become a leader in politics. He comes of Democratic stock and has always been true to the Democratic standard, and hence enjoys the fullest confidence of his party. As early as 1881, when but twenty-three years of age, he was elected Alderman of his district, the Sixth, and received the cognomen of "the School-Boy Alderman," which position he held for two years, and labored assiduously for his district with good effect. In 1890 he was chosen Assemblyman for the same district by a large majority over his opponent, Hon. James S. Erwin. The duties of this office he discharged with ability till the Hon. Leon Abbett, having discovered his fitness for the honors and responsibilities of the bench, in April, 1891, appointed him to succeed William P. Douglass as Judge of the First District Court of Jersey City. As a jurist he fully met the high expectations of his friends, presiding with marked dignity, ability, justice, and decision.

Judge Puster is a member of Grant Lodge, No. 89, K. of P., of Unique Council, R. A., and of the Order of Good Fellows; Past Grand of Lincoln Lodge, No. 136, I. O. O. F.; and representative to the Home for Aged Indigent Odd Fellows of New Jersey, of which institution he is a Director and formerly President. He has also served several years as the representative to the Grand Lodge of Odd Fellows of New Jersey. He is one of the managers of the Aged German Home, known as the Raymond Roth Altenheim, under the management of the German Pioneer Verein, as well as counsel for the same institution. He is also counsel for five different building and loan associations.

On the 24th of January, 1883, Judge Puster was married to Miss Julia A. Wenner, daughter of John C. Wenner, for many years past a leading business man and manufacturer of Jersey City. They are blessed with four daughters, in whom Judge Puster has a great and fatherly pride.

He became associated in partnership with Hon. Robert S. Hudspeth, ex-Presiding Judge of the Hudson County Court of Common Pleas, and has a suite of finely appointed offices in the Davidson Building, Jersey City. Judge Puster is still a young man, having only reached the prime of life, and has every prospect of a brilliant future before him.

THE FIRST OF THE MABIES in America wrote the surname Meebji. He was Casparus (Jasper) Mabie, and of French origin, though from what particular part of France he hailed does not appear. He was a Huguenot, and either he or his ancestor had fled from France to Amsterdam, in Holland, from which city he emigrated to America about 1692 with his wife, Elizabeth Schuerman, and three children: Christina, Sophia, and Peter. The family went to New Harlem, where Casper bought lands of Daniel Tournure, and where he became a considerable landholder. On September 29, 1696, he was elected Constable of Harlem, the duties of which office he discharged for one year. In 1700 he sold part of his farm and in 1709 the balance, and removed to Bergen County, N. J., where in 1710 he purchased of Captain Lancaster Symes a large tract on the west bank of the Hudson, extending westward to Closter. Here he settled, and here he died about 1720. His children were Christina (married Joost Albert Zabriskie), Sophia (married Matthew Conklin), and Peter, all born in Holland, and Jeremia, Abraham, Frederick, and John, baptized at Harlem. Of these Peter married Catelyntie Johns Bogert and had issue at least thirteen children, all baptized at Tappan. Peter located at Old Tappan. The descendants of his children spread over Bergen County, and many of them are still residents.

THE MERSELES FAMILY is still numerous in Hudson and Bergen Counties. They trace their lineage to Pieter Marcelisen (Marcelis), a native of the little Town of Beest, near Leerdam, in the Province of Utrecht, Holland. He left Amsterdam in April, 1661, with his wife, four children (aged, respectively, twelve, six, four, and two years), and two servants, on the Dutch West India ship "Beaver," and arrived at New Amsterdam on the 9th of May of the same year. The ship's register shows he paid 232 florins passage-money for the family of eight persons, all of which goes to show that even then he must have been a man of considerable means. He removed to Bergen, where he settled, and where his wife died in 1680, and he followed her in 1681. His issue were James, Jannekie, Pieter, Merseles, Elizabeth, and Hillegond. These all married and remained at Bergen. Peter, the eldest son, died wealthy. Some of his descendants settled in Rockland County, N. Y., and in the north end of Bergen County.

THE VANDELINDA FAMILY.—Pieter Linde was a native of Belle, a town on the road from Bruges to Ghent in Flanders. He was a physician, and came to America in 1639 with his wife, Elsie Barents. The shipping records show that, on April 18, 1639, he paid to David Pietersen de Vries and Frederick Pietersen de Vries 140 Carolus gelders ($56) for passage for himself and wife to New Amsterdam, where he settled and followed his profession until the death of his wife in 1643. On July 1, of the following year (1644), he entered into a marriage contract with Martha Chambers, or Ekomberts, of New Kerck, in Flanders. She was the widow of John Manje, or Monnye. The marriage knot was tied July 10, 1644, at New Amsterdam. After this marriage Vandelinde removed to Brooklyn, where he became the owner of the patent of his wife's first husband. This he sold January 23, 1652, to Barent Joosten. He owned several other pieces of property, both at Brooklyn and New Amsterdam, and in 1655 was tobacco inspector of the latter city. After Linde's death his descendants assumed the name of Van der Linde.

His son, Joost Van der Linde, removed to Bergen, N. J., in the fall of 1670, where, on January 30, 1671, he bought about 90 acres of land of Pieter Jansen Slote between Constable's Hook and Bergen Point. Here he resided until his death. His children of the third generation were John (died in 1696), Roelof, Jannetie (married Peter Laurens Van Buskirk), Hendricke (married Laurens Laurens Van Buskirk), and Machtelt (married Albert Zabriskie). All of these except John removed to Bergen County. Roelof resided with his father at Bergen, where, on October 2, 1682, he married Susanna Hendricks Brinkerhoff. He removed to Hackensack in 1686, where he helped to organize and became a member of the Dutch church. He became joint owner with his brothers-in-law, Laurence and Peter Van Buskirk, in the New Hackensack patented lands, and also bought of the New Jersey proprietors large tracts of wild land west of the

Pascack River in Washington and Midland Townships in Bergen County. His first wife having died in 1700, he married (2) Rachel Cresson, widow of John Peters Durie, who survived him, but by whom he had no issue. He was a man of wealth, and died in New York City early in 1709, leaving a will dated September 6, 1708, proved February 13, 1709. His issue of the fourth generation were Peter, Henry, Classie, Maritie, Sophia, and Geesie.

Peter, by the will of his father, received his father's plantation at New Hackensack, and Henry all the lands on the Pascack and Saddle Rivers, in the northern part of the county. Hendrick resided at Polifly, below Hackensack. The numerous descendants of Peter and Henry (4) have become scattered over a large area of territory, including Bergen and Hudson Counties.

GEORGE LOURIE WILEY, a well known electrical engineer and a prominent resident of Arlington, N. J., was born in St. Louis, Mo., on the 12th of May, 1849. He is the son of George W. Wiley and Elmira M. Gregg, a grandson of James Wiley, Jr., and Margaret Sutherland and of James Gregg and Abagail Wright, and a great-grandson of John Wiley and Matilda Lourie and of Joseph Wright and Mary Sinclair. The Sutherlands and Louries were of royal Scotch blood and the Greggs and Wrights on his mother's side were members of the Society of Friends or Quakers. His father, George W. Wiley, was a stock broker and well known in Wall Street twenty-five years ago; he was an esteemed and prosperous citizen, and died in Chicago in 1899, having retired from business in 1878.

Mr. Wiley was graduated from the St. Louis (Mo.) City University and afterward spent one year in a classical and technical course under a private tutor. In 1868 he became a clerk in the New York Gold Exchange Bank, where he remained one year. He then associated himself with the Gold and Stock Telegraph Company of New York, and continued with that corporation for eleven years (1869-1880), serving successively as clerk, Assistant Superintendent, and Superintendent. In 1880 the Gold and Stock Telegraph Company's telephone business, which was then under his charge, was consolidated with that of the Bell Telephone Company of New York, forming what is now the New York Telephone and Telegraph Company. Mr. Wiley continued under the consolidation of the new company as General Superintendent for two years, resigning in 1882 to become President and General Manager of the Central Telephone Company in Mexico. He sailed for that country June 22, 1882, and continued with that company in Mexico for three years, until it was put on a paying basis. In 1885 he returned to New York and became manager of the Standard Underground Cable Company, manufacturers of electrical wires and cables, with offices in New York, Pittsburg, Philadelphia, Chicago, and San Francisco, and factories in Oakland, Cal., Pittsburg, Pa., and Perth Amboy, N. J. He is also President of the New York Electric Construction Company, a Director in several important electrical enterprises, and a member of the American Institute of Electrical Engineers and of the New York Electrical Society.

In these various positions Mr. Wiley developed great executive ability, and not only achieved success, but gained a reputation in electrical circles which extends throughout the country. He also has a wide reputation as an inventor and electrical expert. Though an active, energetic, and patriotic citizen, he has always avoided public or political office, having devoted his entire time to the important duties which have devolved upon him and which he has discharged with ability and satisfaction. He is a Mason, an Odd Fellow, a Past Regent of the Royal Arcanum, and a member of the Loyal Additional. He holds membership in America Lodge, No. 1304, R. A., and in Arlington Council, L. A. He was raised in the Presbyterian Church and has affiliated with that faith. His career has been an active and successful one, and in both business and social relations he is highly esteemed and respected. As a resident of Arlington, N. J., he has contributed much to the growth and development of that attractive borough, and is prominently connected with many of its leading institutions.

GEORGE L. WILEY.

On Christmas Day, December 25, 1873, Mr. Wiley was married to Josephine Griffiths Polhemus, of New York, a lady well known in literary circles. They have six children, three sons and three daughters, the eldest, a son, being twenty-two years of age.

THE PEACK FAMILY.—John Peeck (as he spelled it), the common ancestor of the Pake and Peak families of Bergen County, still quite numerous, was of English parentage, but whether he came to New Amsterdam from Holland or England does not appear. He must have come over in

1649 or 1650, for his marriage to Maria Vlockers (widow) is recorded in the New Amsterdam church records as of February 20, 1650. This entry, unlike most of the other entries, contains no reference to the place of his nativity. As the name Peeck does not appear in any of the New York or New Jersey records prior to this, he must have been the first of the name in New Netherlands at least. The couple lived in New York, where he died in 1659. His children were at least four: Ann, 1651; John, 1653; Jacobus, 1656; and Maria, 1658.

John Peeck married in New York, July 18, 1683, Elizabeth, daughter of Dr. Gysbert Van Emburgh, the American ancestor of all the Van Emburghs of Bergen County. Dr. Van Emburgh was from Amsterdam, and began as a shopkeeper and book-vender in New Amsterdam, but went from there to Albany to reside. From there he removed to Kingston, where he practiced medicine successfully, and was scheppen from 1663 to his death in 1665. His son, John, was a physician, and married a daughter of William Sandford, of Bergen County. He bought considerable land in Bergen County, where he eventually settled.

John Peeck had eight children by his wife, Elizabeth Van Emburgh, all of whom settled in Bergen County, principally in the localities called Schraalenburgh and Kinderkamack, where his descendants still flourish.

THE POWLESS FAMILY, still very numerous in Bergen County, trace their descent from Paulus Pietersen, who was born at Merwen, Holland, in 1632, and emigrated to this country in 1656. His wife, Tryntie Martens, was among the emigrants who came over from Holland in the ship "Gilded Beaver," in 1658. The marriage of Paulus Pietersen and Tryntie Martens is that announced on the records of the old Dutch church in New York: "Paulus Pietersen j.d. Van Merwin int Stiff Aken in lant van Gilbert Sept 1, 1685." Merwin is a small town in Holland, and Aken a town in Prussian Saxony, on the left bank of the River Elbe. Paulus Pietersen located at Bergen, N. J., where he soon became a prominent man in all town affairs. In 1663 Governor Stuyvesant appointed him one of the commissioners to fortify the town (at what is now Bergen Square, Jersey City) against the depredations of the surrounding Indians. In the same year he obtained patents for several parcels of land in and about the Town of Bergen, containing in all thirty-seven acres. After the occupation by the British (May 12, 1668), Governor Carteret confirmed Pietersen's title to his Bergen lands. In 1764 these lands passed to the ownership of Garret Newkirk. Paulus Pietersen died December 18, 1702, and his wife's death preceded his on May 19 of the same year.

They had issue seven children, who took the surname of Powleson and Powless. Most of them remained at Bergen, but Martin Powless, the third in point of age, born in 1663, bought lands and settled near Hackensack. He married Margaretta Westervelt and reared a large family. They scattered throughout the county, and the descendants of Paulus Pietersen are numerous to-day in both Hudson and Bergen Counties.

DANIEL RUTAN was located at Esopus on the Hudson River prior to 1700. The place of his nativity does not appear, but he was no doubt a Hollander. His sons, Abraham, Daniel, Jr., and Peter, came to New Jersey and located at Aquackanonck (Passaic) as early as 1702. In 1703 Abraham married, at Hackensack, Mary Rutan, probably a near relative of his. In 1710 Daniel married Ann Hanse Spier, of Bergen, whose parents were then living at Passaic. In November, 1713, Daniel's brother Peter located at New Barbadoes (west of Hackensack), where he married Gertrude Vanderhoff. The Vanderhoffs and Rutans came to Bergen County from Albany about the same time. Probably they were related. The Rutans settled west of the Saddle River in the Hohokus and Paramus sections of Bergen County, where many of them still reside.

THE SCHUYLER FAMILY.—The New Jersey branch of the Schuyler family, now very numerous in the western and northern parts of Bergen County, are descended from Philip Pietersen Van Schuyler, born in 1628 at Amsterdam, Holland, who, with his brother David, emigrated to America in 1650 and settled first at Fort Orange (Albany), N. Y., on December 12, 1650. Following his arrival at Albany he married Margaretta Van Schlectenhorst, of Nieuwkirk, Holland, her father being then manager of the Colonie of Van Rensselaer. He was a magistrate at Albany in 1656, 1657, and 1661. In 1662 he received permission to plant a village on the Esopus River. He died March 9, 1684. His children were six, one of whom was Arent Schuyler, born June 25, 1682, who married and came to New York while yet a young man. In 1793 he went to Pequannock (then in Bergen County), and with Anthony Brockholst purchased 4,000 acres for mining purposes. He also bought large tracts of land in Orange County, N. Y., but in 1710 he purchased land of Edward Kingsland on New Barbadoes Neck, where he resided and where he opened a copper mine. He became a wealthy man. His issue were eight children, several of whom became famous Jersey men, and their issue scattered over Bergen and Hudson Counties.

SCHUYLER ARMS.

JOHN J. KENNEDY, glove manufacturer of West Hoboken, is an example of what one man can accomplish by his own indomitable efforts united with untiring industry, constant application, and original methods. Born and reared in the town, and educated in the local schools, he has paved his way to success and reputation through those channels which would appal a less courageous man, but which, nevertheless, are the only true means of laudable endeavor. His present position, as proprietor of the only glove manufactory of the kind in the country, is all the more noteworthy because it is the result of his personal labors, after years of difficulties and perseverance.

He is the eldest son of Andrew and Mary (Kelly) Kennedy, both natives of Ireland, and a grandson of James and Bridget Kennedy, who came from Ireland to this country when Andrew was about nine years old. They settled in Weehawken, N. J. Andrew Kennedy followed the trade of mason and bricklayer during his active life, and is now retired. His wife died May 6, 1897. Their children are John J., Thomas A., and Mary (Mrs. John Curran), all of West Hoboken, N. J. John J. Kennedy was born

March 21, 1858, attended the public and parochial schools of his native town, and at the age of fifteen entered the office of the old *Highland Sentinel*, in West Hoboken, with a view of learning the printer's trade. After an experience of two years in this capacity and another year as a fisherman he turned his attention to fine glove cutting, associating himself with a Dane named Gustav Elgeti, who claimed to be the first man to learn the French glove cutting system in Copenhagen, Denmark. Mr. Kennedy was the first native of this country to learn French glove cutting, and, so far as can be ascertained, is the only man in the trade who has

JOHN J. KENNEDY.

mastered and follows that excellent but little known system in its entirety.

In 1880 he engaged in the manufacture of fine gloves in West Hoboken, on Hill Street, near Palisade Avenue. He started on a very small scale, in one or two rooms, and with only two or three assistants, whom he was obliged to teach the system, as he has, in fact, all those who have ever entered his employ. Numerous difficulties, principally the introduction of his goods, were met, fought, and overcome, but not without indomitable perseverance and constant endeavor on his part. Competition being keen and general, it was some time before he got his product into the chief centers of the glove trade, but when once it was there no scheming nor maneuvering by rival manufacturers could prevent its instant success. In 1883 he invented and patented a re-inforcement for the opening slit which proved at once valuable, practical, and economical, and in 1890 he obtained another patent which has become famous as the Kennedy patent cut glove.

Mr. Kennedy steadily overcame all obstacles, numerous though they were, and successfully introduced his gloves into every State and territory in the Union, where they now have a very high reputation, selling side by side with the most celebrated makes in the world. He employs about eighty people and manufactures about $60,000 worth of fine street and driving gloves annually. The product is all sold through Wilson Brothers, of New York, Chicago, and Paris, the largest dealers in men's furnishings in the world. Mr. Kennedy has revolutionized the glove business, both in manufacturing and in selling. His success is due entirely to the genuine merit of his goods, together with his personal efforts and tact in placing them before the public. One point of superiority which distinguishes his gloves is the fingers, which are straight and of equal length. In 1883 he originated a picture of two elephants pulling a glove, typifying strength, which has been widely copied by clothing manufacturers and others, though often in different designs. The idea was his.

One can regard Mr. Kennedy's success only with feelings of respect and wonder, for his is one of those very few instances where a man, imbued with a single idea, steadily and persistently hews to the line and eventually achieves the goal of his ambitions. His whole life has been spent in the town of his birth. His labors have been directed toward one object—the manufacture of the best gloves in the market. And the wonderful result of his efforts is seen in his present factory, a large and finely equipped brick building on or near the spot where he made his first start, nearly twenty years ago, and very near the home in which he was born and reared. No man is worthy of more respect than he who carves out his own fortune, unaided save by his hands and brain, and this Mr. Kennedy has done. He stands among the leading glove manufacturers in this country. He has devoted himself strictly to business, to the exclusion of all political or public preferment, and belongs only to St. Michael's Catholic Church, the Holy Name Society, and Palisade Council, No. 387, Knights of Columbus. The object of the Holy Name Society is to suppress swearing. He takes a deep interest, however, in the affairs of his town and county, and never fails to bear the responsibilities of a progressive, patriotic citizen.

Mr. Kennedy was married June 24, 1885, to Nellie, daughter of John and Julia Lucey, of Jersey City Heights, N. J. Of their nine children two died in infancy; the others are John, Mary, Ellen, Julia, Alice, Andrew, and Salome.

THE QUACKENBUSH FAMILY in Bergen and Hudson Counties are descended from Peter Quackenbush, of Oostgeest, Holland. His son, Rynier Pietersen Van Quackenbosch, came to America in 1673-74 and located at New Amsterdam, where he married, March 2, 1674, Elizabeth Jans, of Flushing, L. I. He was a carpenter by trade, and pursued that calling in New Amsterdam. His wife having died in 1691, he married, the following year, Classie Jacobse. He had a large family of children, among whom were Abraham, Jacob, and John. Abraham settled at Schraalenburgh in Bergen County and married Susanna, a daughter of Samuel Hellings (Helms), by whom he had issue ten children. His brother John married Lena Van Houten, and his brother Jacob married Ann Brower. John and Jacob both located in the northerly part of Bergen. Abraham, John, and Jacob each reared large families, from whom have sprung numerous descendants now scattered over Bergen County.

THE RYERSONS are the most numerous to-day of any family in the western part of Bergen County. The original surname of the family was "Reyertzoon." The family were numerous in Amsterdam, Holland, as early as 1390, in which year one William Reyertzoon was Burgomaster of the city. Another member of the family filled the same office in 1414 and 1418. Members of this family held prominent positions in Amsterdam up to 1585. Many of them took an active part in the expulsion of the Spaniards from Holland, for which two of them were banished by the Spanish king, and another, Albert Reyertzoon, was beheaded April 12, 1537. The family coat-of-arms, as registered in Amsterdam, is described as follows: "Eradicated arz; 1 and 4 Sa, a tree withered and eradicated Arz; 2 and 3 Arz; three halberts bend ways and in bend sinister, the middle one longer than the others, sa, the blades vert; Surtout, az. a martlet, or, *Crest*, a swan roussant. *Motto* Voor God en Faderland." The fact that the family had a coat-of-arms, of course, indicates that some of them belonged to the nobility of Holland.

Martin Reyerson, with his brother, Adriaen Ryerson, emigrated from Amsterdam, Holland, in 1646, and settled at Brooklyn, where Martin married, May 14, 1663, Ann, daughter of Joris Jansen Rapeljea. He resided at Brooklyn until 1685. He joined the Dutch Church there in 1677, was elected a magistrate in 1679, and constable in 1682. In 1685 he removed to Flatbush, L. I., where he was one of the patentees of that patent that year. His issue were Marritie, Joris (George), Ryer, Catalyntie, Sarah, Cornelius, Jacobus, Geertie, Helena, and Franz.

Joris (George), baptized September 19, 1666, married, August 11, 1691, Ann Schouten, widow of Theunis Dircksen Dey, of New York. In 1695 George, in company with Anthony Brockholst, Arent Schuyler, Colonel Nicholas Bayard, and John Meet, all of New York, and Samuel Berry, Henry McDonna, and David Mandeville, of New Jersey, purchased from the Governor and Council of East New Jersey 4,000 acres of land in what was then Bergen County (now Passaic), extending northward from the junction of the Pompton River with the Passaic River. Of this large tract George Reyerson eventually became the owner of the greater part, on which he settled. His issue, baptized in New York, were Martin, 1698; Helena, 1701; George, 1703; Lucas, 1704; and Blandina, 1706. There were probably other children born in New Jersey. The descendants of these children are still numerous in Bergen and Hudson Counties. Many of them have held positions of trust and honor in the councils of the State.

THE SICKLES FAMILY had much to do with the early settlement of Hudson and Bergen Counties. Zacharias Sickles, the common American ancestor of the family, was a native of the City of Vienna, Austria, who soon after reaching manhood drifted to Amsterdam, Holland, where he entered the military service and was sent with a fleet on a cruise to Curaçoa, where he remained until 1655. In the service he attained the rank of Adelborst or Cadet. In 1655 Governor Stuyvesant paid a visit to the island where Sickles was on duty. The latter accompanied the Governor to New Amsterdam and soon after attached himself to the garrison at Fort Orange (Albany). In 1658 he became a tapster at New Amsterdam, and upon the surrender by the Dutch to the British in 1664 he married Anna, daughter of Lambert Van Vaelkenburgh, and went to work to gain a livelihood as a carpenter. In 1670 he was elected "town herder," which office he held for thirteen years on a salary of 18 gelders a head for the season. He was appointed rattle-watch, so called from the rattle used to give warning in making his nightly rounds. He was also for some time crier to call the people together on needed occasions, and porter or keeper of the city gates, to close them at night and open them in the morning.

In 1669 he purchased a lot of land in Bergen, N. J., on which his eldest son, Robert, settled. The children of this son scattered through Bergen County, where many of Zacharias's descendants still reside. He had nine children, the eldest of whom was Robert, who married Gertrude Reddenhause and located at Bergen, where he was a prominent resident, and left a large family. His son William, born in October, 1704, married Elizabeth Cooper, and removed to Rockland County, N. Y., from which locality his numerous descendants spread south into Bergen County, where their descendants are still found.

JAN ADRAINSE SIP was at Bergen as early as 1684, where, on April 22 of that year, he married Johanna Van Voorst. He bought several lots at Bergen during the next fifteen years, and became an important and influential person in the town. His issue were eleven children, among whom were Ide, John, Cornelius, Abraham, Henry, and Helena. Most of them married and became residents of Bergen. Their descendants are still numerous in Hudson County.

AARON STOCKHOLM BALDWIN, of Hoboken, comes from one of the oldest families of New England, his ancestors emigrating from the mother country with the early colonists. From New England they moved into Eastern New York, and there raised the standard of their race, conquered the primeval forests, and exemplified in their lives the sterling traits of industry, integrity, and progress. Like the subject of this sketch, many of them achieved prominence in public and business affairs, wielding a potent influence for good, and leaving behind them the memories of an honorable name.

Mr. Baldwin was born in East Fishkill, Dutchess County, N. Y., June 8, 1839, being the son of Elisha S. Baldwin and Aletta C. Stockholm, a grandson of Daniel Baldwin, of Lake Mahopac, Putnam County, N. Y., and of Aaron Stockholm, of Fishkill, from whom he was named, and a great-grandson of Elisha Baldwin, a pioneer of the Hudson River Valley. His father was born at Lake Mahopac, and during his active life followed successfully the dual occupation of farmer and live stock dealer. Mr. Baldwin attended the East Fishkill public schools until he was twelve years old, when he entered Pingree Academy at Fishkill, where he remained five years. Afterward he spent five years at what is now Drew Seminary in Carmel, Putnam County, graduating in 1860. His studies in these institutions were in every way worthy of the broad and receptive intellectual qualities which he manifested as a boy, and which have served him well in business and public relations.

Having received a thorough classical training, he returned home, and in September, 1863, went to Chicago to accept a position with the American Express Company, which he held until July, 1870. At that date he moved to Weehawken, N. J., and engaged in the live stock storage business as general live stock agent for the Erie Railroad, and continued in that capacity until 1898, when he organized and incorporated the Weehawken Stock Yard Company, of which he is President and Treasurer and a Director.

Mr. Baldwin has been an active Republican ever since he cast his first vote and almost ever since the organization of the party, and for about a quarter of a century, with the exception of one or two years, has been a leading member of the Hudson County Republican Committee; and he is now Chairman of its Organization Committee, which has been asked to

AARON S. BALDWIN.

devise ways and means by which the party can be re-organized in the county. He was a member of the Hudson County Board of Chosen Freeholders in 1881, 1882, and 1883, from the Tenth Assembly District, and for seven years served as a member and Chairman of the Board of Tax Commissioners of Hoboken, where he settled in April, 1886, and where he still resides. He is now one of the commissioners appointed by Governor Voorhees to inquire into the expediency of consolidating the several municipalities of Hudson County into one great city. This commission was formally organized June 14, 1899. Mr. Baldwin is also one of the commissioners in Hoboken to adjust the taxes in arrears under the Martin act. He has been a delegate to almost every State, district, county, and local Republican convention for upward of twenty-five years, was an alternate delegate to the Republican National Convention of 1880, and in 1896 was his party's candidate for Sheriff of Hudson County, and, though defeated by about 1,100 votes, carried Hoboken by over 500 and not only reduced the usual Democratic majority to an insignificant figure but changed entirely the complexion of the Democratic vote and raised the standard of the Republicans.

His activity and prominence in the ranks of the Republican party and his long and honorable connection with the live stock markets of New Jersey and New York have won for Mr. Baldwin an extensive acquaintance, among whom he is universally respected and esteemed. He is one of the most popular men of Hudson County. He is a member of the Benevolent and Protective Order of Elks of Hoboken, and has always supported with a liberal hand every movement designed to promote the general welfare.

Mr. Baldwin was married, June 30, 1869, to Elizabeth Janet Watson, daughter of George L. Watson, of Auburn, N. Y.

THE SLOTE FAMILY.—The first American ancestor of the Slote family was John Pietersen Slot, a native of the Province of Holstein in Denmark, who came to America about 1650 with his two sons, John and Pieter, and settled at Harlem, where he bought lands and became a prominent and useful citizen, filling the important office of magistrate from 1660 to 1665. In 1665 he bought of Governor Stuyvesant and located on lands on the Bowery in New Amsterdam, remaining there until 1686, when he bought and occupied a house in Wall Street. In 1703 he removed to the south ward of the city, where he died. His son John, married in 1672 Judith Elsworth, and made his residence in New Amsterdam. Some of his children removed to Hackensack. His brother, Peter Jansen Slot, bought, May 14, 1657, fifty acres at Communipaw, in Bergen County, N. J., on which he located in April, 1665, having first married (1663) Maritie Jacobs Van Winkle, of Bergen. He joined the Dutch church and remained there until 1671, when he sold his Bergen lands and removed to New Amsterdam, remaining there until 1677, when he removed to Esopus, N. Y., and followed his trade as a builder. Returning in 1683, he again located at Bergen, but was soon back in New Amsterdam, living near the Stuyvesant Bowery. He died there in 1688, and his widow married John Demarest and removed to Hackensack, whither also all except one of Peter's children went and settled. Peter's issue were John, 1665; Jacobus, 1669; Tryntie, 1671 (married Nicholas Lozier); Aeltie, 1678 (married Adam Van Orden and Cornelius Banta); and Jonas, 1681. The descendants of these are thickly scattered over Rockland County, N. Y., and Bergen County, N. J.

THE SMITH FAMILY.—A branch of the Smith family, which is still numerous in the northern and western parts of Bergen County, is descended from Lambert Ariaense, who was a native of the Province of Gelderland, in Holland. He emigrated to America when young and settled at New Amsterdam, where, on the 9th of April, 1682, he married Margaretta Garrets Blawvelt, a daughter of Garret Hendricksen Blawvelt, of Deventer, Holland. In 1686 Lambert Ariaense became, with his brothers-in-law, the Blawvelts, and others, a purchaser of the Tappan patent, a large part of which was in Bergen County, N. J. Lambert received a large portion of this patent at each of the divisions. Rev. David Cole in his "History of Rockland County" says:

"Lambert and his two sons located at the 'Green Bush,' where he built a stone house, near where the burying-ground now is. This house was torn down after the Revolution and a new one erected on the same spot by Gerret Smith. Lambert had three sons. The eldest, Garret, was settled, by his father, south of the swamp. Abraham, the second, stayed on the old place, and the third, Cornelius, built on what was then called the Ridge, just west of the present Erie Railroad. Garret, the eldest, was great-grandfather of Gerret Smith, the philanthropist and friend of the slave. Lambert's descendants soon grew so numerous that it was necessary to distinguish one from the other, and as he was a smith by profession it became convenient to designate him as Lambert Ariaensen Smidt. This name continued for several years, most of the branches dropped the Ariaensen entirely, and the family was known by the name of 'Smith.'"

The descendants of Lambert, the smith, spread south into New Jersey, some of them retaining the surname Ariaensen, hence the Auryaunsen family.

THE SNEDENS of Bergen County are descendad from John Sneden, a native of Amsterdam, Holland, where his family had lived for many generations. On the 23d of December, 1657, John Sneden, his wife, Gretie Jans, his two children, Carsten and Grietie, and his brother, Claes Sneden, set sail from Amsterdam in the ship "St. John Baptist," bound for the Colony of New Amstel, on the Delaware River. Three years later Claes Sneden removed to New Amsterdam, and John to New Harlem, where the latter purchased two town lots on which he permanently located, and where he died early in 1662. Beginning on the 25th of March, 1662, his estate was sold at public auction. The house, lands, and standing crops brought 135 gelders and the household effects 185 gelders. After the payment of debts 42 gelders remained for the widow and two orphaned children, Carsten and Grietie, of whom, on April 28, 1662, Philip Casier and Lubbert Gerritsen were appointed guardians. Grietie married, August 13, following, Jean Guenon (Genung), and went to reside at Flushing, L. I. Carsten entered the service of Daniel Tourneur, January 15, 1668, for a year, to have at its expiration 300 gelders and "a pair of shoes and stockings." His uncle, Claes Sneden, resided at New Amsterdam, where he had by his wife, Maria ——, several children. John Sneden (supposed to have been a grandson of Carsten), about 1740, bought of Henry Ludlow and settled on a large farm at what is now Sneden's Landing, on the west side of the Hudson River. This farm was partly in Bergen County, N. J., and partly in Rockland County, N. Y. John's sons, Dennis (who died unmarried) and John, became the owners of his lands at his death, and John's descendants are still numerous in the northerly part of Bergen County.

FRANK H. MELVILLE, of Bayonne, Hudson County, was born in England on the 7th of July, 1840. He received his education in that country, and then came to the United States. For twenty years he was successfully engaged in the paper and paper bag business. Later he engaged in manufacturing sample mailing boxes and rust preventive in New York City.

In public as well as in business affairs Mr. Melville has long been a prominent figure. He has always been an active Republican, and has served as President of the Third Ward Republican Club, as President of the Republican City Committee of Bayonne, and as Secretary of the latter organization. He was twice elected Supervisor of Taxes, and received the unanimous nomination of his party for Freeholder and member of Assembly. Under McKinley's administration he became Postmaster of Bayonne, where he has resided for a number of years. He is a member, Trustee, and Treasurer of the Fourty-fourth Street Methodist Episcopal Church, a member of the Hudson County Republican Committee, a member of the Bayonne City Republican Committee, and a member of the Union League Club, the Masonic order, and the Improved Order of Red Men. In every capacity he has displayed great patriotism, sound judgment, and unfailing public spirit,

FRANK H. MELVILLE.

and is highly respected and esteemed by all who know him. He has discharged the various public duties he has been called upon to fill with notable zeal.

In 1869 Mr. Melville married Philena A. Smith, and of their four children two survive, namely: Florence, born in 1872, and Francis Lorne, born in 1880.

JESSE W. FERDON.—Thomas Ferdon (he spelled it Verdon) emigrated to America as early as 1645. It was probably a sister of his, Magdalena, who married, March 19, 1645, Adam Brower, at Flatlands, L. I. The Ferdons came of a French family which had for some time resided in Holland. Thomas settled in the Gowannus section of Brooklyn, on a farm late of one Anthony Hulse. He married Mary Dadge, a daughter of Aeltje Bredenbend (widow of William Bredenbend) by a former husband, by whom he had one child. Thomas Ferdon (2) was born about 1654. The elder Thomas was a magistrate in Brooklyn in 1661, 1662, 1663, and 1664, and is recorded there as having taken the oath of allegiance to King Charles in 1687. His son Thomas (2) was thrice married, his first wife being Yte (or Elsie) Jurianise (or Jeuriens), widow of Tunis Ten Eycke. By his second and third wives he had no issue. He is enumerated in the census of Brooklyn in 1687 as having only three persons in his family. He was an Ensign in the Kings County militia in 1715, and both he and his first wife were members of the Dutch Church at Brooklyn. When he took the oath of allegiance, in 1687, he was described as a "native" and as residing at Gowannus, owning and occupying the homestead of his father. He was a constable in 1664. In 1718 he is set down as residing at New Utrecht, where he was a deacon in the Dutch Church and where he died. One child, Jacob Ferdon (3), by his first wife, was his only issue, born at Brooklyn, March 19, 1656.

Jacob (3) Married, May 17, 1678 (at New York), Femmetye Williams, of Flatlands, L. I., a native of Meppel, Holland. The couple lived at Flatbush, where they joined the Dutch Church in 1694. Jacob bought a farm at New Utrecht, to which he must have removed, as his name appeared on the assessment roll there for that year and in the census of 1698. The census recites that he had then seven children. In 1709 his name appears on a petition for an additional ferry to Brooklyn. His children were Barbarba, Wilhelmus, Thomas, Maria, Jacob, Jannetje, Femmetje, Dirke, and John.

Of these nine Wilhelmus (4) transplanted the name in New Jersey. He was born at Flatbush in April, 1680, and married Elizabeth ———, of New Utrecht, L. I., where he resided until his removal to this State. On the erection of the new church at New Utrecht, in 1700, he was allotted three men's and three women's seats. In 1726 he was a deacon, and in 1738 an elder, in the same church. He removed to Bergen County, N. J., as early as 1743. On the 10th of March, 1749, he made his first purchase of a tract of 470 acres of land at Closter from Henry Ludlow. On this tract he settled and built his family mansion west of the present residence of Ben S. Smith, northeast of Closter. He bought other lands of Ludlow north and east of his home tract, until he owned over 1,000 acres. The surname of his wife and the date of his death are unknown. His children were John, William, Elizabeth, Dirke, Abram, John (2), and Phebe. His farm after his death passed to the ownership of his three sons, John, William, and Abram, and his numerous descendants spread over Bergen and Rockland Counties.

Of the above children, John Ferdon (5), born at Closter, August 5, 1760, died there July 29, 1827, married, December 20, 1784, Marytie (or "Marishy," as she was called) Sickles, born August 31, 1764, died June 11, 1824. John was a farmer and always lived on part of his father's farm. His children were Braekie (married John A. Haring), Nicholas, and Abram (dead).

Nicholas Ferdon (6), born October 18, 1787, died December 22, 1862, married, in 1809, Jemima Westervelt, born October 10, 1791, died February 19, 1870. By the will of his father all the latter's lands, including the old homestead of his father, went to Nicholas.

Abraham N. Ferdon (7), son of Nicholas (6), was born at Closter, October 5, 1810, and died there in 1883. He married (1) Maria Demarest and (2) Leah Ferdon. He was a farmer and resided on the old homestead at Closter.

His children were eight—six by his first wife and two by his second wife: Caroline, John D., Margaret, Abraham, William, Martha, Jesse W., and Samuel.

Jesse W. Ferdon (8), the subject of this sketch, was born at Closter, N. J., October 14, 1848. He has been a life-long resident of Bergen County. He was educated in the public schools at Closter, leaving, however, at the age of fifteen to earn his own livelihood. When eighteen years old he left farm work, at which he had been employed, to learn the carpenter's trade, and by steady application soon mastered every branch of carpentering, joining, and building. But circumstances and inclination finally led him, after some four years, to abandon the trade and return to farming, which he has since followed with success.

As a resident of Bergenfield, Bergen County, Mr. Ferdon has been more or less active in public affairs, but has invariably declined to accept political office, even when urged to do so by hosts of friends. He is deeply interested in every problem or movement affecting the welfare of the community, and in a quiet, unostentatious way contributes liberally for the support of all worthy objects. In religion he is a member of the Dutch Reformed Church, and in all the relations of life has displayed great mental ability, unswerving integrity, sound judgment, and a patriotic spirit.

Mr. Ferdon married Miss Leah Westervelt, a member of one of the old Bergen County families, and by her has had three sons.

EDMUND W. WAKELEE, a prominent lawyer of New York City and Englewood, Bergen County, N. J., was born in Kingston, N. Y., on the 21st of November, 1869. He is the son of Nicholas and Eliza C. (Ingersoll) Wakelee, a grandson of Joseph and Susan (Curtiss) Wakelee and of Justus and Esther (Stow) Ingersoll, and a great-grandson of David and Hannah Ingersoll and David and Anna (Perkins) Stow. His father, Nicholas, was a prominent business man in Kingston.

Mr. Wakelee received his education at Kingston Academy and at the University of the City of New York, and subsequently entered the law office of Bernard & Fiero, then of Kingston, but now of Albany, N. Y. He was admitted to the bar of both New York and New Jersey in 1891, having graduated from the University of the City of New York in that year. Since then he has been actively and successfully engaged in the practice of his profession both in Bergen County, N. J., where he resides, and in New York City.

During the past seven years Mr. Wakelee has been active in politics in Bergen County as a Republican leader, and has been President of the Republican Club of Harrington Township. In November, 1898, he was elected a member of the New Jersey General Assembly, in which he gained distinction as an able debater. He was re-elected to the General Assembly in 1899 and was selected as the leader on the floor of the Republican majority. He has always been a Republican. As a lawyer he has achieved eminent success, and in the many important cases with which he has been connected has displayed marked ability and high legal qualifications. He is a member of the Bergen County Bar Association, of the Englewood Club, of the Tenafly Club, of the Phi Delta Phi and the Delta Upsilon fraternities, of Northern Valley Lodge, Knights of Honor, of Tenafly, and of Alpine Lodge, No. 77, Free and Accepted Masons, of Closter, N. J. He is also President of the Demarest Firemen's Association, and is a life member of the New Jersey State Firemen's Association. He is unmarried.

ERNEST KOESTER, of Hackensack, N. J., Prosecutor of the Pleas for Bergen County, was born at Norristown, Pa., April 28, 1858, the son of G. F. and Mary B. Koester. He attended the excellent schools of that place and afterward the High School in Philadelphia. He then went to Germany and studied three years in Heidelberg University, and on returning to his native State entered Allegheny College at Meadville, from which he was graduated A.B. in 1876, receiving the A.M. degree in course in 1879. He studied law at Meadville, was admitted to the bar of Pennsylvania August 17, 1881, and was elected District Attorney for McKean County, Pa., on the Republican ticket in 1884. After the expiration of his official term (January 1, 1888) he practiced law in McKean and adjacent counties until 1894, when he came to Hackensack, N. J., where he at once entered upon the work of his profession throughout Bergen County and soon secured a lucrative practice. He was admitted to the New Jersey bar at Trenton June 6, 1895.

On coming to Bergen County Mr. Koester immediately took an active in-

MAIN STREET, NORTH OF PASSAIC STREET, HACKENSACK.

terest in Republican politics and soon became one of the most prominent leaders of his party. While his political convictions and partisan action are consistent there is nothing of what is called bitter partisanship in his make-up. He is one of the ablest lawyers and most respected citizens of the community. In February, 1900, Governor Voorhees appointed him Prosecutor of the Pleas for Bergen County for the usual term from March following. Mr. Koester's high standing in his profession and his qualifications for the prosecutorship are unquestioned. He was not inexperienced in the duties of that office, and his effort to make the administration of justice by the courts in Bergen County impartial, efficient, and economical is noteworthy. He is married and has two children.

ALEXANDER CASS, of Englewood, was born at Carlisle, Schoharie County, N. Y., November 20, 1825. His maternal ancestors were Germans and Hollanders, while those on his father's side were English, the ancestral lines going back to 1686. Hon. Lewis Cass, United States Senator from Michigan, was a member of this family.

Mr. Cass's father died when he was about eighteen months old, and some two years later his mother remarried and moved to Carthage, Jefferson County, in that State, where she died in 1852. Alexander was left, after his mother's marriage, with his maternal grandparents at Carlisle, where he spent his early life on a farm, attending the district school. At the age of twelve he was sent to Albany as clerk in a grocery store, but a year later he returned to his grandparents, and for two years attended Schoharie Academy. Afterward he attended the select school of Professor A. Smith Knight, who was also a civil engineer and lawyer, and there he studied surveying and acted as amanuensis. On April 1, 1842, he became the teacher of the Carlisle school (District No. 4, or the Little York district), where he continued for two and a half years, when he went to the adjoining (Rockville) district, remaining there five and one-half years. In the meanwhile, from 1848 to 1850, he spent a part of his time in the law office of John H. Salisbury, of Carlisle.

In November, 1850, Mr. Cass entered the law office of T. & H. Smith, of Cobleskill, N. Y., and there pursued his legal studies until September, 1852. In April, 1853, he was graduated from the Law Department of the University of Albany, and in the same month was admitted before the Supreme Court to the New York bar as attorney and counselor, being at that time associated with his old preceptor, Thomas Smith, who had moved to the capital city.

Mr. Cass moved to Bergen County, N. J., May 22, 1853, and on August 6 assumed charge of the Upper Teaneck public school. He continued as teacher there and at Lower Teaneck in all thirteen years, and was instrumental in building up the schools to the standard of excellence which those districts have long maintained. In 1845 he was elected Town Superintendent of Public Schools at Carlisle, N. Y., but on account of his youth could not qualify. In 1846, however, he was re-elected and served two terms. He moved from Teaneck to Englewood in 1865, and in 1867 was appointed the first School Superintendent for Bergen County, serving two terms, or six years. Since retiring from that position he has acted as civil engineer and in public capacities. He was elected a Justice of the Peace in 1864 and is now serving his fifth term. From 1859 to 1865 he was Town Clerk of Englewood. He was Assessor for Englewood Township in 1876 and 1877, Coroner from 1878 to 1881 and from 1892 to 1895, Commissioner of Appeals for several terms, and one of the two examiners and visitors of the public schools of Bergen County in 1858-60. In all of these positions he displayed sound judgment, marked ability, and great executive energy.

July 4, 1855, Mr. Cass married Maria Louisa Halleck (now deceased), a native of Delaware County, N. Y., and a lineal descendant of Fitz Greene Halleck, the noted author of "Marco Bozzaris." They had two children: Willard Cass, the subject of the following article, and Hattie E., who died at the age of sixteen months.

WILLARD CASS, the well known civil engineer of Englewood, N. J., has been a life-long resident of that town, where he was born January 5, 1861. He received an excellent public school education, and subsequently studied civil engineering, which profession he has followed successfully in Englewood. He has been connected with many important engineering enterprises, and in every instance has displayed eminent qualifications and a thorough mastery of the business. Public spirited, progressive, and enterprising, he is one of the most respected citizens of Englewood, and has always taken a deep interest in the general walfare of his section. Mr. Cass was married in 1895 to Isabella Taylor, of New York City.

ISAAC L. NEWBERY, of Arlington, is the son of Joseph H. Newbery and Emily Ann Rockefellow Sharp, daughter of Matthias and Catherine (Willet) Sharp, and a grandson of William Newbery, all natives of England. His father, Joseph H. Newbery, came from London in early life, settling in New York City, and there successfully carried on business as a hatter until his death in 1865. His wife died in 1866.

Mr. Newbery was born in New York City on the 27th of August, 1854, and there received an excellent public school education, graduating in 1867 from Grammar School No. 32. In the same year he engaged in the custom house brokerage business, in which he has ever since continued, achieving marked success and gaining a wide reputation. He moved to Arlington, Hudson County, in 1881, and in that attractive suburb has erected a beautiful home which he now occupies.

Although Mr. Newbery has devoted himself assiduously to his business interests he has been active in public affairs, and since taking up his residence in Arlington has become prominent in various important capacities. A Republican in politics, he was a member of the Township Committee in 1885, 1886, 1896, and 1897, serving in 1896 as Chairman of that body. He is President of the Kearny Building and Loan Association, having held that position during the last nine years. This is one of the largest and strongest corporations of the kind in Eastern New Jersey, and under Mr. Newbery's able and energetic management has made an excellent

ISAAC L. NEWBERY.

record. Mr. Newbery is an honorary member of Company G, N. G. N. J., a member and Past Master of Triune Lodge, A. F. and A. M., and a member and Past Regent in the Royal Arcanum. In 1882 he organized the Society of Foresters in Arlington, of which he is Past Chief Ranger. He is also Past Grand of Pilgrim Lodge, I. O. O. F., and has long been a member of the Volunteer Fire Department of Kearny, which he first served as Foreman and Assistant Chief for two years each. In these various capacities as well as in all business relations Mr. Newbery has displayed marked ability, sound judgment, and great enterprise. As a citizen he is highly esteemed and respected. He is thoroughly identified with the affairs of his adopted town and county, active and influential in promoting every worthy object, and thoroughly interested in all movements which promote the general welfare.

Mr. Newbery married Jennie Sinclair, and their children are Agnes L. (wife of H. L. Frazee), William A., Arthur N., Jennie S., Isaac L. (deceased), Joseph H. (deceased), and Emily S.

JAMES WRIGHT MERCER, Freeholder of Bergen County and Postmaster of Lodi, N. J., was born in Scotland on the 10th of May, 1866, his parents being James Mercer and Ann Coverun. James and Ann Mercer were born and married in Scotland and came to the United States in 1882, locating in Lodi.

Mr. Mercer was educated in the public schools of his native country, and shortly after the arrival of the family in Lodi entered the employ of the Susquehanna Railroad as agent at that place. Afterward he engaged in the coal business, which he still follows, having built up a large and successful trade.

In public life Mr. Mercer has displayed the same ability, integrity of character, and enterprise which have marked his business life. He was for three years, or one term, Councilman of the Town of Lodi, and for five years was a member of the Republican County Committee. He is now (1900) Freeholder of Bergen County and Postmaster of Lodi, and is discharging the duties of those offices with characteristic energy and satisfaction. Mr. Mercer is a member of Passaic Lodge, No. 387, Benevolent Order of Elks, and of the Crescent Social Club of Lodi. He was married, November 8, 1893, to Jennie Langford, of Lodi, N. J.

JACOB L. VAN BUSKIRK.—The founder of the Van Buskirk family in this country was Lourens Andriessen, who, after his emigration to America, took the surname of Van Buskirk, the *Van* signifying "from," and Bos Kerck meaning "church in the woods." He was a native of the Province of Holstein, in Denmark, a tanner by trade, and came to America in 1655. Although a single man when he arrived, he set to work at his trade, which he soon abandoned for that of a draper. On June 20, 1656, he bought a lot on Broad Street. Soon afterward he went to Bergen and purchased about 170 acres of land in what is now the Greenville district of Jersey City, on which he settled, and there he took the oath of allegiance to King Charles in 1665. He soon became a man of prominence and wielded great influence in the affairs of Bergen. On September 12, 1658, he married Jannetie Jans, widow of Christiaen Barrentsen, who brought him, as is said, besides four sons by a former husband, about 1,400 florins, heavy money, and ten wampum beads for one stiver. Mr. Winfield adds: "When the country was recaptured by the Dutch and the people expected a for-

GENEALOGICAL

feiture of the lands he and John Berry, Samuel Edsall, and William Sandford appeared at Fort William Henry, August 18, 1673, to request that their plantations be confirmed in the privileges which they obtained from their previous patroons." When a contest arose between the Town of Bergen and the inhabitants on the south of them, concerning fences and the support of a schoolmaster, he again appeared before the council to plead the cause of his neighbors.

Under the act of November 7, 1668, for the marking of horses and cattle, he was appointed recorder and marker for Minkakwa, April 6, 1670, and marker-general for the Town of Bergen, October 8, 1676. On that day he was also appointed ranger for Bergen, with power to name deputies to range the woods and bring in all stray horses, mules, and cattle. He was commissioned a member of the Bergen court February 16, 1677, and February 18, 1680, and President of the same August 31, 1681, and President of the

ANDERSON PARK, HACKENSACK.

County Court August 31, 1682. He was a member of the Governor's Council for a number of years, appointed first March 18, 1672, and held the first commission to administer crowner's quest law in the county in 1672. On January 6, 1676, jointly with the Bogerts, Bantas, and others, he bought a large tract of land north and east of Hackensack, known as New Hackensack, upon which he resided as early as 1688. His issue of the second generation were four children: Andries A. (1660), Lawrens A., Peter A., and Thomas. Of these Peter and Thomas remained at Bergen, while Andries (2), who married in 1717 Jacomina Davids Demarest, and Laurens (2), who married in 1716 Hendricke Vandelinda, bought and settled on extensive tracts of land on the east side of the Saddle River.

Andries's grandson John (4) was born at Saddle River in 1741 and died in 1815. He was a farmer, and was known as "Decke Jan" (thick John), because he weighed some 400 pounds. His grave is in the old Blue Mills graveyard at Saddle River. His wife Sarah is buried at the Lutheran

Church. Their issue of the fifth generation were John, 1777 (died), Andrew, 1779, Hannah, Jemima, and John.

John (5), last above named, was born at Saddle River in 1786 and died in 1873. His wife, Elizabeth Ackerman, was born in 1790 and died in 1860. He and his wife are both buried in the Lutheran cemetery at Saddle River. This John was a farmer. His issue of the sixth generation were John, Adelaide, Sarah, David, Eliza, Jasper, Charity, Andrew, and Jemima M.

John (6) was born at Saddle River August 13, 1809, and died at Hackensack October 18, 1866. His wife was Eliza Huyler, of Tenafly. Both are buried at Cherry Hill near Hackensack. This John was a butcher by occupation. His issue of the seventh generation were seven children: Sarah Ann, Euphemia, John H., David, William H., Alvin, and Jacob L., the last named being the subject of this sketch.

Jacob L. Van Buskirk (7) was born at Saddle River, N. J., July 29, 1851, and received his education in the district schools at New Bridge and Hackensack, after which he learned the trade of a blacksmith, which he followed successfully for nine years. He then took up the calling of a butcher in Hackensack, which he still pursues. Some years ago he was elected Freeholder from his township, which office he faithfully filled for six years. For three years he was Director of the board. He was elected Sheriff of Bergen County in 1898 by a majority of 709 votes over his Republican competitor.

He married Miss May E. Naugle, of Arcola, who was born May 11, 1851. The couple have issue of the eighth generation three children: Margaret F., George, and Henry C., the first two of whom are married, and each have one daughter of the ninth generation.

Mr. Van Buskirk is a member of Hope Encampment, I. O. O. F., of the Order of American Foresters, of the Order of Red Men, and of the Order of United Workmen; President of the Exempt Firemen's Association; Treasurer of the Firemen's Insurance Company; and a member of the Liberty Steam Fire Engine Company, the Democratic Club, the Wheelmen's Club, and other organizations.

CHARLES A. SCHINDLER, Sr., son of Christian Henry Schindler and Catherine Keller, was born July 5, 1827, in Hesse-Darmstadt, Germany, where his father, who died in 1839, was a prominent furniture manufacturer and upholsterer. He was educated and learned the trade of upholstering and decorating in the Fatherland. In 1848 he took part in the revolution, and in consequence was obliged to flee to America, in company with many other fellow patriots, and here he was extensively engaged in manufacturing furniture and upholstering in New York City until 1870. In that year he moved his business to West Hoboken, N. J., where he has resided since 1860.

Mr. Schindler is one of the oldest and most esteemed German citizens in North Hudson County, a man of the loftiest integrity, and in every relation of life has gained the confidence as well as the respect of the community. In politics he is a Republican from conviction, especially on National issues, but in local affairs he is independent, casting his influence in favor of matters promising the greatest good. He is a prominent member of the Patriots' Society of 1848 and '49 of New York.

In May, 1852, he married Sophia Ziegeler, daughter of Daniel Ziegeler, of Hamburg, Germany. She died in October, 1898. Of their ten children six are living, viz.: Charles, Jr., Cora, Sophia, Otto, Thekla, and Rose.

CHARLES A. SCHINDLER, JR., eldest son of Charles A. Schindler, Sr., and Sophia Ziegeler, was born January 3, 1857, in West Hoboken, N. J., where he has always resided, and where he received a public school education. After leaving school he learned the cabinetmaker's trade in the establishment of Brunner & Moore, of New York, where he remained five years, or until about 1884. Since then he has been engaged in business for himself, making a specialty of fine cabinet work and of election appliances, such as booths, registry cases, ballot boxes, etc. He is located at 287 Palisade Avenue, West Hoboken, where he resides with his father, being unmarried.

CHARLES A. SCHINDLER, JR.

In the prosecution of his trade Mr. Schindler has achieved marked success and a wide reputation, and by industry, honesty, and enterprise has built up an extensive business. He is a public spirited, patriotic citizen, a Republican in politics, and a man universally esteemed and respected. For two years—1894 and 1895—he served as Recorder of his town. He was one of the principal organizers of the old Hillside Boat Club, of which he was for nine years the Captain, and was one of the founders and organizers of the Lincoln Club of West Hoboken, of which he is President, having held that office during the last ten years. These and other connections attest his popularity as well as the deep interest he takes in the progress and welfare of the community. He has a fondness for horticulture, and all the fine shrubbery around the old homestead was propagated by him.

WILLIAM D. EDWARDS, a leading lawyer of Jersey City, was born in Greenpoint, Long Island, N. Y., December 17, 1855. In 1860 he removed with his parents to Jersey City, the family settling in that part known as Lafayette. Mr. Edwards received his rudimentary education in the Jersey City public schools and in 1867 entered Hasbrouck Institute, where he was prepared for college. In 1871 he entered the University of the City of New York, from which he was graduated with honor in 1875. Immediately afterward he became a student at the Columbia College Law School, New York City, and was graduated from that institution with the degree of LL.B. in 1878. During the three years which he spent at the law school he was also a student in the office of William Brinkerhoff, of Jersey City. He was admitted to the bar of New Jersey as an attorney in June, 1878, and in 1879 formed a partnership with Hamilton Wallis, under the firm name of Wallis & Edwards. William G. Bumsted was admitted to the firm in 1888, and since then it has continued under the style of Wallis, Edwards & Bumsted.

Mr. Edwards has been for twenty years one of the active and influential leaders of the Democratic party of Hudson County, and in various official capacities has displayed great executive ability and political sagacity. He was Secretary of the Hudson County Democratic Committee in 1879, Chairman of that organization in 1880 and 1881, and in the latter year was elected Corporation Attorney of Bayonne, which office he held for five years. In 1886 he was elected State Senator from Hudson County to succeed William Brinkerhoff, and during his senatorial term framed the bill which gave Jersey City its new charter. He was appointed Corporation Counsel of Jersey City in 1889, and filled that responsible position with marked energy and ability until the spring of 1894. In 1889 he was unanimously nominated by the Democratic party for a second term as State Senator, but declined the honor, preferring to devote his attention wholly to professional work. Mr. Edwards is one of the ablest members of the Hudson County bar, and since his admission to practice has maintained a high standing among his associates.

BAKER B. SMITH is a descendant of Michael Smith, an Englishman, who, while quite young, came to America with Captain John Berry, Major William Sandford, and the Kingslands from the Island of Barbadoes, W. I. Michael first settled at English Neighborhood in Bergen County, N. J., where he married Francina (Frances), a daughter of Major John Berry. Michael was a man of intelligence and business capacity. He was the first High Sheriff of Bergen County and also held a commission as Lieutenant in the colonial militia, of which his father-in-law was Major. Michael purchased from Samuel Edsall a large farm at English Neighborhood fronting on the Hudson River. His children of the second generation, by Frances Berry, were at least two: Frances and John, the latter of whom married Debora, daughter of Thomas Laurens, of Newtown, L. I. Frances married Debora's brother, Thomas Laurens. The dates of birth of Frances and John Smith are unknown, but they were both baptized in the Hackensack Dutch Church in July, 1695. Michael Smith's land in Bergen County, at his death, and which he had bought in 1679, jointly with John Berry, passed to his son and heir, John Smith. John's children of the third generation were Francis, born in 1712; Michael, born in 1714; and John, born in 1716.

Michael Smith, third generation, married Maria Smith, but the date of the marriage does not appear. Their children, so far as known, were twins, John and Abel Smith, born at English Neighborhood, N. J., July 19, 1750. Abel and John subsequently became largely interested in Secaucus lands.

Baker B. Smith, the subject of this sketch, is descended from either John or Abel, above named. His father, Baker Smith (whose father's name was Enoch Smith), married Elizabeth Sickles, of Bergen, prior to 1803, and settled at New Durham, Hudson County, N. J., where Baker B. was born November 29, 1817. Baker Smith died in 1857, at the age of sixty-eight, and his wife at the age of eighty-six. Their children were Mary, Enoch, Eliza, Phœbe, Abram, Baker B., Rebecca, and Philip. Baker B. Smith has always lived at New Durham and is one of the most prominent citizens of that village. For many years he was successfully engaged in the business of shad-fishing, at the same time carrying on farming enterprises. He has been for some time retired from active business pursuits. While he has always been a stanch Republican since the organization of that party, he has neither sought nor accepted office of any kind.

Mr. Smith was married to Sarah Ann Haslett, by whom he had three children: Clarinda H., who became Mrs. A. H. Rider, and is now deceased; Philip H. Smith, now deceased; and Anna M. Smith. Mrs. Smith died March 12, 1895, at the age of seventy-seven. She was an earnest Christian, and an active member of the Reformed Church of New Durham.

CORNELIUS W. BERDAN.—During the religious persecution in France, Jan Baerdan (as he wrote his name), one of the persecuted Huguenots, fled to Amsterdam and from thence came to New Amsterdam sometime prior to 1682, with his wife and one son, Jan Baerdan, Jr. The elder Berdan (as his descendants now spell the name) bought land and settled at Flatlands, Brooklyn, L. I. His wife dying soon after, he married again and had issue by his second wife two daughters.

Jan Berdan (2) and his stepmother could not agree, so John left home and went to Hackensack sometime previous to the year 1693, for on May 20, 1693, under the name of Jan Bordet or Boudet, he was married at Flatlands, L. I., to Eva Van Sicklen, of that place. His place of residence at the time of his marriage is given as Hackensack, N. J. The person who wrote the record of his marriage very likely either mispelled or misunderstood the name. The baptism of his eldest child was recorded in the "Church on the Green" in 1695. He bought a large farm at what is now Maywood, extending from the Hackensack River to the Sprout Brook, on which he lived and spent his life in agricultural pursuits. He bought lands west of the Saddle River, and one or more tracts in the Wieremus section of Bergen County of the Romeyns. His issue of the third generation were ten children: John, 1695; Eva, 1697; Ferdinand, 1700; Albert, 1701; Willimina, 1704; Rynier, 1706; Elena, 1708; Dirck, 1712; David, 1714; and Annatie, 1718.

David Berdan (3), who married, May 12, 1738, Christyontjin Daniels Romeyn, resided on the homestead at Maywood, and had issue eleven children: Eva, Mary, Geesie, Annatie, Margaret, John, Daniel, Lena, Daniel, Mary, and Daniel.

John Berdan (4) was born at Maywood, N. J., in 1749, and died there in

1818. His calling was that of a farmer. He married Ursula Van Voorhis, by whom he had eleven children of the fifth generation: Albert, Isaac, Daniel, John, Peter, David, Peggy, Anna, Christian, Hannah, and Maria.

David Berdan (5), born April 3, 1786, married twice. By his first wife he had children Jane and Sally, and by his second wife, Abagail Bean, he had seven children: John, James, Albert, Harriet, Ann, Rachel, and Christina, all of the sixth generation.

James Berdan (6) was born at Maywood, March 10, 1818, and died there September 6, 1862. He was a farmer, and married Mary Wortendyke, by whom he had issue of the seventh generation Abagail L., Mary E., Cornelius W., and Walter, of whom Cornelius W. is the subject of this sketch.

Cornelius W. Berdan was born in New York City, December 24, 1850. While yet a mere lad his parents removed to Maywood in Bergen County, where Cornelius attended the district school. He subsequently finished

COURT HOUSE AND GREEN, HACKENSACK.

his education at Professor Williams's private academy at Hackensack. At seventeen years of age he became a clerk in a New York broker's office, and later entered the employ of the American News Company, where he remained until 1874, when he entered, as a law student, the office of the late Judge Manning M. Knapp, at Hackensack. A year later he entered the office of Garret Ackerson, Jr., then the most prominent lawyer in the county. Mr. Berdan was admitted to the bar in February, 1878, and has been successfully practicing his profession ever since.

He married, October 15, 1879, Mary Pond O'Connor, daughter of John C. and Elizabeth O'Connor, of Milford, Conn., by whom he has issue a daughter, Elizabeth H., born May 20, 1883. He is a member of Pioneer Lodge, No. 70, F. and A. M., of New York Council, No. 348, Royal Arcanum, of the Hackensack Club, of the Hackensack Golf and Wheelman's Clubs, and of Relief Hook and Ladder Company, of Hackensack. He is also counsel for three townships and two boroughs.

ROBERT CHAPMAN, of Arlington, N. J., who has been associated with the Citizens' Insurance Company of New York since 1871, is the eldest son of Captain William Osborn Chapman and Harriet J. Telfer, and a grandson of Darius Chapman and Millicent, his wife. His grandfather, a native of New York City, was for many years a prominent carpenter and builder. Captain William O. Chapman was born in New York in 1826, and for about twenty-four years was actively associated with the Anchor Steamship Line. He enlisted in 1861 in the famous Seventh New York Regiment, and three months later re-enlisted in the Ninety-fifth New York Volunteers and served until the close of the War of the Rebellion, being Captain of his company. In 1866 he took up his residence in Jersey City Heights, N.J., and about 1890 removed from there to Arlington, Hudson County, where he still lives. He is prominent in Grand Army circles, being a member and Past Commander of Zabriskie Post, of Jersey City. He has five children: Robert, Millicent, Fannie, Carrie, and William Osborn, Jr.

ROBERT CHAPMAN.

Robert Chapman was born in New York City November 4, 1852, and received his early education in the New York public schools. When thirteen years of age he entered the employ of the old Indemnity Insurance Company, of which Colonel Emmons Clark, now Secretary of the New York Board of Health, was Secretary. He remained with that corporation until it failed, about two years later, when he associated himself with the Harmony Insurance Company, which he left in 1871 to accept a position with the Citizens' Insurance Company of New York. Since then he has been actively and prominently identified with that company, having charge at the present time of its loss department.

Mr. Chapman's career of nearly thirty-five years in the fire insurance business has given him an unusually broad experience in underwriting, and the various positions which he has held have enabled him to gain a practical knowledge of every branch. An expert mathematician, he is recognized as authority, not only in the lines with which he has been most intimately connected, but in the business generally, and in every capacity he has achieved eminent success. In politics he is an ardent Republican. He is a member of the Insurance Clerks' Association of New York, of Lafayette Camp, Sons of Veterans, of New York City, and of the Seventh Regiment Veterans, having been an active member of the Seventh Regiment, N. G. N. Y., from 1873 to 1878. In 1890 he settled in Arlington, N. J., where he still resides, and where he has wielded no small influence in advancing the best interests of the town.

September 10, 1874, Mr. Chapman married Josephine, daughter of Joseph and Mary Pollock, of Jersey City Heights, N. J., and their children are Walter Robert and Florence.

VEDDER VAN DYCK, a well-known resident of Bayonne, N. J., and a lawyer in New York City, is descended from Hendrick Van Dyck, who came to this country from Holland with the first Dutch settlers before 1630. These Dutchmen first settled at Communipaw, N. J., but soon found their way over to Manhattan Island.

Hendrick Van Dyck was an ensign in command of the Dutch forces in their early wars with the Indians. He was the first Schout Fiscal—a sort of judge and sheriff—in New Amsterdam, and held his office until 1652. He was one of the original grantees, from the West India Company, of plots of land at New Amsterdam, his lot being on the west side of what is now Broadway, below Trinity Church, and running to the North River. His son Cornelius removed to Albany, N. Y., where he practiced his profession as physician. This Cornelius had a son, Jacobus Van Dyck, also a physician, who settled at Schenectady, N. Y., and was the surgeon at the fort there at the time of the burning of the town, by the Indians, in 1690. Jacobus died at Schenectady in 1759. He left several children one of whom was Lieutenant-Colonel Cornelius Van Dyck, of the First New York Regiment, commanded by Colonel Goose Van Schaeck, during the Revolutionary War. From one of the other sons Vedder Van Dyck is descended, his grandfather being Jacob and his father Peter Van Dyck. His mother, Eleanor Vedder, was also a descendant of the earliest Dutch settlers who came to New Amsterdam.

Vedder Van Dyck was born at Schenectady, N. Y., on the 22d day of January, 1842, and there received his early education, first in the public schools and subsequently at Union College, being in the class of 1865, but leaving college in 1862 to join a New York regiment during the Civil War. He continued in the service until the war was over, and then entered Harvard Law School, leaving there in 1867 and being admitted to the bar of his native State. Since 1867 he has been engaged in the practice of his profession in New York City, having an office at No. 15 Wall Street. Since 1885 he has resided in Bayonne, Hudson County, N. J., where he has served a term of three years as School Trustee, and since 1894 has been one of its Health Commissioners. He married Emily Adams in New York City in 1877.

ROBERT OSCAR BABBITT was born in Mendham, Morris County, N. J., November 5, 1848, and is the son of Robert Millen Babbitt and Henrietta Jolley. On his father's side his first American ancestors were from England and on his mother's side from France. He received his early education

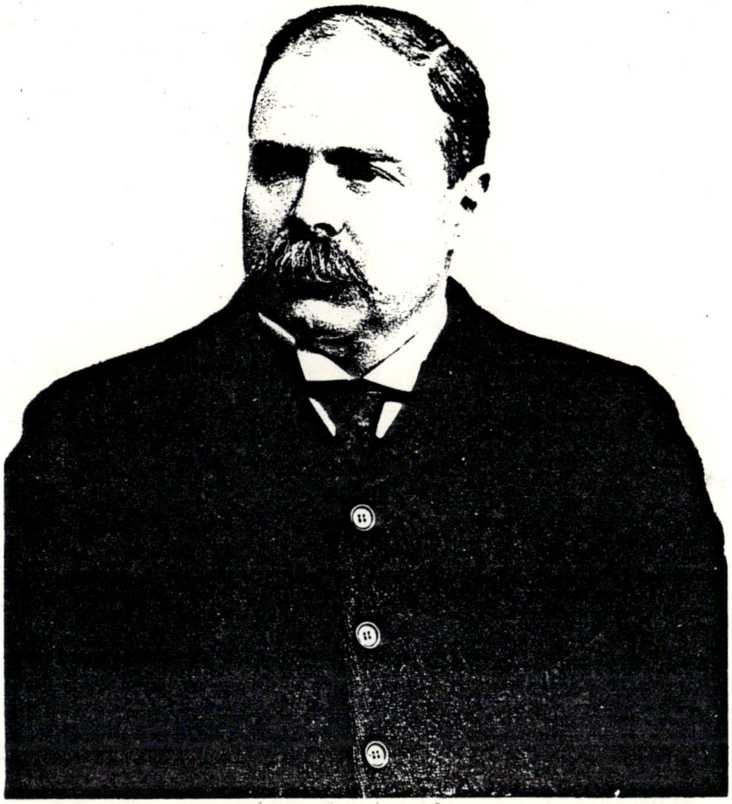

R. O. Babbitt

in the district schools and in the academy of William Rankin, at Mendham, preparing for Princeton College, although he did not enter that university. He studied law for two years with Frederick G. Burnham, of Morristown, N. J., and removing to Jersey City, in 1871, entered the office of Potts & Linn. He was admitted to the New Jersey bar as an attorney in February, 1873, and as a counselor in November, 1878.

After his admission to the bar Mr. Babbitt became a member of the firm of Potts & Linn, with whom he had pursued his studies, and continued his association, under the firm name of Potts, Linn & Babbitt, for one year, after which the firm was re-organized as Linn & Babbitt, and so continued for seven years. However, in 1882, he formed a partnership with Robert Linn Lawrence, which continues to the present time.

Mr. Babbitt has devoted himself exclusively to his profession, applying his leisure to miscellaneous reading, and as a result of his application and legal abilities enjoys a high standing at the bar and commands a large and lucrative practice. He is independent in politics, and has never accepted public office.

Soon after his admission to the bar Mr. Babbitt set himself to the task of mastering the Spanish language, to fit himself for the transaction of the business of certain corporations who had connections in Mexico and other Spanish-speaking countries. His professional duties in this direction, therefore, have afforded him the opportunity for extensive travel in Mexico and other American countries. Mr. Babbitt is a member of the Lawyers' Club, of New York City, and of the Carteret and Union League Clubs, of Jersey City. He was married June 9, 1875, to Mary Elizabeth McCrea, of Middletown, Orange County, N. Y.

REV. JOHN JUSTIN, pastor of the Dutch Reformed Church of the Town of Union, Hudson County, since 1865, was born in Germany in 1842, the son of Peter and Margaret Justin. He spent his early life in hard study. In 1858 he came to this country, crossing the ocean in forty days, and first settled in New Brunswick, N. J. There he entered Rutgers College and afterward the Theological Seminary, from which he was graduated with honors. In the meantime Mr. Justin spent much of his leisure with the renowned musicians Schneeweiss, Fischer, and Mohlenhauer, and later became organist of one of the New Brunswick churches.

In 1864 Mr. Justin moved to Union Hill, and the next year was installed pastor of the Dutch Reformed Church on Columbia Street, which position he continues to hold. The church was then in a very poor condition, but he gave it a new impetus and in 1868 had the satisfaction of rebuilding it. In 1883 the edifice was thoroughly renovated and in 1890 it was enlarged, and at the present time it is one of the most prosperous churches in Hudson County. This is almost entirely due to Mr. Justin's efforts. Bringing to his work great native energy, unusual ability, and unfailing enthusiasm, he has steadily advanced the church and congregation to a point of more than local importance, and has imbued them with his own spirit of courage and usefulness. He has had frequent calls to distant places, but has preferred to give to this society the efforts of his life.

He has traveled extensively, making several trips to the West and two abroad, including one to Asia and Africa, and is an earnest promoter of education. He married Catharine, daughter of Henry and Louise Westerfeld, and has graduated his children from some of the best institutions in the East.

JOHN CLEMENT JUSTIN, M.D., of Guttenberg, N. J., son of Rev. John Justin and Catharine Westerfeld, was born in the Town of Union, Hudson County, September 26, 1868. He began his education in the public schools of his native town, spent a year and a half in the employ of the Equitable Life Assurance Society, and was graduated from Hasbrouck Institute, Jersey City, in 1885, and from New York University in the arts and sciences with the degree of B.A. in 1889. In 1891 he began the study of medicine at the Medical Department of the University of the City of New York, from which he was graduated with the degree of M.D. in 1893. He

JOHN CLEMENT JUSTIN.

immediately entered Heidelberg Hospital in Germany, where he remained one year, and then took special courses in the Würzburg hospitals. Afterward he traveled through the principal cities of Germany, visiting hospitals, and thence went to Switzerland, Italy, France, and England.

Returning to America, Dr. Justin substituted for Dr. Exton, of Arlington, for a period of two months, and in the fall of 1894 began the practice of his profession in Guttenberg, and afterward built his present residence in West New York, Hudson County, where he continues to reside.

Dr. Justin has already achieved success as a physician and surgeon, and throughout the section in which he has acquired an extensive practice is

ERRATA

On page 201, in sketch of Garret T. Haring, change as follows :

In 13th line from top, last word, read Rensie instead of " Reusie " as printed.

The next paragraph should read as follows :

Thomas E. Haring (8), born March 3, 1808, died February 16, 1870, married Rachel Taylor, and had issue two children : Sarah E. and Garret T. Haring, the latter being the subject of this sketch.

In next to last line read Anne G. Hasbrook instead of " Anne A." as printed.

highly esteemed and respected. His ability, integrity, and genial good nature have won for him the confidence of the community. He is a member of the Royal Arcanum, of the Knights of Honor, of the Order of American Mechanics, and of the Foresters of America.

November 26, 1895, Dr. Justin married Ottilie Katherine Kothe, daughter of William and Ottilie Katherine (Fuchs) Kothe, of the Town of Union, N. J. They have one son living, viz.: John Clement Justin, Jr., born October 10, 1897.

GARRET T. HARING is descended in the ninth generation from Jan Pietersen Haring, the emigrant from Hoorn, Holland. The line of descent is the same as that of Garret A. Haring (see page 61) down to the fifth generation.

Garret Johns Haring (5), a son of John Cozine Haring (4) and Aeltie Van Dolsen, born April 28, 1725, married, in 1751, Cornelia Lent, and had issue of the sixth generation eight children: Aeltie, Peter, Frederick, James, Catharine, Elizabeth, John, and Abraham.

John Garrets Haring (6), born at Tappan in 1752, married Rensie (Garrets) Eckerson and had issue of the seventh generation four children: Altie, Garret, Altie, and Margaret.

Garret Johns Haring (7), born January 24, 1779, died May 25, 1849, married Elizabeth Eckerson, and had issue of the eighth generation Rensie and Thomas E.

Thomas E. Haring (8), born March 3, 1808, died July 6, 1870, married Rachel Taylor, and had issue several children, one of whom is Garret T. Haring, the subject of this sketch.

Garret T. Haring (9) was born at River Vale, Bergen County, February 22, 1851, and received a good education in the local schools. Leaving school at the age of nineteen, he began active life on his father's farm, and subsequently engaged in the business of breeding and dealing in horses, in which he has since continued with substantial success.

Mr. Haring is one of the best known men in Bergen County, and for a number of years has been prominent and influential in public affairs. He has served most efficiently as a member of the Board of Chosen Freeholders for nine years, has also officiated as poormaster of the Borough of Old Tappan, and is a member of the Reformed Church. He is an active, progressive, and public spirited citizen, and highly esteemed by all who know him. He married Anne A. Hasbrook and has two children: Sarah C. and Thomas G.

HENRY G. HARING is a descendant in the eighth generation from Pieter Haring, of Hoorn, Holland, for a sketch of whom and of his sons and grandsons see page 61. This branch of the family always resided around Tappan, Hillsdale, Westwood, and Pascack, in Bergen County. Henry G. Haring's line of descent from Pieter, of Holland, is as follows: Pieter Haring (1), of Hoorn, Holland. Jan Petersen Haring (2), of Hoorn, Holland, the first emigrant to America, married Margaretta Cozines (widow), and had issue of the third generation six children, one of whom was Cozine Johns Haring (3). Cozine Jansen Haring (3), born in 1669, married Margaretta Jans Bogert, and had issue of the fourth generation eight children, of whom one was John Cozine Haring (4). John Cozine Haring (4), born in 1696, married Altie Van Dolsen, and had issue eight children of the fifth generation, one of whom was Garret Jansen Haring. Garret Jansen Haring (5), born in April, 1725, married Cornelia Lent, and had issue of the sixth generation eight children, one of whom was Jacobus Garrets Haring (6). Jacobus Garrets Haring (6), born in October, 1764, married, about 1789, Rachel Fredericks Haring, and had issue of the seventh generation John, Rachel, Garret (died), Cornelia, Altie, Ann, Garret J., Maria, Catrina, and Frederick.

Garret Jacobus Haring (7), born near Tappan, November 30, 1801, died November 19, 1869, married Caroline, daughter of Henry P. and Adeline (Smith) Westervelt, and had issue of the eighth generation Adeline, Henry (died), Henry G., and others.

Henry G. Haring (8), the subject of this sketch, was born in Hillsdale, N. J., December 5, 1837, and received his education in the public schools of Bergen County. Leaving school at the age of eighteen, he engaged in teaching and so continued for five years. During that period he gained a broad practical experience and established an excellent reputation. He then worked on his father's farm at Hillsdale for ten years, and since then has been actively and successfully engaged in business for himself as a civil engineer and surveyor. In this profession as in all other connections he has displayed marked ability, sound judgment, and great enterprise, and is widely respected as a public spirited citizen and upright man.

Mr. Haring has also been prominent in the affairs of his town and county. He served at various times as Town Superintendent, Town Clerk, and Assessor, was a member of Assembly in the sessions of 1868 and 1869, and from 1881 to 1886 held the office of Under Sheriff. At the present time he is Overseer of the Poor. He is a Mason, a member of the Improved Order of Foresters, and an attendant of the Reformed Church.

His wife, Christina de Baun, is descended from the French Huguenot family of De Bauns who are noticed elsewhere in this work. They have had three children: Annie, Harry, and Garret (deceased).

ANDREW H. HARING is descended in the ninth generation from Jan Petersen Haring, the emigrant from Hoorn, Holland. The line of his descent is the same as that of his uncle, John T. Haring (see page 154), down to the seventh generation. Tunis J. Haring (7) and his wife, Elizabeth Perry, had issue four children of the eighth generation, one of whom was Abram B. (8).

Abram B. Haring (8) was born May 20, 1811, and married (1), April 18, 1835, Ann Eliza Haring, who died April 9, 1841. He married (2), in 1843, Mary, daughter of Peter Hopper, born September 16, 1819, died May 31, 1853. He married (3), May 3, 1857, Margaret Demarest. The issue of Abram B. Haring of the ninth generation are, by the first wife, Elizabeth, Ann, John A., Teunis A., Martha, and Kate; and, by the second wife, Andrew H. and May.

Andrew H. Haring (9), the subject of this sketch, was born at River Vale, Bergen County, N. J., October 10, 1852, and received his education in the local schools and at Fergusonville, N. Y. At the age of seventeen he started to learn the drug business, and after continuing in that line for two years entered the employ of A. T. Stewart, of New York, with whom he remained three years. He then returned to Bergen County and took charge of the homestead farm, which he conducted for twenty years with marked success. A few years ago he accepted a position with the West

Shore Railroad and still continues in the employ of that line. He has also been engaged in the coal business at Harrington Park and Tappan.

Mr. Haring early took an active interest in public affairs, and during his entire life has wielded a wholesome influence in the community. He served for ten years as Township Collector, and is now Marshal of the Palisade Protective Association. He attends the Dutch Reformed Church at Tappan.

He married Sarah W. Westervelt, also a member of an old New Jersey family, and they have two sons and three daughters.

LUTHER A. CAMPBELL.—William Kempbell (Campbell) was born in Ireland, July 20, 1718, and came to America in the spring of 1735. He settled in the Schraalenburgh section of Bergen County, where, on August 19 of the same year, he married Elizabeth Samuels Demarest. She was born April 3, 1716, and died July 9, 1797. The couple lived at Schraalenburgh, and had issue of the second generation seven children, one of whom was John W.

John W. Campbell (2) was born July 31, 1746, and died at Pascack, N. J., March 15, 1826. He married Letitia Van Valen, of Closter, who was born May 14, 1751, and died June 25, 1841. John W. Campbell (2) early in life located at Pascack, where he established a wampum factory, and for years conducted an extensive business, supplying the United States government Indian agents and traders of the day with Indian money. His descendants, until quite recently, continued the manufacture of wampum. John W. had issue eight children of the fourth generation, of whom one was Abraham J.

Abraham J. Campbell (4) was born at Pascack, October 13, 1782, and died there March 6, 1847. His wife, Margaret Demarest, whom he married May 9, 1807, was born October 16, 1779, and died October 15, 1834. He had issue of the fifth generation John A., Peter A., James A., David A., and Abram A.

David A. Campbell (5), born January 10, 1812, died June 20, 1893, married Sally Haring, of Pascack (born March 6, 1814, died June 12, 1899), and had issue of the sixth generation Ritie, Margaret, Elizabeth, Daniel H., John A., James A., and Abram D.

WAMPUM.

Abram D. Campbell (6) was born at Pascack, October 10, 1842. He was educated in the public schools of his native place and at Hackensack, and after teaching for a short period, during which time he was elected School Superintendent of his township, he resigned and entered the State Normal School at Trenton, from which institution he was graduated in 1863. After leaving school he engaged in teaching until 1865, when he entered the office of Colonel Garret Ackerson, Jr., at Hackensack, as a law student. He was admitted as an attorney at the June term in 1869 and as a counselor in 1875. A few months after his admission as an attorney he opened an office in Hackensack, and on August 7, 1870, was appointed Prosecutor of the Pleas, to fill the vacancy caused by the resignation of Colonel Ackerson, and on September 1, of the same year, he was appointed by Governor Randolph to fill that office until the close of the next session of the Legislature. On April 5, 1871, he was appointed for the full term, and by subsequent appointments held the office for twenty-five years.

Having enlisted in Company C, Second Battalion, N. G. N. J., October 8, 1872, he was commissioned Quartermaster of the battalion with the rank of First Lieutenant January 14, 1873, and on March 15, 1876, received the commission of Captain. He served during the railroad strike of 1877, and retired with the rank of Brevet-Major December 16, 1890.

Mr. Campbell was married, September 22, 1869, to Ann E. Hopper, daughter of Jacob Hopper and Lydia Bogert, of Hackensack, born August 5, 1846. They had five children of the seventh generation: Luther A., Eva, David (deceased), Harry (deceased), and N. Demarest Campbell.

Luther A. Campbell (7), the subject of this sketch, was born at Hackensack, November 28, 1872. He was educated in the public schools, and was graduated with honors from the Union Street High School, of which Dr. Nelson Haas was Principal. Immediately after leaving school he began the study of law in his father's office, and in June, 1894, was admitted to the bar as an attorney; subsequently he became associated with his father under the firm name of A. D. & L. A. Campbell. In 1894, at the organization of the Improvement Commission, Mr. Campbell became counsel and clerk of that board, and was also for several terms clerk to the Grand Jury, by appointment of Judge Dixon, but was forced to give up his position because of growing business in general practice. He has also been chosen counsel in several townships and boroughs in Bergen County. He is a member of Hope Encampment, No. 33, I. O. O. F.

He was married, April 22, 1895, to Mae E., daughter of Richard P. Paulison, of Hackensack. Their children of the eighth generation are Ruth Debaun, born March 5, 1897, and Clarendon, born March 7, 1899.

DAVID W. McCREA has been actively and successfully engaged in the practice of law in Jersey City since 1882, and through his ability and integrity of character has achieved distinction and honor. He is the son of James W. T. McCrea and Harriet E. Schroeder, and was born in New Hampton, N. Y., on the 3d of February, 1861. There he spent his early life, laying the foundation of a sound physique, and gaining in the district schools a rudimentary English education. He also pursued his studies at Middletown (N. Y.) Academy, and later at the private school of Dr. Henry Warren.

From his father's ancestors Mr. McCrea inherits those sturdy Scotch characteristics which distinguish the race, while from his mother, who was of German descent, he likewise inherits high intellectual attainments. Even before completing his studies he had decided upon the law as a profession, and after leaving school began active preparation for admission to the bar. In due time he found himself prepared to enter upon the active practice of the profession, to which he has since devoted his energies with uninterrupted success. Mr. McCrea was admitted to the bar of New Jersey at the February term of the Supreme Court in 1882, and ever since then has been actively and successfully engaged in practice in Jersey City. He is a public spirited, enterprising, and progressive citizen, deeply interested in the affairs of his adopted city and State, and highly esteemed and respected by all who know him.

He was married on the 12th of January, 1899, to Emma Fenner Smith, of Jersey City, N. J.

DAVID W. LAWRENCE, of Jersey City, N. J., was born in the City of New York, November 10, 1850. While a child his parents moved to Pike County, Pa., and continued to reside there and in the contiguous County of Monroe until 1863. That region was then (and is still) a wilderness. While the family lived at Shawnee, Monroe County, the Civil War broke out, and Mr. Lawrence's two older brothers enlisted. In 1863 the family returned to New York, and Mr. Lawrence's father also enlisted. He was wounded in the battle of the Wilderness, taken prisoner, and subsequently died in Andersonville military prison. This left Mr. Lawrence, then a boy of thirteen, as the main support of his widowed mother and two brothers younger than himself. He obtained employment in a retail store, attending school at night.

In 1868 Mr. Lawrence moved to Jersey City and engaged in a mercantile business until 1872, when he accepted an appointment in the New York postoffice, where he remained eight years, discharging his duties with ability and satisfaction, and being promoted to Assistant Chief Clerk of the Registry Department, which position he resigned in 1880. In 1877 he was elected a member of the Board of Aldermen in Jersey City over ex-Mayor John B. Romar, a popular Democrat. He declined a renomination in the spring of 1879, but accepted the nomination for Assembly in the fall and was elected over David J. Post, receiving more majority than his opponent had votes. He was re-elected in 1880 and 1881. At the session of 1881 he was appointed Chairman of the House Committee selected to represent the State of New Jersey at the centennial celebration of the battle of Cowpens at Spartanburg, S. C. At the session of 1882 he was the Republican nominee for Speaker of the House. Prior to the close of the session he was elected in joint session of the Senate and House of

DAVID W. LAWRENCE.

Assembly a Police Justice for Jersey City for the term of three years. At the expiration of his term of Police Justice Mr. Lawrence decided to retire from political life. Two days later, however, he was appointed by the Board of Finance and Taxation, at the request of a Citizens' Committee, Assessor for the Fifth Aldermanic District. This position he filled for three consecutive years, each year being unanimously elected President of the Board of Assessors. In 1888 he was nominated as a Republican and citizens' candidate for Sheriff of Hudson County. Though not elected, he received a very gratifying indorsement. In 1889 he was appointed by Mayor Cleveland, under the new city charter, a member of the Board of Tax Commissioners for the long term of three years, and while he was the minority member his associates unanimously elected him President of the board. Before the expiration of his term he publicly announced that he would not accept any other political office. But on the request of Justice Lippincott he has served on several commissions appointed by the court.

He was formerly a member of Monticello Lodge, No. 140, I. O. of O. F., of the Orion Rowing Association, and of the Palma, Berkeley, and Jersey City Clubs. He is also a member of Bergen Lodge, No. 47, F. and A. M., of Jersey City Consistory, No. 51, of the Hopatcong Club, of the Union League, and of the Lincoln Association, and a life member of the Carteret Club. He is also one of the managers of the Provident Institution for Savings, a Trustee of the New Jersey State Home for Boys at Jamesburg, and is trustee and executor for a number of important estates. He has been faithful and popular in every position he has held, and few business men in Jersey City have been more successful, and none more highly trusted and respected. He is still engaged in the real estate and insurance business, which he established in 1885, and is a large real estate owner in Jersey City.

ABEL I. SMITH, one of the leading lawyers of Hudson County and District Court Judge of Hoboken, is descended from one of the oldest families of East Jersey. In 1732 Abel Smith, his ancestor, settled on a large tract of land in Secaucus, which was then included with Hoboken in old Bergen County. This land was conveyed by deed to Mr. Smith by Israel Horsfield on October 24, 1732, and has ever since been owned and occupied by a member of the Smith family. Daniel Smith, son of Abel, served in the Revolutionary War as a soldier in Colonel Oliver Spencer's cavalry regiment of the Continental Army—a regiment, by the way, noted for its efficiency and bravery. John Smith, son of this patriot Daniel, had a son, Abel I. Smith, Sr., who was the father of the subject of this article, and who served as a private in the War of 1812, afterward holding many positions of trust and honor in Hudson and Bergen Counties, and being one of the most prominent and best known men in that section until his death in 1865. He was one of the few persons honored by Robert Stevens with a pass for life over the Hoboken ferries. The original pass, in the handwriting of Mr. Stevens, is still in the family, and reads: " Abel I. Smith and his wife, if he gets one."

Judge Smith represents the fourth generation of his family after they settled in Hudson (then Bergen) County. He is the son of Abel I. Smith, Sr., and Prudence Cary, his wife, and was born in North Bergen, N. J., June 12, 1843, on the land conveyed to the original Abel Smith in 1732 by a deed describing him as " a gentleman." There he received his preliminary education in the public schools. He was for eight years under the able tutorship of the Rev. William V. V. Mabon, D.D., later a professor in the New Brunswick Theological Seminary. In 1862 he was graduated with honor from Rutgers College, and the same year began his legal studies in the office of J. Dickerson Miller, of Jersey City, being admitted to the New Jersey bar as an attorney in June, 1866, and as a counselor in June, 1873. He has practiced his profession in Hoboken since 1868, coming there from the Town of Union, Hudson County, and by the exercise of great natural ability has achieved eminent success and a high reputation.

He has also filled several important positions. In 1869 he was elected as a Republican to the Legislature from the old Eighth Assembly District, comprising Bergen, West Hoboken, Weehawken, and the Township of Union, and served in the session of 1870. He was the first Republican elected from that district and the only Republican from Hudson County in the session of that year. He declined a renomination. In 1888 he was appointed Judge of the District Court of the City of Hoboken by Governor Green and served until April 1, 1891, and in 1898 he was again appointed to the same position by Governor Griggs. A fact of special interest in connection with his first term on the bench is that, of the many cases which he decided, few were taken to higher courts for review, and all but two so taken were affirmed. His present term expires in 1903.

Judge Smith has been a life-long resident of Hudson County, and for more than thirty years has been actively identified with the growth of the City of Hoboken. He is an able and talented lawyer, one of the acknowledged leaders of the Hudson County bar, a learned, fair-minded, and conscientious jurist, and a public spirited, progressive citizen. His practice has been largely confined from the first to civil suits in the Court of Chancery, in the Circuit, Supreme, and Orphans' Courts, and in the Court of Errors and Appeals, and also in the United States Circuit and District Courts of New Jersey, to the bar of which he was admitted in 1894. He was counsel in the matter of the crossing of the new county road by the Lehigh Valley Railroad Company, and also for three of the most important and noteworthy improvements in Hudson County, namely: the "Bull's Ferry Road," the "Bergen Line Road," and the "Bergen Wood Road." For ten years he was counsel for the Township of North Bergen; for three years he was counsel for the Jersey City, Hoboken, and Rutherford Electric Railway Company; and in a legal capacity has also been connected with many large estates and interests in the County of Hudson. For four years he served as President of the Hudson County branch of the State Charities Aid Association of New Jersey, being also a member of the Committee on Laws of the State Association.

Few men have achieved the distinction in both professional and public life which Judge Smith enjoys. He has long been an active and influential Republican and a recognized leader of the party, and in the various positions which he has filled he has displayed great executive ability, sound judgment, and commendable foresight. At the bar and on the bench he has gained a merited eminence. Well versed in the science of the law, and firmly grounded in the loftiest principles of practice, his untiring efforts and legal attainments have placed him among the foremost lawyers of East Jersey, and in the possession of an extensive and successful practice. Since 1885 John S. Mabon, a son of his early tutor, has been his law partner, the firm name being Smith & Mabon. Judge Smith is also an antiquarian of no little reputation, and at his home has a large and valuable collection of continental money, rare old coins, etc., several of which have been in the family since their settlement in America. His collection includes gold pieces of various countries from 1632 to 1800 and a number of continental coins which were exhumed a few years ago at or near the site of the Smith homestead in Secaucus. He also has a large library, which includes the old family Bible containing the date of the birth of Mary Bailey, one of his ancestors, in St. Philip's Parish, Bristol, England, in 1653. He is a member of the Palma and Union League Clubs of Jersey City, and for years has been identified with many of the leading institutions of his county.

Judge Smith was married December 7, 1870, to Laura Howell, daughter of Martin A. Howell, a prominent resident of New Brunswick and popularly known throughout New Jersey, being a Director of the New Jersey Railroad and Transportation Company, the Camden and Amboy Railroad Company, and other important corporations. They have three children: Abel I. Smith, Jr.; Eliza Howell, wife of James Brown Mabon, of the firm of Kingsley, Mabon & Co., brokers, Wall Street, New York; and Dorothy Gailbraith Smith.

THE VAN BUSSUM FAMILY.—Egbert Van Borsum was a native and resident of Emden, a little town between Groningen and Delfsyle, Holland. There was born, about 1605, his son, Egbert Van Borsum, Jr., who emigrated to America in 1639 and settled at New Amsterdam, where, on December 11 of the same year, he married Antie Hendricks, a native of Sweden. Van Borsum was a sailor and captain, or skipper, of the ship "Prince William" in 1664. On July 15, 1654, he obtained a patent for two lots at the ferry in Brooklyn, and on March 12, 1666, he bought another lot adjoining his first purchase. On these lots he resided. He leased and operated the ferry between New York and Brooklyn, June 1, 1654, and in 1657 was assessed ten gelders toward supporting the salary of Dominie Polhemus. Prior to 1660 he belonged to the New Amsterdam Dutch Church, and took the oath of allegiance to the English King. In 1670 he appears to have resided at Flatbush. He is said to have died on Long Island. His issue were Herman, 1640; Cornelius, 1642; Henry, 1648; Tyman, 1651; Janneken, 1653; and Ann, 1656.

Cornelius married, September 1, 1669, Sarah Roelofse, widow of Hans Kierstead. He was then residing at the ferry at Brooklyn, where he had previously married Grietie Gysberts. August 6, 1668, he was allotted lands at Canarsie, but he probably resided on a farm at Flatbush, which he and Paulus Richards had bought in 1654. On June 28, 1678, he was at Bergen, N. J., and purchased from Anthony Verbruggen a lot of meadow land on the Hudson River at Weehawken, since known as Slaugh's meadow. He afterward became interested in the Saddle River patent in Bergen County. Herman Van Borsum, a descendant of Egbert, Jr., settled at Hackensack in 1748 with his wife, Abagail Furbis. Others of Egbert's descendants settled at Aquackanonck and south of Hackensack, and their descendants have become widely scattered over Bergen County.

GEORGE WAKEMAN WHEELER, of Hackensack, N. J., was born in Easton, Conn., on the 15th of October, 1831. He is the son of Hon. Charles Wheeler and Jerusha Bradley. His father was a Judge of Probate in Connecticut and a member of the Legislature in that State.

Mr. Wheeler received his preparatory education at the old Easton (Conn.) Academy and at Dudley School at Northampton, Mass. Afterward he entered Amherst College, from which he was graduated in the class of

1856. He spent much of his early life teaching school, and in Mississippi, where he resided for a time, filled the position of Superintendent of Schools with acknowledged ability and satisfaction.

Settling finally in Hackensack, N. J., Mr. Wheeler soon came into prominence as a man of energy and public spirit, and as Chairman of the Hackensack Board of Education rendered important service to the community. He also served for some time as Judge of the Court of Common Pleas. His business has been mainly that of an insurance broker, although he has been interested in various financial enterprises. He is Treasurer of the Hackensack Cemetery Company and Vice-President of the Bergen Turnpike Company. In politics he is a Democrat. He is a member of the Episcopal Church, a Royal Arch Mason, and a Past High Priest in the Masonic order. He has traveled extensively in this country as well as abroad.

In 1859 he was married to Lucy Dowie. They have two sons: Hon. George W. Wheeler, Jr., a Justice of the Superior Court of Connecticut,

ANDERSON STREET, LOOKING EAST HACKENSACK.

and Henry D. Wheeler, a commission merchant of New York City.

Mr. Wheeler is a member of the State Geological Board of New Jersey, of the Geological Survey, and of the Forestry Committee, and a life member of the New Jersey State Forestry Association. He was President of the Hackensack Hall and Armory Association for ten years, and has been actively associated with every movement and project which had for its object the welfare and advancement of the community.

THE SPEER FAMILY.—Hendrick Jansen Spiers, the common ancestor of the Speers of Bergen and Hudson Counties, emigrated from Amsterdam to America with his wife, Madeline Hanse, and two children, on the Dutch West India ship "Faith," in December, 1659. It is not doubted that he was a native of Holland. He located at New Amsterdam, where he was known as Hendrick Jansen Spiering, and where three of his children were baptized. In the spring of 1668 he removed to Bergen, N. J., where, on the 12th of May of that year, he obtained from Governor Philip Carteret a patent for about fifty acres of land (extending across the neck from Newark Bay to New York Bay), to which he added by subsequent purchases. He died prior to 1680, and his widow married, in 1681, Aertsen Van der Bilt. His issue were five children, only three of whom survived him. These were John (married Maritie Franse), Hans (married Tryntie Pieterse), and Barent (married Cathelyntie Jacobs).

John Hendricks Spier became largely interested in the Aquackanonck (Passaic) patent, on which he located about 1692. His children were Henry, Franz, Gertrude, Maddeline, Jannetie, Rachel, and Maritie, of whom the following were married in the Hackensack Dutch Church: Henry to Rachael Teunis Pier, 1708; Franz to Dircke Cornelis, 1705; Gertrude to Arent Laurense Toers, 1704; Jannetie to Roelof Cornelis Van Houten, 1715; and Maritie to John Reyerson in 1716. The numerous descendants of these are now spread over Bergen and Passaic Counties, while the descendants of the family who remained at Bergen are numerous in Hudson County.

THE TERHUNE FAMILY is another whose members are widely scattered over Bergen and Hudson Counties. They are descended from Alberts Albertse, Sr., a ribbon weaver by trade, who is said to have been a native of Hunen or Huynen, in Holland. The date of his emigration does not appear, but he was residing at New Amsterdam for some time prior to 1657. In that year he removed to the Nyack patent in New Utrecht, L. I., where in January, 1662, he obtained a patent for a farm which he sold, April 3, 1664, to Nathaniel Britton, of Staten Island. In 1660 and 1665 he bought lands at Flatlands, L. I. Subsequently he, with Jaques Cortelyou and others, obtained the Aquackanonck (Passaic) patent of about 5,000 acres on the Passaic River, in New Jersey, in which the Van Winkles, Gerretsons, Spiers, and many other families became interested. His children were John, Albert, Heyltie, Ann, Styntie, and Sarah. All of these settled near Hackensack in Bergen County. Albert, the second, born in 1651, married (1) Hendricke Stevens Voorhis, and (2) Levina Brickers. He resided at Flatlands, L. I., until 1676, when he removed to Hackensack, where he was one of the leading spirits in the Dutch Church, and was sent to the Colonial Legislature in 1696. He bought a large farm of Captain John Berry, extending from the Hackensack to the Saddle River. His issue were Willempie, Albert, John, Antie, Gerrebrecht, Willempie, Stephen, Maritie, Gertrude, and Rachel. Except the Demarests and Harings probably not one of the early emigrants has as many descendants in Bergen County as Albert Alberts Terhune. The name Terhune was adopted after the removal to Bergen County. In New Amsterdam and Long Island it was Albertsen.

THE CHURCH AT FLATLANDS.

GEORGE STEVENS, of Jersey City, was born in Paterson, N. J., April 15, 1854. He is the son of George T. Stevens and Caroline, daughter of Abram and Cynthia Stager, and a grandson of Ephraim Stevens and Ruth Doughty. His ancestors were early Massachusetts people.

Mr. Stevens's entrance into Jersey City was marked by his entrance into Public School No. 2, under the celebrated Yerrington. He was an apt scholar, his keen, quick perception proving his ability to comprehend any task set before him. Leaving school, he became a messenger boy for the Western Union Telegraph Company, under the supervision of Charles Cary, and afterward accepted a similar position for the Erie Railroad Company. After serving for thirteen years in the capacity of clerk and bookkeeper in Wall Street, New York, he cast about for something else. His father having died when he was about eighteen, he was obliged to assist the rest of the family, and from that time manifested a tendency for entrance into business for himself.

The opportunity came. During his employment in Wall Street he often visited a friend in an undertaking establishment, and carefully noting all the preparations required in the work of trimming caskets and other details soon found that he possessed sufficient insight into the business to make it his life work. And for five years he devoted himself to studying the business in all its branches.

GEORGE STEVENS.

On June 1, 1880, Mr. Stevens engaged in the undertaking business for himself, at 617 Jersey Avenue, Jersey City, and in 1890 moved to No. 605 Jersey Avenue, where he still continues, having built what is without exception one of the most complete and commodious establishments in the State of its kind.

He owes his success to his own personal characteristics, as he possesses all the qualifications that go to make up honesty and fixed purpose. No detail in the requirements of his business are unknown to him. The appointments of his establishment are modern in every respect, beautiful in appearance, and wholly devoid of that grewsome air which often characterizes such places. In brief, they are particularly arranged so as not to present any unpleasant feature to the most delicate-minded observer. His business is large and lucrative, and exclusively among the better class of people, as those with whom he is closely associated attest. His entire establishment is the consummation of his own ideas and designs.

As a citizen Mr. Stevens is known to foster a just pride in his surroundings, and is an active participant in any movement that will advance local improvement. He is a member of St. Paul's Methodist Episcopal Church, of Jersey City, of Rising Star Lodge, No. 107 F. and A. M., of Rising Star Lodge, No. 210, I. O. O. F. (which was named upon his suggestion), of Harmony Encampment, 47, I. O. O. F., and of the Union League Club.

Mr. Stevens married Melvina Wayne, daughter of George Wayne, and a native of New York City. They have no children.

THE TOERS FAMILY.—The first of this family in New Jersey were Laurence Arents Toers and Claes Arents Toers, and, no doubt, they were Hollanders. They were at Bergen as early as 1672, where, on August 15th of that year, Laurence married Francyntie Thomas. Claes married, July 8, 1684, Jacomina Van Neste. Both bought land at Bergen in 1677 on which they permanently located. Laurence's issue were twelve children, among whom were John, Thomas, Mary, and Aaron. Claes, who died in 1730, had eight children, among whom were Judith, Pietertie, Arent, Nicholas, and George. Of Claes's children only three survived, among them being Arent, who received his father's property. Arent married, in 1699, Ann Spier, and reared a large family. The descendants of Laurence and Claes are still quite numerous in Hudson County.

THE VANDERHOFF FAMILY.—In 1711 Cornelius Vanderhoff, John Vanderhoff, and Gertrude Vanderhoff came from Albany, N. Y., to Hackensack. They are said to have been the children of Cornelius Vanderhoff (or Vander Horen, who came to America from Horen, a village in Gelderland, Holland, and first settled at Bedford, L. I., from whence he removed to Albany). Cornelius, John, and Gertrude Vanderhoff settled in the Saddle River district of Bergen County. Cornelius married (1712) Elizabeth Laurence Ackerman. John married (1714) Lea Mathews Hopper. Gertrude married, a little later, Peter Rutan, of Esopus, to which place she probably removed. Cornelius had issue Geertie, Catharine, Jacob, Cornelius, Egbert, and Jannetie.

John Vanderhoff had issue John, Geertie, and probably Catharine, Dorothy, Jacob, and Jacobus, but this is uncertain. The descendants of Cornelius and John are still quite numerous in Bergen County.

GEORGE WILKINSON STORM was for many years, and until recently, one of the most prominent and public spirited citizens of Hackensack, Bergen County. His successful career is the product of energy, enterprise, and integrity in business and private life, on the part of one determined to make his own way in the world, with the capabilities resident in himself as the resources to be depended upon. His success is an encouragement to others, and a brief outline of the facts is here given with that end in view.

Mr. Storm enjoyed the advantage of excellent ancestral antecedents—an advantage which no doubt it is often difficult exactly to estimate. Certainly the inheritance of a disposition of mind and heart, which provide a solid foundation for the development of capacity and character, is beyond price: the richest legacy from parent to child. The son of Edward Storm and Helen, daughter of George and Sophia Wilkinson, and the grandson of John A. and Catherine Storm, the subject of this sketch descended from strong American strains on both the paternal and maternal sides. His first American ancestor was Dirck Storm, a native of Utrecht, Holland, who emigrated from Holland to the New Netherlands during the early Dutch period. Mr. Storm's father was a member of the Holland Society of the City of New York. On the maternal side his ancestors were long seated in New England, and came originally from England.

George Wilkinson Storm was born in Poughkeepsie, Dutchess County, N. Y., in July, 1856. He attended St. Mark's School at Southboro, Mass., and completed his education at Harvard College. Having determined upon a business career, he engaged in the manufacture of elevators and thoroughly learned the business. Having original ideas of his own, and having acquired patent rights, he engaged in manufacture on his own account in

ANDERSON STREET, LOOKING EAST, HACKENSACK.

1889. His business has continually developed and extended to the present time. The Storm elevator has become a well known standard make. Since 1889 the factory has been in Newark, N. J., while for nine years from that date Mr. Storm resided at Hackensack. He now resides in Orange.

Mr. Storm has been active in a social way, and in connection with church work and general philanthropy. He is a member of various social clubs and of the Episcopal Church. He interested himself in the cause of education in Hackensack, and in various interests in the community. He married, in New York, in October, 1879, Isabel T. Abeel, and has two children.

THE VAN DUSEN FAMILY.—The Van Dusens and Van Dusers are descended from Abraham Pietersen Van Deusen, a miller by trade and a native of Deusen in Holland, where he was born about 1602. He came to New Amsterdam prior to 1641 with his wife, Tryntie Melchiors, and several children. In that year he was appointed one of the "twelve men" of the city, and in 1643 one of the "eight men." In 1657 he was admitted to the rights of a burgher. His children were Levina, Peter, Abraham, Isaac, Catharine, and Henry. Of these Isaac Abraham, Sr., was born in Holland in 1634. He came over with his father and settled in New Amsterdam, where he married in 1659 Jannetie Jans, widow of Adam Van Sandt, from Arnheim in Gelderland. He eventually removed to Albany, N. Y., where his son, Abram Isaacsen Van Deusen, married, in 1682, Ann, daughter of Zacharias Sickels. His son, Isaac Abrahamsen Van Deusen, born at Albany in 1688, married, April 5, 1713, Ann Waldron, and had issue, among other children, Daniel, who married Lea Hertie and settled at Tappan in 1735. John Bernard Van Dusen, probably a brother of Isaac's, married a La Roe, and settled in Washington Township, Bergen County, N. J. From these two brothers are descended the Van Dusens of Bergen County.

AUGUSTUS A. RICH, who has successfully practiced law in Hudson County since 1876, is the son of Samuel A. Rich, a native of Genoa, Italy, who followed the sea all his life, leaving home at the age of thirteen. His mother was Ellen E. Stephens. Mr. Rich was born in Brooklyn, N. Y., December 28, 1851, and in 1854 moved with his parents to Hoboken, N. J. In 1860 the family settled in West Hoboken, Hudson County, where the subject of this article has since resided, and where he received a good public school education.

Mr. Rich studied law in New York City with the well known firm of Van Schaick, Gillender & Thompson, and was admitted to practice in that State in 1873. He was admitted to the bar of New Jersey as an attorney in November, 1874, and as a counselor in February, 1878. He began the active work of his profession in Hudson County in 1876, and for many years has been the leading lawyer in West Hoboken. Following without interruption a general law practice, Mr. Rich has achieved eminent success as well as a high reputation, which is by no means confined to his immediate locality.

He has also held several positions of trust and honor. In 1882 and again in 1883 he represented West Hoboken in the New Jersey Assembly, and served both years as Chairman of the Committee on Revision of Laws and as a member of the Judiciary Committee. During these two terms he introduced a number of bills of local importance and was active and influential in all legislative matters. Since then he has drafted several important measures, including the general act for the government of towns, under which Kearny, West Hoboken, West New York, and other boroughs were incorporated and organized, and which served as the model upon which the general act for cities in New Jersey was drawn. In this respect Mr. Rich has gained wide distinction. Having made a special study of town and municipal governments, and endowed with rare good judgment and great legal ability, he is regarded as an authority on these matters, and his prominence in connection with them attests his standing and usefulness. During the past eighteen years he has served as corporation attorney for West Hoboken, and at present he is also attorney for the Townships of West New York and Weehawken. Since 1895 he has been Chairman of the Hudson County Board of Elections, and in May, 1899, he was appointed a member of the committee whose object is the promotion and ultimate incorporation of Greater Jersey City, to include all or nearly all the cities, boroughs, and townships in the County of Hudson. He is a Democrat in politics, and has distinguished himself as a public spirited, progressive, and patriotic citizen. He is unmarried.

ROBERT F. LORD, of Kearny, Hudson County, is the son of John and Jane Lord, and a grandson of Robert Lord and James and Sarah Lang. His ancestors on both sides came to this country from the North of Ireland. Mr. Lord was born in Newark, N. J., on the 22d of January, 1853, but was taken by his parents when young to Kearny, Hudson County, where he received his education. For twenty-five years he has been actively

ROBERT F. LORD.

associated with the Stewart Hartshorn Company, the well known manufacturers of shade rollers, of Harrison. During that period he has filled nearly every position in the establishment, being at the present time the efficient and successful manager of the company's New York office at 486 Broadway.

Mr. Lord has displayed marked executive ability and business capacity, and during his long connection with the great Hartshorn Company he has discharged his duties with credit, honor, and satisfaction. In politics he is an ardent Republican. He has been for many years one of the most active men in the affairs of his municipality, which he served for a term of two years as a member of the Board of Aldermen, and upon the incorporation of Kearny as a town he was elected a member of the first Common Council, a position he now holds. He has also been active in the Kearny Volunteer Fire Department and is a member of the Masons and the Heptasophs.

Mr. Lord married Miss Martha Coulson, of Jersey City, N. J., by whom he has had four children: Bella, John, Robert J., and William J.

THOMAS H. CUMMING, a prominent business man and Justice of the Peace, of Hackensack, was born in New York City on the 6th of November, 1839. He received his education in his native city, and after completing his studies entered a large dry goods store, where he remained three years, laying the foundations of a successful career. On severing his connection with that house he formed a copartnership with his father, and actively engaged in the business of contracting, chiefly in New York and New Jersey, the former being mainly in the line of building sewers. Among other important contracts which they secured and executed was that for the construction of the Lodi branch of the New Jersey and New York Railroad, and another for the line running from Essex Street to Woodbridge.

In 1861 Mr. Cumming engaged in the oil trade in Greenwich Street, New York, and so continued for two years. Following this he was for six years engaged in the leather business. At the end of that period he removed to Hackensack, N. J., where he still resides, and engaged in contracting. In each of these lines of industry he has achieved marked success and a wide reputation for honesty and uprightness.

THOMAS H. CUMMING.

Mr. Cumming is also a Commissioner of Deeds and a Notary Public, and since 1885 has held the office of Justice of the Peace. He has always taken an active interest in the Hackensack Fire Department, serving faithfully and efficiently as a member of Hook and Ladder Company, No. 2, for twenty-six years, a part of the time as its Foreman. He is now an honorary member of that organization. For a number of years he has been President of the Hackensack Relief Association, and during the last thirteen years has served as Collector of License for the Hackensack Commission. He is an active and influential Republican, being Vice-Chairman of the County Executive Committee. He is also a member of the Royal Arcanum and a charter member of the National Union. His father, Thomas Cumming, Sr., was for many years a Lay Judge of Bergen County.

Mr. Cumming married a daughter of the late John H. Banta, of Hackensack, and has three sons.

FRANK B. POOR, President of the Hackensack Board of Trade and one of the most enterprising citizens of Bergen County, was born in Hackensack, N. J., about thirty years ago, and is the son of E. E. Poor, formerly President of the Park National Bank of New York City. He has spent nearly $250,000 in beautifying Hackensack and advancing its interests. He erected the Hamilton Building in 1899-1900 at a cost of $50,000. He formed the Bergen County Ice Company, which recently erected a $50,000 plant. He organized the Golf Club, which is erecting a $12,000 club-house, and he was instrumental in organizing the Hackensack Trust Company, which built in 1900 a $75,000 structure. His aim is to see Hackensack advance.

As was recently said of him: "Mr. Poor has done more for our town in one year than has been done by many men during a generation. One evidence of his ability was the consolidation of the gas and electric light companies in Bergen County, which corporation now supplies thirty-three towns. Their product will be cheapened, and not a single stockholder in the old companies has lost a cent by the change. Mr. Poor is spending money lavishly and intends to turn over to the town many miles of macadamized streets, with sewers, etc., without a cent of expense to the town. Such enterprise is unprecedented, and it is done for the best interests of his birthplace."

JAMES H. BLACK, who has been successfully engaged in business as a blacksmith and carriage-maker in Harrison, Hudson County, since 1888, was born in Belleville, Essex County, N. J., January 15, 1863. He is the son of James V. Black and Elizabeth Vreeland, and a great-grandson of Benjamin Vreeland, a member of one of the oldest families of this State. His first maternal ancestor in this country was Michiel Jensen, who left Holland, October 1, 1636, in the ship "Rensselaerwyck," with his wife and two children, and originally settled opposite Albany, N. Y., but a few years later removed to New Jersey. He was one of the first magistrates of the new court at Bergen, and, although he bore the surname of Jensen, was the founder of the Vreeland family in Eastern New Jersey. Mr. Black's father, James V., was a native of Arlington, N. J., while his mother was born in Moonachie in this State. They were married in New Durham, Hudson County, and in 1857 removed to Belleville, where the subject of this article was born and educated.

James H. Black received the educational advantages which the excellent public schools of Belleville afforded, and after completing his studies became a bookkeeper in a large grocery house. Subsequently he interested himself in the manufacture of iron chains and later engaged in business for himself as a blacksmith and carriage-maker at Woodside, N. J. In 1888 he removed to Harrison, Hudson County, and has since followed that business with constantly increasing success. He is widely known, not only for his mechanical skill and ability, but also for his public spirit, enterprise, and great force of character.

Mr. Black is an independent Republican in politics, and takes a deep interest in every movement that affects the welfare of the community. He is thoroughly identified with the best interests of Harrison, has contributed materially to the success of many worthy objects, and is highly esteemed and respected. He is a member of Harrison Camp, No. 66, Fraternal Legion, of Sylvania Council, No. 5, Golden Star Fraternity, of Newark, and of the Master Horseshoers' Association, No. 67.

On Christmas Day, December 25, 1887, Mr. Black married Lillian Seaver, daughter of Joseph B. and Annette (Sexton) Seaver, of Newark, N. J. They have two children: Ruth Black and Annette Black.

LOUIS FORMON, manager of the People's Safe Deposit and Trust Company of the Town of Union and Treasurer of the Town of Union, is the eldest of five children of William and Louisa (Siedentopf) Formon, natives of Germany, who came to America about 1850 and first settled in New York. There William Formon engaged in ship blacksmithing until just before the outbreak of the Rebellion, when he moved with his family to Secaucus, N. J., and devoted himself to farming. He soon returned to his trade, however, in which he achieved marked success, and died in Union Hill in 1872, widely respected and esteemed. He was a man of great strength of character, of unquestioned integrity and enterprise, and gave to his children the rich inheritance of a good name. His wife died January 7, 1898.

Louis Formon was born in Brooklyn, N. Y., July 24, 1854, and received his education in the public and German schools of New York City. Being the eldest child, and at the time of his father's death the only one of the family old enough to work, the support of his widowed mother and her children devolved almost entirely upon his energies, and though but eighteen years of age he took up his new responsibilities with commendable courage and marked success. Leaving school, fairly well equipped with a literary training, he engaged in the trade of piano making, which he followed successfully for eighteen years, supporting his mother and educating the younger children. He mastered every detail of piano construction; his skill and mechanical ability won for him a high rank among his associates, while his untiring attention to duty, his constant application, and his great care and practical devotion to the interests of his employers gained their appreciation and confidence.

As a resident of the Town of Union, N. J., he early came into prominence, displaying a broad public spirit and winning a deserved popularity. He has taken from the first an active interest in the welfare of the community, and has filled several offices of trust and honor. In the spring of 1890 he was elected Town Clerk of the Town of Union, and served six years, being twice re-elected without opposition; and so faithfully and satisfactorily did he discharge the duties of that position that when he resigned in 1896, to accept the post of manager of the People's Safe Deposit and Trust Company of the Town of Union, he was given a handsomely engraved gold watch, bearing the following inscription: "Presented to Louis Formon by the Officials and ex-Officials of the Town of Union, N. J., for efficiency and faithful service as Town Clerk from April, 1890, to May, 1896." This is a silent but potent evidence of the esteem in which he is held by his fellow-citizens, and especially by those who represent the leading interests of the town. Mr. Formon is still manager of the People's Safe Deposit and Trust

Company of the Town of Union, whose main office is in Jersey City, and which has a capital of $100,000. It is one of the leading fiduciary institutions in Eastern New Jersey, and under Mr. Formon's able and energetic management the branch in the Town of Union has developed to a point of wide usefulness and efficiency. He has distinguished himself as a safe financier of marked ability and sagacity. In 1897 he was nominated and elected Treasurer of the Town of Union for a period of three years. For fourteen years Mr. Formon has been actively identified with the Fire Department of the Town of Union, holding every office within the gift of his company, such as secretary, assistant foreman, and foreman. During the last eight years he has been a member of the department's Board of Representatives and a Vice-President of the State Firemen's Association. He has rendered valuable and appreciative service in developing the Fire Department of the town, and has been instrumental in placing it upon its present efficient basis. He is a member of the Royal Arcanum, and a public spirited, progressive, and highly respected citizen.

Mr. Formon was married on the 25th of February, 1879, to Miss Elizabeth A. O'Brien, daughter of Michael and Mary (Foley) O'Brien, of the Town of Union, N. J. They have eight children: Louisa, Martha, Mary, Louis, Jr., Elizabeth, Henry, Frederick, and August.

MAX HECHT, M.D., Ph.G., of West Hoboken, is the son of Ansel Hecht and Rachel Jacobs, both natives of Hanover, Germany. Ansel Hecht came to this country when a young man and first settled in Baltimore, Md., whence he soon removed to New York City, where he was for many years a large manufacturer and importer of lace goods, collars, and cuffs. He resided in the meantime in Hoboken, N. J. In 1866 he moved to West Hoboken, Hudson County, and purchased the present family homestead on the corner of Palisade Avenue and Courtlandt Street, where he died in March, 1876. His wife still resides there. He was a member of Doric Lodge, F. and A. M., of West Hoboken.

Dr. Max Hecht was born in Hoboken, N. J., January 4, 1865, but has spent practically his whole life in West Hoboken, moving there with his parents when he was one year old. After attending the West Hoboken public schools he entered Cooper Union Institute, New York, from which he was graduated in 1883. Subsequently he took a full course at the New York College of Pharmacy, graduating with the degree of Ph.G. March 13, 1886, and then matriculated at Bellevue Medical College, from which he received the degree of M.D. March 30, 1891. Thus equipped with a thorough literary and professional training, he immediately began the active practice of medicine in West Hoboken, opening and ever since continuing an office in the old family homestead on Palisade Avenue, corner of Courtlandt Street. During the first year of his practice he was also actively connected with the Bellevue Dispensary in New York.

In the twofold relations of physician and citizen Dr. Hecht has already gained no little distinction, even outside of his town and county. He is widely known as a practitioner of recognized ability and skill and has a very extensive acquaintance. Steadily developing his talents in every branch of medicine, he has been successful from the start, and, although a young man, has gained a high reputation. For about one year he was health inspector of West Hoboken, resigning on account of the increasing duties of his practice. He is a member and physician to the Independent Order of Foresters, the chief medical examiner in West Hoboken for the Prudential Life Insurance Company of Newark and the Equitable Life Assurance Society of New York, and a member of the Odd Fellows and of the Hudson County Medical Society. He has been quite extensively interested in real estate in the immediate vicinity of his home, where he has recently completed a handsome residence.

Dr. Hecht was married, March 8, 1898, to Clara Elizabeth Heath, daughter of Joseph A. Heath, of Hoboken, N. J., and a descendant of an old English family.

JOHN FRANCIS MARION, of Jersey City, is the son of John Marion, who came from Ireland to Jersey City, N. J., when thirteen years old, and soon removed to Key West, Va., where he was engaged for a time in the cattle business; he returned to Jersey City, and for many years was in the employ of the Pennsylvania Railroad Company, and died here in 1879, aged forty years. John Marion married Ellen Brady, whose father, James Brady, came to Jersey City from Ireland about 1830 and died here in 1879, having been long employed by the Pennsylvania Railroad Company.

John F. Marion was born in Jersey City, N. J., on the 7th of June, 1867. He attended St. Peter's Parochial School and then entered St. Peter's College, Jersey City. Afterward he read law with Hon. J. Herbert Potts and Frederick Frambach, Jr., in his native city, and was admitted to the bar in November, 1891. Since then he has been actively and successfully engaged in the general practice of his profession in Jersey City. He was a partner of Thomas H. Kelly, Collector of the Port of Jersey City under Cleveland's first administration, until Mr. Kelly's death in 1895, the firm name being Kelly & Marion. He practiced one year alone, and then formed a partnership with Daniel P. Byrnes, under the firm name of Marion & Byrnes, which continued until January 1, 1899. Since then Mr. Marion has practiced alone. He has built up a large and successful legal business and is regarded as one of the able members of the Hudson County bar. He probably has charge of more law work for Catholic institutions than any other lawyer in Eastern New Jersey. He is counsel for St. Peter's College and St. Peter's Church of Jersey City, for the Sisters of Peace of New Jersey, and for St. Joseph's Church of Guttenberg, and one of the counsel for St. Francis Hospital, Jersey City.

Mr. Marion has not only achieved success at the bar, but has also gained distinction for those qualities of citizenship which characterize an energetic, patriotic, and progressive man. In 1895 he received in a post-graduate course the degree of Ph.B. at St. Francis Xavier College, New York City, and for a time wrote many special articles for the New York *Catholic News*. He is a prominent member of the Knights of Columbus, and one of the charter members of the council in Jersey City, of which he was elected first financial secretary. He is also a member of the Catholic Club of Jersey City, of the Third Ward Democratic Club, and of the Catholic Benevolent Legion. In politics he is an active and ardent Democrat.

Mr. Marion was married, October 27, 1897, in St. Peter's Church, Jersey City, by his former preceptor in chemistry, Francis de Fullerton, to Miss Belle Priest, daughter of George and Fannie R. Priest, natives of Boston, Mass.

J. HERBERT POTTS, Justice of the Police Court of Jersey City, was born in Trenton, N. J., July 3, 1851. He was educated at Laurenceville High School, at which institution he graduated in 1868 and prepared for college. For two years he was a member of the Princeton class of 1872. Returning to Trenton at the end of that period, he entered the law office of Hon. Edward T. Green, subsequently a Justice of the United States Circuit Court. Mr. Potts was admitted to the bar of New Jersey as an attorney February 5, 1874, and in the same year began the active practice of his profession in Jersey City, associating himself with a relative, Joseph C. Potts. He has continued in the active practice of law here, except when holding official positions.

In 1873 Judge Potts was appointed Assistant Clerk of the House of the

J. HERBERT POTTS.

Assembly at Trenton, and in 1880 and 1881 he was a member of that body, representing the Sixth Assembly District of Hudson County. In the session of 1880 he was Chairman of the Committee on the Revision of Laws, and in the session of the following year was Chairman of the Judiciary Committee. He was again elected to the Assembly in 1889, 1890, and 1891, representing in the new re-apportionment the Second Assembly District of Hudson County, and being the only Republican Assemblyman from the county in 1892. During that year he was the party (minority) leader on the floor of the House and served on many important committees, including the Judiciary, Revision of Laws, and Treasurer's Accounts. In the autumn of 1892 he was nominated by the Republicans for State Senator from Hudson County, and, although defeated, reduced the Democratic majority from 8,000 to 3,000. This fact illustrates the popularity which he has always enjoyed.

In 1894 he was appointed Justice of the First District (Criminal) Court of Jersey City, which position he still holds, having been re-appointed in 1897. In the spring of the latter year he was a candidate for Mayor of Jersey City and was defeated by Mayor Hoos by the very small majority of about 3,000 votes.

Judge Potts has achieved distinction at the bar as an able and talented lawyer, and on the bench has displayed great dignity, broad and accurate learning, and acknowledged judicial qualifications. He is especially popular in social circles, prominent in the councils of the Republican party, a member of the Carteret Club, of which he was Vice-President two years, a member of the Union League, and a member of the Palma Club, having served the latter four years as a Trustee. For a number of years he has been a leading and influential member of the Republican County Committee of Hudson County.

In 1876 Judge Potts married Miss Louise Bechtel, daughter of Charles Bechtel, who was for many years the publisher of the *State Gazette* at Trenton. They have three children.

HARRY MARTIN CONOVER was born in Manalapan, Monmouth County, N. J., on the 18th of March, 1867, and descends from some of the oldest and most respected families in the State. He is the son of William Stephen Conover, the grandson of Stephen Conover, a great-grandson of John P. Cowenhoven, and a great-great-grandson of Peter Cowenhoven, who was the son of William Cowenhoven, who was the son of John William Cowenhoven, who was the son of William Gerrets Couwenhoven, who was the son of Gerret Woolferts Couwenhoven, who was the son of Woolferts Garretson Van Couwenhoven, who came to this country from Amersfoort, Province of Utrecht, Netherlands, in 1630, who was superintendent of farms for the Patroon of Rensselaerswyck, now Albany, and who subsequently bought a farm at Amersfoort, L. I., and settled there. Mr. Conover's mother was Nancy P. Martin, and on her side he is the grandson of John S. Martin, a great-grandson of Ephraim S. Martin, and a great-great-grandson of Ephraim Martin, who was an officer in the Revolutionary War.

It will thus be seen that Harry Martin Conover descends from some of the oldest families in this country, each generation having distinguished itself in official or private capacities. From these lines of ancestors he inherits those sturdy characteristics which the Holland immigrants brought with them to their new homes, and which still characterize the race. Mr. Conover received his education in Monmouth County, N. J., and in Brooklyn, N. Y. At the age of sixteen he entered the employ of the New York Life Insurance Company in New York City and has been associated with that great corporation ever since, holding positions of trust and honor and gaining for himself the confidence of his associates and superiors.

Mr. Conover served for five years as a member of the Twenty-third Regiment, National Guard of New York, receiving an honorable discharge. He was with the regiment in Buffalo during the well known strike riots of 1894. He is a member of the Dutch Reformed Church.

September 28, 1893, Mr. Conover married Louise Ferdon Kipp. They have two children: David Kipp Conover and Albert Stephen Conover.

JOSEPH FRANCIS XAVIER STACK, M.D., was born July 6, 1871, in Hoboken, Hudson County, N. J., where he still resides. He is the son of Maurice Stack and Mary Carmody, and a grandson of Martin Stack, who married Mary Kelly. His ancestors on both sides descended from Irish emigrants who, since their settlement in this country, have been prominent in both business and civil life. His father, who is now retired, was for twenty-eight years a member of the police force of Hoboken, where the family settled in July, 1863.

Dr. Stack was educated at St. Peter's College in Jersey City and at Bellevue Hospital Medical College, New York, graduating from the latter institution with the degree of M.D. in March, 1896. He then served in the Out Patient Department of St. Vincent's Hospital, New York City, for two years, and on November 2, 1897, engaged in the active practice of his profession in Hoboken, opening his present office at 212 Garden Street. In May, 1898, he was appointed City Physician, which office he still holds.

He is physician to Court Castle Point and Christopher Columbus Lodge, Ancient Order of Foresters of Hoboken, a member of Council No. 99, Royal Arcanum, of Hoboken, and a member of Court Harmony, A. O. F., of the Riverside Athletic Club, and of the Knights of Columbus. Dr. Stack, though a young man, has achieved an excellent practice and a recognized standing in the community, and enjoyed a wide acquaintance and popularity. He is deeply interested in public affairs, is a public spirited, energetic, and progressive citizen, and one of the leading young physicians of Hudson County.

JOSEPH F. X. STACK, M.D.

CHAUNCEY H. SILLIMAN was born in New Bedford, Mass., December 24, 1855, and is the son of Joseph Silliman and Electa J. Miller, a grandson of John Leeds Silliman and Catherine Lockwood, and a great-grandson of Joseph Silliman. Some of his ancestors were conspicuous in the Revolutionary War, among them being Arnold, Wooster, and Silliman, who repulsed Tryon in the Tory raid at the battle of Bennington. The family is an old one in this country, and for generations has been active and influential in local affairs and honored and respected for their sterling qualities, patriotism, and progressive spirit.

Mr. Silliman received a preparatory education in the Betts Military Academy on Strawberry Hill, Stamford, Conn., and subsequently entered Columbia College, from which he was graduated in the class of 1876. He then entered upon a successful business career as assistant freight agent of the Fall River line of steamers; was subsequently associated with Lord & Taylor, of New York, for ten years; and in 1895 engaged in the express

CHAUNCEY H. SILLIMAN.

business, in which he still continues, under the style of the Suburban Parcel Delivery. His field of operation embraces about twenty-five square miles radiating from Arlington, and affords employment to some thirty horses and thirty men. In this business Mr. Silliman has been very successful.

He is a Democrat in politics, having cast his first vote for Samuel J. Tilden. As a member of the Board of Education and Town Council of Arlington he has rendered most efficient service to that borough, and is noted for his public spirit, patriotism, and energy. He is a member of the Masonic order, a Presbyterian by birth, and a liberal contributor to the church of that denomination. He married Lutie Lainhart, by whom he has two children: Florence E. and Chauncey H., Jr.

SAMUEL AUSTIN BESSON, member of the well known law firm of Besson & Spohr, of Hoboken, and one of the foremost attorneys and advocates in Hudson County, was born in Everittstown, Hunterdon County, N. J., April 6, 1853. His great-great-grandfather, Francis Besson, a French Huguenot, came to this country in the latter part of the seventeenth century and settled in the Township of Amwell, in Hunterdon County, where he was an extensive landowner. In that vicinity the family has been established for several generations, always wielding a potent influence in public affairs and taking a prominent part in all matters affecting the welfare of the community. Mr. Besson's great-grandfather, John Besson, Sr., was an ensign in the American Revolution and present at the siege and capture of Yorktown, and at the close of the war married Margaret, daughter of John Opdycke. Their son, John Besson, Jr., had a son William, who, by his wife, Margaret A. Case, was the father of Samuel Austin Besson, the subject of this article. Mrs. Margaret A. (Case) Besson was the daughter of Godfrey and Elizabeth (Welch) Case and a descendant on her father's side of one of the oldest families in the southern part of Hunterdon County.

SAMUEL A. BESSON.

Mr. Besson attended the public schools of Everittstown, the State Normal School at Carversville, Pa., and Lafayette College at Easton, from which he was graduated in 1876. During his college course he was Principal of the Franklin (Pa.) High School for one year, and immediately after his graduation became Principal of the High School at Phillipsburg, N. J. In 1877 he moved to Hoboken, and for three years read law in the office of his brother, Hon. John C. Besson, one of the leaders of the Hudson County bar and one of the ablest lawyers in the State. It was Mr. Besson's intention to complete a course of study at the Columbia Law School in New York, but business matters compelled him to abandon this hope. Under his brother's instruction, however, he enjoyed, practically, the full benefits of such a course, and when he came to the New Jersey bar as an attorney in June, 1879, he was well fitted for the general practice of his profession. Entering at once upon his legal career in Hoboken, he soon displayed qualifications of the highest order, and in May, 1882, was appointed Corporation Counsel.

At this time he was a Republican. He served as Corporation Counsel one year, when there was a complete change in the political offices of the city. During his term, however, he rendered valuable and important services to the municipality in various cases, including those which raised the question of the waterfront rights. In 1886, finding the majority of the Republican party hopelessly under the influence of the liquor dealers and the Democratic politicians, Mr. Besson resigned his membership on the Hudson County Republican Committee, and in that year, and again in 1887, was the candidate for Mayor of Hoboken on the Prohibition ticket. In 1888 he was the candidate of the same party for member of Congress; and though defeated in each campaign, he demonstrated his popularity by polling a very flattering vote. Subsequently he returned to the Republican party, and has ever since actively associated himself with its interests and exerted himself for its welfare, and until a year past has been an influential member of the Hudson County General Republican Committee.

As a lawyer he enjoys an extensive general and corporation practice. He was counsel for the Hoboken Land Improvement Company, and the Hoboken Ferry Company until March, 1898, the First National Bank of Hoboken until 1894, and is yet counsel of the Hudson Trust and Savings Institution and various other important corporations and financial enterprises. He was a member of the law firm of J. C. & S. A. Besson from the time of his admission to the bar until the death of his brother, John C. Besson, December 15, 1894, when the firm of Besson, Stevens & Lewis was organized, which continued until April 1, 1898, when by request of Mr. Besson that firm was dissolved, and Mr. Besson took as a partner John R. Spohr, a young lawyer of good reputation, the present firm name being Besson & Spohr, with offices in the Hoboken Savings Bank Building on the southwest corner of Washington and Newark Streets in the City of Hoboken. Mr. Besson devotes considerable time to the study of political economy, history, English literature, etc. He is a close student, a man of broad culture and accurate learning, a sound and able lawyer, a public spirited, progressive citizen, and a ruling elder of the First Presbyterian Church of Hoboken. He was one of the two founders and one of the first Trustees of the Columbia Club of Hoboken, of which he is still a popular member; and is also a member of Columbia Lodge, No. 63, I. O. O. F., of Euclid Lodge, F. and A. M., and of the Hudson County Bar Association, which he has served as President.

Mr. Besson was married on the 10th of November, 1881, to Arabella, daughter of Joseph M. Roseberry, of Belvidere, N. J. Their children are Henrietta and Harlan.

JOHN CASE BESSON, brother of Samuel Austin Besson, was born in Alexandria Township, Hunterdon County, N. J., April 30, 1838. He received his rudimentary education in the public schools of his native village, completing his studies at the Pennington Seminary. After leaving the latter institution he taught school for a short time. Afterward he studied law in the office of Edward R. Bullock, of Frenchtown, N. J., where he remained for one year. He then took a thorough course at the New York and National Law School at Poughkeepsie, N. Y., where he was graduated LL.B. in the class of 1860. After his graduation he entered the law office of Abraham Van Fleet, of Flemington, N. J., where he remained until February, 1863, when he was admitted to the bar as an attorney. Mr. Besson then opened his own office, locating at Millville, Cumberland County, N. J. His first month's revenue amounted to fifty cents, and the succeeding nine months were but little better. He removed to Flemington, where he formed a copartnership with George A. Allen, which continued for one year. He then removed to Clinton, N. J., opening an office, where he remained for two years. In February, 1866, he was admitted as a counselor. On May 1, 1867, he located in Hoboken and opened an office on Washington Street, in the old Reed house, and began a practice which became one of the largest in Hudson County. In 1883 he formed a copartnership with his brother, Samuel A. Besson.

Mr. Besson married Miss Hasseltine Judson Nice, daughter of Rev. George P. Nice, a prominent Baltimore clergyman. They had two sons. Mr. Besson died December 15, 1894.

He was a Director of the First National Bank, the Hudson Trust and Savings Institution, the Hudson County Gas Light Company, the New Jersey Title Guarantee and Trust Company, and the North Hudson County Railroad Company. In 1875 he published *Besson's New Jersey Law Precedents*, which has been adopted as authority by the general legal profession. He was a member of the Quartette, Columbia, and Union Athletic Clubs, was for six years the Corporation Counsel, and served as Assemblyman in 1885-86.

JOSEPH JOHN HASEL, pastor of St. Joseph's Catholic Church in West Hoboken, was born in Newark, N. J., on the 4th of February, 1861. His parents, Joseph Hasel and Kunigunda Dettinger, were natives respectively of Westphalia and Wurtemberg, Germany. The former came to America in 1820, before his marriage, and had six children: Francis, John, Lena, Clement, Frances, and Joseph J., the subject of this article.

Father Hasel was educated at St. Benedict's College, Newark, at St. Vincent's College in Pennsylvania, and at Seton Hall, Newark, and was ordained to the priesthood April 11, 1886. He was successively assistant pastor of St. Teresa Church, Summit, N. J., of St. Peter's, Newark, and of the Holy Family Church in the Town of Union, in the meantime attending St. Joseph's in West Hoboken, Hudson County. December 1, 1889, he was appointed pastor of St. Joseph's Church, West Hoboken, where he is now doing a most commendable work in both church and school. Father Hasel's pastoral career is rich in good deeds, and one of which he may well feel proud. A worker as well as a student and scholar, he has labored with great zeal and energy for the best interests of his parish, and is beloved and respected by all. His labors in St. Joseph's parish have resulted in the erection of a parsonage, sisters' house, and handsome church, which will cost $75,000, and these improvements were instituted and carried to completion by him. The corner-stone of the new church was laid July 31, 1898, and solemnly dedicated July 2, 1899, by Rt. Rev. W. M. Wigger, D.D.

Father Hasel has also greatly increased the communicant membership of the parish and enlarged the parochial school connected therewith, giving to both a new impetus, a very large measure of his own enthusiasm, and that hearty support which emanates from a pure heart and honest endeavor. He organized the Sacred Heart Society, the Young Ladies' Society, and the Children of Mary, and also the Young Men's Katolischer Gesellen Verein, which is incorporated, and of which he is President. These societies have wielded a powerful influence for good, and under his able and efficient direction are carrying on a work second only in importance to that of the church.

EDWARD C. STRIFFLER, a prominent citizen of Harrington Park, Bergen County, N. J., was born in New York City on the 1st of November, 1868. He is the only son and child of Christian Striffler and Mary Herzog and a grandson of John Striffler, all natives of Würtemberg, Germany. John Striffler was a soldier in Napoleon's army, and a farmer. Christian Striffler came to New York City when a young man and was married here. He established himself in the hardware business on the Bowery about 1868 and in 1873 moved to Ninth Avenue, near Forty-seventh Street, where the firm of C. Striffler & Co., which was formed about 1889, still carries on a thriving business and is one of the important hardware stores of New York. Mr. Striffler was a member of the Knights of Honor, and at one time a Sergeant in the New York militia. In 1884 he moved his family from New York City to River Vale, N. J., where his wife died August 12, 1894, and where his death occurred May 25, 1899.

Edward C. Striffler received his education in the public schools of New York City. He left school at the age of seventeen and entered his father's hardware store, with which he has ever since been identified, becoming a member of the present firm of C. Striffler & Co. upon the retirement of his father in 1893, the other partner being Emil Rudolph, his cousin. This is one of the oldest and most successful general hardware, iron, and steel houses in New York City, and has occupied its present location on Ninth Avenue, near Forty-seventh Street, since 1873.

Mr. Striffler has been active and influential in the community where he resides, and as the successor of his father's business and affairs has developed marked ability. He has served as a School Trustee of Harrington Township, Bergen County, since 1896, and in various other important capacities has displayed the highest attributes of the citizen. In politics he is a Democrat.

Mr. Striffler was married on the 22d of June, 1892, to Elenore Banta, daughter of the late Garrett H. Banta. They have two children: Willard C. and Helen M.

JOHN G. FISHER, formerly County Clerk of Hudson County, was born in New Brunswick, N. J., January 22, 1843, and is the son of J. G. Fisher, of New Brunswick, and his wife, Julia, daughter of Captain William Henry, of the merchant marine. Mr. Fisher received his education in the public schools, and after leaving school became a clerk in a clothing store in his native town. In June, 1862, he enlisted as a volunteer in the Fourteenth New Jersey Volunteers, being mustered out in August, 1864, with the rank of First Lieutenant. He was severely wounded during the battle of Cold Harbor. In 1867 he entered the law office of Judge W. T. Hoffman, of Jersey City, with whom he remained for several years. In 1874 he accepted a position under County Clerk John Kennedy, and continued to serve through several succeeding administrations. When County Clerk Dennis

McLaughlin entered the office Mr. Fisher resigned and entered a real estate office, but subsequently resumed his position at Mr. McLaughlin's request. He was elected a member of the Board of Aldermen of Jersey City in 1873. Later he was elected a Justice of the Peace. In 1895 he was elected County Clerk of Hudson County and served five years. He cast his first vote for Abraham Lincoln, and from that time to the present has been an active and zealous Republican. He is a prominent member of Zabriskie Post, No. 38, Grand Army of the Republic.

Mr. Fisher married Jennie E. Baldwin, of Newark, N. J., and has two sons and two daughters.

WILLIAM M. VAN SICKLE, Supervising Principal of Schools of the Town of West New York, Hudson County, was born on a farm near Peters Valley, Sussex County, N. J., March 15, 1854, and there spent his boyhood days. His father, Benjamin P. Van Sickle, was one of the best known farmers in that county and took special pride in his work.

William M. Van Sickle received his early education in the country school near where he was born. When he was a mere lad he received a license to teach, and for a period of three months engaged in the profession. From this first school he entered the New Jersey State Normal School, and after finishing a course there he took a special course at Cooper Union, New York. He has taught school all along the line since he completed his studies at Cooper Union, teaching at the country cross-road, afterward at the rural village, then going to the town, and is now the Supervising Principal of Schools at West New York, where he has successfully filled the position the past eight years. These schools are now among the best in the country, and have a full complement of studies ranging from the kindergarten to the high school.

Aside from public school work Mr. Van Sickle has been more or less identified with the local interests of the several communities in which he has lived, holding at different times the offices of United States Census Enumerator, Town Clerk, County Committeeman, etc. He has also been connected with the press for a number of years, furnishing many special articles on the questions of the time.

He is also co-editor with Superintendent A. J. Demarest, of Hoboken, in writing the famous system of reading known as "The Synthetic Phonic Word Method of Teaching Reading," which will in time be universally adopted throughout the country. Mr. Van Sickle is now President of the Hudson County Teachers' Association, and he is also one of the members of the Hudson County Teachers' Examining Board.

He was married in March, 1886, to Miss Harriet Brown, of Stockholm, N. J., and has two children: Roscoe and Edith.

ANDREW J. DAVIS, formerly Treasurer of the Town of Weehawken and ex-Chairman of the Board of Council, was born in Albany County, N. Y., March 9, 1843, the son of Howland Davis and Lorinda, daughter of Thomas Craft. His ancestors came originally from Wales and Holland, settling in this country several generations ago. His maternal grandfather, Thomas Craft, of Albany County, N. Y., was a soldier in the patriot army during the Revolutionary War.

Mr. Davis acquired his education in the public schools of his native county. At the age of twenty he became a sailor on the Hudson River, running between Albany and New York. In 1863 he was engaged by the

Camden and Amboy Railroad as a deckhand and subsequently, in 1869, he was raised to a pilot, running between New York and South Amboy. In 1873 he was engaged by the Erie Railroad as Master of the "General McCallum," where he has since remained.

His career has been an eminently successful one. As a Republican, Mr. Davis has long taken an active part in political affairs and is recognized as one of the party's foremost leaders. He has served as Treasurer of the Town of Weehawken, has been a member of the Town Committee, and was Chairman of the Board of Council and Chief of Police. Mr. Davis has also held various other minor offices. He is a progressive, patriotic citizen, a man of the highest integrity, and has long wielded a commanding influence in the affairs of Weehawken, N. J., where he has resided since 1883, having resided for six years in Guttenberg prior to that year. His prominence and popularity have been attested by the several positions which he has been called upon to fill, and the duties of which he has always discharged with fidelity and satisfaction.

Captain Davis married Amanda W., daughter of Samuel R. and Jane (Caruthers) Houston, of Englishtown, N. J. They have had three children: Lillian (deceased), Jesse A., and Lester L. Jesse A. was graduated from Stevens Institute and is now in the Navy Department as an inspector of steel. He was born in 1873 in South Amboy, N. J.

WILLIAM CLAYBORN MARION, of Arlington, N. J., has achieved special distinction in the manufacture of gold pens, a business he has followed for fifty-two years. Born in Lexington, Ky., April 12, 1834, he is the eldest son of Captain William C. and Caroline (Elserth) Marion and a grandson of Alfred M. Marion and Mary, his wife, who settled in Kentucky in the eighteenth century, all being Americans of French extraction. As pioneers in the famous Blue Grass region the family wielded an important influence and distinguished themselves for their artistic taste and mechanical genius, and Mr. Marion seems to have both inherited and developed these traits with peculiar success. His father was a Captain in the Mexican War and was killed in the battle of Churubusco in 1846. His mother died the same year.

Breathing in his father's house a wholesome mechanical atmosphere, and having received at the district schools a good rudimentary education, he left home at the age of fourteen and apprenticed himself to Andrew J. Berrian, a maker of gold pens at 75 Nassau Street, New York. Mr. Marion remanied there three years, and became so skillful in the art of pen making that he secured, at the early age of seventeen, a position as journeyman in the shop of Albert G. Bagley, on the corner of Duane and Centre Streets, New York. Mr. Bagley is credited with being the inventor of the gold pen. After his death the business changed hands, but Mr. Marion continued to act as foreman for thirty-three years, when the plant was purchased by Edward Todd. Mr. Bagley was long the leading gold pen maker of the world, and Mr. Marion not only became deeply interested in his work, but devoted much of his spare time after working hours to the study of difficult mechanical problems connected with the trade, and as a result of this close application he achieved a national reputation as an expert gold pen maker, orders for difficult work being sent to him from all parts of the country.

In 1884 Mr. Marion formed a partnership with G. Armeny and engaged in business on Nassau Street in New York City under the present firm name of Armeny & Marion. Mr. Marion is without doubt or question the oldest living working gold pen maker in the world, his successful and active career extending over a period of more than fifty-three years. He is still in active service, and enjoys a reputation unequaled by anyone in his line of business.

Mr. Marion has carved out his own fortune and paved his own way to success. Coming to New York a small boy, without money, he steadily and courageously went to work, first in Burton's old theater in Park Row and soon afterward in Bagley's pen factory, and when the War of the Rebellion broke out bade good-by to wife and children and enlisted in the Union

WILLIAM C. MARION.

cause. In the summer of 1861, with James Miller, he recruited a company which became a part of the Fifty-second New York Volunteers, Shepard Rifles. He enlisted, however, in Company I, Ninth New York Volunteer Infantry, in the fall of 1861, as a private, and served nine months, participating in the battles of Ball's Bluff and Edward's Ferry. At the latter place he was wounded in the right hand. After this service in Maryland and Virginia he was detailed on recruiting duty in New York City, as a Sergeant, and continued in that line for about one year and three months. In November, 1863, he was honorably discharged.

On his return from the war Mr. Marion resumed the trade of gold pen maker. In his business relations as well as in private life he is regarded with great affection and as a benefactor. Sincere and true in all he attempts, he is a thorough gentleman, universally esteemed and respected as a public spirited, enterprising citizen, and worthy of the confidence which is reposed in him. Mr. Marion lived in Brooklyn for many years. In August, 1889, he moved from that city to Arlington, N. J., where he now resides. He is a Democrat in politics and for several years was President of the Arlington Democratic Club, resigning with all the other officers when the free silver question came to the front in 1896. He attends the Presbyterian Church, is a member of Chancellor Walworth Lodge, F. and A. M., and holds membership in the Scottish Rite bodies, 32°, of New York City. He was a member of Tribune Lodge, No. 159, F. and A. M., of Arlington. He is a member of Pilgrim Lodge, I. O. O. F., of Arlington, which he served as Noble Grand two terms, has been a delegate to the Masonic and Odd Fellows Grand Lodges of New Jersey, and as a member of the Jamaica Bay Yacht Club.

January 29, 1855, Mr. Marion was married in New York City to Caroline Patten, daughter of Susterry and Sarah (Long) Patten, of Nantucket, Mass. They have had ten children: Frank W., an actor; Harry W., who is connected with the firm of A. G. Spalding & Co., of New York; Bertha (Mrs. Edwin Lewis), of Brooklyn; William C., Jr., the New York manager of the Morgan-Wright Company; Alfred P., foreman for Armeny & Marion; Daisy I. (Mrs. Harry Stover), of Brooklyn; Sidney T., who is employed by his father in the factory; Emma, unmarried; and Edwin and Winfield, deceased.

WILLIAM H. VOORHIS has always resided in Schraalenburgh, Bergen County, N. J., where he was born on the 6th of November, 1870. He is a direct descendant of Steven Coerts Van Voorhees, the emigrant (see sketch on page 83), of the seventh generation. His father is John W. Voorhis. The Voorhis family has given many eminent men to the State; its members have been conspicuous in the professions, in military and civil life, and in the quieter pursuits of business and the trades for many generations. His mother was Sophia Vross, daughter of James Vross; her family also came originally from Holland.

Mr. Voorhis acquired his early education in the public schools of Schraalenburgh. Leaving school at the age of fourteen, he entered upon the active duties of life. He learned the carpenter's trade, which he followed as a journeyman for three years, when he engaged in the business for himself. Since that time he has steadily and successfully prosecuted his chosen trade, executing many important contracts, and adding materially to the general advancement of his town. His services have also been called into requisition as a public official. For two years he was a valued member of the Town Council. He is a member of the Dutch Reformed Church, an enterprising, public spirited citizen, and a man of acknowledged influence and standing.

Mr. Voorhis married Minnie Yereance, and they have two children: Ethel, born in 1891, and Arthur, born in 1897.

EDWARD EARLE, known as Edward Earle, Jr., came to Bergen (now Jersey City, N. J.) early in the spring of 1676, from Maryland. He was an Englishman, or of English descent. On the 24th of April, following his

ERRATA

On page 232, in sketch of William H. Voorhis, first paragraph, 8th line, read Sophia Bross, daughter of James Bross, instead of "Vross," as printed.

arrival at Bergen, he purchased Secaucas Island, taking a deed therefor from Samuel Edsall and Peter Stoutenburgh, executors of the will of Nicholas Varlett, who first purchased it from the Indians. Earle's deed recites that the area of the island was about 2,000 acres. Three years later he sold one-half of the island to Judge William Pinhorne for £500, including one-half of all the stock, "Christian and negro servants." A schedule attached to this deed discloses what improvements and personal chattels were on the island at this time, and enumerates "one dwelling house, containing two lower rooms and a lean-to-below-stairs and a loft above, five tobacco houses, one horse, one mare, two colts, eight oxen, ten cows, one bull, four yearlings, seven calves, thirty or forty hogs, four negro men, and five Christian servants." Edward Earle died December 15, 1711. He married, February 13, 1688, Elsie Vreeland. After his death his widow, Elsie Vreeland, went to Hackensack, where, on the 24th of June, 1716, she married Hendrick Meyer, by virtue of a license from the Governor of New Jersey, dated May 8, 1716. Edward, Jr.'s children by Elsie Vreeland were seven in number: Edward, born in 1690; a son, born 1692; Hannah, born in 1685; Marmaduke, born in 1696; John, born in 1698; a son born 1703; and a daughter born in 1704. All of these children eventually settled within the limits of Bergen County and mostly at English Neighborhood.

SAMUEL E. EARLE, the subject of this article, is of the sixth generation from Edward Earle, Jr., who came from Maryland, as stated in the foregoing sketch. His father, Samuel E. Earle, Sr., a life-long farmer, was born in old English Neighborhood, now Ridgefield, filled the offices of school trustee, road master, etc., and died March 12, 1898, at the age of ninety-seven years and fourteen days; his father was Nathaniel Earle, also a farmer. The wife of Samuel E. Earle, Sr., was Eliza McDonald, who was born in North Bergen, and who died there March 28, 1898, aged eighty-seven. She was of Scotch descent. Her paternal grandmother lived to be over one hundred years old. Mr. and Mrs. Earle were both endowed with great force of character and with attainments of a high order, and during their lives were universally respected and esteemed for those sterling qualities which distinguish their race. Of their eight children three are living, namely: Matthias T. Earle, of Jersey City Heights, N. J.; Samuel E. Earle, of North Bergen; and Abraham McDonald Earle, of Brooklyn, N. Y.

Samuel E. Earle was born December 15, 1848, in North Bergen, Hudson County, N. J., where he has always resided. After attending the public schools of his native town he took up his father's vocation, that of farmer, which he has since followed, engaging also from time to time in contract work on roads and streets. He has been Road Commissioner of North Bergen for nine years and a member of the North Bergen Board of Education since 1892. In politics he is an independent Democrat. Mr. Earle has filled every position with ability and satisfaction, and during an active career has won and maintained the confidence of his fellow-citizens. His interest in township affairs, his faithful attention to the trusts committed to his care, and his unfailing public spirit and patriotism, together with his industry, enterprise, and activity, have gained for him universal esteem and respect. He is a member of the Royal Society of Good Fellows.

November 4, 1880, Mr. Earle married Miss Mary S. Rodgers, daughter of Abiatha and Rhoda Rodgers, of New York City. They have two children: Rhoda Ann and Fred Reed.

JAMES SMITH, Treasurer of the City of Hoboken, N. J., since May, 1888, is the son of James Smith, Sr., and Elizabeth Eaton, and was born in County Meath, Ireland, May 5, 1848. In 1850 he was brought by his parents to America. The family settled in Hoboken, Hudson County, and there Mr. Smith has ever since resided, identifying himself with the growth and advancement of the city and contributing materially to its general welfare. He attended Hoboken Public School No. 1, being one of its first scholars, and finished his studies at St. Francis Xavier College in New York City. Subsequently he engaged in the provision trade in Hoboken, and for thirty years has followed that business with constantly increasing success.

In politics Mr. Smith has always been a Democrat. He was elected Treasurer of the City of Hoboken in May, 1888, and by successive re-elections has ever since held that office with great credit and honor to himself and entire satisfaction to the people. That he is popular, trustworthy, and universally respected is attested by the fact that he has had no opposition at the polls since his first election, and even then his opponent for the office was nominated on an independent ticket and polled a very small vote. Mr. Smith has discharged his duties as Treasurer of the city with unceasing fidelity, and with such marked ability and integrity that in 1896 he was the Democratic nominee for the State Treasurership. He is public spirited, enterprising, and patriotic, prompt and exact in the discharge of every obligation, genial and affable in manner, and popular among all who know him. He is a member and one of the founders of the Columbia Club of Hoboken.

Mr. Smith married Miss Minnie Judge, whose father was one of the original Police Commissioners of Hoboken. They have three sons and two daughters.

EUGENE VAN ARTSDALEN MAGEE, of Hoboken, was born in Jamesburg, N. J., December 21, 1852. He is the son of Joseph C. and Elizabeth (Van Artsdalen) Magee and a grandson of Jonathan Magee and Daniel Van Artsdalen, and springs from a family whose members have long been active and prominent in the State.

Mr. Magee was educated at Freehold Institute in Freehold, N. J., and for a time was in the First National Bank of Jamesburg. In 1871 he went to New York City, where he added to his practical knowledge of business affairs. He engaged in the business of clothiers' trimmings in 1880, and so continued with marked success until 1894, when the death of his brother-in-law caused a change in his commercial relations. He then associated himself with his father-in-law, William H. Harper, in the real estate and insurance business in Hoboken, of which he is the manager and proprietor. This agency dates back to 1860, and conducts an extensive business through-

EUGENE VAN ARTSDALEN MAGEE.

out Hudson County. Mr. Magee is an expert in all matters connected with real property and, whenever differences of opinion in respect to values arise, his judgment is accepted as final. He is a resident of East Orange, a gentleman of excellent social and financial standing, and is held in much respect by all with whom he has business or personal relations. He is a member of the Munn Avenue Presbyterian Church of East Orange. He married Minnie Harper and has two children.

WILLIAM WILLIAMS BANTA, of Hillsdale, N. J., numbers among his ancestors some of the most distinguished men of Bergen County. The

Bantas, the Demarests, the Duries, and other prominent families came over from Holland and were original settlers of the county, and to their energy, activity, and enterprise is due much of the county's prosperity, as well as the growth and development of the eastern part of the State.

Mr. Banta is a lineal descendant of Epke Jacobse Banta, a well-to-do farmer who emigrated to America from Harlengen in the Province of East Friesland, Holland, in 1659. The register of the ship "De Trouw" shows that Banta with his wife and children: Seba, aged six years, Cornelius, aged four years, Henry, aged two years, and Weart, aged nine months, left the port of Amsterdam, February 13, 1659, and in due time reached New Amsterdam, from whence Banta went to Bergen in New Jersey, where he took an active part in town affairs, and in 1679 was there appointed one of the Judges of the Court of Oyer and Terminer. The same year he bought a tract of land near Hackensack. His son Dirk bought lands adjoining his father in 1681, and in 1695 four of the sons, in company with other persons, bought a large tract at English Neighborhood in Bergen County. The sons all married, reared large families, and became prominent and influential in county affairs, principally in Bergen.

William W. Banta is of the eighth generation from Epke Jacobse Banta, the emigrant, and is the son of John J. Banta and Margeretta Demarest, and a grandson of Jacob J. and Maria (Williams) Banta, and on his mother's side of David and Margeretta Durie Demarest. He was born at Old Bridge, Bergen County, N. J., on the 20th of July, 1857, and received his education in the public schools of River Edge in the same county. He subsequently spent ten years in teaching, first as Principal of the Hillsdale Public School and later as teacher of Public School No. 2, at Teaneck. From 1887 to 1896 he conducted a general store at Hillsdale, serving also as Postmaster during that period. In 1897 he again accepted the principalship of the Teaneck school, which he still holds.

Mr. Banta is a teacher of acknowledged ability, and during many years' service in that occupation has been eminently successful. He has brought to his duties great intellectual capacity, liberal ideas, and a broad educational training, and the schools under his management have experienced unusual prosperity. He was one of the Assessors of Washington Township in 1894 and Clerk of the new Township of Hillsdale in 1898, and is a Steward and Trustee of the Hillsdale Methodist Episcopal Church. In every capacity he has won the respect and confidence of all who know him. He married Emma Hopper, daughter of Abram A. and Margaret Hopper, of Hillsdale, N. J.

THE VAN HORN FAMILY.—The first American progenitor of the Van Horn family in Hudson and Bergen Counties was Jan Cornelissen, who came to America from his birthplace, the City of Hoorn, Holland, previously to the year 1645. Mr. Winfield, in his "History of Hudson County," thinks this emigrant was under twenty-one years of age when he arrived at New Amsterdam, and cites as proof the fact that, on October 4, 1647, a power of attorney was executed by him for the purpose of collecting money due him from his guardian in Holland. He sided with the English in 1664, and took the oath of allegiance to the king the same year. One of his sons, named Joris, married, March 11, 1663, Maria Rutgers, of Amersfoort, L. I., and had eight children, one of whom was Rutgert Jansen Van Horn, baptized at New York, January 5, 1667. This Rutgert married, April 25, 1697, Neeltie Van Vechten. Another son was Cornelius

Jansen Van Horn. In 1697 both Rutgert and Cornelius went to Schraalenburgh, where Cornelius married Jacomina Demarest, widow of Samuel Helling, and settled east of Closter, where his descendants still reside. Rutgert returned to Bergen and purchased lands at Bayonne, where he resided until 1711, when he bought a farm at Communipaw, where he spent his days, and where he died May 15, 1741. Rutgert's descendants spread over Hudson County, and those of Cornelius over Bergen County.

THE VAN HOUTEN FAMILY.—Boele Roelofsen Joncker, a native of the Province of Gelderland, Holland, and his wife and four children, besides his wife's sister and a boy, came to America, in February, 1659, and settled at New Amsterdam. His wife's surname was Teunis. The names of the children he brought with him were Halmagh, Cornelis, Teunis, and Matilda, and after his arrival in New York he had two more children baptized there: Henry, February 6, 1661, and Catharine, October 8, 1662. Roelofsen's children after his death removed to and settled at Bergen, N. J. Halmagh married, September 3, 1676, Jannetje Peters, a daughter of Peter Merselis, of Beest, Holland. Cornelis married, November 14, 1677, Magdalena Rynese Van Giesen. Teunis married, January 8, 1678, Catharine Claes Kuyper (Cooper). Matilda married, July 22, 1683, John Hendricks. No further mention is made of the other two children. Halmagh's children, baptized at Bergen, were ten: Roelof, Peter, Cornelius, Catelyntie, Jacob, Dirck, Geertie, Elizabeth, John, and Jannetie. These all remained at Bergen, where their descendants are very numerous. Cornelius went to Aquackanonck, where, on March 16, 1684, he and several others purchased and settled on a large tract known as the Aquackanonck (Passaic) patent. His children were Grietie, Roelof, Rynier, Drickie, John, and Cornelius. These remained at Passaic, and their descendants are numerous in Passaic County and in the western and northern parts of Bergen County. Teunis removed to Rockland County, N. Y. (then Orange County), where he purchased lands and located, and where he became somewhat noted. In 1689 he was a Justice for Orange County, and the same year he was a member of the Committee of Safety to deal with the treason of Governor Leisler at New York. He had thirteen children, some baptized at Bergen, some at New York, and some at Tappan. Their names were Grietie, Rolof, Ann, Claes, Jannetie, Vroutie, Cornelia, John, Vroutie, Elizabeth, Pietartie, Grietie, and Anetie. Many of these married and their descendants spread over Rockland County, N. Y., and southward into Bergen County, N. J.

THE VAN GELDER FAMILY.—The numerous Van Gelders in Bergen County are descended from Johannes Van Gelder, who came from Gelderland in Holland about 1661 and settled at New Amsterdam, where he had issue Hester, 1662; John, 1664; Hermanus, 1666; Elizabeth; Maria; Abraham, 1673; Cornelia; Emmerdus; and James. John married in 1686 Effie Roos. Hermanus married in 1689 Catharine Teunis. Abraham married, in 1695, Catalyntie Elias. James settled at Hackensack, N. J., in 1705, and married Susanna Devoe, a widow. Abraham's son John, born about 1702, married Catalina Vanderbeck, and about 1730 settled at Pompton, then in Bergen County. From these two, John and James, there are numerous descendants living in the western part of Bergen County.

ABRAM C. HOLDRUM.—The Holdrums of Bergen County are of Holland extraction. The first to come to America was John Holdrum (or, as he spelled it, Holdron). The exact date of his arrival at New York is not known, but it must have been early in 1708, for in that year he married Miss Cornelia Van Tienhoven, a daughter of Director-General Cornelius Van Tienhoven, of New Amsterdam, where she was born in the fall of 1678.

John Holdrum and his wife resided in New Amsterdam for five years after their marriage, during which time three children were born to them. In 1713 John and his family removed to Tappan, N. Y., where they seem to have resided, neighbors to the Coopers, Eckersons, Harings, and Straatmakers, some of whom were living within the limits of Bergen County. Of what part of Holland John Holdrum was a native does not definitely appear. It is known that he styled himself "yeoman," which signified he was a man possessed of some property, and that he sailed from Amsterdam. He was an agriculturist, and must have been a man of respectability to obtain an introduction into such an aristocratic family as the Van Tienhovens. His children of the second generation were William, Elizabeth, and Lucas, born in New York City, and Elsie, Sarah, John, and Cornelius, born at Tappan, N. Y., the last of whom married Antje Meyer, and had five children.

William Holdrum, of the second generation, born in New York about 1710, married, in 1734, Margrietie Peters, daughter of Claes Peters, of Rockland County, N. Y. William purchased lands in Harrington Township, Bergen County, just south of the State line, about 1745, but what area does not appear, the deed never having been recorded. On December 18, 1760, he purchased from Dominie Benjamin Vandelinda a tract of 258 acres west of the Hackensack River, adjoining the State line. On this William resided all his lifetime, following the occupation of a farmer. His children of the third generation were: John, born in 1735, married Catharine Lepper (and had three children); Cathelyntie, born in 1737; Cornelia, born in 1739; Claes, born in 1740; William, born in 1742; Maria, born in 1745; Abraham, born in 1747; Cornelius, born in 1749; and Catharine, born in 1751. One of these last (Cornelius, third generation) married Elizabeth Haring. He died May

ABRAM C. HOLDRUM.

31, 1831. They had a son, James C. Holdrum (4), born December 21, 1785, who married Margaret Demarest. He died October 5, 1877, and she died March 30, 1870. One of their children was Cornelius J. Holdrum (5), who married Elizabeth De Pew, and had children, one of whom was Abram C. Holdrum (6), the subject of this sketch.

Abram C. Holdrum was born at Orangeburgh, Rockland County, N. Y., September 23, 1837. He received his education in the local public schools of his town, and, after finishing the usual course, was duly appointed to a scholarship in the New York Normal School at Albany, where he completed a thorough classical training. Subsequently he was engaged in business in New York City for nearly twenty years, retiring in 1872 and removing to Bergen County, where he has since resided. From that time to the present he has been honored by almost every local office of trust within the gift of the county and State.

He is and has been for many years a commissioner of deeds and a notary public for New Jersey, Pennsylvania, and New York. He has served as a member of the Board of School Trustees of Washington Township for more than twenty years, being district clerk most of that period. In 1879 he was elected to the Bergen County Board of Chosen Freeholders, and was the first Republican representative from the Township of Washington. He was appointed to take the United States census in 1880 and again in 1890, and in the latter year was appointed by the Governor a member of the Bergen County Board of Elections, of which he served as Secretary until his election to the New Jersey Legislature of 1897. In 1895 he was commissioned Postmaster of Westwood, N. J., and held that office four years.

Elected to the Assembly of 1897 by a plurality of 3,633 over Van Emburg, the highest Democratic candidate, Mr. Holdrum served on the Committees on Game and Fisheries and Revision of Laws, and was re-elected for the session of 1898, his majority over Mr. Fellows, the Democratic nominee, being 808. His entire legislative career was marked by a careful, comprehensive, and intelligent attention to the business of the House, and especially to those measures which affected his town or county, and gained for him a high reputation as well as a wide and intimate acquaintance.

Mr. Holdrum has been a leading member of the Republican County Executive Committee of Bergen County for many years, and in 1896 became the committee's Vice-Chairman. He has been President of the Bergen County Farmers' Mutual Fire Insurance Company since 1891, has been Vice-President of the Bergen County Board of Agriculture and a delegate to the State board for some time, and is also President of the Progressive Building and Loan Association, of Hillsdale, N. J. In all these capacities he has displayed great business ability, sound judgment, and unerring foresight, united with manly courage, indomitable industry, and honest effort. He has faithfully and honestly discharged the duties of every trust. He is a member and past officer of City Lodge, F. and A. M., of New York City, and a member of Rockland Chapter, R. A. M., of Nyack, N. Y.

He married, in January, 1872, Miss Mary Leah Hopper, and has two children living: Bessie C., born in 1876, and Garret S. M., born in 1881, and resides in Westwood, Bergen County.

THE VAN DIEN FAMILY has numerous members in the central parts of Bergen County. Their common ancestor was Gerret Cornelise Van Duyn (said to have been a native of Zwolle in the Province of Overyssel in Holland). In 1649 he emigrated from Niewkerk in Zealand to New Amsterdam and married Jacomina Swarts. He settled at Brooklyn, where he plied his trade of a carpenter and wheelwright. He was fined there in 1658 for refusing to pay toward supporting the minister. On August 10, 1670, he obtained permission to return to Holland, and, with his wife, kept house at Zwolle, but, not prospering, he returned in 1679 in the ship "The Charles," on board of which were several leaders of the sect known as Labadists. He finally located on a farm on Long Island, between New Utrecht and Flatbush. He bought other lands at Flatbush. He was among the Flatbush patentees in 1686 and 1687, took the oath of allegiance in 1687, and was a magistrate in 1687-88 and a justice in 1689-90. He died in 1705, leaving issue Cornelius, Garret, Denys, William, Dirck, Cornelia, Abraham, Aeltie, and Jacomina.

Cornelius removed to Somerset County, N. Y. Abraham settled on the Raritan River in New Jersey, and later went to Cecil County, Md. All the others except Garret settled in Somerset and Middlesex Counties, N. J. Garret went to Bergen, where he settled, and died in 1686. He married Gertie Hopper, and bought lands in 1662 from Governor Stuyvesant, on the Saddle River. His children wrote their names Van Dien. Among his issue was Gerret Van Dien, who married Vroutie Verwey, and lived west of the Saddle River. His issue were Dirk, Cornelius, Hendricka, Albert, and William, and the descendants of these children are now numerous in Bergen County.

THE VANDERBECK FAMILY is among the most numerous of any in Bergen and Hudson Counties. Paulus Vander Beek, the common ancestor of the family in America, was a native of Bremen, in Germany, and came to America about 1643, stopping first at New Amsterdam, where, on October 9, 1644, he married Maria Thomas (or Baddie), a widow who had previously been the wife of Thomas Farden and William Arianse Bennett, of Gowannus. Paulus Vander Beek appears to have been of a roving disposition. In 1655 he was living at Brooklyn. In 1660 he was following the calling of a butcher in New Amsterdam. In 1661 he was farming the excise of Long Island, and in 1662 he was ferry-master. On October 24, 1663, he bought plantation lot No. 17 at Graves End. He was enrolled as a taxpayer of Brooklyn in 1675, and was one of the patentees of the Brooklyn patent in 1677. In 1679 he sold half of a farm at Gowanus for 3,000 gelders. He resided on the farm at Gowannus, late of Garret Bergen. He died in 1680. His children were Conrad, 1647; Aeltie, 1649; and Paulus, Hester, Isaac, and Catharine. Paulus Vander Beek (2), baptized at New Asterdam, November 17, 1650, married, June 13, 1677, Sarah Schouten. He resided at Gowannus, where he died about 1690. His issue of the third generation were Sarah, Maria, Paulus, Sarah, Lucas, and Janneken.

Paulus Vanderbeck (3), baptized at Gowannus, November 6, 1681, married Jannetie Springsteen, and settled at Hackensack, joining the church there September 30, 1710, which is about the time he went there. He bought land in what is now Midland Township and at Paramus, where he settled. His cousin, Paulus Vanderbeck, son of Conrade (2), married (1) Jannetie Johannes, widow of Jacob Culver, and (2) June, 1703, Catryn Martens, widow of Samuel Berry. He likewise settled near Hackensack. Paulus (3) had issue Abram, 1708, and Isaac, 1712, and Paulus (3), son of Conrad, had children Conrad, Jacob, Elsie, Paulus, and Catharine. From these residing about Paramus and Hackensack have sprung a numerous host, scattered over Bergen and Hudson Counties.

HENRY ISAAC DARLING, of Jersey City, was born in County Meath, Ireland, on the 7th of June, 1847. He is the son of James Darling and Susan Ffolliott and a grandson of Hiram Darling and John Ffolliott. He received his education at Santry College, in Dublin, and in 1865 came to New York City, where he began his active career. In 1866 he went to California and spent four eventful years in San Francisco and Sacramento, gaining a wide experience and a full knowledge of business generally. Returning east in 1870, he was in the great Chicago fire of 1871, and the next year (1872) returned to New York, where he was employed for several years in the wholesale dry goods business.

Mr. Darling removed to Hoboken, Hudson County, N. J., in 1875 and lived there nine years. In 1884 he moved to the Hudson City section of Jersey City and engaged in real estate business and building operations. He was the first in his section of Jersey City to inaugurate the system of building a detached house on a lot and selling the whole property on easy terms, thus enabling working people of moderate means to get possession of their homes and pay for them in the easiest possible manner. In this line of operation Mr. Darling has been eminently successful, and a large number of families to-day are enjoying homes which he has provided for them on this basis. Among the buildings which he has erected up to the present time are one hundred and thirty-five houses by actual count in Hudson County, nearly all of which he has sold to families now occupying them. Most of these homes have been built within the past six years, thus bringing into the county property to the value of over $300,000.00, and improving lands which would still be unproductive and of small value as a taxable asset. Numerous builders and contractors have followed his example of building detached houses for homes for working people and have been very successful, yet the inception and inauguration of the plan is due wholly to him, and in this particular line he is the acknowledged leader. Blocks of houses all over the Hudson City and Bergen sections of Jersey City, on

HENRY I. DARLING.

Weekawken Heights, and in West Hoboken attest his design of working people's homes. Mr. Darling makes a specialty of one and two family houses, and he justly claims that he never built a house but what he could sell easily.

As a business man and citizen Mr. Darling has achieved an excellent reputation. He has been successful in all his efforts, for in their inception and execution he has displayed the highest abilities, untiring industry, and superior judgment. He was at one time a member of the Republican County Committee of Hudson County and also served a five years' term as Justice of the Peace, but with these exceptions has never held public office. Though a public spirited citizen, deeply interested in the welfare of the community, and thoroughly identified with its interests, he has never taken a very active part in politics, his extensive business interests demanding and receiving his entire attention. He is a member of Hoboken Lodge, F. and A. M., of Unique Lodge, A. O. U. W., and of the Berkley Club. Both he and his family were prominent in the Ascension Protestant Episcopal Church, New York Avenue and South Street, Jersey City, for many years; they now attend St. John's Church on Summit Avenue, Jersey City.

Mr. Darling was married in Hoboken, N. J., in 1875, to Miss Martha J. Dowden. They have one son, Benjamin J. Darling, now a law student in the office of Henry A. Gaede, of Hoboken, and a member of the afternoon law class of New York University, 1901, and two daughters, Elizabeth and Isabel Letitia.

THE VAN GIESEN FAMILY.—One Reynier Bastiaensen Van Giesen, from Giesen, a village in North Brabant, Holland, came to New Amsterdam with his wife, Dircke Cornelis Van Groenland, prior to 1660, and settled at Flatbush, L. I. He was a schoolmaster, and the first one at Flatbush, as appears from an agreement dated June 6, 1660, which he signed between himself and the consistory of the Dutch Church of Flatbush. He resided at Flatbush in a house which he sold in January, 1663, and was an officer in attendance upon the court. From Flatbush he went to Bergen, and from thence to Hackensack, where, in September, 1699, he married his second wife, Hendrickie Buys, of Bergen. At this time he had dropped the Bastians from his name. His issue were John; Jacob, 1670; Gysbertie, 1673; Bastianse, Abraham, Henry, Isaac, Rynier, Isaac, and perhaps daughters. Of these Isaac married Hillegond Claesen Cooper and Anna Breyand. Henry married Sara Romeyn. Rynier married a Van Dien. All these settled at Hackensack, and later their descendants settled in the western part of Bergen County, where the name is now common.

THE VAN SAUN FAMILY.—The Van Sauns are a numerous family to-day in Bergen County. Jacob Van Zauwen came to America in 1677 and settled at New Amsterdam. There, the following year, he married Jennetie Lucas. The entry of this marriage discloses the fact that the groom was a native of Ransdorp in Holland.

One of his sons, Jacob Van Saen (as he wrote it), born in New Amsterdam about 1683, went to Hackensack in 1705, and married Rachel Bogert. He purchased lands in the Paramus district of Bergen County, where he finally settled. He and his wife joined the Hackensack Dutch Church in 1726. His issue were Jacob, 1706; John, 1709; John, 1711; Jannetie,

1714; Isaac, 1717; Angenitie, 1719; Lucas, 1722; and a daughter, 1725. These intermarried with the Bantas, Demarests, Goetschius, and other families, and scattered over the Counties of Bergen and Passaic.

FREDERICK W. HORSTMAN, of East Newark, Hudson County, was born in Newark, N. J., on the 9th of January, 1843. He is the son of Henry Horstman (son of William and Margaret Horstman), a native of Hanover, Germany, who came to America in 1837 and settled in Newark, where he was married in 1841 to Wilhelmina Luderson, daughter of Frederick Luderson, and where he spent the remainder of his life as a manufacturer of steel springs.

Mr. Horstman received a thorough public school education in his native city, and at an early age learned the machinist's trade. On Lincoln's first call for troops in 1861 he enlisted in Company E, First New Jersey Volunteer Infantry, in which he served three months, when he was honorably discharged. He subsequently associated himself with the firm of Hughes & Phillips, manufacturers of machinery, of Newark, N. J., with whom he remained thirty years, being foreman of their establishment during twenty years of that period. In politics Mr. Horstman is an ardent and consistent Democrat. He has for many years taken an active part in the affairs of the community, having served as Town Committeeman and as a member of the School Board of the Town of Kearny—a part of which now comprises the Borough of East Newark, of which he is at the present time Borough Recorder. He is a member of the Masonic fraternity and of the Knights of Honor, an honorary member of the Aurora Singing Society of Newark, and President of the People's Building and Loan Association, with which he has been actively identified for more than twenty-seven years. Mr. Horstman is a public spirited, enterprising, and progressive citizen, has filled every position with acknowledged ability and satisfaction, and is highly respected by all who know him. He has always enjoyed the entire confidence of the community, and in both business and public capacities has achieved an excellent reputation.

FREDERICK W. HORSTMAN.

Mr. Horstman's wife, Bertha Meis, whom he married in Newark, N. J., came from Germany in 1865. Their children are Henry J., Frederick W., Jr., Bertha, Ida, Julia, Minnie, Sophia, Grace, and Franklin G. The family reside in the Borough of East Newark.

THE VAN VOORST FAMILY.—The first American of the Van Voorsts, of Bergen and Hudson Counties, was Cornelius Van Vorst, who came to America between 1634 and 1636, as is supposed, from the little town of Voorst, in the Province of Gelderland, Holland, near the River Yssel; but as there was a town of the same name in the Province of Antwerp, in Belgium, there is some doubt about Van Voorst's birthplace. He arrived at Bergen (while the Lord of Achtienhoven was still the patron of Pavonia, and Wouter Van Twiller, Director-General of New Netherlands), and settled at Ahasimus. The evidence makes it likely that before his advent at Ahasimus he was engaged in commerce between Holland and the New Netherlands. He appeared at Pavonia in 1636 as superintendent of Michael Pauw's plantation at Pavonia. The name of his first wife does not appear, but his second wife's name was Vroutie Ides. He died in the summer of 1638, and she died in the spring of 1641. His issue were Hendrick, John, and Ann, born in Holland, and Ide, born in New York. The latter is reported to have been the first white male child born and married in New Netherlands. Ide was captured by the Indians in 1643 and taken to Tappan, but was ransomed by Captain John de Vries and others. Ide married, October 18, 1652, Hilletie Jans, of Oldenburgh. He resided at Ahasimus, where, as a farmer, he accumulated wealth and eventually became the owner of nearly all of Michael Pauw's domains. He braved the dangers of border life, and exposed himself, his property, and family to attacks by the savages. In 1656 he took refuge in New Amsterdam, but returned to Bergen when peace was restored. Several times he was obliged to flee from the savages. His children of the third generation were Vroutie, Ann, Cornelius, Pietartie, Cornelius, and Joanna. From these are descended the Van Vorsts of Bergen and Hudson Counties.

THE VAN ORDEN (VAN NAERDEN) FAMILY is said to have originated at Naerden, a town in North Holland, from whence, as early as 1639, one Claes Jansen Ruyter emigrated to America. The surname Ruyter was bestowed on him because he was, as the name signifies, a good horseman. His children dropped the "Ruyter" and went by the name of Jansen. He and his wife, Pietertie Jans, are said to have gone first to Esopus, but, not liking that locality, located at Brooklyn, where in 1645 Claes bought 42 acres of land adjoining the farm of Peter Van Delinde. Claes was an Indian interpreter in 1660. His son, Claes Jansen, married in New York in 1676 Cornelia Williams, of Esopus. He was then registered as being from Esopus. By his two wives he had a large family of children.

Claes's son John married and reared a large family, among whom were Andries (Andrew), Albert, and Adam. These came to Hackensack about 1700, where, on August 31, of that year, Andries married Rachel, eldest daughter of David Demarest (2), by whom he had a son, John. Rachel Demarest died in 1708, and Andries married, August 12, 1710, Antie la Roux, a granddaughter of Jaques la Roux, the emigrant. Andries's children were Jacobus, Elizabeth, Jannetie, Peter, and Wybrig. Albert, brother of Andries, married in 1717 Margaret Mattys, of Hackensack, by whom he had issue. Many of the children of Andries and Albert settled on lands now in Washington, Midland, and Hohokus Townships, where the name is frequently met with to-day.

EDWARD McDERMOTT, for more than twelve years a leading architect and builder of North Hudson County, was born July 31, 1866, in West Hoboken, N. J., where he has always resided. He is the son of John McDermott and Elizabeth McClure. He received his education in the West Hoboken public schools, and after completing his studies turned his attention to architecture, for which he had decided taste. Having gained a prac-

EDWARD McDERMOTT.

tical as well as a theoretical knowledge of the profession, he opened an office for the active practice of architecture in West Hoboken, in 1886, and through his ability and skill has gained an extensive business. He has designed and erected many of the finer structures, including numerous dwellings, in the northern part of Hudson County. His work shows great originality, broad professional knowledge, and marked artistic taste, as well as a thorough comprehension of structural problems. His success is the result of his own efforts.

Mr. McDermott has also been active and influential in public affairs, filling several positions with the same ability and satisfaction which have characterized his professional career. Elected a member in 1890 and Treasurer in 1891 of the Board of Fire Trustees of West Hoboken, and Tax Assessor of the town in 1892, he still holds the latter office, discharging his duties with ability, faithfulness, and honor. He is a member of Cosmopolitan Lodge, No. 351, I. O. O. F.

THE VAN WAGENEN AND GARRETSEN FAMILIES.—Garret Gerretsen was a native of Wageningen, an ancient town near the Rhine River, and about ten miles west of Arnheim in Gelderland, Holland. This town stood on marshy ground, was walled, and was a place of considerable strength during the Thirty Years' War. Garret Gerretsen left his native town with his wife, Annetie Hermanse, and child, Gerret (then two years old), in November, 1660, on the ship "Faith" (commanded by skipper Jan Bestevaer), and reached New Amsterdam on December 23, following. The fare for himself and family was ninety florins. Gerretsen brought with him a certificate of the mayor and scheppens of his native town that he and his wife "have always been considered and esteemed as pious and honest people, and that no complaint of any civil or disorderly conduct has ever reached their ears." Gerretsen went to Bergen, where, on May 12, 1668, he bought of Philip Carteret eight parcels of land in the Town of Bergen. He resided in what is now the Communipaw section of Jersey City, where he died, in October, 1696. His wife died September 7, 1696. His issue were seven children: Garret, Jannetie, Sophia, Herman, Aeltie, Henry, and John.

Some of these took the name of Van Wagenen, while others retained that of Gerretsen, from the name of their father. Garret Gerretsen's descendants, going by the surname of Garretson, Garrison, Van Wagenen, and Van Wagner, are to-day numerous throughout Bergen and Hudson Counties. One of them is Hon. Abram Q. Garretson, just (1900) appointed Associate Justice of the New Jersey Supreme Court.

THE VAN WINKLE FAMILY.—Mr. Winfield has written in reference to the origin of this family: "This name is derived from *winkel*, a corner, square, shop. Winkelier was a shopkeeper. The ancestor was a shop or storekeeper. Its present orthography is comparatively modern. The family settled at Harsimus shortly after their arrival in this country. They came from Middleburgh, the capital of the Province of Zealand, in Holland. This city was on the Island of Walcheron, about forty miles southwest of Rotterdam, well built and populous, with a fine harbor and a prosperous trade.

"I have not ascertained the names of the parents of the three boys and two girls who seem to have made up this family. Their names were Jacob, Waling, Symon, Annetie, and Grietie; their patronymic being Jacobse—children of Jacob. Jacob was the founder of the family in Hudson County. Waling and Symon were of the company from Bergen who, in 1679, purchased and afterward settled 'Haquequenunck,' Aquackenonck, now Passaic." They were the founders of the family in New Jersey, and their descendants are very numerous in the western part of Bergen County as well as in Hudson County. Jacob's son Jacob married Egie Paulis in 1702, and Symon's son married Antie Saunders in 1703. Both of these settled at Hackensack, and so spread the family name through the central parts of Bergen County.

GENEALOGICAL

THE WHITE FAMILY in the northern part of Bergen County are descended from a family of shepherds, for many generations located near Avon, and not far from Bristol, in Somersetshire, England. Here William White was born in 1735 and his wife, Mary, in 1739. William was reared in the calling of his ancestors, and married in 1762. They were hard-working, industrious people. William's wife died in 1792, and he survived her until 1802. Their issue of the second generation were eight children, all born near Bristol: Ann, October, 23, 1763; Isaac, November 17, 1769; George, March 24, 1771; James, September 17, 1774; Thomas, December 20, 1775; Benjamin, 1777; Jonas; and Solomon, December 23, 1781.

Ann (2) married William Tucker and, emigrating to America, settled in Canada, where she died, leaving children: Solomon, Mary, Jacob, Ann Maria, George, Jonas, Joseph, Esau, Harriet, and Benjamin, whose numerous descendants abound in Southern Canada. George (2) served twenty-one years in the British Army, and was severely wounded. Thomas (2) came to America and married. He died October 6, 1823, and his wife, Maria, followed him September 13, 1836. Solomon (2) died, aged twenty-three, unmarried. All the others except Jonas (2) remained in England. Jonas (2), born near Bristol, November 3, 1779, came to America in 1822, and located on "The Flatts," in what is now Palisade Township, Bergen County, N. J., where he married, December 24, 1808, Mary (daughter of Peter Lozier), who was born at Schraalenburgh, July 19, 1778. She dying a few years later, he married (2) Jane Westervelt (widow). He bought lands at "The Flatts," where he spent his time farming until late in life, when he removed to New York, where he died May 10, 1856. His issue of the third generation by his first wife were William, 1814 (died); Mary, 1818 (died); and Peter J.; and, by his second wife, William.

Peter J. White (3) was born at "The Flatts," February 17, 1812. His occupation was always that of a farmer. Until his marriage he resided at "The Flatts." The rest of his days were spent at Closter, where he died, January 28, 1895. He married, March 10, 1841, Sarah (daughter of Abraham J. Zabriskie and Susanna Helms), born at Paramus, May 28, 1806, died at Closter, N. J., October 16, 1875. Their issue of the fourth generation were David S., July 25, 1842; Charity, May 3, 1845; Mary Frances, October 29, 1848; and Lydia Zabriskie, January 24, 1852. These all have children of the fifth generation.

Though a farmer by occupation, Mr. White was for many years foremost in the development of the religious, educational, and material interests of the community in which he lived. In 1862 he organized the first church at Closter (Reformed), in which he was for some time an officer and member, giving liberally to its maintenance and to the support of the minister, Rev. Eben S. Hammond. The latter was a sturdy and outspoken Unionist in a congregation in which anti-war sentiment predominated. Mr. Hammond's advocacy of the war made him enemies, and in the end he was compelled to retire. Mr. White and his wife, an active and energetic woman, supported the clergyman to the end, and, on the latter's retirement, transferred their membership to the North Church at Schraalenburgh. Both strongly upheld the Union cause, and their only son served a term in the Union Army. Mr. White took a lively interest in public improvements, and, in 1865-66, was instrumental in having several new roads laid out and opened in Harrington Township. To the cause of public education he was a liberal patron. He gave his children the best educational advantages. His family were at all times the friends and defenders of schools and school teachers. He was generous and hospitable almost to a fault, for which reason he was often imposed upon by those whose motives were purely selfish.

JOHN W. ROCHE, of Kearny, Hudson County, was born in Elizabeth, N. J., May 17, 1863, and is the son of John and Ellen (Dorran) Roche, and a grandson of John and Martha (Crawford) Roche and of Simon and Mary (Forestel) Dorran, all natives of Ireland. His parents came to America in 1861 and settled in Elizabeth, where his father died in 1894. His mother still survives and resides in Kearny.

JOHN W. ROCHE.

Mr. Roche was educated in the schools of Elizabeth, where he resided until he was sixteen years old, when he removed with his parents to Kearny. As a boy he served his time as a machine moulder, and continued in that avocation until about the year 1887, when he engaged in the hotel business. In 1889 he built his present hotel, the Windsor House, at 345 Kearny Avenue, in Kearny, a commodious structure of three stories Under his management that well-known hotel has had a prosperous and successful career.

Aside from his business connections Mr. Roche has for a number of years taken an active and leading part in public affairs, and from its organization until 1897 was a member of the New Jersey Naval Reserve. In politics he is a Democrat. He has served as a member of the Democratic County Committee of Hudson County, and in 1898 was the regular party nominee for Freeholder, but being in a district where the Republicans have a nominal majority of over 700 he was defeated by about 50 votes. He is a member of the Red Men and Foresters, active and progressive in the affairs of the community, and prominently identified with many public movements.

Mr. Roche married Delia C. Smith, daughter of Owen Smith, and by her has had eight children: John and James, both deceased, and Catherine, Helen, Thomas, Margaret, Mary, and John, who are living.

HERMAN WALKER, Mayor of the Town of Guttenberg, is one of the most prominent citizens of Hudson County, N. J. This is true alike of his business career and influence, and of his activity in political and public life. Since 1878 he has been extensively engaged in the real estate business, acquiring property throughout Northern Hudson and Southern Bergen Counties. He became chief owner of such well known tracts of land as Highwood Park, Eldorado, Grand View, Hudson Heights, Bergenwood Park, Cliffside Park, and others, having just taken title to the Van Vorst tract in West New York, containing 345 lots. He was chiefly active in the creation of what now constitutes the choicest section of Union Township. He was President of Eldorado, the famous amusement resort, and was one of its originators and second largest stockholder. He is President of the North Hudson Land Company, of the New York and Rochester Steel Mat Company, and of the Hudson View Land Company. He is an officer and stockholder in many more corporations. In 1890-91 he was Vice-President of the New Jersey State Firemen's Association. He is a member of the Union League Club and other organizations.

Mr. Walker is one of the most influential leaders of the Republican party in Hudson County. He has been a delegate to nearly every New Jersey Republican State Convention since 1871, and for twenty years he has been a member of the Hudson County Republican General Committee. As the candidate of the Republican party and Jeffersonian Democrats for County Clerk of Hudson County in 1889 he was rightfully elected, but was one of those who were defrauded by the notable election frauds of that year. In Democratic Guttenberg, however, his popularity is such that he has never failed of election to any of the many offices for which he has been a candidate. In 1878 he was Assessor and Clerk of the Joint Committee to set off the Town of Guttenberg from the Township of Union. From 1878 to April, 1886, he was Town Clerk of Guttenberg. From 1881 to 1886 he was Town Recorder, and again, from 1888 to 1895, held the same office. He was a member of the Board of Councilmen in 1886, 1887, 1897, and 1898, and held the position of Chairman of the board in 1886 and again in 1897 and 1898. He was Justice of the Peace from 1879 to 1899, and as Chairman of the Board of Councilmen is by courtesy called Mayor.

The son of Frederick and Barbara Walker, natives of Germany, Mr. Walker was himself born in New York City, April 21, 1850. He attended the schools of New York City and Guttenberg—his parents having removed to the latter place in 1860—until he was fourteen years of age, when he entered the office of his father, who conducted in New York a successful business as a manufacturer. At seventeen years of age Mr. Walker assumed the management of this business, in which he showed marked ability. He began investing in real estate in Hudson and Bergen Counties, however, and since 1878 has devoted himself exclusively to this business. On August 26, 1875, he married, at Guttenberg, Diana H., daughter of John and Diana Behrens, and has four sons and two daughters.

Throughout his business career Mr. Walker has exhibited a remarkably progressive and enterprising spirit, and has been active in securing and suggesting the execution of projects of great public interest. He conceived the plan of preserving the Palisades by the construction of a grand boulevard along the entire edge of the bluff, making the most magnificent driveway in the world. He also conceived the plan of the consolidation into one large municipality of the various towns and villages in Northern Hudson and Southern Bergen Counties. He was one of the large donators of land for the building of the present loop of the County Road, under the act requiring a donation of two-thirds of the right of way before the work could be undertaken. At his suggestion the route was changed so as to pass through Highwood Park, instead of through West Hoboken, as originally contemplated. Some time ago he acquired a brewery in Guttenberg, with thirteen lots and buildings, which had been inactive for several years, but through his efforts a New York syndicate was formed and the plant sold to a stock company and is now successfully operated.

JOHN J. WESTERVELT is descended in the seventh generation from Lubbert Lubbertsen (Von Westervelt), who with his wife and children left their home at Mepple, in the Province of Drenthe, Holland, and emigrated to America on board the ship "Hope" in April, 1662 (see page 99).

John J. Westervelt is the grandson of Peter and Matilda Westervelt, and a son of James P. Westervelt and Margaret Demarest, daughter of John Demarest. He was born at West Woodcliff, N. J., October 14, 1829, and obtained his education in the schools of Bergen County. He left school at the age of thirteen and went to work on his father's farm, where he remained until he attained his majority. He then engaged in the trucking business in New York and so continued until he reached the age of forty-six, when he returned to Bergen County and has since devoted himself to agricultural pursuits. He is one of the best farmers in his section, a member of the Dutch Reformed Church, and honored and respected by the entire community.

He has been twice married, first to Helen Ely, who died in 1878, leaving two children: Margaret and John. In 1884 he married, for his second wife, Margaret Brinkerhoff, a member of an old New Jersey family.

MAURICE J. STACK, County Clerk of Hudson County, was born in Hoboken, N. J., May 20, 1865, and has lived there all his life. He attended the public schools in that city and sold newspapers during much of his boyhood.

Mr. Stack was appointed a patrolman in the Hoboken Police Department July 1, 1886, when only twenty-one years old. In 1890 he was promoted to be a roundsman. Two years later he was made a sergeant. In December, 1892, at the request of the late Prosecutor Charles H. Winfield, the Hoboken Board of Police Commissioners detailed Mr. Stack as a detective in the Prosecutor's office to take the place of Mayor E. R. Stanton, of Hoboken, who gave up the position as Prosecutor's detective when appointed Sheriff

GENEALOGICAL 251

of Hudson County to fill the vacancy caused by the death of Sheriff John McPhillips. Mr. Stack continued as Prosecutor's detective until the death of Mr. Winfield. In 1899 he was elected County Clerk of Hudson County and has filled that office with characteristic ability and satisfaction. He has three children—two sons and a daughter.

EDWIN RAYNOR CASE has been a life-long resident of Jersey City, Hudson County, where he was born on the 7th of April, 1855. He is the son of Menzies Raynor Case and Amanda Malvina Coon, a grandson of

MENZIES R. CASE.

Moses and Charlotte (Miller) Case and of Samuel and Hannah (Negus) Coon, a great-grandson of Josiah Case and Robert Negus, and a lineal descendant of John Case, who came from England and settled in Simsbury, Conn., in 1650. He is also a direct descendant on the maternal side of Anne Hathaway and of Commodore Perry, his great-grandmother, the wife of Robert Negus, being a Perry. Mr. Case's father was director of the Jersey City Board of Education for five terms, his associates in the board, during that time, being Joseph McCoy, James L. Davenport, and A. S. Jewell. He was also, for sixteen years, superintendent of Old Trinity M. E. Sunday School in York Street.

Edwin R. Case was educated at Public Schools Nos. 1 and 13, in Jersey City, and at Hasbrouck Classical and Commercial Institute, which he left in January, 1872, to engage in the tea brokerage business with his father. He continued in that employment until September 10, 1873, and from that time until November 1, 1899, was associated with the People's Gas Light Company of Jersey City, first as a clerk and from October 12, 1880, to October 31, 1899, as Secretary and Treasurer of the company. From the leasing of the gas company to the United Gas Improvement Company,

EDWIN R. CASE.

in September, 1886, to the present time, he has been engaged in the stock and bond brokerage business.

Mr. Case has been a member of the Jersey City Club since 1884, and is also a member of Unique Council, No. 434, Royal Arcanum, and of Vigilant Council, No. 43, Loyal Additional Benefit Association. He is public spirited, active and influential in the community, a man of superior business ability and sound judgment, and highly respected by all who know him.

September 25, 1876, Mr. Case married Emily Fay Hoyt, and they have had three children: Caroline Hoyt Case, Edwin Raynor Case, deceased, and Herbert Hoyt Case.

Add to sketch of Edwin Raynor Case, pages 251-252, the following:

Mr. Case is President and Director of the Fidelity Gas Light Company of Hoosic Falls, N. Y., of the Monroe County Gas Company of Stroudsburg, Pa., and of the New Paltz and Poughkeepsie Traction Company of New Paltz, N. Y. He is also Trustee of the Lakewood (N. J.) Gas Company.

HAMILTON WALLIS, one of the leading members of the New York and Hudson County bars, was born in New York City on the 25th of November, 1842. He is the son of Alexander Hamilton Wallis and Elizabeth Geib, a grandson of John and Mary Ann (Geib) Wallis and of John and Margaret (Lawrence) Geib, and a great-grandson of Joseph and Sarah (Tatterson) Wallis, of John and Rebecca (Shrimpton) Geib, and of Thomas Lawrence, whose wife was a Bogardus, a descendant of "Dominie" Bogardus, the first Dutch minister in New Amsterdam. Joseph Wallis, John Geib, Jr., and Mary Ann Geib were natives of England, the first reaching this country about 1775 and the latter two in 1797. John Geib, Sr., was a native of Staudernheim, Germany. Alexander Hamilton Wallis was President of the First National Bank of Jersey City and was a well known New York lawyer before his removal to Jersey City more than half a century ago. He served as a member of the Jersey City Board of Aldermen and was twice United States Collector of Internal Revenue for the Fifth District of New Jersey.

Hamilton Wallis received his preliminary and preparatory education under the tutorship of W. L. Dickinson, at public school No. 1, and in Hasbrouck Institute, all in Jersey City. He subsequently studied under Charles M. Davis, of Bloomfield, N. J., and under Rev. Samuel Jones, of Bridgeport, Conn., and entering Yale College was graduated from that institution in 1863. He took a course at the Columbia College Law School, graduating with the degree of LL.B., and was admitted to the bar of New York in May, 1865. He was admitted to practice as an attorney in New Jersey in February, 1875, and as a counselor in November, 1878, and is also a member of the bar of the Supreme Court of the United States.

Mr. Wallis has practiced his profession in New York City ever since his admission to the bar there in 1865, and has also had an office in Jersey City since 1875. His rise in the profession was steady and rapid. He early displayed legal abilities of the highest order, and before a court and jury as well as in office work exhibited those striking characteristics which mark the successful lawyer. Possessed of sound judgment, great force of character, and wonderful intellectual capacity, he has been connected with some of the most important litigations in the courts of New York and New Jersey, and the many victories he has won stamp him as an attorney and counselor of unusual ability. In New York he is a member of the well known firm of Wilson & Wallis, and in Jersey City is senior member of the firm of Wallis, Edwards & Bumsted.

While Mr. Wallis has always taken a deep interest in public and political affairs and in all questions which affect the welfare of his city, State, and Nation, he has never sought nor accepted political office, preferring to devote his entire time and energy to the practice of his profession. As a citizen, however, he has long wielded an important influence upon all public matters, and is universally esteemed and respected. He has achieved a wide reputation as an able, conscientious, and reliable lawyer, and through his many excellent qualities has always had the confidence and respect of all who know him. He is a member of the Down Town Association of New York City, of the Carteret Club of Jersey City, and of the Lake Hopatcong Club of New Jersey. He is also a distinguished member of the Lodge of the Temple, No. 110, F. and A. M., of Jersey City, of which he was Worshipful Master in 1873. He was Grand Master of Masons in New Jersey in the years 1879 and 1880, and in these important official capacities has rendered valuable service to the fraternity in the State. He is

President of the Board of Trustees of the Brick Presbyterian Church of East Orange, N. J., and to the duties of all these positions he has brought the same ability and integrity which have contributed so largely to his success and eminence at the bar.

Mr. Wallis was married on the 13th of October, 1868, to Alice Waldron, and their children are Emeline Waldron (Wallis) Dunn, Alexander Hamilton Wallis, Nathaniel Waldron Wallis, and Clinton Geib Wallis.

CHARLES DE CLYNE, until his death a leading citizen of Hudson County, and the father of Gustave and Emil de Clyne, prominent business men of New Durham in the same county, was born in Schwarzburg, Sonderschausen, Saxony, June 24, 1821, and died at his residence in New Durham, N. J., November 5, 1886. He was the eldest of five brothers,—Charles, Theodore, William, Frederick, and John,—who were the sons of George de Clyne and Dorothea Teschner, both natives of Schwarzburg, Saxony. George de Clyne followed the business of an agriculturist and was inspector of a large estate. He was, in turn, the son of Albert de Clyne, a farmer, who was at one time Burgomaster of Schwarzburg, and who was the descendant of a Huguenot family which fled from France on the revocation of the Edict of Nantes, one branch of it settling at Schwarzburg, Saxony.

Charles de Clyne received his education in a school of forestry, becoming proficient as a civil engineer, mineralogist, and botanist. Following his course at this school, he also continued his studies under private tutelage. Like Carl Schurz, Oswald Ottendorfer, and other liberty-loving Germans, he became involved in the revolutionary movement of 1848 and was compelled to flee. He came to America, but soon after re-crossed the ocean for a sojourn in France. During this visit he was impressed by the superiority of the Belgian pavement, and securing a contract for its introduction in New York City, returned to America. He failed to realize from this project through complications with a partner, although the pavement was subsequently introduced in New York. He then entered upon the study of chemistry with the celebrated Dr. Liebig, and was so engaged when the Civil War began. He at once enlisted in the New York State volunteers as a member of the Third Battalion (artillery), which was subsequently re-organized as the Fifteenth Regiment Heavy Artillery. He remained in the service until the close of the war, taking part in many actions. He was commissioned Lieutenant and assigned to the staff of General Thomas D. Doubleday; subsequently he was commissioned Captain, and by General Halleck was appointed Inspector-General of defenses south of the Potomac.

Upon the termination of the Rebellion he established a large manufactory of glue in Hudson County, N. J., which is still owned and conducted by his family. While an active member of the Republican party, he refused to become a candidate for public office, holding only some such unremunerative trusts of honor as school trustee, etc. He established his residence at New Durham.

December 13, 1855, he married Helen, daughter of Christian Klien, of North Bergen, Hudson County. Their children were Caroline (who became Mrs. Abram Kittel), born October 25, 1856; Theodore, born November 26, 1857; Gustavus, born December 29, 1858; Emma, born March 31, 1861, who married Thomas Alcorn, of New Durham; Helen, born August 20, 1866, who married John Henry Outwater, of Washington Grove, Bergen County; and Emil and Clara (twins), born May 15, 1869. Clara, the last named, married

Francis A. Kilgour, of Passaic, N. J. Of the three sons, Theodore, a graduate of Columbia College, is a veterinary surgeon, while Gustavus and Emil conduct the large business established by their father.

Upon the death of their father in November, 1886, the brothers Gustavus and Emil de Clyne assumed the active management of the manufactory, and under their supervision it has grown to be one of the largest and most successful concerns manufacturing sizing and gold gum in the country. They have two plants, one being located in New Durham and the other in Homestead. The former is a familiar landmark of North Bergen and comprises several large buildings, covering a floor area of over 50,000 square feet. That at Homestead was established by them in 1897 for the purpose of grinding mica and has been a great success.

WILLIAM THOMPSON, a prominent resident of Marion, Hudson County, and President of the New York Pie Baking Company, of New York City, was born in Goshen, Orange County, N. Y., February 19, 1826, his parents being James A. Thompson and Catherine Kay. The Thompsons were originally from Ireland, emigrating to America at the time of the religious rebellion, settling first in Orange County, N. Y., subsequently removing to Long Island, and finally locating in Bedford, Westchester County, N. Y. They have been engaged in farming and dairying for several generations. The Kay family, his mother's ancestors, came to this country from Scotland.

Mr. Thompson was educated in the old Brick Church which stood on the site of the present *Tribune* building in New York City, and well remembers that locality as it is now portrayed in history. He also attended Horace Greeley's free lectures. At the age of thirteen he left home under very adverse circumstances, with nothing but a will and determination to succeed, finding himself in New York City without a cent. He obtained employment in a bakery, where he worked for five years and thoroughly mastered the business. When eighteen years old he started on his own account in the baking business, with which he has ever since been identified. His career in this line of industry has been an eminently successful one and stamps him as a man of unusual ability, of great force of character, and possessed of that self-reliance and perseverance which characterize the man of affairs. In 1872 he organized the business now conducted at 82 Sullivan Street, New York City, by the widely known New York Pie Baking Company, of which he is President. This extensive establishment employs one hundred and fifty people and sixty horses, has a capacity of producing from eighteen to twenty thousand pies daily, and is a model in its workings in every respect. It is the largest pie baking establishment in the United States, and under Mr. Thompson's able and energetic management has achieved a phenomenal success as well as a prominent place among the leading manufacturing institutions of New York City.

In this connection James M. Gray, M.D., writing in the *American Journal of Health*, published in New York, says:

"The average home-made pie, owing to improper equipment and lacking facilities, is almost invariably a disease breeder instead of a health help. The pies offered by some of the smaller bakers as evidence of their constructive ability are even worse as a rule. In every large city, fortunately, there are large concerns which have reduced pie-making to an exact science and whose product is not only appetizing, but is deserving of all praise from a health standpoint. The New York Pie Baking Company of this city is a fitting example to illustrate the point in question. This house possesses every facility, every convenience, and every advantage necessary to the production of an article for household consumption which is above criticism. Their establishment is a model of cleanliness, and as they use only the finest grades of high-priced flour and richest and purest milk, cream, and lard obtainable, and combining these with fruits and berries of most superior quality, it naturally follows that the product is all that could be desired by either the epicure or the hygienist.

"There may be, and probably are, in other cities throughout the coun-

WILLIAM THOMPSON.

try, manufacturers whose goods are as wholesome as the New York Pie Baking Company's pies, but a most searching investigation of this special product enables us to write advisedly concerning its merits as a health food."

A. N. Talley, Jr., M.D., in an article in the *United States Health Reports* for August 1, 1899, says:

"The evolution and development of the American pie, like all great industries, has created a positive demand for a standard of excellence, both intrinsically and commercially, Americans being satisfied only with the best of everything. This demand has been ably filled by the New York Pie Baking Company, of No. 82 Sullivan Street, New York City, who have established the reputation, justly deserved, of producing the best and greatest number of pies of any firm in the United States.

"In the rigid inspection and examination made by our experts great care was taken to thoroughly note the physical environments and hygienic conditions of the entire plant and establishment of the company, all of which were found to be in the highest possible state of cleanliness, with the added fact of complete compliance with all sanitary requirements.

"The final reports of our experts have been compiled and unanimously approved by our medical staff, showing so high a grade of merit that we are pleased to extend to the product of the New York Pie Baking Company, for the protection of patrons, the official recognition of the *United States Health Reports*."

Mr. Thompson's vast fund of reminiscence is well known. A most interesting article in a recent number of the *Hotel and Restaurant Magazine*, entitled "Reminiscences of New York in the Forties; Gleaned from an Interview with One of the Most Prominent Business Men in the Metropolis," contains this allusion to his ability to recall past events:

"He who wishes to spend a profitable and interesting hour knows full well that the reminiscent conversation of the old resident has a special zest in which the present is linked with the past, and the institutions of the day contrasted with those of former times. In a recent conversation with Mr. William Thompson, well known to the New York business public as the President of the New York Pie Baking Company, the writer was entertained for several hours with a graphic portrayal of incidents in Mr. Thompson's experience back in the forties. Unhappily, written language fails to give the inflections of verbal narration; it fails also to portray the expression of the features when the mind of the narrator is recalling the events of half a century past. The reader can assist in obtaining a clearer comprehension of these reminiscences if he will give free vent to his imagination and draw a mental picture of Mr. Thompson, a hale and hearty gentleman, although seventy years of age, sitting in his cozy office with a far-away look in his eyes, living over again, as it were, the days that are gone. As recollections crowded each other for utterance his countenance would glow with enthusiasm in the one moment and be saddened in the next as he referred to companions who have passed away. Being requested to give some of the factors which entered into his notable business success, he said: Perhaps the most valuable factor in my success was the experience back in the forties. At that time there was a great rivalry among pie-baking establishments—every one was trying to obtain the reputation of making the best old-fashioned pie. The public was a critical one, and a good pie was in great demand. I entered into the business contest with vim and started an establishment, on a much smaller scale, of course, upon the site we now occupy. There was one bridge which carried me to success, and I have never forgotten that it is essential to keep in mind that fact in order to continually maintain our supremacy in the pie business. That bridge was first-class material. I personally purchased and inspected every ingredient which entered into a pie, and under no consideration would I permit any adulterated products or second grade goods to enter my doors. I gave close attention to the minutest details. Those who bought our pies knew they could thoroughly rely upon every pie at all times, and that no effort to secure trade by a good article and then afterward furnish an inferior grade would be made. The best testimonial to the ironclad rule, ' never to have one inferior pie leave our doors' is contained in the fact that Dolan—you know him, of course—of P. Dolan & Nephew, and also Hitchcock, of Oliver Hitchcock & Son, have been my customers for forty years. Well, of course, if anybody in New York ought to be good judges of things to eat, then Dolan and Hitchcock are those men, as the public fully knows.

"Another factor which has aided materially in our success is the fact that our large patrons, when visiting this establishment, are at perfect liberty at any and all times to go through the various departments—we have no special ' exhibit ' days, when extra clean utensils, floors, etc., are put forward for inspection; every day is inspection day, for every employee knows full well that scrupulous cleanliness is a rule that can not be infringed upon more than once."

In politics Mr. Thompson has always been a Republican. Deeply interested in the affairs of his country and prominent as a citizen and business man, he is especially well informed upon almost every current topic. He is a life member and was one of the founders of the Carteret Club of Jersey City, and is also a member of New York Lodge, No. 330, A. F. and A. M.

In 1866 Mr. Thompson married Matilda Robinson, by whom he has had six children: James A., William, Lydia Ann, Matilda, Rachel (deceased), and Catherine.

GEORGE W. BLAWVELT is descended in the seventh generation from Gerret Hendricksen (Blawvelt), the emigrant, and the progenitor of all the family in New Jersey. His parents were Isaac Blawvelt and Mary, daughter of John Hopper, and his grandparents were Cornelius Blawvelt and Mary Lydecker. He was born on Staten Island, N. Y., February 9, 1847, but removed to Bergen County when young, and there received his education. At an early age he entered the employ of the well known dry goods house of Lord & Taylor, of New York City. Subsequently he engaged in the general trucking business in New York for James Ackerman, in which he continued until 1875, when he established himself in the sugar and molasses trade. In this line he remained until 1895, when he retired, and has since been engaged in the real estate business at Ridgewood, N. J., where he resides.

Mr. Blawvelt has achieved success in every business relation, and during his entire career has enjoyed the confidence and respect of all who know him. He is a public spirited citizen, a Mason, a member of the Knights of Honor, and a member of the Methodist Episcopal Church. He married Annie E. Chisholm, and of their three children one, Annie, is living.

PETER W. STAGG.—The earliest of this name to settle in Bergen County was John Stagg, who is described as " a young man born at Bergen, East N. Jersey." The Bergen records, however, make no mention of him. His marriage to Mary (daughter of Cornelis Jans Bogert) was registered in the Dutch church at Hackensack, March 14, 1697. The marriage of William Stegg, described as " a young man born at New Barbadoes Neck," was to Magdalena Peters Demarest, registered in the same church, October 23, 1697. John and William were probably brothers, but where they came from does not appear. The New York church records throw no light upon the question. John's wife must have died soon after their marriage, as

GENEALOGICAL 259

on November 26, 1698, his marriage to Cornelia Verwey was registered. By his first wife he had no issue, but by Cornelia Verwey he had issue Thomas, 1703; Margaretta, 1710; Isaac, 1712; Jacob, 1715; George, 1717; and William, 1719. There were probably others whose baptisms were not noted on any record.

The record shows that William Stegg and Magdalena Peters Demarest had only one child, Magdalena, born in 1723, but he had a daughter, Elizabeth, who married John Ackerman at Schraalenburgh in 1728. John and William Stegg (Stagg) settled in the vicinity (south) of Hackensack on parts of the Berry tract. Abram Stagg, of Hackensack, settled at Schraalenburgh when he married Maritie Bogert in June, 1732. It was his brother (probably), Cornelius Stagg, a widower, of New Barbadoes, who also settled at Schraalenburgh and married Ann Christie in January, 1734.

It is said that in the start three brothers came to America from Hol-

ESSEX STREET, LOOKING EAST, HACKENSACK.

land, one of whom settled in New York City, another at Sicamac in Bergen County, and a third " went west." However that may be, a John Stagg was known to have settled at Sicamac in Bergen County much more than a century ago, where he married a Miss Van Houten and prospered as a farmer. His son, James Stagg, was born and resided for a time at Wyckoff, Bergen County. He also followed agricultural pursuits. His wife, Sally Westervelt, was born at Tenafly in 1800. The couple eventually moved to Teaneck, where they bought a part of the old Brinckerhoff farm, on which they spent their days. They had issue John, Joseph, James H., Sarah E., and Letty.

John was born in New York City, but was brought up at Teaneck. He married (1) Sally Westervelt and (2) Jane Voorhis. By his first wife his issue were James and Peter W., and by his second wife his issue were Edward, Henry, Jesse, and John, of whom Peter W. is the subject of this sketch.

Peter W. Stagg was born in New York City October 24, 1850. His childhood and early life, however, were spent in Cresskill, N. J., where he attended the public school. In 1875 he went to Jersey City and became a student at law in the office of the late Charles Schofield, and there he remained two years, after which he moved to Hackensack and entered the office of Ackerson & Van Valen, continuing with them until 1879, when he was admitted to the bar at the June term. Immediately after being admitted he opened an office for the practice of his profession, in which he rapidly built up a good business.

At the June term of 1883 he was made a counselor at law. He served as assistant clerk to the House of the Assembly at the sessions of 1891-92, and in 1895 was appointed by Governor Werts as Prosecutor of Bergen County for a term of five years. Prior to the time at which Mr. Stagg became Prosecutor Bergen County had been infested with poolroom and green-goods gangs. These the new Prosecutor drove out, in addition to conducting the ordinary criminal business.

Mr. Stagg is a member of Bergen County Lodge, I. O. O. F., and has been Grand Master of the State of New Jersey, having in 1897 the care and jurisdiction of two hundred and forty-nine lodges in different parts of the State, comprising a membership of 25,000 Odd Fellows. He is also a member of the Fire Patrol. His oldest son, Arthur, was a member of the Second Regiment, New Jersey Volunteers, in the late Spanish War.

Mr. Stagg was married January 14, 1875, to Jennie E. Westervelt, of Bergenfield. His issue are Arthur A. (a law student), Warren H. and Charles W. (both electricians), Elmer, and Harry G.

GEORGE CADMUS.—The Cadmus family are numerous in Hudson and Passaic Counties, New Jersey. Cornelius Cadmus (Cadmuys) was living at Aquackanonck (Passaic) as early as 1718, for the records of the Hackensack Dutch Church register the fact that in April of that year Arientie Cadmus, of Aquackanonck, and Ide Sipp, of Bergen, were married at Hackensack. It is more than likely that Dirk (Richard) Cadmus (who Mr. Winfield thinks was the first of the name in Hudson County) was a son of Cornelius, of Passaic. This Dirk was at Bergen before 1718, for on June 20th of that year he married Jannetje Van Horn. Early in the spring of 1731 he bought of John McEvers and wife a tract of 380 acres of land at Tappan (now in Bergen County), extending from the Hackensack River to the Pascack River. The deed describes him as "Dirck Cadmus of the towne of Bergen." Some or all of it he soon after sold to the Blawvelts, of Tappan. He seems to have remained in Bergen, for in November, 1740, he bought lands of his father-in-law, Van Horn, at Constable's Hook. He died November 8, 1745. He was beyond doubt a Hollander, but when he emigrated or what part of that country he hailed as his birthplace are questions which the early records do not answer. By Jannetje Van Horn he had issue of the second generation Rutgert, Catrina, Frederick, John, Cornelia, and Joris (George). He must have had other children.

Joris Cadmus (2), born at Bergen, married (1) Jannetie Vreeland and (2) Jenneke Prior. She died January 29, 1795, and he died April 2, 1781. Their issue of the third generation were Jannettie, Jannettie, Jannettie, Joris, Metie, Dirck, Casparus, and Jenneke.

Casparus Cadmus (3), born at Bergen, August 16, 1770, died September 23, 1845, married Cathlantie Johns Dodd, born January 27, 1768, and died

October 11, 1822. Their issue of the fourth generation were thirteen: Sara, Joris, John, Casparus, Jannetie, Seeltie, Martha, Martha, Michael, Richard, Cathrina, Andrew, and Eleanor.

Richard Cadmus (4), born November 22, 1803, died October 16, 1873, married Cathaline (daughter of Michael de Mott), died, and had issue of the fifth generation, one of whom was George Cadmus, the subject of this sketch.

George Cadmus (5) was born April 12, 1840, in Bayonne, N. J., where he still resides. He was educated in the schools of Bayonne and Bloomfield, in his native State, and has spent his active life as a farmer. He now lives on the old family homestead at Bayonne. In politics he is a Republican, and in every capacity he has displayed marked ability and won for himself the confidence and respect of his fellow-citizens. He married, first, Cornelia B., daughter of William N. Smith, of New Brunswick, N. J., formerly of New York. She was born October 15, 1839, and died in 1867. They had one child, Henry S. Cadmus, born April 30, 1865, died February 1, 1867. Mr. Cadmus married, second, June 11, 1889, Mrs. Lillie A. (Jones) Abbott, of Bayonne, and has two children of the sixth generation, namely: Clarence W. and May.

DANIEL DRAKE BRYAN was born in New York City on the 2d of December, 1864. He is the son of James H. and Nancy (Hall) Drake, his father being of English and his mother of Holland Dutch descent.

Mr. Bryan was educated in the public schools of New York, and has spent the most of his active life in the custom house brokerage business in that city. He is a Republican in politics, a member of the Royal Arcanum, and a public spirited citizen. In Arlington, N. J., where he resides, he has taken a deep interest in local affairs, and in both business and social relations is highly esteemed as a man of integrity and enterprise.

He married Mary Hay Berry, of New York City, and has one child, Edna Drake Bryan.

DARIUS S. JOHNSON is of English descent. Forty years ago John P. Johnson went from New York (where he was born October 8, 1819) to Pascack (now Park Ridge in Bergen County) and established a passenger stage line between Pascack and Closter. This he operated successfully until the construction of the New York and New Jersey and the West Shore Railway lines did away with all cross-country stage lines. Mr. Johnson then removed to Closter and established a livery business, which he continued until his death, June 7, 1882. He married (1) Ellen de Baun, who was born May 13, 1822, and died August 18, 1859. He then married (2) Maria Christopher, born May 22, 1827, died April 4, 1882. Mr. Johnson's issue of the second generation were Euphemia, Maria, Henry D. B., Margaret (died), Delia, Darius S., Carrie (dead), George, and Maggie—five by his first wife and four by his second.

Darius S. Johnson (2) was born May 4, 1863, in Closter, Bergen County, where he has always resided, and where he received his education. Leaving school at the age of thirteen, he clerked for two years in a grocery store and then entered his father's livery stable. When eighteen years old he engaged in business for himself, becoming a member of the firm of Taveniere & Johnson, which still continues.

Mr. Johnson has achieved success in both business and public affairs. He served one term as Township Collector for Harrington Township and during the past ten years has been Road Commissioner. He is a member of the Dutch Reformed Church and highly respected by all who know him. He married Blanch Pearsall and has two children: Hazel and Martha.

JESSE KIMBALL VREELAND, for many years one of the leading contractors and builders of Hudson County and from 1864 a resident of Bayonne, was born in Rahway, N. J., on the 15th of October, 1835, his parents being Jesse Kimble Vreeland, Sr., and Lockey Brant. His family is one of the oldest in the State, the branch in Hudson County descending from Michael Jansen, who came from Broeckhuysen (North Brabant). He left Holland, October 1, 1636, in the ship "Rensselaerwyck," with his wife and two children. He settled at what is now Greenbush, opposite Albany, as a *boercknecht*, or farm servant. It was not long before he grew weary of agricultural pursuits and the narrow road thereby opened to wealth, and engaged in the fur trade, in which "he made his fortune in two years." Such private speculation being prohibited by law, he was soon brought into difficulty with the authorities. He thereupon abandoned his farm and came to Manhattan. The date of this change is not known, but he was a resident in New Amsterdam November 4, 1644, on which date he empowered Arent Van Curler to settle with Patroon Van Rensselaer all accounts and differences. In 1646 he came over to Communipaw and settled on the bouwerie, owned by Jan Evertsen Bout. For this "Bouwerie" and part of the stock on it he paid Bout the good round sum of 8,000 gelders. In the years 1647, 1649, and 1650 he represented Pavonia in the Council of "Nine," and joined his associates in their crusade against Governor Stuyvesant. In 1649 he was appointed one of the delegates to Holland against the Colonial administration, but owing to the unsettled state of his business he declined the appointment. It was at his house in New Amsterdam that the journal of Van der Donck entitled "Vertoogh" was written. It was seized, and it

JESSE K. VREELAND.

was suspected upon information furnished by Michael Jansen. He was a signer of the application for the first municipal government in New Netherland, July 26, 1649.

During the troubles of 1655 the Indians drove him from his home, when, on September 15, they made a raid on Pavonia and killed every man there, except the family of Jansen. From the dangers and uncertainties of border life at "Gemoenepa" he took refuge on Manhattan. On January 22, 1658, he asked for permission to return to Pavonia and to be relieved from certain tithes. In September, 1661, he had become a man of "competence," living on his bouwerie at Gemoenepa. He was one of the first magistrates of the new court at Bergen. In December, 1662, he joined his neighbors in asking the governor for a minister of the gospel, and for whose support he subscribed twenty-five florins. He died in 1663. His wife was Fitje Hartmans, and they had eight children, from whom are descended various branches of the family now represented in Eastern New Jersey.

Jesse Kimball Vreeland was of the seventh generation from Michael Jansen and his wife, Fitje Hartmans, the emigrants. His parents were both born and married in Rahway, where he received his education in the public schools. Afterward he spent several years in the South. He finally removed from Rahway to New York City and thence, in 1864, to Bayonne, N. J., where he was long prominent in both business and public affairs. After leaving school Mr. Vreeland identified himself with the building and contracting business, which he thoroughly learned and successfully followed. He built a large number of public and private buildings, which stand as monuments to his skill and industry, and stamp him as a man of originality as well as enterprise.

Mr. Vreeland was also prominent in military and civil life. He served throughout the War of the Rebellion, being connected with the Quartermaster's Department at Port Royal. He also served as Chief of the Fire Department at Bayonne, as a member of the Bayonne Common Council, and as a Commissioner of Appeals, and discharged his duties in each position with acknowledged ability and satisfaction. In politics he was a Democrat, and in religion a member of the congregation of the Dutch Reformed Church. His life was one of constant activity and in every way successful, and during his entire career he won and maintained the confidence of all with whom he came in contact. He died July 23, 1900.

Mr. Vreeland married Emma J. Meyer, of Charleston, S. C. They had nine children: Jennie, Emma, Henrietta, Rachel, Jesse, Frederick, Chester, Clarence, and Edna.

WILLIAM SCOTT FERDON is descended from Thomas Verdon, the emigrant, who came to America about 1645 (see sketch on page 184). The line of descent is as follows: Jacob Ferdon, of the third generation, had issue seven children of the fourth generation, as has been stated. One of these, Jacob Ferdon (4), baptized in New York in 1687, was known as Jacob Ferdon, Jr. He married Maria Flierboom, April 8, 1720, and remained on Long Island until 1730, when he removed to Schraalenburgh, N. J., where he bought lands and died about 1752. He had issue of the fifth generation several children: Jacob, Jannetje, Servaes (died), Servaes (died), Maria, Servaes (died), and Catharine.

Jacob Ferdon (5), born on Long Island about 1723, married at Schraalenburgh, May 5, 1748, Helena Van Blarcom. They resided at Schraalenburgh and had children of the sixth generation Jacob, Henry, Servaes, Jacobus, Jacob, Ann, Maria, and Peter.

Henry Ferdon (6) married Jannetje Archbold, lived at Schraalenburgh, and had children of the seventh generation David, James, Lena, Henry, and Jannetie.

Henry Ferdon (7), born at Schraalenburgh, March 10, 1790, died February 27, 1855, married, August 2, 1814, Effie Banta. She was born March 22, 1795, and died August 27, 1879. They left issue, among whom were Samuel B. Ferdon (8), who married Sarah M., daughter of Daniel and Rachel Christie, and had issue, among other children, William Scott Ferdon of the ninth generation.

William Scott Ferdon, the subject of this sketch, was born in New York City on the 29th of July, 1858, and there received a public school education. For several years he has been successfully engaged in the coal and lumber business at Dumont, N. J., succeeding in May, 1899, the firm of De Coster & Ferdon. He is a member of the Dutch Reformed Church, a public spirited citizen, and actively identified with the affairs of his section.

On August 18, 1880, Mr. Ferdon married Jemima Christie, and they have two children: Sadie M. and Myra C.

JULIUS BERGER was born in Davenport, Iowa, March 20, 1860, his parents having emigrated to this country from Germany in 1857. His mother's family was wealthy and influential in the Fatherland, but none of the wealth ever crossed the ocean. His father served for three years in the Civil War, receiving an honorable discharge.

Mr. Berger acquired a limited education in the public schools of Davenport, but in the harder school of practical life he laid the foundation upon which he has built a successful career. The death of both of his parents in 1873 threw him upon his own resources at the tender age of thirteen, and from that time to the present he has relied upon himself. Anxious and willing to work, endowed with plenty of pluck and energy, and determined to pave a way to success and reputation, he entered, in April, 1873, a manufactory of hats and furs in his native city, where he soon gained a valuable experience, which supplemented the earlier training he had obtained in the public schools.

In June, 1880, he removed from Davenport, Iowa, to Jersey City, N. J., and entered the employ of the firm of Harris & Russack, of New York City, manufacturers of fine furs, remaining with them until 1889. On June 22, of that year, he opened his own manufactory of hats and furs at 368 Central Avenue, Jersey City, where he has since continued. He started with a capital of $150, but with pluck, perseverance, and practical business knowledge acquired from his long association with his former employers soon built up an extensive trade.

Mr. Berger was the founder of the Hudson City Business Men's Association and was its President for two terms. He was also President of the Hudson City Turn Verein in 1888 and 1896, and was very active for the welfare and advancement of both organizations. He is also a member of the Jersey City Board of Trade. He was appointed a member of the Board of Education of Jersey City in May, 1899, by Mayor Hoos, and has continued to hold that position. He is a public spirited citizen, active in the affairs of the community, and respected by all who know him. Mr. Berger married Marie Bechtoldt, daughter of George Bechtoldt, a veteran of the Civil War.

GENEALOGICAL

ANTHONY JACOB VOLK has gained the reputation of being one of the best known and most enterprising undertakers in Hoboken, N. J., where he was born November 21, 1865. In a measure he inherits this from his father, Jacob Volk, who, at the time of his death, on August 3, 1874, was the oldest and foremost undertaker in Hudson County, and who, professionally and privately, was universally respected and esteemed. But his reputation is not altogether inherited from his honored father. It is very largely the result of his own efforts, and of a natural ability developed from boyhood.

He is the son of Jacob Volk and Rosa Raab, both natives of Germany,

ANTHONY J. VOLK.

who came to this country when young and were married in New York City. They settled in Hoboken, and were well known throughout the County of Hudson. Mr. Volk attended the public schools of Hoboken and also Hoboken Academy, where he received a thorough classical training. Leaving school at the early age of fourteen, he entered the employ of the National Express Company, and in this and in the office of the American Express Company, both of New York, he spent three years. In 1874 his father died, leaving a large and successful undertaking business to the care of his wife, the mother of Anthony J. Volk, and the latter, when seventeen, assumed its immediate management. Though but a boy, he displayed marked business ability, excellent judgment, and great sagacity, and soon won the respect and confidence of the community. His success was practically instantaneous and uninterrupted. In addition to the undertaking establishment he conducted a large livery stable, and combining the two was necessarily a very busy man. In 1886 he purchased the entire business, which he still continues.

Mr. Volk is independent in politics, firm in his convictions, trustworthy in all the relations of life, and influential and active in the best interests of the community. In the autumn of 1893 he was elected Coroner of Hudson County by the handsome plurality of over 4,400, the county usually giving a Democratic majority of about 6,000. This office he filled with great credit and satisfaction for three years. He is a member and past officer of Hudson Lodge, No. 71, F. and A. M., of Hoboken, and also a member of Protection Lodge, No. 634, Knights of Honor, of Lady Washington Lodge, No. 414, Knights and Ladies of Honor, of the American Legion of Honor, of Guiding Star Lodge, No. 189, I. O. O. F., of Hoboken Council, No. 99, Royal Arcanum, of the Germania Schuetzen Bund of New Jersey, of the Hoboken Schuetzen Corps, of the Hoboken Quartette Club, of the Hoboken Independent Schuetzen Corps, and of the Mannergesang Verein Lyra. For a time he was also financial secretary of the Undertakers' Association of Hudson County. He is a member of the German Lutheran Church, and active in various other organizations.

Mr. Volk was married on the 12th of September, 1888, to Anna M. Kaiser, daughter of John Henry and Anna M. Kaiser, of Hoboken. They have two children: Florence M. and Anthony J., Jr.

JAMES H. STEPHENS, of Closter, is descended from John Stephensen, an Englishman, who came to America about 1670 and located at Fort Orange (Albany), where he followed his profession, which was that of a school teacher. On October 4, 1673, he married Elizabeth Lucas, who, the record states, was from New Orange. The couple must have resided in New Amsterdam for some time, as seven of their children are recorded as having been baptized there, in the Dutch church, up to 1693. His first wife died in New Amsterdam and he married (2) Maria ———. He had children of the second generation: Elizabeth, Lucas, Mary, Steven, Jenneke, Cornelius, Catalyna, John, Peter, Nicholas, Roeloff, Abraham, and Gertrude.

Lucas Stephens (2) married and had issue, among other children, Abraham (3), born about 1730, who married, in 1757, Sarah Peters O'Blenis, of Clarkstown. They resided at Clarkstown, N. Y., and had seven children of the fourth generation: Elizabeth, 1759; Peter, 1760; Maria, 1763; Elizabeth, 1765; Abram, 1767; Jannetie, 1769; and Hendrick, 1771.

Hendrick (4), born at Clarkstown, June 11, 1771, married Ann de Clark, born at Clarkstown, December 11, 1771, died there December 25, 1843. Hendrick died there October 25, 1834. They had issue, among other children, James H. Stephens of the fifth generation.

James H. Stephens (5), born at Clarkstown, N. Y., August 28, 1804, died at Closter, N. J., August 28, 1867, married (1) Catharine Pye in 1824 and (2) Ida E. Pye, widow of Edmund Irish. James H. Stephens was a carpenter, and for many years followed his occupation in the City of New York, where he acquired a competence in constructing frames for buildings which were at that time being shipped to California. Early in the fifties he purchased a large farm in Monmouth County on which he devoted his time to the production of fruits, for which he found a ready market in New York. In 1867 he sold his Monmouth farm and removed to Closter, N. J., on the farm formerly owned by David A. Demarest. He died there five months after his arrival. His issue by Catharine Pye were two sons, Abraham and John H. Stephens, and by Ida E. Pye two children, Edmund and Catharine.

John H. Stephens (6) was born in Bank Street, New York, February 8, 1831, and died at Closter, N. J., September 8, 1887. He learned the carpenter's trade with his father in New York and married Rachel D. Huyler, daughter of Barney and Maria (Demarest) Huyler. In 1858 he removed to Closter, N. J., bought lands, and followed carpentry until the opening of the railroad in the following year, when he built a store (the first one in the place) and began to speculate in real estate. He was station agent for twenty-five years, Postmaster for thirty years, held many town offices, and was the promoter and leading spirit of the village. In fact he may justly be called the father of Closter. His issue of the seventh generation are James H., Eugene, and Percy.

James H. Stephens, the subject of this sketch, was born in Closter, N. J., September 19, 1860, and received his education in the public schools of Bergen County. Leaving school at the age of eighteen, he first engaged in the sugar business in New York City, in which he continued four years. He was then engaged in the meat business in Closter for seven years, and subsequently, after a retirement of two years, associated himself with the Mutual Life Insurance Company of New York.

Mr. Stephens has been successful in every connection, and as a public spirited citizen has taken a deep interest in local affairs. He is a member of the Reformed Church and identified with other organizations in his native county. He married Elizabeth M. Ferdon and has one child, a daughter, E. Marion Stephens.

CALVIN DEMAREST, of Hackensack, is descended in the eighth generation from David des Marest, the emigrant and first American ancestor of the family, for a sketch of whom see page 64. Calvin's grandfather, Thomas Demarest (of the sixth generation from the first David), was born July 18, 1757, and died April 27, 1829. He married, in 1782, Lena Naugle. Their issue of the seventh generation were Sarah, Cornelius T., William, Vroutie, and perhaps others.

Cornelius T. (7), born January 23, 1786, died December 26, 1862, married Margaret Lydecker, born August 1, 1791, died June 27, 1883. She was the daughter of Cornelius Lydecker. Cornelius T. was graduated from Columbia College in 1804, studied for the ministry with Rev. Dr. Froeleigh, was licensed to preach at Paramus in March, 1807, and preached at White House, N. J., from 1808 to 1813, and at English Neighborhood, N. J., from 1813 to 1824. He organized the new church at English Neighborhood and preached in it from 1824 to 1839, and also preached at Hackensack and English Neighborhood from 1839 to 1851 and in King Street, New York, in the True Reformed Church, from 1851 until his death. His children of the eighth generation were fifteen: Helen, Cornelia, Leah, Thomas W., Cornelius Lydecker, Christiana, Penelope, Maria, Calvin, 1st., Charles, Calvin, Garret B., Peter, James H., and Margaret.

Calvin Demarest (8), the subject of this sketch, was born in New York City on the 15th of July, 1825, and received his education in Bergen County. He left school at the age of fourteen and went to work on his grandfather's farm in Bergen County, where he remained fourteen years.

Since then—for a period of forty-six years—he has been successfully engaged in the general trucking business in New York City. He resides in Hackensack, is a member of the Reformed Church, and for years has taken a deep interest in the affairs of Bergen County. Mr. Demarest married Mary Lozier and has two children living: Walter and Myra.

WALTER KISSAM BIRDSALL, a rising young lawyer and a member of the Board of Education of Jersey City, is the son of David and Susannah A. (Clyde) Birdsall, and a descendant of the Birdsalls in the vicinity of Leeds, England. His parents were born in New York State, but came to Jersey City in 1849, where his father, David Birdsall, established the Jersey City Iron Works, in which he is still interested.

Walter K. Birdsall was born in Jersey City, N. J., on the 2d of January, 1869, and received his education in that city, attending Public School No. 1 and the Jersey City High School. He was graduated from Yale University in the class of 1891, and during his senior year there took a year's course in elementary law in the Yale Law School. Subsequently he spent four years in the office of William A. Lewis, as a student, and was admitted to the New Jersey bar at the February term of the Supreme Court in 1895. Since then he has been actively and successfully engaged in the practice of his profession in Jersey City.

WALTER K. BIRDSALL.

In politics Mr. Birdsall is a Republican. He has taken an active interest in the affairs of his party, has contributed largely to its success, and among its younger members is recognized as a leader. On May 1, 1899, he was appointed a member of the Board of Education of Jersey City for a term of two years, and is now serving in that capacity with the same marked ability which he has displayed in professional life.

He is a member of Jersey City Lodge, No. 74, Free and Accepted Masons, of William T. Sherman Council, Royal Arcanum, of the Zeta Psi Greek

Letter fraternity, and of the University Club. He was formerly a member of the Palma Club of Jersey City.

Mr. Birdsall is a prominent, patriotic, and public spirited citizen. He has already achieved a high reputation, and through his liberality, integrity of character, and activity is universally esteemed and respected.

Mr. Birdsall was married on the 24th of August, 1897, to Fannie E. Watson, of Perry, Wyoming County, N. Y.

JOHN HILLRIC BONN, the founder of the present system of street railways in North Hudson County, and one of the most enterprising and successful men of his day, was born in the City of Norden, East Friesland, in the extreme northwest of Germany, September 14, 1829. There he received his early education under private tutors and at the national and classical high schools. He sprung from an honored and respected family, his parents being people of great energy and force of character, and as a boy developed those strong intellectual and moral traits which characterized his entire life. His father was for many years a successful master of vessels in the East India trade, and with him Mr. Bonn visited the East Indies as a youth. This enabled him to acquire, at an impressionable period, a liberal knowledge of the world.

Subsequently he attended a nautical school near Amsterdam, Holland, passed the difficult and intricate examination before the Royal Examining Committee in that city, and was awarded the first degree. But he was not destined for a life on the ocean. From the autumn of 1845 to October, 1850, he was employed by a firm in Emden, East Friesland, which conducted an extensive commercial, shipping, and banking business. In October, 1850, he left Germany and came to New York City, where he accepted a position as bookkeeper and English and French correspondent in a large Greek shipping-house. Two years later, having saved some money, he invested in real estate in North Hudson County, N. J., and also became a permanent resident there, and as soon as he could legally do so he became a citizen of the United States. These relations soon resulted in making him a man of commanding influence. In 1856 he spent considerable time in traveling in America and Europe, and in October of that year was married to Miss Angelina Bonjer, of Emden, East Friesland. In April, 1857, he brought his bride to this country and took up his residence in Weehawken, Hudson County, whence he later removed to Hoboken. They returned to Weehawken in 1867 and made that city their permanent home, settling on the spot formerly owned by Daniel Webster, the statesman. There Mr. Bonn died on the 15th of November, 1891.

Mr. Bonn probably did more than any other one man to develop and improve Northern Hudson County, and to stimulate enterprise and the growth of population. He was untiring in his efforts to secure for that section those permanent improvements which to-day make it so easy of access and so attractive to both residents and visitors. He was a founder and a prominent member of the first Board of Regents of the Hudson County Hospital. In 1868 he was appointed by the late Hon. Joseph D. Bedle one of a commission of seven authorized by the New Jersey Legislature to lay out and improve the public streets on the heights of Hudson County, which include West Hoboken, Union Hill, West New York, and other territory. Upon the organization of this commission Mr. Bonn was unanimously chosen chairman by his colleagues. For various reasons the plan which had been contemplated by the commissioners was not carried out, although the inception and construction of the magnificent Hudson County Boulevard issued from the movement. In 1872 Mr. Bonn also became chairman of the Board of Commissioners which supervised the improvement of the Bull's Ferry road from Nineteenth Street in Hoboken, northerly, and which also built the main sewer in Hoboken to the Hudson River, this public work being completed in 1875.

But his most notable work, and one to which he devoted the best energies of his life, was in connection with the surface and elevated railways of the northern half of Hudson County. He was the founder, originator, and father of the present system of transit. He commenced the construction and operation of street railways in 1859, and soon had lines radiating in every direction from the Hoboken ferry. His investment in this enterprise proved wonderfully successful. He was the first, and indeed the only, President of the various original corporations; and when these were consolidated in 1865, forming the North Hudson County Railway Company, he became the first President of that corporation, and so continued until his death in 1891, a period of twenty-six years. During that time the several lines were extended and improved, new roads were built, and the system placed upon its present efficient basis. In 1874 he built the first steam elevator in Hudson County, and with this the street-cars, with the horses attached, were lifted to the top of the bluff, the process requiring but one minute. In 1884 he erected the elevated railway from Hoboken to Jersey City Heights, an iron structure ranging from fifteen to nearly one hundred feet high. This road was originally operated by cable, and was the first elevated road so operated in the United States. All these roads have adopted electricity as the motive power. In 1890 the great Weehawken elevators, of which Mr. Bonn was the originator, were begun, and on their completion, on October 23, 1891, he made the first trip in them with several other gentlemen. The elevators were formally opened to the public April 26, 1892. These great railway and elevator enterprises may be regarded as the best work of his life, though they were by no means the sum total of his remarkable achievements. As important and necessary public works, however, they represent a man whose foresight and energy proved the wisdom of his judgment.

Mr. Bonn had no inclination for and never held political office, except that of Superintendent of Public Schools in the old Township of North Bergen, to which he was elected in 1857, on both tickets. He held this position one year. He held the respect and confidence of the entire community, and was noted for his benevolence, kindness, and generosity.

Mr. and Mrs. Bonn were members of the German Lutheran Church of Weehawken, and were active in both religious and charitable work. Of their eleven children four died young, and two sons, John H., Jr., and Hillric J., are mentioned in the following sketches. Mr. Bonn was chiefly influential in bringing out the *German-American Encyclopedia*, a work of eleven volumes, and the first of the kind in the United States.

HILLRIC JOHN BONN, eldest son of the late John Hillric Bonn and Angelina Bonjer, was born, October 10, 1858, in Bonnsville, North Bergen Township, Hudson County, a village named in honor of his father. He attended the public schools, and in 1878 was graduated with the degree of Mechanical Engineer from Stevens Institute at Hoboken. Afterward, for several years, he followed his profession with success in Scranton, Pa., Hoboken,

N. J., New York City, Pittsburg, Pa., and Chicago, and was assistant engineer during the construction of the North Hudson County Elevated Railway. On the death of his father in 1891 he was elected Vice-President of that corporation.

JOHN HILLRIC BONN, JR., another son of John H. and Angelina (Bonjer) Bonn, was born in Weehawken, N. J., May 15, 1871, and received his education at Hoboken Academy and Stevens High School, from which he was graduated in 1889. In 1891 he was graduated with the degree of LL.B. from the Law Department of the University of the City of New York, and then took a post-graduate course at that institution, graduating as Master of Laws in 1892. He also read law one year in New York in the office of Brainerd, Davenport & Brainerd, and for a time in Hoboken with Hon. Abel I. Smith and John S. Mabon, and was admitted to the bar of New York in 1893, and to the New Jersey bar as an attorney in February, 1895. In the latter year he opened offices in both Hoboken and West Hoboken. He subsequently gave up his Hoboken office, but still continues the one in West Hoboken, where he has a large and successful general practice. In 1898 he was attorney for the Township of Weehawken. He is a master in chancery, a member of the Phi Delta Phi legal fraternity, and an ardent Republican.

Mr. Bonn was married January 26, 1898, to Marguerite L., daughter of Thomas and Jane Fisher, of Jersey City. They reside in Weehawken.

LIVINGSTON CONKLING, the founder and President of the Associated Justices of the Peace and Constables' Protective Association of Hudson County, is a descendant of some of the oldest and most distinguished families in this country. His paternal ancestors came from England and Ireland in 1735, settling first in New York and removing thence in 1750 to Hackensack, Bergen County, N. J. He is the great-great-grandson of Alfred and Hannah (Marshall) Conkling, a great-grandson of Nathaniel and Hortley (Schrone) Conkling, a grandson of Matthew and Frances (Brickel) Conkling, and a son of Matthew H. and Elvina (Van Ripen) Conkling, his mother being a daughter of Jacob Van Ripen and Katherine Van Drouf, a granddaughter of Isaac and Martha (Goetschins) Van Ripen, and a great-great-granddaughter of Jacob and Mary (Vreland) Van Ripen. Her ancestors came from Holland in 1649 and were among the earliest settlers in Eastern New Jersey. Through his grandmother Mr. Conkling is a great-grandson of Sir Alfred Brickel, of Manchester, England, and though his father he is closely related to the late Hon. Roscoe Conkling, whose ancestors came from Kent County, England. His grandfather, Matthew Conkling, was one of the famous drummers of his day. In 1854 he was presented with the first silver drum ever made. He was the first Poormaster in Hoboken and active during the Civil War. Matthew H. Conkling, the son of Matthew and father of Livingston, was the organizer and leader of Conkling's famous New Jersey Brass Band in 1870, and ably represented the family, which has been prominently identified in the politics of Hudson County for upward of sixty years. Mr. Conkling's mother's cousin, Hon. Garret D. Van Ripen, was Mayor of Jersey City, while another relative and namesake, Jacob Livingston, represented his district in the State Senate.

Livingston Conkling's full name is Matthew Livingston Conkling. He was named after his father, but because of the similarity of the names of his father and grandfather, both of whom bore the name Matthew, he dropped the Matthew and has continued to use only the middle name, Livingston. The family name was, originally, Conklin, and not Conkling, but a number of the descendants added the y, thus giving the name its present form. On the paternal side the family is of Irish and English descent.

Livingston Conkling was born in Hoboken, N. J., on the 10th of May, 1861, and inherited all the sturdy characteristics which made his ancestors so famous in the early and subsequent history of this section of the State. Receiving an excellent public school education in his native city, he learned the trade of decorating and painting, and at the present time is senior mem-

LIVINGSTON CONKLING.

ber of the well known firm of L. Conkling & Co., painters and decorators, 115 Clinton Street, Hoboken, and 125 Eighth Avenue, New York City. Mr. Conkling has achieved marked success in business and is popularly known as a man of ability, integrity, and great force of character.

He has also achieved prominence and distinction in public life, and in this connection bears with credit and honor the eminence which the family has maintained for so many generations. He entered the National Guard of New Jersey as a private in the old Ninth Regiment, and from 1880 to 1889 served as Sergeant in the Second Regiment, N. G. N. J., and from 1889 to 1892 he was Captain of the old Columbia Guards in New Jersey. In political affairs he has been for several years one of the ablest leaders of the Republican forces in the county. He has served efficiently as a member of the Hudson County Republican General Committee for six years, was a member of the Republican Executive Committee of Hoboken for a time, and Vice-President of the Ninth Assembly District Republican Committee for one year. He has been a delegate to numerous city, county, and congressional conventions and always wields a potent influence in party councils and in campaign affairs. He was Secretary of the Garfield Club in 1893, President of the McKinley Club of Hoboken four years, orator of Achaean League, No. 2, of Hoboken, Commander of Christian Woerner Post, No. 1, Sons of Veterans, in 1888, and Judge Advocate-General of the National Department, Sons of Veterans, U. S. A., in 1889. In 1899 he organized the Associated Justices of the Peace and Constables' Protective Association, of which he is President.

Judge Conkling is serving his second term as Justice of the Peace, having been first elected in 1894 and re-elected in 1899, and represents the third generation of his family who has held that office in the City of Hoboken, his predecessors being his father and grandfather. He is also a Commissioner of Deeds and a member of the Knights of Honor, and in every capacity has gained the confidence and esteem of the entire community. He is an energetic, progressive, and public spirited citizen, and a man of broad intellectual attainments.

June 30, 1889, Judge Conkling married Miss Julia Hetzel. They have six children: Irving, Raymond, Gertrude, Roscoe, Isabel, and Matthew Livingston, Jr.

JOHN H. LINDEMANN.—The Lindemann family is among the most numerous and important in Germany. Many of them have, within the last century, attained wealth and distinction in the United States. Henry Lindemann was born in 1799, near Bremen, in the Kingdom of Hanover, Germany, where he married Anna C. Butts and established himself in the dual business of baker and grocer. His only son and child, William L. Lindemann, was born at Bremen and adopted the business of his father. In 1840 William L., the son, came to America and married Johanna Waetge in 1846. His father, Henry, followed him to America in 1845, and the two, having bought a part of the old Naugle farm at Closter, in Bergen County, N. J., adopted farming for a livelihood. Henry, the father, died in 1867, intestate, and his lands descended to his son William L., who in time became one of the largest landholders at Closter. He built and owned the first hotel in the village and was instrumental in organizing the Lutheran Church, the fire company, the Building and Loan Association, and other enterprises for the improvement of the town. He died October 8, 1899, respected by all who knew him. He married Johanna, daughter of Diedrich Waetge. His children of the third generation were William L., Ernest, and John H.

John H. Lindemann (3), the subject of this sketch, was born at Closter, N. J., August 29, 1859, and received a public school education. Leaving school at the age of fifteen, he has since remained on his father's farm, which he has conducted with marked success. He has served on the Town Committee, has been Collector of Harrington Township, and is a member of the Dutch Reformed Church. In every capacity he has displayed ability and integrity of character, and is highly respected by the entire community.

Mr. Lindemann married Amelia Waetge and has three children: Hermiena, Dorothea, and Alien.

ANDREW H. BRINKERHOFF is a descendant in the eighth generation from Joris Dircksen (Brinkerhoff), the first American progenitor of the New Jersey branches of the family. Joris (George) Dircksen (1) was a native of the grazing and stock raising Province of Drenthe, Holland (from whence came so many of the pioneer families of the New Netherlands), where he was born about 1590. Early in life his family removed to Vlissingen (Flushing), a seaport on the Island of Walcheron in Zeeland, at which city many persons were fleeing from religious persecution. Here Joris married Susanna Dubbelo. In 1638 Joris, with his wife, emigrated to America. He first settled on Staten Island and is said to have entered into a contract with one Cornelius Melyn, the owner of the island, to reside there, but on August 16, 1641, owing to the numerous murders committed in the neighborhood by the Indians, he obtained a release from his contract. The same year he settled at Brooklyn, where, on March 23, 1646, he obtained a grant of thirty-six acres of land. On this he seems to have built his home and resided until his death, January 16, 1661. He must have been a man of ability and respected by his neighbors, otherwise he would not have been elected a magistrate in 1654 and re-elected annually thereafter until 1660. He helped to organize the Dutch Church at Brooklyn and was an Elder in it at the time of his death. His issue of the second generation were Derrick (killed by the Indians), Hendrick, Abraham, and Aeltie.

Hendrick (2), born in Holland about 1630, married Claesie (a daughter of Cornelius Jans) Bogert (see sketch on page 105), then of Flatbush, L. I. He lived at Flatbush until 1685, was a magistrate of Brooklyn in 1662-63, and became a member of the Colonial Assembly in 1665. On June 17, 1685, with Jan Cornelise Bogert, the Bantas, and others, he removed to Bergen County and purchased a large tract of land between the Hackensack River and the Overpeck Creek, on which Hendrick settled, and where he died in 1610 or 1611. A stone marks the spot where his remains are buried in the cemetery of the "Church on the Green," at Hackensack. Of this church he was one of the founders, and for many years a leader and officer in it. He held other responsible positions, and was one of the most active and useful members of the new colony. His issue of the third generation were Greetie, Margrietie, Cornelius, Joris, Derrick, and Jacobus.

Cornelius Hendricksen Brinckerhoff (3), born on Long Island, married Aegie Vreeland, of Bergen, May 28, 1708. He was a member of the Hackensack church, and died September 1, 1770, aged ninety-seven. Derrick Brinkerhoff (3) married (1) Margaret Sibse Banta and (2) Abagail Ackerman, and Jacobus (3) married Angenitie Hendricks Banta. The descendants of the last three named have spread over Hudson and Bergen Counties and are still numerous.

Andrew H. Brinkerhoff (8), the subject of this sketch, is a descendant of one of these, and was born at Boiling Springs, Bergen County, October 13, 1847. He is the son of George C. Brinkerhoff (7) and Kezia H. Hopper, daughter of Andrew P. and Anna Hopper, and a grandson of Cornelius G. (6) and Hannah Brinkerhoff. He was educated in the district schools and at Packard's Institute, New York, and with the exception of a few years spent in farming has followed the banking business since leaving the latter institution, being at the present time the Cashier of the Rutherford National Bank. Rising step by step to this responsible position, he has displayed from the first great executive ability, sound business judgment, and a thorough knowledge of financial affairs.

In public life he has also been active and prominent. He has served efficiently as Collector of Taxes, and in 1890 was elected a member of the Borough Council, serving two years, and in 1899 was again elected to that office for a term of three years. He is a member of the Knights of Pythias and of the Board of Trustees of the First Presbyterian Church of Rutherford, of which he is a regular attendant and liberal supporter.

Mr. Brinkerhoff was married on July 12, 1868, to Jennie M. Brinkerhoff and has five children: George C., Henry A., James H., Kezia H., and May.

ISAAC A. HOPPER.—The Hoppers in Bergen and Hudson Counties are descended from Andries Hopper, who, with his wife, Grietie Hendricks, emigrated to America in 1652 and settled at New Amsterdam, where he was enrolled and granted the privileges of a small burgher in 1657. He acquired considerable property, but did not live to long enjoy it, as he died within a year. He had entered into an agreement with Jacob Stol to purchase the Bronx lands, but death cut off both him and Stol before a deed could be signed. His widow married (2) a man named Van Tricht in May, 1660, thereby securing to each of her three children two hundred gelders. These three children were William, born 1654 (married Minnie Jurcks Paulus); Hendrick, born 1656 (married Maria Van Blarcom); Matthew Adolphus, born 1658 (married Anna Jurcks Paulus). Matthew and Hendrick settled in New Jersey.

Isaac A. Hopper is descended in the eighth generation from Andries Hopper and Grietie Hendricks, the emigrants. Matthew Hopper married Aedtje Peters (see sketch on page 71). This Matthew Hopper (3) had a son, Andries (4), who married Elizabeth Bros and had a son, Peter (5). Who this Peter married the Paramus church records may show, but Peter (5), it is said, had three sons: Garret P. (6), Andrew P. (6), and Henry P. (6). Andrew P. was born about 1772, married, July 23, 1797, Anne Voorhis, and had issue, among other children, Henry A. Hopper (7), who married Helen, daughter of Isaac Ackerman, and had issue, besides other children, Isaac A. Hopper (8), who is the subject of this sketch. His father was Sheriff of Bergen County and a member of the New Jersey Legislature.

ISAAC A. HOPPER.

Isaac Ackerman Hopper (8) was born at Boiling Springs, now Rutherford, N. J., April 24, 1843. He received a district school education at "Small Lots" (now Fair Lawn), and, completing his studies at the age of fifteen, has followed farming when not serving the community in official capacities. During the Civil War he enlisted as a volunteer soldier in Company E, Twenty-second New Jersey Regiment, and participated in the battles of

Chancellorsville, Fredericksburg, the Wilderness, and Gettysburg, where his regiment formed a part of General Meade's reserves.

After the war Mr. Hopper again engaged in agricultural pursuits on his father's farm, and soon became active and prominent in local public affairs. He served for six years as Assessor, and in 1881 was elected Sheriff of Bergen County, which office he filled with ability and satisfaction for three years. He was again chosen Assessor for the Township of Saddle River and served ten years, and in 1892 was elected County Collector, serving for four years. Afterward he was for four years Treasurer of Bergen County.

Mr. Hopper is a stanch friend of public improvements, has been especially persistent and successful in his efforts to secure improvement of public roads, and is highly respected by all who know him. He is a member of Gabriel Paul Post, G. A. R., a Democrat in politics, and a member of the Reformed Church of Ridgewood.

November 25, 1868, he married Maria, daughter of Garret A. Hopper, a prominent citizen of Bergen County. They have had one child, deceased.

THOMAS J. POST is descended in the eighth generation from Captain Adriaen Post, the emigrant and common ancestor of all the Post family in Bergen and Hudson Counties (see sketch on page 72). He is the son of Thomas Post and Lucretia Merseles, and was born at Westwood, N. J., April 29, 1862. In the schools of Bergen County he acquired a fair education, and by industry and perseverance has achieved success. Leaving school at the age of sixteen, he engaged as an employee in manufacturing chairs, which he followed for fifteen years, when he established himself in that business. He has built up a large and successful business in this line, and is widely known as a man of integrity, enterprise, and energy.

Mr. Post is a member of the Board of Education of the Borough of Westwood, a member of the Westwood Union Church, and Superintendent of the Westwood Union Sunday School. In every capacity he has discharged his duties with honor, fidelity, and satisfaction. He married Catharine A. Conklin and has one son, Percy A.

WILLIAM WILLCOX VOORHIS is descended in the eighth generation from Steven Coerts Van Voorhis, the first American ancestor of the family. The line of descent is the same as in the sketch on page 83. As will be seen, Lucas Alberts Voorhis (3) had issue several children of the fourth generation, among whom was Hendrick Lucas Van Voorhis (4), born February 11, 1731, died March 6, 1803. He married Wybsie Laroe, who was born November 28, 1736, and died June 8, 1813. They lived northwest of Hackensack, and had issue ten children of the fifth generation: Abram H., Lucas H., Albert H., John H., Annatie, Nicholas H., Jacobus H., Catharine, Magdalena, and Henry H.

Jacobus H. (5), born November 2, 1769, died April 13, 1833, married Mary Demarest, who was born July 14, 1783, and died August 14, 1849. Three generations of the above are buried in the old Voorhis graveyard on the west bank of the Hackensack below New Milford. Jacobus H. Voorhis (5) and Mary Demarest had issue, besides other children, Albert J. Voorhis (6), who married Rachel Hopper. She was born October 5, 1809, and died April 19, 1877. They had issue, among other children, Peter A. H. Voorhis (7), who married Cecelia C. Smith, and who was the father of William Willcox Voorhis (8), the subject of this sketch.

William Willcox Voorhis (8) was born November 27, 1865, in Hackensack, N. J., where he received his education. He left school at the age of sixteen and engaged in business with his father, continuing in that relation until the latter's death. He then retired and has since devoted his energies to the management of the estate.

In public as well as in business affairs Mr. Voorhis has achieved distinction. He served for a time as President of the Board of Council of the Borough of Westwood, is a life member of the New Jersey Society for the Prevention of Cruelty to Animals, and is a member of the Reformed Church. He is public spirited, enterprising, and active in promoting every worthy movement, and thoroughly identified with the affairs of his native county.

Mr. Voorhis married Leanora Westervelt, a member of an old Bergen County family, and they have two children: Cecelia Marguerite and Marie Louise.

JOHN ENSTICE has achieved as a contractor a measure of success which stamps him as one of the most prominent men in his line of business in Eastern New Jersey. His reputation and high standing are doubly merited, because it is through his own efforts, his indomitable perseverance, and his unquestioned integrity and ability that he has paved the way to a place among the leading contractors of the State. He comes from the sturdy old Enstice and Giles families of Cornwall, England, where he was born March 20, 1867, his parents being James Enstice and Annie Giles and his grandparents John Enstice and Maria Norway. His mother, who still survives, is the daughter of James and Amelia Giles, of Cornwall. On both sides he inherits the admirable characteristics of people whose broad and liberal attainments had a most important influence upon the community in which they lived, and who raised by deed and word the high standard of industry, honesty, and fearless fidelity that marks their descendants in both the Old and the New World.

Mr. Enstice has been a resident of New Jersey since he was four years old. In May, 1871, the family bade adieu to the Cornwall home of their ancestors and emigrated to America, to seek, in broader fields, a fortune for themselves and their children. They first located in Dover, N. J., where the father, James Enstice, successfully prosecuted his business as a contractor until shortly before his death, which occurred on the 9th of March, 1883. He had five sons and two daughters, John, the subject of this article, being the third son.

John Enstice attended Public School No. 2, at Mine Hill, near Dover, Morris County, N. J., until he was sixteen, and as a boy manifested and developed those energetic mental qualities which have since won for him so much honor and distinction. Having laid the basis of an active career in studies best fitted for a business life, he became an apprentice to the carpenter's trade in Dover, and there and in Morristown, N. J., followed his vocation with constantly increasing success, winning the respect and confidence of all with whom he came in contact. In the spring of 1886 he moved to Kearny, Hudson County, where he prosecuted his trade for two years, being in charge of important work most of the time. In 1888 he engaged in the business of contracting and building on his own account. His first attempts were modest and unassuming, but the high reputation which he had made soon followed him to his new field of operation, and within a very short time he occupied a foremost place among the prominent contractors in that section. He associated himself with his brothers,

William and Edward J., under the present firm name of Enstice Brothers, and many of the finest and most imposing buildings in Kearny, Harrison, Newark, the Oranges, and other towns are the result of their efforts. Dwellings, public edifices, and a variety of work have been erected by them, and bear the distinctive stamp of their skill and energy and thorough workmanship. In 1899 they completed extensive government contracts at Sandy Hook, which they had commenced in February, 1897, and their work there is among the largest and most important military posts along the Atlantic coast.

JOHN ENSTICE.

In the business and financial as well as in the constructive department of the firm's business Mr. Enstice has been the leading figure, bringing to the management and detail work great executive ability, untiring energy, sound judgment, and unusual foresight. His success in handling the largest contracts, in securing and carrying them to completion, is tangible evidence of his courage and enterprise. His achievements are the result of his own efforts, of constant application, and of the broad and progressive ideas of an able man. As a citizen as well as a contractor he is prominent. In May, 1900, he formed a partnership with John Bohenna, and under the firm name of John Bohenna & Co. engaged in the real estate and insurance business. Mr. Enstice is public spirited and universally esteemed, and in the growth and prosperity of the Township of Kearny he has taken an important part, having been a liberal supporter of its chief institutions and lending his influence in favor of every commendable object. For two years he was a member of the Kearny Board of Education. He is a member of Kane Lodge, No. 55, F. and A. M., and of Union Chapter, No. 7, R. A. M., both of Newark. He is a charter member of Ethic Lodge, Knights of Pythias, of Harrison, and was for three years an Elder and for two years Treasurer of Knox Presbyterian Church of Kearny. He is a Director of the Harrison and Kearny Building and Loan Association, a Republican in politics, and in all the relations of life has displayed the highest attributes of a loyal, energetic, and useful citizen.

Mr. Enstice was married, June 8, 1899, to Nellie May Decker, daughter of Thomas W. and Martha (Van Duyne) Decker, of Kearny, formerly of Pine Brook, Morris County. Soon after his marriage he removed to South Orange, N. J., where he now resides.

JAMES T. LILLIS, Surrogate of Hudson County, is the eldest son of Martin and Catherine (McCarthy) Lillis, both natives of Ireland, who came to this country about 1849 and settled in the north part of the County of Hudson. His father, one of the prominent and extensive truckmen of his time, died in Jersey City on the 1st of January, 1879. His mother's death occurred there August 21, 1887.

Surrogate Lillis was born in West New York, Hudson County, March 6, 1853, and when about four years old his parents moved to Jersey City. He there acquired his early education in public and parochial schools. Entering Rutgers College at New Brunswick in 1870, on a scholarship granted him by the freeholders after he had passed the required examination, he was graduated with the degree of B.S. in 1873, and the same year entered the Hudson County surrogate's office in Jersey City, with which he has ever since been connected. The probate history of Hudson County during the past twenty-seven years is practically a history of Surrogate Lillis's life, and *vice versa*. From a clerkship he rose steadily to the post of Assistant Surrogate, and in November, 1896, was elected Surrogate on the Democratic ticket over his Republican opponent, Hon. P. F. Wanser, then Mayor of Jersey City, receiving a flattering majority. Surrogate Lillis still holds that office, and has discharged its duties with ability and satisfaction. Having had more than a quarter of a century's uninterrupted experience in general probate matters, it is not strange that he should be everywhere regarded as the man best qualified to perform the work coming before a surrogate, and during a life-long devotion to his labors he has achieved an enviable reputation as well as signal success. Genial, sympathetic, and able, thoroughly versed in every department of probate law, and methodical in all his efforts, he is one of the most popular of Hudson County's citizens, and prominent in both political circles and private capacities.

For many years he has been a leading member of the Hudson County Democratic Committee, and for some time he served as its Secretary. He is also a member of the Robert Davis Association of Jersey City, of the Berkeley and University Clubs of the same place, of the Knights of Columbus, of the Benevolent Order of Elks, and of other bodies. He has resided in Jersey City for more than forty years, his present residence being at 208 Palisade Avenue.

Surrogate Lillis was married June 3, 1877, to Alice Dooley, daughter of Felix Dooley, of Poughkeepsie, N. Y. They have four children: Martin J., James T., Jr., John, and Anna.

WILLIAM SEBASTIAN STUHR, of Hoboken, one of the ablest and foremost lawyers of Hudson County, was born in Williamsburg, N. Y., October 1, 1859. At a very early age he moved with his parents to Hoboken, N. J., where his father exerted for many years a commanding influence in political and public affairs.

Mr. Stuhr has, therefore, spent his active life in Hoboken, and to the growth and welfare of the city and also to many of its leading institutions he has contributed some of the best elements of his life. There he acquired his elementary education. He also studied for three years at a prominent institution of learning in Germany, and by the time he had reached early manhood had gained a good classical knowledge as well as a liberal knowledge of the world. Upon his return to the United States in 1874 he entered the Law Department of New York University, from which he was graduated with honor in 1879, receiving the degree of LL.B. He subsequently continued his legal studies in the office of James W. Vroom, of Hoboken, and was admitted to the bar of New Jersey as an attorney in November, 1880, and as a counselor in November, 1883.

WILLIAM H. STUHR.

Since 1880 Mr. Stuhr has been actively and successfully engaged in the practice of his profession in Hoboken. He rose rapidly to a leading place at the bar, not by any sudden freak of circumstances, but by his own efforts, by the exercise of recognized legal ability, and by those honest, straightforward paths which inevitably lead to an honorable end. Careful and painstaking in the preparation of each case which was intrusted to his charge, industrious and indefatigable in collecting both facts and evidence, and sincere in all his arguments before a court and jury, he soon gained an enviable reputation for skill and ability, and for several years has been regarded by his associates as well as his fellow-citizens as a leader of the Hudson County bar. He is one of the ablest and strongest advocates in the trial of causes in the State. Few lawyers have in this respect a higher or wider reputation. His masterful presentation of cases before courts and juries has frequently been noted. He is especially strong in argument, keen and adroit in the examination of witnesses, and a public speaker of admitted prominence and eloquence. A man of unquestioned integrity, he possesses scholarly as well as legal attainments of a high order, and at the bar and in public and private life has been eminently successful.

Mr. Stuhr was Corporation Counsel of the City of Hoboken from 1883 to 1885 inclusive, and served as Assistant Counsel to the Board of Chosen Freeholders of Hudson County in 1888. In these capacities he materially magnified an already high reputation, and discharged his duties with characteristic ability. From boyhood he has been deeply and actively interested in the advancement of his adopted city. He has always been a prominent Democrat, and for several years was President of the Jeffersonian Democracy of Hudson County. In 1889 he was nominated by that party as their candidate for State Senator, and also received the indorsement of the Republicans, and after one of the most exciting campaigns in the history of his county was declared defeated. But he was not one to abide by this decision, which appeared at once to have been brought about by unfair means. He therefore determined to make a contest, and did, with the result that he was seated in the Senate in May, 1890, just as the Legislature was about to adjourn. Probably the most significant and important result of the testimony taken at this time was the indictment by the grand jury of more than fifty election officers of Hudson County, forty of whom were tried and convicted. These were among the most flagrant and noted election frauds ever discovered and prosecuted in New Jersey.

Senator Stuhr was not permitted, however, to actively fill the position which he had so honestly and dearly won. In January, 1891, the Democrats, gaining control of the Senate, unseated him, but not until he had made on the floor of the Senate one of the ablest and most brilliant defenses on record in New Jersey. For three hours on the 15th of that month, immediately after the election of officers, he defended his seat with a zeal and courage which challenged the admiration of his political adversaries and gained for him a host of friends from all parties. Packed galleries at first attempted to interrupt him, but after five minutes all were quiet, and he was given the closest attention to the end. His quiet dignity, his manly courage and commanding presence, his brilliant argument in defense of his rights, not only awed his hearers, but in numberless instances convinced them of the justice of his cause. Even the adherents of McDonald, his opponent, who crowded the Senate and galleries, accorded him their highest respect as a result of his logical and eloquent speech. The vote was taken in silence, but no argument was or could be advanced to show the constitutionality of the action of the majority. The Trenton *Times*, characterizing it as "The First Revolutionary Act," says:

"It was unconstitutional, revolutionary, and entirely without precedent, and can only serve to inflict injury upon the party which performed the act. Senator Stuhr, it will be remembered, was seated by the Senate after a long and tedious investigation. In that investigation it was shown that the frauds of Hudson County were so great that they must have tainted the result and affected the seat of Senator McDonald. Whether wise or unwise, the Senate Election Committee decided then not to call a new election, but to declare that Mr. Stuhr had probably received a majority of the votes cast, and should be sworn into office, and the Senate solemnly, on its own responsibility as a judicial body, so adjudicated."

Again the same paper, in speaking of Mr. Stuhr's brilliant effort, said:

" Senator Stuhr's address in defense of his seat, yesterday, was at times burning with an eloquence which is rarely heard in the New Jersey Legislature. . . . He has shown qualities of courtesy and manliness which have made for him hosts of friends. He came to the legislative halls a stranger, but his modest demeanor and pleasant manner, proving him at once a gentleman and a fair minded, conservative man, won praise and friendship. He goes back to his home known and appreciated outside of Hudson County."

Mr. Stuhr has continued in the practice of the law in Hoboken, where he is a large real estate owner, and where he is highly respected and esteemed. He is a prominent member of Euclid Lodge, No. 136, F. and A. M., of Hoboken; of the Quartette Club and of the Deutscher Pioneer Verein of Jersey City; and of the Jersey City Arion and the Alumni Association of the Law Department of New York University.

He was married in February, 1886, to Miss Marietta Lindsay Miller, daughter of Thomas Miller, a leading citizen of Flushing, L. I.

WILLIAM H. DANIELSON was born in New Durham, Hudson County, N. J., where he still resides, June 16, 1826, and is of Scotch descent on the paternal side and of Dutch ancestry on the maternal side. He is the son of Joseph Danielson and Rebecca Ackerman and a grandson of William Danielson and Mary Lee. Henry Ackerman, his maternal grandfather, was an old resident of New Durham, a soldier in the War of 1812, and a descendant of the old Dutch family of Ackerman of Bergen and Hudson Counties.

Mr. Danielson received his education in the schools of New Durham, and has since followed the occupation of a farmer. He has been a successful agriculturist and an influential member of the Democratic party, and has served as Town Committeeman of New Durham. He has been a supporter of the Baptist Church and of various kindred interests, and is highly respected and esteemed.

He married, first, Rachel Riker, by whom he has four children: William H. (born in 1850), Anna M., Joseph, and Ella. He married, second, for his present wife, Caroline Wilmington.

AUGUST SEITZ was born in Kay, near Herrenberg, Wurtemberg, Germany, November 24, 1815. He studied for the ministry, but owing to the war of 1830 was obliged to give up his studies. In 1836 he went to Paris, engaging in business until 1848, when he came to the United States, locating at New Orleans, and one year later in New York. In 1852 he settled in Hoboken, N. J., and resided there until his death, May 13, 1899. He was a Mason for more than forty years, and for twenty-two years held a responsible position in the Astor House in New York.

He married, April 22, 1843, at Paris, France, Miss Athenias J. A. Grivel, daughter of Joseph and Rose (Rottier) Grivel. She died in Hoboken, February 23, 1899. Mr. Seitz was an Elder for many years in the German Lutheran Church of Hoboken, one of the organizers of the Hoboken Academy, and a member of the old Volunteer Fire Department. Of his seven children two are living. His brother Charles was knighted for services to the king of Wurtemberg. Another brother, William, succeeded his father as keeper of the king's forests, was recently retired, and is still living. His nephew was one of the Government architects at Stuttgart, Germany.

Israel Seitz, father of August, Charles, and William, was descended from an old and honored Lutheran family of Wurtemberg, Germany, who had held the office of king's forester for several generations. Their integrity of character and honesty of purpose made them conspicuous in the Fatherland.

ARTHUR SEITZ, son of August and Athenias J. A. (Grivel) Seitz, was born in Hoboken, N. J., December 6, 1855, and received his education in the public schools and Hoboken Academy, and under a French tutor. At the age of sixteen he entered the silk house of Linneman, Wehry & Co., of New York City, and remained one year. He then entered the shipping house of Salter & Livermore, in New York, and later the employ of the Hamburg-American Packet Company, as collector. Soon afterward he associated himself with the Domestic Sewing Machine Company as note clerk, and later in Hoboken with Charles S. Shultz, lumber dealer. In April, 1882, he engaged in business for himself as a dealer in coal and building materials, under the firm name of Seitz & Campbell (Herbert P. Campbell). In 1883 they opened the Hoboken free stores, the first of the kind there, which are still in existence, under the name of the Campbell stores. Mr. Seitz was the first President of this corporation.

Selling out his interest in these stores in 1886, he again engaged in the building material and coal business with Charles Fall, as Seitz & Fall, and soon afterward they began extensive building operations. Mr. Fall withdrew and Thomas H. Mickens became a partner as Seitz & Mickens. This firm continued about five years. Since then Mr. Seitz has been engaged in the contracting and building business alone, and for the last two years in appraising property almost exclusively. In February, 1899, he became one of the organizers of the North River Light, Heat, and Power Company, of Hoboken, of which he was Treasurer.

Mr. Seitz has always been a strong Republican, as was his father before him. He has served two terms as a member of the Hoboken Board of Education, is Vice-President of the Hoboken Free Library Commission, is President of the Hoboken Tax Commission, and is President of the Board of Trustees of the First Presbyterian Church of Hoboken. He is also Past Master of Advance Lodge, No. 24, A. O. U. W., having served four terms, and is now Representative to the Grand Lodge of New Jersey. He is a member of Hoboken Council, No. 99, Royal Arcanum, was Vice-President and one of the organizers of the Hoboken Chess Club, and was the organizer and one of the first officers of the Philatelic Society of Hoboken, and is still a prominent collector of stamps. He was for several years a member of the Hudson County Republican Committee, has been a delegate to local and State Republican conventions, and has been Chairman of the Hoboken City and Ward Republican Conventions. In April, 1900, Mayor Fagan appointed him a commissioner for Hoboken to the State Exposition to be held in Newark in 1902.

Mr. Seitz was married to Miss Helen Jamieson Borthwick, of Hoboken,

N. J., April 14, 1887. He is a public spirited citizen, active and influential in all the affairs of the community, deeply interested in American shipping, and highly respected by all who know him.

JOHN ZELLER is one of the foremost men of Hudson County and an acknowledged leader of the Democratic party. Having lived in the Township of North Bergen since he was one year old, he is actively identified with public and political affairs, and through his integrity, ability, and genial good nature has gained a wide popularity. He was born in New York City on the 16th of December, 1855, the son of Gottfried and Margaret Zeller, both natives of Germany. His parents came to this country from the Fatherland and first settled in New York. When John was less than one year old they removed to North Bergen, Hudson County, N. J., settling in the vicinity of Guttenberg. At the outbreak of the War of the Rebellion, in 1861, Gottfried Zeller enlisted in the Fifty-sixth New York Infantry Volunteers, and served two years and six months, when, having received an honorable discharge, he reënlisted in the Third New Jersey Cavalry. He remained with that regiment until the close of the war, gaining distinction for bravery in action and honor and acknowledgment for high soldierly qualities which he displayed in action.

JOHN ZELLER.

John Zeller obtained a public school education in the Guttenberg section of North Bergen, and in early manhood learned the trade of barber and hairdresser, which he has followed more or less down to the present time. In politics he has always affiliated with the Democratic party, and from his youthful days has taken an active and influential part in its councils. For many years his prominence and popularity in party affairs have made him a recognized leader, while his sound judgment and great executive ability have won the confidence as well as the respect and admiration of the entire community, which has frequently honored him with election to offices of responsibility and trust. He was Assessor for the Town of Guttenberg from 1883 to 1886, a member of the Guttenberg Town Council in 1890 and 1891, and a representative to the New Jersey Legislature in 1892 and 1893 from the Eleventh District, comprising the Townships of Union and North Bergen, the Towns of Union, West Hoboken, and Guttenberg, and the north part of the Township of Weehawken.

In each of these capacities Mr. Zeller displayed those broad and brilliant qualities which have made him so popular throughout Eastern New Jersey, and which have won for him an extensive acquaintance and hosts of friends. His legislative career was marked by close attention to duty, by valuable and efficient work both in committee and on the floor, and by constant usefulness in the interests of his constitpents. Socially, politically, and fraternally he is widely known and universally esteemed, and if the past is an indication of the future there are yet higher honors in store for him.

DANIEL G. BOGERT, JR., is of the ninth generation from Cornelis Jans Bougaert (see sketch on page 65), who was the first American ancestor of the several branches of the Bogert family in New Jersey. Among his children were two sons, John Cornelise and Guilliam of the second generation.

John Cornelise Bougaert (2) emigrated with his father about 1662 and first settled in the Wallabout section of what is now Brooklyn. He seems to have been a farmer and well-to-do, as he wrote " yeoman " after his name. As has been said in the sketch referred to, he married Angenetie Strycker, daughter of a wealthy Long Island farmer, and in 1686 removed to Hackensack, where he had previously (with the Bantas, Van Buskirks, and others) purchased a large tract called " New Hackensack." He and his wife joined the Dutch Church there in 1686. He was elected a Deacon of the church in 1696. He is presumed to have died about 1715, as his name does not appear on the records after that date.

Guilliam Bougaert (2), the other son of the emigrant first named, came over with his father about 1662 and also settled in the Wallabout section. He married a widow, a Mrs. Bergen, who was the first white child born on Long Island. Their issue was seven sons and three daughters who settled in different localities.

Guilliam (3), one of the sons, settled in Teaneck, Englewood Township, Bergen County, N. J., in 1697, where he built a log cabin, which he occupied for a number of years (on the site of the present Bogert homestead). He then built a stone house nearer the Teaneck road which stood until 1840. His issue was five sons: John, Jacob G., Cornelius, Henry, and Stephen.

Jacob G. (4), the second of these children, married Sarah Van Voorhiss and settled on a farm one-half mile north from his father's farm. Their issue of the fifth generation were Maria and Albert J.

Albert J. Bogert (5), born July 29, 1765, married Sophia Westervelt, and continued on his father's farm. His children were Sarah, Jacob, Albert, Jane, Gilliam, Henry, and Belinda.

Gilliam Bogert (6), born March 3, 1797, bought his great-grandfather's farm and married Maria Demarest, a direct descendant of north of France Huguenot stock. They had issue of the seventh generation Albert G.,

Sarah, Sophia, Daniel G., John G., Hannah D., Marie B., Andrew D., Belinda, Jacob G., and Elsie.

Daniel G. Bogert (7), son above named, was born October 13, 1825. He is a farmer in Teaneck, near the old Bogert homestead. He has served as Assessor for several years, as a Freeholder and Deputy Sheriff, and as Census Enumerator in 1864, 1865, 1866, 1870, 1880, and 1890. He married Sarah A. Bogert, of Paramus, and had nine children: Gilliam D. (born August 16, 1849), John A., Mary Emma, Cecelia, Daniel, Lillian, Estelle, Arthur, and Edith.

John A. Bogert (8), born in Teaneck, October 12, 1850, married Emily, daughter of Stephen G. Hopper, of Hackensack, and has two children living: Charles A. and Stephen G. He is engaged in the lumber business in Englewood with Andrew D. Bogert.

Gilliam D. Bogert (8) is a carpenter and builder of the firm of Gilliam D. Bogert & Brother, which operates in Englewood and Leonia. He married Mary E. Christie, daughter of Peter and a granddaughter of Dower Christie, of Schraalenburgh, and has two children: Daniel G., Jr., and Sarah A., of the ninth generation.

This family of Bogerts have ever since their settlement in New Jersey lived at Teaneck, Englewood, and vicinity. The old Bogert homestead at Teaneck is now owned by the William Walter Phelps estate.

Daniel G. Bogert, Jr. (9th gen.), was born in Englewood, N. J., December 27, 1877. He was educated in the Englewood public schools, graduating therefrom June 27, 1894, and since then has been engaged in the publishing business in New York City.

EDMUND E. JOHNSON has been a resident of Secaucus, Hudson County, since 1854, and is one of the most prominent and highly respected citizens of that community. A Republican in politics, he has held such local offices of honor and trust as Town Committeeman and School Trustee. He was born on Staten Island, N. Y., December 9, 1824, and was educated in the public schools of New York City. He is the son of William Johnson and Catherine Martling, his father being a volunteer soldier in the United States Army during the War of 1812.

Early in life Mr. Johnson engaged in the hotel and restaurant business in partnership with his brother. Later he organized the firm of Jaques & Johnson, of New York City, dealers in pianos, organs, and other musical instruments. Subsequently he resumed the hotel and restaurant business, was very successful, and in 1863 retired from active business. He has since successfully speculated in real estate in New York City, Westchester, Long Island, Jersey City, and Secaucus, where, as already stated, he has had his residence since 1854. He has always taken an active interest in public improvements, and is known as an enterprising and public-spirited citizen. He is an Odd Fellow, and while a resident of New York City was identified with the South Baptist Church. He is now identified with the Reformed Church. In 1847 he was a member of the Carbine Rangers (cavalry) and participated in quelling the Astor Place riot.

Mr. Johnson married Loretta B. Delavergne, of Dutchess County, N. Y., by whom he has four children: Eliza B. (wife of A. S. Engle), William E. Johnson, Alvah W. Johnson, and Marie Louise, wife of George H. Dentz. The eldest son, William Edgar Johnson, who resides at Homestead, Hudson County, is in the Registry Department of the New York Postoffice, where he has been for the past eighteen years. He was born in 1852, and married Mary Olson, by whom he has five children. Mrs. George H. Dentz resides at Jersey City Heights and has five children. Mrs. A. S. Engle resides at Kearny and has three children. Mrs. Johnson died February 7, 1899. Florence Delavergne, daughter of Mr. and Mrs. Dentz, died September 26, 1898. William Delavergne, son of William E. Johnson, died February 12, 1899.

IVINS D. APPLEGATE, Chief Engineer of the Fire Department of Hoboken, Hudson County, was born in that city on the 14th of May, 1853.

IVINS D. APPLEGATE.

He is the son of Ivins D. Applegate, Sr., and Susan Deas Whitney, and a grandson of John B. and Nancy (Anderson) Applegate and John and Mary (Ludlam) Whitney.

Mr. Applegate was educated in Public School No. 1, in Hoboken. In 1870, at the age of seventeen, he went to sea with his father, who was master and part owner of a sailing vessel engaged in the coasting trade. In 1874 he was promoted to the position of first mate, and in 1876 he became master of the same vessel. Afterward he entered the employ of William N. Parslow, a prominent undertaker in Hoboken, with whom he remained until June 1, 1891, when the paid fire department was organized and he was made its Chief Engineer. Mr. Applegate became a member of the old Hoboken Volunteer Fire Department by joining Engine Company No. 1 in May, 1877, and continued in that company until the department was disbanded. During this time he represented his company two terms of one year each in the Board of Representatives of the Widows' and Orphans' Relief Fund, and during five terms of one year each was the company's foreman. He served as Chief Engineer of the Volunteer Fire Department during the years 1889 and 1890, until the organization of the present paid department on June 1, 1891, when he was appointed Chief Engineer, which position he still holds, having been three times elected Chief to succeed himself. He was the last Chief of the old Volunteer Fire Department and the first Chief of the present paid department of the City of Hoboken, and has probably done more than any other one man toward placing the department upon a substantial basis and affording the city that excellent protection from fires which has long been its pride. He is one of the leading fire chiefs in the State, being well known not only in this section but throughout New Jersey for his efficient executive ability and courage. He was influential in bringing about the movement which resulted in the organization of the present paid fire department of Hoboken, and from the first has been indefatigable in making it one of the best protective bodies in the State. He is a member of Euclid Lodge, No. 136, F. and A. M., a public spirited and progressive citizen, and actively identified with the public and social life of his native city. During his entire career he has maintained the confidence, respect, and esteem of the community.

Mr. Applegate was married on the 2d of September, 1884, to Evanglyn Parslow, sister of his old employer, William N. Parslow, of Hoboken. They have seven children: Ivins D., Whitney Parslow, William Nassau, Susan Elizabeth, Evanglyn Mary, Ruth Alga, and Arthur Knox Banta.

JAMES W. PEARSALL, President of the New Idea Pattern Company of New York City, which he organized, and of which he is the owner, has long been a resident of Ridgewood, Bergen County, N. J., where he has been prominent in church and Sunday school work and in connection with various other interests. His business success has been entirely due to his own energy and talents.

Mr. Pearsall was born in New York City, October 17, 1839, and is the son of Silas Pearsall and Ellen, daughter of Alonzo Parker. His father was also born in New York City, while the ancestral line on the paternal side was long established in America. Ellen Parker was born in Waterford, Ireland. Having been educated in the New York public schools, about 1856 Mr. Pearsall entered the employ of James V. Freeman in the wholesale butter trade at 101 Front Street, New York City. Afterward he was with W. H. Phillips, his successor, with whom he remained for nearly eight years. He then removed to Hempstead, Long Island, where for something more than two years he was engaged in the retail grocery business. Returning to New York City, the next ten years were also spent in the wholesale butter trade in the employ of S. W. & J. I. Hoyt. During the subsequent two years he engaged in the same line on his own account.

Mr. Pearsall then formed a connection which eventually led to his present business. He entered the employ of the Domestic Sewing Machine Company in New York, and remained with them for eighteen years, until the company failed. During the last seven years of the eighteen he had been manager of the pattern department of this concern, and he recognized the existence of needs in the pattern trade which no one had undertaken to meet. Thus having severed his connection with the Domestic Sewing Machine Company, in April, 1894, he organized and secured the incorporation of the New Idea Pattern Company, of which he is President and chief owner. This business has been recently described as follows:

"When the New Idea Pattern Company was started, about six years ago, it had practically no cash capital, but what was even more valuable than a bank account was Mr. Pearsall's experience in the pattern business, his acquaintance and good standing among New York houses, and, most important of all, a plan for selling patterns that proved an instantaneous success. This plan or idea is threefold, or has three salient features, which are, briefly: (1) a uniform price, (2) the requirement of no contract, and (3) no minimum limit to the amount of goods to be purchased by a retailer.

"Working on these principles and other innovations to the pattern trade, the upbuilding of the company's business has been of the record-breaking order. Five times in these years it has been necessary to move the head office in New York into larger quarters. Now it has fifty feet frontage on Broadway, with a depth of two hundred feet, and has over one hundred people on its pay roll. There are now over 3,000 agencies established among retail merchants, and distributing offices are located in Chicago, Toronto, and seven other large cities, Chicago being the principal distributing point in the West. The company is incorporated and the stockholders, besides Mr. Pearsall, are his three sons and a son-in-law."

Mr. Pearsall married Hannah W. Myers, and has three sons and three daughters: Ella L., William F., Edgar L., Silas E., Lina G., and Laura C. Pearsall. During the past twenty-five years he has been an active member of the Methodist Episcopal Church, and for a number of years has been a Sunday school superintendent. He is Chairman of the Ridgewood Township Sunday School Association, a member of the Board of Education of Ridgewood, and a Director of the First National Bank of Ridgewood. For fifteen years he has also been a member of the Knights of Honor, and in 1899 held the position in this order of Grand Dictator of New Jersey.

MILTON DEMAREST, of Hackensack, N. J., is descended in the eighth generation from David des Marest, the French emigrant, concerning whom see p. 64. The line of descent is as follows: David des Marest and his wife, Maria Sohier, the emigrants, had issue of the second generation several children, of whom one was Samuel (2), who married Maria Dreuns, and had issue eleven children of the third generation: Magdalena, David, Samuel, Peter, Jacomina, Judith, Sarah, Simon, Rachel, Susanna, and Daniel.

Samuel Demarest (3), of Schraalenburgh, married Annatie Van Horn and had issue of the fourth generation Samuel, Jannetie, Cornelius, Samuel, David, Elsie, Daniel, and Maria.

David Demarest (4) removed to Rockland County, N. Y., where, in 1729, he married Catherine Van Houten. He resided near Tappan, N. Y., where they had issue of the fifth generation Annatie, David, Geertie, Peter, William, Elizabeth, Samuel, Geertie, Lydia, Jacobus, and Garret.

Jacobus Demarest (5), born at Tappan, August 20, 1748, married, in 1784, Rachel, daughter of Cornelius C. Smith, who was born at Tappan, May 14,

1756. She died April 28, 1825, and he died October 9, 1844. They had issue of the sixth generation Cornelius J.; Jacobus, 1789; Sarah, 1792; Elizabeth, 1795; and Joost, 1797.

Cornelius J. (6) was born at Orangetown, N. Y., May 24, 1785, and died September 27, 1863. His wife, Catherine Holdrum, was born June 30, 1787, and died August 31, 1852. Both are buried at the cemetery at Tappan.

Among the children of Cornelius J. (6) and Catherine (Holdrum) Demarest was John C. Demarest (7), who married Isabella, daughter of Daniel D. Tallman, and had issue, among others, of the eight generation, Milton Demarest, the subject of this sketch.

Milton Demarest (8) was born in Rockland County, N. Y., June 8, 1855. He spent his boyhood days in attendance upon the public schools at Nyack, N. Y., and finished his education in the private school of Professor William Williams and at Hackensack Academy, his parents having removed to

ORITANI FIELD CLUB, HACKENSACK.

Hackensack when he was quite young. After completing a thorough academic course he entered as a student the law office of M. C. Gillham, at Hackensack, where he completed a full course of study. In June, 1877, he was admitted to the New Jersey bar as an attorney, and three years later as a counselor. He practiced his profession until the summer of 1879, when he formed a law partnership with Walter Christie, of Hackensack, which lasted for one year. From that time until 1894 he practiced alone, and then associated himself with Abram de Baun, with whom he has since carried on an extensive and lucrative practice.

From 1872 to 1877 Mr. Demarest served as a member of Company C, Second Battalion, N. G. N. J. He has served seven years as counsel and clerk of the Hackensack Improvement Commission, and is a member of the New Barbadoes Board of Education, of which body he was elected President in March, 1900. He is a member of Pioneer Lodge, F. and A. M., of Bergen County Lodge, I. O. O. F., and of the Oritani Field Club, and has served as a Deacon and Elder in the First Reformed Church at Hackensack. In politics he is a Republican. He ranks high in his profession, and is popular socially.

He has been twice married, (1) to Carrie W. Christie and (2) to Adaline B. Christie. His issue of the ninth generation are Lottie, Carrie I., and Edith.

SAMUEL BURRAGE REED, one of the oldest and most prominent architects in this country, was born in Meriden, Conn., on the 7th of January, 1834. He is the son of Samuel Francis Reed and Sarah Tharp, and the grandson of Solomon and Bessie Reed and Joel and Sarah (Darling) Tharp. On his paternal side his ancestors came from Holland during the Revolutionary War, and his great-grandfather took an active and conspicuous part in that conflict. At the close of the war he settled in the fertile valley or pass which for upward of one hundred years has been known as "Reed's Gap," between the mountains that skirt the easterly boundary of Wallingford, Conn. The Air Line railroad between New York and Boston runs through this "Reed's Gap," as will be noted on their published tables. On his maternal side, the Tharps (three brothers) came from Leeds, England, and were among the first settlers in New Hampshire. One of the brothers (William), about the year 1760, removed to Meriden, which at that time was a part of Wallingford, Conn. Here he established himself on a farm which still remains in the family, and here it was that Joel Tharp (an only child) was born December 10, 1778. The buildings have all twice gone to decay, and the third have since been erected within a few feet of the original site. The elder Tharp was respected and served as adviser and administrator of the laws under the "Charter of King Charles II.," of which he was the keeper. The copy of this "Charter with the Acts and Laws for the English Colony of Connecticut, in New England in America," is now in possession of the subject of this sketch, and is prized by him as a family relic.

Following an old custom, Joel Tharp deeded all his property to his only son, Gideon, leaving three daughters with nothing, or risking that in life's lottery they would find companions that would care for them and bear their burdens. This worked all right for the majority, but badly for the minority. Sarah was the eldest, and from the time she was seventeen, when her mother died from sunstroke, she took entire charge and care of the family. Her two sisters married first, and married well, while she remained single until she was thirty years of age, when she married Samuel F. Reed, a builder, aged thirty-two years, on March 24, 1833. Their married life was short, for he died on the 12th of the following October, so Mr. Reed, the subject of this sketch, entered this world as a posthumous child. His mother was able to care for her child until he was seven years of age, when she was advised to part with him, and send him "West" to those she trusted would care for him. She did not realize that she was virtually sending him out of the reach of civilization. At the age of seven he was sent to parties she had known years before, who had settled in the "Black River Country" (Leyden, Lewis County, N. Y.), which was then mostly a wilderness, with occasional settlements miles apart along what was known as the "State Road." There were no schools in that section, and consequently no means of enjoying those educational advantages which the youth of to-day have at their doors. In this frontier region Mr. Reed spent seven years of his boyhood with an aged couple who had nearly worn themselves out on a partly-cleared farm of two hundred acres. Being large for his age, very much of the work fell to his lot. There were no idle hours to waste away, nor had he any companions to divert him from his tasks. He acquired a rugged physique, grew to be self-reliant, learned to think for himself, obtained valuable experiences, and developed an individuality which has remained with him and characterized his life.

Seven years was a long time for him to have charge of all the matters on this farm, but at last relief came when his mother suddenly appeared in her anxiety to learn of his situation. At first he did not recognize her,

S. BURRAGE REED.

having forgotten her features. They very soon became acquainted again. He then showed her over the place, the hundred sheep and other animals, the amount of work he had to do and how he did it. It was easy for him to explain to her that this was no place for him; that while here he would always be a drudge and wear the tow-cloth frock and strap. She saw that his complaints were well founded and determined to find means to take him East with her. A few weeks after she took him to Meriden, and apprenticed him to learn the builder's trade. His first work here was done on the famous mansion of Moses Y. Beach (then proprietor of the New York *Sun*). This structure was erected from designs furnished by Architect Austin, of New Haven. Its cost was sixty thousand dollars, which was a great deal of money in those times when one dollar paid for one day (of twelve hours) of skilled labor. It was while learning his trade that he realized and felt the importance of an education. Just at this time a popular clergyman delivered a lecture on "The Powers of the Mind," in the school-house near by. The matter of this lecture made a deep impression on Mr. Reed, then about fifteen years of age. The lecturer had a trunk with him, containing various articles which he used in illustration during the lecture; along with these were books, some of which he discarded while closing his trunks. Among them were catalogues of publications, of which up to this time Mr. Reed had no knowledge. These books he gradually obtained, read, and re-read, until he thoroughly knew what they contained. His habits of study had attracted the attention of a physician (Dr. David Allen), who gave him access to his library and offered to guide him in his studies. At once his theme was medicine, and after two years' study he appeared before Dr. Sperry, of Hartford, for an examination and a certificate, which he obtained. He was still an apprentice and had some time yet to serve, which prevented the practice of his profession except during spare hours.

Gradually the subject of medicine became a secondary matter. As his skill in his trade developed he became intensely interested in its problems, and finally at the age of twenty-one with his chest of tools he settled in Flushing, L. I. He took his books with him and continued his studies, determined that he would not allow himself to be in ignorance on any subject. He very soon made the acquaintance of Prof. Howard Osgood (now of Rochester University), who kindly offered to give him instruction in the Greek language. This offer was gladly accepted and *Strong's Epitome*, as his primer, and *Antigone*, as a classic, were soon mastered. At the age of twenty-four he possessed an extensive library, including the works of Comb, Spurzheim, Lavater, Gall, Comte, Wayland, Nott and Gliddon, Dick, Koch, Gill, Dowling, Cavallo, Mattison, Silliman, Hale, Home, Plutarch, Good, Dodd, Esdale, and many others of like character, which he had studied industriously and become thoroughly familiar with.

A course of lectures by local talent having been proposed during the following winter, Mr. Reed consented to deliver one entitled "Mental Science." The subject attracted the faculty of a nearby institution that attended the lecture. At its close an interview was requested and arranged for. The purpose of the interview was not stated, but turned out to be an examination, and unfolded the plan of establishing a class in mental philosophy with a request that he assume its leadership. Mr. Reed, though flattered by this request, could not with his retiring disposition enter a curriculum with which he was entirely unfamiliar, and believing that the walls and rules of such an institution would be too narrow and restraining for him declined the offer. He had discovered however, that with perseverance, industry, and indomitable energy he had acquired a broad and accurate knowledge of those studies and sciences which are usually taught only in colleges, and through his own efforts and personal exertions had secured a splendid education and laid the foundation of a most successful career.

For several years he was engrossed in the building business, which up to this time he regarded as his legitimate calling. Designing structures became an interesting part of his work, and to perfect himself in this branch he took a course of instruction under Prof. James McLean (brother of Judge McLean, of Ohio), who for twelve years was a designer on government work in Washington.

Now being fully equipped by practice and experience in designing as well as construction, his plans were sought after until his entire time was devoted to their execution. It must be gratifying to him in his travels in any direction to point out the works of his hands that stand as monuments of his taste and skill. For thirty years he has been located at No. 245 Broadway, New York City, opposite the City Hall, where he has planned an average of upward of one full set of original designs per month during the whole time. Buildings in every style and for all purposes are included in the list. He was the first to develop what has so long been known as the "Queen Anne Style," or more properly "Cottage Style." The Pinard cottages in Newport, R. I., represent his first work in that style. Mr. Reed is a fellow of the American Institute of Architects, and is the author of five publications on architecture specially intended to assist in the erection of convenient and comfortable cottages. How well this laudable endeavor to aid the deserving classes has been appreciated is best told in the fact that the sales of his first book outnumbered any other architectural work ever published.

For about twenty years his labors have been devoted to more elaborate structures. The residence of James A. Bailey (successor to P. T. Barnum) on St. Nicholas Avenue, New York City, is an interesting and distinct type. Bloomingdale Church, Sixty-eighth Street and Broadway, New York City, was where limestone was first used in that city. Collegiate Church on Second Avenue is a beautiful decorated Gothic. Mention of many other buildings of similar character that are now standing in many parts of the country might be made, but it is needless to extend the list here. We should mention his latest work as the Passaic County court house, at Paterson, N. J., which Mr. Reed secured in a competition, including forty-eight architects from all the principal cities. This beautiful structure is in classic design, of white marble, fire-proof throughout, surmounted with a dome, and will require four years for its construction.

We have entered at some length into the details of this story and life-work because of its lesson and tendency to inspire determination, hope, energy, and industry in the face of misfortune and disadvantages, and as an example it may be of infinite value to the younger readers. Mr. Reed started without the help of either father or mother, absolutely without means or friends to advise with, and could hope for nothing from his surroundings. In spite of all these adverse conditions he determined to work up and win at least the respect of intelligent men, and this he has done as all who know him will testify. His business has been his constant pleasure and to its development he has devoted his best energy. In early life he had no chance to join in sport with other boys, and to this day has never seen a ball game, shot a gun, worn a skate, or gone a fishing. He does, however, enjoy table games and is especially fond of chess. He has decided convictions concerning any action, believing in any case that there is but one right way to act. Serving as the "balance wheel" between clients and contractors in more than four hundred cases, he has been able to fully cover each case both professionally and judicially. We are sure no other living architect has such a record.

For several years Mr. Reed has resided in Woodcliff, N. J., where he has taken an active part in public affairs. He was twice elected Mayor of

Woodcliff, and afterward was elected Justice of the Peace. Subsequently he was appointed Commissioner of Deeds. The two latter positions he now holds. Mr. Reed is an interesting talker on religious matters, and for seven years served as a Deacon in the Baptist Church in Flushing, L. I. For seven years he was an Elder in the Reformed Church in New York City, and for the same period a member of the Classis of New York.

Mr. Reed has been twice married, his first wife being Eliza A. Wright, of Flushing, L. I., and his second Lizzie Lowerre, of Brooklyn, L. I. He has five children—four daughters and one son.

CORNELIUS CHRISTIE, train master of the West Shore Railroad at Weehawken, N. J., is distinctively a railroad man, having spent his entire business life in that line. He is descended in the sixth generation from James Christie, the Scotch emigrant, concerning whom see sketch on page 106. The line of descent is James Christie (1), the emigrant, who married Magdalena Samuels Demarest, of Schraalenburgh, and had issue of the second generation thirteen children, one of whom was William Christie, who married Catelyntie Demarest and had issue of the third generation ten children, of whom Captain James Christie, of Revolutionary fame, married Maria Banta, and had issue of the fourth generation seven children, one of whom, David Christie, born December 1, 1789, married Anna Brinkerhoff, and removed to New York City, where he made a fortune as a stone cutter. In 1835, having bought the farm of Garret Mayer at Ridgefield, N. J., he retired from business. He had issue of the fifth generation, one of whom was Albert B. Christie, who married Lydia A. Christie (a distant relative) and settled at Ridgefield Park about 1830. He left issue of the sixth generation, of whom one was Cornelius, the subject of this sketch.

Cornelius Christie (6) was born at Ridgefield Park, September 24, 1864, and was educated in the public schools, graduating from Washington public school, No. 32, Hackensack, in July, 1881. Beginning business as a telegraph operator in the office of the New York, Susquehanna and Western Railroad, in May, 1881, he continued in their employ until June, 1883, when he entered the office of the West Shore Railroad Company as telegraph operator. He so continued until March, 1888, when he was promoted to the position of train despatcher, which he held until April 1, 1895, when by a second promotion he became train master. Mr. Christie has about five hundred men under his supervision, directly and indirectly, more than half of whom may trace their examination, discipline, and employment to his management.

Mr. Christie was married, October 12, 1898, to Miss Selena Wells, of Goshen, N. Y., only daughter of James E. Wells, for many years Supervisor of the Town of Goshen and General Superintendent of the Orange County Agricultural Society. Their bridal trip extended over nine thousand miles through the Western States.

CORNELIUS DOREMUS, a prominent lawyer of Hackensack and New York City, was born at Arcola, Bergen County, N. J., on the 22d of January, 1862, his parents being Jacob W. Doremus and Sophia E. Van Dien. He is descended in the fifth generation from Johannes (John) Doremus, who was born at Middleburg in the Island of Walcheron, in Zeeland, Holland, about 1698. He came to America in 1709, and located at Acquackanonck (Passaic). From there he went to Hackensack, where, in August, 1710, he married Elizabeth, daughter of Abraham Ackerman. The date of the registry of the marriage is August 19. He bought lands in the limits of the Ramapo patent at Preakness and on the Saddle River near Paramus. Joris (George) Doremus, probably his son, lived at Passaic. He married Mary, daughter of Jan Berdaen (Berdan). John and George had each several children, whose descendants have become numerous throughout Bergen and Passaic Counties. On his mother's side Mr. Doremus is descended from Dirck Garretsen Van Dien, of Utrecht, Holland. His grandparents were John B. and Margaret (Westervelt) Doremus and Cornelius G. and Susan E. (Post) Van Dien.

Mr. Doremus received his primary education in the public schools of Bergen County, and after graduating therefrom, in 1878, entered Stevens Institute in Hoboken, where he completed his academical studies. In 1880 he began the study of law as a student in the Law Department of the University of New York, from which he was graduated in 1883, being ad-

HACKENSACK RVcR.

mitted to the New York bar in the same year. He was admitted to the bar of New Jersey as an attorney in 1884 and as a counselor in 1889, and has successfully practiced his profession in Hackensack, Bergen County, and at 120 Broadway, New York City, for a number of years. He has been counsel to the Board of Chosen Freeholders of Bergen County, which position he held for four years. He has been also counsel for Ridgewood village and the Township of Ridgewood and is now counsel for Saddle River, Maywood Borough, and other municipalities.

Coming to the bar well equipped for the duties of a professional career, Mr. Doremus has been eminently successful and in a number of important cases has displayed the highest legal abilities and qualifications. He has devoted himself unceasingly to the interests of his clients, and during the sixteen years of his practice has built up a large and lucrative business, both in New York City and in his native county. He has never aspired to public office, but in 1895 was induced by his friends to accept the nomination for

State Senator. He is a member of the Reformed Church of Ridgewood, N. J., where he resides, and is a loyal and public spirited citizen, thoroughly interested and identified with the affairs of the community, active in promoting every worthy object, and highly esteemed and respected by all who know him.

Mr. Doremus was married on the 6th of December, 1885, to Jennie M. Lake, of Monsey, N. Y., and their children are Florence L., born September 23, 1886, died July 25, 1887; Mabel, born June 14, 1888; and Nellie Budlong, born September 26, 1891.

HAMILTON VICTOR MEEKS is one of the most successful business men of Hudson County, N. J. He is President of the Gardner & Meeks Company, which controls large lumber interests at Union Hill and Guttenberg. He is a Director and Vice-President of the Hudson Trust Company of Hoboken and West Hoboken, of which he was one of the original incorporators. In 1891 he organized the Woodcliff Land Improvement Company, and has been its Secretary and Treasurer to the present time. To his business abilities and energy are chiefly due the remarkable success of this company in building up the beautiful village of Woodcliff-on-the-Hudson. The Grand Boulevard, constructed by Hudson County at a cost of $3,000,000, runs through the edge of Woodcliff, on the crest of the Palisades, and from this elevated point a remarkable view of New York City is spread before the eye. Whether it be viewed by day, or whether it be identified by its myriad lights by night,—an impressive spectacle,—the great metropolis is unfolded to the eye like a huge panorama. The site of Woodcliff is historic ground, and for nearly half a century it has been in the possession of the Meeks family,—one of the interesting old families of New York City and New Jersey.

Joseph Meeks was a prominent citizen of New York City prior to the American Revolution. He was one of the founders of " The Baptist Society," as it was then called, and its first meetings were held at his home. His name appears in the poll list of the electors of the City of New York in 1761.[1] He was a patriot, and his three sons, John, Joseph, and Edward, all fought in the patriot cause during the Revolution.

Captain John Meeks, the eldest son, married, in New York City, Susanne Helene Marie de Molinars, of an old French Huguenot family. She was the daughter of Jean Joseph de Molinars, and a granddaughter of Jean Joseph Sieur Brumeau de Molinars, who was at one time assistant to the Rev. Louis Rou of L'Eglise de Saint D'Esprit of New York City. John Meeks held the commission as Captain during the Revolution in the famous regiment known as " The Hearts of Oak." He owned a country place at Morristown, N. J., adjoining Washington's headquarters, and his wife acted as interpreter for Washington and Lafayette during the time of their stay there. As a reward for his services during the Revolution Captain John Meeks received a grant of land near Syracuse, N. Y., which his descendants have never claimed. He had several sons and a daughter.

Joseph Meeks, the second son, was a prominent citizen of New York City. At the age of twelve he assisted in tearing down the British flag from the top of a greased pole erected in Battery Park. Subsequently he was a soldier in the War of 1812. He was one of the founders of the original Tammany Society, from which Tammany Hall has sprung. He married Sarah, daughter of Colonel John Van Dyke, an officer of the Revo-

---

[1] See James Grant Wilson's *Memorial History of the City of New York*, vol. ii., p. 322.

lution and a descendant of one of the best known old Dutch families of New York. They had several sons and two daughters.

John Meeks, father of the present Mr. Meeks, was the eldest son of the preceding. He married Elizabeth Bush, granddaughter of Richard Bragaw, of Revolutionary fame. Mr. Meeks became a resident of Hudson County, N. J., and in 1851 acquired about one hundred and fifty acres of land,—the present site of Woodcliff,—purchasing from nineteen different titles. It is upon this land that, through the enterprise of Hamilton V. Meeks, the present beautiful village of Woodcliff has sprung up within less than a decade. As already stated this land has an interesting history. A portion of it was once the property of Commodore de Kay, one of the most remarkable characters in the history of Hudson County. Again, the point of land jutting into the Hudson from the Woodcliff property is no other than the identical Block-House Point, of Revolutionary fame, where "Mad Anthony" Wayne made his unsuccessful sortie against the British in the winter of 1779-80. Unfortunately the only fruits of General Wayne's prowess on this occasion consisted in the capture of a herd of cattle, and this performance became the inspiration of the satirical poem, "The Cow Chase," published in New York City by the ill-fated Major André just previous to his capture and execution for acting as a spy in connection with the treason of Benedict Arnold. In Winfield's *History of Hudson County* the reader will find a full and careful account of the attack upon the block-house, with Major André's poem in full.

Hamilton V. Meeks was born in New York City, December 19, 1850. His father was a member of the New York firm of J. & J. W. Meeks, cabinet-makers, which had been established by their father, in turn, in the early part of the present century. This business was originally established on Broad Street, and barely missed destruction in the great fire in New York in 1835, being just on the edge of the burned district. Mr. Meeks received his education in the New York public schools and the College of the City of New York, being graduated from the latter in 1872. On November 4, 1874, he married Euretta Eleanor, daughter of Robert E. Gardner, of an old family of Hudson County, N. J., and the same fall engaged in business with his father-in-law under the style of Gardner & Meeks, lumber dealers, of Union Hill and Guttenberg. This business had been originally founded by the firm of J. & R. Gardner, which became, successively, Robert E. Gardner and Gardner & Meeks. Upon the death of Mr. Gardner in 1895 the Gardner & Meeks Company, of which Mr. Meeks has since been President, was incorporated.

Mr. Meeks resides at New Durham, and is an Elder in the Grove (Dutch) Reformed Church of that place. He is also a member of the Columbia Club of Hoboken, and is on its entertainment and library and picture committees. His college fraternity is the Chi Psi, Kappa Chapter. He is an independent Republican, broad-minded and liberal in his views, and has never held any public office. He has been a generous promoter of every movement looking to the public interests, and is one of the gentlemen whose liberal donation of two-thirds of the right of way alone enabled the construction of the Grand Boulevard, on the crest of the west bank of the Hudson, overlooking New York City, to be carried into execution.

Mr and Mrs. Meeks have three children, two sons and a daughter: Howard Victor Meeks, Clarence Gardner Meeks, and Euretta Eleanor Meeks.

Yours very Respy.
Flavel McGee

FLAVEL McGEE was born April 6, 1844, in Frelinghuysen Township, Warren County, N. J. He prepared for college at Newton Collegiate Institute, Newton, N. J., and Blair Presbyterial Academy, Blairstown, N. J., and was graduated from Princeton College in June, 1865. Three years later he received the degree of A.M. He studied law in Belvidere, and was admitted to the bar of New Jersey in June, 1868. He began practice in Jersey City, forming a partnership with William Muirheid, under the firm name of Muirheid & McGee. The degree of counselor-at-law was conferred upon him at the June term of the Supreme Court, 1871, the first term possible under the rules. At the same term that he was admitted he argued two cases in the Supreme Court and one in the Court of Errors and Appeals. Two of these afterward became leading cases. One was that of the International Life Insurance and Trust Company *v.* Haight, in which it was held for the first time in New Jersey that in estimating the assets of a corporation for taxation United States securities and mortgages not liable to taxation must be deducted. The other was the case of Ransom *ads.* Ruckman, wherein the Court of Errors settled the law on the doctrine of arbitration. Within the first year after his license as a counselor he was employed in important railroad litigation, and since that time has at all times been extensively employed by corporations, notably railroad, banking, and insurance corporations. He was one of the earliest members of the New Jersey bar to engage in the practice of admiralty.

In the year 1876 the late Governor Bedle was added to the firm, which was known as Bedle, Muirheid & McGee until 1888, when Mr. Joseph D. Bedle, Jr., was added to the firm under the style of Bedle, Muirheid, McGee, & Bedle, Jr. This continued until the death of Mr. Muirheid in 1892, when the firm became Bedle, McGee & Bedle. On the death of ex-Governor Bedle in October, 1894, the firm was changed to McGee, Bedle & Bedle, Mr. Thomas F. Bedle being added. The latter retired from the firm in 1899, when the firm name was changed to McGee & Bedle. Recently Robert L. Lawrence has been added, the firm name remaining unchanged.

Upon the death of the late Mr. Justice Bradley, Mr. McGee was put forward by the bar of New Jersey for the position of Justice of the Supreme Court of the United States, and upon the death of the late Chief Justice Beasley his name was urged for the position of Chief Justice of the State. He holds commissions as Master in Chancery, Supreme Court Commissioner, and Advisory Master of the Court of Chancery. He is also a counselor of the Supreme Court of the United States.

He has always been a Republican, and in important elections has frequently taken the stump. In the contest for the United States Senatorship, in which the late Governor Abbett was defeated by Rufus Blodgett, Mr. McGee took an active part with his then partner, Governor Bedle, in opposition to Mr. Abbett's candidacy. In the canvass, which resulted in the nomination of the Hon. John W. Griggs for Governor of New Jersey, Mr. McGee was in the beginning one of the few Griggs men in Hudson County, but he was able to go into the convention with forty-one votes from Hudson County unalterably pledged to Griggs, which resulted in the casting of the whole vote of Hudson County for Griggs, thus securing his nomination.

On the death of the late Charles H. Winfield, Governor Griggs offered to Mr. McGee the position of Prosecutor of the Pleas of the County of Hudson, and earnestly urged its acceptance. The latter declined, however. He has been offered by his party the nomination for almost every important office within the gift of the party in Hudson County, all of which he has declined. He is Vice-President of the Republican County Committee and a member of the Executive Committee. He is a member of the Union League Club of Hudson County, the Carteret and Palma Clubs of Jersey City, the Union League Club of New York, the Society of the Cincinnati, and the Sons of the American Revolution of New Jersey. He was an Elder in the Presbyterian Church of Jersey City up to the time of its consolidation with the First Presbyterian Church of Bergen, since which time he has been an Elder in the First Presbyterian Church of Jersey City.

Mr. McGee married Julia F. Randolph, daughter of the late Judge Bennington F. Randolph and Eliza Forman, of Jersey City, and a granddaughter of Francis C. F. and Phebe H. (Crane) Randolph, of Belvidere, and John B. and Hope Forman, of Freehold, N. J.

CHARLES CLARKE BLACK, one of the leading members of the bar of Jersey City and a member of the State Board of Taxation of New Jersey since April 1, 1891, was born on Wigwam Farm near Mount Holly, Burlington County, N. J., July 29, 1858. He is the son of John and Mary Anna Black and grandson of John and Sarah Black, on his father's side, and of Charles and Rachael Clarke, on his mother's. They were all prominent citizens of this State. His ancestry is an old and honorable one.

Mr. Black received his preparatory education at Mount Holly Academy. He was graduated from Princeton University in the class of 1878, after a regular four years' course, and then entered the law office of Colonel James N. Stratton, of Mount Holly. Afterward he studied for a time in the office of Coult & Howell, of Newark, N. J., and then entered the Law Department of the University of Michigan at Ann Arbor. He was admitted to the Michigan bar by the Supreme Court of that State in 1880, and to the New Jersey bar before the Supreme Court as an attorney at the June term, 1881, and as a counselor at the June term, 1884. Since his admission to the bar of his native State Mr. Black has successfully followed his profession in Jersey City. For nearly twelve years he has been a member of the well known law firm of Randolph, Condict & Black. He is a man of broad and accurate learning, an attorney and counselor of acknowledged ability, and during his legal career has displayed those high qualifications which stamp him as a leader.

Mr. Black served for five years as a member of the Hudson County Board of Registration under the ballot reform law, and on the 21st of March, 1891, was appointed a member of the New Jersey State Board of Taxation for a term of five years from the 1st of the following April. In 1896 he was re-appointed to that office for a second term of five years, and is discharging his duties with the same ability, integrity, and conscientious attention to duty which have made him so prominent at the bar.

Outside of his law practice and official duties Mr. Black has found time to indulge in literary work, for which he has decided talents. In his *Taxation in New Jersey* and *Law and Practice in Accident Cases* he has made two valuable additions to legal literature, and won for himself a reputation as a writer which extends beyond his native State. He is a member of the Palma Club, of the Princeton Club of New York, of the University Club of Hudson County, of the Hudson County Bar Association, of the New Jersey State Bar Association, of the Knights of Pythias, of the Independent Order of Odd Fellows, and of the Ancient Order of United Workmen. In religion he adheres to the faith of the Society of Friends.

On the 12th of February, 1890, Mr. Black was married to Alice G. Hazen, at Flushing, L. I. They have no children.

FRANK P. McDERMOTT, one of the prominent members of the bar of Jersey City, was born on the historic battleground of Monmouth, N. J., October 23, 1854. For more than a century the family name has been prominently identified with that locality. His great-grandfather, William McDermott, served as a soldier in the Revolutionary War, and after the decisive battle of Monmouth settled in Monmouth County, where his descendants have ever since resided.

Mr. McDermott received an excellent preparatory education, attending first the common schools and subsequently Freehold Institute. He was obliged, however, to abandon the cherished hope of a college course, and, turning his attention to the law, entered the office of Acton C. Hartshorne and Chilion Robbins, both skillful, studious, and eminent advocates. Mr. McDermott pursued his legal studies under their instruction, and in November, 1875, shortly after attaining his majority, was admitted to the bar. He began the active practice of his profession at Freehold, Monmouth County, N. J., and there his abilities as an advocate, his broad and accurate knowledge of the law, and his devotion to the interests of his clients soon won for him a leading place among the prominent lawyers of that section. The law and equity reports of the State contained many important cases argued by him, and not a few of them determined difficult legal principles. His practice at the Freehold bar soon outgrew the limits of his native county, and, desiring a more central point and a wider field for the exercise of his energies, he removed his office, in the fall of 1894, to Jersey City. There, as in his native county, he has built up a most excellent reputation. He is a member of the Lawyers' Club of New York, a public spirited and enterprising citizen, and a man of unswerving integrity and great strength of character.

In March, 1880, Mr. McDermott married Elizabeth Thompson, daughter of Dr. Joseph C. Thompson, of Monmouth County. They have three sons and one daughter.

JOHN H. Du BOIS.—The Du Boises are of French origin, and are descended from Louis Du Bois, who was born at Wicres, near the City of Lisle, now in the Province of Artois, France, October 27, 1626, and married October 10, 1655, Catharine Blancon. The couple fled from Lisle to Mannheim in the Lower Palatinate to escape persecution shortly after their marriage. In 1660 they emigrated to America, and located, or attempted to locate, at Hurley, Ulster County, N. Y. In 1667 Louis Du Bois led a colony for the settlement of New Paltz, from which place he removed to Kingston in 1687. His wife, at one time, was captured by the Indians, but was afterward rescued by her husband. She died in 1706. Their children were Abram, Isaac, Jacob, Sarah, David, Solomon, Louis, Matthew, Rebecca, and Rachel.

John H. Du Bois is lineally descended from the emigrant, Louis Du Bois, in about the seventh generation. He was born in Kingston, N. Y., April 22, 1841. His father, John S. L. Du Bois, was a native of Hurley, N. Y., and his mother, Margaret Van Gaasbeck, was born in Kingston, N. Y. These as well as their worthy ancestors exemplified the sterling characteristics of their race. Mr. Du Bois is now one of the foremost citizens of Weehawken.

John H. Du Bois obtained his education in the Kingston public schools. After completing his studies he found employment as a bargeman for the Delaware and Hudson Canal Company, with whom he remained until he attained his majority. Subsequently he was for four years the master of a coal barge, and at the end of that period came to Weehawken as an overseer of men for the same corporation. At the present time he has

JOHN H. DuBOIS.

charge of all outside work, including all shipments of coal, for the Delaware and Hudson Canal Company.

Through his faithfulness, integrity, and untiring devotion to duty Mr. Du Bois has won the confidence of not only his associates, but of all the company's officials and of the community in which he is an honored citizen. He is universally esteemed for those qualities of manhood which distinguish his race, and which deserve the trust and respect of every honest man. Being a Republican in politics, he has taken an active interest in local public affairs, and was elected by his townsmen a member of the Board of Town Council and subsequently Chairman of the board for a term of three years. He is also a prominent member of the Lincoln Club, a leading Republican organization of Weehawken, and a member of the First Methodist Episcopal Church of Hoboken. Progressive, patriotic, and enterprising, and imbued with the highest principles of manly courage and devotion, he has always supported every movement designed to advance the community and its people.

Mr. Du Bois was married, on the 28th of December, 1864, to Miss Alice R. Howland. They have two sons: George H. and Charles H., and reside in Weehawken, N. J.

WILLIAM LEWIS STEWART, formerly Postmaster of Arlington, Hudson County, and a veteran of the Civil War, is descended from a long line of Scotch-Irish ancestors. His father, Edward Stewart, son of John Stewart, died in Arlington, November 15, 1894, aged eighty-four years. His mother, Maria (Hoyt) Stewart, died May 1, 1895, at the age of eighty-three. Both were Presbyterians, the father being an Elder in that church and otherwise connected with the churches at Muscatine, Ia., Brooklyn, N. Y., and Arlington, N. J. They had two sons: William L., the subject of this article, and John E. Stewart, of Plainfield, N. J., senior member of the firm of Stewart, Warren & Co., stationers, 29 Howard Street, New York City.

Mr. Stewart comes from Revolutionary stock. He was born in Middletown, N. Y., April 18, 1843, and received his education in the district schools of Iowa, whither the family removed while he was young. After leaving school he engaged in farming in Iowa, and subsequently became a practical sugar planter in Louisiana, where he remained seven years. He removed to Brooklyn, N. Y., in 1875, and thence in 1876 to Arlington, N. J., where he has since resided. He was successfully engaged in the stationery business in New York City from 1877 to 1894. He served as Postmaster at Arlington from 1894 to December 31, 1899.

Mr. Stewart served with distinction in the War of the Rebellion. He was mustered into Company E, Eighteenth Iowa Infantry, August 6, 1862, and served on the frontier division of the Southwest under Curtis, Schofield, and Steele, his regiment being a part of the Seventh Army Corps. He participated in a number of important engagements, notably those at Springfield, Mo., second Pea Ridge, Poison Springs, and Camden, Ark., and was honorably discharged from the service in August, 1865.

Returning from the war, Mr. Stewart entered upon an active business life. He is a member of the Union Veteran Legion and of the Veteran Association. He is a member of the Union Veteran Legion and of the Veteran Association of Arlington, and respected as a man of ability, enterprise, and public spirit.

Mr. Stewart married, in 1884, Lydia B. Miller, daughter of James Burt, of Warwick, N. Y. They have no children.

JOHN HENRY MACDONALD has been a life-long resident of Bayonne, N. J., where he was born on the 15th of February, 1844. He is the son of John Macdonald and Hanna Everson, and a great-grandson on his mother's side of a soldier in the Revolutionary War. His parents were both born and married in Hudson County, N. J., where the Macdonalds and Eversons have resided for many years.

Mr. Macdonald attended the Bayonne public schools, acquired an excellent rudimentary education, and then engaged in the oyster business in his native town. Afterward he became lighthouse keeper at Bergen Point, N. J., under President Lincoln. He enlisted in 1861 and served nine months in Company C, Twenty-first New Jersey Volunteers, participating in the battles of Chancellorsville, Fredericksburg, and other engagements, and being honorably discharged from the service in 1862.

Mr. Macdonald is now the proprietor of the Riverside House in Bayonne, and is one of the most popular citizens of Southern Hudson County. He is patriotic, public spirited, and progressive, active in the interests of the community, influential in promoting local prosperity, and respected and esteemed by all who know him. In politics he is a Republican, and in religion a Methodist. He is a member of Van Houten Post, Grand Army

JOHN H. MACDONALD.

of the Republic, of Jersey City, and prominently identified with other important organizations and enterprises in his native county.

He was married on the 24th of December, 1865, to Ann L. Barnes, daughter of Stephen D. and Judith Barnes, of Port Richmond, Staten Island, N. Y. They have three children: John S., Emma J., and Charles W.

JAMES PRENTICE NORTHROP, a member of the well known law firm of Wallis, Edwards & Bumsted, of Jersey City, N. J., springs from some of the oldest families of New England, his paternal ancestors coming over in 1630 and his mother's in 1640. Both lines were among the earliest settlers of Massachusetts and Connecticut, and were represented in the Colonial and Revolutionary wars, as well as in the professional and business affairs and in the civil life of the colonies and States. Mr. Northrop is the only child of James R. Northrop and Catherine S. Prentice, daughter of Nathan and Alice (Spencer) Prentice. His father was the only son who attained maturity of Rev. Bennett F. Northrop, a graduate of Yale College and of the Albany Theological Seminary, and a well known Congregational clergyman of Connecticut, and who was the only son of Joshua Northrop, of Litchfield, Conn.

James P. Northrop was born in Springfield, Mass., on the 5th of August, 1856, and received his education in the common schools of Connecticut and New Jersey. He read law in Jersey City in the offices of Hon. William A. Lewis, Raymond P. Wortendyke, and Wallis & Edwards, successively, and was admitted to the bar of New Jersey as an attorney at the November term of the Supreme Court in 1880 and as a counselor at the February term in 1892.

Since 1880 Mr. Northrop has been actively and successfully engaged in the general practice of his profession, and is now a member of the law firm of Wallis, Edwards & Bumsted, of Jersey City. He resided for a time in Bayonne, Hudson County, where he served for two years as City Attorney. He is now a resident of North Plainfield, N. J. Mr. Northrop is an able lawyer, a man of broad attainments, and respected and esteemed by all who know him. He is a member of Enterprise Lodge, No. 147, F. and A. M., of Jersey City, a member of the Hudson County Bar Association, and a member of the Park Club of North Plainfield.

September 27, 1883, Mr. Northrop married Harriet R. Wilson, daughter of Milton B. and Harriet (Metcalf) Wilson, of Danielson, Conn. Both the Metcalfs and Wilsons are among the oldest families of that State. Mr. and Mrs. Northrop have one daughter, Norma.

FRANCIS DOUGLAS JACKSON, of Hoboken, one of the leading produce commission merchants in Hudson County and a Major in the Spanish-American War, was born in Brooklyn, N. Y., on the 19th of August, 1841. He is the son of Charles Jackson and Eliza M. Castle and a grandson of Amasa and Mary (Phelps) Jackson and of William and Sarah (Marvin) Castle. His great-grandfather, Colonel Michael Jackson, was Colonel of the Eighth Massachusetts Infantry in the American Revolution and was brevetted Brigadier-General for meritorious service. His great-great-grandfather, Jonathan Jackson, was the first Collector of the Port of Boston, Mass., while his first ancestor, Edward Jackson, came to New England about 1630 and settled near Boston. The family has always been prominent and influential in all the affairs of life, active in promoting every worthy object, and distinguished in public and other capacities. The name has figured prominently in the history of New England for generations.

Major Jackson was educated in the schools of Brooklyn, N. Y., where he resided until 1870, when he moved to Hoboken, Hudson County, N. J. During the past thirty years he has been actively and successfully engaged in the commission business, dealing extensively in farm and dairy products, with his office in Hoboken. He owns five creameries in different localities and is one of the largest shippers in Hudson County.

In military affairs Major Jackson has achieved special distinction. He served in the Civil War in 1862 and 1863, in Company H, Seventh New York Infantry. Afterward he was active in the New Jersey militia, becoming

First Lieutenant and Adjutant in the Ninth Regiment December 20, 1881, Captain of Company E, Second Regiment, April 6, 1886, Captain of Company L, Fourth Regiment, May 31, 1892, and Major of the Second Regiment May 22, 1893. He was Major of the Second New Jersey Infantry in the Spanish-American War, being attached to General Fitzhugh Lee's corps, and was honorably mustered out of service November 17, 1898. Major Jackson is a member and Trustee of the Columbia Club of Hoboken, a member of the Seagirt (N. J.) Rifle Club, a member of the Spanish-American War Veterans' Association, and a member of the Naval and Military Order of the Spanish-American War. He is one of the best known men in Hudson County, universally respected and esteemed, and active in promoting local objects. In business he has been eminently successful; in military affairs he has achieved special distinction, having risen from private to commanding officer. He is and has been for several years a Vestryman in St. Paul's Church, Hoboken.

Major Jackson married Lizzie H. Gaunt, by whom he has had six children: Gertrude, F. Douglas, Charles Phelps, Edward, Nathalie, and Oliver.

MARTIN LAWLESS, Police Justice of Harrison, Hudson County, since 1894, and for many years a leader of the Democratic party, was born in Newark, N. J., April 6, 1850, the son of James Lawless and Ellen Sims. His parents were both natives of Ireland, but were married in this country, his father coming over about 1845. James Lawless was associated with Obert, Meeker & Co., of Newark, for about thirty years, and later was made attendant on the Harrison Avenue free bridge. He died in 1879.

Judge Lawless attended the public schools of Newark, and then learned the trade of mason and bricklayer, which he followed for several years. About 1887 he engaged in business for himself, and as a contractor and builder erected a large number of important buildings, including the first carbonizing furnaces for Thomas A. Edison in Harrison, the Sacred Heart Convent, the Goodman building, the Hartshorn factory, and many others in Harrison and vicinity. His work stands as monuments to his industry and enterprise. His success was merited, because it was the result of his own efforts.

He also found time for political activity, and as a Democrat served on the Board of Aldermen of Harrison for four years and in the New Jersey House of the Assembly during the sessions of 1892 and 1893. In both of these capacities he exerted a potent influence and made honorable records. In 1894 he became Police Justice of Harrison, where he resides, and he has continued in that office, discharging its duties with ability, courage, and satisfaction. Judge Lawless is a man of sound judgment, of great force of character, and of fearless energy and directness. In the councils of the Democratic party he is a trusted and valued leader. He is a prominent member of the Robert Davis Association, of the Knights of Columbus, and of the Master Masons' Association, and in religion is a Catholic. He has never married.

JAMES SHUART, of Ramseys, Bergen County, is the grandson of Adolphus Shuart, who fought in the War for Independence. His maternal grandfather, John Sutherland, was in the War of 1812, and received a pension of $12 per month up to the time of his death. The Shuarts are of German ancestry, but have made their home in Bergen County since coming to America.

Mr. Shuart is the son of Henry A. Shuart and a grandson of Adolphus Shuart, and was born in Hohokus Township, Bergen County, August 19, 1844. After receiving a limited education in the common schools he began business in the dry goods and grocery trade in Orange County, N. Y. This proved successful, and in 1870 he came to Ramseys, where he opened a meat market. This also became a profitable business, and in 1896 he retired. Mr. Shuart is a Free Mason and a prominent Odd Fellow. He served three

JAMES SHUART.

years as a member and President of the Board of Education, and was recently elected to serve three more years in the same capacity. He has also served as Assessor and Road Commissioner of Hohokus Township for three years. In politics he is a Democrat. He and his family attend the Lutheran Church.

Mr. Shuart was married at the age of seventeen to Susan Jane Hunter, daughter of David Hunter, of Orange County, N. Y. They had one son,

Franklin Shuart, of Ramseys. Mr. Shuart's first wife died in 1868, and he married, in 1872, Miss Eleanor N. Litchult, of Brooklyn, N. Y. They have had four children: Elizabeth, who married Albert G. May, of Ramseys; Eva R., who married S. G. Conklin, of Newburgh, N. Y., and died at the age of twenty and one-half years; Harry, formerly a student at Peddie Institute and now a student at Yale College; and Edna, at home.

HENRY HOPE VANDERBILT, of Hoboken, descends from the noted Vanderbilt family of Staten Island, N. Y. The first ancestor of this family in America was Jan Aersten Van der Bildt, who came from Holland about 1650. He was married three times. His son, Jacob Janse Van der Bildt, was married, August 13, 1687, to Maritje (Mary) Van der Vliet (" of the stream "), and their son Jacob, born in 1692, married Neeltje (Cornelia) Denyse. In 1718 the last named Jacob purchased a farm on Staten Island and removed thither from Flatbush, Long Island. From him descended the famous " Commodore " Vanderbilt, the distinguished Vanderbilt family of New York, and numerous branches of the family in different sections of the country.

Henry H. Vanderbilt was born in Williamsburg, N. Y., April 8, 1862, but has spent nearly all his life in Hoboken, N. J., whither he came with his parents when a small boy. His father, Jacob Vanderbilt, and his mother, Angelina C. Hope, inherited the sterling characteristics of their ancestors, and instilled these traits into the minds of their children. He attended the Hoboken public schools, improved every opportunity that came in his way, and early displayed high mental and physical qualifications. His training was practical as well as theoretical. Soon after completing his studies he established himself in business, dealing in coal, masons' materials, and drain pipe, and has built up an extensive trade. His office and yards are on Willow Avenue and Seventeenth Street, Hoboken.

Having devoted his energies strictly to business, Mr. Vanderbilt has never sought nor held public office, but as a public spirited citizen, deeply interested in the affairs of his town and county, he has contributed to the general welfare by casting his influence on the side of right and justice, and is respected for those virtues and attributes which mark the successful man. He is a member of the Columbia Club of Hoboken. He married Miss Lavinia E. Taft, and resides on Garden Street, Hoboken.

JOHN SIDNEY DARLING, one of the most prominent residents of West New York, formerly the Township of Union, Hudson County, was born in New York City, July 29, 1853, the son of James Darling and Mary Adams. He is of Scotch descent, his father having been born in Glasgow, while his mother was born in Edinburgh. His parents were married in New York, having come to this country in 1850 and 1844, respectively. For eighteen years his father was engaged in business in that city as a plumber and gas fitter. Subsequently he was a collector for the Manhattan Gas Company of New York. He moved to West New York (Taurus postoffice), N. J., in 1860, and died there September 22, 1867, from the effects of a shot fired by burglars. His mother was born in the City of Edinburgh, December 25, 1820, and died in West New York, N. J., July 8, 1900.

John S. Darling was educated in the public schools of New York City and in New Jersey in what is now West New York. He served an apprenticeship as a bricklayer, and then engaged in the business of bleaching and refinishing lace curtains in West New York. Disposing of this business in 1889, he became Secretary and Treasurer of a corporation which operated the so-called sanitary laundry trays, subsequently, also, becoming manager of the plant. Having disposed of his interest in this enterprise, he next engaged in manufacturing music-boxes, under the name of the American Music Box Company, of West New York and later of Hoboken. Since 1893, however, his business has been that of a real estate and insurance operator, and in this line he has been remarkably successful, having offices on Bergenline Avenue in West New York, opposite the town hall.

JOHN S. DARLING.

Mr. Darling was a member of the Hoboken regiment of the National Guard, Ninth New Jersey Volunteers, and was honorably mustered out as Sergeant at the expiration of his term of enlistment of seven years. He is a charter member of the Empire Hook and Ladder Company and was its Foreman for two years, and belongs to Mystic Tie Lodge, No. 123, F. and A. M., to Cyrus Chapter, No. 23, R. A. M., to Pilgrim Commandery, No. 16, K. T., of Hoboken, to Mecca Temple, A. A. O. Nobles of the Mystic Shrine, of New York, to the Order of the Elks Lodge, No. 74, of Hoboken, to the Foresters of America, of West New York, to Oak Cliff Council, No. 1,748, Royal Arcanum, and to Palisade Lodge, No. 128, Knights of Pythias. He has held various official positions in these orders. He is also a member of the Dutch Reformed Church.

Mr. Darling has been conspicuous in various public capacities. He is a Democrat, and an active leader of the party. He was Township Clerk of the Township of Union (now West New York), being in fact its first Clerk, and served three years. For four years he was Tax Collector and Treasurer of the same township, being successively elected without opposition. For two years he was Chief of Police of the Township of Union. He was also both Tax Collector and Disbursing Officer of the school funds of the Township of Union, and is now the Tax Collector of West New York, being elected on the organization of the town in 1897 and re-elected in 1899 for a term of three years. He is also a Commissioner of Deeds and a Notary Public.

He married, September 17, 1893, Abigail B., daughter of James and Sarah Crossley, of Fairview, N. J., by whom he has one child, Sidney Louis Darling, born August 9, 1894.

STEWART LOWRY, a well known hotel proprietor of Secaucus, Hudson County, has been a life-long resident of that place, having been born there on the 31st of March, 1854. He is the son of Robert Lowry and Margaret Foley, both natives of Ireland, who came to this country in early life and took up their home in Secaucus.

Having received a good practical education in the Secaucus public schools, Mr. Lowry engaged in the business of a hotel keeper and farmer, which he has since followed with uninterrupted success. He has also served his fellow-townsmen in various important capacities, among them that of Constable. He is a member of the Royal Society of Good Fellows and the Foresters of America, and as a citizen is highly respected for his integrity, enterprise, and sound common sense.

Mr. Lowry married Miss Annie Price and has six children: Margaret, Nellie, Stewart, Jr., Humphrey, Isabella, and Mary.

ISAAC D. BOGERT, Mayor of Westwood and a leading merchant of that borough, is descended in the eighth generation from Cornelis Jansen Bogaerdt, the Dutch emigrant, concerning whom see the sketch of Daniel G. Bogert on page 132. The line of descent is as follows: Cornelis Jansen Bougaert (1), the emigrant, and his wife, Geesie Williams, had issue of the second generation Wyntie, John C., Classie, Roelof, Maritie, and Peter.

John C. Bogert (2) married Angenetie Strycker, of Long Island, and settled at Hackensack, N. J., where he had issue of the third generation Roelof, Lammetie, Claes, John, Cornelius, and Albert.

Albert Bogert (3), of Hackensack, born about 1690, married, February 17, 1713, Martha Bertholf, and had issue of the fourth generation John, Guilliaem, Isaac, Jacobus, Angenitie, Henry, Cornelius, Cornelius, and Angenitie.

Isaac Bogert (4), born in 1718, married, June 4, 1742, Lea, daughter of John Demarest, and settled near Westwood, N. J., on a farm purchased in 1765. His issue of the fifth generation were Albert, Jacobus (who died in the Revolutionary cause), John, and Martina.

Albert Bogert (5) inherited his father's homestead, married, and had issue of the sixth generation, one of whom was Isaac A. Bogert, born about 1766, who married, May 31, 1788, Margaret Durie. They resided on the old homestead and had issue of the seventh generation two children: David and Lea.

David Bogert (7), born July 2, 1800, married Hannah Ackerman, and resided at Westwood, where he had issue of the eighth generation, one of whom was Isaac D. Bogert, the subject of this sketch.

Isaac D. Bogert (8) was born on the old Bogert homestead at Westwood in 1834. Having spent his early life in school, he continued on the farm until 1869, when he began a mercantile career, which he has since followed, having been the head of the firm of Bogert & Van Emburgh from the time the business started. Besides the grocery business he was Postmaster for twenty years. The firm also maintained a large trade in lumber and coal.

Mr. Bogert has been selected by his fellow-townsmen at various times to represent their interests in official capacities. He was Freeholder for six years, during a part of which time he was Director of the county board. He also filled the office of Collector for Washington Township, and in 1899 was elected the first Mayor of Westwood. In conjunction with Richard Hopper, Abram B. Bogert, and others he organized the Reformed Church at Westwood in 1887, and has filled the office of Elder since that time. Mr. Bogert is a member of the Grand Army, but aside from this his relations in life are domestic. He is public spirited, and through his kindly aid the village has received great help. In 1894 he generously donated for public use two acres of valuable ground in the center of the borough for a park, in which are twenty-seven sugar trees of his own planting.

In 1852 Mr. Bogert married Anna Van Wagoner, daughter of John Van Wagoner, of Oradell, N. J. They have no children.

ADDISON D. WHITE, a veteran of the Civil War and now a Justice of the Peace in Harrison, Hudson County, was born on Staten Island, New York, April 9, 1846. He is the son of Richard White and Ann Simonson, and a descendant of ancestors who came to this country several generations ago, both his parents being natives of Staten Island.

Mr. White acquired, as a boy, a good public school education, and had scarcely finished his studies when, impelled by the patriotism which distinguishes his race, he enlisted in the One Hundred and Thirty-second New York Volunteer Infantry for service in the War for the Union. He served three years, participating in Sherman's historic march to the sea and in numerous battles and skirmishes, in all of which he bore a conspicuous part.

Returning home at the close of his service, with an honorable discharge and a brilliant record for bravery in action, Mr. White devoted himself to active business pursuits. In 1870 he removed to Harrison, N. J., where he has since resided, and until 1875 was successfully engaged in real estate operations. He is now connected with the Domestic Sewing Machine Works. In politics Mr. White is an ardent and influential Democrat, and for several years has been active in the interests of his party. He is now (1900) serving his second term as Justice of the Peace. He is a member of the Junior Order United American Mechanics and of the Daughters of Liberty. He married Miss Margaret Martin and has three children.

ORD DARLING, a prominent citizen of West New York (Taurus post-office), Hudson County, and a brother of John S. Darling, whose sketch appears on page 308, was born on Forty-second Street in New York City, on the 13th of April, 1857, and moved with his parents to West New York when about seven years old. He was educated in the public schools of the latter place, and when sixteen entered his father's bleachery, where he remained until he reached the age of twenty, learning and mastering every branch of the business.

In 1873 Mr. Darling entered the employ of the National Wood Manufacturing Company, of New York. He continued with that concern as outside man, laying parquet floors, until 1878, when he became superintendent of lighters for the West Shore Railroad. About 1885 he resigned that position, but after a year spent in a bleachery returned as ferry master at the old ferry, where he continued from 1886 to 1890. He was subsequently foreman of the Union Granite Company until 1893, and since that time has been State agent for New Jersey of the Climax Powder Company, of Emporium, Pa., having his office in West New York (Taurus postoffice).

ORD DARLING.

In public life Mr. Darling has been prominent for a number of years. He was a member of the Board of Council of the Township of Union for one year, Chairman of the board for two years, Police Sergeant of the Town of Union for two yeras, and Township Treasurer one year. At the present time he is serving his second term as a member of the Hudson County Board of Chosen Freeholders from West New York. In politics he is an active and influential Democrat. He has been a member of the Democratic County Committee from his district since about 1895.

Mr. Darling was a charter member of Court West New York, No. 29,

Foresters of America, has been Chief Ranger for three successive terms, and has served as District Deputy for Court Fort Lee and Court Palisade. He was one of the organizers and is still a prominent member of the Fire Department of West New York, and was most active and useful in the organization of that township. He is also a member of the Royal Arcanum and of the Elks.

In these and various other capacities Mr. Darling has displayed great executive ability and native energy, and throughout his life he has retained the confidence and respect of all who know him. He has always been a progressive citizen, ready to promote every worthy enterprise, and active in the affairs of the community. It was while serving as Sergeant of Police, at the Guttenberg race track, that he saved the life of Michael Buckley, a constable, while the latter was attempting to arrest a noted desperado and criminal.

Mr. Darling was married, in March, 1880, to Alice, daughter of John and Alice White, of West New York. They have nine children: Ord, Jr., Jennie, John, Harry, Alice, Gertrude, Erastus, Mary, and James.

JOHN JAMES TOFFEY, of Jersey City, for two terms Sheriff of Hudson County and State Treasurer of New Jersey from 1875 to 1891, was born in Pawling, Dutchess County, N. Y., on the 1st of June, 1844. He is the son of George A. Toffey and Mary D. Cooke and the grandson of Daniel and Betsey Toffey.

In 1854 he removed with his parents to Hudson County and since then he has been a resident of Jersey City. He received his education in the public schools and in the University of the City of New York. He took an active part in the War of the Rebellion, enlisting, August 21, 1862, at the age of eighteen, in the Twenty-first Regiment, New Jersey Volunteers. After serving with that regiment for nine months, and taking part in all its engagements, he was mustered out of service, but immediately re-enlisted in the Thirty-third Regiment, New Jersey Volunteers, and was commissioned First Lieutenant of Company G. On November 23, 1863, during an engagement at the battle of Missionary Ridge, Tenn., he was severely wounded, which disabled him from further service in the field. President Lincoln afterward commissioned him a Lieutenant of the Veteran Reserve Corps, and he performed duty until June, 1866, when he was honorably discharged from service. He received from Congress a medal of honor for " gallantry at the battle of Missionary Ridge."

Returning to civil life, Mr. Toffey engaged in active business as a live stock dealer, and so continued from 1866 to 1874, being connected with the well known firm of Daniel Toffey & Co., one of the first in this country to engage in shipping dressed beef to Europe.

Mr. Toffey has always been an active Republican, prominent in public affairs, and one of the most distinguished men in his section. He was a member of the Board of Aldermen of Jersey City in 1874 and 1875, and in the fall of 1875 he accepted the nomination of his party for the Fifth District for Member of Assembly and was elected by a large majority. He was again elected in 1876. He served as Sheriff one term, and in 1885 was elected State Treasurer of New Jersey by joint session of the Legislature, and served in that capacity six years. In 1891, both Houses of the Legislature being Democratic, he was succeeded by Hon. George R. Gray, but his services were acknowledged and recognized by the following resolution, passed March 9, 1891, the Legislature being Democratic in both branches:

"WHEREAS, The retiring State Treasurer, Hon. John J. Toffey, has discharged the duties of his office in a manner honorable to himself and greatly to the benefit and advantage of the State;

"*Resolved* (the House of Assembly concurring), That we hereby express our recognition and appreciation of the services of our retiring Treasurer, and congratulate him upon the excellent record he has made for himself and the State."

In 1893 Mr. Toffey was again elected Sheriff of Hudson County by over 6,000 majority, and served another three years. In 1867 he organized Company D, Fourth Regiment, New Jersey Rifle Corps, which became a part of the National Guard, and of which he was Captain. He was elected Major of the new regiment, and later was elected Lieutenant-Colonel, which position he held until 1876, when he resigned.

Colonel Toffey is one of the most popular men of Hudson County. He is a member of G. Van Houten Post, No. 3, G. A. R., and of Pennsylvania Commandery of the Military Order of the Loyal Legion. He is Past Master of Bergen Lodge, No. 47, F. and A. M., and a member of Mount Vernon Chapter, R. A. M., of Hugh de Payen Commandery, K. T., and of New Jersey Consistory, Scottish Rite. He is a member of the Union League, Palma, Carteret, and Jersey City Clubs, and of the Medal of Honor Legion, and is also an Elder in the Bergen Reformed Church.

Colonel Toffey was married, May 17, 1870, to Mary Elizabeth Sip, granddaughter of Colonel Garret Sip and great-granddaughter of Peter Sip, one of Hudson County's first Judges. They have had four sons, three of whom survive: George A. Toffey, John J. Toffey, Jr., and William V. Toffey. He resides at 155 Magnolia Avenue, Jersey City. His son, John J. Toffey, Jr. (1900), is First Lieutenant in the Fourth United States Infantry at Manila, Philippine Islands, having been in many of the engagements in that place. His brother, Daniel Toffey, was an officer on board the United States steamer "Monitor" during the historical engagement with the Confederate steamer "Merrimac" in the Civil War.

JOHN E. OTIS, the first Chairman of the new Town of West New York and one of its leading business men, is the son of Patrick Henry Otis and Margaret Gillorly, natives of Ireland, who came to this country in the spring of 1853 and settled in New York City. There Mr. Otis was born on the 20th of September, 1853, soon after their arrival. The family removed shortly afterward to Philadelphia, where Patrick H. Otis engaged in business as a distiller, rectifier, and wholesale dealer in liquors, which he conducted with success for several years. He died in Jersey City Heights about 1875.

Mr. Otis was reared in Philadelphia. He attended St. Michael's Parochial School until he was ten years old, when he entered St. Michael's Academy, where he remained until he reached the age of twelve. Afterward he attended De la Salle College at Philadelphia until he was fifteen, when he moved to Brooklyn, E. D., N. Y., and continued his studies a short time. He was then employed by his father as bookkeeper and assisted in managing his business. Subsequently he was associated with his father in Jersey City Heights, N. J., until 1875, when his father died. In 1876 the family moved back to Philadelphia, when Mr. Otis was employed by Gould & Co., wholesale milk dealers, of Washington, to manage their dairy during the Centennial Exposition. In 1877 the family moved to Baltimore, Md., where Mr. Otis engaged in mining, which business he followed successfully in New Jersey, New York, Maryland, and Georgia. For four years he was in the service of the West Shore Railroad. In 1888 he established himself in the hardware trade at West New York, where he has since resided.

Few men have contributed more to the growth and welfare of a community than Mr. Otis has to the section in which he lives. He has not only given it an important impetus in business affairs, but has also been

JOHN E. OTIS.

active and influential in its very foundation as a town as well as in its organization and advancement. As Clerk for one year, as a member of the Board of Council, and as Acting Chief of Police of the Township of Union he took a prominent part in all local affairs, and it was through him that the Town of West New York was set off and legally incorporated July 5, 1898. He was the principal founder and organizer of the new town, and in the spring of 1899 became its first Chairman, which office he now fills. He is also Acting Chief of Police under the new charter, Treasurer of the Firemen's Relief Association, and Foreman of the Empire Hook and Ladder Company, having organized the first fire department in West New

York. In these various capacities he has displayed patriotism and enterprise, and is universally respected and esteemed as a public spirited, energetic, and progressive citizen. His popularity is attested by the confidence in which he is held and by the honorable standing which he has attained in the town and county. He was a Commissioner of Appeals in the Township of Union for about three years and Financial Secretary of the West New York Lodge of Foresters of America for about five years, and in various other connections has been a useful and valued citizen and a trusted business man.

Mr. Otis was married in 1883 to Emma Hoppelsberg, daughter of Frederick August Hoppelsberg, of Guttenberg, N. J. They have five children living: Henry George, Charles Carhart, John Edward, Walter William, and Cecelia.

CLEMENT De R. LEONARD, of Hoboken, attorney and counselor at law, is the son of Francis De P. Leonard, a grandson of John Leonard, and a great-grandson of Joseph Leonard, who was High Sheriff of the Colony of New Jersey in 1771, and who died in 1779. His paternal ancestors were French Huguenots, and, coming to this country about the time of the Huguenot War, figured prominently in the civil and military affairs of New Jersey. Mr. Leonard's father is an old and well known citizen of Red Bank. His grandfather, John Leonard, was a warm personal friend of Thomas Jefferson, and was by him appointed United States Minister to the Court of Spain, a position he held for thirty years, achieving distinction as an able and talented diplomat and gaining the confidence and respect of his countrymen as well as the esteem and friendship of the Spaniards. His mother, the wife of Francis De P. Leonard, was a member of the distinguished Lippincott family of Monmouth County, N. J., whither her ancestors came from Holland in the early settlement of the territory. Like the Leonards, the Lippincotts have been conspicuous and prominent in nearly every capacity in the State, and have contributed much to its professional, civil, and military welfare.

Mr. Leonard was born in Red Bank, Monmouth County, N. J., February 18, 1846, and inherited the sturdy Holland Dutch and Huguenot characteristics of his race. He received his early education at St. Charles College near Ellicott City, Md. Subsequently he took a full classical course at Seton Hall College in Orange, N. J., and was graduated therefrom with honor in the class of 1869. During the next three years he read law in the office of Charles H. Trafford, of Red Bank, and then became assistant to Hon. Robert Allen, Jr., Prosecutor of the Pleas for Monmouth County. In these offices he gained a wide and valuable experience. He was admitted to the New Jersey bar as an attorney in June, 1873, and as a counselor in June, 1876, and in 1877 removed from Red Bank to Hoboken, where he has ever since practiced his profession. He is one of the ablest lawyers in Hudson County, and the many important cases with which he has been connected as counsel attest his legal skill and attainments. He has built up a large general practice, and enjoys the confidence of the entire community.

A Republican in politics, Mr. Leonard has long been active in the welfare of his party. He was a delegate to the Republican State conventions of 1888, 1892, and 1896, a delegate to all the Republican congressional and county conventions in his district from 1888 to 1896 inclusive, and Chairman of the City Republican Executive Committee of Hoboken in 1894, and did excellent work. In 1895 he was President of the Ninth Assembly District Committee, and at present (1900) he is Chairman of the First Ward Association of Hoboken. In 1896 he was elected to the New Jersey Assembly by the handsome plurality of 2,429 over his Democratic opponent. He is also President of the Governor Griggs Battalion, an active and aggressive Republican organization. In 1898 he was the choice of his party for District Judge, but declined the nomination. As citizen, lawyer, and party leader he is universally respected and esteemed, and in every capacity his ability and sound judgment have won for him an enviable record.

EDWARD SMITH, of Bayonne, N. J., was born in Clarkstown, Rockland County, N. Y., on the 4th of September, 1847. His parents, Peter D. W. Smith and Sarah Pye, were both natives of Rockland County, where they were married.

Mr. Smith received his educational training in the Clarkstown district schools and early displayed those business attainments which have since marked his life. He first engaged in the grocery trade at Closter, N. J., and subsequently in the livery business at Nyack, N. Y. On the 1st of April, 1875, he removed to Bayonne, Hudson County, and established himself in business as a butcher, in which he was very successful. For a number of years he has been engaged in the liquor business in Bayonne.

In politics Mr. Smith is a consistent Democrat, active in public affairs, and prominent in campaign work. For three terms he was one of the School Trustees of Bayonne, and in that capacity rendered efficient service to the city and to the cause of local education. He is the founder and President of the Edward Smith Association, one of the leading political organizations in Hudson County. He is also Vice-President of the Liquor Dealers' Association, of Bayonne, a member of the Exempt Firemen's Association, and a member of Bayonne Lodge, No. 99, F. and A. M., and of Bayonne Council, No. 695, Royal Arcanum. His religious affiliations are with the Dutch Reformed Church.

Mr. Smith is a prominent and enterprising citizen, active in promoting every worthy object, prompt in the discharge of duty, and thoroughly identified with the best interests of his section. He is an acknowledged leader of the Democratic party in Bayonne and for many years has wielded an important influence in shaping the political destinies of his party there.

On June 23, 1876, Mr. Smith married Emily Gilhooley, daughter of R. G. and Eliza (Hoffman) Gilhooley, of Nyack, N. Y. They have four children: Frank, Ellen Tallman, John, and Mary.

LOUIS ALBERT MENEGAUX, a leading plumber of Union Hill, N. J., and a member and formerly President of the West Hoboken Board of Education, was born in Philadelphia, Pa., June 14, 1868. His parents, Charles Frederick Menegaux and Louisa Petchin, were natives of France and descendants of old and respected families; his paternal grandfather, Frederick Menegaux, being Mayor of Dembenois, Canton of Audincourt, where Charles Frederick was born. The latter came to America in 1853 and settled in Philadelphia, where he was for many years engaged in furniture manufacturing, and where he died in August, 1868. His wife, Louisa Petchin, who still survives, came over in 1855, and they were married in Philadelphia. He was a man of great enterprise, and highly respected and esteemed.

Louis A. Menegaux received a thorough education and a military training in Girard College, Philadelphia, from which he was graduated with honor in 1885. He also spent a few months in a public school in West Hoboken, N. J. His father having died when he was only six weeks old, he was reared by his mother, a woman of great force of character and of a peculiarly sweet disposition, and to her able guidance he owes much of his success in life. On leaving college he spent a year in his native city learning the trade of plumber and gas and steam fitter, which he finished in Union Hill, Hudson County, with Albert Thourot, removing there in August, 1886. He remained with Mr. Thourot for about five years, mas-

LOUIS A. MENEGAUX.

tering every detail of the business, and in 1891 he purchased the establishment and still conducts it. Mr. Menegaux is a man of recognized ability, and as a plumber has achieved eminent success. He has one of the finest and most complete establishments in his section of the State, and the many important contracts which he has executed attest his skill and enterprise. Few men of his age have gained the popularity and high reputation which he enjoys, and fewer still are better or more widely known.

As a citizen he is public spirited, energetic, and progressive, encouraging all worthy movements, and liberally and cheerfully supporting every commendable enterprise. In politics he is an ardent Republican. He resides in West Hoboken, where he has been a member of the Board of Education since 1895, being the only Republican elected to that body in that year, and being re-elected in the spring of 1899 without opposition. He was President of the board in 1897 and 1898, and in that capacity and as a member has rendered most efficient service to the cause of local education. Mr. Menegaux is a member of Hoboken Lodge, No. 74, Benevolent and Protective Order of Elks, and of Palisade Lodge, No. 128, Knights of Pythias, in the uniform rank of which he holds a captain's commission. He is also a member of Mystic Tie Lodge, No. 123, F. and A. M., of Cyrus Chapter, R. A. M., of Pilgrim Commandery, No. 16, K. T., and of Mecca Temple, A. A. O. Nobles of the Mystic Shrine. He was appointed United States Grand Juror for the September term, 1900.

JOSEPH ELLIOTT WRAGG, a prominent retired manufacturer and ice dealer of North Bergen, N. J., descends from a distinguished family of England, one of his ancestors, John Wragg, being buried in Westminster Abbey. He is the son of James Wragg and Hannah Hodkins, and was born in Chesterfield, England, on the 18th of April, 1828. When a boy—not four years of age—he came with his parents to America, and in 1839 settled in Bergen County, N. J. In 1859 he removed to English Neighborhood, Hudson County, where he still resides, and where he was engaged with his brother, John Wragg, under the firm name of James Wragg's Sons, in the manufacture of worsted, linen, and horse-hair oil press-cloths for linseed, cotton seed, rape seed, mustard seed, sperm, and stearine. He continued in this business with success until 1870, gaining a wide reputation for ability, sound judgment, and executive skill. From 1869 to 1882 he was engaged in the ice business, building up a large and successful trade.

He had received, as a boy, a good private school education in Williamsburg, N. Y. In public affairs, and especially in the development of the community, he has always taken a deep interest, but never aspired to office or political preferment. He has exerted an important influence in various directions, and by courage and perseverance has achieved a high reputation in all the relations of life.

Mr. Wragg was married, October 10, 1859, to Catharine Fisher Tracy, widow of William Henry Tracy, daughter of Michael Fisher and Martha Engle, and granddaughter of Lieutenant Andrew Engle, a distinguished Revolutionary soldier, and Janette Strachan, his wife. Mrs. Wragg died May 15, 1898. She had two daughters by her first husband, viz.: Margaret M. Tracy and Ellie M. Tracy. The family reside at Fairview, N. J.

MICHAEL FISHER was for many years one of the most prominent and best known men in Hudson County. His influence was felt in both public and private affairs, and in the various positions which he filled he rendered very efficient service. He was born on April 29, 1794, and died on the 15th of November, 1880. He received a common school education. On October 13, 1814, he married Martha Engle Banta, daughter of Andrew Engle and Janette Strachan, and settled in New Durham, Hudson County, where he resided until his death November 15, 1880. He held several offices of trust, including those of County Treasurer for many years and Freeholder from North Bergen in 1846 and 1847. His ability and integrity, his broad executive qualities, his strength of character and genial habits made him popular and esteemed, while his long and intimate connection with public interests gained for him the confidence of the entire community.

Mr. Fisher left three daughters, the youngest of whom, Catharine, was married twice, and is survived by two daughters: Margaret M. and Ellie M. Tracy. The former was born in English Neighborhood, N. J., March 4, 1844. Both are daughters of William Henry Tracy and granddaughters of Ephraim Tracy and Elizabeth Youmans.

Mrs. Martha Engle Banta Fisher's father, Andrew Engle, enlisted at Philadelphia, October 1, 1776, as Ensign in the Twelfth Pennsylvania Regiment, Continental Army, and served in the American Revolution with distinction, being promoted to a second lieutenancy in Brigadier-General Conway's brigade. He saw considerable service, and at the battle of Monmouth his regiment was nearly destroyed. Being reduced to a mere skeleton by exposure and severe fighting, it was incorporated with the Third Pennsylvania under Colonel Thomas Craig, and on December 20, 1778, Andrew Engle was made a captain's lieutenant. His original commission, signed by John Jay, is still preserved by his descendants. After the close of the war he purchased a farm in English Neighborhood, N. J., where he died June 2, 1810, from the effects of a wound received at the battle of Monmouth. He left three sons and four daughters. The youngest son, James Engle, was educated at West Point and served in the United States regular army.

ELIJAH STRONG COWLES, one of the prominent members of the bar of Jersey City and New York, was born in Coventry, Vt., on the 30th of April, 1836. His ancestors came to New England at a very early day and for generations have been active and influential in all the affairs of life.

Mr. Cowles received his educational training in the public schools and at St. Johnsbury (Vt.) Academy, where he fitted for Dartmouth College. Illness, however, prevented him from entering the latter institution and he therefore turned his attention to the study of law, entering the office of Hon. Ephraim Paddock, one of the Justices of the Supreme Court of Vermont. Mr. Cowles was admitted to the bar of his native State and for two years practiced in Coventry, where he was born. He came to New York City and practiced his profession for about two years, or until 1868, when he removed to Jersey City, N. J., and entered the law office of Washington B. Williams. Here he formed the acquaintance of Edward B. Wakeman, then a prominent lawyer and resident of Jersey City, who soon retired from active practice.

Mr. Cowles entered Mr. Wakeman's office and upon the latter's retirement succeeded to his business. In 1875 he associated himself again with Washington B. Williams under the firm name of Williams & Cowles, which continued for about twelve years, and was one of the best and foremost law firms of Eastern New Jersey. About 1895 Mr. Cowles formed a copartnership with William H. Carey, formerly a professor in Hasbrouck Institute, Jersey City, and the law firm of Cowles & Carey is now actively and successfully engaged in the practice of law in both Jersey City and New York.

Mr. Cowles has achieved an eminent reputation at the bar, and during his entire career has maintained the respect and confidence of all who know him. He is a lawyer of ability, industry, and unimpeachable integrity. As a citizen he is thoroughly identified with the affairs of his city and county, and active and influential in every movement which affects the welfare of the community. He is interested in an important corporation known as the Automatic Fire Alarm Company, of New York City, of which he has been for several years President. Much of his time has been devoted to the organization and development of Christian and charitable work and especially in connection with the Young Men's Christian Association of Jersey City, of which he was one of the founders and which he served for five years as President. In politics he is an ardent and consistent Republican, taking at all times an active part in political affairs.

Mr. Cowles's first wife was Miss Sarah L. Persons, of Coventry, Vt., who died in 1871. They had two children, both deceased. In 1875 he married

ELIJAH S. COWLES.

Miss Sarah E. Woodward, of New York City, who died in 1893. January 3, 1895, he married Miss Anna Banta, of New York City, and they have one daughter, Sarah Banta Cowles.

CHARLES KINSEY CANNON, for nearly thirty years one of Hoboken's leading lawyers and formerly Corporation Attorney of the city, was born in Bordentown, N. J., November 12, 1846. He is the son of Garrit S. Cannon, a grandson of James Spencer Cannon, and a great-grandson of William Cannon, all of whom were distinguished citizens of West Jersey. On his mother's side he is likewise descended from one of the old New Jersey families, being a great-great-grandson of John Kinsey, a great-grandson of James Kinsey, and a grandson of Charles Kinsey, whose daughter Hannah married Garrit S. Cannon. James Kinsey was for some time Chief Justice of the Supreme Court of New Jersey.

Mr. Cannon obtained his early education at Burlington, N. J. He was graduated with honor from Yale College in the class of 1867, and then took up the study of law, graduating from Columbia College Law School in New York City with the degree of LL.B., in June, 1870, and being admitted

CHARLES K. CANNON.

to the New York bar at the same time. He was admitted to the bar of New Jersey as an attorney in November, 1870, and since then has been actively and successfully engaged in the general practice of his profession in Hoboken, Hudson County, where he also resides. In November, 1873, he was admitted before the Supreme Court as a counselor. Mr. Cannon has been in constant practice for thirty years, and during that period has tried a large number of important cases in the various courts of the State which have won for him a recognized leadership at the bar. He is a lawyer and advocate of unusual ability, of marked judicial qualifications, and of keen discrimination and ready perception, and both in the office and before a jury displays those qualities which have long held him among the foremost legal practitioners in Hudson County.

His energies have been devoted almost uninterruptedly to the duties of his profession, in which he has achieved eminence and success; yet he has been called upon to fill several important trusts and positions, among them that of Corporation Attorney, of Hoboken, from May, 1877, to May, 1878. He has been Vice-President of the Columbia Club of Hoboken since 1895, and is also a Director of the First National Bank and a Vestryman of Trinity Church, Hoboken. In every capacity Mr. Cannon has exhibited that public spirit and consummate ability which characterized his ancestors, from whom he inherits peculiar legal qualifications and forensic skill. A man of the strictest integrity, he is universally respected and esteemed, and during a long and honorable career has maintained the entire confidence of the community.

Mr. Cannon was married on the 22d of April, 1880, to Miss Agnes R. Herbert, who died March 22, 1897. They had two children: Garrit S. and Agnes H., who are still living.

CHARLES LUXTON, one of the earliest real estate operators in Hudson County, was born in London, England, and came to America when five or six years of age, with his parents. The family settled in New York City, where he received his education, and where he learned and subsequently engaged in the business of ship carpenter and joiner. In 1850 he moved to Jersey City Heights, N. J., and at once became a large landowner and real estate operator, being one of the very first to make that business a distinctive feature in the industries of Hudson County. No man was more prominent or active in promoting the growth of that section, or in developing its resources and contributing to its prosperity. He secured the charter incorporating old Hudson City on the 11th of April, 1855, furnishing the money for the purpose out of his private means. He also organized the old Hudson City Fire Department and was its first Chief Engineer. He was a leading Democrat, for some time Tax Collector, and the principal mover in the inception and construction of the first walk across the meadows from the foot of Congress Street into Third Street, Hoboken. His liberality and enterprise were prime factors in building up the young and growing city. He developed the section formerly known as Luxtonville, from Bowers Street to the Paterson Plank Road and from Palisade Avenue to Central Avenue, and opened large tracts of land in North Bergen, Clarendon (Secaucus), and Greenville (South Bergen) as well as in old Hudson City. He was also heavily interested in lumbering and lumber mills in Pike County, Pa. Possessing great mechanical genius, he invented several important appliances, including a post socket, a machine for manufacturing peat into fuel, and others. He was a prominent, active, and influential citizen, a man of great foresight and sagacity, and a generous benefactor. As a charter member of Eagle Lodge, F. and A. M., he took a deep interest in local Masonic matters, and out of his own funds built the lodge rooms. He also contributed liberally to church and school, and to all projects designed for the advancement of the community.

He died in Jersey City Heights in March, 1889, at the age of sixty-five, and is survived by his widow, who was Susan Hopper, and who is now eighty-one years old, and by an only son, George J. Luxton, and three of his four daughters.

GEORGE JOHN LUXTON, only son of Charles and Susan (Hopper) Luxton, was born in New York City on the 20th of February, 1844. In 1850 he moved with the family to New Jersey, and there, in the public schools of old Hudson City, received his education, which was practical and calculated to fit him for a business career. At the age of nineteen he associated himself with his father, and so continued until the latter's death in 1889, since which time he has engaged in real estate operations alone. Mr. Luxton's experience of thirty-six years in the real estate and insurance business makes him the oldest operator in Northern Hudson County, and one of the oldest west of the Hudson River in Eastern New Jersey. Probably no other man in the State has been more heavily identified with real estate matters nor more prominent and active in developing suburban property, improving it for factory and residential purposes, and converting it into handsome homes, than has Mr. Luxton during the last ten or fifteen years. He opened and built up, in Jersey City Heights, the Leinau tract, a tract of 102 lots, between Nelson and Tonnelly Avenues, and two tracts of 82 and 95 lots each, representing a total valuation of about $150,000; the Indian Spring property of about 90 lots, the Buse tract on Malone and Spring Streets, and the Van Amberg tract, 118 lots, on Central and Summit Avenues and Shippen Street, in West Hoboken; Tyler Park, 145 lots, between Grand and Tonnelly Avenues north and south of Hamblet Place, in North Bergen, at a cost of $40,000; and Weehawken Heights in Weehawken. The last named tract represented property valued at about $400,000, and under the name of the Palisade Land Company Mr. Luxton converted it from a field, overgrown with brush and trees, into one of the finest and most thickly settled sections of the county. The houses which adorn it cost from $4,000 to $18,000, and the whole was developed between 1894 and 1897.

Mr. Luxton's extensive real estate operations are best illustrated by the fact that he has built up sections comprising about one-half of Jersey City Heights, one-third of West Hoboken, practically all of Weehawken Heights, and a considerable part of North Bergen. His method has been to buy the land, lay it out into city lots, streets, and avenues, cause modern improvements to be carried out, and place the property in the market on terms which have enabled the workingman as well as the capitalist to own and occupy his home. And in nearly every venture he has been successful. He is one of the prominent and enterprising, as well as one of the oldest, real estate operators in Hudson County, and is widely respected as authority in all matters pertaining to the business. His knowledge of land titles is broad and comprehensive, giving him the position of a recognized leader among his fellow-citizens. He settled in West Hoboken in 1893, and has offices at 470 Palisade Avenue, Weehawken, and 596 Palisade Avenue, Jersey City.

Mr. Luxton has also been interested since 1898 in the North River Company, in connection with real estate matters, and is a member of Doric Lodge, F. and A. M. In politics he is a Democrat. He has long been a prominent and useful citizen. His patriotism led him to enlist, January 30, 1865, in Company E, Fortieth New Jersey Volunteers, with which he served in Virginia, West Virginia, and North Carolina, participating in numerous skirmishes in following up Lee's army, including Farmersville, New Store, Danville, and others, and being present at the surrender of Lee at Appomattox. He was honorably discharged July 13, 1865.

Mr. Luxton married Louisa C., daughter of Charles and Margaret Coltier, natives of France, who moved to this country and settled in Jersey City. Of their four children two are living: George and Emily Marion.

WILLIAM HENRY WILHELM has been a life-long resident of Harrison, Hudson County, N. J., where he was born on the 4th of November, 1853, his father being Peter Wilhelm, a native of France, while his mother, Mary Hasson, was born in Ireland. They came to the United States when young and first settled in Harrison, N. J., where they were married. During their long and eventful careers they enjoyed the respect of all who knew them. They were industrious, progressive, and patriotic people, whose native characteristics impressed themselves upon the community in a remarkable degree.

Mr. Wilhelm received his educational training in the public schools of Newark and Harrison, and after completing his studies engaged in the brewing business with his father, who then conducted a large brewery in Newark. Leaving his father's employ, he accepted a position with the Peter Hauck Brewing Company, of Harrison, N. J., with which he has been actively associated during the last twenty years, and of which he is now Superintendent. The success and reputation of this well known corporation is due in no small measure to Mr. Wilhelm's efficient and energetic management. He has been identified with the business

WILLIAM H. WILHELM.

from boyhood, possesses a practical knowledge of every department, and is thoroughly qualified for the duties which he has so admirably and successfully performed.

He is one of the most popular citizens of Harrison, a man of broad and liberal attainments, thoroughly identified with the progress of the community, and actively interested in those affairs which affect the municipality and its people. He is a prominent and influential Republican, and for seven years served with marked ability as a member of the Harrison Board of Aldermen. His services in this and other capacities have won for him an excellent reputation and stamp him as a trustworthy leader. He is a prominent member of Copestone Lodge, No. 147, F. and A. M., of Kearny, of Harrison Lodge, No. 120, I. O. O. F., of Newark, of Lodge No. 21, B. P. O. E., and of the Arion and Aurora Singing Societies, of Newark, and as a citizen is public spirited, patriotic, and enterprising, and deeply interested in the welfare of his native town.

Mr. Wilhelm was married on the 12th of May, 1889, to Tilley Haas, daughter of Frederick and Josephine (Bridgem) Haas, of Newark, N. J. They have one child, Hazel Wilhelm.

ALONZO WORDEN LETTS, a well known lawyer of Hoboken, descends from some of the oldest families of New Jersey and New York. He is the son of William Henry Letts and Gettie Jane Clum, a grandson of William and Ann (Runyon) Letts and of Sylvester and Catherine (Hover) Clum, and a great-grandson of John Letts, whose wife, Mary Bennett, was the daughter of Uriah Bennett. The Letts and Bennett families were early settlers of Manahawkin, Ocean County, N. J., while his paternal grandmother, Ann Runyon, was a native of Lakewood, in the same county, and the daughter of Richard and Deborah (Runyon) Runyon. His great-great-grandfather, Benjamin Letts, was the son of Nehemiah Letts, a soldier in the War of the Revolution and a nephew of John Letts, also a soldier in the Revolution. William Letts, the earliest known ancestor of the family in this country, was an original settler of Elizabethtown, N. J., and ever since his arrival the name has been conspicuous in the history of both the Colony and State. It is prominently mentioned in the Town Book of Middletown as early as December 30, 1667, as well as in the Congressional records now in the library of the New Jersey Historical Society. Their ancestry is Holland Dutch. The Bennetts came originally from England, and both families were among the early settlers of Ocean County. The Clums and Hovers, who were also of Holland Dutch descent, have lived in Columbia County, N. Y., for many generations, and from the first have been prominent and influential in all local affairs. Sylvester Clum, the maternal grandfather of Alonzo W. Letts, was the son of Jonas and Gettie (Stahl) Clum, while his wife, Catherine (Hover) Clum, was the daughter of Jeremiah Hover and Amanda Waters.

William Letts, the grandfather of Alonzo W., was born in Manahawkin, Ocean County, N. J., January 29, 1827. At the age of thirteen he left home and for many years followed the sea. In 1850 he settled in Hoboken, Hudson County, where he has since resided, being successfully engaged in the ice business. William Henry Letts, his son, and the father of Alonzo W., was born in Hoboken on the 13th of November, 1852, and has always lived in that city. He was educated in the Hoboken public schools, and for many years has been actively and successfully engaged in the ice business. He was a leading member of the Hoboken Volunteer Fire Department, serving for two years as Assistant Foreman and for three years as Foreman of Excelsior Engine Company No. 2. In 1882 he was elected, on the Republican ticket, Freeholder from the Ninth District, a Democrat stronghold, and for five years was annually re-elected to that office. This indicates at once his popularity and the confidence in which he is held by both Republicans and Democrats. In 1887 he was elected to the New Jersey House of Assembly, and being re-elected in 1888 served two terms in that body with great honor and ability. In 1892 he was appointed Fire Commissioner of Hoboken. In 1897 he received the appointment of Clerk of the Hoboken District Court, which position he still holds, having for three years discharged its duties with acknowledged ability and satisfaction. He is one of the best known citizens of Hoboken, where he has spent his life.

Alonzo Worden Letts was born in Hoboken, N. J., May 28, 1876. As a student in Public School No. 2 and later in the Hoboken High School he developed a strong inclination for professional life as well as decided scholarly ambitions, and after leaving the latter institution entered the Law Department of New York University, from which he was graduated with the degree of LL.B.

On the 21st of February, 1898, Mr. Letts was admitted to the New Jersey bar, and at once began the practice of law in Hoboken. On the 22d of the following March he was appointed a Master in Chancery by the late Chancellor Alexander T. McGill. Mr. Letts came to the bar well equipped for the duties of a lawyer, and has already displayed those legal abilities and qualifications which win success. He is a member of Hoboken Council, No. 99, Royal Arcanum, and of the Columbia Club of Hoboken, and actively identified with the affairs of his native city. He was married July 21, 1898, to Marie C. Koch, of West Haven, Vt.

THOMAS B. USHER, of West Hoboken, Secretary of the New Jersey State Board of Taxation since its inception in 1891, is descended from sturdy Scotch ancestry, being connected with the family of which the Very Right Rev. James Usher, D.D., Archbishop of Armagh, Ireland, was a distinguished member. James Usher, his father, was born in Edinburgh, Scotland, came to America about 1842, and first settled in Canada, whence he removed in 1860 to West Hoboken, N. J. He was a genealogist and writer of family history. His large and valuable library, comprising more than three thousand volumes, covered nearly every phase of the history of this country, and was regarded as one of the best and finest in its line in the United States. He died in West Hoboken. His wife, who also died there, was Harriet Birks, daughter of John Birks and a native of England, and their children were James Usher, of the Town of Union, a member of the New Jersey Assembly in 1894 and 1895 and in the latter year the leader of the Democratic minority and the party nominee for Speaker of the House; Thomas B. Usher, the subject of this article; Walter Scott Usher, a Captain of the police force of West Hoboken; and Wallace Bruce Usher, of West Hoboken.

Thomas B. Usher was born in Bonnsville, Hudson County, N. J., on the 30th of March, 1861. He received a common school education in West Hoboken, supplemented his literary studies by a business course at Cooper Union, New York, from which he was graduated at the age of nineteen, and then became a clerk in the book store of Alexander Denham, of the latter city. Subsequently he entered the employ of Bradley & Smith, brush dealers, of New York, where he remained until 1890, when, having been elected a member of the New Jersey Legislature from West Hoboken, he took his seat in the House of the Assembly and served with honor as Chairman of the Committee on Labor and Industries and as a member of the Revision Committee and of the Committee on Towns and Townships. In 1891 he served a second term and held the same positions on those committees. Mr. Usher had long made a serious study of those vital problems which affect the welfare and liberty of the people. His studies and observations were along original lines, principally in the field of moral and municipal reforms, and on entering the Legislature he at once took a prominent part, not only in the measures coming before that body, but also in the introduction of various bills, which soon gained for him a recognized leadership, especially in reform legislation. Among these bills was one separating prisoners confined in the State prisons on a basis according to their moral standing, and, although it was defeated, the measure attracted wide attention and received the support of the better elements of society. He also introduced a bill allowing a will to be probated during the lifetime of the testator, thus eliminating the chances of a legal contest and permitting the testator to see that his or her intentions were carried out. He originated and secured the passage of a bill authorizing the floating of the American flag on public school houses, another providing for the establishment and maintenance of free reading rooms in different cities, and many others of equal note and importance.

On the organization of the New Jersey State Board of Taxation in March, 1891, Mr. Usher was appointed by Governor Leon Abbett the Secretary of that body, and has ever since discharged the duties of the office with credit and ability. To him is due in a large measure the board's constantly increasing usefulness.

Mr. Usher is a Democrat in politics, has served as a member of the Hudson County Democratic Committee, and enjoys the confidence and respect of the entire community. He was married in September, 1882, to Dora Beegen, daughter of William and Mary Beegen and a descendant of old Holland Dutch stock. They reside in West Hoboken, and have two sons: James and Edward, both students at Blair Presbyterial Academy, Blairstown, N. J.

JOHN SEELEY, of New Durham, Hudson County, is one of the best known citizens of that section. He was born in Oxford, England, April 4, 1819, the son of Job Baker Seeley and Elizabeth Willis, his ancestors having been long established in the City of Oxford. When the present Mr. Seeley was a boy his father came to America, settling in North Bergen, N. J., where he engaged in the shoe business. He died in New Durham in 1855, when sixty-three years of age. His wife subsequently died in Ohio.

John Seeley was educated in the public schools and then engaged in the manufacture of shoes, in which business he was successful. He subsequently engaged in real estate speculation, chiefly at New Durham, Hudson County. For a time he was also engaged in the grocery business in Hoboken. He is a Democrat, and held the office of Town Treasurer for a period of twenty-one years. For a great many years he has also been connected with the Fire Department. He is a member of various clubs and societies. He is a member of the Episcopal Church, and a liberal supporter of church and educational interests and of all worthy local enterprises.

Mr. Seeley has been twice married. By his first wife, Sarah House, of Schenectady County, N. Y., he has five children: Mary, Kate, John, William, and James. He married, second, Augusta Blythe, by whom he has two children, Frederick and Howard.

GEORGE M. SNYDER, one of the most prominent and public spirited citizens of West Hoboken, Hudson County, is a native of Germantown, Columbia County, N. Y., where he was born January 29, 1842. He is the son of George W. Snyder and Margaret Rouse, a grandson of Samuel and Lydia Snyder, and a descendant of German Palatinates who settled in New York near the beginning of the eighteenth century.

Mr. Snyder attended the district schools of Greene County, N. Y., and the Claverack Institute, of Columbia County. He became a deck hand on a steamer plying on the Hudson River, and a little later was fireman on the same vessel. At the age of twenty he came to New York City and engaged in the produce commission business in Washington Market. This business he followed for twenty-eight years, being very successful. Through his early steamboat experience he also became interested in the project of the Catskill line of boats on the Hudson River. He was at first a Director in the corporation owning this line, but presently became its President and Gen-

GEORGE M. SNYDER.

eral Manager, and has continued in this position for twenty-two years, to the present time. Under his management the business of this line has grown, and five boats are now kept in commission, instead of two boats, as formerly. Among the well known boats of this line are the "Escort," now the "City of Hudson"; the "Walter Brett," now out of commission; the "City of Catskill," which was destroyed by fire in the winter of 1884; and the "Kaaterskill," one of the finest steamboats on the Hudson, now in active service. The "Escort" was rebuilt and lengthened and rechristened the "City of Hudson." The steamers "W. C. Redfield" and "Thomas McManus" were purchased under the present management. In 1898 the "Onteora" was built by W. & A. Fletcher, of Hoboken, is entirely new, with steel hull, and has proved to be one of the fastest and ablest boats on the river.

Mr. Snyder has long resided in one of the most elegant mansions on Palisade Avenue, West Hoboken. He built this edifice, and has also erected twenty-four other residences in West Hoboken. He is also well known for his public spirit in other directions, has taken great interest in the public school system, has contributed to its development, and is likewise conspicuous in connection with other public institutions and public movements. He is a leading member of the First Presbyterian Church of West Hoboken, with which he has been officially connected for about thirty years. He has been a stanch supporter of the Republican party since it was organized, and has been one of its liberal financial assistants and influential in its councils.

Mr. Snyder married, in 1864, Anna E., daughter of Captain John Gould, who commanded some of the vessels since owned by his son-in-law. Of the four sons of Mr. Snyder the eldest, Rev. Joseph G., is a Presbyterian minister in Brooklyn. Another, Edwin H., is his father's successor in business, and is President of the Board of Education of West Hoboken. The third son, George W., is cashier of the firm of A. F. Young & Company, a produce commission house of New York City. The youngest son, John H., is now attending the Law School of Columbia University, New York City.

FREDERICK WILLIAM FARR, one of the rising young lawyers of Bayonne, Hudson County, N. J., was born there on the 16th of April, 1874, and is the son of William C. Farr and Dora Schmidt. His parents were both natives of Germany, but came to the United States when young and were married in Bayonne, where they have spent their active lives.

Mr. Farr received an excellent private school education in his native city and at St. Matthew's Academy, New York City, and as a youth displayed those intellectual qualifications which early led him into the law as a profession. He pursued his legal studies under the tutelage of Horace Roberson, counselor at law, one of the leading lawyers of Bayonne, and at the New York Law School, and was admitted to the New Jersey bar in 1895. Since then he has been actively and successfully engaged in the general practice of his profession in Bayonne.

May 3, 1897, he formed a copartnership with William W. Anderson, under the style of Anderson & Farr, which still continues. In politics he is a Republican, and in religion a member of the Lutheran Church. He is public spirited, progressive, and enterprising, and actively identified with the best interests of his native place.

Mr. Farr was married on the 7th of November, 1895, to Louisa Burkhardt, daughter of Ludwig and Augusta Burkhardt, of Newark, N. J. They have one son, William C. Farr.

SAMUEL HESS, of New Durham, Hudson County, was descended from one of the oldest and most respected families in Pennsylvania. His maternal grandfather, Adam Hart, was a soldier in the War of 1812 and was wounded and lost a finger in action. He was a radical Democrat, a prominent farmer in Lycoming County, Pa., and lived to the great age of one hundred and three. The Hart and Hess families were all substantial residents of Lycoming County. W. W. Hart, uncle of the subject of this article, is a practicing lawyer in Williamsport, Lycoming County, Pa., having a large and lucrative clientage. Two other uncles, Davis Hart and John Hart, enlisted as members of a Pennsylvania cavalry regiment in the Union Army at the outbreak of the War of the Rebellion and served three years, being honorably discharged. Davis became a Captain in the service. He was in Andersonville prison for a time and made a most honorable record. J. T. Hess, a brother of Samuel Hess, enlisted in the War for the Union at the first call for troops and after six months' service was discharged on account of sickness.

Samuel Hess, son of Reuben and Jane (Hart) Hess, was born at Montgomery Station, Lycoming County, Pa., January 10, 1850, and received his education in his native State. His early life was that of the average farmer's boy. At the age of eighteen he began to learn the carpenter's trade, at which he served a two years' apprenticeship. In 1870 he engaged in railroading, becoming a fireman on an engine. After three and a half years of this service, running on the Eastern Division of the Philadelphia and Erie Railroad, a branch of the Pennsylvania line running to Sunbury, Renova, and Harrisburg, he was made a locomotive engineer and continued in that capacity until 1883, when he resigned. He then entered the service of the West Shore Railroad as a locomotive engineer and remained with that company until 1896, when failing health compelled him again to resign and give up railroading. He then engaged in the hotel business at New Durham, in the Town of North Bergen, Hudson County. During his long and active service on the railroad Mr. Hess made a first-class record, never being suspended, and always discharging his duties with the utmost fidelity, energy, and satisfaction. He was respected by both employers and employees, and gained a high reputation.

Mr. Hess was a prominent Democrat and for several years took an active part in politics. In 1878, while a resident of Sunbury, Pa., he served as a member of the Common Council. In 1896 he was elected a member of the Board of Education of North Bergen Township, Hudson County, N. J. His brother, J. T. Hess, was Clerk and Recorder of Lycoming County, Pa., while his uncle, Frederick Hess, also held important offices there. Samuel Hess was a member of the Sunbury (Pa.) lodges of Odd Fellows and Knights of Pythias, of the Masonic fraternity, of West Shore Council, Royal Arcanum, of Cyprus Chapter, No. 32, Royal Arch Masons, of Union Hill, and of the Brotherhood of Locomotive Engineers of Sunbury, Pa., until 1896.

Mr. Hess married Miss Gertrude Hasbrouck, of Ravena, Albany County, N. Y., by whom he had one daughter, Mary, who died in infancy.

JOHN GEORGE SYMS, who with his father, the late John Syms, has done so much for West Hoboken and Hudson County, was himself long established in business in New York City. His grandfather, John Syms, was born and lived in the Town of Torquay, Devonshire, England, where his ancestors were long seated. About 1814 John Syms, the father of John George Syms, came to New York City, established himself in the shoe business, in Chatham Street, and acquired a comfortable fortune. He bought a large tract of land on the present site of West Hoboken, then known as the Indian Spring woods and subsequently as the Syms woods, and another tract from Palisade Avenue to Central Avenue. In 1843 he removed to West Hoboken, which remained his residence from that time until his death in 1868. John Syms was very active in connection with public improvements. He was one of the builders and owners of the Jersey City Plank Road, joining with Mr. Armstrong and others in the execution of this project. He was also very prominent in establishing the public school system of West Hoboken, and always took a lively interest in educational matters. He was the founder of what was known as the Syms Library. He built the original church edifice of the First Baptist Church, of West Hoboken, of which he was long the leading member, and by his will left a large sum of money to be devoted to the erection of the present church structure. He was active and successful in efforts to secure the observance of the Sabbath-day, and to prevent its desecration. He was a stanch and leading member of the Whig party, and one of the most eminent and public-spirited men in the history of Hudson County. He died in 1868, at the age of seventy-eight. His wife, Grace Lakeman, also a prominent member of the First Baptist Church, of West Hoboken, and active in church and benevolent work, died in 1859, at the age of sixty-seven.

John George Syms was born in New York City, November 25, 1826, and received his education there and in institutions in Connecticut. He was long engaged in business on Chatham Street, New York City, as a dealer in guns and firearms, but retired in 1870 from active business in this line. Since that time he has been engaged in attending to his large real estate interests in Hudson County.

He has resided in West Hoboken since 1843, with the exception of the years from 1848 to 1856, and, like his father, has been prominent in connection with matters affecting the general welfare of the community. He was conspicuous among the original number who secured from the New Jersey Legislature the act authorizing the improvement of the streets of West Hoboken, to run parallel and at right angles, widening them, and making a tax map which is still in use. He has held for many years such positions of local trust and responsibility as Treasurer of West Hoboken and member of the Township Committee. Prior to the beginning of the Civil War he was a member of the Whig party, and since that time has been a Republican and a leader in party councils. He is a member, an officer, and one of the most liberal supporters of the First Baptist Church of West Hoboken. He donated $15,000 to this church to enable it to carry out certain improvements.

Mr. Syms married Louisa Gordon Brown, and has six children living: John B. Syms, Grace Lakeman (wife of James R. Whaples, a native of Connecticut), Mary Louisa (wife of Thomas Reynolds, of Rhode Island), Winfield H. Syms, George N. Syms, and Louisa G. (wife of William E. Warner, of New York City). All of his children are members of the First Baptist Church, of West Hoboken, with which Mr. Syms and his father have been so prominently identified, while some of them hold official positions in connection with it.

ERNST G. ASMUS has spent his active life as a florist and horticulturist, and from a small beginning has built up one of the largest and most successful establishments in the United States. Born in Hamburg, Germany, on the 27th of November, 1844, he is the son of Christian A. and Elizabeth (Bade) Asmus, both natives of that city. There he obtained his preliminary education. In 1852 he came with his parents to this country and first settled on Staten Island, New York, but soon moved to the present Town of Union, N. J., where he completed his studies.

After leaving school Mr. Asmus engaged in business as a florist. He started in a very small way and with comparatively little capital, but by industry, perseverance, and economy, soon gained a foothold and a ready market for his products. He made a close study of plants and flowers, noting especially the conditions under which they attained the highest degree of perfection, and observing from a scientific standpoint the rules which produced the best results. In brief, he thoroughly mastered every detail of horticulture and floriculture and soon became a recognized expert. He also studied the market, the tastes of the people, and the best interests of his patrons, and steadily acquired an extensive trade, which has grown to be one of the largest in the United States. His grounds, located on the Hudson Boulevard in the Town of North Bergen, cover an area of twenty acres, five of which are under glass, and his output includes every variety of ornamental plants indigenous to the climate or in demand for home decoration.

Mr. Asmus is a public spirited, patriotic citizen, and thoroughly alive to the interests and welfare of the community. He is a Democrat in politics, a prominent member of the Association of American Florists, and a communicant of the Protestant Episcopal Church.

He married Miss Josephine Lung and has three sons: Adolph E., born in 1875; Edward R., born in 1878; and Grover E., born in 1885.

AUGUST FRANK, a leading druggist of the Town of Union, is the son of Gottfried Frank and Maria Odenwälder and a grandson of John Frank, all members of prominent families of Germany. His parents came to America in 1881. They were thrifty, respected people, and gave to their children the rich inheritance of a good name.

Mr. Frank was born in Stuttgart, Germany, August 28, 1869, and there received his preliminary education. Coming to this country with his father and mother in 1881, he turned his attention to the drug trade, and in

1888 was graduated from the New York College of Pharmacy with the degree of Graduate of Pharmacy. Afterward he held a clerkship in and subsequently became the Manager of the large drug store of F. W. Hille, remaining until 1894, when he purchased the business for himself, adding to this pharmacy the one located at 146 Bergenline Avenue in the Town of Union, which he still continues. With a large and practical experience in the trade he has achieved a high reputation. He has devoted his undivided attention to a constantly increasing business, and by studying the demands of the time has kept abreast of every condition. As a business man he has displayed marked ability. His excellent judgment, his unquestioned integrity, his genial nature have won for him a deserved popularity as well as the confidence of the entire community. In the growth and welfare of the town he has exercised much influence. Public spirited, patriotic, and progressive, he has taken an active interest in various movements of local importance, and has contributed much to the general advancement of the place.

In politics Mr. Frank is a stanch Democrat, and in religion a Protestant. He is a member of West Shore Council, Royal Arcanum, of Jefferson Lodge, I O. O. F., and of the Independent Order of Foresters. In all of these he is prominent and influential. He is also a member and Secretary of the Schuetzen Corps of Union Hill, and a member of the Turn Verein, of the Uncle Sam Bowling Club, and of other social and political organizations.

Mr. Frank was married, April 8, 1896, to Miss Tillie Beier, daughter of Florian and Carolina Fransisca Beier, of Germany. They have one son: Richard August Frank, born January 29, 1897.

GEORGE BRUCE has been a resident of Hudson County, N. J., since 1857, and throughout this period has had his home at North Bergen, with the exception of the years from 1861 to 1864, when he resided at Jersey City Heights (then Hudson City). He is of Scotch descent and the son of a shipbuilder.

Mr. Bruce enjoys the unique distinction of being the leading restorer of oil paintings in the United States. He has restored many valuable public and private collections, including the Trumbull and Jarvis collections for Yale College. In 1888 he restored the collection of historic portraits in the Governor's room of the City Hall, New York City. His success in this delicate work is of course only possible because he is a talented artist, and has executed many original studies in oil of high merit. In 1857 he met the late Alexander H. Taylor, the celebrated restorer of oil paintings, and started with him to learn the art. His business relations with Mr. Taylor remained very close, and upon the latter's death in 1878 Mr. Bruce became his successor.

Mr. Bruce has been honored with many local trusts. He was elected a Town Committeeman of North Bergen in 1867, when the board consisted of three members. For twelve consecutive years, beginning with 1873, he was a member of the Board of Education and District Clerk of School District No. 3, North Bergen. He served as township Assessor continuously from 1878 to 1900, when he declined further service. He is a Democrat and has been prominent in the councils of the party for many years. For twelve years he was a member of the Democratic County Committee of Hudson County. He took a prominent part in perfecting the new method of voting at the primaries. He was the first Treasurer of North Bergen Township, and has served efficiently as commissioner on many important improvements in the northern part of Hudson County, including the Paterson Avenue and Secaucus road, the Hudson County Boulevard, the joint outlet sewer from the Town of Union, and a number of others. He has also been useful in various other capacities, being an active member of the Fire Department in Hudson County from 1863 to April, 1900, when he resigned. He is prominent socially, and at his home in New Durham has a rare art collection, including valuable oil paintings, prints, engravings, and curios. He is a member of Hoboken Lodge, No. 35, F. and A. M., of Pentalpha Chapter, No. 11, R. A. M., of Pilgrim Commandery, No. 16, K. T., and of Mecca Temple, A. A. N. O. M. S., of New York City.

GEORGE BRUCE.

Mr. Bruce married Catherine, daughter of Major John S. Sexton, of Bull's Ferry, a veteran of the War of 1812. Of their five children two are living, namely: John S., of the Town of Union, and George, Jr., of Weehawken.

CARL HENRY RUEMPLER, Sheriff of Hudson County, was born in Germany on the 12th of March, 1848, his parents being George Martin Ruempler and Dorothy Egoets, both natives and descendants of ancestors of the Fatherland.

Mr. Ruempler was educated in the public schools of Germany and then learned the carpenter's trade, which he followed for several years. In 1873 he came to this country, arriving in Jersey City on the 6th of September. Immediately afterward he took up his trade as carpenter and continued the same until March, 1875. On the 1st of May of that year he established himself in the liquor business in Jersey City and so continued until 1881, when he became proprietor of the Court House Hotel, formerly Allen's Hotel, which he continued until May 29, 1899.

Soon after coming to this country Mr. Ruempler identified himself with the political and public life of Hudson County. He declined political preferment until 1895, when he was elected to the New Jersey Assembly by a majority of 4,447. He served one term in that body and gained a high reputation. In November, 1899, he was elected Sheriff of Hudson County for a term of three years, his majority being 9,951—the greatest majority ever received by any Sheriff of Hudson County.

Mr. Ruempler is a public spirited and patriotic citizen, deeply interested in the affairs of his adopted city and State, and thoroughly identified with its business and political prosperity. He married, in 1884, Elizabeth Landwehr, and has two children: Elsie and Minnie.

J. WILLIAM GRIFFIN, Superintendent of the New York and New Jersey Water Company and a respected citizen of Arlington, Hudson County, was born in Washington, D. C., on the 23d of September, 1860. His ancestors were Virginians, and for many years were conspicuous in the history of that Colony and State. His mother's maiden name was Jane Anderson. His father, Dennis Griffin, served with the celebrated Home Guards at Washington during the War of the Rebellion.

Mr. Griffin acquired his educational training in the public schools of New York City. He became an expert in mathematics, and early displayed a strong desire for a profession. After leaving school he took up the study of civil engineering, and from books and active practice soon achieved the reputation of an expert. That he has put his broad and accurate knowledge to practical use is evident from the responsible position he now holds, that of Superintendent of the New York and New Jersey Water Company at Arlington. He has discharged the duties of this important office with ability and satisfaction. Mr. Griffin is a public spirited citizen, and takes a deep interest in every movement affecting the welfare of the community. He resides at Arlington, Hudson County, where he is held in high esteem, not only for his professional achievements, but also for those eminent qualifications and personal attributes which distinguish the successful man. He is a member of the Royal Arcanum and prominent in other connections.

Mr. Griffin married Miss Hanna Engelsheim, and has two children: Weldon Dominick and Herbert Lauris.

JAMES HENRY SYMES, a leading resident of West New York, Hudson County, and for many years a Captain in the National Guard of New Jersey, was born in Somersetshire, England, April 21, 1847, being the youngest but one in a family of ten children of James Symes and Jane Dally. His father was a carpenter. His mother was the daughter of John Dally and a sister of William Dally, the founder of what was called Dallytown on Union Hill, the place being named in honor of him.

In 1849 the family started for America in a stanch sailing vessel. When off the cove of Cork, Ireland, the ship was wrecked, and Captain Symes's father, his twin brother Henry, another brother Albert, and a sister Ellen died during the trip, which lasted four months. Undaunted, however, by this terrible disaster, which included also the loss of nearly all their goods, the brave mother continued the voyage, arriving in New York January 17, 1850, with her remaining seven children: John Symes, now of Elmira, N. Y.; Louisa, wife of Joseph Steffens, of Sacramento, Cal.; Emma, wife of William W. Whitman, of Oakland, Cal.; Cecelia Symes, also of Oakland; Aaron Symes, of California; and Sarah, who died in 1888. Arriving in this country, with scarcely a friend or acquaintance, and bereft of her husband

JAMES H. SYMES.

and three children under circumstances at once sudden and sad, the mother lost no time in establishing a home for her family in what is now the Town of Union, then North Bergen, N. J. She died there in September, 1881, aged seventy-four. Her life was one of great self-sacrifice, of genuine heroism, and in every respect exemplary. The manner in which she reared her fatherless family attests the goodness and purity of her character.

Captain Symes was educated in the public schools of the Town of Union and at the Free Academy in New York City, and at the age of seventeen entered a New York broker's office, remaining there from 1862 to 1867.

He was then made teller of the New York Gold Exchange Bank, an institution doing a gold clearing house and banking business, and continued in that capacity until after the memorable Black Friday of September, 1869. This experience has been of inestimable value to Captain Symes, and is one that he regards with peculiar satisfaction. It enabled him to acquire a broad and liberal knowledge of general business matters as well as of the intricacies of banking, and by strict industry and perseverance he gained an honorable record. His fondness and skill in mathematics made him an expert, while his ability and sound judgment attracted no little attention.

The panic of 1873, however, turned the course of his life into channels outside of banking, and, becoming active in political affairs as a member of the Democratic party, he served as Town Clerk of the Town of Union for three terms between 1871 and 1876. He was also Town Recorder for two years and a Justice of the Peace. About 1878 he entered the office of Speelman & Bruch, map publishers of Hoboken, and assisted them on the surveys and in the publication of maps for New York City and Hudson County for three years. He not only did much of the selling, but also acted as financial man and confidential clerk.

In 1881 he purchased property in West New York, Hudson County, and took up his permanent residence there, and there, in September, 1882, he established a lumber yard and at once entered upon an energetic business. He was successful from the first. Starting on a modest scale, he gradually and steadily built up an immense trade, aggregating over $100,000 a year— a sum not exceeded and probably unequaled by any similar business in North Hudson County. He conducted this business with uninterrupted success until the spring of 1898, when, having acquired other large and important interests, he sold it to the Dodge & Bliss Company, the present owners.

During the decade between 1885 and 1895 he also purchased large tracts of land in the Towns of West New York, North Bergen, and Weehawken, which he laid out into lots, streets, and avenues, with all the modern improvements, and upon which he built many houses, factories, etc., thus contributing materially to the growth and development of those communities. He has developed properties amounting to over 1,000 city lots, and has built up and sold over a quarter of a million dollars' worth of holdings. He still owns large properties, principally real estate, to the development of which he is devoting all his time and energies. With a number of other gentlemen he is actively interested in a project having for its purpose the establishment of a grand railroad terminal, with coaling and other facilities, on the Hudson County Boulevard in North Bergen, at the head of Main Street.

Captain Symes has always been actively interested in educational matters, in politics, and in every movement affecting the future of his town and county. He has always been one of the most generous and benevolent of men, giving liberally of time and means to every worthy object. Though often urged to accept public office he has generally declined to do so, on account of engrossing business cares, yet he has never failed to discharge with promptness and fidelity all the duties of a citizen. In 1896-97 he was a prominent member of the Board of Council of West New York, being the only Democrat in that body. He has also been a delegate to many town, county, district, and State Democratic conventions.

He has been especially prominent in the National Guard of New Jersey and in rifle practice, being widely known as an expert marksman. In 1867 he joined Company B, First Battalion, N. G. N. J., as a private, and was successively promoted to be Corporal, Sergeant, Second Lieutenant, and, in 1872, Captain, and served until 1877, when he resigned, the battalion in the meantime becoming the Ninth Regiment. He declined a Major's commission in order to take care of his company, which he built up, and which gained the reputation of being one of the best disciplined companies in the State. In 1878 and 1879 Captain Symes acted as Quartermaster of the regiment, and at the end of that period he took command of Company E, a position he was urged to accept to save and re-organize the company, which had scarcely enough members to give it a standing. About this time the Ninth became the Second Regiment, N. G. N. J. He was Captain of Company E for about three years, and recruited and re-organized it, put it in good shape, and then resigned. When James A. Garfield was inaugurated President he induced the regiment to go to Washington, where it received the honor of being the largest and best military organization in line. In 1888 Captain Symes was persuaded by Colonel Edwin A. Stevens and the other officers of the Second Regiment, and by the members of Company B, to accept the captaincy of that company, which he did, although he had retired from the other command with the intention of devoting himself entirely to private affairs. The company had run down to a membership of about fifteen, but under his able guidance it was soon recruited to its full quota and became one of the "crack" companies of New Jersey.

Enthusiastic, patriotic, and popular, he gained the love of his men and the respect and esteem of his superior officers, and was noted as a good disciplinarian. In rifle practice he was expert and proficient. He was a member of the State team of 1880, which won the Hilton trophy, a statue of the "Soldier of Marathon." This match occurred at Creedmore, and was open to every State in the Union and to the United States regular army. In 1881 Captain Symes won the first prize—a rifle—a prize offered by the Governor in a match open to all line officers in New Jersey, five shots each, the distance being from 200 and 500 yards. He has also won many other honors as an expert marksman, both in military and in private contests.

He is a close student of natural history and science, an expert mathematician, and deeply interested in all questions of current import, and has a large and valuable collection of scientific works. His travels include two trips to California, one to the Yellowstone Park, and another with team through the entire Adirondack region. He is a member and Past Master of Mystic Tie Lodge, No. 123, F. and A. M., and a member of Cyrus Chapter, No. 84, R. A. M.

Captain Symes was married, April 19, 1873, in the Town of Union, N. J., to Matilda, daughter of Henry F. Maackens, a native of Holland, and Matilda, his wife, who was born in Germany. Mrs. Symes was born in the Town of Union in 1853. She died March 1, 1892, leaving three children: Jane Victoria, wife of Arnold H. Rippe, of the Town of Union; Henry Frederick Maackens Symes; and Matilda Symes. Two other children died young.

LOUIS DIEHM, Jr., the well known ice dealer of West Hoboken, N. J., was born in that town July 16, 1865, and has always resided there. He is the son of Louis and Lizzie Diehm, both of whom came to this country from Germany.

Mr. Diehm obtained his education in the public schools of his native town, and, like most young men, found various employments until he was twenty-five. In 1890 he engaged in the ice business, which he has continued with marked success to the present time, having his headquarters in West Hoboken. He is an active, enterprising citizen, deeply interested in public affairs, and thoroughly alive to the needs of his town and county. For some time he served as a member of the West Hoboken Town Council. He is a member of the Independent Order of Odd Fellows and of other organizations.

Mr. Diehm married Miss Leonie T. Thourot and has four children: Emilie, Lucy, Edward, and Harry.

DAVID DAVIS, of Kearny, overseer of the Marshall Thread Mills, is the son of William Davis and Mary Morrison, both natives of Wales and descendants of old and prominent Welsh stock. He was born in Shrewsbury, England, February 1, 1870, and there received his education in public schools. After leaving school he turned his attention to the linen thread business, and by energy and perseverance has mastered every detail, becoming a recognized expert.

In 1887 Mr. Davis came to the United States and settled in Kearny, N. J., where he at once associated himself with the well known Marshall Thread Mills, of which he is now overseer of one of the departments. This position he has filled with practical ability and satisfaction. He is thoroughly conversant with every branch of thread manufacture, having grown up in the business.

Mr. Davis is an ardent Republican, and for some time served as Town Clerk of the Town of Kearny, where he resides. He is a member of the Masonic fraternity, of the Independent Order of Foresters, of the Benevolent Order of Redmen, and of the First District Republican Club.

He married Miss Helen Connett and has one son, William Gladstone Davis.

THOMAS JEFFERSON DOBBS, a member of the old family which gave its name to Dobbs Ferry-on-the-Hudson, is the son of Frederick Fowler Dobbs, who was born at Dobbs Ferry, N. Y., in 1800, was engaged in the business of shad-fishing, and died at North Bergen, Hudson County, February 14, 1854. Frederick F. Dobbs's wife, Leah Carling, whom he married in 1836, died March 10, 1888. His parents were Jerry Dobbs and Jane Fowler, daughter of Vincent Fowler, of Dobbs Ferry, with whom Aaron Burr stopped for a time after his celebrated duel with Alexander Hamilton in 1804. The site of this duel is near the present residence of Thomas J. Dobbs, in Weehawken. Thomas J. Dobbs's maternal grandfather, Michael Carling, lived at Kingston, N. Y., and married Margaret, a daughter of John Bartholf. Force of circumstances compelled John Bartholf to serve the British during the Revolution, and he was instrumental, while carrying powder, in defeating General Wayne's attempt to capture the block-house, just north of Guttenberg, on the Hudson, opposite New York City. Mr. Dobbs's paternal great-grandfather was a pilot and ship's carpenter, who served the patriot cause during the Revolution, building batteaux for Washington across the Hudson. Dobbs Ferry was named after him and his family. Mr. Dobbs's grandfather, Jerry Dobbs, was also a carpenter, and was killed by accident at Tappan, Rockland County, N. Y. The present Mr. Dobbs is a worthy descendant of this interesting family, and enjoys the highest esteem of a wide range of friends and acquaintances throughout Hudson County and beyond its boundaries.

Thomas J. Dobbs was born in North Bergen Township, now West New York, Hudson County, March 7, 1841, and received his education in the public schools at Bulls Ferry. He worked with his father until the latter's death, February 14, 1854, following the calling of a shad-fisherman. After working for a time with others in the same business he established himself in 1860 in the business of quarrying pavement stones, which he conducted for many years. On July 26, 1864, he enlisted in the United States Navy,

THOMAS J. DOBBS.

and was honorably discharged July 6, 1865. He was on blockade duty at Wilmington, N. C., and on the James River, and was in action at Howlett House and other engagements. His two brothers, Henry and Richard, also served in the Union Army during the Rebellion, the former in the Twenty-second New Jersey Volunteers and the latter in the Sixth California Infantry.

At the close of the Civil War Mr. Dobbs resumed the quarrying business which he had established, and successfully carried it on for some time. Afterward he was engaged in the ice business, about seven years, in which he was no less successful. He sometimes put up as much as

3,300 tons of ice in a winter. Still later he followed successfully the business of piledriving, while he served as inspector and timekeeper for John H. Bonn, in connection with the piledriving for the old iron bridge or viaduct at the West Shore ferry in Weehawken. Mr. Dobbs has also established a considerable reputation as an inventor. His important inventions include an apparatus for clearing spiked cannon, an unconnectable harness, and other devices. He is a member of Ellsworth Post, No. 14, G. A. R., of Union Hill. He has long been one of the prominent leaders of the Republican party in Hudson County, and has held a number of local offices. In the Town of West New York, where he resides, he has served with credit in the positions of Collector of Taxes, Town Treasurer (two terms—1867 and 1878), School Trustee (several years), and Town Committeeman (three years). For several years he was a court officer in Hudson County.

On July 29, 1880, he married Eliza Wiley, daughter of John M. Wiley and Matilda Young, of West New York. They have four children: Leah, Thomas Jefferson, Jr., Aaron B., and Matilda Dobbs.

GABRIEL B. REID, Treasurer of the Town of Kearny, N. J., and one of the leading real estate men of that section of Hudson County, was born in Glasgow, Scotland, on the 15th of May, 1851. In 1853 his parents, James Reid and Elizabeth Menzies, came to this country and settled in Newark, N. J., whence they removed, in 1873, to Kearny, where both died—the mother in 1884 and the father in 1897. James Reid, a compositor by trade, held positions on different newspapers. He and his wife brought from their native land all the sterling attributes of their race and transmitted the same to their children, together with an honorable name.

Gabriel B. Reid received his early education in the public schools of Newark, and for a time, while the family were on a visit to Scotland, attended the schools in Glasgow. There he also began active life as a merchant. Upon his return to America in 1872 he was for twenty-five years connected with the Clark Thread Company in Newark, N. J., and during the last two years has been successfully engaged in the real estate business. He is a typical Scotchman—a man of excellent character and sound judgment, and a public spirited, enterprising, and patriotic citizen, being one of a family of ten children brought to this country by his parents. He has relied from a very early age upon his own resources, and enjoys the distinction of being a fearless and conscientious exponent of the higher characteristics of the Scotch race.

Mr. Reid is a prominent and active Republican, and has filled several positions with ability and satisfaction. He was Town Committeeman of Kearny for three terms, Town Clerk two years, and Treasurer of the town in 1897 and in 1899 was again appointed to that position, which he still holds. He is Past Master of Copestone Lodge, No. 147, A. F. and A. M., and was one of its charter members. He is also a member of the Knox Presbyterian Church of Kearny, where he resides. Mr. Reid married Miss Jennie Tannehill, also a native of Scotland, and they have five children: James M., Gabriel B., Elsie J., John W., and Annabel G.

JEREMIAH CLARE WHITTLES, one of the Sinking Fund Commissioners of Kearny, Hudson County, N. J., is the son of Abram Whittles and Mary (Jones) Whittles and a grandson of Abram Whittles, Sr., and was born in Rochdale, Lancashire, England, April 25, 1859. There his ancestors

ERRATA

In sketch of William Keudel Leicht, pages 343-345, read as follows:

Charles K. Leicht was born in 1851 instead of "1854" as printed (first date in 4th line from bottom, page 344).

William K. Leicht was born October 4, 1853, instead of "October 1, 1854," as printed (4th line from top of page 345).

had lived for many generations, his father being superintendent of woolen mills. Mr. Whittles was educated in his native town, and from early in life has been actively identified with cotton and woolen manufacturing. Learning the trade as a boy, he devoted himself to it with energy and mastered every detail. Coming to America, he interested himself in the manufacture of machinery for cotton and woolen industries, and in 1893 invented and patented an automatic cloth-feed appliance which has met with great success. This appliance is entirely different from anything heretofore made. It does not tear the most delicate cloth, and yet it works with wonderful rapidity and in some respects revolutionizes the work for which it is intended and which was formerly done by hand.

Mr. Whittles has not only achieved prominence as an inventor and manufacturer, but has also taken an active interest in public affairs, and as a Republican has filled several positions with credit and satisfaction. He served for two years as a member of the Kearny Board of Education, and is now a member of the Sinking Fund Commission of that city. His activity in politics covers a period of five years, during which time he has rendered efficient service to his party and town. He is a prominent member of the Masonic fraternity, of the Independent Order of Odd Fellows, of the Knights of Pythias, of the Improved Order of Redmen, and of the Episcopal Church. Having spent five years in a technical school in England, and being of an inventive turn of mind, Mr. Whittles has gained a wide reputation in the industry to which he has devoted his active life. He is a public spirited, patriotic, and progressive citizen, a man of unswerving integrity, and highly esteemed in the community.

Mr. Whittles married Miss Elizabeth Emily Dixon, of Carlisle, England, and they have five children: Mary Ellen, Frank, Camilla, Ethel, and George.

WILLIAM KEUDEL LEICHT.—At Schottenstein, a town in the Kingdom of Bavaria, early in the nineteenth century, resided Andrew Leicht, the earlier home of whose ancestors was in the Tyrol, an Austrian province on the southwestern frontier of Germany, from whence some of their descendants found their way into Bavaria and settled at Schottenstein many generations back of the nineteenth century. Andrew Leicht and his wife, Eva Barbarie, had issue, among whom was Andrew Leicht (2), born at Schottenstein, June 5, 1817. At twenty years of age the latter came to America and located at Hudson, Columbia County, N. Y., where in 1840 he met, wooed, and married Miss Maria Semler (daughter of John and Anna Semler), who had come to America in 1829, from the village of Gross-Felda, in the Grand Duchy of Hesse-Darmstadt, where she was born May 1, 1822.

After his marriage Andrew Leicht (2) embarked in the butcher business at Hudson, N. Y., continuing successfully for sixteen years. In 1856 he sold out and came to New York City, and the following year removed to Hudson County, N. J., where he purchased a valuable tract of land west of Hoboken on what was then known as " Van Vorst Heights." On this tract, in the following year (1857), he built and equipped a large brewery plant, and with John Roemmelt, his son-in-law, began the manufacture of lager beer under the firm name of Roemmelt & Leicht. The business was continued with varying success until the death of the partners. During the first twenty years of its existence the lager beer industry of the country was in its infancy, and Roemmelt & Leicht's products were known far and wide. Mr. Roemmelt, who was a native of Schwanfelt, in Bavaria, died in 1884, and Mr. Leicht's death occurred in 1885. In his lifetime Mr. Leicht was one of the best known and most prominent men in Hudson County. He took an active part as a Democrat in the political affairs of old Hudson City before it was swallowed up by Jersey City, being twice elected Alderman and once Freeholder of the ward in which he resided. He was active, energetic, scrupulously honest, and possessed sterling integrity, blended with good business capacity, which qualities made him popular with and

WILLIAM K. LEICHT.

respected by a large circle of his fellow-citizens. His widow, a lady of cheerful disposition and kind and matronly instincts, survives him, having passed the seventy-eighth mile post of life. The issue of the third generation of Andrew Leicht and Maria Semler (all born at Hudson, N. Y.) are five children: Andrew E., born in 1842; Amelia, born in 1843; Charles K., born in 1854; William K.; and John M., born in 1856. Of these Andrew E. married (1852) Louise Miller and is a retired brewer with two children in Chicago, Ill. Amelia married John Roemmelt (now deceased) and has had ten children (now in Jersey City). Charles P. married Kate Mahoney and with four children is in Newburgh, N. Y. John M. married Eugenia Veyresset and with two children is at Cleveland, Ohio.

William K. Leicht (3), the subject of this sketch, was born at Hudson, Columbia County, N. Y., October 1, 1854, and came with his parents to New Jersey in 1857. He obtained a thorough education in the German academy at Hoboken, at a high (grammar) school in New York City, and at Columbia College, from which institution he was graduated. He read law in the office of the late Attorney-General Robert Gilchrist in Jersey City, and was admitted to the New Jersey bar as an attorney in February, 1875, and as a counselor in February, 1878. He then formed a law partnership with C. B. Harvey, of Jersey City. A few years later this partnership was dissolved, since which time Mr. Leicht has maintained an office and successfully practiced his profession at No. 328 Palisade Avenue, Jersey City, making real estate law and conveyancing specialties. As one of the executors and trustees under the will of his wealthy uncle, Joseph Rubsam, of Stapleton, Staten Island, Mr. Leicht has been kept busy since 1890 managing a large estate, and for the past five years he has been Secretary of the Rubsam & Horrmann Brewing Company, at Stapleton, a position which requires much of his attention and from which he receives a handsome salary. He is a great lover of travel, and notwithstanding his many business responsibilities has found time to travel all over the United States, Mexico, South America, the West Indies, the Bermuda Isles, and through every country in Europe as far north as "the land of the midnight sun." In 1900 he made an extended trip through Scotland and Ireland. He is sociably inclined and genial in his disposition. Extensive travel and observation have made him an agreeable conversationalist. He is a member of but one club—the Berkeley, of Jersey City. He has never married.

JAMES G. WALLACE, senior member of the well known real estate brokerage and insurance firm of Wallace & Limouze, of Union Hill, is the son of Lawrence W. Wallace and Mary Golden. He has always resided in the Town of Union, Hudson County, N. J., where he was born December 3, 1865. There he received a public school education, graduating at the age of twelve. He then accepted a position as clerk in the banking house of James G. King's Sons, the widely known Wall Street firm which has since retired from business after a continuous existence of over a century. Mr. Wallace rose from office boy to a position of trust and responsibility, and during the fifteen years of his connection with the firm handled millions of dollars, became an expert accountant and penman, and had the advantages of a thorough business training in foreign and domestic banking. The broad and valuable experience which he obtained in that institution has served him in various capacities and brought him into prominence as an able, conservative business man.

In 1893 Mr. Wallace formed a copartnership with George Limouze, under the firm name of Wallace & Limouze, and since then he has been actively and successfully engaged in the general real estate brokerage and insurance business in the Town of Union, their office being at 165 Bergenline Avenue. He is an ardent Democrat, and was one of the founders and organizers of the Democratic Central Organization, of which he is still a leading member, and which he served for a time as Secretary. He is also a member of the old Third (now First) Ward Democratic Club, formerly Vice-President and now President of Columbia Hose Company of Union Hill, and a member and the present Advocate of Palisade Council, No. 387, Knights of Columbus. He was one of the organizers in 1898 of the Hamilton Building and Loan Association of Union Hill, and is its Secretary. He is also an enthusiastic member of the Foresters of America, a Commissioner of Deeds, a Notary Public, and a Justice of the Peace, which office he has held since 1891, having been re-elected in 1896 for a second term of five years.

He was married, May 16, 1888, to Miss Katherine H. Walker, daughter of the late James Walker, of the Town of Union, N. J. They reside at 266 Palisade Avenue, Union Hill, and have three children living: Katherine Walker, Ethel May, and Marguerite Mary Wallace.

THOMAS F. BULGER, member of the Board of Aldermen and one of the leading manufacturers of Harrison, Hudson County, was born in Newark, N. J., March 25, 1857. His parents, John and Mary (Eustis) Bulger, were natives of Ireland, but came to the United States when young, and in 1854 were married in Newark. In 1858 they moved across the river and took up their residence in Harrison, Hudson County.

As a boy Mr. Bulger attended the parochial schools of Newark and Harrison. He not only acquired a good practical education, but developed a rugged physique, and when he arrived at man's estate he entered upon the career which has won for him both honor and success. After leaving school he engaged in the business of manufacturing wire cloth, which he has ever since followed, building up a large and successful industry. He stands among the leading manufacturers of Hudson County, and through his own indomitable efforts, applied with intelligence, united with skill and ability, has achieved an honorable reputation.

His public life has been equally conspicuous. An ardent and enthusiastic Democrat, he was for seven years a member of the Harrison Board of Education and is now (1900) a member of the Board of Aldermen, representing the First Ward. His services in these and other capacities have brought him into more than local prominence as a man of ability, integrity, public spirit, and enterprise. He is a member of the Knights of Columbus and of the Catholic Church.

Mr. Bulger married Ellen McPhillips. Of their eleven children eight are living, namely: Henry J., Joseph, Kate E., John, William, Thomas F., Jr., George, and May. Three—Charles, James, Mary Lizzie—died young.

DAVID ST. JOHN, M.D., of Hackensack, one of the leading physicians of Bergen County, was born in Berne, Albany County, N. Y., in March, 1850, his parents being David St. John and Mary Johnson. His mother was of Scotch descent. He is descended from Matthias St. John (Sention), who came from England in 1635 and settled in New England. His grandfather, Noah St. John, moved to New York State upon his marriage to Elizabeth Waterbury, of Waterbury, Conn.

Dr. St. John pursued a preparatory course of study in the Albany schools and then began to fit himself for the profession of medicine, entering the office of Dr. H. W. Bell, of Berne, N. Y., and afterward the office of Professor James H. Armsby, then the leading surgeon of Albany. He took a course of lectures at the Albany Medical College, the Buffalo Medical College, and the Bellevue Hospital Medical College, graduating from the latter institution with the degree of M.D. in 1875.

Upon graduation Dr. St. John settled in Hackensack, N. J., where he has since resided, and where he has acquired one of the largest and most successful practices in Eastern New Jersey. He is not only prominent in

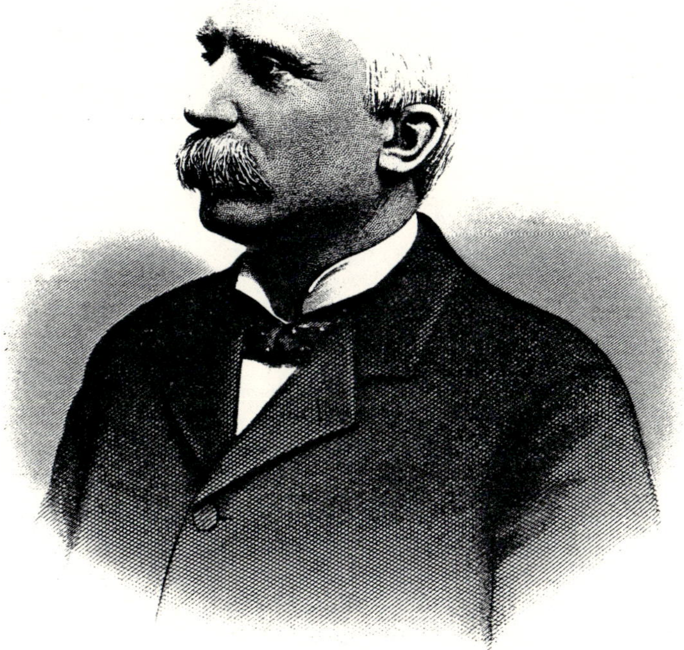

D. B. John M. D.

the profession of medicine and surgery, but has also been closely identified with all matters of local or public interest. He was the first to realize the need and advantages of a hospital for the better treatment of a class of medical and surgical cases, and in 1888 was instrumental in organizing the Hackensack Hospital, one of the most useful institutions in Bergen County. While his energetic and untiring efforts in its behalf have been ably seconded by all classes of citizens, his indefatigable labors have been the primary cause of its success, and under his able direction as President of the Medical Board and visiting physician and surgeon the hospital has outgrown its present quarters and is being replaced by a much larger structure, which will be one of the best equipped institutions of its class in the State. One wing of the new building, consisting of two wards, will be known as the St. John wards, Dr. St. John having assumed the cost of this part. Another wing will be the Frank B. Poor wards, that gentleman having given the amount necessary for its construction. Dr. St. John is a member and former President of the Bergen County Medical Society, and a member of the New Jersey State Medical Society, the New York State Medical Association, the New York Academy of Medicine, and the American Medical Association. He was appointed by Governor Griggs one of the managers of the New Jersey State Hospital for the Insane at Morris Plains, and is surgeon for the Erie Railroad. He also does a great deal of surgical work in the western portion of Bergen County outside of his hospital practice. Associated with him is Dr. A. A. Swayze, a graduate of the College of Physicians and Surgeons of Baltimore, Md.

Dr. St. John is First Vice-President of the Hackensack Trust Company, a Director of the Hackensack Bank and of the Gas and Electric Company of Bergen County, and President of the Hackensack Heights Association, owners of a large tract of valuable real estate on Hackensack Heights.

Courteous, dignified, and sympathetic, Dr. St. John has achieved marked success in his profession and enjoys the confidence and respect of his numerous patients as well as of the entire community. He was married in 1879 to Miss Jennie Angle, second daughter of John H. Angle, of Scranton, Pa. They have three children: Olive Graham, Fordyce Barker, and Florence Angle.

CHARLES W. WYCKOFF, carpenter and builder, of West Hoboken, is the son of George and Margaret Ann (Snook) Wyckoff and a grandson of Jacob Wyckoff, a native of Holland and later a leading farmer of Wertsville, Hunterdon County, N. J. George Wyckoff was born in Wertsville and followed the trade of blacksmith until the War of the Rebellion, when he enlisted in the Thirty-fourth New Jersey Zouaves. He was wounded in a skirmish near Atlanta and died at Rome, Ga., while in the service.

Mr. Wyckoff was born in Wertsville, Hunterdon County, N. J., October 19, 1848, and received his education in the adjoining County of Mercer, attending the public schools. He learned the trade of carpenter in Hopewell, N. J., which he followed as a journeyman for ten years, principally in Princeton and Asbury Park. During the last twenty years he has been actively and successfully engaged in business for himself as a carpenter, contractor, and builder, beginning in Asbury Park and continuing since August, 1887, in West Hoboken, N. J. More than one hundred dwellings in Asbury Park and Ocean Grove and an equal number in Hudson County are the result of Mr. Wyckoff's energy and enterprise, and all bear evidence of his skill, thorough workmanship, and executive ability. He has also erected many other buildings of note, including the old elevated structure of the West Shore Railroad in Weehawken.

He is an ardent and consistent Democrat, and during the past six years has served as a member of the Board of Education of West Hoboken, where he resides, having his home at 722 Dubois Street. In May, 1865, he enlisted in the Thirty-fourth Regiment, United States regular army, and for eighteen months was connected with the Freedman's Bureau in Texas, thus gaining an active experience in the great reconstruction problem. He then became a civilian, and remained there in all four years, when he returned North and took up the trade of carpenter. Mr. Wyckoff is a member of Mystic Tie Lodge, No. 123, F. and A. M., of Union Hill, of Columbia Lodge, No. 151, K. of P., and of West Shore Council, No. 1097, R. A. He is widely respected, not alone because of his prominence in contracting and building circles, but also on account of the active interest he has taken in local affairs and especially in all matters affecting the public welfare.

He was married June 29, 1870, to Abbie Britton, daughter of Stephen Britton, of Rocky Hill, N. J., the ceremony being performed by the late Rev. Alexander T. McGill, D.D., LL.D., professor in Princeton Theological Seminary. They have eight children: Sarah Elizabeth, Margaret Annie, William A., Charles W., Jr., Joseph H., Abbie, Louie, and May.

HALLOWAY WHITFIELD CLOUSE, of Kearny, was born at Four Bridges, Morris County, N. J., February 21, 1839. His parents, Stephen Clouse and Susan Sliker, were both born and married in Morris County, and were descended from some of the oldest families of the State, his mother's ancestors having served in the Revolutionary War.

Mr. Clouse received his education in the public schools at Four Bridges, and subsequently learned the carpenter's trade, which he still follows. He removed from Morris County to Kearny, N. J., when a young man, and for many years has been actively and prominently identified with the progress of that town. For thirty-three years he was associated with the Delaware, Lackawanna, and Western Railroad Company, holding a position in the carpentry and building department. He is one of the oldest and best known carpenters in Eastern New Jersey.

Mr. Clouse has always been a Republican in politics, active and influential in party councils, and foremost in promoting the welfare of his community. He was a member of the Board of Education of Kearny for nine years, and in that capacity rendered efficient service. He is now an election officer of that town. He is a member of Friendship Lodge, No. 111, Independent Order of Odd Fellows, of Newark, and of the Knights and Ladies of Honor of the Golden Star, of East Newark, and in religion is a Presbyterian.

Mr. Clouse married Martha Jane Bennett, daughter of Moses D. and Mary B. Bennett, of Mendham, N. J. They have three children: Warren C., Louis E., and Morris W.

JACOB GUNSET, of North Bergen, is one of the substantial business men of Hudson County, where he has resided for more than forty-five years. He has had a successful career, is highly esteemed and respected in the community, and is now engaged in farming and market-gardening. In politics he is independent, and has never cared to become a candidate for any political office. He is a member of the Evangelical Association.

Mr. Gunset is the son of Philip and Elizabeth Gunset, and was born February 27, 1833, in Alsace, now a part of Germany, but at that time a part of France. Having been educated in the public schools of his native place, he came to America in 1853, and originally settled in New York City, but shortly afterward removed to North Bergen, where he has since resided.

He married Mary Glock, and has nine children: Katie, George, Maggie, Jacob, Elizabeth, Charles, Emma, Fred, and Mary.

A substantial citizen in the community in which he lives, Mr. Gunset belongs to the number of foreign-born citizens who came to America out of love for its free institutions, and on account of their appreciation of the

JACOB GUNSET.

great advantages which this country affords to the worthy and the enterprising. He was for nineteen years a School Trustee in North Bergen Township, Hudson County, and was the prime mover in the establishment of Public School No. 5. He has always been active in school work, was District Clerk of the School Board, and hired the first teacher in District No. 5.

EDWARD WILLIAM BERGER was born in Liverpool, Onondaga County, N. Y., July 17, 1871. His grandparents, Andrew and Elizabeth Berger, were substantial residents of Ettlinger, Baden, Germany, the former being a large and successful brewer. His father, Edward William Berger, Sr., a native of Ettlinger, came to America at about the age of eighteen, and was married in New York City to Margaret Hensel. Afterward he moved to Liverpool, and with two brothers engaged in the salt business, then the leading and most promising industry in Central New York. He died at the early age of twenty-nine, in New York City. His wife survives him, and resides with the subject of this article in Weehawken.

Edward W. Berger was educated in the public and high schools of New York City, graduating from the latter in 1883. He then entered Packard Institute in New York and took a full course in mechanical engineering, meanwhile holding a position with the Ingersoll Rock Drill Company, at that time the largest manufacturers of all kinds of mining machinery in the world. In the dual capacities of student and employee he obtained not only a theoretical but a practical knowledge of the profession in which he has achieved success. He was graduated from Packard Institute with the degree of M.E. in 1889, and remained with the Ingersoll Rock Drill Company from 1883 to 1895, having for several years full charge of all inside detail work in connection with the machinery. Resigning this position in February, 1895, he engaged in the machine, hardware, and plumbing supply business in the Town of Union, N. J., where he soon made a record as an able, substantial, and enterprising business man. In April, 1896, he built his present store and home on the corner of Bull's Ferry road and Fulton Street in Weehawken, and there he has continued his business operations on the same lines, building up an extensive trade. He conducts the largest business in the line of machine, hardware, and plumbing supplies in North Hudson County, and has supplied some of the heaviest contractors in connection with all the principal work in that section. With him are associated his half-brother, Frederick G. Baumann, and step-father, Frederick C. Baumann.

He is possessed of excellent judgment, foresight, integrity, and energy. He is an ardent Democrat, a member and formerly (for one year) President of the Northern District Democratic Club of Weehawken, a member of the North Hudson Business Men's Association, and assistant foreman of Clifton Hose Company of Weehawken. For three years he was a prominent member of the Board of Commissioners of Appeals of the Township of Weehawken, and during two years of that period served as its Chairman. He is also a member of the Union Hill Schuetzen Corps, of the Zweivelberger Bowling Club, and of the Robert Davis Association of Jersey City. He is unmarried.

FRANK H. DENNIS, of Arlington, Hudson County, N. J., was born in Pittston, Pa., July 29, 1850. His parents, John Dennis and Mary A. Arthur, were both born and married in England and came to the United States in 1849. His grandfather was James R. Dennis, a man of marked ability and enterprise.

Mr. Dennis received his education at Wyoming College in Kingston, Pa. He associated himself at an early age with the Atlantic Cable Company and at the present time holds a responsible position with the Commercial Cable Company in New York City. He resides in Arlington, Kearny Township, Hudson County, where he has for several years taken a leading part in political and public affairs. He has filled with acknowledged ability the office of Township Tax Commissioner, and in various other capacities has displayed sturdy qualifications and characteristics. Mr. Dennis was for several years Secretary of the Royal Arcanum and the Foresters of America. Public spirited, patriotic, and enterprising, he is prominently identified with the community and enjoys the respect and esteem of all who know him.

In 1872 Mr. Dennis was married in New York and has two children: Frank H., Jr., of Denver, Col., and Mary Elizabeth.

WILLIAM GREEN, one of the prominent business men and public officials of Kearny, Hudson County, was born in Bath, Somerset, England, July 31, 1845. He is the son of James Green and Ann Williams and a grandson of James and Mary (Williams) Green, all of whom, together with their ancestors, were noted for their longevity, living to an unusual age. His grandmother, Mary Williams, died at the age of one hundred years. His mother, Ann Williams, moved from Wales to England when young and was married in Bristol, England, to James Green.

In 1866 William Green left his native country and came to the United States, locating first in Greenville, N. J., and moving thence to Kearny, Hudson County, in 1872. He had already received a good practical education in the public schools of England, and after completing his studies engaged in the butchering business in Bristol. This he followed for some time, even after coming to New Jersey, although his principal business was market gardening. While in Kearny he became one of the most successful market gardeners of that section. Later he gave up that business and engaged in the business of real estate and contracting, which he has since followed in Kearny with uninterrupted success.

WILLIAM GREEN

Mr. Green is one of the most enterprising, public spirited, and patriotic citizens of Hudson County, and for a number of years has been prominently identified with its political and business affairs. He is an ardent Republican, a man of great strength of character, and deeply interested in every worthy movement. For six years he served most efficiently as a member of the Town Committee of Kearny. He was Street and Water Commissioner of Kearny for two years, a member of the Board of Chosen Freeholders of Hudson County for four years, a Director of the board for one year, and Assessor for Kearny for two terms. These positions he filled with marked ability and satisfaction, and gained the respect of all classes, irrespective of party affiliations. Mr. Green is a member of Copestone Lodge of Free and Accepted Masons, of West Hudson, and of Fort Laurel Lodge of Foresters of America, of Arlington, and is also a communicant of the Episcopal Church.

Mr. Green was married, September 20, 1869, to Emily Sweet, daughter of Isaac and Susan (Lear) Sweet, of Bristol, England. They have one son, William Norvin Green.

JOSEPH L. WILLIAMS, one of the leading business men of Bayonne, Hudson County, is the son of Jacob B. and Margaret E. (Morrison) Williams, and was born in Pittsburg, Pa., on the 20th of April, 1864. His parents were both born and married in that city, and through several generations inherit those sturdy characteristics which have marked their lives.

The public schools of Pittsburg furnished the early educational advantages which Mr. Williams enjoyed and upon which he laid the foundations of his career. Subsequently he pursued a thorough preparatory course at the college in his native city, and then accepted a position as agent of the Allegheny Railroad of Pennsylvania in Pittsburg. Afterward he became bookkeeper of the Ocean Oil Company in his native city.

In 1881 he removed to Bayonne, Hudson County, N. J., where he engaged in the coal and contracting business with marked success. Four years later, however, he sold out this business and established himself as a truckman and liveryman, in which business he is still actively and successfully engaged. He is also Superintendent of the Kill von Kull Ice Company, of Bayonne.

Mr. Williams has achieved success in every business enterprise. He is esteemed for those qualities which distinguish the successful man and enjoys the confidence of all who know him. In politics he is an ardent Republican, and in a quiet way has rendered efficient service to his party and community. For a number of years he was Secretary of the Board of Trade of Bayonne. He is a member of the Newark Bay Boat Club and of the First Methodist Church of Bayonne, and is actively identified with the best interests of the community.

WILLIAM H. HUBER, of Secaucus, Hudson County, is the youngest son of Frederick and Christina Huber, both natives of Bavaria, Germany, who came to this country in 1845. They first settled in Jersey City, but in 1852 removed to Secaucus, where they imparted to the community the sterling qualities of their race and to their children the substantial training of thrift and industry. Their children were Cornelius and Frederick, Jr., both deceased, Elizabeth, Jacob F., Louisa (deceased), Cornelia (wife of Rev. Leopold Mohn, D.D.), Fredericia (wife of John H. Post), William H., Wilhelmina, and John L.

Mr. Huber was born in Jersey City, N. J., December 21, 1850. Two years later he removed with his parents to Secaucus, Hudson County, where he received his early education, attending the public schools. He completed his studies, however, in Hoboken, and since then has been actively and successfully engaged in farming and market gardening in Secaucus. Through his perseverance, industry, and enterprise Mr. Huber has achieved a high reputation, is esteemed and respected as a man of unquestioned integrity, and is recognized as one of the best farmers and gardeners in East Jersey.

He has also taken an active part in local affairs. In brief, he is one of the substantial citizens of Hudson County. He is a member of Excelsior Council, Royal Arcanum, of Jersey City.

Mr. Huber married Elizabeth Greenleaf, daughter of Abram and Lucretia Greenleaf. They have two children: Cornelius M., born August 11, 1882, and Lucretia L., born June 17, 1886. Mrs. Huber, a woman of refinement and cultivation, descends from an old and well known American family, her ancestors being among the early colonists of New England.

HENRY F. COLLINS, of Granton, was born in Guttenberg, Hudson County, N. J., April 28, 1843, and is the son of John Collins and Ann Redmond and a grandson of Henry Collins. He received his education in the public schools of New Durham, N. J., learned the carpenter's trade, and has since followed the business of a carpenter and builder, in which he has been very successful.

Mr. Collins has also held various offices of trust. He was Township Clerk for three years, and for five years he served as a Justice of the Peace. He was subsequently appointed to the office of Recorder. In these as well as in every other capacity he has displayed marked ability and enterprise.

WALTER F. COURTMAN, of West Hoboken, N. J., was born in London, England, December 24, 1858, the son of Joseph Courtman and Mariah Barker. He received his education in the schools of London and vicinity, and came to America in 1872, settling in New York City. Since 1888 he has been a resident of West Hoboken. He engaged in the preparation of bronze and vault work, chiefly along artistic lines, and did extensive work for Tiffany & Co., of New York. For about nineteen years he was foreman of the bronze and chandelier works of J. F. Palmer & Co. Subsequently he was with John Williams, who did the bronze work for the famous Vanderbilt marble mansion at Newport, R. I., and also for the residence of the late C. P. Huntington in New York City.

Since 1893 Mr. Courtman has been engaged in business on his own account, in West Hoboken, as proprietor of architectural iron works. He has recently been engaged in erecting improvements in connection with St. Michael's Monastery and St. Joseph's Church, of West Hoboken, and St. Joseph's Church at Jersey City. He is a Democrat, and a member of the Holy Name Society, of the Catholic Benevolent Society, and of Palisade Council, No. 127.

Mr. Courtman married Mary Mooney, of New York City, and has two children: Walter and Margaret.

SIMON KELLY is one of the most energetic, enterprising, and progressive citizens of Weehawken, and no one is more prominent and widely known, not merely in Hudson County, but throughout the State of New Jersey and the City of New York. The son of John Kelly and Margaret Brennen, he was born in Ireland, August 22, 1848, and was brought to this country by his parents when a child. He received his education in the public schools of Hoboken, N. J.

The famous road house at Weehawken, of which Mr. Kelly is the proprietor, is one of the most notable political headquarters of the Democracy of New Jersey, while its owner is everywhere recognized as one of the most skillful of political leaders. He has filled with credit every office of any importance in the gift of the Town of Weehawken. In 1871 he was elected Town Poormaster, and was re-elected for 1872-73. Some fourteen years ago he was elected to the Town Council, and was made its Chairman. He is also a Freeholder. He served for fourteen years as Chief of Police of Weehawken, distinguishing himself for his efficiency in this office, as he has in every position which he has held. Subsequently he was also elected Mayor of Weehawken, and was one of the most popular and progressive

SIMON KELLY.

mayors in the history of the town. For six years he was President of the School Board, and he reigned as a king in the hearts of the children on account of the many treats and pleasant surprises which he contrived and carried through to enliven the drudgery of school-work, and make the thought of school less obnoxious to the little ones.

In the councils of the Democratic party Mr. Kelly has been no less prominent and energetic. Continuously during the twenty-nine years since 1871 he has been a member of the Hudson County Democratic Committee, and during the same time has been an active member of the Executive Councils.

His influence as a political leader has been felt throughout New Jersey as well as in the City of New York.

It must also be emphasized that Mr. Kelly is distinctly the founder of St. Lawrence's Parish, Weehawken, which is now one of the most thriving parishes in the State. It was upon his suggestion that Colonel E. A. Stevens gave one-half of a block of land to this parish, while Mr. Kelly's influence brought other gifts, in addition to his personal generosity. He was also largely instrumental in securing to Weehawken its handsome model school-building, a large and finely appointed brick structure. He is charitable, and every Christmas during the last fifteen years he has seen that every poor family in Weehawken has had a good dinner.

He married Annie Fouttrell, and has living four children of the seven that have been born to him.

JOHN M. FITZPATRICK, member of the Common Council of Hoboken and one of the prominent masons and builders of Hudson County, was born in Hoboken, N. J., on the 14th of May, 1870. He is the son of Michael and Ann (Bowden) Fitzpatrick, and a grandson of John and Margaret (Hines) Fitzpatrick and John and Ellen (Hamilton) Bowden, all natives of Ireland. His father came to America in 1858 and his mother in 1859. They were married in New York City, and soon afterward settled in Hoboken, Hudson County, where they still reside.

Mr. Fitzpatrick received his education in the parochial and public schools of his native city, and at an early age began life as a clerk with Toby & Kirk, stock brokers, of New York City, with whom he remained two years. Subsequently he learned the trade of mason and builder, which he had mastered at the age of nineteen. He then formed a partnership with his father, which continued until 1894, since which time he has been engaged in business as a mason and builder on his own account. Mr. Fitzpatrick has executed with ability and satisfaction a large number of important contracts, and has established for himself a reputation which stamps him as a man of energy and enterprise.

He is a popular citizen of Hoboken, a prominent and active Democrat in politics, and respected in both social and business circles. He has served as a member of the Democratic City Committee of Hoboken and is now (1900) a member of Hoboken Common Council. His public spirit and patriotism have frequently been displayed on important occasions, and in every capacity he has faithfully and conscientiously discharged the duties committed to his care. He is a member of the Catholic Benevolent Legion, of the Knights of Columbus, of the Benevolent and Protective Order of Elks, and of the Hoboken Turn Verein.

Mr. Fitzpatrick married Miss Honore Quinn, and they have five children: Mary, Ellen, John, Anne, and Cecelia.

WILLIAM T. HOWE, a well known coal merchant of Kearny, N. J., is the son of John Howe and Esther Jane Somerville and a grandson of William and Margaret (Pollock) Howe. His ancestors on both sides came to this country from Ireland. He was born in Harrison, Hudson County, on the 19th of June, 1854, and there received his education. Afterward he was for twenty-three years a bookkeeper for different concerns and in that capacity gained a broad and practical knowledge of business affairs. In

1894 he engaged in the coal, ice, and wood business in Kearny, and has since built up a large and successful trade in that line.

Mr. Howe was for some time a member of the First Infantry Regiment, New Jersey State Militia, receiving an honorable discharge. He is a Prohibitionist in politics and is now serving as a Justice of the Peace. He is a member of the Knights of Pythias, of the Ancient Order of United Workmen, of the Temple of Honor, of the United Order of the Golden Cross, of the New Jersey Coal Dealers' Association, and of the Presbyterian Church, and was one of the founders and for many years an enthusiastic member of the Kearny Fire Department.

WILLIAM T. HOWE.

Mr. Howe married Mattie D. Wilbur, daughter of Andrew and Elizabeth (Doty) Wilbur, and has five children: Ida Somerville, Essie J., George T., Clarence D., and Charles W.

JAMES J. BOWE, a successful and well known builder of Guttenberg, Hudson County, and one of the prominent and influential leaders of the Democratic party in Eastern New Jersey, was born in that town (Guttenberg) on the 30th of December, 1861. His parents, Thomas and Ellen (Carroll) Bowe, were natives of Kilkenny, Ireland, and shortly after their arrival in this country settled in Guttenberg. Both were respected for those sterling and sturdy virtues which characterize their race.

Receiving a good practical education in the Guttenberg parochial schools, Mr. Bowe engaged in active business pursuits, becoming a contractor and builder. His success has been the result of his own efforts. Many important buildings in Northern Hudson County attest his skill and ability, while the esteem and confidence in which he is held by his fellow-citizens represent in a measure his popularity throughout his section. In politics he has been an ardent and consistent Democrat since he cast his first vote. He has been Assessor of the Town of West New York since 1897, and clerk of the Board of Education of Guttenberg for three years, serving in each capacity with ability and satisfaction. He has also been Chairman of the Democratic Town Committee of West New York. Mr. Bowe is regarded as one of the ablest Democratic leaders in his locality, and has rendered efficient service in the interests of his party. He is a member of the Royal Arcanum and other social, fraternal, and political organizations.

Mr. Bowe married Miss Mary Knight, and they have had seven children, namely: Katharine, Nellie, James, Richard, May (who died young), Angus, and Florence.

HENRY ANDES, of North Bergen, N. J., has lived in North Hudson County since he was six months old, and in various positions has contributed to its growth and prosperity. His parents, Henry Andes and Theresa Morton, were natives of Germany, and from them he inherited all the sturdy intellectual and physical characteristics of his race.

He was born in Paterson, N. J., June 30, 1867. When six months old the family moved to West New York, Hudson County, where he obtained a public school education. At the early age of ten he left school and began to earn his own living, finding employment as a "reeler" in the Givernaud silk-mill at Homestead. He was a foreman over twelve other young men when only fifteen, and at the age of sixteen became a freight checker on the West Shore Railroad. Six months later, however, he began to learn the trade of mason and plasterer, which he has followed ever since with the exception of two years, when he was a special policeman at the Guttenberg race track. In 1891 he engaged in business for himself, and was the first builder to erect a three-story brick house in West New York. This building stands on King Street, near Pierce Avenue. In 1897 he built no less than thirty-three houses, some of which are his own property, and eleven of them were cottages at Highwood Park.

Mr. Andes is one of the most successful contractors and builders in the northern part of Hudson County. He is thorough in every detail, energetic and practical in carrying out his contracts, and prompt in all he undertakes. His foresight, integrity, and sound judgment, and his capacity for business, have brought him into more than local prominence. In politics he is an ardent Republican. He was elected a member of the North Bergen Board of Education from District No. 5 in 1891, and was re-elected in 1893 and again in 1894, the last time for a term of three years, receiving 388 out of the 401 votes cast. He was one of the principal organizers and the first Foreman of the American Hose Company of North Bergen, which he has served as Treasurer, and is a member of the Germania Schuetzenbund, Sergeant of the First Battalion of New Jersey, and a member of the Independent Order of Foresters and of the Merry Owls.

He was married, February 21, 1893, to Miss Sophia Menkel, of West New York. They have two children: Henry, Jr., and Gertrude, and reside on Robert Street, North Bergen.

CHARLES SINGER, JR., Town Clerk of the Town of Union, is the son of Charles Singer, Sr., and Caroline Kiefer, and a grandson of George and Catherine Kiefer, both natives of Germany, who settled in Buffalo, New York, more than sixty years ago. For three generations the family has held high rank among our most industrious, honored, and respected Ger-

CHARLES SINGER, JR.

man-American citizens. His father, Charles, was for many years a noted chef, holding responsible positions in some of the leading hotels in this country, including the famous Astor House of New York. He is now retired, living in Union Hill. George Kiefer was a non-commissioned officer in the Civil War, enlisting in a regiment raised in Buffalo, and died there in 1877.

Mr. Singer was born on Union Hill, Hudson County, N. J., July 13, 1868. There his parents have resided for over thirty-two years, and the property owned by his father, at the corner of Palisade Avenue and Franklin Street, was the scene of the first mass meeting held for the purpose of hearing the town charter publicly read. When Charles was three years old the family moved to Utica, N. Y. Later they lived in Syracuse and in Buffalo in that State, and in San Francisco, Cal., but when he was eleven years of age they returned to Union Hill, N. J., where they have since remained. Mr. Singer was graduated with honor from the public schools of his native town in 1882, and also attended a private school, developing in these institutions a naturally bright and quick intellect, and, despite his fun-loving disposition, being always studious and observing. After leaving school he entered the employ of the great silk manufacturing firm of Givernaud Brothers, where he remained fourteen years. During the greater part of this period he held a most responsible position as one of the managing clerks of the concern.

He has been a member of the Democratic Town General Committee since he attained his majority (1889), and for five years he has been President of the First (old Third) Ward Democratic Club of the Town of Union. He was also an organizer and the first Secretary and is still a member of the Democratic Central Organization. In politics he has always been a leader of recognized ability, but never sought office. He declined all political preferment until April, 1896, when he was urged to accept the nomination for Town Clerk, which he did, though much against his wishes. He was elected by a large majority, and in April, 1899, was re-elected for a second term of three years without opposition. In accepting this office he sacrificed, in a measure, the bright and promising prospects which appeared open for him in a business career, but the selection of him as a candidate has more than justified the wisdom of the choice. He has conducted the town's affairs in a thorough, business-like manner, creditable to himself and his constituents, and most satisfactory to all classes of citizens irrespective of party. With characteristic energy and application he entered upon his duties as Town Clerk, which he has discharged for more than four years with great fidelity and honor. He has proven himself more than equal to his task, and is acknowledged to be one of the best clerks the Town of Union ever had.

Though a young man, Mr. Singer has achieved a high reputation for ability and perseverance. He is a public spirited citizen, imbued with an exalted sense of patriotism and progressiveness, and by action and example has exerted a wholesome influence in the community, whose respect and confidence he enjoys to the utmost. He is one of the most popular and best known men, not only in his town, but in Hudson County. He was one of the principal organizers of Palisade Council, Knights of Columbus, of Union Hill, and was chosen its first Grand Knight, which office he still holds. He is also an honorary member of St. Paul's Lyceum of Jersey City Heights, and a leading member of the Emil Groth Association, of the John J. Eagan Association, of the Union Hill Turn Verein, of the All Bees Bowling Club, and of the Hamilton Wheelmen. Being an expert accountant, he is or has been an officer in most of these bodies. He has proven his efficiency in every capacity, and is justly recognized as one of the ablest accountants as well as one of the most popular young men in Hudson County. He is unmarried.

JOHN P. WILHELM, one of the leading market gardeners of Hudson County, residing in Kearny, was born in Harrison, N. J., May 16, 1857. His parents, Peter and Mary (Hasson) Wilhelm, were natives of Germany, and, like many other enterprising, freedom-loving citizens of the Fatherland, left that country and came to America. Settling in Harrison, N. J., they became respected and honored citizens, and exerted in the community a wholesome and enterprising influence.

Mr. Wilhelm acquired his education in the public schools of Harrison, and there laid the foundation upon which he has built a successful and honorable career. He has been engaged all his life in the healthful occupation of market gardening, and to-day is widely known and respected as one of the leading agriculturists of Hudson County. Although never aspiring to political office, he has taken a deep interest in public affairs, and in the community in which he has so long resided is honored and esteemed for commendable traits of character and qualities of thrift. He liberally encourages every worthy object and has often been called upon to exert his influence in matters of importance to the community, a fact which at once attests his popularity and the confidence in which he is held.

Mr. Wilhelm married Miss Jessie Van Emberg, of Harrison, a descendant also of German ancestry, and a woman of great energy and force of character.

EZRA K. SEGUINE, a prominent lawyer and citizen of Jersey City, was born at Delaware Water Gap, Slateford, Pa., on the 18th of November, 1858. He descends from a Huguenot family who settled at Seguine's Point, Staten Island, on their arrival from France, and who represented all that is good in French social life. He is the son of William P. and Sarah E. (Kennedy) Seguine, a grandson of Jacob and Martha (Ward) Seguine and of Charles and Martha (Twining) Kennedy, and a great-grandson of Jacob Seguine, Sr.

Mr. Seguine was educated in the local schools of his native town and at Mt. Dolia Academy in Glen Gardner, N. J., and at an early age entered mercantile life in New York City. Subsequently he read law in the office of Charles E. Scofield, of Jersey City, and was admitted to the bar of New Jersey in November, 1879. After the death of Mr. Scofield in 1878 Mr. Seguine closed out his extensive bankruptcy practice, and since his admission to the bar in the following year has been actively and successfully engaged in the practice of law in Jersey City.

In addition to his extensive law business in all the courts of the State he is interested in iron and coal mining properties in Eastern Tennessee and is the head of the Seguine-Axford Veneer Company of Jersey City and Harriman, Tenn. Both as a lawyer and business man he has gained a high reputation.

Mr. Seguine was married, July 30, 1884, to Emma C. Small, daughter of John Small, of Jersey City, who was for many years prominently identified with the Morris Canal in New Jersey. They have two children: Charlotte and Maude.

JOSEPH FRANKLIN CROWELL, for several years Corporation Counsel of the Town of Kearny, N. J., where he resides, was born in New York City on the 17th of October, 1855, his parents being Gilbert Lafayette Crowell and Matilda Du Rie Allaire, both natives of New York City. On his mother's side he is connected with the Du Ries and Christies, two old families of Bergen County. He is also, on the maternal side, a lineal descendant of Alexander Allaire, the Huguenot, of Rochelle, France, who came to New York in 1680 and founded the Town of New Rochelle in Westchester County. The Crowells were among the very earliest settlers of this State. They came originally from England and settled in Cape Cod, Mass., whence they removed to New Jersey and settled in Woodbridge, Middlesex County, about 1675. They have been prominently identified with the development of the State and its history ever since. Mr. Crowell's paternal great-grandfathers, Edward Crowell and Asher Fitz Randolph, were Revolutionary soldiers, both serving in the New Jersey State troops throughout the War for Independence. He is the possessor of an interesting Revolutionary relic—a gold ring, presented to his ancestor, Captain Asher Fitz Randolph, for a special personal service, by

JOSEPH F. CROWELL.

General Lafayette, upon whose staff Captain Fitz Randolph served during the Revolution. Mr. Crowell's grandfather, Joseph Crowell, who removed from New Jersey to New York in 1808, was a veteran of the War of 1812, and for many years lived in old "Greenwich village" in the corporate limits of New York City. Here in the old ninth ward, as it was afterward known, Mr. Crowell, the subject of this sketch, was born. His parents moved to Arlington, N. J., in 1878.

Having received a thorough preparatory education at Mount Washington Collegiate Institute in his native city, Mr. Crowell entered Columbia College and was graduated with high honors in 1878, standing sixth in his class, and with membership in the Phi Beta Kappa fraternity. He then entered the law office of John Clinton Gray, of New York City, now a Justice of the New York Court of Appeals, and was graduated LL.B. from Columbia College Law School in 1880, being admitted to the bar of New York as an attorney and counselor in May of the same year. In February, 1886, he was admitted to the bar of New Jersey, and since then he has successfully practiced his profession in Hudson County, residing in Arlington.

Mr. Crowell has taken an active part in the affairs of his adopted town, and for a number of years has been one of its leading citizens. He was Town Clerk of Kearny in 1888 and 1889 and Corporation Counsel in 1890 and from 1896 to 1899 inclusive. In these and various other capacities he has distinguished himself as a man of ability, integrity, and great force of character. He has achieved marked success in his profession and stands high as a lawyer and advocate. He has been a member of the Democratic County Committee of Hudson County since 1889 and one of its Executive Committee since 1896, and is also a member of the Robert Davis Association of Hudson County, of the Delta Kappa Epsilon fraternity and the Delta Kappa Epsilon Club of New York City, and of the Columbia College Alumni Association.

February 7, 1882, Mr. Crowell was married in Salt Lake City, Utah, to Miss Ida MacArthur, daughter of Heman MacArthur, of Ripon, Wis. They have four children: Mima, Gilbert Lafayette, Joseph Franklin, and Matilda Du Rie.

RICHARD VEALE, of Kearny, Hudson County, was born in Cornwall, England, on the 7th of July, 1864. He is the son of Nicholas Veale and Lucy Esterbrook and a grandson of Richard and Nancy Veale and Nicholas and Mary Jane Esterbrook. Mr. Veale came to America with his parents in 1871. The family first settled in Morris County, N. J., where he received a public school education at a place called Mine Hill. Subsequently they removed to Maine, thence to the State of New York, and in 1885 to California.

In 1887 Mr. Veale located permanently in Kearny, Hudson County, N. J., where he has since become prominent as a business man and public spirited citizen. In early life he learned the carpenter's trade, and while in California was successfully engaged in mining. For thirteen years he was associated with the Delaware, Lackawanna and Western Railroad Company in the capacity of carpenter. In 1898 he engaged in the grocery and provision business in Kearny and still continues in that line of trade.

Politically, Mr. Veale is a strong Republican, active in politics, and deeply interested in all public affairs. He was for seven years a Director in the Harrison Building and Loan Association, has served as Chairman and Secretary of the Town Republican Committee, and is Secretary of the District Club. He has also been a member of the Kearny Town Council, in which he served on the Ordinance Committee. He was a delegate to the State Republican Convention that nominated Governor Griggs, and was for many years a member of the Mutual Benefit Association (a railroad organization). He is Past District Deputy of the Knights of Pythias and Junior Deacon of Copestone Lodge, F. and A. M. In every capacity he has displayed marked ability, integrity, and enterprise, and is highly respected by all who know him.

Mr. Veale married Sarah Bone, daughter of John Bone, of Mine Hill, Morris County, N. J. They have three children: Sadie, Richard Clifford, and John Wesley.

URIAH ALLEN, one of the oldest and best known business men in Jersey City, was born in New York City on the 6th of July, 1825, his parents being James P. and Mary Allen. On his father's side he is of Scotch and on his mother's of Holland descent and springs from some of the oldest families in this part of the country.

Mr. Allen received a good practical education in his native city and from boyhood has been a very active business man. For many years he was a successful merchant in New York, conducting a large commission business and making an independent fortune. Retiring from that, he established himself in the furnishing business in Jersey City, which he continued for a period of twenty-one years. At the present time he is actively and successfully engaged in the art business in Jersey City, having always been identified with that line as a side issue.

Besides devoting his energies to an extensive business Mr. Allen also took an active and influential part in public affairs, and from early life has been an enterprising, public spirited, and progressive citizen. He was one of the original founders and chief supporters of the Republican party in Jersey City in 1856, and ever since then has been intimately identified with its affairs and prominent as one of its acknowledged leaders. He has not, however, sought or accepted public office, preferring to devote his time wholly to business. For eight years he served in the New York State National Guard as a member of the Seventh Regiment, one of the most noted military organizations in the country.

Mr. Allen married Susanna Elizabeth Thompson, daughter of John Thompson, an old resident of the Seventh Ward, New York City. She died in 1894, leaving four children: Halsey W., Morris S., Horace G., and Jessie E.

JOHN JOSEPH FALLON, Assemblyman for Hudson County, residing in Hoboken, was born in New York City, December 19, 1870. His father, John James Fallon, born November 12, 1840, in County Roscommon, Ireland, came to America when twelve years of age. When the Civil War broke out in 1861 he enlisted in the Thirty-seventh Regiment, Irish Rifles, for two years, at the end of which time he received an honorable discharge. He was engaged in many battles and received a silver medal of honor from Major-General Phil. Kearny, under whom he served. His father, John Fallon, who resided in County Roscommon, Ireland, was a prosperous leather merchant. He had several brothers who were grain merchants, one of whom, Michael Fallon, had three sons, one of whom, Rev. Martin Xavier Fallon, was pastor of St. Paul's Roman Catholic Church at Wilmington, Del., for more than twenty-five years. He died in 1900. Another brother, Richard Fallon, a resident of New Rochelle, N. Y., is a well known contractor and builder. John Fallon married Mary Tumulty, of County Roscommon, Ireland. They were the grandparents of John Joseph Fallon, the subject of this article.

The latter's mother, Mary Ellen Fallon, is a descendant of the well known Fitzgerald family, among which was her uncle, John Fitzgerald, M.D., of London, for many years a member of Parliament, and Rev. John Fitzgerald, of County Roscommon, Ireland. Her parents were Colonel Patrick Fitzgerald and Mary Fitzgerald, of County Roscommon.

John Joseph Fallon, when not quite one year old, removed with his parents to Hoboken, where he has since resided. His early education was received in St. Mary's Parochial School, Hoboken, from which he was graduated.

He then attended the public schools of Hoboken, graduating in 1885. He obtained employment in a broker's office in New York City, where he remained but a short time, and then worked in a wholesale drug house for a year. He was afterward employed by the Western Union Telegraph Company as a messenger, and rapidly advanced to the position of receiving and

delivery clerk in the Maritime Exchange office, which position he held until 1890, when he resigned because of ill health and a desire for outdoor employment. He then entered the employ of the Metropolitan Life Insurance Company of New York as an agent in the Hoboken district, which position he occupied for one year, when he was promoted to the position of assistant superintendent, which he held for four years. In 1892 he enrolled as a student in the Metropolis Law School, which has since been merged with the University Law School of the City of New York, attending the evening sessions and graduating therefrom in 1895. He was admitted to the New Jersey bar as an attorney at law and solicitor in chancery at the June term, 1895, and as a counselor in November, 1899. He is also a master in chancery by appointment of the late Chancellor Alexander T. McGill and a member of the bar of the United States District and Circuit Courts.

Subsequent to his admission to the bar the officers of the Metropolitan Life Insurance Company offered him the position of superintendent, which offer was declined by Mr. Fallon, he having determined to practice law, and in February, 1896, he severed his connection with the company and formed a copartnership with ex-Judge William E. Skinner and Assemblyman John J. Marnell, under the firm name of Skinner, Marnell & Fallon. This partnership continued for two years, when it was dissolved. Mr. Marnell and Mr. Fallon thereafter formed a copartnership under the firm name of Marnell & Fallon, and they have offices in the Second National Bank building, Hoboken. Mr. Fallon has been active in politics for a number of years. In every political campaign for the past seven years his voice has been heard in advocacy of the Democratic party, but he never sought nor accepted office until 1899, when, at the earnest solicitation of his friends, he accepted the nomination for member of the General Assembly of the State of New Jersey, and on November 7 of that year was elected by a majority which attested at once his popularity and the confidence in which he is held. In that office as well as at the bar he has displayed marked ability and energy.

Mr. Fallon is affiliated with numerous societies, among which are Hoboken Lodge, No. 74, Benevolent and Protective Order of Elks, Hoboken Council, No. 159, Knights of Columbus, Court Castle Point, No. 54, Foresters of America, the Robert Davis Association, and the M. J. Coyle Association.

He was married December 20, 1893, to Mary L., daughter of Patrick Kelley, of Hoboken. They have two children: John J. Fallon, Jr., and Marguerite Fallon.

ADDISON ELY, a leading lawyer of Rutherford, Bergen County, and Captain of Company L, Second Regiment New Jersey Volunteers, is the great-grandson of Captain Levi Ely, a hero of the Revolutionary War, who was killed in the battle of Mohawk, and who is buried in West Springfield, Mass., under a monument erected to his memory by public spirited citizens in recognition of his patriotism and worth. The family has been prominent in the Connecticut Valley, and particularly in Massachusetts, for many generations, while a number of its branches have wielded a potent influence for good in other sections of the country. Captain Addison Ely's mother, Emeline Harrison, was the daughter of Seth Harrison, who was a cousin of President William Henry Harrison, the grandfather of President Benjamin Harrison. This family has also been a prominent one in Western Massachusetts.

Captain Ely is the son of William and Emeline (Harrison) Ely, and was born in Westfield, Mass., May 23, 1853. On the death of his mother, in 1862, he came with his father to Bloomfield, N. J., an aristocratic suburb of Newark, and here and in the vicinity he has ever since resided. He fitted for college at the Brooklyn Polytechnic Institute and at Phillips

Andover Academy. It was his ambition and intention to enter Harvard University, but circumstances compelled him to abandon a collegiate course and begin life as a teacher, which he did at the age of eighteen. He taught a district school at Connecticut Farms, Union County, N. J., and subsequently became Principal of the Caldwell High School in Essex County, and during this connection, and afterward, he also studied law with a view of being admitted to the bar.

In 1879, however, he temporarily relinquished this intention and accepted the principalship of the public school at Rutherford, N. J., which he filled with marked ability and satisfaction for several years, gaining a high standing for thoroughness and excellent discipline. Many of his pupils are successfully settled in the arts and professions in or near Newark, and owe their first inspiration and early training to his efforts, and he continues to hold their respect, love, and confidence.

Having thoroughly prepared himself in legal study, Captain Ely was admitted to the bar of New Jersey as an attorney at the February term of the Supreme Court in 1888 and as a counselor in February, 1891, and has continuously and successfully practiced his profession in Bergen County. He rapidly came into prominence as an able lawyer, and by his untiring energy, industry, and careful preparation has won many notable victories. His practice takes him into all the courts, and has constantly increased, giving him a high standing at the bar and, locally, the position of a leader.

He is an ardent and active Democrat, but has never sought nor accepted political office, preferring to devote his whole time to his profession. He is always ready, however, to bear a loyal citizen's part in public and party affairs, takes a deep interest in all worthy movements affecting the community, and does not hesitate to condemn selfish motives or unworthy schemes. He is especially prominent in military circles, having been Captain of Company L, Second Regiment, N. G. N. J., since 1893, when he was unanimously elected to that office. Under his management and discipline that company has gained a remarkable degree of efficiency. He is a member of the Presbyterian Church and of almost all the leading societies and organizations of Rutherford, including the Masonic order, the Royal Arcanum, the Legion of Honor, and the Union Club.

In 1874, when he was twenty-one years of age, Captain Ely married Miss Emily J. Johnson, of Connecticut Farms, N. J., and they have had seven sons and three daughters, all of whom are living. Their eldest son, Addison Ely, Jr., born in 1876, is a graduate of Columbia College, New York. For two years he edited the *Bergen County Herald*. He was graduated from the Law Department of Michigan University in June, 1900, and now is engaged in active practice with his father.

ALPHONSE THOUROT, a leading plumber and the Postmaster of Taurus in the Town of West New York, Hudson County, was born in West Hoboken, N. J., February 25, 1860. His parents, Louis Thourot and Catherine Perenot, were both natives of France, coming to this country when young. The former served for a time in the War of the Rebellion.

Mr. Thourot was educated in the public schools of West Hoboken. At the age of thirteen he began life as an apprentice to the plumbing and gasfitting trade, which he mastered in some of the best establishments in West Hoboken and New York. In 1881 he engaged in business for himself in West Hoboken, but the next year moved to the Town of Union, where he continued until 1891, when he sold out. During this period he not only achieved success, but also gained a high reputation as a first-class plumber and gas and steam fitter, and came to be regarded as a man of ability and integrity. In 1891 he assisted in the organization of the Union Granite Company, located at the "Old Ferry" in West New York, and for about four years was its President. Under his able management that company laid the foundation of its present prosperity and usefulness.

In 1895 Mr. Thourot removed to West New York and opened his present plumbing establishment, and upon the creation of the postoffice of Taurus, on July 1, 1896, was made the Postmaster, which office he still holds. He was also Recorder of the Township of Union for five years and a Justice of the Peace for a similar period. He is a prominent member of Mystic Tie Lodge, No. 123, F. and A. M., of the Royal Arcanum, and of the Sons of Veterans. In politics he is a Democrat, earnest in his convictions, and active in the councils of his party. Public spirited and patriotic, he is esteemed for those abilities and virtues which mark the successful man.

Mr. Thourot was married on the 24th of August, 1880, to Eleanore, daughter of Gustav and Louise Fermont, of the Town of Union. They have one child, Emily.

JOHN B. WILLIAMS, one of the prominent and enterprising farmers of New Durham, Hudson County, is the eldest son of John Williams and Sarah A. Saunier and a grandson of John Williams, Sr., and Rebecca Smith. Of his paternal grandfather, John Williams, Sr., but little is definitely known. He was an honored resident of New Durham, and is supposed to have been lost on the Hudson River. By his wife, Rebecca Smith, he had children as follows: Leah, wife of Henry Post; Phoebe, wife of Job Smith; Margaret, wife of William Berry; John, Jr., who succeeded to the New Durham homestead; Ann, wife of Garret Van Giesen; and Rebecca, wife of John Green. John Williams, Jr., the only son, was a life-long resident on the family homestead, being born there in 1804, and dying there in 1881. He was always a farmer, an old-time Whig, and a useful, enterprising citizen, universally respected for those virtues which distinguish an honest man. His wife, who died May 14, 1886, was Sarah Ann Saunier, daughter of Mitchell and Eliza (Vreeland) Saunier, of New Durham, and a descendant of Pierre Paul Saunier, a celebrated botanist who was sent to America by the French government to gather natural products of this country for transplanting in Europe; he came over with André Michaux, a French botanist and trader. Mr. and Mrs. Williams had seven children, as follows: Ann Eliza, who married Henry H. Van Glahn; John B., the subject of this sketch; Mitchell; Angeline; Margaret, who married Bryant Stephens; Mary Emma; and George E. Of these only John B., Mitchell, and Mary Emma are living.

John B. Williams was born December 15, 1836, on the old family homestead in New Durham, Hudson County, on which he has spent his entire life. His education was obtained in the common schools of the neighborhood. After completing his studies he learned the trade of bookbinder, which he followed as a business, in conjunction with farming, until 1864. Since then he has devoted himself to agricultural pursuits, building, and real estate, achieving eminent success in every sense of the term. He is regarded as one of the best farmers in his section of the State. Industrious, enterprising, and practical, he is universally respected for those broad and sterling qualities which mark the honest man. The esteem in which he is held is attested by his popularity, and by the confidence reposed in his sound judgment and unimpeachable character. He is a man of the highest integrity, faithful to every trust, just and conscientious in all the relations of life, and modest and unassuming, though true to his convictions and fearless in discriminating between right and wrong. A keen sense of justice is one of his strongest characteristics. He is a Republican in politics, but has never sought political preferment or publicity of any kind. On the contrary he has declined official positions, though often urged to accept them, accepting only the position of State Visitor to the Agricultural College at New Brunswick, N. J. While he adheres to party lines on State and na-

JOHN B. WILLIAMS.

tional issues, he is strictly independent in all local maters, casting his vote and influence in favor of those candidates and movements which promise the greatest good, and which have the public welfare at heart. Born and reared on the farm, and educated in the practical school of experience, he developed a strong constitution, great mental energy, and high physical and intellectual abilities, and during a long and successful career has maintained the confidence of the entire community.

Mr. Williams was married in 1866 to Gertrude Edsall, daughter of Samuel and Isabella (Christie) Edsall and granddaughter of John Edsall and Gertrude Lydecker. They have had four children: John Walter Williams, who is engaged in business in New York City; Annette; Samuel Edsall Williams, deceased; and Sarah Isabell Williams.

Mrs. Williams is a member of the Sons and Daughters of the Revolution. Her brothers and sister are John S. Edsall, Sarah A. (Mrs. Cornelius J. Westervelt, of Bergen County), and Samuel S. Edsall. The children of her paternal grandparents, John and Gertrude (Lydecker) Edsall, were Samuel S., Hannah (Mrs. Joel M. Johnson), Naomi (Mrs. John H. Brinckerhoff), Mary Agnes (Mrs. Samuel de Groot), Garret L., and Gertrude (Mrs. Isaac R. Vreeland). Mr. and Mrs. Williams represent two of the oldest and best known families in East Jersey, as well as several allied families of prominence and distinction.

WALLACE WHITE, M.D., of West Hoboken, Hudson County, N. J., where he is in the enjoyment of a large professional practice, and holds the office, in the line of his profession, of Town Physician, is universally regarded as one of the most enterprising and public spirited gentlemen in the community. Although he has been engaged in practice in West Hoboken but about five years, he has become one of the best known physicians and surgeons in Hudson County, and has among his patients members of many of the oldest and wealthiest families in the county. Dr. White has established a wide reputation for skill as a surgeon, having had remarkable success with this class of cases. His work in connection with diseases of children has also been especially notable. His office is completely equipped, moreover, with electrical appliances for every form of treatment of diseases of the ear, nose, and throat. He also conducts a general practice. He is enthusiastic in original scientific investigation, and is progressive and enterprising. In illustration of this trait it may be noted that he is the only physician in Hudson County who has equipped himself with a complete electrical outfit for taking photographs by means of the Roentgen rays, or "X-ray." He has succeeded in a number of cases, by means of this device, in locating bullets or other foreign matter in the bodies of patients, in cases where no other expedient known to medical science would have been successful.

He is a native of Paterson, N. J., where he was born during the progress of the Civil War. He attended the public schools of Paterson and Princeton Preparatory School, and in 1893 was graduated from the New York College of Physicians and Surgeons—the Medical Department of Columbia University. After his graduation he took a special course in midwifery in the Sloane Maternity Hospital of New York. Later he was in charge of the Outdoor Patient Department of Roosevelt Hospital in the same city, while he was likewise in charge of the Outdoor Children's Department of Bellevue Hospital. In 1895 he was the successful competitor among twelve candidates who engaged in competitive examination for the position of House Physician in Christ Hospital, Jersey City Heights. In this position he established such a reputation for skill that wealthy patients who had been treated by him at the hospital prevailed upon him to engage in private practice in West Hoboken.

GUSTAV W. SCHOLP, ex-Mayor of North Bergen, Hudson County, is one of the most progressive and popular citizens of that community, of which he has been a resident since 1881. He is a Democrat, and has been one of the active leaders of the party and prominent in local affairs. He was a candidate for Township Committeeman in 1892, but was unsuccessful in the convention. He was elected a member of the Board of Education of North Bergen in 1894, became clerk of the board, and, having subsequently been re-elected for another term, was made President of the Board of Education by his colleagues. In 1896 he received the Democratic nomination as Township Committeeman, defeating in the convention the gentleman by whom he had himself been defeated in 1892. His election to the committee followed. Mr. Scholp was elected to the office of Mayor at the end of a contest which demonstrated his popularity, defeating Charles Pinnell, who had held the office for more than twenty years.

Mr. Scholp was born in the City of New York, March 31, 1861, and is the son of Charles Scholp and Mary, daughter of Henry Barringer. He is of German descent. Up to the age of fourteen he attended the public schools of New York City. During the next six years he mastered every branch of the art of glass engraving, being in the employ of William Van Hofe, of 33 Murray Street, New York. During the next fifteen years, however, he was engaged as a salesman with W. M. Schwenker, of New York, dealer in brewers' supplies. He is now successfully engaged in business for himself in the same line.

Mr. Scholp married Sophie Lehnig, December 2, 1883, and owns the handsome home in which he resides on Hudson Boulevard, North Bergen. He is President of the Merry Owl Association, Past Master of Mystic Tie Lodge, F. and A. M., and a member of the Elks of Waterbury, Conn., and of Hoffman Lodge of Union Hill, Hudson County, N. J.

JOSEPH SAUNDERS PARRY, who has been actively and successfully engaged in the practice of law at Hoboken, N. J., since November, 1886, was born in Warminster Township, Bucks County, Pa., April 8, 1857. He is the son of Thomas and Lydia (Conard) Parry, a grandson of Isaac and Mary Parry and Jonathan and Hannah Conard, and a descendant of the Parry family who came to America about 1681, and who, being followers of William Penn, settled near Philadelphia. Both the Parrys and Conards have been prominent in the history of Eastern Pennsylvania, being from the first substantial citizens, and exerting in their respective communities a wholesome influence. Being members of the Society of Friends, their standards of honesty, integrity, and industry, as well as their purity of character and love of liberty, were moving factors in the general growth and development of the region and are still firmly implanted in local associations.

Mr. Parry was educated in the common schools, at the Friends' Central School in Philadelphia, and at the Pennsylvania State Normal School at Millersville, from which he was graduated in 1879. Between 1879 and 1882 he was engaged in teaching in Pennsylvania. He pursued his legal studies in the office of Judge Joseph H. Gaskill, of Mount Holly, N. J., and remained there until his admission to the bar as an attorney at the June term of the New Jersey Supreme Court, 1886. In February, 1890, he was admitted as a counselor. Mr. Parry entered upon the active practice of his profession at Hoboken, Hudson County, in November, 1886, and by close attention to business has acquired an honorable standing at the bar.

Mr. Parry takes a deep interest in public affairs, and liberally encourages every object which has the welfare and prosperity of the community at heart. He is a public spirited citizen, a man of acknowledged ability and enterprise, a Past Master of Euclid Lodge, No. 136, F. and A. M., and a member of the Columbia Club of Hoboken, in which city he resides. He was married, on the 31st of March, 1897, to Miss Sarah P. Willets.

JAMES ALLAN, member of the Board of Aldermen of Kearny, Hudson County, N. J., and formerly a member and President of the Board of Education of that town, was born in Lochwinnoch, Scotland, January 17, 1843. His parents, James and Mary (Harvey) Allan, were both natives of that place and were married there.

Mr. Allan received his education in Johnstone, Scotland, and then learned the patternmaker's trade, which he has ever since followed. In 1879 he came to the United States and settled in East Newark, N. J., whence he subsequently removed to Kearny, where he now resides. He is, and has been since his arrival in this country, actively and successfully engaged in business as a patternmaker and carpenter, and to his skill and enterprise are due many of the finer buildings of this section. His work gives evidence of great talent. He has superintended the erection of many important buildings, including one of the linen thread mills in Kearny.

Mr. Allan has not only achieved success and prominence in business affairs, but has also taken an active interest in public life, and has filled several positions with characteristic energy and satisfaction. Before coming to America he served eight years in the volunteer army at Johnstone, Scotland, receiving an honorable discharge. He is an ardent Republican, a public spirited, energetic, and patriotic citizen, and for four years was a member of the Board of Education of Kearny, being President of that board two years. At the present time he is a member of the Board of Aldermen of Kearny, and is also a member of the Masonic fraternity and of the Independent Order of Odd Fellows. He is a member of the North Reformed Church of Newark, and in all the relations of life has achieved both success and honor.

November 4, 1873, he married Miss Mary Gillies, of Glasgow, Scotland. They have three children: James, Janet, and Bessie.

JAMES ALLAN.

JAMES O'BRINE, of West Hoboken, is a son of the late Felix and Mary O'Brine, and was born in West Hoboken, N. J., on the 22d of March, 1855. There he received a public school education. Felix O'Brine was a well known mason and builder, and after leaving school James associated himself with his father and mastered every detail of the trade. Upon the death of his father, in 1880, he succeeded to the business, which he has successfully conducted to the present time. Among the buildings which he has erected, or assisted to erect, and which stand as monuments to his skill and industry, may be mentioned Public School No. 3, Hoboken, and the Fritz Reuter Home for Aged and Infirm People in Schuetzen Park, North Bergen. Many other prominent buildings in Hoboken and vicinity have also been erected by him. Mr. O'Brine is a public spirited and enterprising citizen, a prominent Democrat, and one of the leading citizens of West Hoboken.

VALENTINE DENZER, of West Hoboken, was born in Manheim, Bavaria, Germany, September 18, 1834, the son of Valentine Denzer, Sr., born September 29, 1799, and Elizabeth Becker, his wife, and a grandson of Albinus Denzer. In November, 1834, he was brought by his parents to America, and for nearly three years the family lived in New York City. In August, 1837, they moved to Washington County, Ohio, but in the fall of 1844 returned to New York, retaining, however, their property in the West. The father was a miller, and in New York was engaged for six years in the grocery business at 500 East Fourth Street. In May, 1856, they returned to the old home in Ohio, where Valentine Denzer, Sr., resided until May, 1876, when he once more came East, and died in West Hoboken, N. J., August 23, 1878. His wife died in 1884, aged seventy-six.

Valentine Denzer, the subject of this article, attended school in a log school house in Lowell, Ohio, until he was nine years old. Afterward he attended the public schools of New York City, and when sixteen took a private course of study for the purpose of entering Columbia College. This ambition, however, was not gratified. At the age of eighteen he became bookkeeper in a large establishment at 57 Elm Street, New York, which position he held until 1854.

In 1855 he associated himself with Sands & Nathans in the athlete and circus business, and continued with them and their successors—including P. T. Barnum, Barnum & Bailey, and others—for seventeen years, traveling from St. John, New Brunswick, to Denver, Col., three times in a buggy, and also from St. Paul to the City of Mexico with a team. He visited every State and territory in the Union, and being a close observer gathered an immense amount of information. His work brought him into contact with all classes of people and enabled him to gain a liberal knowledge of the country, which, with his remarkably retentive memory, makes him an interesting and instructive conversationalist. Mr. Denzer became one of the best known showmen in the United States. After leaving the business he formed a copartnership with his brother-in-law, Valentine Schneider, and Charles H. Medicus, and opened a furniture store in New York City. The financial panic of 1873, however, forced them to retire, and Mr. Denzer returned to his old profession of bookkeeper, which he still follows. He is an expert mathematician, methodical and accurate, and his books are models of neatness.

In 1875 he took up his present home in West Hoboken. He is a member, a Trustee, and a Past Master of New York Lodge, No. 330, F. and A. M., and a member of Manhattan Chapter, R. A. M., of New York City, and of Commercial Lodge, Knights of Honor. He served two years as Master of New York Lodge of Masons, and when he retired December 26, 1893, was presented with a set of elaborately engrossed resolutions and a handsome sterling silver dinner set, consisting of seventy-two pieces, as testimonials from the officers and brethren in appreciation of his services in the chair, in building up the lodge, and inspiring it with his own enthusiasm.

Mr. Denzer was married in New York, April 21, 1855, to Barbara Schneider, a native of Germany and the daughter of Valentine Schneider, who died in New York of cholera, and Christina, his wife, who died in 1869. They have had nine children, six of whom survive and reside near or with their parents in West Hoboken.

GEORGE VALENTINE DENZER, eldest son of Valentine Denzer, Jr., and Barbara Schneider, was born in New York City, August 21, 1858. He received his education in the public schools of New York, and there, on completing his studies, engaged in the wholesale manufacture of furniture. This venture proved successful. In 1872 he took up his permanent residence in West Hoboken, where, in 1881, having closed up his business in New York, he engaged in the retail furniture trade, which he has since conducted. He has one of the largest, finest, and most complete furniture establishments in Hudson County, and is regarded as an able, enterprising business man and a public spirited, patriotic, progressive citizen. He is prominent and popular, highly esteemed and respected, and maintains the confidence of his fellowmen. He is a prominent member of Palisade Lodge, No. 84, F. and A. M., of the Union Hill Schuetzens, of the Zwiebelberger Bowling Club, of the Junior Order United American Mechanics, and of other organizations of a social, political, and benevolent nature.

Mr. Denzer was married, March 20, 1881, to Miss Eugenia Leuly, daughter of Jacob and Barbara Leuly, of West Hoboken. They have two children: Francis and Florence E.

WILLIAM J. WHITESIDE, of East Newark, N. J., is the son of George W. Whiteside, a merchant, and Eliza Feely, and was born in Belfast, Ireland, February 14, 1846. His mother was also a native of that city, while his father's birthplace was Surrey, England.

Having received a good education in the public schools of Belfast, Mr. Whiteside came to this country in 1867 and settled in New York City, where he found employment with Stewart Hartshorn, the well known inventor and manufacturer of the celebrated Hartshorn window-shade rollers and the founder of the present Stewart Hartshorn Company. Mr. Whiteside has continued in the employ of that establishment, having held various responsible positions, and being now foreman of one of the departments. He removed to East Newark, Hudson County, with the concern in 1871, and still resides there.

Mr. Whiteside is a Republican in politics and a Protestant in religion, and esteemed as a man of integrity, ability, and enterprise. Though giving his attention strictly to business, he takes a deep interest in all public matters and especially in questions of both local and national importance, and his views and opinions are received with respect and confidence.

February 5, 1866, Mr. Whiteside married Sarah Starett, daughter of James and Hannah Starett, of Belfast, Ireland. She is of Scotch descent. Their children are Lillian, Florence, William J., Jr., and Hazel.

JAMES KITCHELL ALLEN, of Kearny, Hudson County, was born in Whippany, Morris County, N. J., on the 20th of August, 1855. His parents, Albert Allen and Sarah E. Loper, were natives respectively of Massachusetts and Morris County, N. J., and were married in this State. Mr. Allen received his educational training in the public schools of Morristown, and subsequently entered upon a business career which has been both honorable and successful. He first engaged in the grocery trade. Afterward he became a florist and horticulturist in Garfield, N. J. During the last fourteen years, however, he has been actively and successfully engaged

JAMES K. ALLEN.

in business as a florist in New York City, where he has built up a large trade.

While Mr. Allen has devoted himself mainly to his large and growing business, he has at the same time taken an active interest in public affairs and has served as a School Trustee of Kearny, N. J., where he resides. In politics he is a Democrat. He is a member of Triune Lodge, No. 159, Free and Accepted Masons, of Arlington, of La Mancha Lodge, No. 24, Knights of Pythias, of Newark, and of the Royal Arcanum, and attends the Methodist Episcopal Church. For seven years he served as a member of the Fire Department of Kearny. He is a public spirited, enterprising, and patriotic citizen, highly esteemed by all who know him, and prominently identified with the growth and prosperity of his adopted town. His success in business is due to his great energy and ability combined with fair dealing, honesty, and integrity; and besides holding membership in the Florists' Club in New York City he is a member of the Society of American Florists of the United States, and is widely known as an expert in horticultural matters.

Mr. Allen married Miss Lucy Smith, daughter of Tibbs and Mary A. Smith, of England. They have three children: Albert William, George James, and Lucy Mary Ellen.

CHARLES C. HENDRICK, M.D., one of the rising young physicians of Jersey City and since 1895 Medical Health Inspector of Hudson County, was born in Phillipsburg, N. J., on the 5th of February, 1871. His father, Christopher Hendrick, was the first engineer to construct and run an engine in Mexico, and for some time was head engineer for the Emperor Maximilian. His paternal grandfather, Thomas A. Hendrick, came to this country from Ireland in 1845, and was a close friend of the late Hon. Thomas A. Hendricks, Vice-President of the United States. There are still in the family many interesting letters written by the latter to the former. Dr. Hendrick's mother was Julia Murphy, a daughter of Michael and Bridget (Dunlavey) Murphy, both natives of Ireland. His paternal grandfather's wife was Mary Dunlavey.

Dr. Hendrick was educated at St. Bonaventure College in Allegany, N. Y., at St. Canisius College in Buffalo, N. Y., and at Seton Hall in Orange, N. J., where he was graduated A.B. in 1891. The same college conferred upon him the degree of A.M. in 1893. Subsequently he took up the study of medicine and was graduated from Bellevue Hospital Medical College in New York City, receiving his degree of M.D. March 26, 1894. Afterward he also studied law and was admitted as an attorney in New Jersey in November, 1897.

Entering upon the practice of medicine in Jersey City, Dr. Hendrick soon gained distinction and was called upon to fill various positions of trust and responsibility. Since July, 1895, he has served as Medical Health Inspector of Hudson County, a position for which he is well qualified and in which he has rendered most satisfactory service. In 1898 he went to Cuba as an Assistant Surgeon in the United States Army and there broadened an already wide and practical experience in both medicine and sanitation. He is one of the ablest sanitary experts in Eastern New Jersey, and though a comparatively young man has already achieved a high position among the leading physicians of Hudson County. In politics he is a Democrat, and a member of the Robert Davis Association and the M. J. Coyle Association.

Dr. Hendrick was married, in December, 1894, to Agnes Nallin, of Brooklyn, N. Y. They have two sons: Thomas and Joseph.

GEORGE H. RUTMAN, of Kearny, Hudson County, is the son of Jonathan Rutman and Ann E. de Mond, both natives of New Jersey and descendants of some of the oldest families in the State, being of Holland Dutch origin. Mr. Rutman was born in Raritan, N. J., on the 16th of October, 1852, but received his education in the public schools of Elizabeth, whither his parents moved when he was young. Since leaving school he has been engaged in several lines of industry, the most important of which is that of painter and decorator, which he has followed successively for twenty-seven years in Elizabeth, Newark, and Kearny, N. J., having had his residence in Kearny since about 1887. His long and active connection with this trade and the large number of important contracts which he has executed have won for him an acknowledged leadership among his contemporaries. Possessing artistic qualities of a high order, he has achieved success and is known as one of the best painters and decorators in Eastern New Jersey. In 1889 he erected his handsome residence on the corner of Bergen Avenue and Elm Street, Kearny.

GEORGE H. RUTMAN.

In politics Mr. Rutman has always been a Republican. He served as Police Justice of Kearny during the years 1897 and 1898, but otherwise has declined political preferment, preferring to devote his whole time to business. He is a member of Ethic Lodge, Knights of Pythias, and of the First Baptist Church, both of Harrison, Hudson County, and is an exempt fireman of the Kearny Fire Department. He enjoys the confidence of the entire community.

On the 24th of May, 1876, Mr. Rutman married Mary Ellen Lackey, daughter of James and Ellen Lackey, of Newark, N. J. They have six children: Mabel, George, Herbert, Ella, Florence, and Garret Hobart.

JOHN CONWAY, President of the Union Granite Company, located at the old Weehawken ferry landing in Hudson County, is the son of Henry Conway and Annie O'Harrow and a grandson of James Conway and John O'Harrow. He was born February 2, 1858, in Renfrew, Scotland, and there obtained a public school education. Completing his studies at the age of fifteen, he entered upon the active duties of life as an apprentice at the tinsmith's trade, which he followed with marked success in Glasgow, where he had charge of a large tin shop.

But his ambitions led him to seek in America a broader and better field for the development of those talents which he has displayed in various business capacities, and which have marked him as a man of ability and enterprise. Landing in New York City on the 29th of August, 1880, he entered the employ of the American Gas Meter Company, manufacturers of gas meters, where he remained twelve years. In 1892 he associated himself with the Union Granite Company as a salesman in the factory, and a year later was made Vice-President and in 1894 President, which office he still holds. This corporation has its office and factories at the old Weehawken ferry landing above Weehawken, in Hudson County, and is one of the largest and most successful of its kind in the United States. The company manufactures sanitary laundry trays, granite, slate, and porcelain wash trays and sinks, combination bath and wash trays, slate mantels and wainscoting, slate stairs, water closets and urinals, vestibules, wood mantels, soapstone washtubs, etc. Mr. Conway's genius is well illustrated in his slate tub and combination bath and washtubs, which he invented and patented, and which have gained a wide reputation. Under his able and energetic management the business of the company has steadily grown to extensive proportions and ranks among the leading industries of Hudson County. Its present standing and successful trade are largely due to his ability, sagacity, and unceasing devotion to the manufacturing and business ends.

Mr. Conway was elected to the Board of Council of the Town of Union for the years 1891, 1892, 1898, and 1899, and during one term was its Chairman. As a Democrat he has been active and influential in party affairs, has frequently served as a delegate to local, county, and congressional conventions, and has been a member of the Hudson County Democratic Committee. He is Chairman of the Third Ward Democratic Club of the Town of Union, where he resides, and was for three years Chairman of the Board of Trustees of the Union Hill Fire Department. He is a member of the Knights of Columbus, of the Royal Arcanum, of the Catholic Benevolent Legion, and of the Columbia Hose Company of Union Hill, which he largely aided in organizing. In all these positions as well as in business affairs he has exhibited ability, sound judgment, and all the qualities which distinguish the successful man.

March 26, 1882, Mr. Conway married Mary E. Foley, daughter of John Foley, of New York City, and their children are Mary, John, Jr., James, Annie, and Joseph.

ROBERT WATERS has achieved distinction in the twofold capacity of author and educator. Born in Thurso, Scotland, May 9, 1835, he is the son of William and Alexandrina (Sutherland) Waters, and came to America with his parents in 1843, settling in Montreal, Canada. Though his father was a loyalist, and preferred Canada to the United States, the family of his mother, who was a daughter of Donald and Mary Sutherland (*née*

Innes), of Braalbin, Caithness-shire, Scotland, seem to have been of a different mind; for two of his granduncles, John and William Sutherland, after sharing the fortunes or misfortunes of the Pretender, Prince Charles, in the Rebellion of 1745, emigrated to the United States, and fought under Washington to the end of the Revolutionary War, when they were mustered out with the rank and honors of commissioned officers. Mr. Waters is not a little proud of these two noble kinsmen of his, one of whom, John Sutherland, settling in Hamilton, Ohio, presented a tract of land to that thriving town for a park, which bears his name, Sutherland Park, to this day.

ROBERT WATERS.

William, writing from Philadelphia in 1797 to another brother in Scotland, speaks of the country as "becoming crowded," and of the best land as being "already taken up!" Many of the Sutherlands of Philadelphia and of parts of Ohio are direct descendants of these two Revolutionary soldiers.

In his thirteenth year Mr. Waters was placed as an apprentice to the trade of printer in the office of the Montreal *Gazette;* and although he had previously attended three different schools, he owed, up to that time, his education almost entirely to his mother, who was a woman of superior character and fine intellectual attainments. At the age of fifteen young Waters removed with the family to New York City, where he worked for several years as a printer in the offices of Harper & Brothers, Thomas B. Smith, and others. It was while working at his trade in these places that he imbibed a passion for study and literature, which he gratified during every leisure moment, devoting himself with assiduity to the study of languages and to the reading of good authors. He made, in this way, a considerable acquaintance with the best works of English writers, mastered the French and German languages, and attended night schools, lyceum lectures, debating societies, etc., of which he gives some account in his well known book, *Intellectual Pursuits.* All this he supplemented with a period of foreign travel, going to Europe in his twenty-sixth year, and spending eighteen months in England and another eighteen in France. The experience he gained abroad, which marked an important epoch in his life, he will probably relate in a forthcoming work. While working as a printer in Paris Mr. Waters met a young American teacher of English who was instrumental in leading him into the profession which he has since honored by many years of useful service. Acting upon this gentleman's suggestion, that he apply for a post, through one of the Parisian Bureaux de Placement, as teacher of languages in a provincial school, he procured a position as *professeur d'anglais et d'allemand* at a large boarding and day school for boys in Saint Quentin, a manufacturing town in the north of France, where he soon found himself in a congenial sphere. His intimate knowledge of French, German, and English, and his natural ability and genial companionship, won for him a warm place in the hearts of his pupils and assured his success from the first. He remained there one year, and then went to Germany, arriving at Munich in August, 1863. Five months later, with a mind filled with pleasant recollections of the art galleries, artists, and lovers of learning of that historic university town, he accepted a position as teacher of English branches in the Commercial School of Offenbach-on-the-Main, a manufacturing center of Hesse-Darmstadt, five miles from Frankfort-on-the-Main. Here, he declares, he first learned what teaching meant. The excellent methods, thoroughness, and broad knowledge of the German teachers contrasted strongly with the weaker and more superficial system of the French, and inspired Mr. Waters with profound respect for and admiration of German methods. Here he taught and studied for four years, learning a great deal of German methods of teaching, of German life and literature, and acquiring for himself considerable knowledge of various important branches of education. He looks upon this period as one of the happiest and most profitable in his career. Finding his duties, his opportunities, and his surroundings so congenial, he relinquished the intention of going to Italy and Russia, and remained much longer in Germany than he had anticipated.

During the last year of his residence in Germany he passed an examination in Darmstadt before the Grand Ducal Council of Higher Studies, which entitled him to teach in any public school in the Duchy of Hesse-Darmstadt, of which Offenbach is the largest manufacturing town; but he never availed himself of this privilege. In 1867 he returned to New York City, where he taught one term in Dr. Gerke's German-American school, and, at the same time, gave lessons in a New York evening school. At the end of that period he accepted an advantageous position from the Board of Directors of the Hoboken German Academy, in Hoboken, N. J., as teacher of languages, history, and literature in that institution. Mr. Waters filled that position with eminent success for more than fifteen years, constantly enlarging his knowledge of the profession and aiding materially in the prosperity of the school. Here, he says, he made the acquaintance of some of the best teachers he ever knew, chief among whom was the late Magnus Schoeder, who had studied in the University of Berlin until his twenty-eighth year, and who was deeply versed in Greek, Latin, metaphysics, and mathematics. With this eminent scholar and teacher Mr. Waters became closely associated, exchanging lessons with him for years, imbibing much of his enthusiasm for the profession, and finding in him the ablest teacher he had ever had. Mr. Schoeder subsequently became Director of the Hoboken Academy, and each year gave Mr. Waters a new branch to teach, which compelled him to enlarge and fortify his own knowledge in various branches. The two worked together in the greatest harmony, and in every difficulty Mr. Waters invariably stood by the side of his chief. Leaving French, finally, to other teachers, Mr. Waters devoted most of his time to English branches, chiefly in the higher classes, and to German by translation into English, with a view of making English clear by comparative grammar. These years in the academy were attended with peace, friendship, and honor, and with a broadening acquaintance with learning and literature, which Mr. Waters now recalls with pleasure. His pupils, many of them, became prominent in professional and public life, and invariably imbibed the enthusiasm, the laudable ambition, and the inspiring spirit of their able and esteemed teacher. Among these pupils may be mentioned Edward Russ, William C. Heppenheimer, and Joseph Wetzlar.

In 1883 Mr. Waters was chosen Supervising Principal of the West Hoboken public schools, which at that time consisted of one school with seven hundred scholars and seventeen teachers. Since then the local system has grown to four schools, 4,000 scholars, and 75 teachers, and under his able and energetic management ranks among the very best in the State or in the country. The seventeen years that he has devoted to these schools have been marked by the introduction of those excellent methods which he has mastered in a wide and varied experience, and by a growing efficiency in every department of education. That this is due to Mr. Waters is a fact which he may regard with pride and satisfaction. He may, without exaggeration, be pronounced one of the ablest educators in New Jersey, and withal a scholar, an untiring student, and a progressive, patriotic man, inspiring his pupils and his teachers with that lofty sense of honor which has characterized his whole career. His integrity, his public spirit and enterprise, and his eminent success as an educator have gained for him universal confidence and esteem.

Mr. Waters is also an author of some note, having written several books which have become widely known. Among these are: *Intellectual Pursuits, Life of William Cobbett, Shakespeare as Portrayed by Himself, John Selden and his Table-Talk, Flashes of Wit and Humor,* and a capital edition of Cobbett's *English Grammar,* all of which have passed through several editions. He has made a number of translations from the French, one of which is entitled *Magical Experiments, or Science in Play*. Mr. Waters has also written for the *Home Journal* a series of chapters on "Culture by Conversation"; for the *Twentieth Century* a paper on the "Career and Conversation of John Swinton" (one of his oldest friends, having worked with him as a printer in the fifties); and for *Frank Leslie's Magazine* an interesting paper entitled "How I Became My Own Landlord." He is a great believer in co-operative land and building societies, whose principles he has practically illustrated, and which he recommends especially to those working for a fixed salary. Of late years, however, Mr. Waters has written comparatively little, his exhaustive duties as Supervising Principal of the West Hoboken public schools leaving him small leisure for this kind of work, for which he is so well fitted.

In 1873 he married Helen, the eldest daughter of Edmund Ferrett, Esq., of New York, by which marriage he has two daughters, Alice and Edith.

JAMES CLARK, the well known contractor and builder of Union Hill, was born in Bathgate, near Edinburgh, Scotland, November 23, 1864, the son of James Clark, Sr., and Ann Swinton, and a grandson of John Clark. He comes from an old Scotch family, residents of the vicinity of Edinburgh for many generations.

Obtaining a thorough public school education in his native Town of Bathgate, he turned his attention to the carpenter's trade, which he mastered, and which he followed there with marked success until the spring of 1885. The field, however, was too limited for one of his energy and enterprise, and in that year he came to America. Settling first in Albany, N. Y., he subsequently followed his trade in and around New York City, and finally, in 1891, took up his residence in the Town of Union, N. J. Here he found an excellent opportunity for the exercise of his talents, and at once took advantage of it. Identifying himself with the growing population, and displaying sound judgment and foresight, he soon came into prominence as a man of acknowledged ability. In August, 1892, he engaged in business for himself, and since then he has become one of the leading contractors and builders in the town. A large number of private residences and other buildings in the northern section of Union Hill are due to his energy and enterprise. He has executed some of the largest contracts in Hudson County during the past few years, and has also had a large business in other cities. With a successful period of eight years behind him, and with the confidence and respect of the entire community, he stands among the leading local contractors and builders. He is a public spirited, patriotic, and progressive citizen.

In politics he is an ardent Democrat. He is a member of Doric Lodge, No. 82, F. and A. M., of West Hoboken, of Unique Lodge, No. 34, A. O. U. W., of Jersey City, and of Cosmopolitan Lodge, I. O. O. F.

Mr. Clark was married, July 5, 1889, to Janet S. McMillan, daughter of Daniel McMillan, a well known citizen of Sydney, Australia. They reside on Fourth Avenue in Union Hill, and have three children: Agnes Ann, Violet, and James Victor.

ALLAN BENNY, of Bayonne, Hudson County, N. J., was born of Scotch parentage in Brooklyn, N. Y., on the 12th of July, 1867. He received a thorough education, took the usual law course, and was admitted to the bar of New Jersey in February, 1889, immediately after attaining his majority. Since then he has been actively and successfully engaged in the practice of his profession in Jersey City, residing in Bayonne.

Mr. Benny has for many years taken a prominent part in the politics of his adopted county and State, and is one of the acknowledged leaders of the Democratic party. He served as a member of the Board of Councilmen of Bayonne from 1892 to 1894, representing the First Ward, and in that capacity displayed abilities which have since brought him into prominence. At the expiration of his term as Councilman in April, 1894, he became a candidate on the Democratic ticket for re-election against the late William J. O'Brien, a former President of the Bayonne Common Council, and Wilson

J. Haver, Republican. The election returns gave Mr. Haver 114 votes, Mr. O'Brien 260 votes, Allan Benny 259 votes, and "Benny" one vote. Mr. Benny claimed that the vote cast for "Benny" should be counted for him and contested the election before Judge Lippincott in the Hudson County Circuit Court. Judge Lippincott decided that he should have the "Benny" vote, but it appeared in the case that his father was a Scotchman and not naturalized here at the time of the birth of his son Allan, and the Judge decided therefore that Mr. Benny was not a citizen of the United States and declared Mr. O'Brien elected. Upon an appeal to the Supreme Court of the State Judge Lippincott's decision was reversed. Mr. Benny was not only declared to be a citizen of the United States by virtue of his birth in this country, but the election was declared a tie (29 Vroom, 36). Mr. O'Brien, who had taken the seat in the Board of Councilmen because of Judge Lippincott's decision, was forced to vacate, and it remained vacant during the remainder of the term.

In November, 1897, Mr. Benny was elected to the General Assembly of New Jersey by a plurality of 8,623 votes over the highest candidate on the Republican ticket. He was re-elected in November, 1898, by a plurality of 8,345, and during the first two terms in the Legislature magnified an already high reputation and won the approval of both party friends and political opponents. Mr. Benny is an able lawyer, a public spirited and enterprising citizen, a man of integrity and force of character, and respected and esteemed.

JOHN B. BRANAGAN, of New Durham, Hudson County, was born in the County of Bergen, N. J., September 25, 1856. He is the son of Michael Branagan and Ann Meehan, daughter of Charles Meehan and Amelia Stewart, who was a first cousin of the late A. T. Stewart, the noted merchant prince of New York City. He is also a grandson of Colonel William Branagan, a brave and distinguished soldier in the Revolutionary War, who won promotion for gallantry in the Continental service.

Mr. Branagan was educated in the public schools. From the time he was eight years old he has earned his own living. At that age he began to spend his summers in boating, earning five dollars per month and his board. When he was sixteen he was mate of a sailing vessel, and a year later he had charge of a vessel with five men under him. At the age of twenty he began steamboating, a business he has since followed, being now classed as a pilot. He knows every part of the Hudson River and the waters around Greater New York, having spent his active life upon them, and is recognized as one of the ablest and most trustworthy pilots in the service.

In 1885 Mr. Branagan settled permanently in New Durham, Hudson County, N. J., where he has been prominent as a public spirited, enterprising, and patriotic citizen. He is a leading Democrat, has been an active and influential member of the Hudson County Democratic Committee, and in 1893 was elected a Justice of the Peace to fill an unexpired term. In 1895 he was re-elected for a full term of five years. At the beginning of both terms Mr. Branagan was appointed, by a resolution of the Township Committee, Police Justice and Recorder of the Township of North Bergen, which positions he still holds. He has also served as Chief of Police. He is a member and formerly an officer of the American Association of Master Pilots and of Sumner Lodge, No. 180, Independent Order of Odd Fellows, of Jersey City. He enjoys the confidence and respect of all who know him.

Mr. Branagan was married, December 29, 1885, to Anna Caroline Teetsel, and they have two sons: John B., Jr., and Edward Paul Clifford Branagan.

CHARLES McGEE, for four terms a member of the Board of Aldermen of Bayonne, N. J., and now a member of the Board of Chosen Freeholders of Hudson County, was born in Ireland on the 12th of November, 1856. His parents, Daniel D. McGee and Annie O'Donnell, were both born and married in that country.

Mr. McGee received his early education in Ireland. In 1871 he came to the United States and settled in Pennsylvania, where he completed his studies, and where he was subsequently interested in mining. The experience he gained in this connection proved of great value to him in the active affairs of life, and especially when he was subsequently connected with the oil business at Bayonne, N. J., where he has resided for a number of years. He is now actively and successfully engaged in the hotel business in that city, and in every capacity is highly respected and esteemed.

Politically Mr. McGee has long been a prominent and influential Democrat, an acknowledged leader in party councils, and thoroughly identified with the Democracy of his section. He served four terms on the Board of Aldermen of Bayonne and is now a member of the Board of Chosen Freeholders of Hudson County. In this capacity, as well as in all the relations of life, he has displayed ability, energy, sagacity, and sound judgment. His patriotism, public spirit, and progressiveness have brought him into prominence throughout the county and stamp him as a man of excellent character.

CHARLES M'GEE.

He is a life member of the Bayonne Democratic Club and a member of the Robert Davis Association of Jersey City. He is also a member of the Ancient Order of Hibernians and of Bayonne Lodge, No. 434, Benevolent and Protective Order of Elks, and for fifteen years has been a member of the Bayonne Fire Association.

Mr. McGee was married, in Bayonne, N. J., on the 24th of June, 1886, to

Catherine Kelly, daughter of James and Annie Kelly, of that city. They have six children: Annie, Charles, Mamie, James, Daniel, and Catherina.

MARTIN W. BODE, the oldest groceryman in the Town of Union, is the son of John Henry Bode and Margaret Ahrnes, and was born in Hanover, Germany, August 15, 1848. His parents were both natives of the same place.

Mr. Bode acquired a good practical education in the public schools of Hanover, and as a youth developed those physical and intellectual characteristics which have contributed materially to his success in life. In 1866 he came to this country, landing in New York City, where he began his career as an errand boy in a grocery store. In 1869 he removed to Union Hill, Hudson County, N. J., and accepted a clerkship in a store, which he held until 1872. On June 2, 1872, he purchased his present store on the corner of New York Avenue and Columbia Street in the Town of Union, and there he has resided ever since, being the oldest and probably the best known groceryman in that section of the county, and especially on the hill. Dealing in groceries, flour, feed, etc., Mr. Bode has been very successful, and by constant attention to business has gained a high reputation. Honest and straight-forward in all his relations, and progressive and patriotic in both public and private affairs, he enjoys the confidence and esteem of his fellow-citizens.

In politics he is a stanch Republican and a prominent factor in the councils of his party. He was a member of the Board of Education of the Town of Union from 1886 to 1889 and from 1892 to 1895, and served one year as Chairman. He is a member of Palisade Lodge, No. 84, F. and A. M., of Jackson Lodge, I. O. O. F., of the Knights of Honor, of the Independent Schuetzen Corps of Union Hill, of the Zwievelberger Bowling Club, and of the German Lutheran Church.

Mr. Bode was married in 1878 to Miss Emma Fausel, daughter of George and Christina Fausel, of the Town of Union, N. J. They have one daughter, Meta C.

JOHN DWYRE, Principal of Public School No. 1, at Harrison, N. J., since 1873, is a native of Ireland, and when a young man came to America with his parents. Having received a thorough education in the public schools of his native country, he began teaching soon after his arrival in this country, first in Elizabeth and subsequently in Newark, N. J. In 1873 he became Principal of Public School No. 1, of Harrison, Hudson County, which position he has since filled.

Few educators have gained the distinction and reputation which Mr. Dwyre has long enjoyed. He is one of the ablest, as well as one of the most faithful, teachers in this section of the State, and during the twenty-seven years that he has been at the head of one of the most important public schools in Harrison he has displayed eminent abilities, great force of character, and a broad and liberal learning. He is thoroughly identified with the public life of Harrison, has written a history of that town, and is a prominent member of the C. B. L. and A. O. H.

Mr. Dwyre married Helena Shannon, and has had six children: John, Stephen, Edward, James (deceased), Mary, and Helena.

JAMES F. PRENDERGAST, for the past twenty-four years a leading educator and for seven years Principal of Public School No. 2, of Harrison, N. J., was born in Limerick, Ireland, on the 11th of July, 1848. There he received his education, passing through the Model School and graduating in 1866. Subsequently he served an apprenticeship at the carpenter's trade, which he followed for six years.

A trade, however, was not Mr. Prendergast's ambition. He early developed marked abilities as an educator and teacher, and, coming to this country, engaged in school teaching, which he has followed successfully. Since 1893 he has been the efficient Principal of Public School No. 2, of Harrison, N. J.

Mr. Prendergast has always taken an active interest in the public affairs of the community, and is regarded as one of Harrison's most enterprising and patriotic citizens. He was Assessor of the Town of Harrison in 1875-76, and is a member of the Catholic Benevolent Legion, of the Improved Order of Redmen, of the Ancient Order of Hibernians, and of the Holy Cross Literary Association. In 1884 Mr. Prendergast married Miss Sarah L. Kearns. They have had six children.

EDWARD SARGENT, general contractor, of Kearny, N. J., and for some time a member of the Board of Chosen Freeholders of Hudson County, was born in Macclesfield, England, September 13, 1856, the son of Robert Sargent and Helen Hall. His parents were both natives of the same place.

He attended the public schools of Manchester, England, and then learned the machinist's trade, which he followed with success until 1879, when he came to America and settled in Paterson, whence he subsequently removed to Kearny. Here he found employment in the machine department of the Clark Thread Mills. Later he became foreman of the spinning department of that corporation. He resigned this position in 1888 and engaged in general contracting, in which business he has been very successful.

Mr. Sargent is a Republican, and for several years has been active and influential in the councils of his party, being recognized as one of its trusted leaders. As a member of the Hudson County Board of Chosen Freeholders from Kearny he has rendered efficient service in the interests of the public and gained for himself a high reputation. He is a public spirited, progressive citizen, a member of the Presbyterian Church, President of the Republican Club of Kearny, and a member of the Hudson County Republican Committee, of the Masonic fraternity, and of the Sons of St. George.

He married Miss Priscilla Wright, and has three children: May, Adda, and Edwin, and resides in Kearny, N. J.

CHARLES OTTO STUMPP, of West Hoboken, is the son of Jacob and Barbara Stumpp, and was born in Germany in March, 1846. In 1866 he left the Fatherland and came to America, settling in New York City. Six years later, in 1872, he removed to West Hoboken, Hudson County, N. J., where he has since resided.

Mr. Stumpp was educated in Germany and France, and upon coming to America entered the employ of a seed house. In this and other employments, by the practice of frugality and economy, he was enabled, in 1885, to engage in business for himself, and since that year has conducted at 88 Gansevoort Street, New York City, one of the most successful seed establishments in the country. He has established a large trade and is widely known as a man of integrity, ability, and enterprise. Mr. Stumpp takes an active interest in the affairs of West Hoboken, where he established himself in the dry goods business in 1875, opening a store at 401 Hackensack Plank Road. He has continued this business in connection with his New

York house with marked success. He is a public spirited, patriotic, and progressive citizen.

Mr. Stumpp married Miss Rebecca Brett, of Fishkill, N. Y., by whom he has four children: Margaret, Otto, George, and Rebecca (Mrs. George Philan). Otto Stumpp is associated with his father, while the other son, George, is engaged in the same line of business in Barclay Street, New York City.

JOHN OLENDORF, title officer of the New Jersey Title Guarantee and Trust Company of Jersey City, was born in Albany, N. Y., on the 14th of June, 1848. His paternal ancestors were Germans, while those on his mother's side came to this country from England. He is the son of John Olendorf and Anna N. Loomis, a grandson of Arnold and Dorcas (Low) Olendorf and William R. and Charlotte (Cary) Loomis, and a great-grandson of Daniel and Catharine (Hoover) Olendorf, who were the founders of the family in this country about 1776. His maternal great-grandparents were Solomon and Prudence (Robbins) Loomis.

Mr. Olendorf received a thorough education at Public School No. 1, Jersey City, at a private school in New York City, at Mount Washington Collegiate Institute, and at Yale College, graduating from the latter with honor in the class of 1869. Subsequently he studied for one year in Berlin, Germany, and thus completed a liberal educational training which has served him so well in active life. Having studied law, he was admitted to the New Jersey bar in 1876, as an attorney, and at once entered upon the active practice of his profession in Jersey City, where he has ever since enjoyed an extensive general clientage. Since 1888 he has also been title officer of the New Jersey Title Guarantee and Trust Company of Jersey City, one of the most successful corporations of the kind in the country.

JOHN OLENDORF.

Mr. Olendorf brought to the bar great force of character, broad intellectual qualities, and all the attributes which make a successful lawyer.

That he has used these gifts with honor to himself and credit to his profession is evident from the standing which he justly holds among his fellow lawyers. He is regarded as an able advocate and counselor, and in the field of real estate law especially has no superiors and few equals. His long and active connection with real estate matters and titles has won for him a high reputation as an expert. He has also taken a prominent part in public life, and in Bound Brook, N. J., where he resides, is a valued member of the Board of Education. He is also a member of the University Club, and as a citizen is progressive, enterprising, and public spirited, deeply interested in the welfare of the community, and respected and esteemed by all who know him.

On the 17th of October, 1878, Mr. Olendorf married Elizabeth Herbert, and they have one daughter, Helen Parker Herbert Olendorf.

FRANK J. STUKE is well known in Hudson and Bergen Counties, especially for his extensive knowledge of real estate. He is the son of John F. Stuke and Johannah Rodenbeck and a grandson of Franz Stuke, a soldier in the Prussian Army about the year 1812. His father settled in New York on coming to this country, and in 1860 was a cavalryman in Company A, First Regiment New York Cavalry.

Mr. Stuke was born in New York City on the 23d of February, 1853, of German parentage. He acquired a good public school education. When he was fourteen years of age his parents removed to Guttenberg, N. J., and soon afterward he took up harnessmaking, which he mastered in every detail. In 1870 he went to Utah and thence to Helena, Mont., in the interest of the Union Brewing Company, and while in the West engaged in gulch mining. Subsequently he resumed his trade of harnessmaker, and in 1872 went to Fort Benton, thence to Sioux City, and finally returned to Guttenberg by way of New York. For three years he had entire charge of the harness department of David Jones, the millionaire maltster, returning again to Guttenberg in 1875. In 1879 he settled in the Town of Union, Hudson County, where he has since resided, and where he was engaged in the harness business for many years, or until the spring of 1897. From 1880 to 1885 he held a position as custom house inspector. He is now, and has been for several years, actively engaged in the real estate and insurance business in Union Hill, where he has contributed materially to the advancement of various interests and institutions. Mr. Stuke has achieved marked success. Social and popular, a lover of a good story, and a general favorite among his associates, his reputation and honorable standing are the result of his own energetic efforts. He is always ready to encourage, with both time and means, every project which promises good to the community. He takes an active interest in public improvements and in municipal enterprises. In 1892 and again in 1897 he was elected a Justice of the Peace.

He has been for many years an active member of the Foresters of America, of the Royal Arcanum, and of the Royal Society of Good Fellows. He is a free thinker, broad and liberal-minded, earnest in all the relations of life, and a man of strength of character and of unimpeachable integrity, and in the town and county in which he has taken such deep interest he is highly respected and esteemed. On real estate and insurance matters he is a recognized authority.

Mr. Stuke married Miss Alice Weis, of New York, and they are the parents of seven children: Frank C., a bookkeeper, born in 1875; Lillian, born in 1880; Robert, born in 1882; John, born in 1886; Alice, born in 1890; Lucy, born in 1892; and Walter, born in 1895.

JOHN DIPPEL, Jr., is one of the prominent, influential, and highly respected citizens of West New York, Hudson County, N. J. He held the office of Tax Collector for two terms, or a period of four years, and also served one term as a member of the Board of Education of West New York. He is an active member of the Republican party, a member of the Republican Association of West New York, a member of Palisade Lodge, No. 84,

JOHN DIPPEL, Jr.

Free and Accepted Masons, and a member of the Ancient Order of Free Smiths and of the Foresters of America.

He was born in New York City, October 7, 1855, and is the son of John Dippel and Wilhelmina Unkenholz, a grandson of John Dippel and Anna Bock, and a great-grandson of John Peter Dippel, who was a soldier during the Revolution and subsequently returned to Europe. Mr. Dippel's father was a soldier during the Civil War, from 1861 to 1865, being a member of Company G, Fourth New Jersey Volunteers.

Mr. Dippel was educated in the public schools of New York City and North Bergen, Hudson County, N. J. Between the ages of eighteen and twenty-one he served a three years' apprenticeship in New York City as a mason and plasterer. During the next ten years he worked as a mechanic in New York City. In 1883 he embarked as a boss mason, and has continued in business for himself to the present time. His work as a contractor has been quite extensive. At the present time he is building twenty-four houses at Highwood Park. Mr. Dippel enjoys the confidence of his fellow-citizens in a marked degree. He married Eva Amanda Weyer, who was born in New York City in 1855.

HENRY J. STILSON, for many years a member of the Common Council and one of the Assessors of Bayonne, N. J., was born in Lansingburg, Rensselaer County, N. Y., April 3, 1852. He is the son of Henry and Jane Stilson and a grandson of Henry and Hannah Stilson and of William and Jane Vanderhoff, his ancestors coming to this country at a very early day.

Mr. Stilson was educated in the public schools and academy of Lansingburg, and at the age of twenty began active life as a clerk in the mercantile business. He continued in this line for ten years, or until he had reached the age of thirty, when he engaged in the wall-paper business for himself. This was in 1882.

In public and political life Mr. Stilson has also gained a high reputation. As a resident of Bayonne, N. J., he has long been prominently identified with the best interests of the place and has taken an active part in promoting its welfare. For two years he was a member of the Bayonne Common Council and for nine years he rendered efficient service as Assessor of the city. He is a member of the Exempt Firemen, having been for many years connected with the old Volunteer Fire Department, and is also a member of the Masonic fraternity and of the Benevolent and Protective Order of Elks. He married Miss Lydia H. le Maire.

JAMES S. HICKEY, Chief of the Fire Department of Bayonne, N. J., was born in New York City on the 12th of October, 1869. He is the son of James Hickey and Elizabeth Walsh, who were born in Ireland, married in England, and came to the United States about 1862, settling in Brooklyn, N. Y., whence they subsequently removed to Bayonne.

Mr. Hickey finished his education in the Bayonne public schools, and soon after completing his studies entered the employ of the Standard Oil Company, with whom he has since been associated. He has also taken an active part in public affairs, and as a Democrat has been influential in party councils and in promoting the best interests of his adopted town. As Chief of the Fire Department he has rendered efficient service in organizing and improving various fire companies. He is a public spirited, patriotic, and enterprising citizen, a young man of deserved popularity, and respected and esteemed by his fellowmen.

JOHN REINHARDT was born in the Town of Union, Hudson County, N. J., August 18, 1874. His father, John Reinhardt, Sr., was for many years one of the most prominent and best known men in the county, serving as Sheriff from 1871 to 1874, and holding other positions of trust and responsibility. His mother was Anna Margaret Reisenweber, a native of Saxony, Germany, while his father, John Reinhardt, Sr., was born in Havre, France.

Mr. Reinhardt was educated in the public schools of Jersey City and West Hoboken, Hudson County, and since completing his studies has been largely engaged in the real estate business. He has taken an active part in political affairs, and is well known as one of the ablest of the local leaders of the Democratic party. He is the founder and President of the John Reinhardt Association of West Hoboken, and is a Justice of the Peace and a Notary Public. He is also Second Vice-President of the Associated Justices of the Peace and Constables' Protective Association of Hudson County (formed August 22, 1899, in Hoboken) and Secretary of its Executive Committee, and Vice-President and a member of the Board of Directors of the Republic Savings and Loan Association of Hoboken. As a citizen he is public spirited, progressive, and patriotic, taking an active interest in the welfare of the

JOHN REINHARDT.

community and liberally supporting and encouraging every worthy project. Though a young man, he has already displayed those qualities and principles of integrity and sound judgment which mark a successful career, and is highly esteemed and respected for the commendable enterprise he has shown in both public and political as well as in business matters.

WILLIAM HAGAN, of Secaucus, was born in New York City on the 12th of September, 1841. He is the son of Edward and Arabella Hagan and a grandson of Edward Hagan, Sr., the family being of Scotch-Irish descent. Mr. Hagan acquired his education in Quackenbush and Forrest College of

New York. He learned the machinist's trade there, and for a few years followed that business as a manufacturer.

In 1863 he came to Secaucus, N. J., with his father, and settled on the place he still occupies, where he has since followed successfully the vocation of a farmer. Enterprising, progressive, and energetic, he is regarded as one of the best farmers in Hudson County, and has always enjoyed the confidence and respect of the community. For many years he has been active and influential in the Democratic party. In 1877 he was elected a Justice of the Peace, and during a period of ten years he filled that office with credit and satisfaction. He was Town Committeeman for three years, and has also served as Notary Public and Commissioner of Deeds. Mr. Hagan comes from a patriotic family, one of his nephews, Edward Field, being a soldier in the War of the Rebellion. He is a member of the Royal Arcanum and of the Royal Society of Good Fellows.

He married Sarah Post, daughter of Cornelius and Eunice Post, of Hudson County, and they have had six children, as follows: William F., Eugene P., Lester (deceased), Grace C., John H. (deceased), and Cornelius E. Cornelius Post, father of Mrs. William Hagan, served in the Civil War as a member of the Tenth New Jersey Infantry. His wife, to whom he was married December 31, 1853, was the daughter of Judge John Sturgis, who was for many years a leading resident of New Durham, Hudson County, dying there at the age of sixty-five. Mr. Sturgis was a Lay Judge for about fifteen years, and was also a Justice of the Peace, a Town Committeeman, a member of the Masonic and Odd Fellows fraternities, and a prominent man of affairs, being highly esteemed for his benevolence and actively identified with the community. Edward de Mott Pequignot is a naval officer on the "Raleigh," and, being in Dewey's fleet, served through the Spanish-American War. He represents the third generation to serve his country, and is a grandson of Judge Sturgis and a nephew of Cornelius Post.

THOMAS J. McMAHON, a member of the Board of Aldermen of Harrison, Hudson County, was born in Newark, N. J., on the 7th of December, 1858. His parents, Patrick and Maria (Clements) McMahon, both natives of Ireland, came to this country in 1848 and were married in Newark, whence they subsequently removed to Harrison.

Mr. McMahon received his educational training in the Harrison public schools, and upon the completion of his studies engaged in the manufacture of trunks in Newark and New York City. He was successful in this business for a time, abandoning it, however, for the wider and more promising field of electrical industry, which he now carries on successfully in Harrison. He is a man of marked business ability, sound judgment, and great enterprise.

In public life Mr. McMahon has also achieved prominence. He is a leading Democrat, has been for several years a power in the councils of his party, and in various official capacities has rendered valuable service to the community. He was for two years a member of the Harrison School Committee, and during the last four years has served as a member of the Board of Aldermen of Harrison. He was one of the founders and a charter member of the Harrison Fire Department and the first President of Neptune Hose Company, and from the first has taken an active interest in the department's prosperity. Public spirited, enterprising, and patriotic, he is esteemed and respected, and has won and maintained the confidence of all who know him.

PETER J. GOODMAN, a well known journalist of Harrison, Hudson County, was born in New York City on the 30th of January, 1861, being the son of Philip Goodman and Ann McDonald and a grandson of Peter Goodman. His ancestors came to this country from Ireland, where some of them still reside. Mr. Goodman was educated in the parochial schools of Harrison and at the Christian Brothers Academy in Newark, N. J. After leaving school he engaged in the general stationery and newspaper business, but during the past twelve years has been actively connected with the staffs of the New York and Newark newspapers. His career as a journalist

PETER J. GOODMAN.

has brought him into wide popularity throughout this section of the State. Energetic, progressive, and possessed of a large fund of general information, he is an able writer, and to the duties of his profession he has brought a thorough practical training as well as great efficiency.

He is a Democrat in politics, a member of the Robert Davis Association of Jersey City, and active in all local affairs. He has been prominently identified with the Fire Department of Harrison since its organization and has held every office in the gift of the department, serving three terms as Chief Engineer. He is a member of the Adjustment Commission of the town and a member of the Catholic Benevolent Legion and the Knights of Columbus.

Mr. Goodman married Mary T. Coburn, daughter of the late Thomas Coburn, of Harrison, Hudson County.

JOHN FROST, retired, one of the oldest residents of Weehawken, N. J., is the son of Isaac Frost and Maria Ward, natives of Wian-Farthing and Yacksam, England, respectively, and descendants of distinguished families. His father dying, his mother married for her second husband Henry Brand, and came to the United States in 1838.

Mr. Frost was born in Yacksam, England, October 11, 1817, and there received his education. Having a desire to embark in a wider field of activity than his country seemed to offer, he left England when fifteen years of age and came to the United States, where he first obtained employment as a farm laborer. Afterward he engaged in the oyster business with considerable success. In 1858, however, he settled in Weehawken, N. J., where he still resides, and where he held for many years responsible positions with the New York, Lake Erie and Western Railroad Company, now the Erie Railroad Company. He discharged his duties with fidelity and ability, and won the confidence and respect of the officials as well as of his associates, among all of whom he was very popular.

In the growth and prosperity of Weehawken Mr. Frost soon gained influence, and through his energy and public spirit has been active in promoting the general welfare. He early took an active part in the councils of the Democratic party, becoming one of its trusted leaders. For ten years he served as a member of the Board of Chosen Freeholders, and for fifteen years he was a Town Committeeman. In these as well as in various other minor capacities he distinguished himself for ability, sound judgment, and patriotism, and contributed much to the advancement of the community. Honest and enterprising, he is a man of the highest integrity, and enjoys the confidence and respect of all who know him. He is a member of the Odd Fellows fraternity and of the Protestant Episcopal Church.

Mr. Frost was married, December 25, 1845, to Miss Catherine Norris, a native of Halifax, Nova Scotia, who came to the United States when young and settled with her parents in Jersey City, N. J. They have six children: John H., Bryan, William, Isaac, Norris, and Joshua. The eldest, John H. Davis, enlisted in 1861 in the regiment known as the Oregon Rifles, and was wounded at the battle of Winchester, serving until the close of the Rebellion in 1865. Isaac Frost, another son, served ten months in the Civil War as a member of the Thirty-ninth New Jersey Volunteers.

JAMES BRIERLEY, the well known undertaker and funeral director of Kearny, Hudson County, was born in England on the 5th of November, 1862, being the son of Joshua Brierley, Sr., and Ellen Tunstall. Having received a thorough educational training in his native country, he came to America at the age of twenty and at once took up his permanent residence in Kearny, N. J. He engaged in the undertaking business, first with his brother and subsequently alone, and now has one of the best appointed establishments in that place. Mr. Brierley has achieved marked success. He is quick to adopt and assimilate new ideas and methods.

Since coming to Kearny in 1882 he has taken an active interest in the welfare and prosperity of the town, and is esteemed and respected as one of its most public spirited, enterprising, and patriotic citizens. His support and encouragement have been the means of promoting many important movements. He is President of the Hudson County Cricket Club and a member of the Knights of Pythias, the Improved Order of Redmen, the Sons of St. George, the Improved Order of Heptasophs, the Knights of the Golden Star, and the Presbyterian Church and leader of its choir. In politics he is an independent Republican, voting for and acting in the best interests of good government.

Mr. Brierley has been twice married, first to Elizabeth Richards, who

JAMES BRIERLEY.

bore him a son and a daughter: Josiah and Margaret. By his second wife, Sarah J. Catlow, he has two sons: William and George.

PHILIP J. ULLMYER, of Secaucus, Hudson County, was born in Bavaria, Germany, May 1, 1838, the son of Jacob Ullmyer and Catherine Kunc. He received his education in the public schools of the Fatherland, and remained there until 1854, when he came to America. He first settled on a farm in South Bergen, Hudson County, N. J., but in 1871 removed to Secaucus, where he still resides, enjoying in quiet retirement the fruits of an active life spent in farming and gardening. For many years he was one of the largest and most successful farmers and gardeners in the County of Hudson, and through his ability, integrity, sound common sense, and enterprise gained the confidence and respect of all with whom he came in contact.

He has also taken an active part in town affairs and especially in local educational matters, and for more than eighteen years has been a valued member of the North Bergen Board of Education, serving most of the time as its Chairman. He is still a member of that body. No man in the town has rendered more efficient service in the cause of its schools. Realizing the necessity of adequate school facilities and the advantages derived by the young from a thorough training in those branches which modern business methods demand, Mr. Ullmyer has thrown his influence into the work of improving and advancing the public schools, and has brought to his efforts great native ability, sound judgment and foresight, and genuine enthusiasm and patriotism. As a member of the Schuetzen Bund of New Jersey he has also been prominent and useful, serving for several years as Vice-President and Trustee, and being for four years Captain of the Secaucus Company. In politics he is a Democrat with independent proclivities. He is esteemed as a progressive citizen, and is one of the substantial men of the county.

In 1866 Mr. Ullmyer married Miss Elizabeth Schott, a native of Germany, and their children are Philip Frederick, Catherine Elizabeth, and Elizabeth.

GEORGE W. CRANWELL, a prominent builder and contractor of West Hoboken, was born in Ireland on Christmas Day, December 25, 1836, and is the son of Edward Cranwell and Elizabeth, his wife. Coming to this country with his parents when very young, he received his education at the Christian Brothers' school in Utica, N. Y., and in 1857 removed to West Hoboken, N. J. In 1866 he returned to Utica, where he resided until about 1886, when he again came to West Hoboken, which has since been his home.

Mr. Cranwell became identified with the building and contracting business while yet a mere youth, and during a period of nearly thirty-five years has followed that vocation with uninterrupted success, becoming one of the best known contractors and builders in the country. He learned the trade of mason and builder in Utica, N. Y., and there erected the most of the German Catholic Church, the Wheeler, Kiernan & Company's stove works, St. John's Protectory (then St. John's Orphan Asylum), and many other buildings of importance. He also built the north wing of Hamilton College in Oneida County, N. Y., St. Mary's Catholic Church at Cooperstown in the same State, many well known structures in Little Falls, and a large part of the buildings erected by Alfred Dolge at Dolgeville, N. Y., during a period of twenty years, and the large public school edifice in that town. These are only a few of the contracts executed by him in a number of towns and cities, including the City of New York, in the Empire State. In New Jersey he has also been active in contracting and building. He erected the original part of the Hoboken Monastery in West Hoboken, the new town hall in the Town of Union, and numerous other private and public buildings in these towns, in Weehawken, and in the City of Hoboken.

Mr. Cranwell's work shows great skill and ability, and stamps him as one of the ablest members of his vocation. Active and energetic, honest and upright in his dealings, thorough and exact in the work committed to his care, and faithful in the discharge of every trust, he is highly respected and esteemed. In politics he is an ardent Democrat.

He married Miss Margaret Fullerton, of Jersey City, N. J., and has five children living, namely: James W., Emma, Ellie, Elizabeth, and Cecelia, the former—the only son—being a partner in his father's business under the firm name of G. W. Cranwell & Son.

HARVEY C. PIERCE, General Manager of the Arlington Manufacturing Company and one of the leading Republicans of Hudson County, is descended from the old Pierce and Henderson families of New England.

HARVEY C. PIERCE.

Born in Pittsfield, Mass., on the 1st of May, 1860, he is the son of William Pierce and Elizabeth Henderson, natives, respectively, of West Boylston, Mass., and of Newport, N. H.

Having attended the public schools, Mr. Pierce prepared for Williams College, Williamstown, in his native State, and there pursued his studies with characteristic zeal and energy. Afterward he became actively interested in the manufacture of articles from celluloid, and, engaging in the business, he has ever since been identified with it in one capacity or another. In 1891 he was made General Manager of the Arlington Manufacturing Company, of Arlington, N. J., which position he still holds.

This is one of the largest and most successful establishments of the kind in this country, and no small degree of its growth and prosperity is due to Mr. Pierce. He has displayed excellent business ability, sound judgment, and great sagacity and foresight, while his knowledge of commercial affairs as well as of the process of celluloid manufacture has gained for him a high reputation.

He has also been prominent and influential in public matters, and especially in politics, and is a leading member of the Hudson County Republican Committee. He is also President of the Arlington Club, a member and Past Master of Triune Lodge, No. 159, A. F. and A. M., and a member of Triune Chapter, No. 257, R. A. M., of Columbian Commandery, No. 1, K. T., and Mecca Temple, N. O. M. S., all of New York City. He is also Vice-Regent of the Royal Arcanum, and President of the District Association. In the councils of the Republican party, with which he has always been actively identified, he has rendered most efficient service, and is regarded as one of its able and trusted leaders. As a resident of Arlington his influence has been felt in every movement affecting the welfare of the community. He is progressive, public spirited, and active in the advancement of all worthy objects, and enjoys the respect and confidence of all who know him.

October 26, 1886, Mr. Pierce was married at Princeton, N. J., to Miss Mattie Perrine, of Jerseyville, Ill., and their children are Arthur, born in 1890, and Gussie, born in 1887.

CLEMENS A. KREBS, of Arlington, N. J., Recorder of the Town of Kearny, was born in New York City on the 12th of August, 1853. His parents, Hubert Krebs and Margaret Schiffhauer, were both natives of Germany—the father of Coblenz and the mother of Baden. Hubert Krebs came to the United States in 1847 and was married the same year in New York City, where he spent the remainder of his life. He died April 8, 1883.

Clemens A. Krebs received a good education in the public schools of his native city, and after completing his studies entered the famous dry goods store of A. T. Stewart, where he remained three years. He then associated himself with his father in the business of stair building, which trade he followed for a number of years, part of the time in New Brunswick, N. J. In 1873 Mr. Krebs entered the postal service as a letter carrier attached to Stations E and K of the New York City postoffice, where he remained until March, 1881, when he entered the United States customs service in the Appraiser's department, Port of New York, of which he became Foreman July 12, 1883, having successfully passed the civil service examination. He continued in that capacity for twelve years, or until November 7, 1895, when the office was abolished. On July 30, 1889, he took up his residence in Arlington, Hudson County.

Mr. Krebs has discharged his duties with fidelity, promptness, and ability. He is an enterprising, public spirited man, deeply interested in the welfare and prosperity of the community, and prominently identified with its best interests and institutions. For several years he was a member of Company H, Seventy-first Regiment, N. G. N. Y., of New York City. In Arlington he has served as Police Justice, Justice of the Peace, Commissioner of Deeds, Notary Public, and Recorder of the Town of Kearny, which office he now holds, having been appointed May 1, 1899, for a term of two years. In October, 1900, he was nominated by the Hudson County Republican Convention for member of Assembly from the West Hudson District. He is a prominent member and Deacon of the First Presbyterian Church of Arlington, a Republican in politics, and a member of Triune Lodge, F. and A. M., and of Americus Council, No. 1304, R. A., both of Arlington.

May 30, 1876, Mr. Krebs married Miss Fannie Warnock, and their children are Clemens A., Jr., born in 1877; William Warnock, born in 1878; Fannie, born in 1880; and Belle Frances, born in 1887.

GEORGE BERNHARDT BERGKAMP, Mayor of West Hoboken and one of the most popular and energetic citizens of North Hudson County, was born in New York City on the 1st of October, 1865. His father, Henry H. Bergkamp, a native of Germany, came to New York when a young man and engaged in farming in what is now Harlem on Manhattan Island. There he married Sophia Schlemme, also a native of Germany. In 1868 they removed to Secaucus, Hudson County, N. J., where he died in 1874. His wife's death occurred in 1871.

Mr. Bergkamp was educated in the public schools of Secaucus, where his parents settled when he was three years old. Reared on the farm, he developed a robust constitution, and early acquired those habits of thrift and industry which have characterized his life. For two years after leaving school he was a clerk in a grocery store in Brooklyn, and afterward he held clerkships in different grocery stores in Hudson County until 1885, when he accepted a position as salesman in a large commission house in New York. There he remained four years. In 1889 and 1890 he was engaged in the hotel business, first in Secaucus and later in New York City. In 1890 he established his present real estate and insurance office in West Hoboken, where he resides.

Few men have contributed more to the growth and prosperity of the City of West Hoboken than Mr. Bergkamp. The development of the north part of the city is largely the result of his untiring efforts. During three years he built no less than twenty-six dwelling houses there. In 1898-99 he erected on the Hudson Boulevard, between Charles and High Streets, an extensive auction mart for the sale of horses, etc., and for the use of a livery and boarding stable business. He is also an auctioneer, a Notary Public, and a Commissioner of Deeds, and in these various capacities has been successful.

Mr. Bergkamp is an ardent Democrat, a recognized leader of his party and a man of unquestioned integrity and great force of character. In 1894 he was chosen by the Eleventh Assembly District Convention a member of a committee to re-organize the Democratic party in Hudson County, and by virtue of this position was a member of the Executive Committee of the Hudson County Democratic Committee. To this duty he brought great energy and ability, and the result attested his foresight and shrewd executive management. In April, 1899, he was elected Mayor of West Hoboken for a term of two years, receiving a handsome majority in spite of strong political opposition. He has also been the President of the North Hudson Business Men's Association since its organization in January, 1897, and is a member of the Royal Arcanum.

He was married, September 30, 1888, to Theresa Rosebrock, daughter of Henry Rosebrock, of New York City. They have five children: George, Henry, Herman, Edward, and Ida.

DAVID NAUGLE.—The Naugles of Bergen and Hudson Counties are of Holland lineage. John Naugle (1), son of Barent Naugle, was born at Groningen, Holland, about 1645, of well-to-do and respectable parentage. Through the influence of his father, who had been in the marine service,

John, at an early age, entered as a cadet the Dutch naval service, and before reaching his minority made several cruises to America. While on one of these expeditions in 1664 he participated in the conflict between the Dutch and English fleets, the result of which was the surrender of the Dutch. Being patriotic and rather hot-headed, young Naugle was so disgusted with the cowardice of the Dutch that he loudly denounced them, left the service, and declared he would leave the country. Not long afterward, however, being in Harlem, he met Miss Rebecca Waldron, the daughter of an English refugee. The smiles and winsome ways of the English maiden influ-

DAVID NAUGLE.

enced him to change his mind and remain at Harlem, where, in 1670, he married Miss Waldron, bought a lot, joined the Dutch Church, and settled down for life, soon becoming an active factor in the new settlement. Taking an interest in politics, he sought office, but, as he still continued to denounce the English, it was not till 1677 that he was elected Constable. Two years later he became a magistrate. It was while Constable that it became his duty to execute the writs in a law suit which drove old David des Marest over to the west side of the river into Bergen County. Later John Naugle was made a Deacon in the Dutch Church. He bought lands at Spuyten Duyvil and at other points on the Harlem River, and became wealthy.

Although somewhat erratic and eccentric, he appears to have been a man of sterling principles and qualities of mind. He died in Harlem in 1689. His widow married, in 1690, John Dykeman. The issue of John Naugle (1) of the second generation were Barent (died), Jannetje, John, Anna, Catrina, Barent, Johanna, Jacobus, Debora, and Resolvent.

Barent (2) and Resolvent (2) were destined to spread the name throughout Bergen County. In 1708 Barent (2) married Sarah Kiersted, and Resolvent (2), on May 9, 1712, married Clarissa Lydecker. Miss Kiersted, the wife of Barent (2), was a New York lady of education and refinement, and particularly versed in the Indian tongues. While in New York she had acted as interpreter for the colonial officials in their dealings with the savages.

On April 10, 1710, Barent and Resolvent crossed the Hudson River into Bergen County, New Jersey, and bought of Captain Lancaster Syms a tract of 1,030 acres of land northeast of Closter, extending from the Hudson River west to the Tiena Kill. The price paid was £225 sterling. They had much trouble to perfect their title to these lands, as other persons attempted to establish an adverse claim to them. In the end, however, the adverse claimants were beaten. The two brothers cleared and tilled portions of their tract jointly and built each his family residence on what is now called the "Rockland road." Resolvent joined the Hackensack Dutch Church and Barent the church at Tappan. A few years before their deaths they divided their original purchase between them, Barent taking the north half and Resolvent the south half. Barent was a Justice of the Peace and held all other town offices. He was also in command of a train band. The issue of Barent Naugle (2) of the third generation were John, Rebecca, William, Henry, Sarah, and Johanna.

John Naugle (3) married (1), in 1729, Elizabeth (Jacobus) Blawvelt and (2) Magdalena Naugle. His children of the fourth generation were Sarah, John, Barent, Catharine, Maria, Elizabeth, Henry, Rebecca, David (died), Elizabeth, and David.

David Naugle (4), the youngest, born in 1750, married about 1775 Dirke Fredericks Haring and had issue of the fifth generation John D., Rachel, Frederick, and Elizabeth.

John D. Naugle (5), born May 9, 1777, died October 22, 1841, married Sarah Mabie, born March 2, 1776, died January 2, 1876 (aged nearly one hundred years). They resided on the old Barent Naugle homestead and had issue of the sixth generation David (died), Sarah, Rachel, and John J.

John J. Naugle (6), born in Closter, N. J., July 1, 1818, died January 27, 1882, married, August 8, 1839, Hannah Maria Eckerson, born May 20, 1821 (dead). Residing at the old homestead they had issue of the seventh generation David, Elizabeth (died), Margaret, Rachel, Elizabeth, Frederick, James, and William H., of whom David Naugle (7) is the subject of this sketch.

David Naugle (7) was born August 2, 1841, in Closter, N. J., where he still resides. He received his education in the Closter public schools and at Delaware Academy, and subsequently taught school for a time. He then studied civil engineering, and subsequently entered the customs service, in which he has continued for twenty-eight years. In this capacity he has established a high reputation.

He has also been prominent in public affairs, having served as Superintendent of Public Schools and Town Clerk of Closter. He is a Republican in politics, a member of the Closter and Republican Clubs, and a member of the Zeta Phi fraternity. He was one of the founders of Alpine Lodge, No. 77, F. and A. M., and belongs to the Dutch Reformed Church.

In 1862 Mr. Naugle married Ella Woodworth, of Delhi, N. Y., daughter of William and Julia Ann (Chase) Woodworth, and their children are Margaret Marvine and Annie.

JOHN J. BATE, of Westwood, N. J., was born in Brooklyn, N. Y., on the 26th of November, 1856. He is the son of John J. and Hanna R. (Stratton) Bate, a grandson of William and Mary (Jones) Bate and of William P. and Rachel (Hoover) Stratton, and a great-grandson of William Bate and William Stratton. His maternal uncle, Hon. Nathaniel P. Stratton, was State Senator from Cumberland County, N. J., in 1860-62, and Lay Judge of that county for a time. His paternal ancestors—the Bates—settled in Camden County, N. J., in 1701, coming there from England.

The schools of Brooklyn, N. Y., furnished John J. Bate with his early educational training. He left school at the age of twenty and engaged in farming in Bergen County, continuing for seven years. He then identified himself with the newspaper business, and after five years in that line he became actively engaged in the real estate business, which he still follows. He resides in Westwood, Bergen County, N. J.

Mr. Bate was not only a successful farmer, but has gained a reputation in real estate affairs. He has also taken a prominent part in the public life of the community in which he has so long resided, having served as President of the Board of Education of Westwood for six years, as Assessor for three years, and as Secretary for the Bergen County Board of Assessors for three years. In 1895 he was Borough Clerk of Westwood, and the next year (1896) was the candidate for State Assemblyman on the Democratic ticket. He is a member of the Reformed Church, a public spirited, progressive, and enterprising citizen, and thoroughly identified with public affairs.

Mr. Bate married Miss Annie Comey. They have four children: Alice L., born in 1882; Edith A., born in 1884; Daisy D., born in 1887; and Arthur C., born in 1888.

EMIL JOSEPH FOERCH, Township Clerk of North Bergen, Hudson County, is the son of John Michael Foerch and Anna M. Schottmiller, both natives of Germany. He was born in New York City on the 1st of August, 1863, and is one of a family of five sons and one daughter, his brothers and sister being Gustavus, Rudolph, Julius, Otto, and Addie.

Mr. Foerch acquired his education in the public schools of the Town of Union, N. J., whither his parents removed when he was a boy. For a time he was successfully engaged in the manufacture of cigars, but subsequently he devoted himself to music, becoming a teacher of the art and a member of the noted Damrosch Musical Union. His tastes, his environment, and his natural inclinations all fitted him for the musical profession, and in prosecuting it as an instructor and student he has scored marked success and won a high reputation.

As a Democrat he has been prominent and influential in public affairs and a recognized leader of the party in North Bergen, where he resides. He was a member of the Board of Education of that town from 1885 to 1888, and in 1894 was elected a Justice of the Peace, which office he held four years. In 1897 he was elected Township Clerk of North Bergen and in 1900 was re-elected without opposition in the primary election and in the general election, and is still discharging the duties of that position with the same ability, fidelity, and integrity which have characterized his life. In 1898 he was appointed Clerk of the local Board of Health and of the Commissioners of Adjustment of Unpaid Taxes. He is also Secretary of the First Ward Democratic Club of North Bergen and a member of the Gustav Scholp Association, of the Merry Owl Benevolent Association, and of the Local Association, No. 3,502, K. of L., and an honorably discharged member of the Second Regiment, N. G. N. J.

Mr. Foerch married Miss Eva Michael. She had eight children, of whom four are living, namely: Emil, Christina, Cecelia, and Julius. His first wife died in 1897, and in 1899 he married Mrs. Emma Gertrude Gebhard, who has three children by her first husband, viz.: Katie, Augusta, and George, all of whom are living.

JACOB RINGGER, senior member of the firm of Ringger & Freiberger, of West Hoboken, is the son of Rudolf and Barbara Ringger and was born in Zurich, Switzerland, February 7, 1847. He is of German descent and education, his studies being pursued in the public schools of Germany. There he also learned the trade of cabinetmaker, which he followed in that country until 1881, being engaged in business for himself during the last ten years. In 1881 he came to America to seek a broader field for the exercise of those talents which have since brought him into prominence.

Settling first in Illinois, he followed his trade with marked success until 1885, when he moved to West Hoboken, N. J., which has since been his home. Besides cabinetmaking he also engaged in carpentering and building, and at times this was his principal vocation. In 1891 he formed a copartnership with Jacob Freiberger, under the firm name of Ringger & Freiberger, and established in West Hoboken a large and successful woodworking business. Five years later, in 1896, their mill was totally destroyed by fire, causing a heavy loss. The proprietors rebuilt on a larger and more modern scale, and now have one of the best equipped woodworking establishments in East Jersey. They employ on an average thirty-five hands, and manufacture sash, doors, mouldings, etc.—in fact, every article used in finishing and ornamenting a house or other wood work. Both members of the firm being practical cabinetmakers and woodworkers and experienced carpenters and builders, their efforts have been very successful. Mr. Ringger attends to the business end, Mr. Freiberger devoting himself to the mechanical or manufacturing operations.

Mr. Ringger is a pronounced Democrat, a man of fine character and high qualifications, and a thrifty, progressive, public spirited citizen. He is a liberal contributor to all worthy local objects, and takes a deep interest in every movement affecting the welfare of the community. Public office and politics, however, he has always avoided.

He was married, in 1868, to Miss Barbara Meile, a native, like himself, of Zurich, Switzerland. They have three children: Jacob, Jr., Minnie, and Emma.

JACOB FREIBERGER, member of the general woodworking firm of Ringger & Freiberger, of West Hoboken, N. J., was born in Würtemberg, Germany, March 30, 1856, the son of George Freiberger and Catrina Barbara Nouffer. He was educated in the Fatherland, and there also learned the woodworking trade in all its branches, becoming an expert.

In 1886 Mr. Freiberger came to America, and five years later, or in 1891, formed a copartnership with Jacob Ringger, under the style of Ringger & Freiberger. The firm engaged in the general woodworking business in West Hoboken, establishing a mill on the corner of Highpoint and Kerrigan Avenues. The venture proved successful from the start. In 1896 a disastrous fire burned their entire plant, but with commendable enterprise and courage they at once rebuilt, and now have one of the best equipped and most modern woodworking factories in their section. Mr. Freiberger attends to the inside or manufacturing work, while Mr. Ringger devotes himself to the business end.

Mr. Freiberger married Miss Amalie Diener, and their children are Amelia, Jacob, Jr., Annie, Rosalia, William, and Emily.

WILLIAM SMITH, of Harrison, Hudson County, N. J., was born of Scotch parentage and ancestry in Paisley, Scotland, October 10, 1858, and

WILLIAM SMITH.

there received a thorough public school education. His parents were also of Scotch birth, and endowed with sterling qualities and sturdy characteristics. His father, William Smith, Sr., died in that country, and in 1882 Mr. Smith came to America with his mother, Ellen (Robinson) Smith, settling in Harrison, N. J., where he has since resided.

After completing his studies in the public schools of Paisley Mr. Smith learned the roofing business in all its branches, and on coming to Harrison engaged in it for himself, and during the past twenty years he has achieved marked success and a high reputation. He is one of the best known roofers in Hudson County. Thorough, prompt, and honest, uniting great energy to acknowledged ability, he has built up an extensive business and won the confidence of the entire community. Much of the important roofing work in Harrison and vicinity is the result of his efforts and skill.

Mr. Smith is a Republican of the independent type, believing in honest government for the masses and in voting, especially in local elections, for the best candidates. He is a member of the Knights of Pythias and of the Presbyterian Church, and a public spirited, patriotic, and enterprising citizen.

He married Miss Grace Green and has six children: William, Jr., Peter, David, James, John, and Maggie.

JOHN JOSEPH MULVANEY, President of the Board of Education of Jersey City and one of the prominent lawyers and citizens of that place, is the son of John Mulvaney and Mary McGee, both of Irish descent. His ancestors emigrated from Ireland to this country about 1848.

Mr. Mulvaney was born in Jersey City, Hudson County, on the 23d of April, 1868, and received his education in the public schools of that place, graduating from School No. 1. In 1889 he began the study of law in the office of Collins & Corbin, of Jersey City, and was admitted to the New Jersey bar as an attorney before the Supreme Court in November, 1893, and as a counselor at the February term, 1899. Since his admission, in 1893, he has been actively and successfully engaged in the practice of his profession in Jersey City, and in the many important cases with which he has been connected has displayed high legal qualities as well as broad and accurate knowledge of the law.

Mr. Mulvaney's well known interest in educational matters was aroused through his having taught in the Jersey City evening schools while studying law, and this interest was recognized and encouraged by his appointment in January, 1898, as a member of the Board of Education. He was re-appointed to the same office in May, 1898, for a term of two years, and in May, 1899, was elected President of the Board. He has taken a special interest in the welfare and progress of the Training School and the establishment of kindergartens as a part of the public school system of Jersey City. As a member of construction committees of new schools he has devoted unceasing attention to the proper sanitation of schools and the adoption of modern methods in heating and ventilation. These efforts on his part have brought him into prominence and won for him a high reputation. In brief, he is an acknowledged authority on matters pertaining to schools and education in his native city.

Mr. Mulvaney has been President of St. Bridget's Lyceum for several terms, and has served as an officer of Jersey City Council, K. of C., and of Father Corr Council, C. B. L., in all of which he is a prominent member. He is also a member of the Catholic Club and of the Palma Club, of Jersey City. He is public spirited, progressive, and enterprising, thoroughly identified with the welfare of his native city, and esteemed and respected in every capacity. He married Esther T. A. Sherlock, and has three sons and one daughter living and one daughter deceased.

HENRY KÜHL, Sr., had the distinction of starting the first conservatory or florist's establishment in North Hudson County. He was born in France of German parents on the 22d of August, 1808, and there received his education. His inclinations and tastes were always for flowers, ornamental plants, and their culture. Coming to this country at an early age, he settled in the present Town of West Hoboken, N. J., where he engaged in business as a florist. He was recognized as the pioneer florist in this section of the State, and during a long and active career achieved eminent success. Through his industry, integrity, and sound judgment he gained a commanding reputation as well as confidence and respect, and was regarded as one

HENRY KÜHL, Sr.

of the foremost men of the community. He died April 7, 1893. Just before leaving France he married Annie Marie, who died April 2, 1893, aged seventy-nine.

HENRY KÜHL, Jr., only son and child of Henry Kühl, Sr., and Annie Marie, was born January 28, 1853. He was a life-long resident of Union Hill, Hudson County, dying there July 31, 1885. He always followed his father's business, that of florist. Though but thirty-two years of age at the time of his death, he gained an honorable reputation for ability, integrity, and enterprise, and was respected and esteemed by all who knew him. His knowledge of floriculture was broad and practical. He not only achieved distinction in his calling, but also won honor and confidence as a public spirited citizen. Like his father, he was an ardent Republican, and a useful, energetic man.

He married Josephine Pierson, daughter of Joseph and Catherine Pierson, natives of France. She died September 15, 1896, aged fifty years. Their children are Catherine (Mrs. Francis Vivarttas), Henry, Julius, and Daisy, all of West Hoboken, the last three occupying the Kühl homestead on the Hudson Boulevard. This beautiful residence was built by Henry Kühl, Sr., but the present improvements, including the greenhouses, etc., were added by Mrs. Josephine (Pierson) Kühl, who was a woman of great business ability, force of character, and rare feminine accomplishments and culture. The business, which has been successful from the start, is now conducted by the four heirs—Mrs. Vivarttas and Henry, Julius, and Daisy Kühl—under the style of the estate of Henry Kühl, and attests the thrift and sound judgment of its founder and his successors.

THOMAS O'BRIEN, Tax Collector of the City of Englewood, N. J., was born in Wales on the 14th of May, 1861, his parents being Charles O'Brien and Ellen Fitzgerald. The family came to the United States in 1873 and settled in Englewood, where they still reside.

Thomas O'Brien received a public school education in England and Englewood, N. J., and subsequently learned the trade of tailor, which he has continuously followed with marked success. He now has one of the leading merchant tailoring establishments in Englewood.

In politics Mr. O'Brien is a Democrat. He was Town Clerk of the Town of Englewood for four years and during the past six years has been City Tax Collector. He has filled both of these offices with acknowledged ability and satisfaction. The esteem and confidence in which he is held by the community have been repeatedly shown in his election to offices. He is a prominent member of the Firemen's Association, of the Royal Arcanum, and of the Catholic Benevolent Association, all of Englewood. His activity in the community, his efforts to promote its welfare, and his prominence among his fellow-citizens stamp him as a man of standing and reputation.

Mr. O'Brien was married, September 7, 1892, to Alice Rath, daughter of Ferdinand and Mary E. Rath, of Englewood, N. J. They have two children: Dudley and Vernon O'Brien.

MICHAEL J. CANNON has been a life-long resident of Hoboken, N. J., where he was born February 20, 1865, the son of John Cannon and Winifred Nolan, both of whom have lived in Hoboken for the past fifty years. He acquired a good education in the public schools of his native city, and after graduating from the high school learned the trade of printer in New York, which he followed successfully for several years. Deciding to adopt the legal profession, he entered a law office in New York City as a student, and subsequently served a clerkship in the law office of Hon. William S. Stuhr, of Hoboken.

Mr. Cannon was admitted to the New Jersey bar at the February term of the Supreme Court in 1896, as an attorney, and at once commenced the practice of law in Hoboken, opening an office at No. 40 Newark Street. Since then he has built up a large and successful business. As a court and office lawyer he has displayed marked ability, broad and comprehensive learning, and sound legal qualifications, and the many important cases which have been intrusted to his care attest the confidence and respect in which he is held by the community. He has also taken an active interest in public affairs. In April, 1892, he was elected a School Trustee from the Fourth Ward of Hoboken, and served as such for three years. He was married on the 20th of June, 1895, to Mary A. V. Code.

SEBASTIAN MAULBECK, the well known surveyor of Hudson County, was born in Schlicht, Bavaria, Germany, on the 16th of March, 1861. He descends from an old and respected family, his parents being Andreas and Anna Maulbeck, his grandparents Franz and Theresa Maulbeck, and his paternal great-grandfather Friedrich Maulbeck. He inherited the sturdy physical and intellectual qualities for which the Germans are noted. His father, grandfather, and great-grandfather were men of great force of character, and contributed to their community the wholesome influences of honored and respected citizenship.

Mr. Maulbeck received a thorough classical and technical education in the Fatherland, attending first the industrial schools in Amberg and Nuemberg and later the Polytechnic High School at Munich in Bavaria. In these institutions he developed those traits of character which predestined him for a professional career, and displayed a special preference for mathematics, in which he became an expert. An apprenticeship of four years at surveying in Bavaria not only determined his future course, but gained for him the technical training which he coveted as a boy and youth. In

SEBASTIAN MAULBECK.

1882 he left Bavarian Germany and came to America, and for a time was employed by the Sanborn-Perris Map Company, of 115 Broadway, New York. Subsequently he was engaged on the surveys of the public parks of that city, especially of Central Park and Morningside Park, and in this capacity achieved a high reputation for ability and efficiency. In 1888 he engaged in general surveying in Hudson County, N. J., where he has since practiced his profession with increasing success. He has been the official surveyor of the Towns of Union and West Hoboken, and has laid out many of the principal streets, squares, and public grounds in that section. An expert mathematician, he is also a man of marked artistic tastes, and in the discharge of his professional duties has displayed signal ability in the line of beautifying nature and laying out public walks and thoroughfares. In other words, he has shown a rare knowledge of landscape engineering as well as a ready and practical skill in the more prosaic affairs of surveying.

Mr. Maulbeck is public spirited and progressive. He enlisted in the Ninth (afterward the Second) Regiment, National Guard of New Jersey, stationed in Hoboken, in which he served under Colonels Hart and Stevens. He is a member of the Independent Schuetzen Corps of West Hoboken, where he resides.

Mr. Maulbeck was married, in 1887, to Miss Theresia Sternbauer, daughter of Wilhelm Sternbauer, of Passan, Bavaria, and they have seven children: Sebastian, Jr., Joseph, Theresia, Anna, Emma, Elsa, and Paula.

JOHN M. MÜLLER, a well known merchant of West Hoboken, N. J., is a native of Hanover, Germany, where he was born on the 9th of April, 1852. He is the son of Lutje Müller and Catherine Sterling. His education was obtained in the national schools of the Fatherland. In 1871 he came to America, and, taking up his residence in New York City, engaged as a clerk in the grocery business. There, in 1880, he established himself in trade, opening first a grocery in Elm Street and subsequently one on the corner of First Avenue and First Street. He was successful from the start. In 1890 he removed to West Hoboken, N. J., and purchased his present store on the corner of Clinton Avenue and Warren Street, where he has built up an extensive trade in groceries, flour, coal, hay, and feed.

In politics Mr. Müller is an ardent Republican. He has never sought nor held public office, but has given his entire attention to a large and growing business. He is a member of West Hoboken Council, Royal Arcanum, of Manhattan Lodge, No. 130, Knights of Pythias, of New York, and of the Court of Foresters of America located in West Hoboken, where he resides.

Mr. Müller was married to Miss Emily Meyering, daughter of Albert and Christina Meyering, of New York City, and they have two children: John Albert and Emily Louise.

MICHAEL FRANCIS MOYLAN, formerly Township Committeeman and now Mayor of New Durham, Hudson County, was born in old Hudson City, N. J., in 1858. His parents settled there in 1853. Mr. Moylan attended old No. 3 school in what is now Jersey City until he attained the age of seventeen, when he entered a large New York jewelry establishment for the purpose of learning the jeweler's trade. When twenty-one years old he became an assistant to his brother, James Moylan, the well known civil engineer, who at that time was engaged on the civil engineering work on the New York Ninth Avenue elevated railway line, and who served as a member of the New Jersey Legislature from Hudson County in 1891 and 1892, representing the Fourth Assembly District of Jersey City.

Upon the completion of this road Mr. Moylan was appointed to a position as one of its locomotive engineers, which he held until 1883, when he entered the service of the West Shore Railroad Company. Since then he has been associated with that corporation as a locomotive engineer, running the Catskill Mountain express, the New York and Montreal express, and other important trains. He is one of the best and most trustworthy engineers connected with the road, and for years has enjoyed the confidence and respect of the officials as well as his associates.

GENEALOGICAL

Mr. Moylan has been a life-long resident of Hudson County. He has lived in New Durham since 1883, and is one of the town's most prominent and influential citizens. A Democrat in politics, he has long been a recognized leader of the party and for some time served as a member of the North Bergen Township Democratic Committee. His activity in political and public affairs dates from the time he was old enough to think and act for himself. In 1897 he held his first office, that of Township Committeeman, and rendered valuable service on the board, having the welfare and general interests of the Township of North Bergen at heart. The next year—

MICHAEL F. MOYLAN.

1898—he became the first Chairman or Mayor of the new Borough of New Durham, and in this capacity has magnified an already high reputation for ability, integrity, and faithfulness. He was one of the chief organizers of the town, and under his efficient guidance it has developed into one of the best local governments in the State. Mr. Moylan was one of the founders and organizers, as he was also one of the first Directors, of the Town of Union Building and Loan Association, one of the strongest institutions of the kind in East Jersey. He is a charter member of West Shore Council, Royal Arcanum, a member of Excelsior Hook and Ladder Company of New Durham, and a progressive, public spirited, and energetic citizen, whose active interest in the community has gained for him universal respect and esteem.

Mr. Moylan was married, in May, 1876, to Miss M. J. Walsh, daughter of Lawrence and Margaret Walsh. She died in 1879, leaving one daughter, Cora G., now a student at the Sacred Heart Academy in Albany, N. Y.

GEORGE CARRAGAN has been a resident of Bayonne, Hudson County, N. J., since 1859. He was born in Saratoga Springs, N. Y., March 7, 1844, and is the son of James Carragan and Mary Vanderwerker and a grandson of Eleazer and Martha (Keech) Carragan and of Sovereign and Lucy (Ross) Vanderwerker. His maternal great-great-grandfather was Rip Van Dam, one of the early members of the New York Colonial Council and subsequently Governor of New York. The name Carragan is of Welsh origin, the original spelling being Cadawgan. The children of James and Mary (Vanderwerker) Carragan were Ella, John, George, and Samuel, the subject of this sketch being the third child and second son.

George Carragan was educated in the common schools of Saratoga Springs and for twenty years was a commercial traveler for the Schieffelin Drug Company, of New York City, in which he is now interested. He is also the financial head of the business of August Kress & Co., importers of grocers' specialties, of 64 Dey Street, New York; a leading manufacturer of badges, stencils, seals, rubber stamps, etc., of 35 and 37 Beekman Street, New York; the head of the wholesale commission house of R. B. Poucher & Co., West Washington Market, New York; and a Director in the Mechanics Trust Company of the City of Bayonne, N. J. These various business associations indicate in a small measure Mr. Carragan's ability and success as a financier. He has been eminently successful, and through his own efforts has built up a reputation for integrity and uprightness of character which is recognized by all who know him.

Though an ardent and active Republican, and influential in the councils of his party, he has never sought nor held political office. His large business interests demand and receive his entire attention. He is a member and Elder of the Reformed Church of Bayonne, Hudson County, where he has resided continuously since 1859. He is also a prominent 32° Mason, holding membership in Palestine Commandery, Knights Templar, of New York City, and was a charter member of the Royal Arcanum of Bayonne, being the orator on the occasion of its organization. He is still active in that body.

Mr. Carragan married Margaret Vreeland, a member of an old and well known New Jersey family, and they have one child, Ella, wife of Charles W. Thomas, of Bayonne.

JAMES F. GAVEGAN, foreman of the shipping department of the Standard Oil Company at Bayonne, N. J., was born in Brooklyn, N. Y., November 6, 1870. His parents, John Gavegan and Cecelia Rush, natives of Ireland, came to the United States when young. They were married in Brooklyn, and finally moved from there to Bayonne, N. J.

Mr. Gavegan was educated in the public schools of both Brooklyn and Bayonne, and upon completing his studies associated himself with the Standard Oil Company, with which he has since remained. He now holds the responsible position of foreman of their shipping department. He is an ardent and active Democrat, a public spirited and patriotic citizen, and for two terms has served Bayonne as a member of the Board of

School Trustees. He is a member of the Foresters of America, of the Benevolent and Protective Order of Elks, and of the Catholic Club.

THOMAS CHARLES McNAMARA, physician and surgeon, of 715 Park Avenue, Hoboken, N. J., was born at Annagh in the suburbs of Ballyhaunis, County Mayo, Ireland. His parents, John McNamara and Bridget Kilduff, were both born in Ireland and are still living. They were brought up in England, where they were married in 1856. Afterward they went to reside at the old family seat at Annagh, where a branch of the Clan McNamara had settled immediately after the memorable convention of the Irish chieftains in 1541. At this convention, when Donogh O'Brien, who was then tanist of Thomond, and to whom the Clan McNamara then paid tribute as their chief, swore allegiance to Henry II. of England, the McNamara clans refused to obey, and hence they were driven out, their castles and possessions being confiscated.[1] Dr. McNamara's mother's ancestors were of Scotch origin, and were fosters of the O'Malleys, princes of Hymania, down to the second half of the last century.

Caisin, a younger son of Cas (founder of the Dalcassian septs of Munster), was ancestor of the Clan Mac-con-Mara, which means the family or descendants of "Son of the Sea-Warrior," anglicised *McNamara*. Caisin was seventh in descent from the renowned warrior Cormac Cas, who in the second century of the Christian era died from spear wounds received in battle from Eochy, King of Leinster. From Caisin the McNamaras, with their correlative septs of O'Grady, O'Hurley, O'Hickey, O'Hea, etc., were called Clan Caisin, but from Callin, seventh in descent from Caisin, it was most frequently called Clan Cullin.

The McNamaras were anciently " Princes " or " High Chiefs " of Tullugh,

THOMAS C. M'NAMARA.

[1] For a more detailed description see *The History of a Clan*, by Major McNamara.

County Clare, ranking also as "lords" of the now Barony of Bunratty, County Clare, and were hereditary marshals of Thomond.

Armorial Insignia.—The simplicity of the heraldic blazon bespeaks its extreme antiquity, containing the single rampant lion of the original Milesian shield. It is tinctured "argent" on the field gules, expressing in heraldic language "wisdom combined with power or majesty." The golden spear heads, placed in chief, commemorates the killing of their remote ancestor, Cormac, by Eochaidh or Eochy, King of Leinster, in the battle of Samhna Hill, County Limerick.

Dr. McNamara received his primary education at the Carrownedan and Ballyhaunis National Schools. From the former he was graduated as a teacher, after having served therein a monitorialship of six years, under the Commissioners of National Education, in 1878. From 1878 to 1880 he took a special course of training in mathematical and mechanical science at Ballyhaunis National School. During all those years of training he was under the direct supervision of Archdeacon Kavanagh, Rector of the famous "Shrine of Knock."

In 1880 he entered as a student St. Jarlath's College, Tuam, which was then under the direction of John, Archbishop McHale, or, as Daniel O'Connell used to call him, "The Lion of the fold of Juda." The inveterate hatred of John of Tuam toward English oppression in Ireland was well grounded in the youthful minds of his students, as recent history has testified. Accordingly, having imbibed his teachings, it is no wonder that in a few months Dr. McNamara found himself allied with the physical force party of Ireland, a branch of which was then ripe within the college. This band of young students carried their principles through the turbulent West, especially among the small tenant farmers of Mayo, with the result of establishing the Land League under the guidance of the ablest tactician and leader of modern times, Charles Stewart Parnell. The part they played in its establishment culminated at the first meeting at Irishtown, but others, such as Michael Davitt, took the credit. During the three years Dr. McNamara spent in Tuam College he was regarded as a close student, and was amply rewarded by carrying off the highest honors in his class in Latin, Greek, English, French, Irish, mathematics, history, and literature. The distinctions he acquired gained for him the approbation of the then Coadjutor, Archbishop McEvilly, who nominated him to study for the Catholic priesthood in 1883. On September 5, 1883, he presented himself for examination at Maynooth College. He took up for study an advanced course on arts, the next year passing into higher mathematics, natural philosophy, and mechanics, while the year after was taken up with moral philosophy (embracing logic, natural theology, and psychology), and in his last year he studied dogmatic and moral theology. The language spoken in Maynooth is more or less confined to the Latin tongue.

About this time his health began to give way and he decided to take a rest from study. In October, 1886, he left Maynooth College, having obtained therein the Order of Tonsure. At his departure he received the following letter from the President of the college:

MAYNOOTH COLLEGE, October 8th, 1886.

DEAR MR. MCNAMARA: I have much pleasure in sending you the testimonial letter you ask. Your conduct, during the four years you have spent in our college has been very good in every way, and gives the strongest reason to hope that, by your attention, application to your business or profession, and your high character for virtue, you will succeed in the secular life on which you are now entering of your own free choice.

I shall be glad to hear of your success, for your honorable career in our college has had the effect of giving your superiors here an interest in your future. I remain, dear Mr. McNamara,

Yours faithfully,

Mr. Thomas C. McNamara,   ROBERT BROWN,
   Diocese Tuam.   President.

About a week after leaving Maynooth Dr. McNamara went to study law under a master of Trinity College, Dublin, but finding the legal profession distasteful, he gave it up in six months, returned home, and acted as manager for his father from 1887 to 1892. During those five years he came into closer relations with many of the Irish Parliamentary party, became a stern advocate of Parnellite principles, politically, and for their advocacy was satisfied to become a voluntary exile in 1892. It fell to his lot to be one of six who lowered into their graves the three greatest men whom the Irish nation produced in the second half of this century: John, Archbishop of Tuam, Celtic scholar, author, preacher, poet, and politician; Charles S. Parnell, the most astute parliamentary and political leader of Ireland; and P. W. Nally, athlete, and organizer and head center of Clan-na-Gaels, who was done to death in a British dungeon a week before his intended release, because he refused to turn informer upon that little band of students which he formed in Tuam College.

Having formed many branches of the League in the West, Dr. McNamara determined no longer to live under the ban of coercion. The detectives of Scotland Yard were ever upon his track since the incarceration of his brother, John, under the Foster Act; but he always evaded arrest. In the spring of 1892 he sailed from Queenstown to make his home

"Where a man is a man, if he's willing to toil,
And the humblest may gather the fruits of the soil."

He took cabin passage in the "City of New York" and in seven days arrived at New York. In the autumn of 1892 he entered Bellevue Hospital Medical College, New York, and from there graduated M.D. on the 25th of March, 1895. On April 17, 1895, he was graduated from the University of the State of New York. He applied for a license to the State Board of Examiners to practice medicine and surgery in the State of New Jersey, which was granted on the 31st of May, 1895. During his years of study in medicine, along with the ordinary college course, he took almost all the private courses of instruction, and did practical work for one year in the outdoor department of Bellevue, in the surgical as well as in the heart and lung wards. In the autumn of 1897, having applied for and receiving a law student's certificate, he entered the New York Law University, remaining one term. By this time his medical practice had grown so extensive that he could not devote much time to the law.

For over five years he has practiced medicine and surgery with excellent results. He was employed as expert witness in the case of the State v. Dr. Colletti, appearing for the plaintiff. In 1897 he received the unanimous vote of thanks from the assembled delegates to the county convention of the Foresters of America, New Jersey. In 1899 he was elected High Court Physician to the State of New Jersey by the Independent Order of Foresters. He was appointed Township Physician in Weehawken on March 29, 1900, and became visiting surgeon to St. Mary's Hospital in Hoboken.

He was the first President of the Shamrock Club, founded by him in 1897, and one of the prime movers in the establishment of the United Irishmen of Hoboken. He was President of the O'Brien Football Club and a delegate to the Gaelic Central Council in Ireland. He is a member of the Hudson County Medical Society, a member of the Society for the Relief of Widows and Orphans of Deceased Medical Men, a charter member of the Knights of Columbus, and a member of the Irish National Club of New York, the Shamrock Club of Hoboken, the Coyles Democratic Club, the Anchor Club, the Hibernians, the Clan-na-Gaels, the Foresters of America, the Independent Order of Foresters, the Companions of the Forest, and the Wood-Choppers. He is examining physician to the U. S. A. Letter Carriers' Mutual Benefit Association, the Ladies' Branch of the Catholic Benevolent Association, the Independent Order of Foresters, the Companions of the Forest, and Courts America, Stevens, Minturn, Pride of Hoboken, and George Washington, of the Order of Forestry.

Dr. McNamara is unmarried. He had three brothers and one sister: Patrick, John, James, and Mary. James died at the age of seventeen. Patrick and John, who are living, married sisters, nieces of Rev. M. Loftus, Rector of Our Lady of Angels' Church, Brooklyn, N. Y., and nephew to Rt. Rev. Anthony O'Regan, third Bishop of Chicago, who was consecrated on the 25th of July, 1854. Mary married John Healy, of Chicago, who at the time of their marriage was an extensive merchant in the Town of Ballinasloe, County Galway.

JAMES WALLWORK, a well known plumber and business man of Kearny and Harrison, Hudson County, was born in England on the 15th of January, 1874. He is the son of Edward and Rachel (Smith) Wallwork and a grandson of James Wallwork, and on both sides a descendant of old and respected English ancestry.

In 1884 Mr. Wallwork, then a youth of ten years, came to America with his father, Edward, and settled in Kearny, N. J., where his parents still reside. There he received a good practical education in the public schools. He early displayed qualities which have won for him marked success. On leaving school he began learning the trade of a plumber, which he mastered in all its branches, and which he has followed in both Kearny and Harrison. He has been successful in this line of industry.

In politics Mr. Wallwork is independent. He is public spirited, patriotic, and enterprising, and though a young man has already achieved distinction in the community and a reputation for ability and integrity. He is prominent in fraternal and social circles, being a popular member of the Knights of Pythias, of Copestone Lodge, A. F. and A. M., of Kearny, of Harmony Chapter, R. A. M., of Newark, and of the Plumbers' Association. He married Miss Mary Boyce, of Harrison, N. J., where they reside.

JUDSON CAMILLE FRANCOIS, the recognized leader of the Democratic party in West Hoboken, N. J., was born in Brussels, Belgium, December 5, 1850, being the seventh in a family of fourteen children of Joseph Francois and Pauline Marie, eleven of whom are actively engaged in business as ladies' hairdressers. Joseph Francois was also a noted ladies' hairdresser until his death in 1890, in what is now Jersey City Heights, whither he came with his family from Belgium in 1856.

Mr. Francois obtained his education in the public schools of Jersey City Heights, finishing in Grammar School No. 2, on the corner of Central Avenue and Congress Street. His studies were designed to meet only the practical requirements of a business life, yet the strength of character and a retentive memory which he possessed gave him, at a very early age, the prestige of a leader among his associates, and he left school fairly well equipped to enter his father's hairdressing establishment. Here his ability and industry soon won for him a complete mastery of the trade. His brothers and sisters have also achieved professional prominence in New York or New Jersey. In 1872 he opened his present hairdressing parlors at 419 Paterson Avenue, West Hoboken, and besides this he also conducted for several years a similar establishment on the corner of Sixth Avenue and Fourteenth Street, New York.

Mr. Francois is widely known as a Democratic leader. He has been active and prominent in his party since 1876, when he was elected Constable, an office he held for sixteen consecutive years, serving as Court Officer during that entire period, gaining a wide acquaintance among the leading men of the county and laying the foundation of a future political career. From the time he assumed the duties of Constable and Court Officer to the present he has been an influential leader of the Democratic party, fearless in his convictions, zealous and active in his party's welfare, and true to the fundamental principles upon which it exists. On January 8, 1889, he was elected to the New Jersey Legislature, from the old Tenth (now the Eleventh) Assembly District of Hudson County, to fill the vacancy caused by the death of Edwin F. Short, who had been elected in the preceding autumn. In the Assembly Mr. Francois at once took a leading position, and as a member of the Committees on Ways and Means, State Prisons, and Miscellaneous Business was instrumental in promoting much important legislation and in defeating measures of questionable value. Among the several bills which he introduced was one giving one policeman for every 800 population in West Hoboken, another providing that a defendant under arrest should have three days' notice before the date set for his trial, and a third authorizing the erection of the present Turn Verein hall in the Town of Union. He also introduced several local sewerage bills, and was the means of defeating the measure which had for its object the consolidation of Arlington, Kearny, and Harrison.

Mr. Francois was elected a member of the West Hoboken Town Council in 1892 and served two years, and since April, 1897, he has held the office of Justice of the Peace. From 1883 to 1889 he was a member of the Hudson County Democratic Committee, and in 1898 was re-elected to that position, which he still holds. He was Treasurer of the West Hoboken Board of Fire Trustees for about four years, and is the founder and standard bearer of the J. C. Francois Association, a non-partisan body in West Hoboken having about 100 members, Alfred S. Franklin being President. Mr. Francois served for ten years in Company B, Fourth Regiment, N. G. N. J., becoming Second Sergeant. He is an exempt fireman, having been for twenty-two years a member of Neptune Engine Company of West Hoboken. He is also a member of the Royal Arcanum. On State and national issues Mr. Francois is a consistent Democrat, voting and acting with his party, but in town and county affairs he is fearlessly independent, working first and last for the best interests of the people, and casting his influence in favor of those matters which promise the most good.

He was married March 3, 1872, to Martha, daughter of Abraham Stilwell and Elizabeth Van Voorst, his wife, whose father, Garret Van Voorst, was descended from one of the oldest families in East Jersey. The Stilwell family were early settlers of Staten Island. Mrs. Elizabeth Stilwell is living with the subject of this sketch. She was born in North Bergen, November 5, 1812, and is one of the oldest surviving residents of Hudson County. Mr. and Mrs. Francois have four children: Joseph Judson, Martha (Mrs. Charles Wase), Alexander, and Edward.

THEODORE J. VOGT is a successful butcher and a recognized leader of the Democratic party, with which he has been actively identified since boyhood. His parents, Theodore and Elizabeth (Nieland) Vogt, were natives of Germany and sturdy representatives of the Fatherland. Coming to this country about the middle of the present century, they were married soon after their arrival and settled in the Town of Union, N. J., where they lived ever afterward. Theodore Vogt was a master carpenter and contractor, the first boss builder on Union Hill, and a man of great energy, ability, and force of character. He retired from business shortly before his death, which occurred in the Town of Union in July, 1886. His wife died there in 1899. Both were members of the Catholic Church, and are buried in the Weehawken cemetery. They had six children, namely: Elizabeth and Annie, both deceased; Frank, a well known hotel proprietor of Kansas City, Mo.; Theodore J., the subject of this article; and Rosa and Lena. Theodore Vogt, the father of this family, achieved distinction in public life as well as eminent success as a contractor and builder. He was a prominent Democrat, active and influential in the councils of his party, a valued member of the Board of Education of the Town of Union, a leading member of the Town Council, and a founder and life-long member of the Liedertafel Society of Union Hill. In brief, he was one of the foremost men of his time, taking an active part in all local affairs, and earnestly supporting every movement which promised benefit to the town and county. Though born and reared in Germany, he and his wife were both imbued with the American spirit of patriotism and thoroughly exemplied that spirit in their deeds and actions.

THEODORE J. VOGT.

Theodore J. Vogt was born in 1859, in the Town of Union, N. J., where he has always resided. There he received his educational training. While a boy he learned the butcher's trade, which he has continuously and successfully followed, building up an extensive business and reputation. His success and prominence in this line are noteworthy.

Mr. Vogt has taken an active part in politics from the time he was a youth, and almost from the day he cast his first vote to the present he has been an acknowledged leader of the Democratic party. His influence in party councils steadily gained in force and extent until now it is felt, not only in his own town and vicinity, but throughout the county. He is a member of the Board of Education of the Town of Union and of the Foresters of America. As a citizen he is esteemed and respected. He possesses great energy and force of character, and, like his father, is public spirited, enterprising, and patriotic, thoroughly alive to the needs of his native town, prompt to encourage those objects having its welfare at heart, and worthy of the confidence reposed in him by his fellowmen.

In 1883 Mr. Vogt married Rosa Valerius, of Elmira, N. Y., by whom he has three children: Edward, Joseph, and Frank.

JOHN CONLEY, to whose energies as a contractor much of the growth of Woodcliff, Hudson County, N. J., is due, was born in New York City in 1853, the son of John Conley, Sr., and Rosanna Goodwin. His parents emigrated from County Monahan, Ireland, in 1836, and settled in New York, where John Conley, Sr., successfully followed his trade as a tailor until his death in 1897. His wife died in 1898. Both were nearly eighty years of age.

Mr. Conley attended the New York public schools, and then learned the hatter's trade, which he followed for a few years. Subsequently he was engaged in the grocery business in that city for about fifteen years, achieving success and gaining a high reputation. He moved to what is now Woodcliff, in the Township of North Bergen, Hudson County, N. J., in 1894, and the next year engaged in contracting and building, a vocation he has since followed with great energy and profit. Many of the finest homes in that attractive village have been erected by him. Being a practical carpenter and mason, his work bears evidence of permanency and stamps him as a man of skill. The dwelling in which he resides is an excellent example of his efforts. He is independent in politics.

Mr. Conley married Miss Anna McNamara and has had six children, three of whom are living, viz.: John, Jr., James, and Sarah.

PETER H. SEERY, Vice-President and Superintendent of the New Jersey Tube Company, is the son of Thomas H. and Mary Seery, a grandson of John and Ellen (Seery) Seery, and a descendant of one of the old Norman-Celtic families of County West Meath, Ireland. Thomas H. Seery, his father, was for more than half a century connected with the Waterbury Brass Company, of Waterbury, Conn., being for thirty years its efficient Superintendent. This connection covered his entire business life. He was recognized as authority on brass manufacturing in every department of the trade, and gained a wide reputation as one of the ablest and most talented brass workers of his time. He died October 18, 1896, at Waterbury, Conn., where his widow still resides.

Peter H. Seery was born in Waterbury, Conn., on the 27th of September, 1859, and received his education in the public schools of that city. He inherited his father's mechanical talents, and early in life took up the work in which the elder Seery achieved such eminent success. He has been actively identified with the brass working trade, and is now Vice-President and Superintendent of the New Jersey Tube Company, one of the largest and most successful corporations of the kind in the country. Mr. Seery has displayed marked ability, not only as a brass worker, but also as executive manager in business affairs, and the success of the New Jersey Tube Company is due in no small measure to his energy and constant application.

He has always taken an active part in local affairs, and as an independent Republican and patriotic citizen has wielded an important influence in the

PETER H. SEERY.

community. Before coming to New Jersey Mr. Seery was for six years a member of Company G, Connecticut National Guard. He resides in Newark and is a member of the North End Club and of the Royal Arcanum. Public spirited, enterprising, thoroughly identified with the best interests of the city, and a liberal supporter of every worthy movement, he is universally respected and esteemed. The business of the New Jersey Tube Company being located in Harrison, he is closely identified with the affairs of Hudson County and is justly esteemed as one of its progressive men.

Mr. Seery was married in Waterbury, Conn., in 1886, to Miss Frances Ellen Fitzpatrick. They have one son, Irving.

HUGO FRANK WALDONS is one of the successful builders in North Hudson County, and in West Hoboken, where he resides, is respected as a public spirited, enterprising citizen. Born in Baden, Germany, August 24, 1865, he is the son of Ferdinand Waldons, deceased, and Susanna, his wife, who survives and resides with the subject of this article. He came to the United States in 1883 and located in New York City, where he completed his education in the high school. He soon returned to the Fatherland. In 1886 he again came to this country and settled permanently in Hudson County, N. J., where he has achieved success as a contractor and builder, having built up an extensive business. He is a thoroughly practical operator in every branch of the trade and proficient in architectural drawing, in which he has developed marked artistic skill. He makes his own blueprints and attends personally to the minutest detail. A large number of the finer buildings in his section are the result of his energies and handiwork, and not a few of them bear evidences of his talents as a designer. Able and progressive, possessed of sound judgment and originality, and energetic in all he attempts, Mr. Waldons is one of the prominent builders of Hudson County.

He takes a deep and often an active interest in the welfare of the community, and in various capacities has contributed much to its growth and advancement. He is a Democrat in politics, a sagacious business man, and enjoys a wide popularity. At one time he served as a fire inspector. He has never sought office, however, preferring to devote his whole attention to his growing business. He holds membership in several social and other organizations, and has also an honorable military record, having served for three years as a soldier in the German Army.

Mr. Waldons was married on the 21st of September, 1895, to Anna Schwiki, a native of Germany. They have two children: Elsie and Arthur.

WILLIAM E. McCARTY, a Councilman of the Town of Union, Hudson County, was born February 5, 1866, in New York City, the son of William and Ellen (Toolin) McCarty, natives of Ireland. In 1868 he was brought by his parents to the Town of Union, N. J., where he has since resided, developing and broadening those sturdy characteristics which have won for him a prominent place in the community. After leaving the public schools of Union Hill, where he acquired a good rudimentary education, Mr. McCarty associated himself with the paper rolling business in New York City, and also learned the trade of blacksmithing and horseshoeing with his father, whose reputation in this line extended beyond the limits of his neighborhood. Subsequently he entered the employ of Gardner & Meeks and soon rose to the position of foreman.

Mr. McCarty identified himself with the Democratic party on attaining his majority, and through his activity and enthusiasm rapidly gained distinction as an able and trustworthy leader. He early won the respect and confidence of his fellow-townsmen, and has exerted from the first an important influence upon local affairs and especially upon his party's welfare. In the spring of 1897 he was elected a member of the Town Council of the Town of Union on the Democratic ticket, and by re-election still holds that office. He is also Clerk of the Board of Trustees of the Free Public Library of Union Hill. He is Past Chancellor of Mount Alverno Council, No. 162, C. B. L.; Past Chief Ranger of Court Palisade, No. 24, F. O. A.; and one of the founders of the Central Democratic Organization, in which he has held important offices. He is also a member of the First Ward Democratic

Club and the John J. Eagan Association. In every capacity his sound common sense, unswerving integrity, and native ability and enterprise have won for him a wide popularity.

OSCAR VERILHAC, the well known florist of Arlington, N. J., is the son of Matthew and Mary (Salee) Verilhac, and was born in Leon, France, on the 19th of April, 1847. His parents were both natives of that country. Mr. Verilhac was educated in the public schools of Leon, and for a number of years was successfully engaged in business as a florist there. He served in the French army during the war with Germany, and in several important battles displayed great courage and bravery.

In 1876 Mr. Verilhac came to New York City, where he resumed his business as a florist. In 1886 he removed to Arlington, Hudson County, N. J., where he still resides, and where he has since been engaged in the same business. He is one of the leading florists in this part of the State, and enjoys a reputation for ability, thoroughness, and fair dealing.

Mr. Verilhac has won success through his own efforts, and since boyhood has displayed those intellectual qualifications of integrity and honor which distinguish the successful man. He has displayed in his adopted country the same degree of patriotism, public spirit, and energy which led him to volunteer as a soldier in the war between France and Germany, and which have always marked him as an exemplary citizen. He is thoroughly identified with the public affairs of the Borough of Arlington, a Democrat in politics, a member of the Presbyterian Church, and respected and esteemed. As a florist and horticulturist he is recognized as an authority. His knowledge of the science is broad and accurate, while the ability and fair dealing which he has displayed in business matters stamp him as a man eminently worthy of the success which he has attained. He was married, in 1884, to Selma Rothe, of Pearl River, Rockland County, N. Y.

OSCAR VERILHAC.

WILLIAM A. CASSIDY, now serving his third term as a member of the Board of Aldermen of Bayonne, Hudson County, was born in England on the 5th of July, 1866, his parents being James and Margret (Sommers) Cassidy. His ancestors on both sides are Irish. The family came to the United States in 1868 and settled in Bayonne, N. J., where young Cassidy received his education.

At an early age he engaged in the meat and grocery business, which he followed successfully for several years. He is now an engineer at the Standard Oil Company's works at Bayonne.

In politics Mr. Cassidy is a prominent and influential Democrat. He served one term as a member of the Board of School Trustees of Bayonne, and is now serving his third term as a member of the Board of Aldermen of that city. In these and other capacities he has displayed all the attributes which mark the successful man of affairs, and which stamp him as a public spirited, patriotic, and progressive citizen. He is a member of the Bayonne Democratic Club, of the Bayonne Fire Department, of the Ancient Order of United Workmen, and of the Catholic Church.

Mr. Cassidy married Miss Catharine Dwyre, of Elizabeth, N. J., and they have three sons: Francis, George, and William.

JOHN M. GILLIGAN, a prominent manufacturer of corsets, was born in Kearny, Hudson County, N. J., where he still resides, on the 14th of April, 1872. He is a son of Isaac Gilligan and Ellen Nolan, natives of Ireland, who came to the United States in 1856, settling in Newark, N. J.

Mr. Gilligan received his educational training in the public schools of Newark and Kearny, and early developed business abilities of a high order. After obtaining experience in the various employments which a boy usually seeks he settled upon manufacturing, and, finding a suitable and congenial field for the exercise of his ambition, engaged in the manufacture of corsets in his native town. He soon established a large and successful trade.

In politics Mr. Gilligan is an ardent and active Democrat. He has served as a member of the Board of School Trustees of Kearny for three terms and is prominently identified with the best interests of the town. He is a member of the Knights of Columbus, of St. Patrick's Alliance, and of the Catholic Benevolent Legion.

THOMAS A. DUFFY, the well known contractor and builder of East Newark, Hudson County, is the son of James Duffy and Mary Smith, natives respectively of Ireland and England, who came to the United States in 1865. He was born in Fall River, Mass., where his mother was visiting, on the 26th of February, 1872, and there received his education in the public schools.

After leaving school Mr. Duffy engaged in business as a contractor and builder, which he has since followed with increasing success, his home and headquarters being in East Newark. Many of the finest and most imposing buildings in that section of Hudson County are the result of his industry and enterprise. His work shows artistic taste and skill as well as a thorough knowledge of structural problems, and stands as monuments to his integrity, ability, and faithfulness. Though a young man, he has achieved prominence in his line, and is esteemed and respected as a man of courage, honesty, and energy.

He has also taken an active interest in public affairs, serving as a member of the Board of Aldermen and of the Board of Chosen Freeholders and as Assistant Chief of the Fire Department. He is an ardent Democrat in politics and a prominent member of various bowling clubs. The popularity and confidence in which he is held by the community are attested by the many important duties which he has so faithfully and satisfactorily discharged.

ADOLPH SCHLEICHER, one of the prominent citizens of West Hoboken, Hudson County, N. J., and since 1896 a member of the Board of Education, was born in the City of Brooklyn, N. Y., August 19, 1868. He is the son of Victor Schleicher and Jacobine Miesel, daughter of Martin and Wilhelmina Miesel, a grandson of Lawrence Schleicher and Carolina Schleicher, and a great-grandson of John and Emma Schleicher. His paternal ancestors were mineowners in Germany during the eighteenth century. The first of the line in Germany bore the surname of De Trayer, and was one of a band of French Huguenots who were driven from France through the persecution of the Protestants in the reign of Henry IV., in the sixteenth century. This ancestor settled in Stollenbey, near Stollberg, Germany, and assumed the German name of Schleicher. The family of Mr. Schleicher's mother is also of French origin. Victor Schleicher, father of Adolph Schleicher, came to America in 1855, enlisted in the Union Army during the Civil War, and was taken prisoner by the Confederates at the battle of Williamsburg, Va. Adolph Schleicher, Sr., namesake and uncle of Mr. Schleicher, served with distinction in the German Army, as an officer of the Royal Guards, and also came to America. For seventeen years he was connected with the police courts of New York City, and for eleven years held the office of Recorder of Union Hill, Hudson County, N. J. Jacob Miesel and Louis Miesel, uncles of Mr. Schleicher, served with distinction in the Union Army during the American Civil War.

Mr. Schleicher was educated in the public schools of Union Hill, N. J., at private schools, and at Cooper Union, New York City. At the age of seventeen he accepted a position with the Weber Piano Company in New York City, received rapid advancement, and remained with this house until it failed. Since that time he has been very successfully engaged in the real estate and insurance business in West Hoboken, N. J. Well known for his public spirit, the only office which he has ever accepted has been that of member of the Board of Education of West Hoboken, to which position he was elected in 1896 and re-elected in 1899.

The military instinct, so characteristic of his family, was displayed in Mr. Schleicher's enlistment, in 1888, in Company B, Second Regiment, National Guard of the State of New Jersey. He rose to the rank of senior Sergeant, and when the Second and Fourth Regiments were consolidated he still continued as an officer. He was honorably discharged in 1894.

He married Miss Lena Biedermann, of New York City. He is a prominent member of the West Hoboken Business Men's Association, of the Columbia Club, of the Palisade Democratic Club, of Cosmopolitan Lodge, Independent Order of Odd Fellows, of Hoboken Lodge, Benevolent and Protective Order of Elks, of Capitol Lodge, K. of H., and of Garfield Council, No 56, J. O. U. A. M.

SAMUEL ARMSTRONG, the popular and well known undertaker of Union Hill, is the son of James Armstrong, a native of Ireland, who came to America when very young, and who served four years in the War of the Rebellion as a soldier in a New Jersey regiment of volunteers. His mother was Mary Ann Carr, whose strength of character and intellectual attainments in every way equaled those of her husband.

Mr. Armstrong was born in Edgewater, N. J., on the 5th of April, 1861, and there received his early education in the public schools. Leaving Edgewater at the age of thirteen, he went to Ridgefield, in the same State, where he remained for ten years, being for five years the sexton of the Protestant Episcopal Church of that town. During this period he also became a church or pipe organist of no mean ability. In 1884 he removed to Orange, N. J., and a little later to Jersey City Heights, where he was married, in 1885, to Miss Margaret Allgaier, of West New York, Hudson County. In the mean-

SAMUEL ARMSTRONG.

time he was learning the business of undertaker, embalmer, and funeral director with Henry E. Taylor, one of the best known and most successful undertakers of New York City. Later, having mastered every detail of the profession, he became the manager of the undertaking establishment of Mrs. Caroline Gschwind, of Union Hill, N. J., where he took up his residence. In this position he developed those active energies and business attainments which have marked his subsequent career, and which have won for him a wide popularity and an honorable reputation. In September, 1889, he opened an undertaking establishment for himself at 213 Bergenline

Avenue, Union Hill, which he still conducts. He also has an office at 317 Humboldt Avenue, in the same town, and resides at 510 Palisade Avenue.

As an undertaker, embalmer, and funeral director, Mr. Armstrong has achieved success and popularity. By his own efforts and untiring industry he has built up an extensive business. He is a man of recognized ability, public spirited, enterprising, and progressive, and liberally encourages every worthy movement. Deeply interested in the welfare of the community, he has contributed to its institutions, and enjoys the respect and confidence of his fellowmen. His popularity is best illustrated by the fact that, at St. Augustine's fair in 1895, he won a gold medal and in 1894 a gold-headed cane offered by the *Dispatch* for the most popular man in Hudson County.

In politics he is an ardent and influential Republican. In 1892 he was a candidate for County Coroner on the party ticket, and, though defeated, received a large and flattering vote. He is a member of Mystic Tie Lodge, No. 123, F. and A. M., of West Shore Council, R. A., of Palisade Lodge, K. of P., of Garfield Council, Jr. O. U. A. M., of Court Palisade, F. of A., of the Royal Society of Good Fellows, of the Uniformed Rank, K. of P., of Germania Schuetzen Bund of West New York, of Ellsworth Post, Sons of Veterans, of the Independent Schuetzens of Union Hill, of Mohawk Tribe, I. O. R. M., and of the Klondike Bowling Club. In all of these he is popular and prominent, and in every capacity he has achieved success and honor.

JOHN O'DONNELL, a veteran of the Civil War and for eighteen years Township Assessor of Weehawken, N. J., was born in Liverpool, England, on the 4th of April, 1842. He is the son of Patrick O'Donnell and Ann McStay and a grandson of Hugh O'Donnell, and descends from a long line of Scotch and English ancestors.

Mr. O'Donnell received his early education in the public schools of Liverpool. In February, 1852, he came with his parents to this country, and, settling in New York, completed his studies in Grammar School No. 11, on Seventeenth Street, in that city. Afterward he was employed there in various capacities. In 1860 he settled in Hudson City, now Jersey City Heights, N. J., and applied himself to learning the carpenter's trade with Charles J. Knighton; but the excitement incident to the War of the Rebellion aroused his patriotism to the point of enlisting in the Union cause, in which he served with honor and distinction. Joining Company F, Twenty-first New Jersey Volunteers, in August, 1862, he was soon transferred to Company I, of the same regiment, and for about ten months participated in the operations in Virginia, including Mary's Heights, Chancellorsville, and other battles and skirmishes.

In 1863 Mr. O'Donnell was honorably discharged from the service and resumed his associations with Mr. Knighton, applying himself to the trade of carpenter and stair builder. Later he entered the employ of David Stagg, of Hoboken, and in 1869 he engaged in business for himself in partnership with Ambrose Gale. Their business was almost exclusively stair building. In 1870 Mr. O'Donnell succeeded this firm, and has since followed the stair building trade, though of late years his time and energies have been very largely devoted to important official duties. As a stair builder, however, he achieved success as well as a high reputation for skill and ability, and is one of the oldest members of that trade in East Jersey. He has always been an active Democrat, prominent in the councils of his party, and recognized as one of its influential local leaders. For about five years he was

Commissioner of Appeals for the Township of Weehawken. In 1876 he was elected a member of the Township Committee, and in 1877 he was re-elected, but the new law reducing the board from five to three members threw him and another associate out. He was again re-elected in 1878, as one of the three members composing the board, but on account of political differences refused to sit, and resigned. In 1881 he was elected an Assessor of the Township of Weehawken. Owing to a tie vote, however, he did not qualify, but in 1882 he was re-elected to that office, and by successive re-elections has continued to hold it to the present time. He is now serving his eighteenth consecutive year, a fact which attests at once his popularity, his faithfulness and fidelity, and the esteem and confidence in which he is held by the community. His long and uninterrupted connection with the assessorship has not only given him a wide experience in real estate values, but has enabled him to gain an extensive knowledge of municipal affairs.

Mr. O'Donnell has been for many years a delegate to township, county, and district Democratic conventions, in which his influence has materially advanced the interests of the party. He has always been a fearless advocate of honest government and sound Democratic principles. As a citizen he is public spirited, enterprising, and patriotic. He was for fourteen years a member of Wadsworth (now Woerner) Post, G. A. R., of Hoboken, and is now a member of Ellsworth Post, No. 14, of the Town of Union, of which he was for a time the Junior Vice-Commander. He is also a member of the Catholic Benevolent Legion.

On June 25, 1868, Mr. O'Donnell married Mary Fottrell, daughter of Patrick and Elizabeth (Tiernan) Fottrell and a native of Dublin, Ireland, who came to America with her parents about 1855. They have seven children living, namely: Mary (Mrs. John Concannon, of Hoboken), William, Elizabeth, Ann, James Patrick, Angelus, and John, Jr. The family reside in Weehawken.

HERMAN HUBERT WOUTERS, Treasurer of the Town of Weehawken and the well known druggist of Weehawken Heights, is the son of Peter and Mary Wouters, and was born in Germany on the 3d of November, 1867. He received a thorough classical education at the school of St. Thomas à Kempis in Kempen-on-the-Rhine, and, coming to America in 1884, finished his studies in New York City. At the age of nineteen he entered the drug store of A. Rogers & Co., on the corner of Bleecker and Jones Streets, New York, for the purpose of learning the business of pharmaceutical chemist, and subsequently served a clerkship in a similar establishment in Jersey City. These associations, together with his own native energy and natural ability, enabled him to master every detail of the trade, and within a few years he had gained the distinction of an expert.

In 1893 he moved to Weehawken, N. J., and purchased the drug business of N. H. Perrine, on the Boulevard, which proved a most fortunate venture. About two years later he opened another drug store on Spring Street in West Hoboken, but subsequently sold it, and in 1896 started still another apothecary establishment at the corner of Palisade Avenue and Dodd Street, Weehawken Heights, which he still continues. In 1897, with William Kyvitz as his partner, he opened yet another drug store and pharmacy on Bergenline Avenue in the Town of Union.

Mr. Wouters is an able, enterprising, and successful business man, and through his own efforts and industry has achieved a high standing, being to-day one of the leading chemists and pharmacists in North Hudson

County. By fair dealing, honesty, and perseverance he has built up an extensive trade. Since he became a resident of Weehawken he has been an active and influential factor in all matters connected with the town, and his fellow-citizens have attested their confidence in him by electing him to positions of trust and responsibility. In the spring of 1894 he was chosen a member of the Weehawken Board of Education and by the board was appointed District Clerk. Three years later, in the spring of 1897, he was elected Township Committeeman for the southern district of Weehawken, running on the citizens' and taxpayers' ticket, and when the

HERMAN H. WOUTERS.

board convened was appointed Town Treasurer, which office he still holds. He has also been Chairman of the Fire Committee, Clerk of the Board of Health, and Chairman of the Board of Council, a position corresponding to that of Mayor, and through his agitations and activity succeeded in getting a fire alarm system placed in operation in the borough. In every capacity he has displayed great ability, sound judgment, and untiring devotion to the best interests of the community in which he is so highly esteemed and respected.

He is a charter member of the Weehawken German Society, of the Lincoln Republican Club, and of the Palisade Hose Company, a member and

Trustee of the North Hudson County Cyclers, and a member of the Odd Fellows fraternity. He married Miss Agnes Mordt, and has four children: Herbert, Adolph, Walter, and Consuelo. They reside at 500 Palisade Avenue, Weehawken Heights.

JAMES A. KELLY, one of the leading real estate dealers of Bayonne, Hudson County, is the son of William Kelly, a native of Ireland, where the latter's wife, a Miss Quinn, was also born. His father served as a member of the Bayonne Common Council for seven terms, or fourteen years—longer than any other official. In the fall of 1899 he was elected a member of the Hudson County Board of Freeholders, in which he is now serving.

Mr. Kelly was born in Bayonne, N. J., on the 4th of October, 1873, and received his education in Public School No. 1, in that place, at St. Francis Xavier College on Sixteenth Street, New York City, and at St. Peter's College and Drake's Business College in Jersey City. After graduating from the latter institution he went to work in the office of the Singer Sewing Machine Company at Elizabethport, N. J., and while there was appointed Assistant Collector of Revenue for the City of Bayonne, which position he held three years. He then engaged in real estate operations on his own account and has since conducted a large and successful business in his native city.

Mr. Kelly has gained an excellent reputation for business ability, integrity, and enterprise. He is actively interested in the welfare of his native city, has contributed materially to its prosperity in various real estate operations, and with Dr. Lucius F. Donohue was largely influential in locating the Babcock and Wilcox Company there. He was one of the organizers of the Fourth Regiment, New Jersey Militia, joining Company I, the first company organized in Bayonne. He is also a prominent member of the Bayonne Democratic Club, of the Young Men's Association, of the Knights of Columbus, of the Jersey City Catholic Club, of Drake's Alumni, of the old New Jersey Athletic Club of Bayonne, and of the Greenville Musical and Social Club.

Mr. Kelly was married, April 19, 1899, to Mary H. Ryan, daughter of Robert H. Ryan, Warden of the Hudson County Almshouse.

ROMEO THOMPSON CHURCHILL, D.V.S., is prominent alike in the practice of his profession as a veterinary surgeon and as a member of the Democratic party. Born in New York City on the 26th of May, 1853, he is the son of Joseph Churchill and Sarah Leviness. The family on his father's side is of English descent. Joseph Churchill was born in Bristol, England, February 22, 1813, and died in Hudson County in 1891. His wife, Sarah, daughter of John and Hannah Leviness, was born in 1818 and died in Middlesex County, N. J., in 1871. They had six children: Joseph P., Sarah M., Samuel A., William L., Romeo T., and George W. Joseph Churchill first lived in Yonkers, N. Y., being engaged as a professional driver for the Livingston family. Removing to New York City, he located on Forty-first Street and subsequently on Forty-eighth Street, and built the first house on the latter thoroughfare. He was engaged in business as a butcher for about two years, and then returned to England, settled his father's estate, and when nearly twenty-one years of age again came to America, settling in New York, where he was married on his twenty-first birthday. In the meantime he had acquired an education which fitted him for the practical affairs of life. He began the practice of his profession as a veterinary surgeon soon after his marriage, and about 1852 purchased the Bloomingdale stage line, which he extended, consolidating it with the Harlem line. He continued this business until 1866, when he sold the franchise to George Ribblett and resumed his profession, which he followed until his death, and in which he gained distinction. He was a Democrat, firm in his convictions, popular with his clientage, and well known throughout the State of New York.

Dr. Romeo T. Churchill received his education in New York City. After graduating from the public schools he entered the New York College of Veterinary Surgery, from which he was graduated in veterinary surgery, both medical and comparative, in 1886, receiving the degree of D. V. S. Since then he has resided and followed his profession at Secaucus, North Bergen Township, Hudson County, N. J. His reputation as a skillful and successful veterinarian extends beyond the county, and in New York, where he has an office, he supervises the veterinary work of several of the largest stables in the city.

In politics, as a leading Democrat, he is one of the best known men in Eastern New Jersey. He was for several years a member of the North Bergen Township Committee, and it is said that the affairs of the township were never in better condition than when he held that office. When he resigned the township treasury contained a surplus of over $30,000. For a number of years he served as Township Collector, discharging the duties of the position with faithfulness and satisfaction. He has also been a member of the Board of Education, a Justice of the Peace, a delegate to various political conventions, and a member of several social, political, and fraternal bodies.

Dr. Churchill is a public spirited and enterprising citizen, and widely esteemed and respected. In the active practice of his profession he has achieved eminent success. He married Miss Eliza J. Dunn.

WILLIAM TOLEN, Chief of Police of Kearny, Hudson County, and one of the best known citizens of Eastern New Jersey, was born in Philadelphia, Pa., June 21, 1851. His parents, George R. and Kate (Smith) Tolen, were natives of Germantown, Pa., and soon after their marriage in that place removed to Philadelphia, whence they came to Newark, N. J., in 1856. They were people of industry and force of character, and transmitted to their children those sturdy qualities of head and heart which invariably pave the way to success.

Coming to Newark when he was five years old, William Tolen spent his boyhood and youth in that city, attending the public schools. After leaving school he learned the trade of carpenter and builder, which he followed in Newark until 1881. He then removed to Kearny, Hudson County, where he has lived ever since, following the same business and engaging quite extensively in contracting. He built Public School No. 5, engine house No. 4, and many other large buildings in Kearny and vicinity, and by close application to business has achieved both success and honor. His work shows the thoroughness and excellence which characterize all of his undertakings, and stands as monuments to his skill, industry, integrity, and enterprise.

Since taking up his residence in Kearny Mr. Tolen has been active and prominent in public life and an important factor in the prosperity of the town. In politics he is a Republican. He was a member of the Town Council one term, Assistant Chief of the Fire Department two years, Commissioner of Appeals three years, and Commissioner of Assessments two years. At the present time (1900) he is Chief of Police of Kearny. In each of these positions he has exhibited marked ability, patriotism, and sound common sense, and has won the approval and confidence of the entire community. His activity in political affairs has brought him into more than local prominence and gained for him an acknowledged leadership in the councils of the Republican party. Mr. Tolen had some experience on a merchant ship under the British flag, on which he served one and one-half years, leaving when he was about fifteen. He remained abroad altogether three years. He is a member of the Methodist Episcopal Church, a man of broad and liberal culture, and a progressive citizen. He is a life member of the New

WILLIAM TOLEN.

Jersey State Firemen's Relief Association and was President of the Kearny Firemen's Association for five years.

In 1876 Mr. Tolen married Ella V. Plum, by whom he has six children: Kate, S. Thornton, Harry S., Robert P., Ella G., and Sadie E.

JAMES CLOSE, President of the New Jersey Tube Company, was born in Paterson, N. J., February 28, 1868. He is the son of Samuel Close and Margaret J. Moore, a grandson of James Close and Rachel King Close, and a great-grandson of James Close. His ancestors came to this country from Ireland and have always been prominent in public and business affairs.

Mr. Close was reared in Belleville, Essex County, N. J., and received his principal education in the adjacent Town of Bloomfield. His active business life began while he was yet a youth. He learned the metal-working business in Belleville with the firm of Hendricks Brothers, and has constantly followed it with marked success. He is now President of the New Jersey Tube Company, of Harrison, Hudson County, which was established in the spring of 1896 for the manufacture of steel and brass tubing, and which has developed into one of the largest and most successful manufacturing concerns of the kind in the country. The employees in their factory at Harrison number about two hundred and thirty-five, and they turn out a superior quality of steel and brass tubing which finds a ready sale throughout the United States.

Mr. Close is an independent Republican, but has never taken an active part in political affairs, his business demanding his entire attention. Though a young man he has achieved success and holds a high place among the leading manufacturers of Hudson County. He resides, however, in Newark, N. J., and is a member of the Masonic order, of the North End Club, and of the Park Side Angling Club, all of that city.

He married Miss Mary Frank Hayward, of Waterbury, Conn., and has two children: Helen Hayward Close and Margaret Moore Close.

OSCAR SANDFORD, father of Mrs. Peter Brandt (see page 431), was born in Kearny, N. J., January 19, 1820. His father, David, was born on the old Sandford homestead at Passaic, N. J., and in his earlier days was a carman in New York City, where he had a large number of men in his employ. He married Calista Brown. Michael Sandford, father of David, was one of the largest landowners and wealthiest men in his section, and at one time owned a number of slaves. He married Jennie Sandford.

Oscar Sandford was educated in Newark, N. J., and in New York City, and during his early life was engaged in the butchering business. Subsequently he followed the japanning trade in Newark, where he also had a livery stable. Later he was the proprietor of the old Halfway House in Kearny, Hudson County. He was a Democrat in politics, a member of the Methodist Episcopal Church, and widely esteemed as a man of integrity, honor, and enterprise. He was successful in all he attempted. As a marksman he was especially noted, being the champion shot of America at the time of his death. He was killed by a Pennsylvania Railroad train in Jersey City, while returning from a business trip to New York, April 20, 1868.

He was married in Newark, N. J., to Catherine B. Easton, a native of Edinboro, Scotland, and had nine children: John, Mary Emma (Mrs. Peter Brandt), Henrietta, Delia, Oscar, Amanda, Oscar (2d), Fitz, and Allan.

LORENZO WOOD, JR., of Kearny, Hudson County, was born in Brooklyn, N. Y., on the 17th of March, 1868. He is the son of Lorenzo D. C. Wood and Mary E. Mahar, natives of that city. There he received his education in the public schools.

After leaving school, equipped with the knowledge which fitted him for the practical duties of life, Mr. Wood engaged in the sugar business, and for several years has held a responsible position with the American Sugar Refining Company of New York City. He resides in Newark, N. J., where he has wielded no small influence in promoting the general welfare and in shaping local affairs. Though never aspiring to public office, he is deeply and actively interested in the prosperity of the town, and liberally encourages all worthy objects. He married Miss Bertha A. Horstmann.

PETER BRANDT, who for many years has been successfully engaged in the ice business in Harrison, N. J., was born in Philadelphia, Pa., on the 22d of November, 1848. His parents, George Brandt, a native of France, and Sarah Kountz, a native of Germany, came to this country when young and first settled in Philadelphia, where they were married. George Brandt was a cavalryman in the Mexican War, sustaining a broken leg and receiving an honorable discharge. He also served in the War of the Rebellion with bravery and distinction. For five years he was official court interpreter in New York. He spoke seven languages—French, German, English, Spanish, Italian, Danish, and Portuguese.

When Peter Brandt was an infant his parents removed to New York City, and there he received a thorough public school education. After completing his studies and gaining such practical experience in life as a boy usually acquires he engaged in the horse business, which he successfully conducted in New York City for several years. In 1860 he removed to Harrison, Hudson County, and since then has been actively and successfully engaged in the ice trade, becoming one of the most prominent factors in that industry in his section.

PETER BRANDT.

Mr. Brandt is a public spirited, energetic, and patriotic citizen, a man of great enterprise and executive ability, and highly esteemed and respected by all who know him. His honesty of purpose and fair dealing have won for him the confidence of the entire community. In politics he is a Democrat and deeply interested in the affairs of his party and town.

On the 10th of August, 1865, Mr. Brandt married Mary Emma Sandford, a descendant of one of the oldest and most distinguished families in New Jersey, and a native of Harrison, Hudson County. Of their ten children four are living, namely: John Dunham, Jane Sanford, George Washington, and Peter Oscar.

CONRAD BICKHARD, only son of Henry and Maria (Stermer) Bickhard, was born in Hesse, Germany, October 12, 1820. In his youth and early manhood he received a thorough industrial training, especially in the line of woodworking, and for several years he made spinning wheels and weavers' looms. He was a natural mechanic, endowed with great artistic skill, and became an expert in all branches of carpentering and cabinet work. His tastes inclined toward the finest workmanship, and even to fine carving, many examples of which are still extant. His grandfather was on a visit to America at the time the Declaration of Independence was signed.

In 1848 Mr. Bickhard left the Fatherland for America, and in New York City, where he lived for about six years, engaged in carpentering and cabinetmaking. In 1853 he became one of the pioneers of what is now West New York, Hudson County, N. J. The story of his settlement there is interesting. He was obliged to cut his way through the woods almost from the ferry to a point about five miles northwest, and on the spot where his widow now resides erected a rude house, which his family occupied until he could build a more comfortable home. His nearest neighbor was more than two miles distant. All around him were forests, yet out of these he carved his home, and lived to see the timber cleared away, houses spring up, and a village grow into activity. Here he followed the trade of carpenter with success, and occasionally gratified his finer instincts by making pieces of household furniture, many of which are still prized for their elegance as well as for their associations. He received a premium for good scholarship in architecture.

Mr. Bickhard served seven months as a member of a New Jersey regiment in the Civil War, being honorably discharged on account of illness. An ardent Republican, he was for many years a School Trustee and District Clerk, and was one of the first five members and founders of the German Reformed Church of the Town of Union. He was also a member of the Harugari, of the old "Seven Wise Men," and of the original fire department in West New York. Mr. Bickhard always took an active interest in the growth and prosperity of his town, was prominent in every movement designed to advance its welfare, and was highly respected by all who knew him. He died October 15, 1875.

He was married in September, 1846, to Catherine, daughter of John and Elizabeth (Mabes) Arnold, of Hesse, Germany, where she was born April 30, 1825. She survives him and resides in the family homestead in West New York which he built. They had nine children, one of whom, Henry Bickhard, enlisted in the United States regular army. Four are living, viz.: Amelia (Mrs. Scommodau), Matilda (Mrs. Lurcott), Charles, and Mary.

HENRY W. SOLFLEISCH, of Homestead, North Bergen, Hudson County, was born in New York City on the 10th of April, 1869, the son of Adam Solfleisch and Margaret Berner. His parents were born in Germany. His father served as a Captain in the German Army, and after coming to this country was a soldier in the Union Army during the War of the Rebellion.

Mr. Solfleisch obtained his education in the New York public schools and then learned the trade of engraving and printing, mastering every branch and becoming an expert. At the age of twenty-one he started in business for himself, and now has, at No. 143 Fulton Street, New York, one of the largest steel and copper engraving and printing plants in the country. His success is the result of his own efforts, properly and judiciously applied, and from a modest beginning he has built up an extensive business.

He has taken an active part in the affairs of North Bergen, and for three years served as a School Trustee of the township. He is a member of the Foresters of America, and as a citizen is public spirited, enterprising, and patriotic. In 1893 he married Miss Elise Kaestner. They have four children.

LOUIS KIESEWETTER, of Secaucus, N. J., is one of the active leaders of the Democratic party in Hudson County. His first vote was cast for General George B. McClelland, the Democratic candidate for President of the United States in 1864, and he has been a consistent Democrat from that time to the present. He was a Freeholder of Hudson County in 1879 and 1880. He has been a member of the Democratic County Committee of Hudson County for many years, and is Chairman of the Democratic Executive Committee of Secaucus.

Mr. Kiesewetter was born in Germany, October 8, 1845, the son of August and Caroline Kiesewetter. In 1846 he was brought to America by his parents. The family settled originally at Greenville, Jersey City, subsequently residing in Hoboken, where August Kiesewetter died in 1883. Mr. Kiesewetter's mother still resides there. He was educated in the public schools of Hoboken, subsequently learning the trade of a butcher, which he has followed since. In 1870 he engaged in business on his own account in Hoboken. Since 1880 he has been a resident of Secaucus. In addition to his regular business he has also speculated largely and successfully in real estate. In the Civil War he served in the Union Army, enlisting in 1862 in Colonel Howard's Marine Artillery. He was subsequently transferred to the Ninety-eighth Regiment, New York Volunteers, with which he served two years and two months. He then entered the Quartermaster's Department and was transferred to Folly Island. He participated in the bombardment of Fort Sumter and in various other engagements, and in 1864 was mustered out of the service. He is a member of the Knights of

LOUIS KIESEWETTER.

Honor, the Ancient Order of Redmen, and the O. D. H. F. Benevolent Society.

He married Francesca Bornawetz, of Hoboken, by whom he has five children, who are living: Ernest, Frank, Otto, Carrie, and Louis.

JAMES EDWIN HULSHIZER, JR., Secretary and Treasurer of the New Jersey Title Guarantee and Trust Company, of Jersey City, was born in Broadway, Warren County, N. J., on the 7th of August, 1869. His father, James Edwin Hulshizer, Sr., one of the most prominent members of the New York Produce Exchange and a leading citizen of Jersey City, died May 15, 1900, in his sixtieth year.

Mr. Hulshizer received his preparatory education at Hasbrouck Institute in Jersey City, graduating from that institution in 1886. He then entered Columbia College, New York City, and was graduated therefrom in the class of 1890, receiving the degree of Bachelor of Arts. While a student at college he gained during vacations considerable experience in business and financial affairs in the employ of the Provident Institution for Savings in Jersey City and in the office of Logan, Cowl & Co., grain brokers and members of the New York Produce Exchange. After leaving college Mr. Hulshizer entered the employ of the New Jersey Title Guarantee and Trust Company, of Jersey City, as a clerk, and steadily rose step by step to the position of Secretary and Treasurer, which he is now filling with acknowledged ability. He is an able business man, a public spirited and enterprising citizen, deeply interested in the welfare of the community, and prominently identified with the affairs of the city and county. His broad and accurate knowledge of real estate titles is well known. He is a member of the Palma and Carteret Clubs of Jersey City.

JAMES E. HULSHIZER, JR.

Mr. Hulshizer married a daughter of William Martin, of Jersey City, and resides there at 78 Madison Avenue.

WILLIAM H. SCHMIDT, one of the substantial citizens of Hudson County, N. J., has been a resident of West New York, in that county, since 1869. From 1873 to 1894 he was actively engaged in the wholesale ice business. In 1894 his extensive plant was destroyed by a cyclone, but he rebuilt on a larger scale. In 1898 he built the well known Schmidt's hygiene ice factory on Harrison Street, near the Hudson Boulevard, in West New York, of which he and his youngest son are sole owners, the firm name being William H. & E. H. Schmidt.

Mr. Schmidt is one of the most extensive property owners in Northern Hudson County. As a Democrat in politics he has been active in public life. For a period of twelve years he was Chairman of the Township Committee, and in this capacity distinguished himself by the display of rare executive ability. For ten years he was also a Justice of the Peace. For six years he was a member of the School Board of West New York. He has also served as Treasurer of the township, having held this responsible position for more than four years. He enjoys the confidence of the community and has established a reputation for integrity and soundness of judgment.

Mr. Schmidt was born in Germany, May 5, 1834, the son of Bernard and Margaret Schmidt, and received his education in that country. In 1851 he came to America, settling originally in New York City. There he resided during the next eighteen years. In 1853 he engaged in the real estate business, and was also connected with a manufacturing enterprise. In 1857 he enlisted in the Fifty-fifth Regiment, National Guard of the State of New York, and when the Civil War broke out, in 1861, he volunteered with his regiment for service in the cause of the Union and went to the front. He saw active service throughout the Peninsular campaign, including participation in the fierce seven days' fight in the Wilderness. On account of disability received in service he was honorably mustered out in 1863. Since the war he has taken an active interest in the Grand Army of the Republic, and is a member of Ellsworth Post, No. 14, of New Jersey.

Returning to New York at the close of his period of service in the Union Army, Mr. Schmidt found that his business interests had practically slipped from his grasp during his absence. But he soon established another successful business, as the proprietor of a woodcarving establishment for the manufacture of piano frames. Meantime, he had acquired real estate holdings in West New York, Hudson County, and thither he removed in 1869. He has since taken great interest in everything affecting the public welfare of West New York and Hudson County.

CHARLES A. HEINS, the well known wholesale dairy produce dealer of West Hoboken, N. J., is the son of Diederick and Johanna Heins and was born in Germany, June 20, 1865. He obtained his education at Bremen, in the Fatherland, and early developed traits of industry, economy, and enterprise which have won for him success in business and private life. Leaving his native country in 1883, he came to New York and engaged as clerk in a grocery store. Subsequently he associated himself with A. R. Reynolds & Co., one of New York's largest cheese firms, and the experience thus gained has served him well ever since.

About 1890 Mr. Heins established his present business at 169 Spring Street, West Hoboken, and through his energy, integrity, and sound judgment, united with great tact, has built up an extensive trade as a wholesale dealer in cheese, butter, and all kinds of dairy produce. Beginning on a small scale, he has enlarged his establishment and improved his facilities until now he has one of the largest and best appointed wholesale houses of the kind in East Jersey.

In politics Mr. Heins is a stanch Republican, but his attention has been devoted to business, to the exclusion of public preferment or political honors. He is a prominent member of the West Hoboken Business Men's Association, of the Schuetzen Association of New Jersey, and of the Odd Fellows. He is a public spirited, patriotic citizen, and enjoys the confidence of all who know him.

Mr. Heins married Miss Lotta Mohr, and has three children: Charles, Lotta, and Florence.

THOMAS HENRY, contractor, truckman, and dealer in masons' supplies, of the Town of Union, N. J., is the son of Thomas Henry, Sr., and Mary Smith, both natives of Ireland. His father came to this country about 1850, settling first in New York City, and subsequently moving to the Town of Union, where he died in 1887.

Mr. Henry was born in the Town of Union, Hudson County, November 28, 1861, and obtained his education there in the public schools. After completing his studies Mr. Henry identified himself with the trucking business, first as an employee and in 1887 as proprietor, and by enterprise, industry, and practical application has gained an honorable standing. In 1887 he engaged in trade as a dealer in masons' building materials, fire clay, coal, drain pipe, etc., on the corner of Palisade Avenue and Gardner Street, the firm name being William D. & T. Henry. They also did a general trucking business. William D. Henry, brother of Thomas and senior partner of the firm, died April 9, 1897, and since then Thomas Henry has conducted the business alone.

Mr. Henry is one of the best known business men in North Hudson County. Enterprising, energetic, and thorough, he has been successful, and through his integrity and force of character has achieved a high reputation. He has also been prominent in public capacities, having served as a Councilman of the Town of Union for four years from May 1, 1895, to May 1, 1899. During three years of that period he was the only Republican on the board and the only candidate elected on the local Republican ticket. This fact attests the esteem and confidence in which he is held by his fellow-citizens. Mr. Henry is a member of the Business Men's Association of the Town of Union, of the Knights of Honor, and of Garfield Council, Jr. O. U. A. M.

He was married on the 27th of March, 1888, to Miss Mary Brems, daughter of Michael Brems, of the Town of Union, N. J. They have one daughter, Clara Henry, and reside in the Town of Union.

ADOLPH WILLIAM WEISMANN, son of August Weismann, was born in Germany, and about 1840 came to this country with his parents, settling in New York City. His father was engaged in the cigar business in New York until 1874, when he retired and moved to what was then Lossburg, in West Hoboken, N. J., where he died in 1895.

Mr. Weismann was for many years associated with his uncle, August W. Weismann, one of the earliest druggists and chemists in New York City, his store being on the corner of Broome and Orchard Streets. In 1874 he engaged in the drug trade on his own account in West Hoboken, where he died in March, 1896, highly respected and esteemed. He was a man of considerable prominence in the community, of great force of character, and of unquestioned honesty and integrity, and always took a deep interest in public affairs. His attention, however, was given wholly to business, in which he was successful.

He married Anna Meyers, daughter of William Meyers, who died in 1888, leaving three sons and one daughter, viz.: Ferdinand, Adolph, David, and Louisa.

FERDINAND WEISMANN, eldest son of Adolph William Weismann and Anna Meyers and a grandson of August Weismann and William Mey-

FERDINAND WEISMANN.

ers, was born in West Hoboken, N. J., June 1, 1874. He was educated in the West Hoboken and Union Hill public and high schools, graduating from the latter in 1891. In the same year he passed the examination before the New Jersey State Board of Pharmacy. Entering his father's drug store at a very early age, he grew up in the business and acquired a practical knowledge of every branch, and in 1894 succeeded his father under the firm name of F. Weismann & Brother, his partner being his oldest brother, Adolph. This copartnership still continues, with two stores: one at 166 Bergenline Avenue in the Town of Union and another at 485 Palisade Avenue in West Hoboken. They have been very successful and maintain an extensive trade.

Mr. Weismann is an ardent Democrat, and since 1896 has been Deputy Register of Deaths for Hudson County. He is also a Notary Public, a member and clerk of the Board of Education, and a member of the Junior Order United American Mechanics, of the Benevolent and Protective Order of Elks, of the Knights of Pythias, and of the Hamilton Wheelmen.

He was married, October 20, 1891, to Tillie Willis Larwill, daughters of John and Matilda Larwill, of Hoboken, N. J. They have two daughters: Edna and Viola Mae.

ADOLPH WEISMANN, second son of Adolph William Weismann and Anna Meyers, was born in West Hoboken, N. J., October 14, 1877. He was graduated from the high school of his native town in 1894, and the same year formed a copartnership with his elder brother, Ferdinand, and engaged in the drug business in the Town of Union and later also in West Hoboken, the firm being F. Weismann & Brother. He passed his examination before the New Jersey State Board of Pharmacy in 1898.

He is a member of the Masonic fraternity, of the Junior Order United American Mechanics, of the Knights of the Maccabees, and of the Hamilton Wheelmen. November 26, 1898, he married Miss Clara Pritchard, of Utica, N. Y.

JOHN OETJEN, one of the oldest German citizens of West New York, N. J., is the son of John and Anna Oetjen, and was born in Hanover, Germany, December 5, 1837. Educated in the public schools of the Fatherland, he learned the trade of carpenter, but later went to London, England, where he engaged in the manufacture of loaf-sugar. In 1861 he came to America and established himself in the same business on the corner of King and Greenwich Streets, New York, where he remained two years, building up a successful trade. In 1863 he removed to what is now West New York, Hudson County, which has ever since been his home.

During the first two years of his residence in West New York he was engaged in distilling and rectifying liquors. Afterward he was long engaged in the wholesale and retail liquor business, retiring in 1894. Mr. Oetjen has always been noted as a man of integrity, industry, and enterprise. Taking from the first a deep interest in local affairs, he was for eighteen years a School Trustee, serving several terms as Chairman of the board, and during one-half of the time acting as District Clerk. He was also for three years a Township Committeeman. In politics he is a Democrat. He has built several houses in West New York, thus contributing to the material growth of the town, and was a member of the old and unique order known as the "Seven Wise Men." He has also been active in other organizations.

Mr. Oetjen was married in New York City in May, 1870, to Miss Mary Hulse, a native of Germany. They have one son, John F. Oetjen, a carpenter, of West New York.

JOHN WHITE has been a life-long resident of North Hudson County, N. J., having been born in the Town of Union on the 22d of January, 1849. His parents, Michael White and Mary McGrane, natives of Ireland, were married in that country and came to the United States in 1848. They took up their residence on Union Hill, where Mrs. White still lives. Michael

White died there in 1863, respected and esteemed for those manly virtues which characterized all his relations.

Mr. White obtained a good public school education in the Town of Union, and as a youth developed strong intellectual and physical qualities. Learning the carpenter's trade, he engaged in business for himself about 1878 as a contractor and builder, and since then has continued in that occupation with signal success. On Union Hill and in West Hoboken, where he now resides, he has contributed to the general growth and prosperity, and many of the finest dwellings and other buildings are the result of his energies. He has built up an extensive business. His ability and enterprise, his integrity and sound judgment, and his sagacity and foresight have won for him a wide popularity, and the respect and confidence of the entire community. He is one of the prominent citizens of North Hudson County, and from boyhood has been active and influential in behalf of the best interests of the public.

In politics Mr. White is a Democrat, and at different times has served as Commissioner of Assessments. For three years he was a member of Company B, Fourth Regiment, N. G. N. J. He is a leading member of the Holy Name Society of St. Michael's Monastery, of West Hoboken, and has been identified with other important social bodies.

Mr. White was married in July, 1881, to Miss Jane Hogan, daughter of John Hogan, of Jersey City Heights, N. J. They have six children: Mary, Jennie, Nellie, James, Joseph, and Addie.

FREDERICK J. BERGMANN, Jr., of Weehawken, is the son of Frederick J. Bergmann, Sr., and Gertrude Zeigeler, and a grandson of John Bergmann, all natives of Germany, his father being born in Bavaria and his mother in Frankfort. The revolutionary events of 1848 drove his parents, with a large number of other German patriots, to America, to seek the home and freedom which the Fatherland denied them. Arriving in the United States in that year, they settled on Staten Island, N. Y., where the subject of this sketch was born May 5, 1870. Soon afterward they removed to Weehawken, N. J.

Here Mr. Bergmann has since resided. Obtaining his education in the Weehawken public schools, he learned the trade of painter and decorator, which he still follows in that town, having established himself in business in 1891. He is one of the leading painters and decorators in North Hudson County, and by industry, perseverance, and honest endeavor has achieved success. His work bears evidence of artistic taste and originality.

While devoting himself assiduously to his profession Mr. Bergmann has not neglected the duties of a public spirited, patriotic citizen, but has served his town in various capacities. For three years he was a member of the Weehawken Board of Education and rendered efficient service. As a member of the Fire Department he has also contributed materially to the progress of the town. He is a member of the Odd Fellows fraternity, of the Foresters of America, and of the Weehawken Cyclers. In politics he is a Republican and in religion a Presbyterian, and throughout the community is highly respected and esteemed.

Mr. Bergmann married Miss Augusta Kleinker. They have one daughter, and reside on the corner of Hudson Avenue and Angelique Street, Weehawken Heights.

JOSEPH ALOYSIUS McCURNIN, now serving a second term as a member of the Board of Aldermen of Bayonne, Hudson County, was born in

Ireland on the 1st of July, 1859, his parents being John McCurnin and Jane McDonald. The family came to the United States in 1866 and settled in Jersey City, where the subject of this sketch received his education in St. Mary's Catholic Institute.

After leaving school Mr. McCurnin entered the employ of the American Standard Paper Company, where he acquired the rudiments of a business training. Afterward he became interested in a commission business in Washington Market, New York City. Leaving this, he associated himself with the Standard Oil Company, and is now foreman of their extensive refinery at Bayonne, N. J. Mr. McCurnin is a man of great force of character,

JOSEPH A. McCURNIN.

endowed with executive ability of a high order, and in every position has achieved honor and distinction.

He has also been prominent in public affairs. As a Democrat he has taken an active interest in politics, and for five years rendered efficent service as a member of the Board of School Trustees of Bayonne. He is now serving his second term as an Alderman of that city. He is a member of the Royal Arcanum, of the Foresters of America, of the Benevolent and Protective Order of Elks, and of the Knights of Columbus.

In 1885 Mr. McCurnin married Miss Mary Burns, of Bayonne, N. J. They have seven children: James, Annie, John, Joseph, Vera, William, and Jane.

THOMAS A. CARBREY has always resided in Harrison, Hudson County, N. J., where he was born April 25, 1869. He is the son of Michael and Ellen (Leonard) Carbrey, natives of Ireland, who came to America when young, were married here, and settled in Harrison.

Mr. Carbrey received a good educational training in the public schools of his native town, and has spent his active life in the wire business, in which he has already achieved marked success. He has also taken an active and prominent part in politics, and as a member of the Harrison Board of Education has rendered efficient service to the town. He is an ardent and consistent Democrat and a public spirited, patriotic, and enterprising citizen. His popularity and reputation are indicated by the fact that he has served as President of the American Wire Weavers' Association.

THOMAS CARROLL, Clerk of the Township of Weehawken since April, 1891, was born in Hoboken, N. J., May 1, 1867. His parents, Patrick Carroll and Johanna Sullivan, and his grandparents, Philip and Mary Carroll, were natives of Ireland, his father being born in Tipperary and his mother in Cork. Philip Carroll came to America with his family soon after 1850 and settled in Princeton, N. J., where he operated a large stone quarry, and where he and his wife spent the remainder of their lives. Patrick Carroll learned the carpenter's trade in New Brunswick, and about 1862 removed to Hoboken, where he had charge of the Hoboken Land Improvement Company's saw-mill for about twenty-eight years. Afterward he moved to Weehawken and died there in April, 1890, being survived by his wife and several children, of whom Thomas is the eldest living son. He was a Commissioner of Appeals for three terms, a member of the Hoboken Ferrymen's Association, and a prominent, active, and influential citizen.

Thomas Carroll was educated at St. Mary's parochial school and the Christian Brothers' school in his native city, and at the age of fifteen entered the employ of the Standard Oil Company, with which he remained about three years. Subsequently he learned the plumbing trade with J. H. Kniffin, of Hoboken, and for more than six years he followed that business with marked success, having an establishment of his own during a part of that period.

In the meantime Mr. Carroll became an acknowledged leader of the Republican forces in Weehawken, taking an active part in local politics and being honored by his party with several positions of trust. Under the old law he was Police Clerk of Weehawken for six years, and in April, 1891, he was elected Township Clerk. The duties of this position, which he has discharged with ability and satisfaction, led him to relinquish temporarily the business of plumber and gas fitter, in order to devote to it his attention and energies.

Mr. Carroll was one of the organizers in 1890 of the old Weehawken Athletic Club, of which he was Secretary. He is an exempt member of Baldwin Hose Company No. 1, of Weehawken, which he served as Secretary for six years. He was a member and Secretary of the old West Side Social Club, and is a member of Glendlaugh Council, No. 214, C. B. L. He is a public spirited, progressive citizen and active in promoting the best interests of his town and county. He is unmarried, and resides with his mother in the family homestead at 14 West Nineteenth Street, Weehawken.

LOUIS C. NEUSCHELER, Collector of Taxes of the Town of Union, Hudson County, N. J., has been a life-long resident of that place, having been born there on the 28th of September, 1867. He is the son of George and Eliza (Wicks) Neuscheler. His father, Captain George Neuscheler, Jr., was for some time Town Clerk of the Town of Union, First Lieutenant in the Fifteenth Regiment, United States Heavy Artillery, and Captain of Company B, Ninth Regiment, New Jersey National Guard, which regiment he organized. He died in 1873, after an active and useful life, respected by all who knew him.

Louis C. Neuscheler's birthplace and early home was on Palisade Avenue in the Town of Union. He received his education in the public schools

LOUIS C. NEUSCHELER.

of the neighborhood, and then became a bookkeeper, a profession he has since followed. His interest in politics and public affairs was manifest even during his youth, and has continued to be one of his chief characteristics. He became a Notary Public and subsequently Collector of Arrears, and is now (1900) the efficient Collector of Taxes of the Town of Union. In these capacities he has displayed marked ability, sound judgment, and great sagacity—qualities which invariably lead to higher honors. Public spirited, progressive, and thoroughly identified with the best interests of his native town, he enjoys the confidence and esteem of the entire community, and as a member of the John J. Egan Association he is prominent and active in politics. He is a member of the Republican Association of the Town of Union, of the Mutual Benefit Association, of the Hamilton Wheelmen, and of the New Jersey Building, Loan and Investment Company. He is unmarried.

EDWARD A. O'CALLAGHAN is one of the rising young lawyers of Jersey City, N. J., where he was born on the 11th of November, 1874. His father, Thomas C. O'Callaghan, was born in Ireland in 1845, and his mother, Ellen Carey, in Quebec, Canada.

Mr. O'Callaghan received an excellent preparatory education and then entered Manhattan College, from which he was graduated with the degree of B.A. in 1895. He received the degree of LL.B. from the New York Law School in 1897 and was admitted to the New Jersey bar in the same year at the February term of the Supreme Court. He is also a member of the bar of New York State. Settling in Jersey City, Mr. O'Callaghan entered upon the active practice of his profession early in 1897. He has steadily gained influence and standing at the bar and among his younger associates already holds a prominent place. He is a member of Jersey City Lodge, No. 211, Benevolent and Protective Order of Elks. His wife, whose maiden name was Charlotte Aherne, is a native of Queenstown, Ireland.

GEORGE WYRILL, of Harrison, N. J., one of the leading citizens of Hudson County, was born in York, England, on the 14th of December, 1865. He is the son of Robert Thomas Wyrill and Sarah Thomas, both of whom were born in England.

Mr. Wyrill received his education in the public schools of his native town, and in 1882 came to the United States. Locating in Newark, N. J., he soon afterward moved to Harrison, Hudson County, and engaged in the ice business, which he still follows with marked success. He is one of the representative business men of Hudson County.

While Mr. Wyrill has devoted his energies and attention strictly to business affairs, he has at the same time taken a deep interest in the questions of the day, and especially in matters affecting the progress and welfare of his adopted town. He is thoroughly identified with the public and political affairs of the Borough of Harrison, a prominent member of the Democratic party, and a liberal contributor to every movement which has for its object the advancement and betterment of his fellowmen. He is a member of the Knights of Pythias and of the Methodist Episcopal Church, and a public spirited, enterprising, and patriotic citizen.

Mr. Wyrill was married on the 24th of November, 1898, to Miss Jennie Porter, of Harrison, N. J.

JOHN NEVIN, A.M., M.D., is one of the prominent physicians and surgeons of Jersey City, N. J., where he was born on the 21st of September, 1863. He is the son of Michael Nevin and Frances Carey, who were for many years honored and respected residents of that municipality.

Dr. Nevin received his preliminary education in the Catholic Institute of Jersey City. Subsequently he entered Manhattan College in New York City and was graduated from there in the class of 1882, receiving the degrees of A.B. and A.M. Deciding upon medicine as his life work, he became a student in 1883 in the Medical Department of the University of the City of New York and after the regular course was graduated from that institution with the degree of M.D. in 1886.

In March, 1886, Dr. Nevin began the practice of medicine in Jersey City, where he soon came into prominence as a physician and surgeon of unusual ability, and where he has ever since conducted a large and successful business. Displaying broad and liberal qualifications, a thorough mastery of the science of medicine, and sound judgment united with a genial good nature, he has gained a wide circle of friends and an enviable standing in the community. Among the younger practitioners of the profession he is an acknowledged leader. As a citizen he is public spirited, progressive, patriotic, and universally esteemed and respected.

Dr. Nevin has filled a number of important positions with ability and

JOHN NEVIN.

satisfaction. In 1892 he was appointed surgeon to the Jersey City Fire Department, which position he resigned. In November, 1896, he was appointed surgeon of the Police Department of Jersey City and has ever since held that position. He is the Medical Director of the Colonial Life Insurance Company of America, a prominent member of the Hudson County Medical Society, and a member of the Medical Society of the State of New Jersey and of the University and Carteret Clubs of Jersey City.

In October, 1887, Dr. Nevin married Nellie Doherty, and they have had two children: Grace Nevin (deceased) and John Nevin, Jr.

WALTER A. WALSH, formerly President of the School Board and Common Council of Kearny, Hudson County, was born in Newark, N. J., June 9, 1850. When five years old he went with his parents, Michael and Rachel (McCarell) Walsh, to Ohio, but returned at the age of fourteen and received a common school education in his native city. His parents were born in Ireland, and in 1848 came to Newark, where they were married in 1849.

Mr. Walsh was successively engaged in the manufacture of buttons, in wood turning and manufacturing moldings, etc., in baking, and in the manufacture of buttons and jewelry, achieving in each business enterprise that degree of success which ability, sound judgment, and faithful attention to detail invariably merit. He also obtained in these connections a valuable experience and a high reputation. In 1891 he engaged in the liquor and hotel business in Kearny, Hudson County, in which he still continues.

In public and political life Mr. Walsh has filled several important trusts. He was a member one year and President two years of the Borough of East Newark Common Council, and has also served as President of the Borough of East Newark School Board. In every capacity he has discharged his duties with ability, fidelity, and satisfaction. He is a member of the Catholic Benevolent Legion, of the Exempt Firemen's Association, and of other social bodies. He married Miss Mary Kenney.

HENRY STOCKFISH, JR., Township Treasurer and an organizer and the first Chief Engineer of the Fire Department of North Bergen, Hudson County, is the eldest son of Henry Stockfish, Sr., and Mary Danker, and was born in West Hoboken, N. J., June 24, 1857. Henry Stockfish, Sr., came from Germany to the United States in 1847, and in 1854 married Mary Danker, by whom he had seven children: Margaret, wife of C. H. Kopf; Henry, Jr., the subject of this sketch; Louisa, wife of John Brady, of West Hoboken; Mary, wife of John Hoffsetter, of North Bergen; Eleanor, widow of John Dahm; Emily, deceased, who married George Schell; and George F., of North Bergen. Mr. Stockfish moved to Secaucus in 1862 and remained there five years, when he settled with his family in the old homestead on the Weavertown road, now the Hudson County Boulevard. He was one of the pioneer retail milk dealers in North Hudson County, a prominent man in the community, and a leading and consistent Democrat. He died in 1898, aged about seventy years. His wife's death occurred in 1890, at about the age of fifty-nine.

Henry Stockfish, Jr., attended the public schools of North Bergen and Packard's Business College in New York, and after completing his studies in 1875 spent ten years assisting his father in business. Afterward he was engaged for about four years in the grocery trade. In 1891 he established himself in business as a retail milk dealer, and by industry and application has built up one of the largest businesses of the kind in North Hudson County.

In politics Mr. Stockfish has been for years a leading Democrat, and in the councils of his party has been very active and influential. He was elected Collector for North Bergen in 1884, and by re-elections held that office for eleven consecutive years, discharging his duties with ability, fidelity, and satisfaction. In 1886 he was also elected a member of the North Bergen Board of Education for three years, and in 1897 he was appointed Treasurer of the Township of North Bergen, which office he still holds. In 1890 he was one of the principal organizers of the North Bergen Fire Department, of which he became the first Chief Engineer, and in which he has ever since taken a deep and active interest. He was also for one year a Justice of the Peace, and is a member of Pioneer Engine Company and of the Foresters of America. Public spirited and enterprising, he is esteemed and respected, and in every capacity has won the confidence of the community.

Mr. Stockfish married Miss Katherine Brown, daughter of Joseph Brown, and has four children: Marie, Lulu, Mabel, and Florence.

JOHN McAULEY, one of the oldest painters and decorators of West Hoboken, N. J., was born in that town on the 19th of December, 1855, the

JOHN McAULEY.

son of John and Helen McAuley, natives of Ireland. There he received his education, attending the public and parochial schools. After completing his studies he learned the trade of a painter, which he has since followed, being in business for himself during the last twenty years.

Mr. McAuley possesses great skill and talent, and in the prosecution of his trade has been successful. In politics he has always been an ardent and active Democrat, taking a prominent part in the councils of his party, and becoming one of its trusted and honored leaders. On August 5, 1898, he was appointed Chief of Police of West Hoboken, which position he now holds. He is a public spirited citizen, and is held in high esteem by the entire community. He has won the confidence and respect of all with whom he has come into contact.

He married Mary Tyndel, daughter of Michael and Margaret Tyndel, and resides where he was born, in West Hoboken, Hudson County.

CHARLES SCHULTZE, member of the Common Council from the Second Ward of Hoboken, N. J., was born in that city on the 4th of April, 1859, and is the son of Emil (who died December 3, 1899) and Anna Schultze, both of German descent. Mr. Schultze received his early education at Hoboken Academy, and subsequently studied for two years at Lausanne, Switzerland. He was for several years engaged in the wine business in Europe, chiefly at Crenznach, Germany, at Rheims, Paris, Bordeaux, and Cognac, France, and in London, England. In this connection he obtained a wide and varied experience as a wine expert and established a reputation which he has ever since maintained. Returning to this country, he identified himself with the same business and at the present time is associated with John Osborn & Co., importers, of No. 20 South William Street, New York City.

Mr. Schultze has achieved success in both business and public capacities. As a resident of his native city he has taken an active part in political affairs, has been prominent in various important relations, and in 1898 was elected Councilman from the Second Ward, which position he still holds. He is a public spirited, patriotic, and enterprising citizen and justly esteemed and respected for those qualities which distinguish his race. In fraternal and social circles he is especially prominent. He is a member of the German Club, of the German Riding Club, of the Valencia Boat Club, of the Royal Arcanum, of the Benevolent and Protective Order of Elks, of the Quartette Club, and of the Lutheran Church of Hoboken.

Mr. Schultze was married in 1883 and is the father of four children— three sons and one daughter.

BARTHOLOMEW FITZGERALD, of West Hoboken, Hudson County, N. J., is now living in retirement from active business life after a successful and honorable career. He is recognized as one of the most substantial and influential citizens in the community. A Democrat in politics, he is a leader in that party. Both in his business career and in his political activities he has always exhibited sound judgment, based upon keen observation of men and things, and has never failed to manifest the courage of his convictions. His personal, business, and political integrity has never been questioned. For six years he held the responsible position of a member and Chairman of the Common Council of West Hoboken, and in this office of trust showed a determination to carefully look out for the best interests of the community.

Mr. Fitzgerald was born near Killeagh, County Cork, Ireland, May 14, 1842, the son of John and Mary Fitzgerald. He is a descendant of the famous Fitzgerald family which for many centuries has occupied so prominent and patriotic a place in the history of Ireland and of her struggles against oppression. The Fitzgeralds were of Norman descent, but, having become established in Ireland, they intermarried with the Irish nobility, and so completely made the cause of Ireland their own that it became a proverb that the Fitzgeralds were more Irish than the Irish themselves.

Mr. Fitzgerald inherited many of the sterling qualities of his ancestors. He was educated in the schools near his birthplace, and in 1862 came to America. During a year or more after his arrival in this country he resided in New York City, but since 1863 he has been a resident of Hudson County, N. J. He engaged in business as a builder and contractor, both in New York City and Hudson County, and for many years conducted a very successful business. He accumulated a fortune.

He married Mary E. Gilligan, by whom he has seven children: Dr. Thomas Fitzgerald, a physician in Jersey City; Henry Fitzgerald, who is engaged in the marble business; and Mollie, John, Morris, Fannie, and Florence Fitzgerald.

JAMES D. FINK, of Hackensack, was born in Orange County, N. Y., March 24, 1833. He is the son of Hamilton Fink and Delia, daughter of James Duryea, and a grandson of Philip Fink, his paternal ancestors having come originally from Germany. Up to about the age of thirteen he attended school in Orange County, and then became a clerk in a grocery store in the City of New York. He continued in this employ for eight years, and during the next eight years he was the cashier of a New York hotel.

In 1871 Mr. Fink engaged in the express business, and since that date has been the proprietor of an express between New York City and Hackensack, Bergen County, N. J. He has long been a resident of the last mentioned place, and is a member of the Hackensack Baptist Church. He married, in 1858, Barbara W. Bogert, by whom he had two children, Harry D. and William M. Fink. She died in 1878, and in 1885 he married Kate M. Seinsoth.

ANDREW GIRSHAM, Postmaster of Guttenberg and a veteran of the Civil War, was born in the South of Ireland on the 22d of April, 1839. He is the fourth in the family of seven children of Andrew Girsham, Sr., a native of Edinburgh, Scotland, and Tomasiana Metlan, his wife, who was born in Ireland, and a grandson of David Girsham and Elizabeth Driscoll. His parents came to this country about 1850 and settled in New York City, where his father followed the business of sign painting. The latter died about 1891, in Brooklyn. His wife's death occurred in New York in 1860.

Andrew Girsham finished his education in the public schools of New York, and there, at the age of fifteen, began learning the trade of paperhanging and staining. His relations for about fourteen years were with Westerberg, Jefferson & Co., and under their able and efficient instruction he mastered every detail of the business. In 1867 he moved to Guttenberg, Hudson County, N. J., where he has since resided and followed his trade.

While Mr. Girsham has gained a wide reputation as a talented paperhanger and stainer, he has also achieved prominence in public affairs. He has always been an ardent Republican, fearless and consistent in party interests, and patriotic and loyal in the welfare of his county and State. In April, 1861, he enlisted in the Eleventh New York Volunteer Infantry, known as Colonel Elmer E. Ellsworth's New York Fire Zouaves, and served for about thirteen months, participating in the first battle of Bull Run and in numerous skirmishes, and being present at Newport News during the historic engagement between the "Merrimac" and "Monitor." In town matters he has been especially prominent. He served as a Constable for nine years, as a Justice of the Peace for five years, as a Recorder of the Town of Guttenberg for three years, and as a School Trustee for twelve years, being district clerk for about five years. On June 22, 1898, he was commissioned Postmaster of Guttenberg, which office he now holds. He has also been an active member of the Republican committees of Guttenberg and Hudson County and a delegate to many conventions, and in every capacity has acquitted himself with credit and honor.

He is a member of Ellsworth Post, No. 14, G. A. R., of the Town of Union, and of the Volunteer Firemen's Association of the City of New York. He is progressive, public spirited, and faithful to every trust, and enjoys the respect and confidence of the community.

Mr. Girsham was married, April 22, 1866, to Mary A. Curley, daughter of Michael and Margaret Curley, of New York, and their children are Thomas J., Andrew J., Robert E., and Tomasiana.

EUGENE DE WITT KNOX, one of the best known real estate and insurance men of Union Hill, is the son of De Witt Clinton Knox and Anna Singleton and a grandson of Isaac Knox and Emma Van Dresar. His paternal ancestors came to New Jersey from Germany before the Revolutionary War, in which some of them served with honor and distinction. His father, a wheelwright by trade, now resides in New York City, while his grandfather, Isaac Knox, was one of the earliest and for many years a leading carriage and wagon manufacturer at Rome, N. Y. On his grandmother's side he is of Holland Dutch descent, her ancestors, the Van Dresars, having come from that country several generations ago, and serving with distinction in the War of the Revolution. His mother, Anna Singleton, was born in England. Some of his ancestors were massacred by the Indians in New Jersey.

Mr. Knox was born May 15, 1870, in Rome, N. Y., where he received a public school education. In 1883 he became a clerk in a shoe store in his native city, and remained there until 1886, when he came to New York and assumed a similar position in an uptown shoe house, which he held for a year and a half. In 1888 he entered the service of Best & Co. on Twenty-third Street, New York, as a shoe salesman, and became assistant buyer in the shoe department. He resigned this position February 24, 1897, and engaged in the real estate and insurance business at Union Hill, N. J., where he resides, having settled there in 1893. He has displayed energy, excellent judgment, and ability, and since he established himself in business he has gained a high reputation and the confidence and esteem of the community. His specialty has been that of building houses and selling them on easy payments. In one year he disposed of no less than twenty-four houses in this way. He has done much toward the building up of the northern part of Union Hill. He is a man of energy, integrity, ability, and keen judgment, and in the prosecution of a constantly increasing business has been successful. As a citizen he is public spirited, enterprising, progressive, and patriotic.

He is Collector of Arrears for the Town of Union, having been appointed in October, 1898, to fill the unexpired term of the late John M. Myer, and elected in March, 1899. He was one of the organizers and the first President (1899) of the new hook and ladder company of the Town of Union, and is a member of the Democratic Central Organization, of the Royal Arcanum, of the Woodcliff Club, and of North Hudson Tent, No. 10, K. O. T. M.

Mr. Knox was married, January 4, 1890, to Rose Donnelly, daughter of James and Rose Donnelly, of New York City. They have had three children: Anna Clinton, Arthur (deceased), and Burton.

GEORGE CUNLIFFE, of Kearny, son of Joseph Cunliffe and Hannah Ainscow, was born in Lancashire, England, the birthplace of his parents, on the 20th of March, 1847. He comes from an old and distinguished line of English ancestors. Receiving a good public school education in his native town, he learned the trade of spinner, which he followed until 1880, when he came to the United States. Here he entered the Clark O. N. T. Thread Mills, in Newark, N. J., and remained there several years, holding responsible positions, and gaining the respect and confidence of both associates and employers.

Subsequently Mr. Cunliffe originated what is known as botanic beer, which he manufactures in large quantities, and in which he has built up an extensive trade, his factory and residence being in Kearny, N. J. In this

GEORGE CUNLIFFE.

business he has achieved success. He is a public spirited, progressive citizen, a Republican in politics, and a member of the Sons of St. George and of the Methodist Episcopal Church.

Mr. Cunliffe married Miss Ellen Pilkington, and has seven children: William Thomas, Joseph, Mary Hannah, Robert, Sarah Helen, Stephen, and Florence.

SAMUEL D. DEMAREST was of the seventh generation in direct descent from David des Marest, the first American ancestor of the family (see sketch on page 64). The line of his descent is as follows: David des

Marest (1), who married Maria Sohier and came from Europe in 1662. His son, Samuel Davids Demarest (2), born in Mannheim on the Rhine in 1653, died at Schraalenburgh, N. J., in 1728, married, August 11, 1678, Maria, daughter of Simon Dreuns. They resided at Schraalenburgh, and most of their descendants have resided there ever since. Their children of the third generation were Magdalen, David, Samuel, Peter, Jacomina, Judith, Sarah, Simon, Rachel, Susanna, and Daniel.

Simon Samuels Demarest (3) married Vroutie Cornelius Haring and had children of the fourth generation Samuel, Caroline, Cornelius, Daniel, Maria, John, David, Peter, Jacob, Jacob.

David Simons Demarest (4), born March 1, 1736, married Jannetje Davids Campbell, March 27, 1758. They had issue of the fifth generation, among others, Simon Davids Demarest.

Simon Davids Demarest (5), born at Schraalenburgh, May 12, 1765, died July 17, 1828, married, December 8, 1787, Hannah Banta, born November 15, 1768, died September 10, 1826. They had issue of the sixth generation, of whom one was David Simons Demarest.

David Simons Demarest (6) was born August 23, 1795, died July 4, 1877, married Margaretta Durie, who was born August 31, 1802, died January 17, 1867. One of their children of the seventh generation was Samuel D. Demarest, the subject of this sketch.

Samuel D. Demarest (7) was born at Bergenfield, N. J., October 13, 1826, and died May 12, 1879. He married Catherine A. Van Antwerp and had three children.

He was educated in the public schools of Bergen County, and at the age of fifteen began active life on his father's farm, where he remained several years. He then learned the trade of shoemaker, which he followed successfully until his death.

Major Demarest was an active man, a public spirited citizen, and highly respected and esteemed by all who knew him. He served nine months in the Civil War as a member of the Twenty-second Regiment New Jersey Volunteers, rising from the post of Captain to the rank of Major. For a number of years he was a Freeholder. He attended the Dutch Reformed Church, and in every capacity displayed sound judgment and acknowledged ability.

ABRAM D. GREENLEAF, a veteran of the War of the Rebellion, is the son of Everett R. Greenleaf and Jane Danielson and a grandson of Enoch Greenleaf and William Danielson. He was born in New York City on the 7th of October, 1828. Coming from old English stock, and from ancestors who settled in this country several generations ago, he inherited the sterling characteristics of his race, and during a long and active career has exemplified the family traits in both private and public life.

He was educated in the public schools of New Durham, Hudson County, N. J., whither his parents removed when he was a boy. There he has resided to the present time, following the occupation of fisherman and the trade of a carpenter. In 1862 he enlisted in the Twenty-first Regiment, New Jersey Volunteers, and served until the close of the Civil War, being detailed in 1864 on the brigadier-general's staff. He participated in both battles of Fredericksburg and at Chancellorsville, and attained distinction as a brave, patriotic soldier.

Mr. Greenleaf is an independent Democrat, a man of great force of character and native ability, and esteemed and respected for his public spirit, integrity, and enterprise. He was a Constable and a Court Officer under Judges Bedle and Randolph, and in religion is a Methodist.

He married Miss Elizabeth Lozier, and has three children: William E., Abram, and Levi L.

CHARLES W. BURROUGHS, of Arlington, Hudson County, was born in Johnsville, N. Y., March 1, 1851. His parents, James Burroughs and Ann Maria Warren, were both natives of that State, the former of Brinkerhoff and the latter of Glenham, their ancestry dating back to colonial times. They were of English descent.

When Mr. Burroughs was a mere boy the family removed to New York City, where he received a good public school education, and where he has spent his business life. After completing his studies he associated himself with the dry goods firm of Wicks & Co. Subsequently he was with S. B. Chittenden & Co. for a short time. In 1877 he accepted a position with the well known house of Lord & Taylor, of New York, with which he has ever since remained, serving in various important capacities, and discharging his duties with ability, promptness, and satisfaction. Having spent his active life in the dry goods trade, Mr. Burroughs has gained a broad and thorough knowledge of every branch of the business, and in many lines is regarded as authority. His integrity, uprightness of character, and faithful attention to duty, united with a genial nature and sound judgment, have gained for him the confidence and respect of both employers and associates.

CHARLES W. BURROUGHS.

He is a member of Triune Lodge, F. and A. M., of the Royal Arcanum, of the Arlington Club, and of the Orange Canoe Club. For many years he has resided in Arlington, N. J., where he has taken a deep interest in public affairs and an active part in the development of the town. Though never aspiring to public office, he has wielded no small influence in behalf of the general welfare, and is one of the promoters of every worthy object.

Mr. Burroughs was married in New York City on the 18th of January, 1882, to Miss Addie F. Rankin, of Bennington, Vt., and their children are Florence M., Edith W., Belle, and Walter F.

WILLIAM BARDSLEY is the son of Thomas and Harriet (Kay) Bardsley, natives of Stockport, England, where he was born February 18, 1852. There he received his preliminary education in private schools. In 1869 he married Miss Harriet Fletcher, and the same year came to this country, locating in New York, where he attended the Mechanics Institute and also studied architecture. Inheriting the sterling mental and physical characteristics of his race, he developed marked ability in the direction of designing and artistic instincts of a high order. His training, especially in New York, was in this line, and his successful career has justified the wisdom of his choice.

He thoroughly mastered the trade of cabinetmaker, which he has followed, either practically or in a business way, from early life. In 1872 he established himself in business at 147 to 151 Baxter Street, New York, and has since continued there under the firm name of Bardsley Brothers. They have an extensive trade, not only in New York City, but in adjacent sections of New York and New Jersey, and through their ability and honest, straightforward dealings stand among the successful firms in the business. Mr. Bardsley is a practical cabinetmaker, thoroughly conversant with every detail of the trade, and an able business man. As a resident of Kearny, Hudson County, N. J., where he settled many years ago, he has exerted an important influence in both public and private affairs, and for seven years was a member of the Township Committee, on which he still serves, having been its Chairman for three years. He is an ardent Republican, and a member of the Republican Club of Kearny, of the Kearny Presbyterian Church, and of Copestone Lodge of Masons, of which he has been Worshipful Master. Public spirited, progressive, and patriotic, he is respected and esteemed by all who know him, and has always maintained the confidence of the community.

Mrs. Bardsley is also a native of Stockport, England. They were married in Manchester in 1869 and at once came to America. They have seven children: Joseph, Lottie, Emilie, Hattie, William, Jr., Elmer, and Harold.

JOHN F. LEE, of Bayonne, was born on West Eighth Street, New York City, November 9, 1874, and is the son of Michael Lee and Ellen Farrell. His father is a landscape gardener by profession, a leading resident of Bayonne, and a representative Democrat in politics. He is of Irish descent on both sides, his parents having come to this country from County Cork, Ireland.

John F. Lee received his education in the parochial schools of Bayonne, Hudson County, N. J., whither his parents removed when he was young. He subsequently pursued a legal course in connection with regular practitioners, holding a position as law clerk. This profession, however, did not suit his taste, and he turned his attention to journalistic work, which he is determined to make his future business and for which he has decided ability and talents. Mr. Lee is a Democrat in politics, and during the past four years has been one of the school trustees of Bayonne. He is a member of Court Winfield, Foresters of America, and of Star of the Sea Lodge, No. 187, Knights of Columbus, both of Bayonne. He is also a prominent member of the Bayonne City Democratic Club, and one of the active and influential younger citizens of that enterprising community.

JOEL W. BROWN, of Jersey City, was born at Rocky Point, Long Island, N. Y., on the 18th of December, 1836, being the eighth of nine children of Isaac W. Brown and Chauy Yarington. He is the grandson of Joseph Brown, Jr., and Miriam Davis, and a great-grandson of Joseph Brown, Sr., and Mehitable Vale. His father was a well known sea captain.

Mr. Brown was educated at Miller's Place Academy on Long Island and at Fort Plain Seminary in Montgomery County. In 1855 he engaged in teaching school on Long Island and during the years 1856 and 1857 he was in Omaha, Neb., engaged in the real estate business and in teaming. He went there, as most emigrants did at the time, in a "Prairie Schooner" across the State of Iowa. From 1858 to 1868 he followed the sea, being master of different schooners sailing along the Southern coast to the West Indies and other places in the Gulf of Mexico. During the War of the Rebellion he was captain of a vessel in the service of the United States Government.

In 1868 Captain Brown abandoned the sea and engaged in mercantile pursuits, purchasing a ship chandlery store in Newburgh, N. Y., which he conducted until 1870. In that year he sold out and engaged in the dry dock business at Newburgh under the firm name of Bullman & Brown, and so continued until 1878, when the business was removed to Jersey City. Mr. Bullman died in 1890 and the concern was incorporated under the style of the Brown Dry Dock Company, of which Mr. Brown has continuously been President. This is one of the most important industries in Jersey City. It gives employment to a large number of men, and under Mr. Brown's able and energetic management has become well known among the shipping interests.

In public as well as in business life Mr. Brown has achieved a high repu-

JOEL W. BROWN.

tation. He is a Prohibitionist in politics, having been actively and prominently identified with that party for about twenty years. He served it as a delegate to the last four National conventions and in other important capacities. He has been its nominee for Mayor, Assemblyman, State Senator, and Freeholder, and for many years has been and still is a member of the State Prohibition Executive Committee. He was a delegate to the National convention at Cleveland in 1888 which nominated General Fisk for the Presidency, and also a delegate to the convention of 1892 which nominated Hon. George Bidwell. He has served for many years as a member of the Prohibition County Committee of Hudson County, and in 1889, 1890, and 1891 was Chairman of that body. For twenty-four years he has been an Elder in the Bergen Reformed (Dutch) Church. Since 1859 he has been a prominent Mason, holding membership in Bergen Lodge of Jersey City. He is also a member of Mount Union Chapter, R. A. M., of Hugh de Payens Commandery, K. T., of Jersey City, of the Maritime Exchange of New York City, and of other social, political, and business organizations. He is a public spirited, progressive citizen, thoroughly identified with the affairs of the community, and respected and esteemed for those qualities which stamp the successful man.

Mr. Brown was married, December 19, 1865, to Hattie E. Woodhull, of Port Jefferson, Long Island, N. Y. They have had three daughters: Ella W. (wife of Arthur Ingham), Lulu W. (who was drowned at Manasqua Beach while trying to save the life of a small boy), and Hattie. The family reside at 53 Duncan Avenue, Jersey City.

WILLIAM BLAIR, of River Edge, N. J., was born in New York City on the 4th of July, 1812, being the son of Ezekiel and Susan (Weinard) Blair, both of Scotch descent. He received his early education at Public School No. 1, which stood opposite the Hall of Records in New York City, but at the age of fourteen started at the trade of sailmaking, which occupation he continued until the age of eighty-one, being, doubtless, the oldest sailmaker in the country at the time of his retirement.

Mr. Blair was a Corporal and Sergeant in the National Guard, and in every capacity achieved a high reputation. At the time of the Mexican War the firm of Blair & Higgins was employed by the Government to fit out the army with tents and covers. They made a swing-cot for General Scott, of whom Mr. Blair was a personal friend. He was Judge of Elections three terms, a Commissioner at the time the Bergen County poorhouse was built, and is a prominent member of and active worker in the Second Reformed Church at Hackensack.

He married Mary Robinson. They have had eight children: William, Jr., Susan, James S., Mary J., and four deceased.

JOSEPH H. PILSON, of Jersey City, was born in Brooklyn, N. Y., September 29, 1858. His father, Alexander Pilson, was of Scotch descent, while his mother, Susan (Barker) Pilson, was of Irish extraction.

Mr. Pilson was educated in the public schools of New York City and afterward entered the printing business with A. J. Doan, remaining with him for four years. The partnership was then dissolved and he continued in the same business in Jersey City. There, in 1893, he started the *Chronicle*, a Republican newspaper, of which he is still the proprietor and editor. In connection with the *Chronicle* Mr. Pilson conducts a large and successful printing establishment whose principal work is printing for the leading lawyers and business men in Hudson County and for most of the public institutions of Jersey City.

He has always been a Republican, but has never held office to any extent. He served three months on the Grand Jury of Hudson City in 1896. He is a member of the Royal Arcanum; of the Loyal Additional Benefit Association; the Odd Fellows; the Knights of Pythias, and of other societies and organizations. As a citizen he is public spirited, progressive, and highly esteemed.

Mr. Pilson married Mary J. Moir, in New York City, and has had five daughters: Jessie, Violet, and Josephine, deceased, and Edith and Hazel, who are living.

J. WYMAN JONES.[1]—It is always interesting to trace the early life of men of energy, for usually there will be found those surroundings which foster a vigorous and independent character. This is aptly illustrated in the life of J. Wyman Jones. Born in the Town of Enfield, N. H., he was subjected throughout boyhood to the hardy and healthful country life of New England; and the rugged aspect of nature, the exhilarating winters, together with a rigorous home training, combined to produce a vigorous and courageous youth, eager for a conflict with the world. His father was a sturdy New England justice, prominent in the affairs of his locality, and several times a member of the State Legislature. His mother was a woman of genuine sweetness and refinement, and a direct descendant of the famous Hannah Dustin. It was the desire of both parents to keep their only son at home, but when his school career at Meriden Academy was ended he pressed onward for Dartmouth College, where he was admitted in 1837. In his class were a son of Daniel Webster, Edward Webster, who died in the Mexican War; Rev. Dr. Leonard Swain, of Nashua, N. H.; and Gardiner G. Hubbard, Esq., of Washington, D. C.

Upon graduation, in 1841, he could not be persuaded to locate at home; and although put wholly upon his own resources, he began the study of law in New York City. In 1843 he was admitted to the New York bar, and for twenty years followed his profession, the latter part of the time in Utica, N. Y. Prior to his removal there he married Harriet Dwight Dana, daughter of James Dana, of Utica, and sister of Professor James D. Dana, of Yale University, who survived until 1882. At Utica Mr. Jones made many warm friends in his profession, including the late Justice William J. Bacon, Senator Kernan, Joshua Spencer, and Senator Conkling.

Advised by his physician that he must lead an out-of-door life, he reluctantly relinquished the practice of law to give himself to rural pursuits, although still retaining his interest and membership in the New York bar. In 1858, by invitation of a former client then engaged in surveying the Northern Railroad of New Jersey, he made an examination of the proposed route, and being impressed by the natural beauty of the country, with characteristic daring determined to throw himself heartily into the development of the region where Englewood is now located. He spent the summer of 1858 in securing property rights from the original owners, and by the autumn of that year had control of nearly all the land now occupied by that village. He proceeded to lay out the town, to name its streets, and to procure a survey and map of its territory. By the spring of 1859 he had moved his family to the new place and had gained for it the support of several valuable friends. In this same spring, at a meeting

---

[1] Adapted from a sketch in the "Memorial History of the City of New York and the Hudson River Valley."

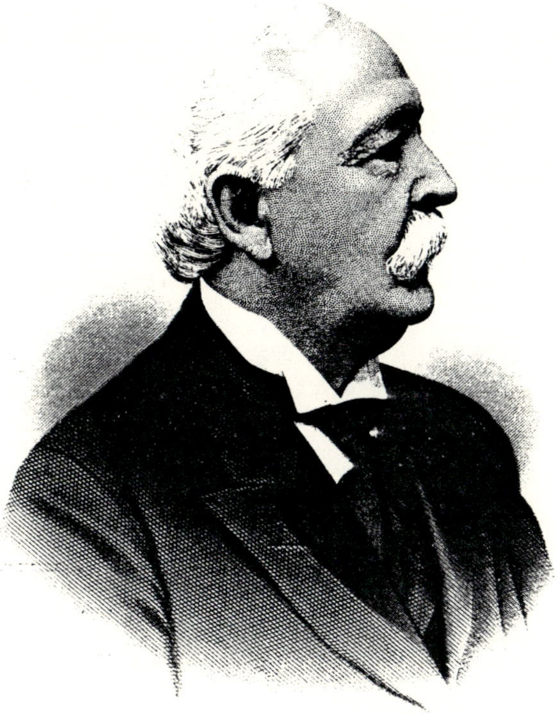

J. Wyman Jones.

of the residents, the name Englewood, suggested and advocated by him, was adopted. Since that time Mr. Jones has been prominent in the secular and religious life of Englewood, and he still maintains a keen interest in its growth and welfare. He has had the satisfaction of seeing it develop, pursuant to the general plan formulated by himself, into a beautiful and progressive suburb of New York City. In addition to the initial work at Englewood he also became largely interested in the neighboring Towns of Closter and Norwood, the latter of which he established and named.

In 1865 Mr. Jones became President of the St. Joseph Lead Company, a corporation manufacturing and mining lead in the State of Missouri; and by persistent energy, overcoming all obstacles, he has raised the company from an almost hopeless condition to its present position as one of the largest lead-producing concerns in the United States. With the lead company are also associated a railway corporation having a road forty-eight miles in length, and a cattle and farming company transacting a large business, of both of which Mr. Jones is President. He is also President of the Doe Run Lead Company. During the thirty years of his presidency of the St. Joseph Lead Company he has spent much of his time at the mines in Missouri, where now there is a prosperous community. During this entire period there has never been a strike among the men, it having been one of the chief concerns of the company, under the leadership of Mr. Jones, not only to treat its employees fairly, but also to aid in every undertaking which promised to contribute to their pleasure, or to their moral or physical welfare.

In politics Mr. Jones has been a Republican since the days of the Free Soil party. At the outbreak of the Civil War, while deep in his work at Englewood, he was an ardent Northerner, frequently speaking at public meetings. He was many years Chairman of the Republican County Executive Committee, and was chosen a delegate-at-large from the State of New Jersey to the Presidential Convention of 1872. In 1876 he was elected a delegate to the State Convention by the Englewood Republicans after he had declared himself friendly to Senator Conkling and opposed to Hon. James G. Blaine, and subsequently by the State Convention was elected a delegate to the Presidential Convention at Cincinnati. There, with five other New Jersey delegates, he refused to vote for Mr. Blaine, and voted on the first and every ballot for Mr. Hayes, who was nominated by the convention. While this course was distasteful to the Blaine adherents, so far as Mr. Jones was concerned it was in accord with the declarations he had previously made, and with the decision of his Englewood constituents. In later years he has taken no active part in politics, but maintains a loyal adherence to his party and an earnest concern for the country's prosperity.

Personally Mr. Jones is a courtly gentleman, thoroughly American, and counts his friends among all classes of men. He possesses a keen insight into human nature, and judges quickly and accurately.

In 1886 Mr. Jones married Mrs. Salome Hanna Chapin, of Cleveland, Ohio. During the winter season they reside at Thomasville, Ga., where they have a Southern home of rare attractiveness. They also have a charming historic home at Bolton, Mass., where Mr. Jones now spends the greater part of each year.

GEORGE FELIX COPIN has been a life-long resident of West Hoboken, N. J., where he was born on the 12th of July, 1861. He is of French descent. His father, Francis Copin, born in Belfort, France, August 10, 1833, came to America in 1853, and for thirty-five years lived in West Hoboken. In 1888 he moved to New Durham, Hudson County, where he died June 17, 1898. His father was Nicholas Copin, and through a long line of ancestors he inherited those broad mental qualities which characterized his life, and which gained for him the reputation of an honest, industrious, and honorable man. He married Christina Arnould, daughter of Jacob Arnould, and a sister of Denis Arnould, a private in Battery G, First New York Light Artillery, and of Joseph Arnould, First Lieutenant in Company E, Fifty-fifth New York Volunteers, both serving with distinction in the Civil War.

George F. Copin received a good practical education in the parochial schools of West Hoboken. His first employment was as a clerk in a large clothing store. Subsequently he accepted a responsible position in the office of Givernaud Brothers, the well known silk manufacturers. In these capacities he developed marked business ability, and by perseverance accumulated some money. In 1884 he established himself in the confectionery business in West Hoboken, in which he has since been engaged with increasing success. As a result of his own indomitable efforts he has built up an extensive trade.

Mr. Copin has also been active in the public affairs of his town, which he served as a School Trustee in 1895 and 1896 and as a Councilman in 1897 and 1898. He is a leading member of the Catholic Benevolent Legion, of the Order of Foresters, of the Catholic Young Men's Lyceum, of the Mozart Choral Union, and of the Monastery Church Choir. He is especially prominent in social and musical circles.

In 1886 he married Miss Annette Guillard, and they have three children: Louise, Christina, and Annette.

JOHN D. BLAWVELT is descended in the tenth generation from Garret Hendricksen Blawvelt (1), the first American progenitor of all the Blawvelts in New Jersey (see page 68). Garret Hendricksen Blawvelt had a son John (2), who married Catharine Cornelius and had issue a large family, one of whom was John (3), who married Margaret Tallman and had a son David (4), who married Maria de Clark and had a son, David D. Blawvelt (5). The latter was born December 31, 1738, and died March 12, 1856. He married Ellen Fowler. They had a son, David D. Blawvelt (6), born at Tappan, May 11, 1768. He died January 7, 1849. He married Maria Haring, who was born September 19, 1772, and died April 25, 1822. They resided at what is now Harrington Park. The issue of David D. Blawvelt (6) and Maria Haring of the seventh generation was a son, Daniel D. Blawvelt (7), born at Old Tappan, September 18, 1794, died there March 20, 1873. He married, in 1817, Effie Demarest, who was born September 13, 1798, and died June 9, 1861. Their children of the eighth generation were David D. and Catharine.

David D. Blawvelt (8), born April 16, 1818, died December 30, 1879. He married, in 1837, Jane Blawvelt, who was born in 1820, and was descended from the same common ancestor and of the same generation as her husband. They resided at what is now Harrington Park, N. J. David D. Blawvelt (8) served in the Union Army in the Rebellion. He recruited the Twenty-second New Jersey Volunteers, and on September 2, 1862, was commissioned Captain, serving with his regiment in the field until it was mustered out of service June 25, 1863. Their children of the ninth generation were Helen M., John D., and Effie Louise.

John D. Blawvelt (9), the subject of this sketch, was born near Tappan, at River Vale, Bergen County, N. J., November 29, 1815, and received a public school education. At the age of fourteen he left school and went to work in his father's sawmill, where he remained until 1833, when he began learning the carpenter's trade. He followed that business successfully until 1845. In the meantime the homestead had been sold, but it was bought back by him in 1841, and after leaving his trade he returned to the old farm and was actively engaged in agricultural pursuits until 1875. He then sold the place, but as the parties who purchased it did not carry out their contract he was obliged to take it back again in 1878. He continued farming on the old homestead for three years, when he sold it, removed to Westwood, and has since lived there in retirement.

Mr. Blawvelt has always maintained an untarnished reputation and the respect and confidence of all who know him. He is a public spirited citizen, active and influential in the community, and a member of the Baptist Church. He married Leah Demarest and has had two children—a son and a daughter—both deceased.

ADOLPH H. BARKERDING, of Park Ridge, N. J., is the son of Henry and Henrietta (Mollenhauer) Barkerding and a grandson of Henry Barkerding, Sr., and Regina Mollenhauer, who came to this country from Hamburg, Germany. He was born in Charleston, S. C., May 22, 1869, and attended the schools of that city until he was fourteen years of age. He then left school to engage in the dry goods business in Charleston, remaining with the same firm for a period of twelve years and rising to the position of general manager. Upon receiving an offer of a position with Mittag & Volger, of Park Ridge, N. J., he resigned his former position and came to New York. He has since that time been associated with them.

He is a member of the Lutheran Church of Park Ridge, a public spirited and progressive citizen, and highly esteemed by all who know him. He married Charlotte J. Police and has one child, T. A. Barkerding.

CHARLES CROZAT CONVERSE, LL.B., LL.D., of Highwood, N. J., was born in Warren, Mass., October 7, 1832. His ancestry is an historical one. Prior to the Norman conquest of England in 1066 the titled family of De Coigneries held a distinguished place among the old nobles of France, its possession of its estates there, and occupancy of its Chateau de Coignir, extending back to, and being lost in, the remotest antiquity. Roger de Coigneries, born in 1010, yielded to the persuasions of his youthful companion and friend, William the Conqueror, joining him in 1066 in his invasion of England and rendering him conspicuous service in the battle of Hastings, having his name, anglicized Coniers, recorded in the roll of Battle Abbey. Throughout William's subsequent contest in subjugating the North of England, De Coigneries accompanied him, and at its close was placed in command of the castle of Durham, one of the most important strongholds in that region, and which, with the domains about it, by Episcopal grants, soon became the seat and castle of the Coigneries family, then known as Conyers, and continued for nearly 600 years as such until the reign of Charles the First in 1625-45. Roger left a son, Roger de Coniers—or Conyers,—to whom the Bishop of Ranulph gave the Manor of Rungstan, in Yorkshire, between 1099 and 1126. He left a son, Roger, who was Baron of Durham and Lord of Bishopton, living from 1134 to 1174. He left a son, John, who lived till 1239 and had the Manors of Sockburn, Bishopton.

Stainton, and Auckland confirmed to him. He left a son, Sir Humphrey, of Sockburn and Bishopton, possessed of lands in Stainton, granted to the Abbey of Rievaulx in 1270. He left a son, Sir John, whose heir was his brother's son, in 1334, and named Sir John, to whom was entailed said manors. He left a son, Robert, in 1395, who left a son, Sir Christopher, who left a son of the same name, who left a son, Sir John, who married Margaret, daughter of Lord Darcey and Meynell, who had his seat at Hornby Castle and was governor of York Castle. In 1460 he joined Richard, Duke of York, against the king. He left a son, Sir John, who married Alice Nevile, daughter of Lord Fauconbridge and heir of the Earl of Kent, and was installed knight of the most noble Order of the Garter in 1484. He left a son, Sir William, Lord Conyers of Hornby, who married Ann Nevile, daughter of the Earl of Westmoreland. Sir John's second son, Reginald, was seated at Wakerley Manor, County of Northampton, and died there in 1514. He left a son, Francis, who married Anne, sister of Sir Richard Blount, and died in 1560. He left a son, Francis, who succeeded to the Wakerley estates. He left a son and heir, Christopher, who left a son and heir, Edward, born January 30, 1590, who came to America with Governor Winthrop in 1630.

Winthrop and his companions reached the shores of New England June 12, 1630, and Charlestown in July following, and there, on July 30th, a church was organized by Winthrop and Conyers. Two years later this church was removed to Boston and ever after was known simply as the First Church of Boston. Immediately after its removal Conyers and others organized the First Church of Charlestown. His son James attained distinction in the French-Canadian War, and was made Commander-in-Chief of the Colonial forces of Massachusetts. He was afterward chosen Speaker of the General Court for three consecutive terms, dying in the third term.

Edward Conyers consecrated himself and his wealth to church and town building. In 1640 he founded the church and Town of Wooburn, now Woburn, calling to its pastorate his English friend, Rev. Thomas Carter. Edward Conyers's son Samuel married Mr. Carter's daughter Judith. He manifested, in his new-world life, those characteristics which marked his long ancestral line. His boldness caused him to be doubtless the first subject of King Charles in this country to suffer arrest for charging the king with popery, he having declined to publish the king's letter sent to him for that purpose, on this ground. Conyers was duly tried for this offense, but was discharged by the court for the reason that "his language did not reflect on his majesty's letter." He shunned whatever savored of the worldly distinctions of his English family. He refused to name Woburn after his old family home. His habit of making the letter "y" very short when writing his name, as noted in his last will and testament, led other persons to calling it Convers, and during the subsequent lapse of over two hundred and fifty years an "e" has been added to it, making it Converse. Edward de Conyers died in 1663. His daughter Mary married, in 1643, Simon, son of James Thompson, of England, who settled in Woburn in 1640. His son Samuel, who was, with his father, a legatee of Simon Thompson, removed in 1710 to Killingly, Conn., and became the first settler of Thompson, named so in honor of James Thompson. Samuel Conyers died in 1669. He left a son, Samuel, who died in 1732. He left a son, Edward, who died in 1784. He left a son, Jacob, who died in 1797. He left a son, Jacob, whose distinction it was to unite, by his marriage, the lines of the Winthrop and Robinson settlements in America, as, after graduation from

Brown University in 1790, he married Miss Ellen Robinson, of Plymouth, Mass., of the family of the Puritan leader, and whose ancestress, of the same name, was an heir of Captain Miles Standish. He died in 1804, leaving a son, Manning, since deceased, whose son, Charles Crozat Converse, LL.B., LL.D., of Highwood, N. J., whose birthplace is near Woburn, Mass., is well known by his contributions to general literature and his success in his profession of the law.

Charles C. Converse also ranks as one of America's leading orchestra composers. Whilst pursuing his literary and legal studies in Germany he took a course of instruction in musical composition under the great harmonist, Richter, and his professional confreres, at Leipsic. Spohr, Dr. Converse's orchestral mentor, Liszt, and other composers highly praised Dr. Converse's orchestral works, which embrace overtures, symphonies, cantatas, etc. Some of his German songs have been published in Leipsic by Brirtkopf & Haertel. His American Concert Overture, for full orchestra, was played at the Boston Peace Jubilee and since then by Anton Seidl in New York and Theodore Thomas in Chicago. His Concert Overture, "Im Fruehling," for full orchestra, has been played several times in New York under the direction of Mr. Thomas. His Psalm Cantata, on the 126th Psalm, for chorus, soli, and full orchestra, was performed at the concert of the American Music Teachers' National Convention in Chicago in July, 1888, also under Mr. Thomas's direction.

On Dr. Converse's return from European study he entered the Law Department of Albany University, graduating therefrom with the degree of LL.B. Since then he received the honorary degree of LL.D. His love for music and musical composition has increased with the lapse of time, as his large accumulation of manuscript works shows.

Dr. Converse was married, January 14, 1858, to Miss Lida Lewis, of Alabama. Mrs. Converse is of the distinguished English family of Axtell. Colonel Axtell, her ancestor, who was King George III.'s official representative in America during the American Revolutionary War, built and occupied, as his official residence, the historic Melrose Hall, in Brooklyn, N. Y., the then finest house on Long Island. She, and their only living child, Clarence, constitute his family, their first child, William, dying in infancy.

There are biographical sketches of Dr. Converse in "Allibone's Dictionary of Authors" under his pen-name of *Karl Reden*, in "Sribner's Cyclopedia of Music," in "One Hundred Years of American Music," with portrait, and in "Appleton's Cyclopedia of American Biography." Dr. Converse assisted in preparing the "Standard Dictionary," in whose vocabulary is the common-gender pronoun invented by him and presented to philologists iu 1858.

JOHN T. CALLAHAN, Chief of Police of Harrison, Hudson County, N. J., was born there on the 1st of October, 1852. His parents, Jerry Callahan and Mary Fallon, were natives of Ireland, coming to the United States when young. They were married in this country.

Mr. Callahan received his education in the public schools of Jersey City, N J. Subsequently he moved to Harrison, Hudson County, where he has been for many years a prominent and influential citizen and one of the leaders of the Democratic party. For a time he was the Keeper of the Penitentiary at Snake Hill, Hudson County, and for two terms served as a member of the Board of Aldermen of Harrison. He is now serving as Chief of

Police of that city. Mr. Callahan has filled every position with ability and satisfaction and is known as a man of integrity, public spirit, and patriotism. He is a member of the Knights of Columbus, of the Ancient Order of Hibernians, of the Royal Arcanum, and of the Davis Association.

Mr. Callahan married Miss Mary Ann Brooks, and they have six children: Mary, Loretta, Catharine, William, John, and James.

FREDERICK H. DRESSEL, the well known florist of Weehawken, N. J., was born in Hesse-Darmstadt, Germany, on the 8th of June, 1861, his parents being Herman Dressel and Eliza Pattberg. His father came to this country in 1848, lived for a few years in New York City, then went to Charleston, S. C., and finally returned to the Fatherland.

Mr. Dressel received an excellent educational training in Germany, in Belgium, and in and near London, England, and early developed those traits of industry, integrity, and practical application which have won for him both success and honor. In 1887 he was sent out by the well known orchid establishment of F. Sander & Co., of St. Albans, near London, to British Guiana in South America to collect orchids. He remained there one year, making a three months' journey from Georgetown to Mount Roraima with a party of seventy-five Indians, being the third white man to ascend that mountain. His experience in this connection was both extensive and valuable, and enabled him to gain a practical knowledge of orchids in their native state. Among the numerous varieties of that plant which he collected and sent home were the *Cattleya Lawrenciana* and *Cyprepidum Schomburgianum*, two of the most valuable orchid species in existence.

FREDERICK H. DRESSEL.

Returning to England, Mr. Dressel came to this country in October, 1888, and for one year represented his former employers, F. Sander & Co., in Jersey City, N. J., where he first resided. Subsequently he lived for a time in Brooklyn, N. Y. In 1890, however, he settled in his present home on Weehawken Heights, Hudson County, where he engaged in business for himself as a florist. His original establishment comprised only two greenhouses, but from this modest beginning he has steadily enlarged the business until now he owns and operates twenty houses and ranks as one of the foremost florists in New Jersey. He gives employment to about eight people.

Mr. Dressel's success is the result of his own efforts united with natural ability, sound judgment, and enterprise. His business, under his able and energetic management, has grown to extensive proportions, and is regarded as one of the most important of the kind in the country. He has traveled extensively in Europe, North and South America, and the West Indies. Possessing mental and physical qualities of a high order, he is a cultivated, courteous gentleman, endowed with great intellectual capacity, and distinguished for his geniality and companionable nature. He has a large and interesting collection of curios which he collected while among the Indians in British Guiana. In politics he is a stanch Democrat. He is a member of Palisade Lodge, No. 84, F. and A. M., of the Association of American Florists, and of the New York Florists' Club, and in all the relations of life has displayed those sterling characteristics which mark the successful man.

June 7, 1893, Mr. Dressel married Emma, daughter of Alfred and Carolina Schmidt, of Hoboken, N. J. They have three children: Frederick Herman, George Alfred, and Carrie.

CHARLES SMITH, of Kearny, was born in Bolton, Lancashire, England, January 10, 1847, and there received a public school education. He is the son of Samuel and Mary (Crompton) Smith, both of whom were born and married in England.

Mr. Smith came to the United States in 1873, landing in New York City on the 12th of April. He went at once to Chicago, Ill., and, on his arrival there, engaged with the Chicago and Northwestern Railroad Company. In 1885 he returned East and settled in Kearny, Hudson County, N. J., on the 30th of June.

Mr. Smith is a machinist by trade, and is engaged at present with the Pennsylvania Railroad Company, having been in the employ of that corporation during the last eighteen years. He served two years as Police Justice of Kearny. He is a Justice of the Peace, and a member of the Kearny Board of Education. He belongs to the Masons and has been Financier of the Improved Order of Heptasophs since its organization. He is a Republican in politics and a communicant of the Protestant Episcopal Church of Kearny.

Mr. Smith was married to Miss Elizabeth Hardman, of England, October 17, 1868. They have no children.

JOHN BEST, of West New York (Taurus postoffice), is of English descent. His grandfather, Jacob Best, lived and died in Cornwall, England. Jacob's wife was Miss Riddell, by whom he had several children, among whom was John, who was born and died in Cornwall, and whose wife was Phillipia Hicks, also of Cornwall. She is still living there. Their children were six sons and one daughter. John Best, Sr., was a builder and contractor, a business he followed all his life. He died at the age of fifty-three.

John Best, the subject of this sketch, was born at Cornwall, West England, April 8, 1846. He remained in England until 1872, receiving a practical education in the parochial schools, learning the trade of carpenter and builder, and becoming especially proficient in stair building. In June, 1869, he was married to Elizabeth Ann Vague, of Cornwall, who died there, without issue, in 1871. In 1872 he came to America and settled in New York City, where he resided until 1890. During a part of that time he was successfully established in business on his own account. In 1874 he married, second, Rebecca C. Opie, who died, also without issue, in 1896, in New York. He married for his present wife Ida Svenson, of West New York, N. J., and they have one child, Ellen, born December 23, 1897.

JOHN BEST.

Mr. Best is successfully engaged in the manufacture of stairs, and in that line has displayed great artistic taste and natural ability. His establishment is located at Nos. 321 and 323 Bergenline Avenue, West New York. In politics he is Republican, and for the past three years has taken an active part in public affairs. He has been a Committeeman for three years, is deeply interested in local education, and is active in everything pertaining to the best interests of the community. He and his wife are attendants of the Grove Reformed Church. Mr. Best, however, was formerly a Methodist and had been brought up a Presbyterian. He acquired much of his education in the night schools of New York City. He is a member of Charles Dickens Lodge, No. 45, Sons of St. George, of New York.

WILLIAM O. ARMBRUSTER, Postmaster of Weehawken, N. J., and one of the leaders of the Republican party, is a son of Joseph E. Armbruster and Amelia Hofer, both natives of Germany. His father came to America in 1846 and engaged in the hotel business, first in New York, subsequently in Brooklyn, and finally in Jersey City, where he died in 1889.

Mr. Armbruster was born in New York City on the 17th of October, 1856. At a very early age he removed with his parents to Brooklyn, N. Y., where he received a good education in Turner's school. When twenty years old the family moved to Jersey City, locating in the old Fourth Assembly District, and there he secured employment as a shipping clerk for Lewis Pattberg & Brothers, novelty manufacturers, with whom he remained eighteen years. In 1884 he removed to the Town of Union and in 1892 engaged in the mantel business, and so continued under the style of the Excelsior Mantel Company until 1898, when he sold out in order to devote his time wholly to official duties. He became one of the successful business men in North Hudson County, and through his industry, integrity, and enterprise built up a large trade.

In politics Mr. Armbruster has always been a stanch Republican, fearless in espousing the best principles of his party, and earnest in his convictions as well as enthusiastic in his efforts. During the past twenty years he has served much of the time as a member of the Hudson County Republican Committee. He was Overseer of the Poor of the Town of Union for two years (1885 and 1886), and a Councilman in 1894, 1895, and 1896, serving as Chairman of the Committee on Streets and Sewers during his full term. In 1896 he was elected to the New Jersey Legislature from the Town of Union by a handsome majority. During the session of 1897 he carefully watched over the interests of his section of Hudson County, introduced several important measures that promised to advance the general welfare, and strenuously opposed others that, in his opinion, would have a contrary effect if passed. In brief, he introduced and secured the enactment of no less than eleven bills affecting North Hudson County. One of these was the Martin Act. He also introduced a racetrack bill, which was defeated, although it contained much-needed reforms.

Mr. Armbruster has always taken a prominent part in town and county affairs, has frequently been a delegate to local, district, and State Republican conventions, and has for many years wielded a potent influence in all public matters. He is esteemed and respected, and has gained the confidence of all with whom he has come into contact. The various positions which he has filled with so much honor and credit attest his popularity. On July 7, 1898, he was commissioned Postmaster of Weehawken, and is now discharging, with ability and satisfaction, the duties of that office. He is an active member of Mystic Tie Lodge, No. 123, F. and A. M.; of Cyrus Chapter, No. 32, R. A. M.; of Summit Lodge, No. 182, I. O. O. F., of Jersey City; of Palisade Lodge, No. 129, K. of P.; of West Shore Council, No. 1097, R. A.; of Garfield Council, No. 56, Jr. O. U. A. M.; of Wahwequa Tribe, No. 188, I. O. R. M.; of Hoboken Lodge, No. 74, B. P. O. E.; of Columbia Hose Company, No. 2, Town of Union; and of the Hamilton Wheelmen, the North Hudson Wheelmen, and the League of American Wheelmen.

Mr. Armbruster was married, December 17, 1881, to Sophie H. Rottmann, daughter of Henry J. and Sophie Rottmann, the former, Henry J., being the first Mayor of the Town of Union, where he settled in 1852. They have one daughter, Sophie Armbruster.

CHARLES McQUILLAN, a prominent member of the Board of Aldermen of Bayonne, Hudson County, and Superintendent of the Standard Oil Company at that city, is the son of James McQuillan and Elizabeth Ross, and was born at Matteawan, N. Y., April 1, 1851. His parents were born and married in Ireland, and in 1844 came to the United States, settling first in Matteawan, N. Y., moving thence to New York City in 1857, and finally coming to Bayonne, N. J.

Mr. McQuillan received his education in New York City, and subsequently learned the machinist's trade. He had hardly more than completed his apprenticeship, however, and thoroughly mastered every detail of the business, when he was asked to accept a position with the Standard Oil Company, with which he has ever since been associated, having now the superintendency of their business in Bayonne. The fidelity and characteristic energy with which he has discharged every duty of this responsible position have brought him into prominence as a man of integrity and ability, and won for him a reputation which extends beyond the limits of his adopted city and county. He is known as a man of public spirit, enterprise, and progressiveness, and has filled a number of positions with ability, honor, and satisfaction.

CHARLES M'QUILLAN.

A Democrat in politics, Mr. McQuillan early identified himself with public affairs and for some time served as Chief of the Fire Department of Bayonne. He is now serving his sixth term as a member of the Board of Aldermen of that city, and in this capacity has rendered efficient service in advancing the interests of the place and developing its resources. He is President of the Bayonne Democratic Club, and a member of the Masonic fraternity, of the Benevolent and Protective Order of Elks, of the Foresters of America, and of the Presbyterian Church.

Mr. McQuillan was married in New York City to Miss Martha Driver, and their children are May, Daisy, and James.

WILLIAM MONTAGUE O'NEILL, who is engaged in the plumbing and house heating business under the firm name of W. M. & E. S. O'Neill, the latter being Edward Sylvester O'Neill, is a prominent citizen of Bayonne, Hudson County. He is the son of Francis and Catherine (Dunn) O'Neill, and was born in New Brunswick, N. J., on the 12th of December, 1859. His parents were both natives of Ireland, coming to this country when young, marrying in New Brunswick, and moving thence to Newark, N. J., and in 1871 to Bayonne. They were thrifty, industrious people and respected and esteemed by all who knew them.

Mr. O'Neill acquired his education at the Christian Brothers' Academy in Newark, and afterward took up the study of law in the office of William Lindsay, of New York City, with whom he remained about one year. Circumstances and tastes combined at that time to divert his attention from a professional to a business life, and he entered the plumbing business established by his father in Bayonne. In 1880 he and his brother, Edward Sylvester O'Neill, succeeded to their father's business and have since conducted it with marked success. They make a specialty of house-heating and plumbing and also carry on a hardware trade.

As a citizen and business man Mr. O'Neill is highly respected and enjoys the confidence of the entire community. He is a Democrat in politics, an exempt fireman of the Fire Department of Bayonne, and a member and Grand Knight of the Knights of Columbus. His activity in promoting the best interests of his section, his honesty and enterprise in all business matters, his genial good nature and integrity of character, have made him one of the popular men of Hudson County.

Mr. O'Neill was married on the 4th of November, 1896, to Mary McAvoy, daughter of Peter and Julia McAvoy, of Elizabeth, N. J. They have one child, Agnes C.

WILLIAM D. DALY, member of Congress from the Seventh Congressional District of New Jersey, was born in Jersey City in 1851, and always resided within the limits of Hudson County. He rose to distinction in the political and legal life of the State. His early education was received in Public School No. 1, Jersey City, where he had as schoolmates several who later became prominent. At fourteen years of age he became an apprentice in Cory's iron foundry in Jersey City, and subsequently was employed in the foundry of the Erie Railroad and still later in Blackmore's foundry. But the young workman was ambitious. The legal profession had attracted him, and in May, 1870, he entered the office of Blair & Ransom in Jersey City. Four years later (June, 1874) he was admitted to the bar as an attorney, and later he was made counselor.

Mr. Daly entered upon the practice of law with the tact and energy peculiar to self-made men. He practiced law in all the courts of New Jersey, represented the defense in more capital cases than any lawyer in the State, and stood in the front rank of criminal lawyers. In the great Erie Railroad strike of 1878 he appeared as counsel for the arrested freight-handlers and secured their acquittal. In 1887 he conducted the defense of the Cigarmakers' Union in Jersey City, whose leaders were charged with conspiracy. In this case also he succeeded in obtaining a verdict of acquittal.

In appreciation of his legal ability President Cleveland, during his first term, appointed him Assistant United States Attorney, and this office he held for three years, handing in his resignation to an incoming administration. In 1888 he was made an alternate delegate to the National Democratic Convention at St. Louis, and again in 1892 to the Chicago Convention. In 1891 he was urged to accept the nomination for member of the House of Assembly from the Eighth District of Hudson County. Elected by a rousing majority, he took his place on the floor of the House as the practical leader of his party. The same courtesy which had characterized his work as a practitioner won for him hosts of friends as a legislator, even from the opposition, and at the close of the session the same Legislature appointed him Judge of the Hoboken District Court. This office he resigned upon his election to the Senate in 1892.

The election which resulted in the choice of Judge Daly to the Senate was won after a most exciting campaign. He was triumphantly elected by 5,645 plurality—the largest vote ever given a Senatorial candidate in Hudson County. In 1895, after an exciting contest, Mr. Daly was re-elected Senator from Hudson County for a term of three years. In 1896 he was a district delegate to the National Democratic Convention at Chicago. During his six years' service in the State Senate he gained a high reputation as a legislator, and for more than half that period was the leader of his party on the floor. He made a brilliant record in 1895, when the riparian rights question was before the Senate, during his opposition to the Creamery Trust, and while serving as a member of the Special Investigating Committee of the Senate. During the Presidential campaign of 1896 he rendered his party valuable service on the stump and also as Chairman of its State Committee. He was a prominent candidate for the Democratic gubernatorial nomination in 1898.

Mr. Daly was elected to Congress in 1898 from the Seventh District of New Jersey, comprising all of Hudson County except the City of Bayonne. He received a plurality of 10,108, the largest ever given to a candidate for Congress in the district. He died, while holding that office, July 31, 1900.

He was a member of various clubs and organizations, including the Bar Association of Jersey City, the Medico-Legal Society, and Rising Star Lodge, No. 109, F. and A. M.

JOHN E. BOWE, contractor and builder of Weehawken, Hudson County, is the son of Thomas Bowe and Ellen Carroll and a grandson of Thomas and Ellen Bowe. He was born at Fairview, Bergen County, N. J., January 2, 1858. His parents were natives of Kilkenny, Ireland, and soon after their arrival in America settled in this State.

Mr. Bowe obtained his education in the public schools of Guttenberg, Hudson County whither the family removed when he was a boy. For a number of years he has been actively and successfully engaged in business as a builder, residing on the heights of the Town of Weehawken.

He has also taken an active part in public affairs, and in the discharge of various official duties has displayed marked ability, sound judgment, and unquestioned integrity. He was a member of the Hudson County Board of Chosen Freeholders one year, has served as Foreman of Clifton Hose Company of Weehawken, and is a member of the Royal Arcanum, of the Union Hill Schuetzen Corps, and of other social and political organizations. In every capacity he has gained the confidence and respect of the entire community. He is progressive, public spirited, and thoroughly interested in the advancement of his town and county, and in many instances has exerted a wholesome influence in furthering the general welfare.

Mr. Bowe married Miss Mary Keefe and has five children: John, Ella, Josephine, Thomas, and Charles Eyper.

GENEALOGICAL 469

FREDERICK A. SCHWARTZ is one of the prominent, enterprising, public spirited, and respected citizens of West Hoboken, Hudson County, and has been honored by his fellow-citizens by election to many offices of local responsibility and trust. He has taken a lively interest in the subject of education and the public school system, and has held the office of School Trustee, faithfully discharging the duties connected with this position. He has also served as Assessment Commissioner, and won the public confidence by his integrity, fairness, and sound judgment. He has been elected to the Council of West Hoboken, and while a member of this body exhibited

FREDERICK A. SCHWARTZ.

concern and care for the welfare of the community. The confidence which his service in these various capacities inspired is evidenced by the fact of his election as Town Treasurer of West Hoboken.

Mr. Schwartz is a native of West Hoboken, N. J., where he was born in June, 1853. He is the son of Frederick Schwartz, whose wife was a daughter of Henry Courvoisier. His grandfather was Frederick Schwartz, Sr. His paternal grandparents were natives of Germany, his father being born in New York City. His ancestors on the maternal side were Swiss, and his mother was born in Switzerland.

Mr. Schwartz attended the public schools and completed his education at

Hoboken Academy. He then became errand boy for a business firm, and he has remained with this same firm during the thirty years since, and is now the manager, in charge of the office and the general business.

Mr. Schwartz married, in 1876, Anita la Stayo. He has been a member of the Volunteer Fire Department of West Hoboken for more than twenty years, and is a member of Neptune Engine Company. He is also a member of the Royal Arcanum and has been First Regent of the West Hoboken Council in that order. He has always taken an active interest in everything connected with the welfare or improvement of West Hoboken.

GEORGE LIMOUZE, junior member of the real estate brokerage and insurance firm of Wallace & Limouze, of the Town of Union, was born in West Hoboken, N. J., July 30, 1866, his father being French and his mother of German descent. He attended the public schools of his native town until the age of twelve, when he began active life as errand boy in a large manufacturing establishment in New York. Since then he has practically earned his own livelihood. Remaining with that concern, and giving strict attention to business, he arose to the post of foreman, which he held for nine years, resigning in 1887 to assume charge of the large real estate interests of W. W. Hitchcock.

In 1889 he associated himself with the Woodcliffe Land Improvement Company as managing agent of its vast property in North Hudson County. Five years later, in 1893, he formed a copartnership with James G. Wallace, and under the firm name of Wallace & Limouze has since carried on an extensive general real estate brokerage and insurance business, their office being at 165 Bergenline Avenue in the Town of Union. During the past three years Mr. Limouze has had entire charge, as resident agent, of the local interests of the Cossitt Land Improvement Company, which has done so much toward the development of the northern section of the Towns of Union and Weehawken.

Mr. Limouze is an able and energetic business man, and in his knowledge of real estate and insurance matters has few equals. His perseverance, sound judgment, and unswerving integrity, together with his faithfulness to duty, have gained for him a high reputation. He resides in a handsome home on the corner of Hudson Avenue and Fourth Street in the Town of Union.

In politics Mr. Limouze is a Democrat. In 1896 he was appointed a member of the Board of Education to fill the unexpired term of a member who had died, and rendered valuable service to both the board and the town. He has been President of the Hamilton Building and Loan Association of the Town of Union since its organization in 1898; is Past Chancellor Commander of Columbian Lodge, Knights of Pythias; a member of Garfield Council, No. 56, Jr. O. U. A. M.; a member of Mystic Tie Lodge, No. 123, F. and A. M.; a Director of the North Hudson Hospital Association; and a member of the First Ward Democratic Club of Union Hill, a Commissioner of Deeds, and a Notary Public. He is also well known as an auctioneer, a business he has followed with marked success.

He was married in 1886 to Miss Catherine Schaeffer, daughter of George W Schaeffer, assistant chief engineer of the Hackensack Water Company. They have one son, Percy.

PETER ANTHONY BROCK has always resided in Jersey City, N. J., where he was born on the 22d of August, 1870, his parents being George P.

Brock and Margaret Ott. His ancestors were natives of Germany and came to this country in 1837. George P. Brock was for many years an active and influential factor in politics, and, though never holding an elective office, was appointed to fill an unexpired term as County Clerk. He was one of the prominent men of Hudson County in his day, and enjoyed the confidence and esteem of all who knew him.

Peter Anthony Brock was educated at St. Peter's College, Jersey City, at St. Vincent's College, Latrobe, Pa., and at Stevens Institute in Hoboken. In 1887 he became bookkeeper for the Phillip Semmer Glass Company,

PETER ANTHONY BROCK.

Limited, of which he is now a stockholder, Director, and Treasurer. In June, 1894, he enlisted in the Second Signal Corps, New York Militia, was warranted Corporal, and on August 22, 1899, was commissioned First Lieutenant.

In political and public matters Mr. Brock has long taken an active interest, and in various capacities has gained special distinction. On November 7, 1899, he was elected to the New Jersey Assembly from Jersey City. He has been for several years especially active in matters of vital interest to wheelmen, and was one of the chief promoters and founders of the organization known as the Associated Cycling Clubs of New York, of which Judge

Sims is President. He was formerly President of the old Metropolitan Association of Cycling Clubs of New York City and the Metropolitan District. The asphalt connections with the Pennsylvania Railroad ferries and the boulevard by the means of York and Mercer Streets are almost entirely due to his efforts and enterprise. Mr. Brock is thoroughly interested in the affairs of his native city, actively identified with almost every public improvement, and a popular, progressive, and patriotic citizen. His experience in business affairs, in the militia, and in social and public life, as well as his prominence in promoting various important movements, have won for him the confidence of the entire community, and a reputation which extends beyond the limits of Hudson County. He is a member of the Jersey City Club, of the Palma Club, and of the Catholic Club, all of Jersey City, and also of the Knights of Columbus and the Robert Davis Association. He is President of the Good Roads Association of Hudson County and Secretary of the National Cycling Association. These connections indicate in a small measure his prominence in the movement for good roads and cycling interests.

On the 21st of September, 1897, Mr. Brock married Charlotte Emma Langler. They have two daughters, Margaret Anna Brock and Charlotte Grace Brock.

JAMES W. MILLER, of Rutherford, was born in Caldwell, N. J., March 13, 1858. He is the son of J. M. Miller and Sarah A. Phillips, both natives of this State and representatives of old families. He received a public school education. He taught school for a number of years and afterward studied law. He was admitted to the bar and is now actively and successfully engaged in the practice of his profession in Rutherford, where he resides.

Mr. Miller was married, in 1894, at Cranford, N. J., to Kate T., daughter of Charles N. and Hannah Drake, of that place. They have one son, Frank Miller.

ROBERT H. WORTENDYKE is of the seventh generation from Corneliese Jacobse (alias Stille), the common ancestor of all the Wortendykes in Bergen County (see sketch on page 91).

Frederick J. Wortendyke (3) and Divertie A. Quackenbush had, among other children, Cornelius (4), born at Pascack, N. J., July 6, 1757, who died there March 31, 1822. He married Anneatie (Hannah) Van Blarcom, born in 1759, died at Pascack, October 16, 1836. The will of Cornelius (4) was proved April 21, 1822. He was a farmer, and his children of the fifth generation were Cornelius, Rynier, Abraham, Mary, Martha, Altie, Sally, Rachel, Sophia, and Jenny.

Abraham Wortendyke (5) married Catharine Demarest. They had children of the sixth generation, among whom was Hon. Isaac Wortendyke, who married Louisa Hoffman, of Claverack, N. Y.

Isaac Wortendyke (6) had children of the seventh generation, one of whom was Robert H. Wortendyke, the subject of this sketch.

Cornelius Wortendyke (4), great-grandfather of Robert H., moved to what is now Wortendyke, N. J., in 1796. Some of the land is still owned by the Wortendyke family. What is now Wortendyke and vicinity was called Newtown for fifty years, a name given to the place in 1800 by Cornelius. The first mill established at Wortendyke (then Newtown) was built by Cornelius Wortendyke in 1812 for a wool-carding mill. Abraham Wortendyke (5) succeeded Cornelius in the woolen business. In 1832 the factory was changed from a wool to a cotton mill. This business was conducted successfully by Abraham Wortendyke until his death in 1857. On September 1, 1811, Cornelius Wortendyke leased a lot of land twenty-three feet square, near the present Methodist Episcopal Church, for twenty-five years, for a school building, which was the first schoolhouse in that locality of which any information can be obtained. The late Isaac Wortendyke (6) was Principal of Claverack Academy at Claverack, N. Y., from 1846 to 1849. From January, 1868, to January, 1878, he was Surrogate of Bergen County, and in 1880 he was elected to the Senate from that county.

Robert H. Wortendyke (7) was born in Brooklyn, N. Y., April 4, 1859. He was educated in the public schools and at Hackensack Academy, and in June, 1879, began his business life as agent for the Liverpool and London and Globe Insurance Company, with offices at Hackensack, N. J. In August, 1897, he moved his office to Ridgewood, Bergen County, where he is carrying on a large and successful real estate, insurance, and loan business, representing several large insurance companies. He has resided since childhood at Midland Park, Bergen County, and has always maintained the confidence and respect of all who know him.

In public as well as in business life Mr. Wortendyke is well known. He was elected a member of the Board of Education at Midland Park (District 46) in March, 1891, and served three years. In March, 1892, he was elected District Clerk of the board. In 1895 he was appointed Postmaster at Midland Park. In March, 1895, he was elected Mayor of the Borough of Midland Park for a term of two years. In each of these capacities he displayed marked ability, sound judgment, and great energy, and performed his duties with honor and satisfaction. He is a member of the Reformed Church of Paramus, N. J., and a public spirited, progressive, and patriotic citizen.

Mr. Wortendyke was married, April 22, 1891, to Eva Glass, daughter of William Glass, of Cleveland, Ohio. They have two children.

WARREN FERDON is descended in the ninth generation from Thomas Verdon and Mary Badye, the first American ancestors of the family. The line of descent is the same through eight generations as that of Jesse N. Ferdon (see sketch on page 184). John D. Ferdon (8), the brother of Jesse N. Ferdon, was born at Closter, N. J., and married Clarissa Gecox, daughter of William Gecox, of Alpine, N. J. One of their children of the ninth generation is Warren Ferdon, the subject of this sketch.

Mr. Ferdon (9) was born in Alpine, N. J., on the 1st of October, 1868. He was educated in the schools of Bergen County, and at the age of seventeen began his active career in the dry goods business. Six months later, however, he became a clerk in a grocery house, in which he remained five years, when he engaged in the grocery and grain business for himself in Closter, N. J., where he still resides. He has continued in this business until the present time (1900), having built up a large and successful trade. He is a member of the Dutch Reformed Church, a public spirited citizen, and highly esteemed by all who know him.

CHARLES FREDERICK LONG is one of the prominent architects of Jersey City, where he was born on the 8th of April, 1871. His father, Charles K. Long, a leading builder and contractor, has resided in that city for forty years and is one of the best known men in Hudson County. His mother, Mary Pickell, deceased, was descended from a line of Holland Dutch ancestors who came to this country many years before the Revolutionary War and settled in New York City. On his father's side he is of Canadian descent.

Mr. Long was educated in the Jersey City Grammar and High Schools and at the New York Art Institute. He early displayed artistic talents and chose architecture for his life work, thoroughly fitting himself for that profession. His studies were broad and practical, and enabled him to gain a wide experience in all branches of the building trades. For four years he was engaged in the practice of architecture in New York City. Since then he

CHARLES F. LONG.

has practiced his profession in Jersey City, where he has gained, by his skill, industry, and acknowledged ability, an enviable reputation and a large acquaintance. He erected Public School No. 19, the Lembeck building, and Public School No. 20, the largest and most approved school of its kind in the State. His work bears the stamp of great artistic merit, and, though a young man, he has achieved a recognized standing in the community.

As the progenitor and organizer of the New Jersey Naval Reserve Mr. Long is known throughout the State and was one of the leading factors in State naval affairs. On May 25, 1898, he was commissioned by President McKinley Ensign in the United States Navy and served on the United

States cruiser "Badger" with the North Cuba blockade squadron during the war with Spain. He was honorably discharged October 8, 1898, at which time he was commanding officer of the Division of Acting Marines. He is a prominent member of the New Jersey Society of Architects, of Amity Lodge, No. 103, F. and A. M., and of the Naval and Military Order of the Spanish-American War.

WILLIAM SUMNER LAWRENCE, of Hasbrouck Heights, N. J., was born in Boston, Mass., October 8, 1854, and was educated in the public schools of that State. In business he has always been connected with the wholesale shoe trade, being with one house in Boston for a period of eighteen years. He is now a stockholder and Director in the firm of Morse & Rogers, 134-140 Duane Street, New York, the largest jobbers in shoes, rubbers, and findings in New York City. He has been with this house about ten years.

He was elected Mayor of Hasbrouck Heights in March, 1897, and was re-elected in 1899. He is a Director of the Hasbrouck Heights Building and Loan Association and a Director of the Star Building and Loan Association of New York City, and has served two terms as President of the Hasbrouck Heights Field Club. He is also a member of the Executive Committee of the Seward League of Hasbrouck Heights, a Republican organization, and has been a member of the Hasbrouck Heights Board of Education two terms. Mr. Lawrence married Lydia A., daughter of Captain Myer Bradbury, of Machias, Me.

EDWARD F. CARBIN, of Bayonne, N. J., was born in New York City on the 31st of October, 1857, his parents being E. C. Carbin and Mary Brady. They came from Ireland to the United States when young and were married in New York, whence they removed to Bayonne in 1867.

Mr. Carbin was educated in the public schools of the Third Ward of Bayonne and afterward engaged in lumbering operations on the Hudson River between New York and Albany. In 1880 he entered the employ of the Pennsylvania Railroad Company, with which he has ever since been associated.

He is a member of the School Board of Bayonne, but aside from this has never accepted public office. He has always taken, however, a deep interest in local affairs, and as a citizen and business man is highly respected. He is a Democrat in politics, and a member of Paurapaugh Lodge, No. 187, I. O. R. M., of Hook and Ladder Company No. 1, and of the Exempt Firemen's Association, all of Bayonne. He was married in Bayonne, November 15, 1880, to Mary L. S. Smeaton.

LAMBERTUS C. BOBBINK, of Rutherford, N. J., was born in Holland on the 11th of April, 1866, being the son of Jacob and Wilhelmina (Gemmenk) Bobbink. His parents were natives of Holland, where they were married.

Mr. Bobbink received his education in the schools of his native country. He came to the United States in 1894 and settled in Rutherford, N. J., where he still resides. Before coming to America he was successfully engaged in the florist business for three years in Holland, an equal number of years in England, two years in France, three years in Germany, and one year in Belgium, thus gaining a large and valuable experience. He now carries on the florist and nursery business on a large scale, under the firm name of Bobbink & Atkins, in Rutherford.

He is a member of the American Florists' Union and of the New York Florists' Union, and served for a year and a half in the army of Holland.

In 1897 Mr. Bobbink married Gertrude Schmidt, of Hoboken, N. J. They have one child, Bertie.

JAMES EDWARD BLACK, one of the popular citizens and largest meat dealers in Bayonne, N. J., was born in that place on the 2d of July, 1868. His parents, John Black and Margaret Gasque, removed to Bayonne from New York State, and for many years have been useful and respected citizens of that municipality.

Mr. Black received his education in the Bayonne public schools, where he laid the foundation upon which he has already built a successful career. After leaving school he associated himself with the T. C. Brown Dry Goods Company, of Jersey City. In 1889 he engaged in the meat business for himself in Bayonne, where he has since built up a large and successful trade in that line. He is one of the most popular citizens of the southern part of Hudson County, an able and substantial business man, deeply interested in the prosperity of the community, and respected by all who know him. In politics he is a Democrat and in religion a Methodist. He is a member of Bayonne Lodge, No. 695, Royal Arcanum, of Bayonne Lodge, No. 571, I. O. H., and of the Improved Order of Redmen.

December 21, 1890, Mr. Black was married, in Nyack, N. Y., to Mary Jane Armstrong, daughter of William K. and Anna Bella (Henderson) Armstrong, of Spring Valley, N. Y. They have one son, Edward Stewart.

JAMES E. BLACK.

GEORGE W. COLLIGNON was born March 14, 1864, in Westwood, N. J., where he still resides. He is the son of Nicholas Collignon and Catherine Demarest and a grandson of Peter and Mary C. (Perrie) Collignon and James Demarest and Jane Wortendyke. His father was First Lieutenant in the Twenty-second New Jersey Volunteers during the Civil War. On the paternal side he is of French descent and on his mother's side of Holland Dutch ancestry, her family having come to this country at an early colonial period. The Demarests and Wortendykes are both noticed at length in preceding pages of this work.

Mr. Collignon was educated in the schools of Bergen County, and at the age of fifteen began active life as foreman in a chair factory. He continued in that capacity for fifteen years and then established himself in the lumber business, starting a sawmill, which he still operates.

He has achieved success in business and is also highly respected as a public spirited, progressive, and enterprising citizen. He has served as Trustee of School District No. 1, for two terms, was Borough Councilman one term, and is a member of the Dutch Reformed Church. He married Lillie Bogert and has two daughters: Mabel and Bertha.

ARTHUR ANDERS, of East Rutherford, was born in Berlin, Germany, July 22, 1859. He is the son of Charles Anders and Wanda Schneider, who were born and married in the Fatherland.

Mr. Anders was educated in his native country, first in the public schools and subsequently in the high school of Berlin. There he also entered a business college, and after completing the course began his career by spending three years in commercial business in that city. He came to America in September, 1884, and occupied various positions in New York business houses, principally as bookkeeper and cashier. In 1890 he settled in East Rutherford, N. J., where he purchased property and still resides.

In East Rutherford Mr. Anders established a general agency business which he continued successfully until 1897, when he turned his attention wholly to real estate and insurance, in which he has been successful. He organized a board for the Metropolitan Savings and Loan Association, a prosperous organization of Newark, N. J.

Mr. Anders was married in New York City, in 1890, to Miss Margaret Mutter, of Berlin, Germany. They have two children: George and Elsie.

CAMILLUS MONDORF, Rector of St. Joseph's Roman Catholic Church of East Rutherford, N. J., was born on the Rhine, near Cologne, Germany, October 21, 1844. While a student he entered the Prussian Army in 1866, and after serving the statutory term resumed his studies, first in Belgium and afterward in Germany. He came to America in 1876, and on January 1, 1877, was ordained a priest by Bishop Wadhams, of Ogdensburg, N. Y. The Rt. Rev. Bishop Wigger selected him in August, 1885, as Rector of St. Joseph's Church in East Rutherford. This church was built in 1873.

JOHN BANTZ, of the firm of Klahre & Bantz, of West Hoboken, was born in Hoboken, N. J., on the 13th of June, 1868, the son of Frederick J. Bantz and Lena Schenck. His father, now a retired citizen of Hoboken, formerly lived in West Hoboken, having emigrated to this country from Germany in 1850; he took an active part in all that pertained to the best interests of the town, and served with ability and satisfaction as Town Treasurer, Town Collector, and Chairman of the Board of Fire Trustees.

John Bantz attended the Hoboken public schools and Cooper Institute, New York, where he pursued his studies for six years. His educational training, therefore, was on broad and liberal lines, and enabled him to gain a practical knowledge of those branches which proved the most applicable to the career he was destined to follow. After leaving school he learned the trade of carpenter, and while yet a youth engaged in carpentering and building with marked success. In 1894 he became a member of the firm of Klahre & Bantz and engaged in the manufacture of window frames, mouldings, mantels, balusters, brackets, etc., in West Hoboken, where they have established a large and successful business. Their trade has developed to extensive proportions. Mr. Bantz is not only a practical carpenter and builder, but also proficient in architectural drawing, original in his designs, and thorough and skillful in all that pertains to artistic woodworking and decoration.

JOHN BANTZ.

He has achieved a high standing, and is respected as a public spirited, progressive, and patriotic citizen. His attention has been devoted strictly to increasing business interests. He is an ardent Republican, and has been active in local political affairs, but has never sought nor accepted public office. His fraternal affiliations are with Euclid Lodge, F. and A. M., Pentalpha Chapter, No. 17, R. A. M., Pilgrim Commandery, No. 16, K. T., and Fraternity Lodge, I. O. O. F., all of Hoboken. He is also an exempt fireman, having served as a member of the Weehawken Volunteer Fire Department. Mr. Bantz has always cast his influence in favor of every movement designed to promote the welfare and advancement of the Town of West Hoboken.

JOHN BOGERT[1] was born April 6, 1839, in Closter, Bergen County, N. J., where he still resides. He is the son of Matthew S. Bogert and Margaret Christie and a grandson of Seba Bogert and David and Maria (Wanamaker) Christie. His paternal grandmother was a Blackledge. His father served as a private in the War of 1812, and his grandfather, David Christie, was for a number of years Judge and Surrogate of Bergen County. All of these families are noticed at length on other pages of this work.

Mr. Bogert received his education in Bergen County. He left school at the age of sixteen and began his career on his father's farm, where he remained two years. He then went to New York and engaged in the trucking business, continuing for six years. At the end of that period he returned to the homestead and followed agricultural pursuits for about four years, when his father sold the farm. He then engaged in business as a dealer in horses.

During his entire life Mr. Bogert has taken an active interest in local affairs and in various capacities has rendered efficient service to the community. He is a Commissioner of Appeals, and a public spirited and progressive citizen. He married Jane Bogert and has four children: David C., Morton, Mabel, and Elmer.

RALPH VAN VALEN.—On the paternal side the Van Valens of Bergen County are of German extraction and on the maternal side French. In 1593 Hans (John) Verveele (1), the son of a prominent German citizen residing in the City of Cologne, is known to have married Catharine Oliviers, daughter of John Oliviers, a prominent French merchant at Cologne. There Hans resided with his wife until the fires of religious intolerance which culminated in the expulsion of all the Protestants drove the couple to Amsterdam, Holland, about 1610. In 1594 Hans and Catharine had a son, Daniel Verveele (2), born to them, who in 1615, five years after their flight from Cologne, married Anna Elkhart and became, like his father, a shopkeeper in Amsterdam. By Anna Elkhart Daniel (2) had four children of the third generation from Hans, the eldest of whom was John Verveele (who wrote the name Vervelen), born at Amsterdam about 1617. John (3) was well raised and educated, as his subsequent career shows. In 1636 he married Anna Jaarsfelt, by whom he had three children of the fourth generation from Hans. Early in 1657 John Vervelen (3) and several others left Amsterdam for New York, with their wives and children, and arrived at the latter place early in April. The first thing John did was to enroll himself as a burgher of the city (April 24, 1657) and to unite with the Dutch church. By two purchases of land on June 4 and May 16, 1664, he became a large landowner. His social habits won him friends and popularity, and he soon found himself at home in the brewery business with Isaac de Forest, a prominent French refugee. In 1660 he was elected Schout, but was defeated the next year. This disgusted him, as we find him joining the Harlem settlement in 1663, whence he was sent as a delegate to the Colonial General Assembly and where he became one of the original patentees of the Harlem patent in 1667. The several important public duties intrusted to him and his long retention therein, particularly as ferry-master, evidence the favor in which he was held. When his second lease of the ferry expired his son, Daniel Vervelen, in his behalf petitioned Governor Dongan (1668) for its renewal. He was told to hold the premises until further orders to the contrary. Four years later Frederick Phillipse

---

[1] This sketch is of the same person mentioned on page 60, in which the middle initial "M" was erroneously used.

brought suit in the New York Colonial Court to eject him from the Island of Paparinima, which Phillipse claimed under a title derived from Vanderbeck. The Council defended Vervelen's title, but, the Governor having proposed to build a bridge across the Spuyten Duyvil, the Mayor and Aldermen ousted Vervelen by an order of the court dated July 19, 1693. Vervelen was then employed to build a bridge connecting Harlem and Phillipsburgh Manor, called King's Bridge, and to collect tolls. He died between 1669 and 1702. His children of the fourth generation were Daniel, Anna, and Maria.

In 1652 Daniel Vervelen (4), then a mere boy, came to America, seven years ahead of his father, John (3). On his way over he was in the care of the Rev. Gideon Schaats, a prominent Dutch divine then seeking an asylum in America. Dominie Schaats had a daughter Alida, to whom Daniel became very much attached, and whom he married three years later. He embarked in trade in 1655, but joined his father at New York soon after the latter's arrival. He joined the Dutch church in 1661. Both he and his father owned lots in Prince (now Beaver) Street. There also they ran an extensive brewery business. Daniel (4) sided with the English in 1667, and was assaulted and severely injured by the Dutch populace. Several years later he removed to New Utrecht, Long Island. Thence he went to Spuyten Duyvil. He died about 1715. His children of the fifth generation were Anna Maria, Johanna, Henry, Bernardus, Rynear, Gideon, Frederick, and John.

On the 5th of March, 1701, four of the sons of Daniel (4): John, Gideon, Rynear, and Bernardus, bought of the heirs of Balthazar de Hart 2,100 acres of land at Closter, in Bergen County, extending west from the Hudson River to the Tiena Kill Brook. Their title was for some years in dispute, and after much trouble Bernardus succeeded in obtaining title to the whole tract in 1708. He settled on it and his descendants have become numerous in the county.

Bernardus (5), born about 1670, married (1) Sophia la Maiter and (2) Jannetie Vanderbeck, and had a number of children of the sixth generation, among whom were Alida, Isaac, Cornelia, Daniel, John, Hester, Frederick, Abram, James, and Bernardus.

Ralph Van Valen, the subject of this sketch, is of the tenth generation from Hans Verveele, first mentioned, and of the fifth generation from Bernardus (5). He is a grandson of Isaac Van Valen and Elizabeth Hern and Abram and Margery (Wortendyke) Post and the son of John Van Valen and Maria Post. He was born at Pascack, N. J., March 27, 1858, and received his education in the schools of Bergen County. At the age of sixteen he began active life on his father's farm, but two years later entered the employ of the New Jersey and New York Railroad, remaining six years. He then learned the painting trade and has since followed that business with marked success. He has served as Constable of the Borough of Woodcliff, where he resides.

SANDFORD BOGERT starts his American ancestry with Cornelis Jans Bougaert, the emigrant (see sketch on page 132), from whom he is of the ninth generation. He is the son of David A. Bogert and Phebe Ann Osborn and a grandson of Albert Bogert and Rachel Blawvelt. He was born at Pearl River, Rockland County, N. Y., November 21, 1841. There he received a public school education. He left school at the age of thirteen and went to work in a tannery, and continued in that business for thirteen years, mastering the tanner's trade in every branch. He then engaged in farming in Hillsdale, Bergen County, N. J., where he still resides.

Mr. Bogert is a public spirited citizen, and has served two terms each on the School Committee and Township Committee of his town. He is a public spirited citizen and thoroughly identified with the best interests of the community. He married Catharine M. Van Riper, a member of one of the old families in New Jersey.

WALTER W. WIEDERMANN has always resided in Hoboken, Hudson County, N. J., where he was born July 8, 1875. His parents, Louis and Rose

WALTER W. WIEDERMANN.

(Hess) Wiedermann, were both natives of Germany, and in 1852 left the Fatherland and came to this country, settling in Hoboken. Louis Wiedermann is now one of the oldest living residents of that city. He was actively and successfully engaged in the grocery business for thirty-seven years, his establishment on the corner of Washington and Ninth Streets, Hoboken, widely known as Wiedermann's Mammoth Grocery House, being one of the largest and most complete in the county. Later it was conducted by his son, Louis Wiedermann, Jr., who died in 1889, after which the father sold out and retired from active business.

Walter W. Wiedermann is the only surviving son of Louis Wiedermann, Sr., and Rose Hess, and although but twenty-five years of age has attained an honorable position in business. He received an academic and public school education, and after a course at the Jersey City Business College entered the employ of Stein & Weidner, real estate and insurance agents at No. 504 Washington Street, Hoboken. This was in 1890. He remained with them four years, laying the foundation upon which he has built a successful career, and gaining a broad and accurate knowledge of business in general and of real estate and insurance affairs in particular.

In 1894 Mr. Wiedermann formed a partnership with Charles von Broock under the style of the Metropolitan Dairy Company, a name which indicates the character of their business. Subsequently he started the Palace Hotel in Hoboken, but in 1898 returned to the real estate and insurance business, purchasing the establishment and interests formerly conducted by J. W. Bremerman, Allison Mather, and Frank Anderson, which he still conducts. Mr. Wiedermann has brought to his various business enterprises ability, sound judgment, and native energy, and by integrity of character and faithful attention to duty has achieved success. He is Secretary of the Mutual Home and Savings Association of Hoboken, and prominently identified with the best interests of his city and county. He is also a member of the Masonic fraternity, the Improved and Benevolent Order of Elks, and the Foresters of America, and a public spirited, progressive citizen.

PETER C. COLLIGNON, of Westwood, was born in Rivervale, Bergen County, N. J., October 19, 1856. He is the son of Claudius O. Collignon and Sarah Cleveland and a grandson of Peter and Mary C. (Perrie) Collignon and Neil Cleveland and Sarah Cole. His ancestors came to this country from France.

Mr. Collignon was educated in the Bergen County public schools, and at the age of eighteen became a bookkeeper in a chair factory. He continued in that capacity until 1890, when he purchased the business and successfully conducted it until 1896. He is a member of the Dutch Reformed Church of Tappan, N. Y., a public spirited and progressive citizen, and honored and respected by all who know him.

He married Isabella E. Ward, by whom he has three children: Raymond, Isabelle, and Viola.

GEORGE DANIEL CANFIELD, of Kearny, Hudson County, was born in Barton, N. Y., on the 30th of September, 1840. He is the son of George W. Canfield and Julia A. Case, both of whom were of English descent.

Mr. Canfield was educated in the public schools of Orange County, in Barton, N. Y., and for over twenty years was successfully engaged in the rubber stamp business in New York City. In 1872 he settled permanently in Kearny, Hudson County, where he has since resided, and where he has been successfully engaged in the real estate business since 1888. He is a Republican in politics, has served with ability and satisfaction as a member of the Kearny School Board, and is a member of the Odd Fellows and of the Fraternal Legion. As a citizen he is public spirited and enterprising. He is actively interested in the welfare of the community and in various capacities has served his fellow-citizens efficiently and honorably.

He married Harriet E. Hadley, by whom he has four children: Jennie M., Burton E., Julia, and Dorothy G., all of whom reside in Kearny.

BURTON EDMUND CANFIELD, of Kearny, was born in Davenport, Iowa, April 24, 1870, being the only son of George D. and Harriet E. (Hadley) Canfield and a grandson of George W. Canfield and Julia A. Case. His maternal great-grandfather, a Hoyt, served in the Revolutionary War.

Mr. Canfield was educated in the public schools of Kearny and at the New Jersey Business College. Subsequently he became a bookkeeper in New York. Resigning that position, he engaged in the real estate business in Kearny, in which he still continues under the firm name of George D. Canfield & Son. He is a stanch Republican, active and influential in party affairs, and served as Town Clerk of Kearny in 1896-97 and Town Treasurer in 1898-99. He is a member and President of the Board of Education, a member of the Davis Memorial Methodist Episcopal Church of Harrison, a member of the Royal Arcanum, and a public spirited, enterprising citizen. Mr. Canfield married Millie B. Remey, by whom he has one son, George R.

JOHN CALVIN GARDENIER, of Hillsdale, was born in Woodcliff, Bergen County, N. J., December 30, 1868. He is the son of Garret H. and Alvina (Post) Gardenier and a grandson of Henry Gardenier and Jane Post. He received his education in the public schools of Hillsdale, Bergen County, whither his parents removed when he was young. At the age of eighteen he established himself in the livery business at Hillsdale, and has since continued in that line, having now one of the best livery stables in the county.

Mr. Gardenier is a public spirited citizen, active in the affairs of the community, and respected by all who know him. He attends the Dutch Reformed Church. He married Clara Ottignon and has one son, Harold Gardenier.

JOHN H. HOLDRUM is of the seventh generation in direct line from John Holdrum, the emigrant (see sketch on page 237). The line of descent is as follows: John Holdrum (1) married Cornelia Tienhoven. Their son, William Holdrum (2), married Margaret Peters. Their son, Cornelius Holdrum (3), married Elizabeth Haring. Their son, James C. Holdrum (4), married Margaret Demarest. Their son, Cornelius (5), married Elizabeth de Pew. Their son, Cornelius C. (6), married Adaline Hopper, and had a son, John H. Holdrum (7), the person named above.

John H. Holdrum was born at Rivervale, N. J., January 16, 1862. He was educated in the public schools of Bergen County, and at the age of eighteen began active life on his father's farm. Five years later he went to New York City, where he was engaged in the ice business for four years with marked success. He then removed to Oradell, Bergen County, and engaged in general contracting, a business he has since followed. He has done about all the general contracting in his section since he established himself in business and is respected as a man of ability, integrity, and enterprise. He is a member of the Dutch Reformed Church, a public spirited citizen, and a worthy representative of one of the old Bergen County families. He married Matilda Westervelt and has one son.

JOHN P. McMAHON, Town Clerk of West Hoboken, N. J., is the eldest son of Bernard and Catherine McMahon, natives of Ireland, who came to America in 1860 and settled in West Hoboken, where they still reside, their other children being Edward and Catherine.

He was born in that town on the 29th of November, 1868, and there obtained his education in St. Mary's parochial school, graduating at the age of seventeen. He then engaged in the retail milk business in West Hoboken. Although a mere youth, he developed ability and sound judgment, and for about ten years conducted a large and successful trade. His popularity is attested by the confidence and esteem in which he has long been held by the community, and especially by his wide circle of friends and acquaintances. As a Democrat he took an active part in politics, and in the spring of 1896 was elected Town Clerk of the Town of West Hoboken, which office he still holds, being re-elected in April, 1899, for a second term of three

JOHN P. M'MAHON.

years. By virtue of this position he is and has been also clerk of the Board of Town Council.

Mr. McMahon has discharged his official duties with singular fidelity, consistency, and success, and has won the respect of all classes irrespective of party affiliations. He is a prominent member of the Robert Davis Association, and takes a deep interest in the affairs of his town and county. On April 27, 1899, he married Mrs. Elise Guarnerio, of West Hoboken, an accomplished and most estimable lady, and resides at No. 501 Spring Street in that town.

PETER M. HOLDRUM, of Rivervale, is of the sixth generation from John Holdrum, the first American ancestor of the family (see sketch on page 237). The line of descent in his case is as follows: (1) John Holdrum married Cornelia Tienhoven; (2) William Holdrum married Margaret Peters; (3) Nicholas Holdrum married Maritie Janse; (4) Cornelius Holdrum married Margaret Sarvent; (5) William C. Holdrum married Letty Merseles; (6) Peter M. Holdrum married Elizabeth Wortendyke.

Peter M. Holdrum, the subject of this sketch, was born at Rivervale, Bergen County, June 24, 1822. He was educated in the Bergen County schools, and at the age of seventeen went to work on his father's farm, where he has ever since continued. He served as Assessor for several years and has held various other local offices, discharging the duties of each with acknowledged ability and satisfaction. He is a member of the Dutch Reformed Church. He is one of the oldest farmers in his section, and during his long and active life has maintained the confidence of all who know him. He married Elizabeth Wortendyke and has one daughter.

EDWARD M. ANSON, of Hasbrouck Heights, Bergen County, was born at Hyde Park, Dutchess County, N. Y., June 4, 1856. His ancestors were English, and for several generations have been residents of this country.

Mr. Anson was educated in the public schools of Lockport, Niagara County, N. Y., and at the age of fourteen was employed as a telegraph operator in the oil regions of Butler County, Pa., later being employed by the Western Union Telegraph Company in Buffalo, Chicago, Cincinnati, St. Louis, and New York. When the St. Louis convention met to nominate Samuel J. Tilden for President he was one of the five operators of Chicago chosen to attend to the telegraphic business of the meeting, and again at the Cincinnati convention, when Rutherford B. Hayes was nominated, he was chosen to act in the same capacity. In 1877 Mr. Anson moved to New York as chief operator in the main office, where he remained twelve years. In April, 1892, he left the service to engage in real estate business, in which he has ever since continued.

He was one of the organizers of the Building, Loan and Savings Association of Hasbrouck Heights, which he served six years as Secretary. He was the organizer and Secretary of the Hasbrouck Heights Land and Improvement Company and the organizer and Secretary of the Lemmermann Site Company. Since beginning business Mr. Anson has built over one hundred houses and brought out from the city more than one thousand residents. While devoting his time and energy to the upbuilding of his borough, although not seeking office or self-interest, he was appointed Postmaster in November, 1893, holding the office for four years. In 1896 he was elected a Justice of the Peace. He is a member of a number of organizations at Hasbrouck Heights, including the Pioneer Club, the Hasbrouck Heights Field Club, and the Royal Arcanum. He is also a member of the Old Time Telegraphic Association, the Telegraphers' Mutual Benefit Association, and the Telegraphers' Aid Society.

Mr. Anson was married to Miss Margaret E. Crawford, of New York City, April 16, 1879. He is a highly esteemed citizen, both in his public life and in his private character.

WILLIAM JOHN DOCKRAY, the youngest man ever elected to the Board of Education of Kearny, N. J., where he resides, was born in Valatia, Columbia County, N. Y., on the 16th of January, 1875. He is the son of

James and Margret (Harrison) Dockray, both of whom were born and married in England, and who came to the United States in 1872 and settled first in Valatia, New York State, moving thence in 1884 to Kearny, N. J.

Mr. Dockray obtained a good practical education in the Kearny public schools, and upon leaving them engaged in the grocery business in that town. This venture occurred when he was but fifteen years of age. He still follows the same business in Kearny, and has gained for himself a wide reputation. He has also taken an active interest in public affairs, and as an ardent and consistent Republican has developed rare political ability and

WILLIAM J. DOCKRAY.

sagacity. He is now (1900) serving as a member of the Kearny Board of Education, being the youngest man ever elected to that important position. Few men at his age have attained the prominence and influence in the community which he has achieved. He has gained success in both business and public affairs and is regarded as one of the representative young men of Hudson County. Public spirited, patriotic, and enterprising, he takes a deep interest in every movement which affects the welfare of the community and in various ways has exerted an important and wholesome influence in advancing local projects. His services on the Board of Education have been marked by strict fidelity to the best interests of the schools of his town. Mr. Dockray is a member of the Knights of Pythias and of the Knox Presbyterian Church at Kearny.

O. G. CAMPBELL'S first American ancestor, William Campbell, was born on the Isle of Man in Great Britain and baptised in Cork London Church, February 9, 1689, as appears by the inscription on his tombstone in the old cemetery at Tappan, N. Y. His parents were probably natives of Ireland. He emigrated to America in 1716 and went to Tappan, where the following year he married Aeltie Minnelly. She was a granddaughter of Minne Johannes, of Friesland, Holland, who came to America in 1663 with his first wife, Rensie Feddens, and settled at Flatbush, Long Island, where he became a person of note. In 1684 he removed to Haverstraw, N. Y., where he purchased and located on 3,000 acres of land. He married a second wife, Magdalena Hendrix, in 1689, and became one of the leading men in what was then Orange County, N. Y. In 1685 he was commissioned High Sheriff of Orange County. He attained wealth and prominence, and died leaving a large and respectable family. His son, Albert Minnelly, married Mensie Jepes and setled near Tappan, where on the 17th of July, 1697, his daughter Aeltie, the wife of William Campbell, was baptised.

William Campbell purchased and settled on a large tract of land near Tappan, where he became wealthy and influential. He died January 7, 1760, and his wife survived him until August 10, 1776. Their children of the second generation, all baptised at Tappan, were Albert, William, Mensie, Ann, John, Abraham, Robert, Arie, Cornelius, Elizabeth, and probably one or two more. The descendants of these children of William Campbell spread north over Rockland County, N. Y., and south into Bergen County, N. J., where they are still numerous.

O. G. Campbell, the subject of this sketch, is of the sixth generation in line of descent from William, the emigrant. He is the son of John E. Campbell, who was born at Nyack, N. Y., and Henrietta Van Valen (a descendant of John Verveele, the emigrant), who was born in Haverstraw. N. Y. He was born at Wallingford, Conn., January 10, 1870, and was educated at Rockland College and at Columbia College, New York. He then engaged in the undertaking business. For a time he was also engaged in bridge contracting. He is a Republican in politics.

THOMAS J. BYRAM.—The Byrams are said to be descended from Nicholas Byram, who with his wife, Susanna Shaw, emigrated from the County of Kent, England, and settled at Dedham, Mass., near the middle of the seventeenth century. It is also said that Nicholas was the son of a titled Englishman.

His son Nicholas (2), born about 1650, married (1) Mary Edson and (2) a sister of James Keith, physician. Nicholas (2) had a son Ebenezer (3), born at Dedham, Mass., in 1692, who married, in 1714, Hannah Hayward.

Ebenezer Byram (3) served in King Philip's War, and on the 18th of June, 1744, led a colony from Massachusetts to New Jersey. The colony settled at Morristown, N. J., where Ebenezer established and was the leader of the first church. He was known as "Captain Ebenezer." He died August 9, 1753, and his wife January 11, 1761.

Their son, Ebenezer Byram (4), born in Massachusetts in 1716, died at Morristown in 1762. He married, in 1738, Abagail Alden, a great-granddaughter of John Alden, of "Mayflower" fame. The descendants of Captain

Ebenezer (3) and his son Ebenezer (4) spread over Morris and Sussex Counties. Two of them, John and Jeptha Byram, were among the first settlers of Sussex County. They organized the Township of Byram and gave it their family name, which it still retains. Jeptha was the first Collector of the township. Jeptha and John owned iron ore lands besides farm lands. Each had about 160 acres, which he tilled, making a specialty of melons. John's lands descended to his son Nicholas and Jeptha's to his son Jeptha. The latter had a daughter, Hannah, who married Asahel Lovell, whose family moved to and settled at Enfield, Tompkins County, N. Y., in 1806.

Thomas J. Byram, the subject of this sketch, is descended from one of these early Byrams. He is the son of Job J. Byram and Mary F. Lyon, and was born at Sparta, Sussex County, October 5, 1868. His parents were also natives of Sparta. He was educated in the Sparta public schools and subsequently learned the carpenter's trade, which he has since followed. He is now in business for himself, residing in Arlington.

Mr. Byram is a Republican in politics, a Methodist in religion, and a member of the Royal Arcanum. He is a public spirited citizen and respected by all who know him. He married Louisa Ryder and has one son, Roy.

ALBERT BORN, of Secaucus, Hudson County, was born in New York City on the 22d of November, 1849. He is the son of George Born, a native of Germany, and Maria Elizabeth Dreiher, who was born in France. He was educated in the schools of Hudson County and subsequently engaged in farming and gardening, a business which he has since followed with marked success.

In politics Mr. Born is an active and useful Republican. He has served for ten years as a School Trustee, being District Clerk part of the time. He is a member of the Royal Arcanum, a public spirited citizen, and respected by all who know him.

Mr. Born married Katherine, daughter of John Kesler, of Homestead, Hudson County, N. J. They have seven children living, namely: Albert, Jr., Etta, Emma, William, Charles, Harry, and Mabel.

WILLIAM NECKER is one of the best known undertakers in East New Jersey. As an embalmer and funeral director he has few superiors. He was born in West Hoboken, N. J., November 12, 1870, his parents, Christopher Necker and Louisa Kienle, being natives of Germany. He is their eldest son. His father came to America about 1866 and settled in West Hoboken, where he followed the bakery business with success for many years.

Mr. Necker obtained his education in the public schools of West Hoboken and Union Hill. Circumstances compelled him, however, to relinquish his studies when he was twelve years old and take up the trade of pianomaking in the establishment of the Braumüller Piano Company, of New York, with whom he remained eleven years. This was a fortunate as well as a very pleasant connection. With energy and adaptability he mastered every detail of the business, learned thoroughly the general construction of pianos, and gained a reputation as a skilled and talented workman. He was popular among both his associates and the members of the firm, and during the last three years had charge of the woodworking department. So well was he liked by Mr. Braumüller, the President of the company, that when the latter's wife died in 1898, five years after he had resigned his position, Mr. Necker was sent for by him to take entire charge of the funeral. This was a compliment, and speaks volumes for Mr. Necker's popularity and integrity, and the esteem in which he is held.

In December, 1892, Mr. Necker resigned his position in the Braumüller establishment and entered the United States School of Embalming in New York City, from which he was graduated in April, 1894. There he received a practical as well as a theoretical knowledge of every branch of embalming and undertaking. Immediately after graduation he opened an office at 251 Bergenline Avenue in the Town of Union. Nearly every one prophesied a failure. But his courage and perseverance never flagged. In

WILLIAM NECKER.

the face of all obstacles, and even of adverse criticism, he struck boldly out upon original lines, and soon acquired a prosperous business. Methodical, enterprising, and energetic, full of sympathy, and appreciating the delicate and exacting duties which necessarily devolved upon him, he steadily won the confidence and respect of the entire community. He was faithful to every trust, diligent in the performance of his work, and availed himself of all legitimate opportunities. He makes it a maxim of treating the poor with the same dignity as the rich.

Mr. Necker's success as an undertaker and embalmer may be said to have been almost instantaneous. At 251 Bergenline Avenue in the Town of

Union, where he resides, he fitted up his present light and attractive office, equipping it with every modern convenience. His practical experience at pianomaking enables him to exercise good judgment in selecting his outfits. He has a taste for the eternal fitness of things, and every detail receives his personal attention. Besides the main office already mentioned, Mr. Necker has branches at 409 Charles Street, West Hoboken, and Sixth Street and Tower Avenue, Guttenberg. He has had many of the larger funerals in Hudson County during the last five years, and has achieved marked success and a high reputation.

Mr. Necker is a progressive, public spirited citizen. He joined the Fire Department of the Town of Union in 1893, and on February 13, 1899, was elected its Chief Engineer, which office he now holds. He is a member of several prominent social and fraternal bodies and a Democrat in politics. He was a candidate for County Coroner in 1896, and, though defeated, received a flattering vote. He is a believer in the power of the press, and in various capacities has exerted a wholesome influence in his town.

Mr. Necker was married on the 4th of March, 1895, to Miss Lilian Gschwind, daughter of John and Eva Gschwind, of the Town of Union. They have two children: William, Jr., and Lilian.

FRANCIS M. McDONOUGH, of Hoboken, was born in New York City on the 9th of August, 1824. When he was one month old his parents removed to Hoboken, N. J., where he laid the foundations of a successful career.

In his youth Mr. McDonough developed a strong inclination for the roving life of a sailor, and in 1837 he shipped as a cabin boy on a vessel bound for Spain. Upon his return he engaged in farming for one year, and then shipped as cook for two or three years. Afterward he was a deck hand on the Hoboken ferryboats until 1844, when he shipped for New Orleans. He worked along shore for a year, shipped on the revenue cutter "Woodbury" under "Bully" Foster, and then engaged in steamboating on the Mississippi for a season. When the Mexican War broke out he was driving a team in New Orleans. He at once enlisted in the Second Regiment, Louisiana Volunteers, and served with credit until he was mustered out at the close of the war. He then resumed his old position driving team.

Returning to Hoboken, Mr. McDonough went to work as a deck hand on ferryboats and was soon promoted to a position as captain. In 1853 he began the business of carting lumber for Brush & Tompkins. He also identified himself with public affairs, and in various important capacities has served the town and county with satisfaction. He was Constable for several years, and when the charter of Hoboken was adopted he was made Captain of Police. He was made Recorder of the city in 1877 and filled the office for twenty-one consecutive years, retiring in 1898. He is a progressive, enterprising citizen, thoroughly identified in all local affairs.

JOHN J. DUPUY, of Rutherford, was born August 6, 1855, in New York City, where he spent his early life. He attended school until he was thirteen years of age, since which time he has been actively and successfully engaged in business affairs.

Mr. Dupuy came to Rutherford, N. J., in 1876, and for five years was employed in a watch factory. During this time he began in a small way to manufacture baseballs and other sporting goods, eventually becoming very successful in this business. His factory was in Rutherford and his salesroom was in New York. At one time he had in all nearly one hundred hands employed and in one season manufactured 365,000 dozen balls. He conducted this business and at the same time a dry goods store in Rutherford until the panic of 1893 caused him to relinquish both enterprises.

As an official Mr. Dupuy's career has also been successful. He served the Borough of Rutherford as Constable from 1880 to 1885, and as Town Collector from 1886 to 1888, being the only Democrat elected on that ticket. He was Coroner from 1887 to 1889, running ahead of his ticket in that election. He was elected Justice of the Peace in 1882, serving five years, and was again elected in 1893. In 1891 he was elected Assemblyman from the Second Assembly District and was re-elected the following year. He has served as Chief of the State Detective Bureau, and has been prominent in fire circles, having served in the department as Foreman, Chief, and President of the organization.

Mr. Dupuy is a member of Boiling Spring Lodge, No. 152, F. and A. M., of Rutherford Lodge, No. 240, I. O. O. F., of Passaic Lodge, No. 387, B. P. O. Elks, of Rutherford Lodge, No. 42, Foresters of America, of Rutherford Council, Royal Arcanum, of United Friends Council, and of other social organizations.

HENRY LEMMERMANN, President of the Mattson Rubber Company, of New York, and a well known resident of Hasbrouck Heights, N. J., was born in Germany in 1848. He came to America in 1863 and for some years was employed in a grocery store in New York City. Subsequently he engaged in the hotel business, in which he continued until 1890, when he became actively engaged in the manufacture of rubber goods. Since then he has been President of the Mattson Rubber Company. Previous to this, in 1884, he bought a farm at Corona (now Hasbrouck Heights), N. J., and in 1891 built his present residence. He immediately began improving the land by opening streets, making sidewalks, planting shade trees, introducing water (the Hackensack Water Company), and supplying electric lights. He then, through the Hasbrouck Heights Land and Improvement Company, built about thirty cottages. In 1893 he organized the Lemmermann Villa Site Company, of which he has been President and Treasurer ever since. He has also been President of the Hasbrouck Heights Building, Loan, and Savings Association since its organization in June, 1890.

Mr. Lemmermann is a Past Supreme Representative of the Knights of Pythias, was Grand Chancellor of the Knights of Pythias of New York in 1878, and is Treasurer of the Pythian Home of New York. He is also a member of the Masonic order and the Royal Arcanum, President of the Pioneer Club of Hasbrouck Heights, and a member of the Commercial Club of New York. He has been Township Committeeman of Lodi Township, a Councilman of the Borough of Hasbrouck Heights, and a member of the Board of Health.

Mr. Lemmermann was married, in 1872, to Miss Wilhelmina Gross, daughter of F. C. Gross, of Hackensack, N. J.

CHARLES R. SOLEY, of Rutherford, is a native of Lyndhurst, N. J. In 1878 he began his business career as a contractor and builder. Subsequently he engaged in steam sawing, turning, etc., and in 1890 he built his factory in Rutherford, N. J., where he carries on a large and successful business, and where he resides.

Mr. Soley has served two terms as Freeholder, one term as a member of the Borough Council, and for several years as Chief of the Fire Department of the Borough of Rutherford. He is a successful business man, a public spirited citizen, and respected by all who know him.

JOHN STEVENS was born in New York City about 1749. He was the son of John Stevens, Sr., who was born there about 1708, and whose father, also named John, came from England in 1699, at about the age of seventeen. The second John settled in New Jersey and was one of the joint commissioners for defining the boundary line between New Jersey and New York in November, 1774. He resigned as Royalist Councilor in 1776, and from August of that year until 1782 was Vice-President of the Council of New Jersey. In November, 1783, he was elected to the Federal Congress, and on December 18, 1787, presided over the State convention that ratified the United States Constitution. He died in 1792.

John Stevens, the subject of this sketch (son of John and a grandson of John Stevens, the immigrant), was graduated from King's (now Columbia) College in 1768, was admitted to the bar, and during the Revolutionary War held several offices, being Treasurer of New Jersey from 1776 to 1779. Afterward he married and resided in winter on Broadway, New York, and in summer on the island of Hoboken, which he then owned. His life was devoted to experiments at his own cost. In 1790 he petitioned Congress for protection to American inventors, which resulted in a law, passed April 10, 1790, that formed the foundation of the American patent law. Having begun experiments in the application of steam in 1788, he now continued them, especially with his associates, Nicholas I. Roosevelt and the elder Brunel, who subsequently built the Thames tunnel.

JOHN STEVENS.

Mr. Stevens, his brother-in-law, Robert R. Livingston, and Nicholas I. Roosevelt built a steamboat and navigated the Hudson River near the close of the eighteenth century, the Legislature of New York having offered a monopoly of exclusive privilege to the owners of a boat that should attain a speed of three miles an hour under given conditions. Their boat, however, failed to develop the required speed, and their joint proceedings were interrupted by the appointment, in 1801, of Livingston as Minister to France. In Paris Mr. Livingston met Robert Fulton and afterward was associated with him in establishing and developing steam navigation.

In 1804 Mr. Stevens built a vessel propelled by twin screws that navigated the Hudson, which was the first application of steam to the screw propeller. The engine and boiler of this steamboat were subsequently deposited in the Stevens Institute at Hoboken. In 1807 Mr. Stevens and his son Robert built the paddle wheel steamboat "Phœnix," which was used on the Delaware River for six years. This boat, according to Professor James Renwick, "was the first to navigate the ocean by the power of steam." Among the patents taken out by Stevens was one in 1791 for generating steam; two in the same year described as improvements in bellows and on Thomas Savary's engine, both designed for pumping; the multi-tubular boiler in 1803, which was patented in England in 1805 in the name of his eldest son, John C.; one in 1816 for using slides; an improvement in rack railroads in 1824; and one in 1824 to render shallow rivers more navigable.

In 1812 Mr. Stevens made the first experiments with artillery against iron armor. On October 11, 1811, he established the first steam ferry in the world with the "Juliana," which was operated between New York City and Hoboken. In 1813 he invented the ferryboat with the paddle-wheel in the middle, which was turned by six horses. This sample of horse-boat was long used on the East River and on the Hudson. In February, 1812, five years before the beginning of the Erie Canal, he addressed a memoir to the commission appointed to devise water communication between the seaboard and the lakes, urging the construction of a railroad. This memoir, with the adverse report of the commissioners, was published at the time, again in 1852, and again by the *Railroad Gazette* in 1882. His plan was identical with that of the successful South Carolina railroad built in 1830-32, which was the first long railroad in the United States.

In 1814 Mr. Stevens applied to the State of New Jersey for a railroad charter from New York to Philadelphia, which he received in February, 1815. He located the road, but proceeded no further. In 1823, with Horace Binney and Stephen Girard, of Philadelphia, he obtained from the State of Pennsylvania a charter for a railway from Philadelphia to Lancaster along the route of the present Pennsylvania Railroad. These were the first railroad charters granted in this country. On October 23, 1824, he obtained a patent for the construction of railroads. In 1826 he built in Hoboken a circular railway having a gauge of five feet and a diameter of 220 feet, and placed on it a locomotive with a multi-tubular boiler which carried half a dozen people at the rate of over twelve miles an hour. This was the first locomotive that ever ran on a steam railroad in America.

ENTRANCE TO CASTLE POINT.

Mr. Stevens's name will ever be linked with the origin and early development of steam as a motive power for water and land transportation, and to him belongs the honor of putting this great force into direct operation. He was also an enthusiastic botanist and amateur gardener, importing and cultivating many new plants. He built Castle Point at Hoboken, and in 1835 replaced it by the present mansion. He died there March 6, 1838.

JOHN COX STEVENS, son of John Stevens, the engineer, was born September 24, 1785, and died in Hoboken, June 13, 1857. He was graduated from Columbia College in 1803, married Maria C. Livingston, December 27, 1809, and was the first Commodore of the New York Yacht Club and commanded the yacht "America" in the memorable race in England in 1851.

ROBERT LIVINGSTON STEVENS, another son of John Stevens, was born October 18, 1787, and died in Hoboken, April 20, 1856. He began to assist his father when only seventeen years old. In June, 1808, he took the "Phœnix" to Philadelphia by sea and subsequently built a number of steamboats. From 1815 to 1840 he stood at the head of his profession in the United States as a constructor of steam vessels and their machinery. In 1821 he originated the present form of ferryboat and ferryslips. He invented the split water-wheel in 1826, the balance-valve in 1831, and the first marine tubular boiler in the same year. He was among the first to use anthracite coal on vessels. He originated the well known T-rail and a bomb that could be fired from a cannon instead of from a mortar. He also built the celebrated Stevens battery, which lay unlaunched in its basin at Hoboken for many years and was the first ironclad ever projected.

JAMES ALEXANDER STEVENS, another son of John Stevens, the engineer, was born in New York City, January 29, 1790, and died in Hoboken, October 7, 1873. He was graduated from Columbia College in 1808 and was admitted to the bar of New York in 1811. With Thomas Gibbons he established the Union Steamboat Line between New York and Philadelphia, which led to the suit of Ogden v. Gibbons—a suit memorable for the decision which placed all the navigable waters of the United States under the jurisdiction of the Federal government.

EDWIN AUGUSTUS STEVENS, another son of John Stevens, the inventor, was born at Castle Point, Hoboken, N. J., July 28, 1795. He learned the profession of civil engineer with his father and his brother Robert L. The two brothers were very closely connected in business affairs. Both were men of great capacity, the elder taking the lead as engineer and the younger as a business man.

Edwin A. Stevens was occupied largely in the management of his father's estate, on which the City of Hoboken now stands. He was also connected with the organization, construction, and operation of the Camden and Amboy Railroad, the charter for which he and Robert L. Stevens obtained from the State of New Jersey in 1830. The road was opened for traffic in 1839-42, Robert L. being President and Edwin A. Treasurer and Manager. The germ of many improvements afterward perfected on other roads can be traced back to the Camden and Amboy line. The vestibule car is a modern instance. While engaged in railroad affairs the brothers still retained their great interests in navigation, made many improvements therein, and were especially prominent in the invention, introduction, and development of appliances for railroads, locomotives, and cars.

In 1842 Edwin A. Stevens patented the air-tight fire-room for the forced draught which had been applied by his elder brother in 1827 to the "North America," and which came into general use at once. This double invention of the brothers is now used in all the great navies of the world. They spent a great part of their lives in devising and effecting improvements in the means of attack and defense in naval warfare, especially for ironclads. Robert had bequeathed the Stevens battery to his brother, and the latter, at the beginning of he Civil War, presented the government a plan for completing the vessel together with another small vessel called the "Naugatuck." This small vessel was accepted by the government, and was one of the fleet that attacked the "Merrimac." The government refused to appropriate the money on the plans proposed by Mr. Stevens, and upon his death he left the vessel to the State of New Jersey together with one million dollars for its completion. Edwin A. Stevens invented the steam plow, which was extensively used for years. He remained the business manager of the Camden and Amboy Railroad for upward of twenty-five years. He founded the Stevens Institute in Hoboken, and bequeathed to it and to the high school a large plot of ground and $150,000 for the building and $500,000 for endowments. His widow, whose maiden name was Martha Bayard,

CASTLE POINT.

afterward devoted $200,000 to religious and charitable institutions, among which was the Church of the Holy Innocents at Hoboken.

DANIEL I. DEMAREST is descended in the ninth generation from David des Marest, the French emigrant, concerning whom see sketch on page 64. The line of descent is as follows: (1) David des Marest married Maria Sohier and had four children; (2) David Davids Demarest, Jr., married Maria Bertholf and had eleven children; (3) Daniel Davids Demarest married Rebecca de Groot and had ten children; (4) Peter Daniels Demarest married Oesseltie Vandelinda and had six children; (5) Peter Peters Demarest married Lydia Hopper and had five children; (6) Peter Peters Demarest married Leah Demarest and had one child; (7) Daniel Peter Demarest married Leah Bogert and had five children; and (8) Isaac D. Demarest, born January 20, 1814, married, December 19, 1833, Margaret, daughter of John J. Van Wagoner. He was a surveyor by occupation, and resided at Oradell, N. J., on part of the farm purchased from the Indians by David des Marest, the emigrant. His brother, Rev. David D. Demarest, D.D., was for many years a professor in the Theological Seminary at Rutgers College. Isaac D. Demarest was an active man in church and civil affairs, in both of which he was honored with positions of responsibility. His children of the ninth generation were Daniel I., the subject of this sketch, and Maria Ann.

Daniel I. Demarest (9) was born at Oradell, N. J., March 16, 1836, and there received his education in the public schools. When eighteen years of age he went to work on the farm, and has ever since been actively and successfully engaged in agricultural pursuits. He has also been prominent in public affairs. For a number of years he served as Postmaster of Oradell, where he resides, and for three years he was a member of the Town Council. For two years he has held the office of Mayor of the Borough of Oradell. In these as well as in other important capacities he has displayed marked ability, sound judgment, and commendable enterprise. He is a member of the Dutch Reformed Church, a public spirited citizen, and thoroughly identified with the progress of the community. He married Ellen Ann Demarest, by whom he had one son, Isaac. She died in 1871, and he married, second, Mattie Robena Wilson, at Hackensack, April 20, 1899, daughter of John William and Robena P. (Ballantyne) Wilson, of New York City.

JOHN H. Z. DEMAREST is descended in the eighth generation from David des Marest, the common ancestor of all the Demarests in New Jersey, of whom see sketch on page 64. David Demarest (1) and his wife, Maria Sohier, had four children of the second generation: John, David, Samuel, and Daniel.

Samuel Davids Demarest (2), born at Mannheim in the lower Palatinate in 1653, married, August 11, 1678, Maria, daughter of Simon Dreuns. He died in 1728. He lived at Schraalenburgh and bought a large tract of land from Governor Lowerie, called the "South West Hook," west of the Hackensack, near Old Hook. He was one of the wealthiest men in his neighborhood at the time of his death. His children were eleven of the third generation, one of whom was Peter Samuels Demarest.

Peter Samuels Demarest (3) married, September 14, 1717, Margarietie, daughter of Cornelius Haring, of Tappan, and had issue of the fourth generation Samuel P., Sophia, Lydia, Caroline, Jacob, Margaretta, Daniel P., John P., and Samuel.

Samuel Peters Demarest (4), baptized June 25, 1724, died March 14, 1808, married, November 19, 1747, Margaret Brinkerhoff, born October 4, 1729, died March 11, 1802. They lived at Schraalenburgh and had issue of the fifth generation nine children: Peter S., Henry S., Cornelius S., Jacob S., Ralph S., Jacob S., Margretie, Maria, and Ann.

Ralph S. Demarest (5), born August 23, 1756, died September 14, 1814, married Maria (daughter of Nicholas and Elsie Demarest), born August 8, 1756, died May 10, 1810. Ralph S. resided on a large farm at Demarest, N. J. His children of the sixth generation were four: Samuel R., John R., Margretta, and Margretta.

Samuel R. Demarest (6), born February 5, 1783, died February 24, 1872, married December 22, 1808, Elizabeth Zabriskie, born February 13, 1789, died May 1, 1875. He resided at Demarest and was a farmer and distiller. His issue of the seventh generation were ten: John Z., Ralph S., Cornelius, John S., Maria, Samuel S., Margaret, Catherine, Garret Z., and Ann Eliza.

Garret Z. Demarest (7), born at Demarest, N. J., January 21, 1829, married, October 18, 1849, Margaret Zabriskie, born October 14, 1830, daughter of John H. and Ann (Winner))Zabriskie. They reside at Demarest, where Garret is a coal dealer and farmer. His children of the eighth generation are John H. Z. and William E. The latter was born June 8, 1861.

John H. Z. Demarest (8), the subject of this sketch, was born at Hackensack, N. J., August 17, 1850, and was educated in the public schools. At the age of eighteen he entered the office of the New York and New Jersey Railroad, but three years later was transferred to the Erie Railroad, where he remained eleven years. He then engaged in business as a member of the stationery and printing firm of Unz & Co., No. 1 Bowling Green and 36 Pearl Street, New York, with which he has since continued. For upward of sixteen years he has been actively and successfully engaged in this capacity. He attends the Dutch Reformed Church of Closter, N. J. In every connection he has achieved success and honor. He married Elizabeth V. Moore and has two children: J. Westerfield and Gretta. They reside in Demarest, N. J.

MILTON G. DEMAREST is of the ninth generation from David des Marest, the French emigrant, concerning whom see sketch on page 64. His line is the same as that of his cousin, Daniel I. Demarest (see page 495) as far as the seventh generation.

Daniel Peter Demarest (7) had five children of the eighth generation, all born at Oradell: Daniel P., Lea, Isaac D., Peter D., David D., and Garret D.

Garret D. Demarest (8) was born at Oradell, N. J., August 23, 1821, and died April 23, 1877. He married, May 19, 1853, Maria, daughter of John D. Demarest, and had issue Lea, Daniel, Margaretta, John, Katie, and Milton G., the last named being the subject of this sketch.

Milton G. Demarest (9) was born at Oradell on the 25th of July, 1871, and received his education in the public schools of Bergen County and at Rutgers College, New Brunswick. Owing to poor health he left school at the age of sixteen and went to California, where he remained two years. Upon his return he entered the employ of Cooper & Demarest, general contractors and dealers in builders' supplies, and has since continued there.

As a resident of Oradell, Bergen County, Mr. Demarest has taken an active part in public affairs. He has served as Clerk of the Borough of Delford, as Secretary and Treasurer of the Delford Land Company and the Delford Sewerage Company, and as Superintendent of the Peetzburg Sunday School. For a number of years he was Superintendent of the Union Sunday School. He is a member of the Dutch Reformed Church, a public spirited citizen, and honored and respected by all who know him. He is unmarried.

JACOB J. DEMAREST, of Closter, is descended in the seventh generation from David des Marest, the first American emigrant and progenitor of the family (see sketch on page 64). The line of descent is as follows: David des Marest (1), of Beauchamp, in Picardy, France, and his wife, Maria Sohier, of Nieppe, in Hainault, had four children of the second generation: David, Samuel, John, and Daniel.

David Davids Demarest (2) married Sara Bertholf, daughter of Rev. Gilliam Bertholf, and had eleven children of the third generation.

Jacobus Davids Demarest (3), baptized May 30, 1705, married (1) Lea de Groot and (2) Margaretta Cozine Haring. He lived at Schraalenburgh and had issue fifteen children of the fourth generation.

John Jacobus Demarest (4), born August 20, 1720, died February 1, 1783, married, March 7, 1744, Rachel Zabriskie, daughter of Joost Zabriskie, who was born March 19, 1725, and died April 16, 1813. They resided at Schraalenburgh and had thirteen children of the fifth generation.

Jacobus Johns Demarest (5), born August 20, 1748, died October 9, 1844, married (1) Rachel Smith, who died April 28, 1825. He married (2), in

1825, Rachel Voorhis, who survived her husband. Jacobus J. Demarest was a surveyor by occupation and lived at Middletown in Bergen County. He had issue ten children of the sixth generation, one of whom was Joost.

Joost Demarest (6), born December 4, 1797, died at Closter, N. J., November 1, 1878. He married, in February, 1823, Margaret, daughter of Frederick Haring, born October 2, 1802. Joost was a cabinetmaker and lived at Piermont, N. Y., until 1825, when he removed to what is now Harrington Park, on the farm now occupied by ex-Sheriff William C. Herring. He served in the War of 1812. His children of the seventh generation were James, Frederick J., John B., Isaac H., Abraham, Vreeland B., Mary M., and Ann Eliza, of whom Jacob J. is the subject of this sketch.

Jacob J. Demarest (7) was born at Piermont, N. Y., March 17, 1834, but has resided in Bergen County since he was one year old, his parents moving to Harrington Park in 1835. There he received his education. He left school at the age of sixteen and began active life on his father's farm. He also taught school about three and one-half years. Afterward he engaged in the hardware business in Closter with his brother Abraham under the firm name of A. Demarest & Brother, and has ever since continued in that trade. He has also been somewhat active in public affairs, having served one year as Assessor and three years as Township Clerk. He is a member of the Dutch Reformed Church and a public spirited, enterprising citizen.

Mr. Demarest married Margaret Durie and has two children: George and Maria.

JOHN KEHOE, of Lyndhurst, N. J., was born in Newark, March 28, 1836. His father, Patrick Kehoe, a native of Wexford, Ireland, came to America when a youth and engaged in the clothing business, which he carried on successfully for forty years. His mother, Mary Anne Hopper, was a descendant of some of the first Dutch settlers of New Jersey. Both of her grandfathers were soldiers in the Revolutionary War.

Mr. Kehoe was educated in the Newark public schools, and previous to going in the army carried on a large meat business in Newark. In the Civil War he went to the front with Company B, Second Regiment, New Jersey Volunteers, in May, 1861, served the full term, and re-enlisted in 1864 in Company H, Thirty-ninth Regiment. He lost his right leg in the battle of Petersburg.

During the next few years he served successively as assistant superintendent of the Soldiers' Home and meat inspector of the City of Newark. Having always had a fancy for horses, he became a veterinarian, being admitted to the New Jersey Veterinary Medical Association on August 12, 1886.

Mr. Kehoe is a Democrat in politics, and has had much to do with the success which has marked the recent career of the Democracy in Union Township. He has actively promoted the many public improvements which have taken place at Lyndhurst since he became a resident there. He is a member of the Union Township Democratic Club and a charter member of Gershom Mott Post, G. A. R., at Rutherford, N. J. He has served as a member of the Democratic County Executive Committee, as a member of the Board of Chosen Freeholders, and for seventeen years was a member of the Township Committee of Union Township.

February 16, 1856, Mr. Kehoe married Sarah Westwood at Cleveland, Ohio. They have eleven children, one of whom, Henry W. Kehoe, is a leading criminal lawyer of Bergen County.

PATRICK SULLIVAN, Chief of Police and Township Committeeman of North Bergen, Hudson County, is the son of John Sullivan and Ann Murphy and a grandson of Timothy and Mary (O'Connell) Sullivan and Patrick Murphy, and was born in Ireland on the 17th of March, 1850. Receiving his preliminary education in the public schools of his native country, he came to the United States in 1868 and finished his studies in New York City, where he was afterward a member of the police force for about five years, and where he was subsequently engaged in the liquor business.

On July 12, 1888, Mr. Sullivan removed to North Bergen, N. J., and opened

PATRICK SULLIVAN.

a hotel near the Guttenberg racetrack, which he still conducts, having achieved that success which industry and faithful attention to business invariably wins. As a Democrat he has been for many years a trusted party leader, and in various capacities has served his town and county with honor and satisfaction. He has been Township Committeeman since the spring of 1898, is now also Chief of Police for North Bergen, and was a member of the Hudson County Grand Jury in 1893 and 1899. Mr. Sullivan is highly respected, and enjoys the confidence and esteem of the entire community.

He was married, in September, 1886, to Miss Ellen Ryan, daughter of Michael Ryan, of Ireland, and has one son, Michael.

JOHN C. BOUTON, of Bayonne, N. J., was born in Rye, Westchester County, N. Y., on the 18th of February, 1852, being the son of Samuel Bouton and Catharine Clark. He received his education in the Christmatic Institute in his native town, and after leaving school studied telegraphy. He was a telegraph operator for several years. In March, 1875, he entered the employ of H. K. & F. B. Thurber & Co. as bill clerk, and was steadily advanced until on February 1, 1884, he became junior partner of the firm of Thurber, Whyland & Co. He was a Director when the company was incorporated and continued as such until the receivers were appointed. He represented the receivers until the final accounting was made, and then became Assistant Secretary of the New East River Bridge Company. He is at present one of the Sinking Fund Commissioners of the City of Bayonne.

Mr. Bouton is a public spirited citizen and highly respected by all who know him. He is a member of Bayonne Lodge, No. 99, F. and A. M., of Bayonne Lodge, No. 434, B. P. O. of Elks, of Bayonne Lodge, No. 695, Royal Arcanum, of the Order of Chosen Friends, of the Independent Order of Foresters, of the Newark Bay Boat Club, and of the Exempt Firemen's Association.

He was married, December 29, 1874, to Mary Louise Webb. They have ten children, all of whom are living.

WILLIAM D. SNOW, of Hackensack, is the son of Josiah Snow, founder of the Detroit *Tribune*. He was born in Massachusetts on the 2d of February, 1832, was educated at Romeo, Mich., and subsequently studied law with Attorney-General Edson, of Dixon, Ill. He was for several years associate editor of the Detroit *Tribune*. He was a strong advocate of anti-slavery doctrines, a frequent contributor to the magazines and journals of that day, and a hymn writer of some note.

Mr. Snow settled at Pine Bluff, Ark., in 1860, and afterward represented Jefferson County in the Constitutional Convention of Arkansas. He was elected in 1865 for the long term to the United States Senate from Arkansas. At the close of his term he declined a re-election, coming to New York City for the purpose of studying law. In 1871, however, Mr. Snow went to Paris, where he spent two years in the study of civil law. In 1875 he was admitted to the New York bar, receiving in the same year the degree of LL.B. from Columbia College. In 1882 he became Secretary and counsel to one of the New York trust companies, but resigned in 1888 to take up general practice. He acted as volunteer aide to General Powell Clayton and Major-General Steele during the Civil War, and was instrumental in the enlistment and organization of three regiments in the State of Arkansas. Governor Murphy afterward tendered him an appointment as brigadier-general of volunteers, which he declined.

Mr. Snow is of retiring and studious habits, and in religion is a Unitarian. He is President of the Unitarian Congregational Society of Hackensack, and a member of the Lawyers' Club, the Bullion Club of New York, and the Oritani Club of Hackensack. Several of his inventions have proved successful, his thermostat being regarded as the most reliable of its kind.

He is now a member of the bar in three States, having been admitted to the New Jersey bar in 1894. After residing in the northern part of Bergen County for more than twenty years, while practicing in New York City, he gave up his city practice in 1896 and removed to Hackensack.

CHARLES LYMAN CREAR, of Rutherford, was born in Albany, N. Y., on the 2d of August, 1847. He is the son of William James Crear and Mary J. Seaton, natives of the Isle of Man.

Mr. Crear was educated in the public schools of New York City, and in 1863 enlisted in the War of the Rebellion, serving about eighteen months in the Seventy-first Militia Regiment, the One Hundred and Second Regiment, and the Fifty-sixth New York Volunteers. During the past thirty-one years he has been associated with the New York News Company, of which he is now cashier.

In public as well as in business life Mr. Crear is well known. He has served three terms of three years each as Councilman of Rutherford, N. J., where he resides, and is President of the Lincoln League, a strong Republican organization. His political affiliations have always been with the Republican party, in which he has taken an active interest. He is a member of the Union Club of Rutherford, of Rutherford Council, Royal Arcanum, of Boiling Springs Lodge, F. and A. M., and of Gershom Mott Post, G. A. R. He is also a member and Treasurer of the Rutherford Athletic Association. As a citizen he is public spirited, progressive, and highly respected.

Mr. Crear married Jessie L. Stewart, daughter of William James Stewart, one of the pioneers of Rutherford, N. J. They have one son, Lyman Durando Crear, who enlisted in Company L, Second New Jersey Volunteers, in the Spanish-American War, and was afterward transferred to Colonel Torrey's "Rough Riders." He is now employed by the North Jersey Title Guarantee and Trust Company, of Hackensack.

GEORGE H. CHAPPELL, of Westwood, was born in Westerly, R. I., July 5, 1844. He is the son of Ahiram J. Chappell and Lucinda Hoxie and a grandson of Elisha and Amy (Steadman) Chappell and Nathan B. Hoxie. His maternal grandmother was a Pollock. On his father's side the family came to this country from England and in this line is included Commodore Perry. His mother's family came from Scotland. Elisha Chappell, his paternal grandfather, was a Captain of artillery in the War of 1812.

Mr. Chappell was educated at Hillsdale College in Michigan. He learned the trade of civil engineering in early life, and during the Civil War served three years with honor and distinction, being a private in Company E, Twelfth Regiment Maine Volunteers, and receiving a commission as First Lieutenant. Afterward he turned his attention largely to inventions. He was the inventor of an engine operated by carbonic acid gas and the organizer of the New Power Company of Illinois, of which he was President. For ten years he was a broker in Wall Street, New York.

Mr. Chappell's career has been an eminently successful one, and from the first he has displayed great executive ability as well as rare inventive genius. He is a member of the Congregational Church, an active and influential citizen, and honored and respected by all who know him.

He married, first, Lettuce Willis, who died in 1888, leaving one son, George H. Chappell, Jr. For his second wife he married Mary Hamm.

CHARLES H. BLOHM was born in Hoboken, N. J., July 20, 1874, and moved to Jersey City when very young. There he was reared and educated. He attended the Jersey City public schools, graduating in June, 1888. He was also graduated from the Jersey City Business College in 1893 and from the New York Law School with the degree of LL.B. June 1, 1896. For four years he had studied law with Hon. Henry A. Gaede, of Hoboken. He was admitted to the New Jersey bar as attorney and solicitor in chancery June 8, 1896. On July 27, 1896, he was appointed master in chancery and on June 12, 1899, he was admitted to practice as a counselor at law. He is also an attorney, counsellor, proctor, and advocate in the United States Circuit and District Courts, being admitted to that bar September 18, 1899.

Although a young man Mr. Blohm has achieved a recognized standing in his profession and is regarded as one of the rising young lawyers of Jersey City. He takes a deep interest in public affairs, and as a citizen is

CHARLES H. BLOHM.

progressive, public spirited, and enterprising. He is thoroughly identified with the affairs of his native county and respected by all who know him.

SEBA M. BOGERT is descended in the seventh generation from Jan Louwe Bougaerdt, for a sketch of whom see page 57. Mr. Bogert's ancestors are also noted on page 60. He is the son of Matthew S. Bogert and Polly Kipp, a grandson of Seba Bogert and Sarah Blackledge, all of Closter, and a great-grandson of William de Graw and Vrouche Blawvelt, his wife.

Mr. Bogert was born in Tappan, now Harrington, Bergen County, N. J.,

October 6, 1825. He received a common school education and afterward was successfully engaged in the produce business. In 1869 he became a member of the New York Stock Exchange and has ever since continued in that capacity.

In public as well as in business life Mr. Bogert has been active and influential. He served as Treasurer of the City of Hoboken and for two terms was a member of the Common Council. He is a Protestant in religion, active and influential in local affairs, and respected by all who know him. As a business man he has displayed marked ability, sound common sense, and great sagacity.

In May, 1843, Mr. Bogert married Lavina Westervelt, who died in 1845, leaving one child, John Westervelt Bogert, who is living. He married, again, April 2, 1857, Catharine Z. Conner, who died July 25, 1900, leaving one child, Mary C. Ford, born June 22, 1862, who survives.

EDGAR H. LOVERIDGE, of West Hoboken, N. J., was born in Jersey City on the 16th of May, 1871, being the son of James W. and Elizabeth F. R. (Hadden) Loveridge and a grandson of James and Elizabeth C. Loveridge and James E. and Jane F. R. Hadden. He received his education in Grammar School No. 7, in Jersey City, studying until fourteen years of age. He then learned the printer's trade and continued in that business about seven years. Afterward he entered the law office of Dickinson & Thompson, of Jersey City, as a student, and remained there until November, 1895, when he was admitted to the bar of New Jersey. In the meantime he attended for two years and was graduated from the New York Law School. After having been admitted to the bar he opened an office in West Hoboken, and has since been successfully engaged in the practice of his profession. He is a member of the Royal Arcanum and of the Foresters of America.

WILLIAM D. SALTER.—The Salter family of what is now known as Hudson County are direct lineal descendants of one Richard Salter, Esq., of English descent, who originally came from Barbadoes to Monmouth County in this State and was a Justice there for many years. His first appearance at Shrewsbury, as appears by the old court records, was on May 23, 1704, and the last entry relating to him is under date of June 23, 1748, when "Justice Richard Salter audited the Overseers' Accounts," as was required by law at that time. The great-grandfather of the subject of this sketch was John Salter, a son of Justice Richard Salter, of Monmouth County. John Salter lived for many years on Staten Island upon a farm near what is now known as Huguenot, and subsequently removed with his family to Hoboken, where he resided at the time of his death. David B. Salter, a son of John Salter and grandfather of William D. Salter, settled in what was then known as Bergen Neck, in Bergen County, in the year 1832, the location being called at that time "Pamrapaugh," an old Indian name meaning "Land of Wealth." His farm extended from the New York Bay on the one side to the Newark Bay on the other, and was adjoined on the south by the farm land of Jasper Cadmus, in old land titles known as "Caspar Codmus," and was included in the second patent granted by Philip Carteret to Thomas Davison, December 12, 1669. Upon this tract grew the Village of Salterville, named from its founder, David B. Salter, and long before the days of railroads and trolley cars upon Bergen Neck the mails were delivered by stage coach from Jersey City to old Salterville postoffice, provided the incoming tides from the New York Bay had not washed away the roadbed of the "Old Bergen Road," which was the only means of ingress and egress; and in that event the village was isolated until the storms abated and the tides receded.

David B. Salter died at the ripe old age of ninety-seven. The latter years of his life were devoted to preaching the Gospel. He erected a church and gathered about him a large congregation of followers. In his firm belief that Christ would return to earth in his lifetime, upon the dates estimated to be the Second Advent, the congregation would gather in the holy edifice to await His coming amid prayer and thanksgiving. All worldly affairs were adjusted, all debts of one to the other were forgiven. Thus he lived and died—a simple hearted, earnest, Christian gentleman. Daniel Salter, a son of David B., was the father of William D. Salter.

The Salter family of Hudson County, formerly of Monmouth County, has furnished its quota of heroes of Revolutionary fame. Lieutenant-Colonel Joseph Salter, Second Regiment of Monmouth County, was breveted for distinguished bravery under command of General Maxwell at the battle of Monmouth. Benjamin Salter, of the Eastern Battalion, a private of "Old Monmouth," was killed on the field of battle September 6, 1779.

William D. Salter was born May 16, 1865, in Bayonne, N. J., where he still resides. His early education was acquired in the public schools of Bayonne, from which he was graduated with high honors in 1881. His education was completed under the personal tutelage of Dr. Hasbrouck, the founder of Hasbrouck Institute, of Jersey City. He subsequently read law in the office of John Linn, of Jersey City, a foremost counsellor of his day, and less than a month after attaining his majority he was admitted to the practice of law in the State of New Jersey on the 3d day of June, 1886. He received his appointment as a Master in Chancery within two months thereafter. For a period of four years from 1891 to 1895 he was Treasurer of the City of Bayonne, and was an efficient, faithful servant, filling his position of trust and great responsibility to the satisfaction of both those who favored and opposed his election. His public life was clean and meritorious.

Mr. Salter was married, February 3, 1898, to Lauretta Greenop, only daughter of Charles William and Martha Greenop. Mrs. Salter's maternal ancestors were lineal descendants of Sir William Wallace, of Scottish fame, and on her father's side a direct descendant of Sir James Scarlett, a celebrated English barrister, whose title was Lord Abinger.

In politics William D. Salter displays that independence of action and thought which characterizes the man, being a stanch Democrat, while all of his family and ancestors are and have been ardent Republicans. He affiliates with the Benevolent and Protective Order of Elks (Lodge No. 211, of Jersey City). He is a Master Mason and a Past Sachem of Pamrapaugh Tribe, No. 187, Improved Order of Redmen. He is a brother of Dr. Joseph E. Salter, deceased, who was a graduate of Bellevue Hospital Medical College of the City of New York, and a physician and surgeon of great ability, who died February 25, 1896, at his home in Bayonne, from pneumonia contracted on shipboard while returning from foreign travels. Dr. Salter was a man greatly beloved by all who knew him. His manners were genial, his spirit broad and liberal. He loved his chosen profession, and gave of his knowledge as freely as it was asked without restraint, regardless of hope of reward. His death was a loss to his patients, still unfilled to them, and a greater one to his family and friends. Such men do not die and become forgotten; they still live in beating hearts and cherished memories.

JOHN B. LOZIER, owner of the celebrated stock farm at Oradell, Bergen County, is descended in the eighth generation from François le Sueur, the French emigrant. The line of descent is as follows: François le Sueur (Lozier) and his wife Jannetie Hildebrand had children of the second generation Jannetie, Hildebrand, John, Jacob, and Nicholas.

Nicholas Lozier (2) married, in 1691, Tryntie Slott (Slote), who died in 1707. He then married (2), in 1709, Antie Dircks Banta. In all he had twenty children of the third generation, to wit: Anthony, Jannetie, Peter, Hildebrand, Jacomina, Marytie, John, Antie, Lucas, Jacobus, Benjamin, Catharine, Hester, Rachel, Dirk, Jacob, Abram, Lea, Margaretta, and Maria.

Abram Lozier (3), born in 1721, married, in 1744, Maria, daughter of William Earle, and had issue of the fourth generation Ann, Maria, Nicholas, Catharine, William, Elsie, Hester, Elizabeth, and Rachel.

William Lozier (4), born in 1757, married, in 1779, Jannetie Benson, and had issue of the fifth generation Ann, Garret, Abram, and Catharine.

Abram Lozier (5), born in 1785, married Kache Ackerman, born in 1778. He died in 1840 and she in 1879. They had issue of the sixth generation, among others, Peter A. and John A.

John A. Lozier (6), born in 1810, died in 1881. He married, June 18, 1835, Charity Baldwin, of Paramus. They resided at Oradell, N. J., and had among other children of the seventh generation David B. Lozier.

David B. Lozier (7), born in 1838, died in 1875. He married Kittie Woodworth Garretson, who was born in 1841 and died in 1866. Among their children of the eighth generation was the subject of this sketch.

John B. Lozier (8) was born at Oradell, N. J., November 28, 1865. His boyhood was spent on the farm, which contributed largely to his splendid physique and his courtly bearing. A public school education supplemented by a course of instruction at Hackensack Academy completed his curriculum of studies.

Mr. Lozier is an artist of considerable ability and taste and has produced many specimens of his own handiwork, especially in decorating china and bric-à-brac. He is also an expert in pen work. He is a musician of no mean attainments, having made a special study of the violin. As a sportsman he excels, having many rare specimens collected by rod and gun while on expeditions to Florida and other shooting resorts. As a writer many interesting articles from his pen have found their way into sporting papers and periodicals, such as the *Turf, Field and Farm* and *The American Field*. His writings are chiefly descriptive and from his own experience.

June 20, 1885, Mr. Lozier married Mary E. Rumsey. They have three children: Claire, Grace, and Mildred. He is a Republican in politics, independent in local matters, and takes great pleasure in his home.

The celebrated Oradell Stock Farm is one of the best establishments of the kind in the State. This farm is located on a high elevation of land overlooking the fertile valley of the Hackensack River on the New Jersey and New York Railroad, eighteen miles from Jersey City. The buildings are modern structures. Excellent water is furnished for the stables from an artesian well 145 feet deep. The land comprising the farm has been owned by the Lozier family since the time of George III., the present owner having now in his possession the original deed of the same. The whole farm, which has been kept intact, consists of three hundred acres, nearly one hundred acres of which is virgin forest.

ABRAM TALLMAN.—In June, 1659, Douwe Harmansen (Tallman) emigrated to America from the Province of Friesland, Holland, on board the Dutch West India ship "Brown Fish," accompanied by his wife and four children. He settled in New Amsterdam, where he remained about nine years, and where three of his children were baptized. In the spring of 1668 he removed to Bergen, N. J., where, on the 12th of May of the same year, he purchased from Governor Philip Carteret several lots in the Town of Bergen. There he settled and there he died in 1678. So far as is known he was an agriculturist. Some years after his purchase at Bergen he purchased one or more large tracts near Nyack, in what is Rockland County, N. Y., on which lands his sons settled. His children of the second generation were Harman, Teunis, Jannetje, Anthony, and Douwe. The three last named were born in New York. By his will, proved in the spring of 1678, he devised his lands to his two sons, Teunis and Harman, who a few years later sold their Bergen lands and settled in Rockland County, N. Y., from whence their numerous descendants rapidly spread southward into New Jersey.

Of the emigrant's children, his son, Harman Douwensen Tallman (2), born in Holland, married, June 1, 1686, Greetie Minnelly, a daughter of Minne Johannes, also a Hollander. Harman's brother, Teunis Douwensen Tallman, married, about 1707, Brechie Peters Haring, and had issue of the second generation Dirk, Grietie, Drikie, Douwe, Maritie, John, Harman, and Brachie.

John Teunis Tallman (3), baptized at Tappan, January 12, 1709, married Helena Isaacs Blawvelt, and had issue of the fourth generation Teunis, Garret, Brechie, and John.

John Johns Tallman (4), baptized at Tappan, September 3, 1751, married Francis Mabie, and had issue of the fifth generation Brechie, Elizabeth, Maria, Teunis, John, and Abraham.

Abraham Johns Tallman (5), born near Tappan, August 3, 1793, married Maria de Ronde, and had issue, among others, of the sixth generation John A. Tallman (6), who married Caroline Conklin and had a son, Abram Tallman, the subject of this sketch. The latter is also connected with many other old Dutch families of this country, including the De Rondes, the Onderdonks, the Harings, and the Blawvelts, of Rockland County, N. Y.

Abram Tallman (7) was born at Tallman's, Rockland County, N. Y., May 6, 1846. His father, John A. Tallman, like most of his ancestors, was a farmer, and Abram's early life was spent on the farm and attending school at Sufferns, N. Y. In 1862, when sixteen years of age, he taught school for a few months at Tallman's, this being the first venture he made in life for himself. In 1863 and 1864 he was employed in a photograph gallery in New York City, but this work proving too trying to his health, he returned to Tallman's and, after six months' rest on the farm, found employment at the Ramapo car shops, at Ramapo, Rockland County, N. Y., where he stayed for the next two years, learning the car building trade. Afterward he worked at the carpenter trade in Sufferns and Middletown, N. Y., and Paterson, N. J., and finally, in 1867, came to Englewood. In 1867 he engaged in the building business in Englewood, and has continued in that line ever since, having built many of the finest residences in the city and being one of the leading builders there.

Mr. Tallman has always taken an active interest in the welfare of Englewood, having seen it grow from a village of about 1,500, in 1867, when he first came there, to a city of about 6,000 inhabitants in 1900. He was a member of the Englewood Township Committee from 1889 to 1893. He was also a member of the Citizens' Committee formed in 1895 to promote the movement for the incorporation of Englewood as a city, and when the place was finally incorporated in 1896 he was elected a member of the first regular City Council and was Chairman of that body from 1896 to 1898.

Mr. Tallman was married, in 1870, to Miss Maria Zabriskie, of what is now Oradell, Bergen County, N. J., whose ancestors were among the earliest settlers of Bergen County. They have one daughter and three sons, of whom one, William Tallman, is a lawyer, practicing in New York City.

WILLIAM TALLMAN was born March 3, 1875, in Englewood, N. J., where he still resides. He attended public school in Englewood from 1880 to 1891, graduating in the latter year, and then spent two years at Drake's Business College, graduating in 1892. In 1894 he received a Regents' academic diploma in New York and in 1897 was graduated LL.B. from the New York Law School. Since 1892 he has been associated with the well known law firm of Betts, Atterbury, Hyde & Betts, of New York, where he was admitted to the bar as an attorney and counselor in June, 1897.

ABRAHAM WILSON DURYEE, A.M., of New Durham, was one of the eminent citizens of Hudson County. For a number of years he was President of the Board of Freeholders of that county, and distinguished himself by the display of executive abilities of a high order. For two years he represented his Assembly district in the New Jersey House of Assembly. For twenty years he was a Township Committeeman. He was also President of the Experimental Station of New Jersey in connection with Rutgers College and of the New Jersey State Board of Agriculture and was an Elder in the Grove Reformed Church of New Durham. In view of these facts, it need hardly be said that Mr. Duryee enjoyed the esteem and confidence of the people of Hudson County to a degree realized by but very few citizens.

He was born in Schuylerville, Saratoga County, N. Y., September 13, 1821, being the son of Rev. Philip Duryee, born in 1775, died in 1850, and Rachel Day, born July 8, 1794. His father, Philip, was Chaplain in the United States Army during the War of 1812. On the paternal side Mr. Duryee was a grandson of Abraham Duryee, who was born May 8, 1743, at Fort Hamilton, and died March 24, 1814, and of Eleanor Nagle, his wife; a great-grandson of George Duryee (born in 1715, died in 1795) and Catherine Schenck; a great-great-grandson of Abraham Duryee (born in 1685) and Elizabeth Polhemus; and a great-great-great-grandson of Joost Duryee (born in 1650, died in 1727) and Magdalene le Fébre, both of whom fled from Paris at the time of the Massacre of St. Bartholomew, coming in 1675 to this country from Mannheim, in the Palatinate of the Rhine. Abraham Duryee, grandfather of Abraham W. Duryee, was born May 8, 1743. He was a member of the first Colonial Council, one of the Sons of Liberty, a member of the New York Revolutionary Committee of Safety, and one of the famous Committee of One Hundred in 1775.

On the maternal side Mr. Duryee was a grandson of Edward Day (born August 21, 1755, died December 10, 1797) and Leah Bourdett (born September 8, 1765, died September 15, 1831); a great-grandson of Peter Bourdett (born May 11, 1735) and Rachel Bush (born in 1745); and a great-great-grandson of Etienne Bourdett. Peter Bourdett (born May 11, 1735), in this line, gave the land for Fort Lee, while he and his slaves built the fort.

Mr. Duryee was educated at a private school at English Neighborhood, N. J., and at Rutgers College, and from the last-mentioned institution received the degree of Master of Arts in 1893. He followed agricultural pursuits on his large estate, and died June 8, 1898. His wife, Caroline, daughter of Garrett Cowenhoven and Annetta Ditmars, lineally descends from Wolfert Garretse Van Cowenhoven, who came to New Amsterdam in 1630, from Amersfort, Province of Utrecht, Netherlands. Mrs. Duryee is still living, aged seventy-six, having been born October 4, 1824. They celebrated their golden wedding in 1894.

DANIEL W. LA FETRA, of Ridgewood, is of English, Dutch, and French descent. His father, William P. la Fetra, born in 1803, died in 1873, was the son of Samuel la Fetra, who was the son of James la Fetra, who was the son of James la Fetra, Sr., who was the son of Edmond la Fetra, who was the son of Edmond la Fetra, Sr., who died in 1687. The La Fetras were French Huguenots, whose blood mingled with that of the Hollanders through the line of Browers to Bogardus, and that of Jansen to Tryn Jansen about 1565. Mr. La Fetra's maternal ancestry may be traced through his mother, Elizabeth T. Woolley, born in 1807, died in 1862, to Daniel Woolley, who married Elizabeth Wolcott, daughter of Benjamin Wolcott, son of Benjamin Wolcott, son of Henry Wolcott, born in 1690, died in 1750, whose father was Peter Wolcott. These maternal ancestors were of English birth.

Mr. La Fetra was born at Eatontown, Monmouth County, N. J., March 31, 1834. He was educated in the public schools of his native county, supplemented by private study at home. When nineteen years of age he engaged in teaching, and has always taken an active interest in public school work. As President of the Board of Education he has for many years been influential in educational matters in Ridgewood, and to his efforts the people are largely indebted for one of the best school buildings in the State. For some years Mr. La Fetra engaged in mercantile pursuits, but for a long time has filled a responsible position in R. G. Dun & Co.'s mercantile agency.

Although deeply patriotic and devoted to his country's interests, he has never sought honor or distinction in military circles. This may be attributed to the fact that he is of Quaker parentage, and that his earlier years were spent under the influence and teachings of that peace-loving sect. He is a member of the Ridgewood Club. Mr. La Fetra married Miss Emma Hendrickson, of an old Long Island family of Dutch descent.

GEORGE A. BERGER was born March 20, 1875, in Hoboken, N. J., where he still resides. His father, Charles Berger, came to this country from Germany in 1862, settling first in New York City and in 1871 in Hoboken, where he resided until his death March 6, 1899. He was for twenty-five years connected with the North Hudson County Railroad and for a number of years was with the Erie Railroad. He was a member of various societies, a popular and influential citizen, and highly esteemed by all who knew him. He was the son of Johannes Berger, also a native of Germany. His wife, Alvina M. Teubner, daughter of Christian C. and Johanna Teubner, still survives.

George A. Berger was educated in the Hoboken public schools and in 1891 was graduated from W. A. Schell's Commercial School of Hoboken. For a time he followed the real estate and insurance business. Afterward he engaged in banking with the Hudson Trust and Savings Institution, of which he was Assistant Secretary for six and one-half years. At the end of that period he resigned and engaged in the real estate business for himself, but afterward sold out and accepted a position as Cashier of the Trust Company of New Jersey at Hoboken, which he still holds. He is a Director of the Mutual Home and Savings Institution of Hoboken, and has gained a high standing for executive ability, integrity of character, and enterprise.

GEORGE A. BERGER.

In politics Mr. Berger is independent. He is a member of the Castle Point Cyclers and of the Riverside Club, and actively identified with the affairs of his native city.

GARRET D. DURIE.—The Durie family, members of which have for two centuries held responsible positions in civil and religious affairs and wielded a strong influence in shaping the destinies of Bergen County, are of French lineage. John Durie (or Durji, as he spelled it) was a French Huguenot, whose birthplace was Picardy, but who had fled with his parents to Mannheim in the Palatinate of the Rhine to escape persecution and death. It has been said that his family was closely related to that of David des Marest (see page 64), for which reason he came to America between 1680 and 1690 and joined the Demarests on the west bank of the Hackensack. He was a blacksmith by trade, and tradition says that, upon his arrival at New Amsterdam, he went directly to Bergen, N. J., whence he walked all the way to the Demarest settlement on the Upper Hackensack. He had with him his four children, but no wife is mentioned and it is presumed he was a widower. Old documents of that period seem to establish the fact that David des Marest, the emigrant, was his uncle. He was present when the will of Demarest was read in 1693, and was then called a cousin of the Demarests. In 1694 he bought from the Indians and from the New Jersey Proprietors 233 acres west of Closter, bounded east on the Tiena Kill and west on the Hackensack. On this he built his family residence and remained until his death. Until within a very few years his descendants owned the old homestead. The house site is now the residence of the late Dr. John L. Terhune.

John Durie (1) was a man of intelligence, sterling integrity, and good business capacity. He had been fairly educated and possessed many accomplishments particularly useful to a pioneer, one of which was that of wielding the pen skillfully, as his signature to official documents shows. He was fond of reading and owned a considerable library, which he disposed of by his will. He was active in all public affairs in the county. He served as arbitrator in many disputes between the settlers and the Indians. He held town and county offices, being Constable, Justice of the Peace, Freeholder, etc. In 1693 he was one of the three County Judges. This was the first county court established in the county. He helped organize the Dutch church at Hackensack and several times held the offices of Deacon and Elder. He also was a member of Captain John Berry's "Train Band." In 1696 he married his second wife, Rachel Cresson, widow of his cousin, David Davids Demarest, who survived him and married again. He died near the close of 1698. His children of the second generation were Jane, Peter, John, and Margaretta.

John Johns Durie (2), born at Mannheim, married, August 20, 1715, Angenatie Johns Bogert. He kept and resided all his life on the old homestead. His children of the third generation were eleven: Rachel, John, John, Mary, Peter, Sarah Peter, Martina, David, Ann, and James.

David Johns Durie (3), born in 1739, died in 1809, married, in 1762, Margaretta Cornelises Van Horn, born in 1747, died in 1827. They had issue of the fourth generation twelve children: Angenitie, Maria, John D., Margaret, Rachel, Sara, Martina, Sara, Martina, Cornelius D., Ann, and Alice.

Cornelius D. Durie (4), born in 1784, died in 1849, married, in 1804, Margaret Brinkerhoff, born in 1782, died in 1856. They had issue of the fifth generation Christina, David C., Elizabeth, Nicholas C., Hannah, John, Cornelius, Richard, and Henry.

Nicholas C. Durie (5), born in 1811, died in 1868, married, in 1830, Maria Demarest, born in 1813, died in 1852. He married, second, Elizabeth Van Houten. His children of the sixth generation were Cornelius N., David N., Margaret, John D., Christina, Hannah, and Ralph C.

Cornelius N. Durie (6), born August 11, 1833, married, February 15, 1854, Rachel A., daughter of Garret I. Demarest. She was born June 18, 1832. He resided at Closter and had issue of the seventh generation Nicholas C., Garret D., and Irving.

Garret D. Durie (7), the subject of this sketch, was born at Closter, N. J., March 20, 1865, and received his education in the schools of Bergen County. At the age of fourteen he entered the employ of the West Shore Railroad. Subsequently he engaged in the shoe business in Closter, continuing seven years. Since then he has been actively engaged in the ice business at that place, building up a large and successful trade.

Mr. Durie has also been active and prominent in public affairs. He served as Postmaster of Closter from 1892 to 1894 and for some time has been a member of the Township Committee of Harrington Township. He attends the Dutch Reformed Church. He married Henrietta Roth and has one son, Roth C. Durie.

EDGAR K. CONRAD, M.D., of Hackensack, is the son of James H. Conrad and Jennie M. Klopp. He was born in Berneville, Berks County, Pa., February 21, 1870, and in 1876 removed with his parents to Chicago, Ill., whence the family went to South Dakota in 1882.

In 1890 Dr. Conrad returned East to take up the study of medicine. He had attended the public schools of Watertown, S. D., graduating from the Watertown High School in 1889. Upon returning East he entered Bellevue Medical College and was graduated from that institution with the degree of M.D. in 1893. He then took up his residence in Hackensack, N. J., and spent one year in the Hackensack Hospital, of which he is now a visiting physician. Since 1894 he has been actively and successfully engaged in the general practice of his profession in that place. He is a Chapter Mason, belonging to Lodge No. 70 and Chapter No. 40, of Hackensack, and a member of Hackensack Lodge, No. 73, I. O. O. F., Hackensack Council, Jr. O. U. A. M., and the Bergen County and State Medical Societies.

ABRAHAM DEMAREST, of Closter, is descended in the seventh generation from David des Marest, the first American emigrant and progenitor of the family (see sketch on page 64). The line of descent is as follows: David des Marest (1), of Beauchamp, in Picardy, France, and his wife Maria Sohier, of Nieppe, in Hainault, had four children of the second generation: David, Samuel, John, and Daniel.

David Davids Demarest (2) married Sara Bertholf, daughter of Rev. Gilliam Bertholf, and had eleven children of the third generation, one of whom was Jacobus Davids Demarest.

Jacobus Davids Demarest (3), baptized May 30, 1705, married (1) Lea de Groot and (2) Margaretta Cozine Haring. He lived at Schraalenburgh and had issue fifteen children of the fourth generation.

John Jacobus Demarest (4), born August 20, 1720, died February 1, 1783, married, March 7, 1744, Rachel Zabriskie, daughter of Joost Zabriskie, who was born March 19, 1725, and died April 16, 1813. They resided at Schraalenburgh and had thirteen children of the fifth generation.

Jacobus Johns Demarest (5), born August 20, 1748, died October 9, 1844, married (1) Rachel Smith, who died April 28, 1825. He married (2), in 1825, Rachel Voorhis, who survived her husband and died in 1835. Jacobus was a surveyor by occupation and lived at Middletown in Bergen County. He had issue ten children of the sixth generation.

Joost Demarest (6) was born December 4, 1797, and died at Closter, N. J., November 1, 1878. He married, in February, 1823, Margaret, daughter of Frederick Haring, born October 2, 1802. Joost was a cabinetmaker and lived at Piermont, N. Y., until 1825, when he removed to what is now Harrington Park, on the farm now occupied by ex-Sheriff William C. Herring. His children of the seventh generation were James, Frederick J., John B., Isaac H., Abraham, Vreeland B., Mary M., and Ann Eliza, of whom Abraham (7) is the subject of this sketch.

Abraham Demarest (7) was born in Harrington Township, N. J., December 14, 1839, and obtained his education in the schools of Bergen County. At the age of sixteen he engaged in the trade of tinsmith, and has ever since continued in that business. He is now at the head of the firm of A. Demarest & Brother, hardware dealers, of Closter.

He is a public spirited, progressive citizen, active in local affairs, and highly respected by all who know him. He served nine months in the Civil War as a private in the Twenty-second New Jersey Volunteers, and is a member of the Dutch Reformed Church of Closter. He married Catherine D. Westervelt, a member of an old and respected New Jersey family.

JOHN CARLSON, of Arlington, Hudson County, was born in Sweden on the 17th of April, 1842. He is the son of Charles and Catharina Carlson, members of old and respected families of that country. Having received a public school education in Sweden, Mr. Carlson came to the United States in 1870, and for a time was connected with the iron manufacturing business in New York City. Subsequently he removed to Arlington, N. J., where he has since been successfully engaged in the coal business.

Mr. Carlson is a business man of acknowledged ability, and during his entire career has maintained a high reputation for probity, integrity, and enterprise. He is a Director of the Kearny Building and Loan Association of Kearny, N. J., one of the oldest and strongest organizations of the kind in the State. In politics he is a Republican. He attends the Baptist Church and in every capacity has displayed great public spirit.

He married Miss Clara Lilljren, of Arlington, Hudson County. They have five children: John, Jr., Minnie, Edith, David, and William.

LOUIS HENRY BRADLEY, of Rutherford, N. J., was born in Brooklyn, N. Y., on the 28th of November, 1874. He is the son of Robert and Ida Frances (Backwood) Bradley, both natives of Brooklyn. He received his educational training in the public schools of that city and began his business career in the real estate business there. Subsequently he became a carpenter and worked at that trade in Rutherford, N. J. He finally engaged in the livery business in the same town, where he has built large and commodious stables for that purpose. He is much interested in the affairs of his adopted town, being a member of the Union Club of Rutherford, of Rutherford Lodge, No. 547, B. P. O. of Elks, of Rutherford Lodge, No. 150, Knights of Pythias, of Rutherford Lodge, No. 240, I. O. O. F., of Rutherford Council, Junior Order United American Mechanics, and of Fire Engine Company No. 2.

Mr. Bradley married Isabell Hunt, daughter of Charles R. and Martha Hunt, of Rutherford. She is deceased.

WILLIAM HENRY BRADLEY, of Hoboken, N. J., was born in Brooklyn, N. Y., on the 10th of September, 1878, being the son of William Henry Bradley, Sr., and Anna Brock. He is of English descent on the paternal side. His maternal ancestors are Germans. The family has resided in Hoboken about sixteen years.

Mr. Bradley attended the Hoboken public schools and studied law in the office of Joseph S. Parry. He was admitted to the bar as an attorney in June, 1899, and is now practicing law in the office of his preceptor.

JOHN SHAFER, of Hackensack, is one of the best known meat dealers in that part of Bergen County. He is also an active and public spirited citizen. The business of which he has been sole proprietor since 1898 was founded in 1872 by Smith & Shafer, Mr. Smith retiring three years ago. His market at 54 Main Street is a model and always well stocked.

Mr. Shafer was Town Commissioner for three years and served as Secretary of the commission. He is one of the best known and most respected merchants in Hackensack. He is an active member of the Hackensack

JOHN SHAFER.

Board of Trade, Past Master of Pioneer Lodge, F. and A. M., Past High Priest of Bergen Chapter, R. A. M., a Noble of the Mystic Shrine (Masons), and Past Grand of the Independent Order of Odd Fellows.

WILLIAM SICKLES BANTA was for many years one of the leading citizens of Hackensack. He was a lineal descendant of Epke Jacob Banta, who was born in Harlingen, West Friesland, Holland, and who sailed from Amsterdam in the ship "De Trouw," for America, February 13, 1659. He settled in what is now Bergen County, N. J., and became one of the Judges of the Oyer and Terminer in 1679. Ian (John) Banta, one of his direct descendants, located at Pascack, in Washington Township, about 1750, and died there, being succeeded by his eldest son, Hendrick Banta, who was born May 27, 1749. The latter died February 15, 1803, leaving about five hundred acres of land in Bergen County which was divided among his five sons. He also had three daughters. His son, Henry H. Banta, born at Pascack, September 30, 1784, was a shoemaker by trade, but spent his active life as a farmer and merchant. In 1832 he removed to Hackensack, and with his brother Teunis carried on a general mercantile business until his death in February, 1849. He was Postmaster of Hackensack for several years, ranked as Adjutant in the State militia, was a Justice of the Peace, and by appointment served as a Lay Judge of the Court of Common Pleas of Bergen County from 1829 to 1834 and 1838 to 1848. He married Jane, daughter of William Sickles, of Rockland County, N. Y., who died in 1870, aged seventy-six. She was descended from Zacharias Sickles, who came originally from Vienna, Austria, to Holland, and thence to Curacoa, one of the West India Islands, where he met Governor Peter Stuyvesant, with whom he came to New York and thence in 1655 to Albany. Zacharias Sickles is regarded as the common ancestor of the Sickles family in America. Judge Henry A. Banta had three children: Margaret (deceased), William S., and Jane (Mrs. John de Peyster Stagg).

William S. Banta was born in Pascack, Bergen County, December 12, 1824. He was educated in the public schools and at the private classical school of Rev. John S. Mabon, in Hackensack, and was graduated from Rutgers College in 1844. He read law with Hon. A. O. Zabriskie, of Hackensack, and was admitted to the bar of New Jersey as an attorney in October, 1847, and as a counselor in April, 1851. He subsequently became a Special Master in Chancery and a Supreme Court Commissioner. In the spring of 1848 he opened an office in Hackensack, where he continued in successful practice until his retirement from the more active duties of the profession in 1868. During this period of twenty years he established a wide reputation as an able and painstaking lawyer. He was Prosecutor of the Pleas of Bergen County from 1860 to 1868, when he resigned. In 1872 he was appointed Law Judge of the County of Bergen to fill the unexpired term of Judge Green, and on April 1, 1873, he was re-appointed for a full term of five years. In 1879 Governor McClellan appointed him Associate Judge of the same court, and he served in that capacity until the expiration of his term in 1884.

Judge Banta, on leaving the bench, retired from the active duties of his profession and afterward devoted his time largely to the care of his private interests. He was widely recognized for his sound judgment, strict integrity, and knowledge of the law. In educational matters he was especially prominent. He was School Superintendent of New Barbadoes, Bergen County, under the old law, and afterward was appointed, with Rev. Alber Amerman, one of the Board of Examiners for teachers of public schools by the Bergen County Board of Chosen Freeholders, a position he held for several years. In 1862 Governor Olden appointed him commissioner of the draft of the County of Bergen, in accordance with orders of the general government, and in this capacity he carried out in a highly creditable manner the provisions of the order by making an enrollment of all persons in the county liable to military duty. Within a month of the time appointed for the draft several companies volunteered, thus filling the quota required for Bergen County. This was a part of the machinery of the State inaugurated and set in motion by Governor Olden, who was pre-eminently the War Governor of New Jersey, and who more than any other man established that system which it was impossible to reverse and which ranked the State among the first in the Union during the entire Rebellion. Judge Banta was also Deputy Internal Revenue Collector for the County of Bergen during a part of the war period. He was a member of the Hackensack Improvement Commission, for several years President of the Hackensack Gas Light Company, and for a long time Secretary of the old Bergen County Mutual Insurance Company. He died May 7, 1900.

May 30, 1850, Judge Banta married Sarah, daughter of John and Caty Ann (Hopper) Zabriskie, of Hohokus, N. J., who died in 1853, leaving a son who died in infancy. In May, 1861, he married her sister, Adelia, who died in 1869. March 16, 1876, he was married to Jane Anne, daughter of Abraham H. and Maria (Anderson) Berry, of Hackensack, and a lineal descendant of John Berry, one of the original patentees of Bergen County. She died February 6, 1900, in the seventy-first year of her age.

WILLIAM MORTIMER CLARK, a prominent business man of Bayonne, Hudson County, N. J., and a veteran of the Civil War, was born in Middleburgh, N. Y., on the 10th of November, 1845. His paternal ancestor, John Clark, came to this country from England, and is interred in Trinity churchyard, New York City, in a vault built in 1790. A number of those in the collateral line emigrated originally from Holland. His parents were Minard H. Clark and Euphrasia Ann Gilbert. The Gilberts were from the North of Ireland and emigrated early to this country, settling at Hudson, Columbia County, N. Y. Their descendants afterward settled at Middleburgh, Schoharie County, where Euphrasia Ann was born. His grandparents were Richard Clark and Christina Dutcher. His great-grandfather was Thomas Clark and his great-great-grandparents were John Clark and Tekie Waldron. The Dutchers and Waldrons were both of Holland descent, and a number of them, like the Clarks, have been residents of this country for many generations. Mr. Clark's ancestors served with honor and distinction in the Revolutionary War, in the War of 1812, in the Mexican War, and in the Rebellion, and from the first have been active and influential in the communities where they have resided.

The Episcopal Chapel at Middleburgh, N. Y., furnished Mr. Clark with the educational training with which he entered upon the active duties of life. After leaving school he served an apprenticeship at the foundry trade, which he has continuously followed. He is the patentee of an acetyline gas generator which has been a marked success. In 1885 he settled in Bayonne, Hudson County, and still carries on the foundry business.

Mr. Clark enlisted in the War of the Rebellion, August 20, 1862, as a member of Company D, One Hundred and Thirty-fourth New York Volunteers, and served until the close of that sanguinary conflict. He participated in the battles of Fredericksburg, Chancellorsville, Gettysburg, Lookout Mountain, and other important engagements, and was with Sherman in his march to the sea. He has always been a Republican, prominent in party and public affairs, deeply interested in the progress of the community, and highly respected for those sterling qualities which distinguish the representative citizen. He is Past Grand Commander of the Knights of Malta of New Jersey, and a member of Mansfield Post, No. 22, Grand Army of the Republic, of Bayonne Lodge, No. 99, Free and Accepted Masons, of Veteran Legion, No. 81, of Jersey City, of Bayonne Lodge, No. 37, Knights of Pythias, of Eastern Star Chapter, No. 21, of Bayonne Lodge, No. 206, Independent Order of Odd Fellows, of Council No. 119, Junior Order of American Mechanics, of Council No. 25, Senior Order United American Mechanics, of Elizabeth, and of Council No. 109, Daughters of Liberty, which he organized. He is also a member of Bayonne Court, Independent Order of Foresters. Mr. Clark is one of the most popular and influential men in the southern part of Hudson County, and in both business and public affairs is widely known. He has achieved success in every capacity, and has discharged with fidelity and satisfaction all the duties which he has been called upon to perform.

On November 9, 1867, Mr. Clark married Julia G. Canfield, daughter of Arza W. and Nancy Canfield, of Palatine Bridge, Montgomery County, N. Y. They have five children: Minard H., William M., Jr., Sylvanus W., Elizabeth A., and Nancy E.

JAMES J. DONNELLY, of Arlington, is the son of John and Ellen (Chester) Donnelly and a grandson of James Chester. His parents came to this country from Ireland, where members of the family still reside. Mr. Donnelly was born June 10, 1866, in New York City, where he received a public school education. He is now engaged in the business of gold and silver plating at 73 Nassau Street, New York.

In politics Mr. Donnelly has been for several years an active and influential Republican. In 1899 he was the representative on the Board of Aldermen from the Fourth Ward of Kearny. He is a member of the Royal Arcanum, of the Independent Order of Foresters, and of the Knights of Columbus, and as a citizen is enterprising, public spirited, and highly respected.

Mr. Donnelly married Margaret Collins, by whom he has four children: Chester, Marguerite, Helen, and Dorothy.

WILLIAM ECKHARDT, a well known real estate and insurance man of Guttenberg, Hudson County, was born in New York City on the 14th of May, 1861. He is the son of Peter Charles and Louise Eckhardt, both natives of Germany. He received a public school education in New York City and afterward went to Salt Lake City, Utah, where he spent five years with his brother, Peter Charles Eckhardt, Jr., in the stock business.

Upon returning East Mr. Eckhardt engaged in the real estate business with his father, and so continued until July, 1890, when he removed to Guttenberg. He then engaged in the real estate and insurance business for himself. In politics he is a Democrat. He was Councilman of Guttenberg one term and is a member of the Democratic Club, of the Royal Arcanum, and of the Ancient Order of United Workmen. In every capacity he has displayed sound judgment and gained an honorable reputation.

Mr. Eckhardt was married, November 7, 1886, to Ellen, daughter of Michael and Catherine McKenna, of New York. They have four children: Peter Charles, 3d, William, Ethel, and Ralph.

PERCY ALMY GADDIS, one of the prominent and successful real estate and insurance brokers of Jersey City, was born in Jersey City, N. J., January 18, 1872, and is unmarried. His great-grandfather, Andrew Gaddis, who was of English descent and a resident of North Branch, Middlesex County, N. J., married Margaret Bergen, a descendant of Hans Hansen Bergen, a native of Bergen, Norway, who came to America in 1633 and settled in the Wallabout section of Brooklyn, where he married Sarah, daughter of Joris Jansen Rapelje. Andrew Gaddis's issue were Jacob B., David A., John Van Dyck, and Catharine Ann. Jacob B., born at North Branch, married Eliza Outcalt, daughter of Judge Outcalt, of New Brunswick. He came to Jersey City in the early fifties, embarked in the lighterage business, and founded the New Jersey Lighterage Company, of which he was President. He died at Ogdensburg, N. Y., in 1886, having had issue

Andrew A., Catharine L., John de F., Theodore F., Margaret, Julia, and Elizabeth.

Theodore F. Gaddis, born at Spottswood, N. J., married Caroline Amelia Ryder, daughter of Brazilla W. Ryder, of Middleboro, Mass., and Hannah Elizabeth Warren, of Darien, Conn. The latter was a lineal descendant of Richard Warren, of the "Mayflower" party. Theodore F. Gaddis came to Jersey City about 1854 and entered Columbia College, but left before graduating to connect himself with the Jersey City Locomotive Works, with which concern he remained until its failure, when he established the Hudson Iron Foundry, with which he was identified until shortly before his death. His issue were Theodore B., James Van Dyck, Percy A., Bertha O., Malcolm L., and Mortimer C.

Percy A. Gaddis, the subject of this sketch, attended the public schools of Jersey City until thirteen years of age, when he entered as a clerk the office of a Wall Street broker in New York. Three years later he became a clerk in the offices of the Erie Railroad Company. Two years later he was employed by C. C. Jewell & Co., real estate dealers. In the fall of 1893 Mr. Gaddis embarked in the real estate and insurance business for himself, near the Hudson County Court House, where he has since success-

GADDIS BUILDING. BALDWIN AV.

fully pursued it. In the fall of 1899 he erected the office building shown in illustration, which he now occupies.

In addition to managing his large and increasing business Mr. Gaddis finds time to devote to religious and political work. As an active member and clerk of the Vestry of the Church of the Holy Cross (Episcopal) of Jersey City he has devoted much time to a study of the history, canons, and traditions of the Church of England, and has had many discussions with eminent divines relative to church doctrines.

He has served on the Republican County Committee, and is a member of the Republican Battery, a crack political organization.

WILLIAM R. REES, of Jersey City, is the son of Rees Rees and Eleanor MacLaughlan, and was born in that city on the 13th of October, 1876. His father is of Welsh extraction and his mother of Scotch-Irish parentage.

Mr. Rees received his education in the public schools of Jersey City, and after leaving school took up the study of the law. He pursued his legal studies in the office of Spencer and Jacob Weart, in Jersey City, was admitted to the New Jersey bar in November, 1897, and is now in partnership with Howard MacSherry under the firm name of MacSherry & Rees. Since his admission to the bar he has had his offices in Jersey City and has been very successful in practice. He was clerk in the Law Department of

Jersey City for three years, and was later called on cases emanating from violations of the health rules by the Jersey City Board of Health. He is a member of the Union League of Jersey City and a prominent citizen, respected by all who know him.

Mr. Rees was married on Easter Sunday, 1899, to Evelyn Eugenie Robinson, of Waretown, Ocean County, N. J.

FRED J. ENSOR, of Arlington, was born in Rugby, England, on the 6th of September, 1873. He is the son of John Flavel Ensor and Esther King.

Mr. Ensor obtained his education in the public schools of Sutton, Cold-

FRED J. ENSOR.

field, and in 1887 left England and came to the United States, settling first in Liverpool, Pa., afterward in Pittsburg in that State, and finally in Wheeling, W. Va. In 1891 he removed to Arlington, Hudson County, N. J., where he has since resided.

For a time Mr. Ensor was successfully engaged in business as a contractor. He is now a dealer in paints, oils, etc., having one of the best known establishments of the kind in his section. In this as well as in other enterprises he has achieved success. He is a public spirited, patriotic citizen, actively identified with local affairs, and a member of the First Regiment, N. G. N. J. He is also a member of Pilgrim Lodge, No. 202, I.

O. O. F., of Americus Council, No. 1,304, Royal Arcanum, and of the Rebekah order of Odd Fellows, all of Arlington. In politics he is independent.

JOHN DE VOE.—The de Voes of New Jersey are of French lineage. Nicholas de Voe, of Rochelle, France, went to Mannheim in Germany in 1645, with his parents and brother Frederick. From thence in 1675 Nicholas emigrated to America and stopped for a while at New Harlem, where he married Mary See. In 1680 he removed to Bergen, N. J., and thence in 1687 to Hackensack, where he purchased lands from the Indians on the west side of the Hackensack and settled near David des Marest. Des Marest claimed title to de Voe's lands, and the latter bought elsewhere. About 1681, his first wife having died, he married (2), in 1682, Margaret Fonda, widow of Jaeck Batton. He died about 1715 and his widow married Henry Karnnega, of Long Island. His children of the second generation were Abraham, Hester (married, in 1698, Henry Brower), Susanna (born at Jersey City, October 11, 1680, married (1), in 1696, Thomas Bricker and (2), in 1695, James Everse Van Gelder), and Mary (married, in 1710, Jacob Buys, of Jersey City). There must have been other sons.

In 1676 Frederick, brother of Nicholas, came over from Mannheim and located at New Harlem, where he settled and resided until his death in 1743. The inventory of his property after his death indicates that he was a man of considerable wealth. His first marriage occurred in 1673, but his first wife died a year or two later, and he married (2), June 24, 1677, Hester Tourneur, daughter of Daniel Tourneur, of Harlem.

John de Voe, the subject of this sketch, is descended in the seventh generation from Frederick or Nicholas, the emigrants. He is the son of James de Voe and Alletta Van Bussum and was born in Saddle River Township, Bergen County, November 6, 1821. He received his education in the schools of his native county, and at the age of thirteen went to work on his father's farm, where he remained three years. He then learned the carriage-making trade, receiving twenty-five dollars a year and his board for five years. This apprenticeship was both practical and valuable. He followed the trade for forty years in New York City and Newark, N. J., and afterward settled in Rivervale, Bergen County, where he has since been engaged in farming. He is a member of the Baptist Church, but for some time has attended the Reformed Church, and in every capacity has gained the confidence and respect of his fellowmen. He married Susan A. Haring.

HENRY KARL, son of John and Wilhelmina (Zeitner) Karl, was born in Germany on the 6th of July, 1869. There he received his education. He came to America with his parents in 1883 and afterward settled in West Hoboken, where he still resides.

His first business was that of a barber in New York City. Subsequently he was a weaver in a silk mill. He is a Democrat in politics, a Justice of the Peace, a Commissioner of Deeds, and a Notary Public. He is President of the Young Democracy of the Third Ward, West Hoboken.

Mr. Karl married Wilhelmina Loehr, daughter of Philip and Catherine Loehr. They have three children: Frederick, Minnie, and Amanda.

CHARLES HOFFMAN, of Carlstadt, N. J., was born in New York City on the 11th of May, 1863. He is the son of Francis and Pauline Hoffman, natives of Germany, who came to the United States in 1870, settling in Carlstadt.

Mr. Hoffman was educated in the Carlstadt public schools and subsequently engaged in the watch-case business. Afterward he became an undertaker, and has since followed that profession with success in Carlstadt, where he resides.

He was elected County Coroner of Bergen County in 1899 and still holds that office. He is a member of several German societies, including the Carlstadt Turners, the Concordia Society, the German Schuetzen, the Carlstadt Schuetzen Corps, the Independent Schuetzen, and the Powder Bowling Club. He is also a member of the Carlstadt Bergen Hose Company, of Carlstadt Lodge, No. 113, Independent Order of Odd Fellows, and of Rutherford Lodge, No. 547, B. P. O. Elks.

Mr. Hoffman was married, May 11, 1893, to Louisa H. Otto, of Carlstadt, N. J. They have two children: Charles and Mary.

BENJAMIN CUMBERLAND STUART, of Hillsdale, is a native of New York City, and the son of Benjamin C. Stuart and Susannah E. Davis, daughter of Thomas Davis, of England. He is a grandson of Thomas Stuart and a great-grandson of Thomas Stuart, Sr., of Scotland.

Mr. Stuart was educated in the schools of Brooklyn, where he resided for several years. After leaving school he took up newspaper work and for a long time served on the staff of the leading New York daily newspapers. He is now and has been for several years President and General Manager of the Standard News Association, with offices in the Postal Telegraph Building, 253 Broadway, New York.

While residing in Brooklyn he was actively identified with the musical affairs of the metropolis and is the author of several musical and literary compositions, including the "Black Diamond Rulers" and other works. He is the eldest brother of a family of newspaper men connected with the metropolitan press, and in both journalism and business has achieved success. He is a member of the New York Press Club, a public spirited citizen, and active and influential in the affairs of Hillsdale, N. J., where he resides.

HORACE ROBERSON, a prominent lawyer of Bayonne, Hudson County, is the son of Samuel Roberson, and was born in Hunterdon County, N. J., May 5, 1858. Although the son of a farmer, Mr. Roberson's inclinations were to educational pursuits. After obtaining a good common school education in the public schools of his own county he entered the New Jersey State Normal School at Trenton, took a full course, and was graduated in 1881. Following this, for five years he successfully filled the position of Principal of the public school at Closter in Bergen County, where he made many friends and was highly esteemed. Having during this time given his spare time to the study of the law, he took a course in Columbia College Law School and was admitted to the New Jersey bar in June, 1887. He was then employed in the office of Counsellor De Witt Van Buskirk at Bayonne for two years. In 1889 he opened a law office in West Eighth Street, Bayonne, and has since successfully practiced his profession in the county and State courts. Having been admitted as a counsellor, he became and is still senior member of the law firm of Roberson & Demarest.

In 1891 Mr. Roberson was elected School Trustee for the one-year term and made a good record on the board. In 1894 he was appointed City Treasurer and served with credit the full term of two years. In 1898 he was elected City Councilman and has served two years. He is solicitor for the Centerville Building and Loan Association. He has always been prominent in the councils of the Republican party, having been a member of the County Committee and Vice-President of the Bayonne City Republican Association. He is devoted to his profession and a zealous worker in everything he undertakes. He is a member of the church and of social societies.

In September, 1890, he married Nettie Marcelia, daughter of Abraham J. Demarest and Eliza W. Lozier, of Closter, N. J. Mrs. Roberson was born at Eastwood, N. J., December 25, 1861. He has two daughters: Elinor W., born December 25, 1894, and Jessie K., born November 1, 1898.

FREDERICK P. VAN RIPER.—Winfield in his "History of Hudson County" says: "This name with its present multitudinous orthography is derived from the Latin *ripa*, and was the name of a city on the north bank of the River Nibbs, sometimes called Nipsick, or Gram. North Jutland (so called to distinguish it from South Jutland or Schleswig), in Denmark, was divided into four dioceses, the most southwesterly of which, lying along the German Ocean, was called Ripen. This diocese was one hundred and forty-two miles in length and fifty-seven miles in width, and was part of Cimbrica Cheresonesus of the ancients, where dwelt the warlike Cimbri, who, at one time, invaded the Roman Empire. The City of Ripen, in the Diocese of Ripen, is situated in lat. 55° 36' north, and lon. 9° 10' east. Next to Wibourg it is the most ancient town in North Jutland. It once had a commodious harbor and profitable commerce; but the one long since filled up and the other sought different channels. Its cathedral was imposing, built of hewn stone, with a steeple of great height, which served as a landmark for mariners. In the Swedish war of 1645 the city was captured, but was recovered by the Danes soon after. From this port, in April, 1663, a vessel named "T'Bonte Koe" (The Spotted Cow) sailed for New Netherlands with eighty-nine passengers, consisting of men, women, and children. Among the number was Juriaen Tomassen, a young man of the City of Ripen. About four years after his arrival he married Pryntje Hermans, May 25, 1667; died September 12, 1695. Some of his descendants took the name of Jurianse—now Yereance and Auryansen,—while others, taking the name of the city from which their ancestors sailed, became Van Ripen."

The children of Juriaen Tomassen were nine of the second generation: Thomas, Gerrit, Aeltje, Christina, Mary, Harman, John, Harman, and Margaret. Of these Harman (2), born December 6, 1686, married (1) Mary Fredericks and (2) Judith Steinmets. Thomas and Gerrit bought lands and settled in Bergen County. The third son, Harman (2), removed to Aquackanonck, where he settled and died in May, 1756. His children of the third generation were Juriaen, Frederick, Abram, Christopher, Mary, Jacob, John, Isaac, Sarah, Jane, Garret, and Thomas.

Frederick (3), born February 22, 1715, married (1) Catharine Hopper and (2) Ann Van Vorst. Frederick resided at Aquackanonck. His grandson, Frederick Jan Van Riper, of the fifth generation, was born August 4, 1782, and died June 7, 1864. He married Mary Van Buskirk, who died November 4, 1873, aged eighty-four years, one month, and seventeen days. Both are buried at the Reformed Dutch Church at Saddle River, N. J. Their issue, among others, was Peter Van Riper of the sixth generation, born December 5, 1808, died November 22, 1880, married Elizabeth Haring, daughter of Isaac and Annie (Post) Haring. She was born May 7, 1809, and died May

26, 1884. They were buried at Pascack, N. J., where they resided. Among their issue of the seventh generation was Frederick P. Van Riper (7).

Frederick P. Van Riper (7) was born at Chestnut Ridge, N. J., July 7, 1832, and received his education in the schools of Bergen County. At the age of seventeen he went to work on his father's farm, teaching school in winter for three years. Afterward he was engaged in the grocery business in Paterson for two years, and since then he has conducted the homestead farm. For nine months he served on the regimental staff of the Twenty-second New Jersey Volunteers.

Mr. Van Riper is a public spirited citizen, a member of the Reformed Church, and honored and esteemed by all who know him. He married Charity Ann Demarest and has had five children, of whom four are living: James D., Anna E., Annetta S., and Peter Elvin.

GEORGE KINGSLAND CAMP, of Jersey City, was born on the manor homestead at Kingsland, Bergen County, N. J., July 15, 1848. He is a direct descendant of Nathaniel Kingsland, to whom the family homestead in Bergen County was originally granted by the Indians during the reign of Charles II. This tract of land extended from the Passaic River to the Hackensack River. He is the son of James Ely Camp and Eliza T. Kingsland, a grandson of Brookfield Camp and George Kingsland and a grandson of Jeannette Ely and Frances L. Ten Eyck.

Mr. Camp was educated in the local schools in what was then Union Township, Bergen County. He also attended Newark Academy and B. T. Harrington's Boarding School in New York. As a boy he began his active life with the Provident Institution for Savings of Jersey City, with which he remained from 1866 to 1872. He then engaged in the real estate business, and subsequently entered the employ of the Relief Fire Insurance Company of New York, with which he continued until 1882. He then returned to the Provident Institution for Savings to accept a clerkship, and is now the Assistant Secretary and Treasurer. He is a man of acknowledged ability, an excellent financier, a patriotic and progressive citizen, and highly esteemed by all who know him.

Mr. Camp was married, February 25, 1892, to Emilie J. Wellner, of New York. They have two children: Kingsland and C. Wellner Camp.

HENRY V. CONDICT was born at Littleton, Morris County, N. J., in 1853. His family was a prominent one in that part of the State, he being the son of Silas B. Condict and a grandson of Hon. Silas Condict, Sr.

Mr. Condict was graduated from Phillips Academy at Andover, Mass., and then began the study of law with Frederick G. Burnham, of Morristown, N. J. After completing his course at the Columbia Law School, New York, he resumed his studies with Robert Gilchrist and the late Chancellor Alexander T. McGill, of Jersey City. He was admitted to the bar as an attorney in November, 1877, and as a counselor in November, 1881. He is now a member of the law firm of Randolph, Condict & Black, of Jersey City.

In 1879 Mr. Condict married a daughter of Ephraim Hudson, late of New York City. Two children have been born to them—Hudson and Edith.

WALTER E. LAFFEY, member of the Board of Aldermen and First Assistant Engineer of the Fire Department of Kearny, Hudson County, and President of the Staniar & Laffey Wire Company, of Harrison, was born in Belleville, Essex County, N. J., January 16, 1864, the son of John Laffey

GENEALOGICAL

and Hannah Staniar. He is of English descent. Receiving a good practical education in the schools of his native town, he entered the establishment with which he is now connected and steadily advanced from employee to proprietor and employer. For more than a quarter of a century his father, John Laffey, was associated with William Staniar, the founder of the wire industry in New Jersey. They erected a large and commodious plant in Harrison, Hudson County, for the manufacture of brass and copper wire and wire cloth, the latter an indispensable factor in the manufacture of paper. The founders and originators of this enterprise successfully

WALTER E. LAFFEY.

conducted the business for thirty years under the firm name of Staniar & Laffey, and became widely known for the excellence of their product and their honorable methods. Finally the senior member, William Staniar, retired, after the death of John Laffey. In 1895 their sons, Walter E. Laffey, J. W. Laffey, W. E. Staniar, and G. W. Staniar, succeeded to the business, incorporating the Staniar & Laffey Wire Company, and are still conducting it with energy, ability, and success. This is not only one of the chief manufacturing industries in Harrison, but one of the best known and most successful of the kind in the country. Its product finds a ready market throughout the Union.

Mr. Laffey, while eminently successful and constantly engrossed in their extensive manufacturing business, has from boyhood taken a deep and at times an active interest in public affairs, and as a resident of Kearny, Hudson County, is prominent and influential in the community. He is a member of the Kearny Board of Aldermen, representing the Second Ward, and was First Assistant Engineer of the Fire Department for two years. He is a member of the Masonic order, of the Knights of Pythias, and of the Royal Arcanum, and as a citizen is public spirited and progressive.

He married Margaret McCloskey, and has three children, namely: Edward, Anna, and Helen.

MICHAEL NEY RITCHIE, of Kingsland and Harrison, was born in County Derry, Ireland, September 18, 1852. He is the son of John Ritchie and Sarah, daughter of John and Mary (Mackel) Ritchie, a grandson of Samuel Ritchie and Nancy McErlane, and a great-grandson of Michael and Catherine (Eccleson) Ritchie and of Peter Ritchie and Mary Diamond. His ancestors came to Ireland from Scotland after the defeat of the Pretender at Culloden in 1745, and settled on the banks of the River Bann, at a place called Creagh, County Derry. They were Scotch Roman Catholics, and since coming to Ireland have been mostly small farmers and fishermen. So far as known none of them became wealthy or distinguished. They were plain, honest people, highly respected, and endowed with sterling traits of character. They participated in the Irish Rebellion of 1798, and one of them was executed for treason at Belfast in 1799. They strongly opposed the British government both in Scotland and Ireland, believing in those principles of liberty which finally led them to America.

Mr. Ritchie was educated partly at the Anahomish National School in Ireland and partly in the public and high schools of Paterson, N. J., having come to this country alone when twelve years old. After leaving the Paterson High School he learned the machinist's trade with Todd & Rafferty, of that city, and as a machinist and millwright traveled over nearly all of North and South America. In this capacity he gained a wide and valuable experience. In 1890 he engaged in the real estate and insurance business. He studied law under the direction of Edward J. Luce, of Rutherford, and was admitted to the New Jersey bar November 4, 1894. Since then he has been successfully engaged in the practice of his profession in Newark, Jersey City, and Harrison, and also at his home in Kingsland, Bergen County, where he settled permanently in 1883. He makes real estate law a specialty.

Mr. Ritchie has also been active in public affairs. He was a candidate for the office of Assessor in 1892, but was defeated by a small majority. He has been counsel for Union Township in Bergen County. Though a firm believer in Christianity he is not a member of any sect or creed, nor of any society of secret organization.

He was married, May 1, 1875, to Julia A. Stalter, and has three sons and two daughters.

AUGUST A. COPIN, the well known florist of West Hoboken and New York City, was born in West Hoboken, N. J., October 4, 1863. He is the son of Francis Copin and Christina Arnould, daughter of Jacob Arnould, who came from Belgium about 1845 and settled in Canada. His paternal grandfather, Nicholas Copin, and his father, Francis, were born in Alsace, France. The family came to America about 1835 and settled in West

Hoboken, N. J. Afterward Francis Copin engaged in business as a florist and gardener in North Bergen, where he died June 20, 1898. His wife died August 26, 1896. George Copin, their eldest son, was born July 12, 1861, in West Hoboken, and received a public school education. He is associated with the well known house of Mouquin, of Fulton and Ann Streets, New York.

August A. Copin received his education in St. Mary's parochial school in West Hoboken. On March 13, 1880, he engaged in business as a florist in New York City, where he has since continued, having his establishment at 222 Sixth Avenue since December, 1888. He also has an establishment at 264 Clinton Avenue, West Hoboken, where he resides. He is an influential Democrat, and has filled a number of positions with acknowledged ability and satisfaction. For three years he was Financial Secretary of the West Hoboken Fire Department, serving in that capacity until May 1, 1899. He is a member of Neptune Fire Company No. 1, of West Hoboken, of St. Michael's Lyceum, of Palisade Council, Legion of Honor, and of the Order of Foresters of West Hoboken.

Mr. Copin was married, January 31, 1883, to Adeline Walsh, of West Hoboken. They have two children: Veronica and Adeline.

PETER HAUCK, one of the foremost men of New Jersey, is known as a leading brewer, a public spirited, enterprising citizen, and a conspicuous member of the Democratic party. Born in Kling Munster, Bavaria, Germany, June 9, 1838, he came to this country with his parents when six years old and located in New York City, where his father engaged in the brewing industry. There he received a good public school education. After completing his studies he entered his father's establishment and thoroughly mastered the profession of brewer, acquiring a practical as well as a theoretical experience in every department of the business.

The brewery established by his father, Adam Hauck, in 1844, on Wooster Street, New York, was a small affair, but the plant was enlarged until it became one of the largest of the kind in the city. In 1869 he removed the entire business to Harrison, Hudson County, N. J., where a substantial building was erected, and where it was continued under the most favorable auspices. Peter Hauck subsequently succeeded his father as sole proprietor, and brought to his duties special qualifications, having been trained up to the business and thoroughly understanding it in every detail. Afterward the firm of Kaufmann & Hauck was formed, and upon its dissolution Mr. Hauck again became proprietor and steadily enlarged his trade. In 1879 the brewery was destroyed by fire, but he at once turned his attention to rebuilding, and in 1880 erected and completed a new plant upon a more extended scale, making it a model establishment of its kind. Giving the new brewery the benefit of his wide experience, he perfected its plans and interior arrangements, and gained for it the concession of being one of the finest-appointed and best-conducted plants in the country. It has a frontage on Harrison Avenue, between Fifth and Washington Streets, of 225 feet, with a depth on Cleveland Avenue of about 400 feet. The main building is a substantial structure, and there is additional accommodation for the malt-house, cooperage, bottling-plant, etc., the whole being equipped with modern improvements, including a 250-barrel brew kettle, ice machines, cellerage, an artesian well, etc. In 1844 three hundred barrels of beer were brewed. When the brewery was moved from New York in 1869 the output had grown to 15,761 barrels. In 1881 the output had increased to 24,612 barrels annually; in 1882 to 28,703 barrels; in 1884 to 35,997 barrels; in 1886 to 50,214 barrels; and in 1889 to 71,589 barrels.

In 1889 the vast interests were re-organized and became a part of the United States Brewing Company, which has a paid-up capital of $5,500,000, and in 1890 the output was 76,309 barrels; in 1893, 86,246 barrels. At present the product exceeds 100,000 barrels per year. Mr. Hauck has continuously retained the management, in which he has displayed ability, executive skill, and sound judgment. He is a Director of the United States Brewing Company as well as Manager of Peter Hauck & Co.'s Hudson County Brewery, a name by which his establishment has long been known. Though founded by his father, it is to him that the growth and success of the concern is practically due.

Mr. Hauck's splendid executive abilities have led him to the discharge of duties on behalf of the public, to which he brought the same skill which has won for him so much success in his profession. He was for a time a member of the Board of Freeholders of Hudson County, and in 1872 and 1873 served in the City Council of Harrison, where he resides. He is a public spirited, enterprising citizen. He has also been a member of the State Democratic Committee of New Jersey.

His eldest son, Peter Hauck, Jr., was born in Harrison in 1872, received his education in Newark Academy, and since 1891 has been actively identified with the business management of his father's brewery. In 1892 he took a full course in the chemistry of brewing at Schwartz College, New York.

FRANK HENRY KIMMERLY, a popular citizen of Bayonne, N. J., and formerly Police Justice of Jersey City, is the son of Alexander H. Kimmerly and Mary Stocker, and was born in New York City on the 23d of March, 1856. His parents were both natives of Germany. They came to the United States when young, were married in New York City, removed to Jersey City, N. J., in 1858, and in 1897 settled in Bayonne.

Mr. Kimmerly was two years old when the family removed to Hudson County, and since then he has lived and labored within the county's limits. Having received a good public school education in Jersey City, he learned the machinist's trade, but soon found that he had no distinct liking for it, and he therefore did not follow it as a business. He took up the hotel business in Jersey City and continued it for several years, after which he engaged in the wholesale liquor business in New York City. He is now proprietor of a hotel in Bayonne and one of the popular and best known citizens of Hudson County.

In politics and in business Mr. Kimmerly has achieved marked success and gained a high reputation. Identifying himself in early life with the Democratic party, he has long been one of its acknowledged leaders and able advisers, and in 1887 was elected a member of the Board of Chosen Freeholders of Hudson County, serving two terms of five years each. From 1890 to 1893 he was also Police Justice of Jersey City. He is a prominent member of the Bayonne City Democratic Club, of the Robert Davis Association of Jersey City, of the Greenville Turners of New Jersey, of Bayonne Lodge, No. 434, B. P. O. E., of Grant Lodge, No. 89, K. of P., of Jersey City, and of Steuben Lodge, Chosen Friends, of New York City. His duties and obligations, both public and private, have been discharged with ability and with that integrity of character which stamp the successful man.

On the 28th of November, 1894, Mr. Kimmerly married Elizabeth Fick, daughter of George and Mary Fick, of Jersey City, N. J. They have one son, George.

FRANK KOCH, of Arlington, was born in Kingsland, N. J., June 7, 1873, his parents being Louis and Amelia Koch, both of German descent. He first attended school in his native town. At the age of ten he entered the Thirteenth Street school in New York City, but a few years later went to Scranton, Pa., and completed his education in the Scranton High School.

When he was twenty years old Mr. Koch entered the office of Addison Ely, of Rutherford, N. J., as a student at law, serving a four years' clerkship. He was admitted to the New Jersey bar in February, 1898. He

FRANK KOCH.

immediately opened an office in Arlington, N. J., where he has since been actively and successfully engaged in the general practice of his profession.

Mr. Koch enlisted at Rutherford, in 1894, in Company L, Second Regiment, N. G. N. J., of which Addison Ely was Captain, and when war was declared against Spain he went to the front with his regiment, which was assigned to the Seventh Army Corps under Major-General Fitzhugh Lee, stationed at Jacksonville, Fla. He was Acting Quartermaster and Ordnance Sergeant of his company. He has been Borough Clerk of the Borough of North Arlington, where he resides, and is now (1900) an active and influential member of the Borough Council. In these as well as in other capacities Mr. Koch has displayed marked ability, and as a citizen is highly esteemed for his public spirit, sound judgment, and integrity of character. He is unmarried.

JOHN MATTHEWS, of Bull's Ferry, North Bergen, Hudson County, is the son of John Matthews, Sr., and Mary Ann Green and a grandson of William Matthews, of Kilowen. He was born at Warren Point, County Down, Ireland, March 7, 1853. In 1867 he came to America, and in New York City, where he landed on December 31 of that year, he finished his education in the public schools. Subsequently he served an apprenticeship at the cooper's trade with Oliver McMahon, 297, 299, and 301 Front Street. He remained there till the summer of 1871, when he went to Chicago, and was in that city at the time of the great fire. This disaster caused him to return to New York, whence he removed on May 24, 1872, to Bull's Ferry in the Township of North Bergen, N. J., where he has since resided. There he has continuously held responsible positions in the cooperage department of the Barrett Manufacturing Company and their predecessors.

Mr. Matthews is a skilled workman, possessing a broad and practical knowledge of every branch of his trade. He is also a prominent, influential, and public spirited citizen, and in various capacities has served his town with credit and ability. A Democrat in politics, he has frequently been called upon to act as a delegate to local party conventions, and since the spring of 1888 has held the office of Justice of the Peace, in which he is serving his third consecutive term of five years. He has also been a Trustee of North Bergen Public School No. 1. He is a Notary Public, a Commissioner of Deeds, and Assistant Chief of the North Bergen Fire Department. He was one of the principal organizers and has continuously been a member and Treasurer of Eclipse Hose Company No. 1, of North Bergen, and during the last two years has been its Foreman. His activity in the formation and development of the Fire Department of his township, his interest in all local affairs, and his efforts in promoting every worthy project attest his public spirit, patriotism, and enterprise. He is a member and Senior Warden of Mystic Tie Lodge, No. 123, F. and A. M., and a member and Vice-Regent of Taurus Council, Royal Arcanum.

June 1, 1874, Mr. Matthews married Miss Eliza Ann Bohne, of Hoboken, N. J., and of their fourteen children seven are living, namely: John Green, Lizzie Maria, Frederick William, Charles Henry, Jane, George, and Florence. The family are members and communicants of Mediator (Protestant Episcopal) Church, of Edgewater, Bergen County.

EMIL SAHNER, of the firm of Sahner & Hauenstein, proprietors of the Union Brewing Company of the Town of Union, is the son of Fritz and Catherine Sahner and a grandson of Carl Sahner, and was born in Dürkheim, Rheinfalz, Germany, in February, 1853.

He received his education in the Fatherland and began active life as a salesman in a large wholesale house in Landau, Rheinfalz, afterward becoming a clerk in a sugar refinery in Croeinfort, Bavaria. At the age of twenty he came to America and started as a salesman in a glassware house in New York City. Subsequently he accepted a position as bookkeeper for the A. Kraemer Brewing Company, of Guttenberg, N. J., and remained there until 1888, when he became bookkeeper for the Union Brewing Company, of the Town of Union, Hudson County. In 1893 he was made collector for that concern. In September, 1897, he formed a partnership with Louis C. Hauenstein, Jr., and under the firm name of Sahner & Hauenstein purchased the entire business, which they still conduct. The Union Brewery, under their able and energetic management, has become one of the largest enterprises of the kind in Hudson County.

Mr. Sahner is a public spirited, progressive, and patriotic citizen, a liberal supporter of every movement designed to advance the general welfare, and a member of the Royal Arcanum and the Ancient Order of United Workmen. He married Miss Louisa Fehr, and resides in the Town of Union.

WILLIAM McKENZIE, of East Rutherford, was born in Glasgow, Scotland, August 22, 1841. From a boy cotton bleaching possessed a strong attraction for him, and he was already proficient in the art when, in 1866, he came to the United States. At Norwich, Conn., and Pawtucket, R. I., he followed the business, winning a high reputation as superintendent in a large concern. He constantly sought opportunities, and in 1875 he took advantage of an opening which has resulted in making him largely interested in East Rutherford and Bergen County, N. J.

Standing by the side of the Erie Railway tracks at Carlton Hill at that time was a large brick building which had become known in the neighborhood as a "white elephant." A cotton bleachery had been established there fifty years before, but its record had been one of ruin for the men who put their money into the enterprise. Mr. McKenzie, whose knowledge of the business was accurate, and who was sanguine of success under right conditions, interested John Ward, a wholesale jeweler, in a plan for starting up the works; the place, including machinery which had been idle for years, was bought, and the successful career of the Standard Bleachery, with a reputation for fine work, was begun. Obstacles, which appeared to be insurmountable, were overcome, and success was fairly forced from apparent failure by the indomitable energy and enterprise of Mr. McKenzie. The bleachery is the most important industry in Bergen County, and gives employment to nearly 500 people.

Mr. McKenzie reached middle age before taking any active part in public affairs. When the call came for him to take a part in the government of his town, which was then Boiling Springs Township, he reluctantly consented, and served two terms as Chairman of the Township Committee. He was induced to run on the Republican ticket for Assemblyman in 1892, the year of the Democratic tidal wave, and was defeated; nevertheless, he headed the ticket. He was still Chairman of the Township Committee when the movement began which resulted in the changing of Boiling Springs Township into East Rutherford Borough. The success of the movement was largely due to him, and he became the first Mayor of the borough. His entrance into the office was marked by a stirring incident, the local election board having unwittingly counted him out in favor of another man. An appeal to Judge Dixon, however, led to a recount, and he was seated. In 1897 he was elected the third time, without opposition.

For many years Mr. McKenzie had served as a member of the Bergen County Republican Executive Committee, and his services to the party were recognized in 1898 by his election as Chairman of the committee to succeed Judge D. D. Zabriskie. He was also Vice-President for the Fifth Congress District of the Republican State League.

Mr. McKenzie took an active part in forming the Rutherford and East Rutherford Board of Trade, of which he was chosen President. He has been re-elected Vice-President of the Rutherford Public Library Association, and is a Director in the Rutherford National Bank, of which he was a founder. For years he has been interested in loan and building associations. He was one of the active organizers of the East Rutherford Savings, Loan, and Building Association, of which he accepted the presidency. The remarkable progress of the association has been due largely to his interest and to the prestige which his name bestowed upon it. He is a governor of the Passaic Hospital, and, in addition to being President of the Standard Bleachery Company, holds the presidency of a paper manufacturing company. He is a member of the Royal Arcanum and of the Union Club of Rutherford.

Mr. McKenzie lives at Carlton Hill, near the bleachery. He is married, and has four sons and a daughter. His eldest son, James J. McKenzie, is actively connected with the management of the bleachery. His only daughter is married and lives near Boston, Mass.

LOUIS C. HAUENSTEIN, JR., one of the proprietors of the Union Brewing Company of the Town of Union, N. J., is the son of Louis C. Hauenstein, Sr., a native of Germany, and Theresa Knand, who was born in New York City. His father came to America in 1856 and first settled in New York, but removed to New Jersey and engaged in the brewing business, having at one time what is now the Standard Brewery in Guttenberg; he is now a prominent real estate dealer and insurance agent of Union Hill, has served as Councilman, and is Recorder of the Town of Union, an office he has held during the past eight years by successive re-elections on the Democratic ticket.

Louis C. Hauenstein, Jr., was born on Morgan Street in the Town of Union, Hudson County, October 18, 1873. He received a good public school education. When seventeen years old he began active life in the establishment of the A. Kraemer Brewing Company, of Guttenberg, and was assistant bookkeeper when the company passed into the hands of a receiver in May, 1893. He then accepted a position as bookkeeper with the Union Brewing Company, of the Town of Union, and continued as such until September 13, 1897, when he formed a partnership with Emil Sahner, under the firm name of Sahner & Hauenstein, and purchased the brewery.

Mr. Hauenstein is a Democrat, and has been prominent in the councils of the party since he cast his first vote. He is a member and since 1893 has served as Treasurer of the Democratic Town Committee of the Town of Union, was one of the organizers of the Democratic Central Organization, and in May, 1899, was elected its Treasurer, and is also a member of its Executive Committee. He was Secretary of the Second Ward Democratic Club and Treasurer of the First Ward Democratic Club. In the spring of 1897 he was appointed a member of the Board of Free Library Commissioners of the Town of Union, of which he has been President since 1898. Mr. Hauenstein is also a member of the Board of Education of the Town of Union and Chairman of its Committee on School Government; a charter member, and receiver since its organization in 1893, of Hoffnung Lodge, No. 62, Ancient Order of United Workmen; a member of the Union Hill Schuetzen Corps and of Garfield Council, Jr. O. U. A. M.; an enthusiastic bowler and a member of the All Bees Bowling Club; and President of the Hamilton Wheelmen, being elected to that office March 1, 1899.

Mr. Hauenstein has displayed marked ability, enthusiasm, and enterprise, and through his integrity and active interest in public affairs is highly esteemed and respected. Although a young man, he is regarded as one of the popular and prominent citizens of North Hudson County.

He was married, October 29, 1895, to Frances, daughter of W. Frank and Susan (McCollum) Trask, of Homestead, N. J. They have one child, a daughter, Viola.

FRANK O. MITTAG, of Park Ridge, was born in Richmond County, N. Y., on the 1st of August, 1855. He is the son of John C. Louis Mittag and Caroline Herms and a grandson of Herman Herms and of Carston J. L. and Caroline (Lammeryer) Mittag. The family came originally from Germany.

Mr. Mittag was educated in the public schools of his native State, and at the age of sixteen engaged in the stationery business in New York City, in which he continued with success for ten years. He then engaged in the manufacture of typewriter supplies, and is now the head of the firm of Mittag & Volger, one of the largest concerns of the class in the country.

In public as well as in business life Mr. Mittag has become well known. He was a member and Corporal of Company A, Thirteenth Regiment, National Guard of New York, and is also a Justice of the Peace at Park Ridge, where he resides. He attends the Protestant Episcopal Church and is actively identified with the affairs of his town. His uncle, Henry C. Wagner, was a near relative of Wagner, the famous composer and musician.

Mr. Mittag married Jennie L. White and has nine children: Florence, Frank, Jennie, Carrie, Ida, Elfreda, Elsie, Lester, and Carter Allen.

JAMES S. MITTAG, brother of Frank O. Mittag and a younger son of John C. Louis Mittag and Caroline Herms, was born in Irvington, N. Y., on the 18th of December, 1860. He received his education in that place, and at the age of thirteen engaged in the human hair business, in which he continued for four years, gaining a large practical experience. For about twenty years he was connected with the stationery business in New York City. He then associated himself with the firm of Mittag & Volger, manufacturers of typewriter supplies, in Park Ridge, N. J., with which he still continues.

He is an active, enterprising, and progressive citizen, and an honorably discharged member of the National Guard of New York, in which he served for seven years. He was a member of the Town Council for six years of Park Ridge, Bergen County, where he resides. He attends the Protestant Episcopal Church, and in every capacity has gained the confidence and respect of all who know him.

Mr. Mittag married Fredericka J. Woelmer and has seven children: Viola, Lottie, Wilfred, Maritta, Zenobia, James S., Jr., and Irving W.

ALBERT LEULY was born in West Hoboken, N. J., on March 15, 1872. He is the son of Jacques Leuly and Barbara Gasser and a grandson of Jacques Leuly, Sr., and Theressa Gasser. He was educated in the West Hoboken public schools, at the Stevens High School, and at the New York University Law School, graduating from the latter institution with the degree of LL.B. in 1894. He was admitted to the bar of New Jersey on the 21st of February, 1895. Immediately afterward he opened offices in the Hudson Trust and Savings Institution in West Hoboken for the practice of his profession, and has since devoted himself to a large and constantly increasing clientage.

Mr. Leuly has already gained a high standing at the bar. He has been connected with several important cases and in every instance has displayed those sound legal qualifications which distinguish the successful lawyer and advocate. He is a member of Palisade Lodge, No. 84, F. and A. M., of the Town of Union, and as a citizen is public spirited, progressive, and highly respected.

He was married on the 16th of June, 1897, to Christine Fisher, and has one son, Albert Melville Leuly.

WILLIAM REED BARRICKLO, a well known member of the New Jersey and New York bars, was born in Jersey City on the 27th of September, 1857. He is the son of Andrew Barricklo and Julia R. Lalor, a grandson of William Reed Barricklo and Jeremiah Lalor, a great-grandson of Farrington Barricklo and Jeremiah Lalor, Sr., a great-great-grandson of Daniel Barricklo and Anderson Lalor, a great-great-great-grandson of William Reed and John Lalor, and a great-great-great-great-grandson of Thomas Wetherell and Barndt de Klyn, who was a son of Leonard de Klyn. He is also a descendant of Nathaniel Fitz Randolph, who in 1750 gave the ground to Princeton University on which Nassau Hall was built and now stands, and who was prominently identified with the movement which resulted in the location of the university at Princeton.

Mr. Barricklo was educated at Princeton University and at the Columbia College Law School. He was admitted to the New York bar in 1880 and to the bar of New Jersey in 1881, and for many years has been actively and successfully engaged in the general practice of his profession. At the present time his offices are at 229 Broadway, New York City. Mr. Barricklo was a member of the New Jersey State Board of Education from 1889 to 1896. He is a member of the Palma Club of Jersey City, of the Princeton Club, and of the New York Athletic Club. In 1897 he married Elizabeth S. Lalor.

ROBERT ALLEN, of Arlington, was born in North Bergen, N. J., August 26, 1849. He is the son of William Allen and Sarah Ann Dorson and a grandson of Robert and Catherine Allen. His ancestors were among the pioneers of North Bergen Township, Hudson County, and for generations have been prominent in both business and public affairs.

Mr. Allen was educated in New Durham, Hudson County, and there began active life on his father's farm. When very young he was thrown upon his own resources. He worked for Michael Fisher, of New Durham, for two years, and for a time was associated with the Old Dominion Steamship Company. In 1875 he settled in Arlington, N. J., and engaged in painting and decorating. Afterward he was engaged in the grocery business. About 1888 he established himself in the real estate business, which he still follows, and in which he has been eminently successful.

In politics Mr. Allen is a Republican. He is active and influential in town affairs, and in various capacities has rendered valuable service to the community. He was one of the organizers of the Arlington Hook and Ladder Company, which has grown to be one of the model organizations of the kind in the State. He was its first Foreman, and brought to his duties the same energy and ability which have characterized his business life. He is a liberal supporter and constant attendant of the Presbyterian

GENEALOGICAL

Church, prominently identified with educational interests, and a public spirited, progressive, and enterprising man. As a citizen he is universally esteemed, having contributed much toward the building up and improvement of Arlington. In this respect he is still very active. He was one of the organizers and for years was officially connected with the Arlington

ROBERT ALLEN.

Building and Loan Association, and is also a member of the Independent Order of Foresters.

Mr. Allen has been twice married, first to Elizabeth McFarland, by whom he had five children, of whom four are living: Jessie May, Robert, Mary Helen and Ethel Elizabeth. He married for his second wife Kate L. Chasmer.

JOHN M. KELLEY, a well known real estate and insurance agent, was born September 2, 1871, in Jersey City, N. J., where he still resides. He is the son of James and Mary A. Kelley. He was educated at Public School No. 8, and for one year attended the Jersey City High School. At the age of fourteen he entered the employ of Peter Semler, with whom he gained a broad knowledge of the real estate and insurance business. In the same year (1886) this business was purchased by Emile Steger, and Mr. Kelley remained with the latter until November 1, 1895, when he established himself in the same business. He now represents four large insurance companies and several estates and controls over $250,000 worth of bonds and mortgages. He is also a Notary Public and a Commissioner of Deeds.

In politics Mr. Kelley is an ardent and consistent Democrat. He was President of the Eleventh Ward Democratic Club of Jersey City, is Past Chief of Court Astley, F. O. A., is President of the Citizens' Building and Loan Association of Jersey City, and is a member of Jersey City Council, K. of C., of Arboret Council, R. A., of the C. Y. M. L. A. of Jersey City, and of the Eleventh Ward Democratic Club. In every capacity he has displayed great enterprise, public spirit, and energy.

Mr. Kelley was married, November 27, 1896, to Miss Nellie Connell, of Hoboken, N. J. They have two daughters.

MUNGO J. CURRIE was born January 24, 1857, in Greenville, now a part of Jersey City, where he still resides. He is the son of James Currie, born in 1800, died 1870, and Ellen Currie, daughter of Robert Currie and granddaughter of John Currie. On his father's side he is a grandson of William Currie and a great-grandson of Mungo Currie. His grandparents were natives of Scotland.

Mr. Currie attended Hamilton Academy at Hamilton, Lanarkshire, Scotland, from 1869 to 1872, and continued his studies in Elizabeth, Union County, N. J., from 1873 to 1875. He was graduated from Princeton College in the class of 1879, and afterward began the study of law in the office of Hon. Henry S. White, formerly United States Attorney for the District of New Jersey. Mr. Currie was admitted to the New Jersey bar, and with the exception of about two years has since been actively engaged in the general practice of his profession. He has had considerable experience in representing landowners in railroad condemnation suits and litigation connected with street improvements in cities. At the bar he has displayed marked ability, a ready grasp of legal principles, and broad and accurate knowledge of law. He is a member of the Princeton Club of New York City, of the Jersey City Golf Club, and of the Jersey City Board of Trade. He is unmarried.

JOSEPH ALEXANDER DUFFY, M.A., of Jersey City, is the son of John J. Duffy, a native of New York, and Mary E. Garvey, of Boston. On his mother's side he traces his ancestry back to Ireland to the year 1792. His father's ancestors came over in 1830.

Mr. Duffy was born December 23, 1874, in Jersey City, N. J., where he still resides. He was graduated from the College of St. Francis Xavier, of New York City, with the degree of A.B., in 1894, and in 1895 received the degree of M.A. from that institution. In 1896 he was graduated from the New York Law School with the degree of LL.B., and in November of the same year was admitted to the New Jersey bar. In 1897 he was admitted to practice at the bar of New York. He is actively and successfully engaged in the practice of his profession in both States, and has already gained distinction for legal ability, sound judgment, and enterprise.

He is a member of the Palma Club and the University Club of Jersey City, and of the Alumni Association of St. Francis Xavier College of New

York. As a citizen he is public spirited and actively identified with the affairs of his native city.

JACOB KUNZ, of Secaucus, was born in South Bergen, Hudson County, June 26, 1857. He is the son of Frank Kunz and Augusta Ochs and a grandson of George Henry Kunz and Genevieve Wippfler. Frank Kunz was born in Bavaria, Germany, December 18, 1817, and came to America in 1845, settling in Jersey City and later removing to South Bergen. Afterward he settled in Secaucus. He was always a farmer and gardener, and was a member of the Masonic fraternity and of the Hariguri. He died in May, 1887. He married Augusta Ochs, a native of Baden, Germany, and had eight children: Frank, Jr., Philip, Christina, Emma, Jacob, Anna, Henry, and Augusta.

Jacob Kunz was educated in the public schools of South Bergen and Secaucus, and, like his father, has always been a farmer and gardener. In that vocation he has achieved success. He is a Democrat in politics and has served efficiently as a member of the Executive Committee of the Hudson County Democratic Committee. He was one of the organizers and is still a member of Washington Hook and Ladder Company of Secaucus, which he has served as Foreman. He is unmarried.

WILLIAM TELL KUDLICH, M.D., was born July 24, 1856, in Hoboken, N. J., where he still resides. Dr. Hans Kudlich, his father, was born in Lobenstein, Austria, in 1823, and was educated in the Gymnasium College of Troppan, Austria. Afterward he spent six years in mastering Latin and Greek, and then studied law in Vienna and medicine in Zurich University. In 1853 he came to the United States and lived for a short time in Greenpoint and Williamsburg. Afterward he located in Hoboken, N. J., and engaged in the practice of his profession, that of medicine, which he had studied in the University of Zurich. He had a large and lucrative practice and gained the confidence and esteem of all who knew him. For years he was a Trustee of the Bank of Savings of Hoboken. He was one of the founders of Hoboken Academy, and after his arrival in America became a strong anti-slavery agitator. He was for many years President of the German Club and a member of the Society of German Physicians. In 1853 he married Louise Vogt, daughter of William Vogt, a celebrated professor of the University of Berne in Switzerland.

Dr. William T. Kudlich was educated at Hoboken Academy and in the Grammar Department of the University of the City of New York. He spent five years in the gymnasium of the college in Zurich, Switzerland, from which he was graduated in 1874. He then returned to Hoboken and during the next three years studied medicine with his father and in the College of Physicians and Surgeons in New York, from which he was graduated with honors, receiving the degree of M.D. After one and a half years spent in the Chambers Street Hospital he again went abroad and for two years was engaged in hospital practice in Vienna. In 1881 Dr. Kudlich located permanently in Hoboken, N. J., and at once entered upon the active and successful practice of his profession. He has built up a large practice and is one of Hoboken's most esteemed citizens. He was Surgeon of the Second Regiment, National Guard of New Jersey, for five years, and is a member of the German Club, of the Academy of Medicine of New Jersey, of the Society of German Physicians of New York, of the Society for the Relief of the Widows and Orphans of Medical Men of

New Jersey, of the Knights of Pythias, the Knights of Honor, and the Royal Arcanum. He is also one of the attending surgeons of St. Mary's Hospital and an alternate examiner of the Equitable Life Assurance Society.

In 1884 Dr. Kudlich married Miss Mary Möhle, of Hoboken, daughter of Adolph Möhle, one of the founders of Hoboken Academy. They have two daughters.

JOHN KUHN, of Closter, was born in Kuhrhessen, Germany, April 16, 1838. He is the son of Henry and Catharine (Block) Kuhn and a grandson of Henry Kuhn, Sr., and John Block. His father served in the Franco-German War.

Mr. Kuhn received his education in Germany. He left school at the age of fourteen and learned the wheelwright's trade, which he followed for two years in the Fatherland. He then came to America and engaged in the hotel business, continuing for some five years. Afterward he took up the carpenter's trade. He settled in Closter, Bergen County, in 1863, and since then has been one of the leading carpenters and builders of that section. He is a member of the Dutch Reformed Church, a public spirited citizen, active and influential in local affairs, and respected by all who know him.

Mr. Kuhn married Sarah Taylor and has had three children: Kate, Libbie (deceased), and Jennie.

DAVID L. LOCKWOOD, of Hillsdale, was born at Park Ridge, N. J., February 2, 1828. He is the son of Lawrence Lockwood and Jane Wortendyke, and on his father's side is of English descent. His mother is a member of the well known Wortendyke family who came to this country at an early colonial period.

Mr. Lockwood was educated in the public schools of Bergen County, and at the age of sixteen began to learn the carpenter's trade in New York City, where he remained six years. He then removed to Yonkers, N. Y., but about five years later returned to New York City, and a few years afterward came to Bergen County and engaged in farming, in which he has since continued. He enlisted as a private in the Twenty-second New York Volunteers in the War of the Rebellion and became a non-commissioned officer. For one term he was a member of the Township Committee of Hillsdale Township, where he resides. He is an active and influential citizen, and highly esteemed by all who know him.

Mr. Lockwood married Elizabeth Holdrum, a member of an old and respected Bergen County family. They have had four children, of whom three are living, namely: Cornelius, William, and Margarette.

WILLIAM C. ENDRES, of Closter, Bergen County, was born in Cassel, Germany, on the 14th of July, 1848. He is the son of Peter Endres and Augusta Heinemenn and a grandson of Nicholas Endres, who was at one time Mayor of Cassel.

Mr. Endres was educated in Germany. He left school at the age of fourteen and learned the business of painting and decorating. In 1866 he came to the United States and the next year settled in Closter, N. J., where he has since resided, and where he has continuously been engaged in the painting and decorating business with marked success. He served as Township Clerk of Harrington Township for three years, and in both business and public capacities has gained the confidence of the community.

GENEALOGICAL

He is a member of the German Lutheran Church and a public spirited, progressive, and enterprising citizen.

He married, first, Johanna Hoffmann, by whom he had five children: William C., Lillie, Mary, Edwin, and Annie. He married for his second wife Mary Eichler, who has borne him two children: Alberta and Johanna.

JAMES M. VAN VALEN, of Hackensack, traces his ancestry to Daniel Van Valen, who came from Holland in 1652 and settled in the present City of New York. In 1657 he was followed by his father, Johannes Van Valen, who settled in Harlem, where he was one of the five original patentees of the Harlem grants and the last survivor of them. His descendants finally removed to Bergen County, N. J., and became extensive landowners. Deeds bearing date 1701 record the purchase of 2,600 acres of land by Johannes, Bernardus, Gideon, and Rynier Van Valen, from Lancaster Syms, comprising all the Palisade lands from the Jay line, extending from the Hudson on the east to Overpeck on the west. Bernardus Van Valen was the great-grandfather of James M. He was a member of the militiamen in the Revolutionary War, and was taken prisoner and confined in the old Sugar House in New York City. A store house built by him is still standing near the railroad depot at Closter. He lived to the age of eighty years and died in 1820, leaving five children: James, Andrew, Cornelius, Isaac, and Jane. James, the grandfather of James M., was for a time a farmer at Closter, but removed to Clarkstown, Rockland County, N. Y., where he died in August, 1786, at the age of twenty-six. He left three children: Barney; Sarah, who became the wife of Henry Westervelt; and Cornelius. Cornelius was born at Clarkstown, May 21, 1786. He in 1867; James M.; and Sarah A., wife of Cornelius D. Schor, of Leonia.

James M. Van Valen was born at Teaneck, Bergen County, N. J., July 21, 1842. He spent his early life attending the public schools. In September, 1861, he enlisted in Company I, Twenty-second New Jersey Volunteers, and served ten months in the War of the Rebellion, being attached

JAMES M. VAN VALEN.

with his regiment to the Army of the Potomac. He then engaged in the book trade in New York and afterward taught school for several years in his native county. He read law with the late Garret Ackerson, of Hackensack, and was admitted as an attorney in November, 1875, and as a counsellor in November, 1878. In 1875 he formed a copartnership with his legal preceptor, Mr. Ackerson, which continued until the latter's death, December 23, 1886. Since then he has practiced alone. April 1, 1888, he was appointed by Governor Robert S. Green as President Judge of the Court of Common Pleas of Bergen County, and on April 1, 1893, Governor Werts re-appointed him to the same office for a second term of five years.

Judge Van Valen has won eminent success and a high reputation as both lawyer and jurist. His opinions, except in two instances, have never been reversed. Beginning active life as a teacher, he has always taken a deep interest in educational affairs, and for eighteen years served as Chairman of the Hackensack Board of Education; he declined a re-election in 1895 on account of professional demands. He became a private in Company A, Second Battalion, N. G. N. J., November 1, 1870, and was transferred to Company C, of the same battalion, October 8, 1872. He was promoted First Lieutenant October 18, 1872, and First Lieutenant and Quartermaster of the Second Battalion April 18, 1876, and resigned June 15, of the same year. He became Captain and Inspector of Rifle Practice February 26, 1883, Colonel and Assistant Inspector-General of Rifle Practice June 8, 1886, and was brevetted Brigadier-General and retired on his own request July 5, 1893. In politics he has always been a Democrat, independent and fearless, never allowing politics even to be hinted at in connection with his duty as judge. In religion he is a member and was formerly a Deacon of the First Reformed Church of Hackensack. As soldier, teacher, lawyer, and jurist he has always been highly respected and enjoys the confidence and esteem of all who know him. He is President of the Bergen County Bar Association, a Past Master of Pioneer Lodge, No. 70, F. and A. M., and Vice-President of the Holland Society of New York, of which he has been a member since its organization.

He was married, June 24, 1874, to Anna Augusta, daughter of Theodore Smith, of Park Ridge, Bergen County, N. J. They have had nine children: James A., Garret A., Emma E., Frederick M., Raymond, George W., Arthur, Howard W., and Anna E.

JOHN HECK, of Westwood, was born in Albany, N. Y., on the 3d of March, 1859. He is the son of Daniel Heck and Susan Christina Kuhn, a grandson of George Heck and Eliza Gobel and of Henry Kuhn and Anna Katherine Bock, and a great-grandson of Justis Heck and John Henry Kuhn. His great-great-grandfathers were Henry Peil and John Bock. His ancestors on both sides came to this country from Germany about the time of the Revolutionary War, in which some of them participated or figured. His parents came to this country about forty-six years ago. His father went direct to Albany, N. Y., where he engaged in the business of painting and decorating.

Mr. Heck was educated in the public schools of Albany and New Jersey. He also attended a seminary. At the age of thirteen he went to work on his father's farm, where he remained until he was twenty-two, acquiring a strong constitution and laying the foundation of a successful career. He then took charge of his father's painting and decorating business, which he has since continued with marked success. He served as Collector of

Washington Township two terms and was appointed agent of township properties and to look after township affairs. He is a member, Steward, and Trustee of the Hillsdale Methodist Episcopal Church and has served as Treasurer for the stewards and Secretary of the Board of Trustees of that denomination. He has also been actively identified with its Sunday School. He is a member of the Board of Education of Washington Township, a member of Hillsdale Lodge, No. 54, A. O. U. W., a charter member of the Westwood Fire Association, and a Director of the Bergen County Farmers' Association. He is in every respect a self-made man, active and influential in the community, and thoroughly identified with those institutions and organizations which contribute so much to the general welfare.

Mr. Heck married Maggie Maurer and has four children: Lizzie M., Martha L., George D., and John Arthur.

MAURICE MARKS was born October 23, 1871, in Jersey City, where he still resides. He is the son of Charles Marks, a native of Germany, and Sarah Heyman, a native of Poughkeepsie, N. Y.

Mr. Marks was graduated from Public School No. 1, Jersey City, in 1884, from the Jersey City High School in 1888, and from the New York University with the degree of LL.B. in 1892. He was admitted to the New York bar as an attorney and counselor in December, 1892, and to the New Jersey bar as an attorney in June, 1893, and since his admission has been actively and successfully engaged in the general practice of his profession, having offices at 170 Broadway, New York, and 76 Montgomery Street, Jersey City.

Mr. Marks is a prominent Democrat, and for several years has been one of the most earnest workers in his party. His services as a campaign orator have been much sought after. He was elected to the New Jersey State Assembly in 1898 and 1899 and was re-elected in 1900, receiving on all occasions large and flattering majorities. Mr. Marks enjoys the unique distinction of having been the only Democratic Assemblyman who ever acted as Speaker while the House was Republican. He is a member of the Robert Davis Association of Jersey City, the representative Democratic organization of Hudson County, a member and Past Master of Columbian Lodge, No. 484, F. and A. M., of New York, and a member of other fraternal and benevolent organizations. Both at the bar and in politics he has gained a high reputation.

GEORGE HOWARD McFADDEN, M.D., of Hackensack, was born in Hollidaysburg, Pa., May 10, 1866. He is the son of Samuel Poole McFadden and Jane Balch, a grandson of Alexander and Leah (McAfee) McFadden and of John and Mary (Potts) Balch, a great-grandson of Jonathan Potts and Deborah Wright, a great-great-grandson of David and Alice (Schull) Potts, and a great-great-great-grandson of Ezekiel Potts and Magdalene Miller. His great-great-great-great-grandparents were David Potts, born in 1670, died in 1730, and Alice Croasdale, born in 1673. His paternal and maternal ancestors were all Scotch-Irish and came to this country from the North of Scotland, Jonathan, David, and Ezekiel Potts coming from Dunblane and Perth, and David Potts, the elder, from Perth, Perthshire.

Dr. McFadden inherited from these sturdy ancestors mental and physical qualities of a high order. He was educated at the high school in his native town, at the Hollidaysburg Academy, at Shortlidge's Academy in Media,

Pa., and at Lafayette College at Easton, Pa. After leaving the last named institution he entered upon the study of medicine with Dr. David St. John, of Hackensack, N. J., and subsequently became a student at Bellevue Hospital Medical College in New York City, from which he was graduated with the degree of M.D. in March, 1889. For four years thereafter he was associated with Dr. St. John in the practice of his profession. On May 1, 1893, he established himself in practice, locating at 281 Main Street, Hackensack, and has since devoted himself to professional work.

He has served as County Physician for six years, as physician to the New Barbadoes Township and Riverside Borough Health Boards, as visiting physician and surgeon to the Hackensack Hospital, and as United States Government Examining Surgeon. He is a member of the Lafayette College Alumni Association, a member of the Bellevue Hospital Medical College Alumni Association, ex-President of the Bergen County Medical Society, and a member of the New Jersey State Medical Association, of the American Medical Association, of the North Jersey Country Club, of the Hackensack Golf Club, of the Oritani Club, of the Hackensack Dramatic Association, and of the Wheelmen's Club. He is the author of medical papers on "Electrolysis in the Treatment of Strictures," "Malarial Poisoning as a Cause for Infantile Paralysis," "Cause and Treatment of Rheumatism," and other important subjects. In his professional work he has achieved a high standing and is well known for his ability and skill. He is a public spirited citizen, actively interested in local affairs, and thoroughly identified with Hackensack and Bergen County.

Dr. McFadden was married, June 2, 1897, by Rev. David Magie, D.D., to Miss Martha Wilcox Stivers, of Paterson, N. J. They have one daughter, Fannie Hobart McFadden, born at Hackensack, June 14, 1898.

GEORGE SWISS, of Kearny, is the son of John J. and Elizabeth R. (Rogers) Swiss, and was born at Passaic, N. J., on the 2d of July, 1852. His father came from France and his mother from Ireland, emigrating to this country when young. They were married in Passaic, and soon after the birth of the subject of this sketch removed to Newark, N. J., where George received his education. In 1862 the latter removed from Newark to Kearny, Hudson County, where he still resides. After leaving school Mr. Swiss engaged in the furniture business in Kearny, in which he continued for several years. He then identified himself with the hardwood finishing business and subsequently engaged in contracting and building, in which he still continues. In this line he has achieved marked success.

Mr. Swiss held a position in the United States Custom House at the Port of New York for some time. He is now Water Surveyor of Kearny. He is a charter and exempt member of Central Hose Company No. 1, of Kearny, and a member of Kearny Lodge, No. 95, I. O. O. F. In politics he is a Republican and in religion a Methodist. As a citizen he is public spirited, progressive, and enterprising, actively identified with all local affairs, and highly respected throughout the community.

July 2, 1872, Mr. Swiss married Sarah J. Corey, daughter of Thomas and Mary (Currier) Corey, of Newark, N. J. They have had ten children: Elizabeth R., John J., George H., Thomas J., Joseph A., William J., Henry E., Eliza W., Martin B., and David J.

G. W. MULLANEY was born in Bayonne, Hudson County, N. J., where he still resides, on the 14th of October, 1861. He is the son of Owen Mullaney and Ann Eliza Hopkins and a grandson of Owen Mullaney, Sr., a native of Ireland, and Susan Thorpe, who was born in Woodbridge, N. J. His parents were born and married in New York, whence they removed to Bayonne.

Mr. Mullaney was educated in the Bayonne public schools and afterward entered the employ of the Pennsylvania Railroad Company. Subsequently he was appointed to a position in the Police Department of Bayonne, with which he is still identified. He is independent in politics, a Methodist in religion, a member of the Royal Arcanum, and President of the Police Benevolent Association of Bayonne. He is thoroughly identified with the affairs of his native city and one of its most popular citizens. He married Cytheria Myers, daughter of G. F. and Mary Myers, of Brooklyn, N. Y.

HASBROUCK INSTITUTE.

HERBERT CLARK GILSON was born February 18, 1878, in Jersey City, N. J., where he still resides. He is the son of Thomas Q. Gilson and Elizabeth Le Con Clark, and a descendant of sturdy English ancestors. His father was senior member of the firm of Gilson, Collins & Co., dealers in lumber and timber on Communipaw Avenue, Jersey City, and died March 27, 1895.

Mr. Gilson was educated at Hasbrouck Institute and at the New York Law School. He was admitted to the bar of New Jersey as an attorney on the 27th of February, 1899, and since then has practiced his profession in Jersey City with marked success. He is a member of Bergen Lodge, No.

47, F. and A. M., of Jersey City, and in every capacity has gained the confidence and respect of all who know him.

WILLIAM B. SMITH, of Park Ridge, was born on Knott's Island, N. C., September 14, 1841. He is the son of Alexander Smith and Mary S. Johnson. His family came originally from England and settled on Roanoke Island.

Colonel Smith was educated at Wake Forest College in North Carolina, which at that time was an institution of considerable prominence. For twenty-five years thereafter, until 1887, he was engaged in the publishing business, and during twenty years of that time was a book publisher, being associated with A. S. Barnes & Company, book publishers, for five years, and with the Authors Publishing Company for another five years. He was the organizer of the latter company. He removed to Bergen County, N. J., in 1882, purchased large properties, and was influential in starting the first building enterprises in that section. He is now engaged in the real estate and insurance business.

Colonel Smith has been very successful, and during his long and active career has maintained the confidence of all who know him. He was Colonel in the Confederate Army, attached to the First Regiment of North Carolina, and serving throughout the war. For eight years he served as a Justice of the Peace. He is a 32° Mason, holding membership in Fidelity Lodge, No. 13, of Ridgewood, N. J. He is a member of the Episcopal Church, a public spirited, patriotic, and enterprising citizen, and thoroughly identified with all local affairs. He married Louise Capsadell.

JOHN F. KLASS, of Hillsdale, was born in Germany on the 9th of October, 1850, his parents being Theodore Klass and Mary A. Kramer. He was educated in the Fatherland and also in this country. At the age of seventeen he left school and began to learn the trade of painting, which he followed for a number of years. He then spent some time in travel and afterward settled in Hoboken, where he entered the employ of the Old Dominion Steamship Company as receiving clerk. He has been associated with that corporation ever since, discharging his duties with marked ability and satisfaction.

Mr. Klass has served in the National Guard of New Jersey and is a member of the Methodist Church. He married Minnie A. Gerke and has had ten children, of whom six are living: John, Esther, Benjamin T., Grace, Minnie A., and Mary A.

WILLIAM HENRY SPEER, of Jersey City, was born February 27, 1838, in Bergen, N. J., his parents being Abraham Speer and Ellen Jane Sharp, both natives of that State. His father was born in Passaic and his mother in Jersey City.

Mr. Speer was educated in the old Bergen school on Bergen Square, now in Jersey City, and for five years was successfully engaged in the dry goods trade in New York. For forty years he has been engaged in the undertaking business in Jersey City, where he resides. In this profession Mr. Speer has achieved marked success. He is one of the oldest and best known undertakers in East Jersey, and during his entire career has enjoyed the respect and confidence of all who know him.

In public and social affairs Mr. Speer has also gained a high reputation. He was a private in Company A, Second Regiment, N. G. N. J., for seven years, and for two years served as Adjutant of that regiment. He was an Alderman of the old City of Bergen for two years, and is a member of the Masonic fraternity, of the Jersey City and Carteret Clubs, of the Knights of Pythias, and of the Reformed Church. In every capacity he has maintained a high standing for ability, public spirit, and integrity of character.

Mr. Speer was married, October 1, 1862, to Eleanor Clendenne Brinkerhoff, a member of an old New Jersey family. They have had five children.

WILLIAM WRIGHT, of Bayonne, was born in London, England, on the 15th of September, 1845. His parents, John Wright and Anna Williams, came to the United States in 1870 and William followed them on June 8, 1874. He was educated in private schools in London and afterward engaged in the liquor business in that city. Subsequently he associated himself with the Great Eastern Railroad of England, with which he continued until he came to America. After his arrival here he entered the employ of the Standard Oil Company, but subsequently engaged in the milk business for himself in Bayonne, in which he still continues.

In public as well as in business life Mr. Wright has become a prominent factor. He served for some time as Commissioner of Appeals and as Supervisor of Taxes in Bayonne. In politics he is Republican. He is an exempt member of Hook and Ladder Company No. 1, of Bayonne, and a member of Bayonne Lodge, No. 99, F. and A. M., of Bayonne Lodge, No. 206, I. O. O. F., of Bayonne Lodge, No. 9, Ancient Order of United Workmen, and of the Royal Arcanum. In religion he is an Episcopalian.

Mr. Wright married Mary Wigley, daughter of Henry and Mary Wigley, of Norwich, Norfolk County, England. They have ten children: Lottie, William, Jr., Harry, Frank, John, James, Joseph, Mary, Mamie, and Lillie.

MILLARD FILLMORE PORTER, of North Bergen, was born in New York City on the 10th of January, 1874. He is the son of John Porter and Jeannette Dobbs and a grandson of F. F. and Leah Dobbs. He was educated at the Academy of the Sacred Heart in Hoboken and has filled clerical positions with acknowledged ability and satisfaction. He has also taken an active part in local affairs and for a time has served as Recorder of the Township of North Bergen, where he resides.

SEBASTIAN MEISCH, of Secaucus, was born in Luxemburg, Germany, April 25, 1862. His parents, Sebastian Meisch, Sr., and Margaret Betz, were both natives of Luxemburg. Mr. Meisch obtained his education in the public schools of his native town. In 1880 he came to America and settled at Greenville in South Bergen. In 1892 he removed to Secaucus, where he still resides.

He has followed farming and gardening since his arrival in this country and has been very successful. In politics he is a Democrat. He was a member of the Executive Committee of the Hudson County Democratic Committee for one year, and in other capacities has rendered valuable service to the community. He married Elizabeth Bender and has three children: Lulu, John, and Adolph.

JOHN H. LACHMUND, Jr., was born November 10, 1871, in Rivervale, N. J., where he still resides. His parents, John H. Lachmund, Sr., and Barbara Beechler, were both natives of Germany. He was educated in the public schools of Bergen County, which he left at the age of fifteen to engage in the grocery business with his father, with whom he continued until 1896. He then established himself in the same business and has since continued in that line, building up a large and successful trade.

Mr. Lachmund has also been prominent in local affairs. He served as Collector for the Borough of Eastwood for two years and for some time has been Clerk of the Borough of Old Tappen, N. J. At the present time he has charge of the postoffice at Rivervale. He is also a member of the Board of Education of the Borough of Old Tappan, having been elected by the people in the spring of 1900. He is a member of the Knights of Honor, the Odd Fellows, and the Encampment of Odd Fellows, and has passed through all the chairs in the Odd Fellows order. On different occasions he has served as a Representative to the Grand Lodge of New Jersey. He has also served as Treasurer of the local lodge of the Knights of Honor since its organization in 1892 and still holds the office, and has been created a Past Dictator for faithful services rendered. He has served on Grand Lodge committees and is now a member of the Grand Lodge of the Knights of Honor of New Jersey. He attends the Lutheran Church, and is recognized as a public spirited, progressive, and enterprising citizen. He married Elizabeth Ryer and has one child, Pearl Lachmund.

PETER F. MAGUIRE, of Jersey City, was born in Ireland, September 20, 1858, his parents being William Maguire and Bridget McManus. He came to this country when young and received his education in Jersey City. Afterward he took up the trade of horseshoeing and carriagemaking, which he has followed with marked success.

Mr. Maguire has also been prominent in public life, having served as a member of the Hudson County Board of Chosen Freeholders. He is a member of the Eleventh Ward Democratic Club, of the Robert Davis Association, of the Young Men's Independent Association, of the Jefferson Club, of the Joseph A. Kerwin Association, of St. Joseph's Lyceum, and of other organizations. He married Ellen Nolan, deceased.

EUGENE WALTER LEAKE was born in Jersey City, N. J., July 13, 1877. He is the son of Thomas W. Leake and Caroline Veyrassat, a grandson of Charles Leake and Eugene Veyrassat, a great-grandson of George Leake and Samuel Veyrassat, and a great-great-grandson of David Leake and Samuel Veyrassat, Sr. His paternal ancestors came from the Town of Leake in Wales, England, while his maternal ancestors, the Veyrassats, were residents of Paris since the French Revolution.

Mr. Leake received his early education in Public Schools Nos. 3 and 12, of Jersey City. Afterward he attended Phillips Andover Academy in Massachusetts, and in 1896 received the degree of LL.B. from the Regents of the University of the State of New York. In 1897 he received his diploma from the New York Law School, winning the first prize in the postgraduate class for excellence in examination and essay. After graduating from the law school Mr. Leake continued his law studies with James B. Vredenburgh and with Blair & Crouse, of Jersey City. He was admitted to the New Jersey bar in 1898, and since then has been actively and successfully engaged in the general practice of his profession, this year (1900) becoming associated with Charles H. Hartshorne and Earle Insley as the junior member of the law firm of Hartshorne, Insley & Leake, with offices in the Provident Bank Building, Jersey City. As a speaker for the principles of the Democratic party of New Jersey he has rendered valuable service to the cause. He is a member of the Players' Club, of the Jersey City Golf Club, of the New York Association of Alumni of Andover, of the New York Association of Alumni of the New York Law School, and of several religious and fraternal organizations.

HENRY STORMS.—The Storms family are of Holland lineage, being descended from Dirck Storms (1), a native of "The Mayory of Bosch" in the Province of Utrecht, Holland. He emigrated to America in 1665, with his wife, Maria Peters, and three children, and settled first in New Amsterdam, where he opened, and under a license, kept a taphouse. On December 25, 1669, he was appointed by the Court of Sessions to the office of Town Clerk or Secretary of Brooklyn, which he held for several years. He was living at Brooklyn in 1675 and 1676, as the assessment rolls for those years show. He joined the Dutch church at Flatbush about this time. In 1677 he went to New Lots, where he taught school in 1680 and 1681. He kept moving about from place to place, was Town Clerk of Flatbush in 1681, and later became a resident of Bedford, Long Island. He went to Tappan, N. Y., in 1691, where he was made clerk of the Sessions of Orange County, which office he held for some time. He is said to have gone from there to Phillipse Manor in Westchester County, N. Y., where he died, and where his descendants became numerous. His issue of the second generation were at least five: Gregoris, Joris (George), Maria, Peternella, and Aeltie, the first three being born in Holland and the last two at Brooklyn. There must have been other children.

Staats Storms (4), a grandson of one of the children of Dirck Storms, married Susanna de Voe and settled at Tappan, N. Y., where he is said to have had sons Jacob, Abraham, Hendrick, and Staats of the fifth generation.

Hendrick (5) married Cornelia Vanderbeck and settled at Paramus, N. J., where he died. Jacob (5), Abraham (5), and Staats (5) remained in Rockland County, whence their descendants spread into Bergen County, N. J. Staats (5) married Christina Ackerson and had a son, John Storms (6), born April 7, 1787, who married Ellen, daughter of John and Maria Blawvelt, and had issue of the seventh generation, among others, Henry Storms (7), the subject of this sketch.

Henry Storms (7) was born at Park Ridge, N. J., where he still resides, on the 18th of October, 1815. He received his education in the schools of Bergen County, and at the age of fourteen entered a cotton mill at Park Ridge, where he remained ten years. Subsequently he spent ten years at Hackensack engaged in the mason's trade. Returning to Park Ridge at the end of that period, he continued to follow the trade of mason for thirty-five years, gaining a high reputation. Afterward he was associated with his son John in the sash and blind business for about fifteen years. He then retired, and is now enjoying the fruits of an active and honorable career. He is a member of the Congregational Church and a public spirited, enterprising citizen. He married Margarette Wortendyke and has one son, John Storms.

CORNELIUS A. ECKERSON.—One of the most intensely interesting chapters of historical delineation extant is Schiller's narrative of what is known as "The Thirty Years' War," that sanguinary and relentless struggle maintained by the Protestant nations of Northern Europe, led by brave Gustavus Adolphus, of Sweden, against the crafty Catholic princes of

Southern Europe, led by Ferdinand of Hapsburgh and Count Wallenstein. The armies of Gustavus passed several times across Holland in their advances to and retreats from their adversaries.

The lusty Swedish youth were sorely tempted by the fertility and productiveness of the soil, and by the prosperity of the people, to make Holland their future abiding place. It is a well known fact that thousands of them, upon the expiration of their terms of military service, yielded to this temptation. Among this number was a youth named Thomas Tomaszen, who had bravely fought under the Protestant banner of Gustavus on the bloody field of Leipsic in 1631. On his way home he chanced to stop at Zell in the Province of Munsterland, where he became so smitten with the country, and with a sprightly little Dutch maiden, that he was constrained to make the place his home. He married the little maiden, of course, and settled down to agricultural pursuits at Zell, where, somewhere about 1640, his son, John Tomaszen, first saw the light of day. It is said that during his youth John learned the trade of blacksmith. If so, he does not seem to have plied it for a livelihood. In the summer of 1665 we find him emigrating to America, landing at New York. The same fall we find him marrying a respectable Dutch lass named Appolonia Cornelisen Siotz and settling on a farm east of the Bowery, not far above where St. Mark's Church now stands. On this farm, which he successfully managed for thirty years, he died in 1692.

He had eleven children, all but one of whom grew to maturity and reared large families. On the baptismal record all these children are entered as being the offspring of John and Appolonia Tomaszen, but it appears that two or three years before their father's death these children adopted the surname of Eckse. During the next twenty years this name, Eckse, passed through as many as a dozen different orthographical variations until at last it became Eckerson. Of late years one branch of the family has supplanted the "E" by "A," making it Ackerson.

Of these eleven Tomaszen children of the second generation Cornelius, the third, was born in New York in April, 1671, and was reared to agricultural pursuits on his father's farm near the Bowery. The woman who became his wife was Miss Wellempie Flierboom, a daughter of Matthew Flierboom, then Judge of the Court at Albany, N. Y. The marriage was solemnized in the Dutch church in New York in August, 1693. Cornelius resided on the old homestead until 1718, when with his wife and five children he removed to Old Tappan, in Bergen County, where he bought of the patentees of the Orangetown patent three hundred acres of heavily wooded land, which he cleared, tilled, and added to by purchase until his death. His descendants of the eighth generation still reside on portions of it. All the Eckersons and Ackersons of Bergen County are descended from him. The old farm originally comprised the Herrick farm, now occupied by A. U. Todd. It also included the farm now occupied by Jacob B. Eckerson, one of his descendants.

Cornelius Eckerson (3) and his wife, Wellempie Flierboom, had issue of the fourth generation five children: Matthew, John, Cornelius, Jacob, and Thomas.

Cornelius (4), born in New York, January 12, 1701, married (1), in 1723, Maria Haring, who died 1727. He married (2), in 1728, Rachel Blawvelt (written Blawfield). Cornelius resided on the old homestead and had issue of the fifth generation twelve children: Garret C., Cornelius C., Wellempie,

NEW AMSTERDAM IN 1656.

Catharine, Maria, John, Abraham, Elizabeth, Rachel, Jacob, David, and Matthew.

Garret C. Eckerson (5), the eldest of the above, was born March 7, 1724, and died May 2, 1798. He married, in 1744, Maria Haring, born January 7, 1724, died December 22, 1798. They resided at Old Tappan, in Bergen County, and had issue of the sixth generation nine children: John G., Maria, Cornelius, Rensye, Cornelius, Elizabeth, Margaret, Abram G., and Brechie.

Abram G. Eckerson (6) was born September 6, 1770, and died May 10, 1847. He married Catharine Smith, born May 24, 1774, died April 17, 1842. Their children of the seventh generation were James A., Garret A., and Cornelius A.

Cornelius A. Eckerson (7) was born at Old Tappan, in Bergen County, July 21, 1801, and died July 28, 1839. He married, February 15, 1823, Catharine Meyers, born in 1803, died in 1892. They had issue of the eighth generation Abram C., Rebecca, and Margaret.

Abram C. Eckerson (8) was born at Old Tappan and married Matilda Demarest, daughter of Garret and Agnes (Westervelt) Demarest. They had children of the ninth generation Catharine, Garret D., Cornelius A., Rachel, Margaret, John A., Matilda, Abram C., and Frederick, of whom Cornelius A. Eckerson (9) is the subject of this sketch.

Cornelius A. Eckerson (9) was born at Harrington Park, N. J., June 7, 1849, and acquired his education in Bergen County. Leaving school at the age of fourteen, he worked for three years on the farm, and then served a four years' apprenticeship at the blacksmith's trade, mastering every branch. At the end of that time he engaged in the blacksmithing and carriage building business for himself and successfully continued in that line for twenty-three and one-half years. He built up a large and profitable trade and gained the confidence of all with whom he came in contact. On December 6, 1893, he was appointed to a position in the New York custom house.

Mr. Eckerson has long been active in local affairs, having served for seven years as Town Clerk of Harrington and for some time as a member of the Board of Education. He is a member of Alpine Lodge, No. 77, F. and A. M., and of the Reformed Church. He married Lurana Wortendyke and has one son, Harry Eckerson, of the tenth generation.

SHELDON TILT, of Demarest, is of English descent. Thomas Tilt, a leather manufacturer from Birmingham, England, settled at West Point on the Hudson about 1750. He purchased property of Benjamin Allison, of Haverstraw, N. Y., August 22, 1777. He signed the Association Articles for Liberty in the Yoost Mabie House (now Andre's Prison), Tappan, N. Y., July 11, 1775, and was Corporal under Colonel Ann Hawkes Hay, his commission being granted February 16, 1776. His children were Daniel, Thomas, Rebecca, and Polly. Thomas (2) married Ann M. Bell, October 15, 1795. He has issue, baptized at Tappan, Catharine, Anna, Thomas, William, Mary, Elizabeth, and Rachel.

William Tilt married Margaret Bogert and had a son, Jefferson Tilt, who married Maria J. Demarest, daughter of the late Ralph S. Demarest and Jane Haring, a granddaughter of Samuel R. and Elizabeth (Zabriskie) Demarest, and a great-granddaughter of Ralph S. and Maria D. Demarest. He had four children, one of whom is Sheldon Tilt, the subject of this sketch. The latter's grandfather, Ralph S. Demarest, was prominent in political matters and represented his district in both houses of the New

Jersey Legislature. His great-great-grandfather, Ralph S. Demarest, served in the Revolutionary War in Captain Christie's company from Bergen County, while his great-grandfather, Samuel Demarest, who was also a soldier in the Revolution, was captured by the English, and confined in the historic sugar house in New York City.

Sheldon Tilt was born in Sparkill, N. Y., March 7, 1868, and received his education in the schools of Bergen County. At the age of seventeen he entered the employ of the Erie Railroad, with which he has since continued, discharging his duties with acknowledged ability and satisfaction. He is a member of the Reformed Church, a public spirited citizen, and respected by all who know him. Being greatly interested in real estate affairs, he was appointed in 1893, by Governor Werts, of New Jersey, as a representative from Bergen County to the World's Fair Real Estate Commission.

JACOB B. ECKERSON, of Rivervale, is of the eighth generation in descent from John Tomaszen, the emigrant and progenitor of all the Eckersons and Ackersons in Bergen County (see sketch on page 53). The line of Jacob B. Eckerson's descent is the same as that of Cornelius A. Eckerson (p. 546) down to the seventh generation: that is to say, down to Abraham G. Eckerson (7) and his wife, Catharine Smith, who had children of the eighth generation James A., Garret A., and Cornelius A. His father served in the Revolutionary War.

James A. Eckerson (8), born August 27, 1806, died March 22, 1875, married (1), in 1830, Elizabeth Blawvelt, daughter of Jacob I. and Rachel (Blanch) Blawvelt. She was born February 11, 1812, and died April 21, 1846. He married (2) Jane Westervelt, born January 3, 1807, died March 12, 1883. James A. Eckerson (8) had issue by Elizabeth Blawvelt five children of the ninth generation: Abram J., Mary, Catharine, Jacob B., and Margaret.

Jacob B. Eckerson (9), the subject of this sketch, was born at Old Tappan, Bergen County, N. J., May 16, 1839. He was educated in the local schools, and afterward, at the age of fifteen, went to work on his father's farm, where he now resides, and which has been handed down from father to son for over two hundred years. In addition to carrying on this old homestead he was also, for about twenty years, engaged in business as a carpenter and builder with his brother.

Mr. Eckerson served nine months in the Civil War as a member of the Twenty-second Regiment, New Jersey Volunteers. He has been a Justice of the Peace for twenty-five years, was also a School Trustee for some time, and for many years was a member of the Town Committee. He has held nearly every local office, including many county offices, and has discharged every obligation with ability and satisfaction. He is a member of the Reformed Church of Tappan and of Gabriel R. Poll Post, No. 101, G. A. R. He married Margaret A. Haring and has two children: Wilbur H. and Bertha.

FRANK HASBROUCK EARLE, a leading civil engineer and surveyor of Jersey City, is descended in the eighth generation from Edward Earle, Sr., the English emigrant, concerning whom and his descendants see sketch on page 232.

Thomas Earle of the sixth generation from Edward Earle, Sr., was born in New York City in 1767. There he lived and died. His wife, Matilda Harrison, of Orange, N. J., survived him and died in Jersey City. His mother was Anna de la Montagne, a descendant of the celebrated French emigrant Johannes de la Montagne, and he was likewise connected by blood and marriage with some of the most wealthy and aristocratic families of New York. His son, Thomas Earle (7), born in New York in 1809, married (1) Euphemia Demarest and (2) Cornelia, daughter of Dr. Stephen Hasbrouck. By his first wife he had issue of the eighth generation two children: Caroline M., who died in infancy, and Ralph D., who is living. By his second wife he had issue of the eighth generation four children: Emma (wife of Daniel Van Winkle, Jr.), Frank Hasbrouck, Ida C. (wife of Willard C. Fisk, of Jersey City), and Annie E. (deceased).

Frank Hasbrouck Earle (8), the subject of this sketch, was born in New York City, May 27, 1852. In 1855 his father and family took up their residence in Jersey City. He was educated in Public School No. 3, Jersey City, and in Hasbrouck Institute, from which he was graduated with high honors. His education completed, he entered the office of Bacot, Post & Camp, then the leading civil engineers of Jersey City. After four years' service there he began the business of surveying and engineering for himself and has been eminently successful therein. In 1886 he formed a business partnership with E. W. Harrison under the firm name of Earle & Harrison, which firm still exists. He has, for over thirty years, been identified with all the most important engineering and surveying projects in Hudson County.

Mr. Earle is a hard worker, thoroughly devoted to his calling, with every detail of which he is familiar. He married, December 29, 1881, Jennie E., daughter of John Baldwin, of Newark, and has four children: Frank Hasbrouck, Jr., and Harold Baldwin (both students in the Newark Academy), Louis de la Montagne, and Donald.

In politics Mr. Earle is a stanch Republican, but he has not aspired to political honors. He is active in church and social matters, being a member of the Roseville Presbyterian Church of Newark, the Roseville Athletic Club of Newark, the Carteret Club of Jersey City, and the General Society of Mechanics and Tradesmen of New York City. He is a Director of the Hudson County National Bank and the New Jersey Title Guarantee and Trust Company, both of Jersey City, and President of the Raritan River Railroad Company. He resides in Newark, N. J.

JOHN W. MOORE is descended in the seventh generation from Samuel Moore, an Englishman, who came with his wife Naomi from the Island of Barbadoes, West Indies, for a sketch of whom see page 118. John W. is the son of Peter D. Moore (6), who married, June 24, 1830, Elizabeth Voorhis.

John W. Moore (7) was born in New York City on the 2d of August, 1847, but received his education in the public schools of Bergen County. Leaving school at about the age of seventeen, he went to work on his father's farm, in what is now Oradell, and has since continued there, succeeding his father upon the latter's death. He is a member of the Dutch Reformed Church, a public spirited citizen, and honored and respected by all who know him. He is a brother of Peter E. Moore, of Schraalenburgh.

JOSEPH J. HANLON has been a life-long resident of Harrison, N. J. He is the son of James Hanlon and Jane Mackel, both of whom were born in Ireland. They came to this country when young and were married in Bloomfield, N. J.

Mr. Hanlon was educated in the public schools of Harrison and at St.

Benedict's College in Newark. Afterward he identified himself with the telephone and electrical business, and rose step by step to the position of Superintendent of the Hudson Telephone Company, which he now holds.

He is a member of the Board of Education of Harrison, being the only Democrat elected to that body and having no opposition in the Fourth Ward. He is a member of the Knights of Columbus, of the Catholic Benevolent Legion, and of the Guard of Honor. In politics he has always been a Democrat. He is popular in his native city and well known for his energy, public spirit, and enterprise.

Mr. Hanlon married Catherine, daughter of Edward and Catherine (Keeshan) Kelly, of Jersey City, on the 15th of November, 1899. Mr. Kelly is a well known building inspector of Jersey City.

JOHN H. ANDERSON.—John Anderson (or "Enderson," as he spelled it) came over to America from Scotland in the fall of 1733, and on the 23d of January, 1734, married Elizabeth (Davids) Demarest. The ceremony was solemnized in the South Church at Schraalenburgh. After their marriage the couple located in the vicinity of New Milford, east of the Hackensack River. John prospered, bought a large area of land, and died well-to-do and respected. His issue of the second generation were Margaretta (died), Margaretta, John J., Sarah, Maria, Annatie, Jacobus, and Lydia.

John J. Anderson (2), baptized October 30, 1743, married, January 27, 1766, Rebecca (Jacobus) Demarest. They had issue of the third generation John J., Jacobus, David, Daniel, Peter, and Sophia.

John J. Anderson, Jr. (3), born December 19, 1767, died April 21, 1841, married, September 20, 1792, Maria Bogert, born April 12, 1770, died January 3, 1845. They resided at Schraalenburgh and had issue of the fourth generation Matthew, James, Sarah, Albert, and John Henry.

Albert Anderson (4), born August 21, 1811 (died), married, November 2, 1833, Margaret, daughter of Henry A. and Lavina (Blawvelt) Voorhis, born November 23, 1812 (died). For many years before his death Albert (4) resided at Closter, N. J. His issue of the fifth generation were John H., Jacob A., Daniel A., Livina, Maria, Lorena, and Alfred.

John H. Anderson (5), the eldest, was born in New York City on the 12th of September, 1834. There he received his education. At the age of twenty he engaged in business as a carpenter, which he has since followed, becoming one of the best known carpenters in his section. He served as Collector of Hackensack Township for four years and for some time has held the office of Assessor of the Borough of Schraalenburgh. In every capacity he has displayed great public spirit, sound judgment, and enterprise. He is a member of the Reformed Church and active in local affairs.

Mr. Anderson married Maria Christie and has three children: James, Margaret, and Matilda.

FRANK S. DE RONDE.—The De Ronde family is of French lineage, as the "de" clearly indicates. Some members of the family had settled at Cortlandt Manor, in Westchester County, N. Y., prior to 1720. Alice de Ronde was married to Sibert Acker at Hackensack in that year, if the marriage records are true. It is stated in the record of her marriage that she was from the "Manor of Cortlandt." Hendrick de Ronde was a French Huguenot. He is said to have emigrated to America long before the beginning of the Revolutionary War and first settled on Long Island. His son, William de Ronde, of the second generation, born May 9, 1778, married Rachel Goetschius and removed to Bergen County, N. J., about 1835, locating in the Teaneck district west of the Hackensack River. He was a farmer by occupation. He died January 21, 1861. His wife, Rachel Goetschius, born April 29, 1784, died May 27, 1866. They had four children of the third generation—three sons and a daughter. The sons were Abram, John W., and William H., of whom Abram and John W. are deceased.

William H. de Ronde, the third son, married Lavinia Doremus, and still survives. He is actively and successfully engaged in the coal business at Englewood, N. J. He has had seven children of the fourth generation, one of whom, Frank S., is the subject of this sketch.

Frank S. de Ronde (4) was born January 24, 1870, at Englewood, N. J., where he still resides. He attended the public schools of Bergen County and New York City until he attained the age of fifteen, when he associated himself with his brother, Abram de Ronde, in the chemical business. Shortly afterward he entered the employ of the Standard Paint Company at 81 and 83 John Street, New York, becoming the business manager and general sales agent. January 1, 1900, he formed the Frank S. de Ronde Company, of New York, of which he is Treasurer and Manager.

He was Captain of Company F, Second Regiment New Jersey Volunteers, from Englewood, in the late Spanish-American War, serving about seven months. As a citizen he is highly esteemed and respected. He is a member of the Presbyterian Church of Englewood and active in all local affairs. He married Kate Bennett.

WILLIAM HACKETT, Jr., son of William and Margaret (Horan) Hackett, was born May 15, 1874, in Jersey City, N. J., where he still resides. His parents came to this country from Ireland in 1860.

Mr. Hackett was educated at St. Paul of the Cross Parochial School and at St. Peter's College in Jersey City. Subsequently he entered the office of the late William C. Spencer and Raymond P. Wortendyke as a student at law. He was admitted to the New Jersey bar at the February term of the Supreme Court in 1897, as an attorney, and since then has been actively and successfully engaged in the practice of his profession in his native city.

JOHN J. CADMUS, of Arlington, is a descendant in the sixth generation from Dirck Cadmus, the emigrant and first American ancestor of the family. The line of descent is the same as that of George Cadmus (see page 260) down to the third generation.

Casparus (Jasper) Cadmus (3) and his wife, Catlyntie Dodd, had issue of the fourth generation twelve children: Sarah, Joris, John, Casparus, Jannetie, Seeltie, Martha, Michael, Richard, Catharine, Andrew, and Eleanor.

John Cadmus (4), born February 21, 1792, died July 28, 1832, married, December 3, 1814, and had issue of the fifth generation seven children: Rachel, Catharine, Jasper, Elizabeth, William, Richard, and Martha.

Jasper Cadmus (5), born October 20, 1821, married, March 12, 1846, Hannah C. Van Buskirk, daughter of James Van Buskirk, and has issue, besides other children, John J. Cadmus, the subject of this sketch.

John J. Cadmus (6) was born in Bayonne, Hudson County, N. J., May 29, 1862. On both sides he descends from old Bayonne families and from a long line of Holland Dutch ancestors. He was educated in the public schools of his native town. Subsequently he removed to Arlington, Hudson County, where he still resides, and where he was engaged in the lumber business from 1888 to 1894. In the latter year, having disposed of that business, he established himself in the insurance business, which he still follows with marked success.

Mr. Cadmus is one of the most enterprising and public spirited citizens of Arlington. He has achieved a high reputation, and enjoys the respect and confidence of the entire community. In politics he is independent. He is a member of the Methodist Episcopal Church of Arlington and active and influential in local affairs.

He married Cora A. Woodruff, daughter of Charles A. and Charlotte A. (Wambold) Woodruff, both natives of Union County, N. J. Their children are Harold J., John A., Ruth A., and Bessie W.

EDWARD HILER, of Ridgewood, is of Holland Dutch descent. He is the son of Lewis B. Hiler and a grandson of John and Ruth (Garrignes) Hiler, all of whom were born near Dover, Morris County, N. J. His mother, Mary L. (Ball) Hiler, was the daughter of Isaac Ball and a granddaughter of Jacob Ball, her mother being a Burnett. Her family were residents of Parsippany, Morris County, N. J.

Edward Hiler was born in Danville, Pa., May 27, 1856, and received his education at Rockway, Morris County, N. J. He left school at the age of fifteen and became a clerk in a country store in Rockaway, Morris County. Afterward he was associated with his father in the iron mines near Kingston, Ontario, Canada, where he remained four years. He then came to New York City, and for twenty years has been actively engaged in the wholesale dry goods business, during eighteen years of which he has been associated with Bacon & Company, 92 and 94 Franklin Street, New York, the last five years as a member of the firm.

Mr. Hiler was a private in the Twenty-third Regiment, N. G. N. Y., of Brooklyn, serving a term of enlistment and being honorably discharged. He is a member of the Reformed Church of Ridgewood, where he has resided for nine years. He married Stella T. Eckman and has five children: Mildred, Lewis, Eddy, Evelyn, and Leslie.

CHARLES EYPPER was born in Strasbourg, Alsace, France, February 13, 1834. He is the son of George and Marian (Beck) Eypper and a grandson of Charles Eypper and Jacques Beck, a soldier in Napoleon's army who perished in the retreat from Moscow.

Mr. Eypper left Strasbourg in 1848 and came to this country. He went to Texas, and from 1856 to 1859 served with a surveying party under Captain Pope, U. S. A., in New Mexico, Texas, and other Western territories. In 1861 he volunteered with the First New York Regiment, Colonel William Allen, and served his full term of enlistment. He participated in the battle of Big Bethel, in the Seven Days' Fight, and in other important engagements, and made an honorable record. He was wounded in the arm by an arrow in an encounter with the Indians when with the surveying party, and during the battle between the "Monitor" and "Merrimac" in Hampton Roads was with a shore battery. Since 1876 he has been engaged in the brewing business.

Mr. Eypper is a public spirited, patriotic citizen, and deeply interested in the affairs of his adopted town. He was Mayor of Guttenberg in 1891 and in every capacity has achieved a high reputation. He married Marguerite Apffel, daughter of Jacques Apffel and Marguerite Bauer. Her father's brother, Henri Apffel, was Director of the Military School at Fontainebleu until 1893, when he died. Prior to that he was a Major in the Engineer Corps. John Apffel, another brother, served in the Franco-Prussian War, was at Strasbourg as Commandant de Place, and was retired as a Colonel in the French Army. Amelie, sister of Mrs. Marguerite Eypper's mother, was Sister Superior of the House of Deaconnesses at Mulhouse, Alsace. All of the family were residents of Weissenbourg, Alsace, France.

WILLIAM J. EYPPER, of Guttenberg, son of Charles Eypper and Marguerite Apffel and a grandson of George Eypper, was born in North Bergen, N. J., December 16, 1868. His eldest brother, George H. Eypper, was born January 26, 1867, in New York City, and is now a prominent resident of Hackensack, Bergen County, being successfully engaged in the wholesale dry goods and commission business in New York.

William J. Eypper was educated in the public schools of Guttenberg and New York City, graduating from Grammar School No. 20, New York, in 1883. He attended the College of the City of New York for one year and then engaged in the life insurance business in New York, continuing until 1892. He then went to Colorado and remained one year. In 1893 he engaged in the real estate and insurance business in Guttenberg with his brother, Charles A. Eypper, who was born in New York, November 11, 1870. Under the firm name of W. J. & C. A. Eypper they conduct a large and successful business and have achieved a high reputation.

Mr. Eypper has served as a Justice of the Peace since 1897. He is a Democrat in politics and active in party affairs. In 1898 he was Recorder of the Town of Guttenberg. He is now Collector of Taxes, having served in that capacity since 1896, and being re-elected in the spring of 1899 for a second term of three years. He is a member of the Franklin Club, of the Hackensack Golf Club, and of the Guttenberg Wheelmen. He is unmarried.

D. M. HENNESSY, of Bayonne, is the son of Michael Hennessy and Elizabeth Devlin, both natives of Ireland, but for a long time residents of Bayonne, where they were married. Mr. Hennessy was born in Bayonne, Hudson County, May 27, 1873, and there received a public school education. Afterward he entered the grocery business and still later identified himself with the hardware trade. He is now successfully engaged in the men's furnishing business and laundry business in Bayonne, where he resides.

In politics Mr. Hennessy is an active Democrat. He has served as Clerk of the Board of Health of Bayonne, and is a member of the Young Men's Association, of the Knights of Columbus, and of the Catholic Benevolent Legion. He is popular and well known, and has displayed ability of a high order.

EDMOND L. GREENIN, of Hillsdale, was born in New York City on the 27th of January, 1872. He is the son of Sampson and Cynthia (Webster) Greenin and a grandson of John S. Greenin and John Webster. His family came originally from England.

Mr. Greenin was educated in the schools of Bergen County, which he left at the age of seventeen. Shortly afterward he came into possession of a valuable estate and for some time has devoted himself to looking after his property. He has, however, been very active in the affairs of the Township of Hillsdale, and is a member of the Township Committee and Chairman of the Board of Health. He attends the Dutch Reformed Church, and is a member of the Knights of Honor and of the Independent Order of Odd Fellows. He married Jennie Gardenier.

LOUIS HAUSSER, of Harrison, Hudson County, is the son of Samuel Frederick Hausser and Caroline Becker, both natives of Germany. His parents were married in the Fatherland, and in 1845 emigrated to the United States, landing in New York City on the 9th of June. They immediately settled in Newark, N. J., which was ever afterward their home, and where Louis was born on the 16th of January, 1848.

Louis Hausser early developed those attributes of thrift and frugality which have served him so well in business affairs. He was educated in the public and German private schools of his native city (Newark), and afterward engaged in the business of butcher, having an establishment in Central Market, Newark. For seventeen years he was actively and successfully engaged in that line of industry. He displayed marked business ability, great patriotism and public spirit, and won the confidence and esteem of a large circle of acquaintances. At the end of seventeen years he abandoned the butcher business and accepted a position of trust and responsibility with the Peter Hauck Brewing Company, of Harrison, which he still holds. He is thoroughly identified with the interests of the community and active in promoting every worthy object.

LOUIS HAUSSER.

Mr. Hausser has discharged every duty which he has been called upon to assume with marked ability and satisfaction. He is a prominent and influential Democrat, an acknowledged leader in the councils of his party, and one of Harrison's most active citizens. For seven years he was Captain of Steamer Company No. 2, of Newark. He is a leading member of various important fraternal and benevolent organizations, including Copestone Lodge, No. 147, F. and

A. M., of Kearny, Damascus Commandery, No. 5, K. T., of Newark, New Jersey Consistory, 32°, Scottish Rite, of Masons, and Mecca Temple, No. 1, Nobles of the Mystic Shrine, of New York City. He is Past District Deputy of the B. P. O. E., of New Jersey, and a member of Newark Lodge, No. 21, of Elks, of Neascoleida Lodge, No. 6, Improved Order of Redmen, of Philadelphia, Pa., of the American Legion of Honor, and of the Heptasophs. As a member of the Germania Singing Society he is prominent in musical circles, and through his membership in the Robert Davis Association of Hudson County and the Joel Parker Association of Newark he is active and influential in political affairs. He is also a member of the original Thirteen Club of New York City.

On the 27th of August, 1871, Mr. Hausser was married to Wilhelmina Truitle, daughter of Jacob and Sophie Truitle, natives of Germany, who came to the United States about thirty-four years ago, settling in Newark, N. J. There Mrs. Hausser was reared, educated, and married. They have three children: Louis Hausser, Jr., Minnie Hausser, and Gussie Hausser.

LEWIS B. PARSELL, M.D.—The Parsell family in Bergen County are of French origin, as the name indicates, it being derived from the French expression of an oath "*Par ciel*," "by the sun." John Parcil, then a resident of Hemdingdon, England, emigrated to America with his wife (whose name does not appear). He first settled at Dutch Kills, Long Island, where he obtained the sobriquet of "John Butcher," for what reason it does not appear, nor do the records disclose the date of his arrival or the name of his wife. His children of the second generation, who must have emigrated with him, were Thomas, William, Henry, John, and Catharine. There were, perhaps, others.

Thomas Parcil (2), born in 1653, married, about 1673, Christina Van Houten. Thomas was a man of some note in his day. Although a blacksmith by trade, he was likewise a practical and experienced farmer and business man. At Dutch Kills he bought and managed a large farm. In 1679 he was made appraiser of several estates at Flatbush. He was one of the original patentees of the Newtown patent in 1686. In 1690 he purchased Great Barents Island for $3,000. At about the same time he sold his Dutch Kills farm for $17,000. He built a house on his island purchase, erected a mill, and lived there until 1723. In the meantime he had bought Hart's Island (then called Spectacle Island), to which he soon removed, and there died about 1731.

William Parcil (2), brother of Thomas, married, in 1694, and had issue of the third generation Nicholas, Thomas, John, and Walter. Nicholas Parcil (3), baptized June 10, 1696, in New York, married Greetie Cole, of Tappan, and removed to and settled at Hackensack.

Walter Parcil (3), baptized in New York, April 1, 1702, went to Schraalenburgh in Bergen County, where, in August, 1728, he married Sophia Riddner, of Bergen. Walter first purchased a tract of land between the Tiena Kill Brook and the Schraalenburgh road, just south of the old Christie farm. This he soon sold and bought a large farm northeast of Closter, fronting on the Hudson River. There he finally settled down for life. Both Nicholas and Walter reared large families and their descendants are widely scattered.

Isaac Parsell, probably a grandson of Nicholas or Walter, married Mary Smock and, dying, left two sons, John and Richard. This Richard married Margaretta Brinkerhoff and removed to Pennsylvania and from thence to

Central New York, finally settling in Cayuga County. There he had at least two children, Isabella (who married Rev. E. S. Hammond) and David (who married Catharine A., daughter of Louis Bevier). The latter resided at Owasco, Cayuga County, N. Y., where on the 16th of April, 1852, was born Lewis B. Parsell, the subject of this sketch.

Dr. Parsell was educated in the high school of Auburn, N. Y. At the age of twenty-one he became an instructor in Fort Plain (N.Y.) Seminary, remaining three years. He then entered the Buffalo Medical College, but later became a student at the Long Island Hospital Medical College, where he completed his medical studies. In 1881 he began active practice in Harlemville, N. Y., but a year later removed to Closter, Bergen County, N. J., where he has since resided. He has built up a successful practice in that section, and both as physician and citizen is highly respected. He has served as physician to the Board of Health of Harrington Township and as President of the District Medical Society of Bergen County. He married Julia M. Hammond.

ROBERT WALLACE ELLIOTT, of Jersey City, was born in Dover, N. J., on the 11th of July, 1856. He is the son of Alexander and Louisa (Wallace) Elliott and a grandson of Alexander and Anna Elliott and William and Elizabeth Wallace. His ancestry is Irish and includes Sir William Elliott, of the English Navy. His father was born in Belfast, while his mother was a native of Mauch Chunk, Pa.

Mr. Elliott was educated at Lehigh University in Pennsylvania, and after completing his studies, in 1872, became the manager of his father's iron mines in New Jersey. He continued in that capacity until 1878, when he was made manager of the Pottsville Iron and Steel Company. From 1880 to 1883 he was manager of the Delaware Rolling Mills at Phillipsburg, N. J. On the 1st of March, 1885, he located in Jersey City, having associated himself with the Gas Improvement Company as Cashier of that corporation. August 1, 1886, when the gas interests of Jersey City were consolidated, he was made the manager and agent of the combined corporations, and on November 1, 1899, he was elected Vice-President and General Manager of the Hudson County Gas Company, which embraces all the gas interests of Hudson County. These positions he still holds.

In the discharge of his duties Mr. Elliott has displayed marked ability, sound judgment, and great energy, and in every capacity has won the approval and admiration of all who know him. He has achieved eminent success, and in public life has also become a prominent factor. He was appointed a commissioner by Governor Green to report upon the advisability of erecting a State Reformatory. For a number of years he has been a prominent member of the Board of Trade of Jersey City and for three years was Chairman of the Board of Trustees of that organization. He is a member of the Manhattan and Twilight Clubs of New York, a member and former Chairman of the Board of Trustees of the Palma Club of Jersey City, and a member of the Carteret Club.

In 1894 he married Mary K. Stockton, a member of an old New Jersey family. They have no children.

FRANCIS W. FORD, of Demarest, was born in New York City on the 14th of July, 1846. He is the son of Isaac Ford and Catharine West, and was educated in the schools of his native city. At the age of sixteen he engaged in surveying in New York and has since continued in that profession. Since 1871 he has served as City Surveyor. He has an office at 8 James Street, New York City, and succeeded a firm which was established in 1809.

Mr. Ford has served as School Commissioner, Road Commissioner, and Police Commissioner, and is a member of the Reformed Church. In public affairs and in private matters he has established a high reputation and is respected and esteemed by all who know him. He married Anna M. Kitching and has six children: Francis K., born in 1877; Howard H., born in 1880; Walter H., born in 1881; Frederick C., born in 1884; Raymond W., born in 1886; and Harold S., born in 1889.

JOSEPH HERRON, of Closter, was born in Ireland on the 17th of April, 1859. He is the son of David and Sarah (Martin) Herron and a grandson of John Herron and William Martin.

Coming to this country when young, Mr. Herron received his education in Troy, N. Y., and at the age of fifteen engaged in clerking. For ten years he followed that avocation in different places and then came to New York City, where he was successfully engaged in business as an exporting merchant for twenty years. At the end of that period he retired from active life and is now associated with his son in the grocery business in Closter, Bergen County, where he resides.

Mr. Herron was especially prominent in the foreign fruit trade, in which he was so long and extensively engaged in New York City, and in that connection gained a high standing for business ability. He is a public spirited citizen, active and influential in local affairs, and a member of the Presbyterian Church. He married Hattie A. Burrows, and has one son, George D., who is associated with his father in the grocery business in Closter.

SAMUEL P. FREIR, of Hasbrouck Heights, was born near Boston in Lincolnshire, England, and in 1882 came to this country. He received a good preparatory and technical education, and is now in the employ of the Western Union Telegraph Company as automatic expert, having introduced the so-called Wheatstone automatic system of telegraphy from England. He has patented several very valuable instruments which his company have in daily use. He has achieved distinction in his profession, is a man of eminent ability, and highly esteemed by all who know him.

Mr. Freir came to Hasbrouck Heights, N. J., in 1892, just at the time that place took on a new lease of life, and has been actively interested in its growth and welfare. He served six years as a member of the Council and in other capacities has contributed to local improvements. In politics he is a Republican. He is a prominent member of the Royal Arcanum and affiliated with all that tends to keep his town on the road to progress.

DWIGHT WHEELER DE MOTTE, of Jersey City, is a descendant in the fifth generation from Mattys (Matthew) de Motte, a native of "Kingston in the Esopus," as the records say, who came from Kingston, N. Y., to Bergen, N. J., in 1704, and on April 4, 1705, was united in marriage with Miss Margriettie Brinkerhoff at Hackensack. On April 4, 1693, Mattys bought of Elias Michaels Vreeland three lots of land at Bergen (Jersey City), the combined area of which was eighty-seven acres. Subsequently at different times he bought other tracts at Bergen and

North Bergen until in a few years he had become a large landholder in Hudson County. He was an active man in the affairs of Bergen, taking a hand in almost everything that came up in the way of improvements. He and his wife belonged to the "Church on the Green" at Hackensack, where nearly all of their large family of children were baptized. Mattys died at Bergen in May, 1759. By his will, proved June 18, 1759, he devised all his Bergen lands to his sons, Michael and George, as joint tenants. His issue of the second generation were John (died), Michael (married Clasie Winne), Henry (died), Ann, John (died December 8, 1744), Henry (married, in 1742, Jannetje Van Wagoner), George (died in 1800, unmarried), Jacob (married, October 11, 1747, Sophia Van Houten), Mary, and Geshy (died in 1744). Michael (2) died November 16, 1799, intestate and without issue, and George (2), by the terms of his father's will, succeeded to the property at Bergen. Henry (2) located at Pompton. John (2) left no issue. Jacob (2) removed to Schraalenburgh, N. J. George (2) left no issue, but a will by which he left all his lands to Michael (3), son of his brother, Henry, of Pompton.

Michael (3) died May 27, 1832, devising his property at Bergen to his children of the fourth generation: Garret, George, Jane (wife of Peter Merseles), Margaret (wife of Richard Vreeland), Maria (wife of James Cadmus), Catharine (wife of Richard Cadmus), and Henry (who had died before his father).

One of these children of the fourth generation had a son, Abraham Huyler de Motte, who married Fannie M. Browning and had, besides other children of the fifth generation, Dwight Wheeler de Motte, the subject of this sketch.

Dwight Wheeler de Motte was born July 14, 1870, in Jersey City, where he still resides. He was educated in Public Schools Nos. 11 and 12 and subsequently took a course at the Law School of the University of the City of New York. He also studied law in the office of Judge Frank A. Newell and was admitted to the New Jersey bar as an attorney in 1897 and to the bar of New York as an attorney and counselor in 1900. He is actively engaged in practice, having offices at 150 Nassau Street, New York, and 259 Washington Street, Jersey City. Though a young man, he has already gained an honorable standing at the bar and is highly esteemed by all who know him. He married Viola Vermilye Mitchell and has one child, Jessie Mitchell de Motte.

JAMES DEMAREST HOLDRUM is descended in the seventh generation from John Holdrum, the first American ancestor from Holland, of whom see sketch on page 237. The line of descent is as follows: John Holdrum (1) and Cornelia Tienhoven had issue of the second generation, of whom one, William (2), born about 1710, married Margaret Peters and had nine children of the third generation, of whom Cornelius C. Holdrum (3), born September 21, 1749, died May 3, 1831, married Elizabeth Haring, who died August 1, 1833. One of their children of the fourth generation was James C. Holdrum (4), born December 21, 1785, died October 5, 1877, married Margaret Demarest, born January 20, 1783. She died March 30, 1870. One of their children of the fifth generation was Cornelius J. Holdrum (5), born March 6, 1806, who married Elizabeth de Pew and had children of the sixth generation, of whom one was James C. Holdrum (6), who married Ellen Maria Holdrum and had issue, among others, James Demarest Holdrum (7), the subject of this sketch.

James D. Holdrum (7) was born at Rivervale, Bergen County, N. J., October 18, 1865, and received his education in the public schools of Washington Township. He also took a commercial course at Packard's Business College in New York City. For a number of years he has been successfully engaged in the grocery business at River Edge, Bergen County, where he resides.

He has also been active in public affairs, being one of the founders of the Borough of Riverside, which he served as Collector of Taxes from the organization until July, 1899. In that year he was one of a committee to further the plans of a church, which was organized September 14, 1899, and of which he is Clerk. He is a member and President of the Pastime Social Club and of the Victa Tennis Club. In every capacity he has displayed great energy, ability, and public spirit, and is respected by all who know him.

Mr. Holdrum was married, April 6, 1896, to Ida May Belle Long at the North Presbyterian Church in New York City. They have one daughter, Marie Rosalind, born January 8, 1899.

WILLIAM TELL La ROCHE, D.D.S., of Harrington Park, was born in Frenchtown, N. J., July 30, 1822. He is the son of Louis F. la Roche and Permelia Hunt, a grandson of John and Anna (Bivens) la Roche and William and Rebecca (Beavers) Hunt, and a great-grandson of Philip Bivens and Joseph Beavers. His ancestors came from Switzerland and France. His grandfather, William Hunt, came from Warren County, N. J., and was a Captain in the War of 1812. His great-grandfather, Joseph Beavers, was Colonel of the Twelfth Regiment of Hunterdon County Militia in 1776, and held that office during the Revolutionary War according to records in the Adjutant-General's office at Trenton. He was of Scotch descent, and settled in Hunterdon County, N. J., before the war. For some time he was a Justice of the Peace. He was remarkable for his love of right doing. His courts were more properly chancery courts than courts of law. His judgments were seldom appealed from and usually not with success. He was for some time a Judge of the Court of Common Pleas for Hunterdon County, carrying out his love of right in all his decisions. If they agreed with his conceptions of justice it was good, law or not law. He was a man of stern integrity and favored no one in doing what he considered to be his duty. Anyone who deserved a reprimand from him and received it did not soon require another from the same source. He deprecated law suits generally, and settled many in a friendly way without costs. He contributed largely to building the Presbyterian Church at Greenwich, N. J., in 1775, of which he was a member. One of the pews of the ancient and orthodox style was built by Judge Beavers. He owned and managed a large farm equal to two at the present time. His family consisted of two sons and thirteen daughters. Joseph, the oldest son, died young. George purchased an estate and became the proprietor of the Pattenburg Mills near Clinton, N. J. The remains of the Christian patriot were interred in the cemetery of Greenwich Church.

Dr. La Roche received his education in Eastern Pennsylvania, in John Vanderveer's school, and at the New York College of Dentistry, from which he was graduated. For fifteen years he was a clinical professor and Trustee of the latter institution. He practiced dentistry in New York City for forty-five years with marked success, and since then has lived in retirement at his country home in Harrington Park, N. J., where he settled in 1855. He is a member of the Episcopal Church and a public spirited citizen. In his profession he established a high reputation, becoming one of the best known and ablest practitioners in New York.

Dr. La Roche married Elizabeth Quackenbush and has four children: William J. (Senator from the Sixth District of Brooklyn, N. Y.), Anna Forrester, Elizabeth Marie, and Louis F. His second daughter married Baron Howland Roberts, first in command of the Queen's Own Regiment, of England.

WALTER J. GREEN, of Kearny, is the son of John Langram Green and Emily J. Pullin, and was born in Bristol, England, on the 16th of September, 1864. His parents were both born and married in that country.

Mr. Green came to this country in 1875 and received his education in the public schools of Kearny, N. J. After leaving school he engaged in contracting, painting, and decorating, and still follows that business, having achieved marked success.

He is a Republican in politics and a communicant of the Protestant Episcopal Church. As a citizen he is public spirited, progressive, and highly esteemed. He was married, October 23, 1887, to Jeanne Morton, daughter of Adam and Mary (Jardine) Morton, and a descendant of ancestors who came from Canada. They have three children: Mary Emily, Lilla Agnes, and Morton Albin.

GEORGE BANCROFT GALE, M.D., of Rutherford, was born in Whiting, Vt., his parents being Daniel A. Gale and Rosetta Austin, both natives of that State. He was educated in the public schools of Whiting and Sudbury, Vt., and also in Springfield, Mass., and subsequently attended the Philadelphia School of Anatomy and the Medico Chirurgical College of Philadelphia, class of 1896.

Dr. Gale practiced medicine in Philadelphia, Pa., until 1898, when he removed to Rutherford, N. J., where he has since resided. He has built up a large and successful practice and is highly respected, both as a physician and citizen. He is a member of Boiling Spring Lodge, No. 157, F. and A. M., of Rutherford, of Vigilant Lodge, No. 155, I. O. O. F., of Philadelphia, of the Ancient Order of United Workmen, of Rutherford Lodge, No. 150, Knights of Pythias, of the Bergen County Medical Society, and of the Tithonian Senate, Order of Sparta, of Philadelphia.

January 30, 1886, Dr. Gale married Sarah A. Trask, daughter of Benjamin B. and Laura (Hare) Trask, of Springfield, Mass. They have two children: Laura and Austin.

GEORGE FRANKENSTEIN, of Jersey City, is the son of Julius Frankenstein and Hedwig Blumenthal, and was born in Berlin, Germany, July 20, 1874. His father was a merchant in that city. He was educated in the Berlin Imperial Gymnasium and in the public and high schools of Jersey City, having come to this country when young. After leaving the Jersey City High School at the age of sixteen he studied law and in November, 1895, at the age of twenty-one, was admitted to the New Jersey bar. Since then he has practiced his profession in Jersey City, making real estate and commercial law a specialty. He was married in June, 1899, to Jessie P. Drumm, of Camden, N. J.

CHARLES H. WESTERVELT, of Bergenfield, is descended in the ninth generation from Lubbert Lubbertsen (Von Westervelt), who with his wife and children left their home at Meppel in the Province of Drenthe, Holland, and came to America on board the ship "Hope" in April, 1662 (see page 99).

He is the son of Cornelius D. Westervelt and Margaret Demarest and a grandson of Cornelius Westervelt and Rev. Cornelius T. and Margarette (Lydecker) Demarest, and was born in New York City on the 15th of May, 1860. He was educated in Bergen County, and at the age of fifteen began to learn the printing trade in Englewood, N. J., where he remained three years. He then entered the employ of De Baun & Morgenthaler, one of the leading printing establishments of New York City. After continuing with them for twelve years he engaged in the printing business for himself, establishing his present office and plant at 71 Maiden Lane, New York. In this line he has been very successful.

Mr. Westervelt is a public spirited, enterprising citizen, and in Bergenfield, Bergen County, where he resides, has been active in promoting a number of worthy objects. He has served as a Trustee of the School Board of Bergenfield and is a member of the Reformed Church. He married Tenie Christie and has two children: Estelle C. and Florence A.

WILLIAM C. HERRING, ex-Sheriff of the County of Bergen and one of the prominent citizens of Harrington Park, is descended in the seventh generation from Pieter Jansen Haring, the Holland emigrant, concerning whom and his son see sketch on page 61. The line of descent is as follows: Pieter Jansen Haring (1), of Hoorn, Holland, had, among other issue of the second generation, a son, Jan Pietersen Haring (2), who married Margrietie Cozine and settled in the northern part of Bergen County, where he had issue of the third generation Pieter, Vroutie, Cozine, Cornelius, Brechie, Margrietie, and Abraham.

Cornelius Haring (3) married Catelyntie Fleerboom and had issue of the fourth generation John, Grietie, Sophia, Vroutie, Daniel, Cornelius, Jacob, and Abraham.

Daniel Haring (4) married, April 28, 1726, Margaretta Banta. He resided at Schraalenburgh and had issue of the fifth generation Cornelius, Jannetie, Catelyntie, Jacob, John, Henry, Maria, Cornelia, Daniel, and Maria.

Jacob Haring (5) married Susanna Livingston and had issue of the sixth generation Henry J., Willempie, Daniel J., and Cornelius J.

Cornelius J. Herring (6), born April 5, 1797, married Ann D. Riker in New York City, where she was born. Both died several years ago. Their issue of the seventh generation were Henry C., Jacob C., John R., James, Daniel C., William C., Mary Jane, and Susan Ann.

William C. Herring (7), the subject of this sketch, was born at Schraalenburgh in Bergen County about fifty-nine years ago. He obtained his education in the schools of his native township and has always followed farming as an occupation. He has been active in politics as a leader in the Republican party. In 1895 he was elected Sheriff of the county on the Republican ticket. In 1862 he enlisted as Orderly Sergeant of Company I, Twenty-second New Jersey Volunteers (commanded by Captain Thomas H. Swenarton), and served nine months, being honorably discharged with his regiment. Since the expiration of his term as Sheriff Mr. Herring has led a quiet life on his farm at Harrington Park.

He married Mary Elizabeth Demarest, daughter of Cornelius E. Demarest, of Norwood, N. J., and has issue of the eighth generation two daughters: Sophanna, who married George D. Herron, of Closter, and Florence, who married William Barker, Jr., of Troy, N. Y., both of whom have issue of the ninth generation. Mr. Herring is an active member of Gabriel Paul Post, G. A. R., of Westwood, and of one or more political organizations.

GEORGE RIESENBERGER, proprietor of one of the best known hotels on the Hudson County Boulevard, was born in Rosendale, Ulster County, N. Y., on Christmas Day, December 25, 1851. His parents, Nicholas Riesenberger and Catherine Blatz, came from Germany to this country about 1843, settling in Ulster County, where the former was employed as foreman of a large cement factory. About 1859 the family moved to the Town of Union, N. J., and here, on what is now the Hudson County Boulevard, Nicholas Riesenberger was for thirty-five years a leading florist. He was a prominent, public spirited citizen, an active member of the old "Wide Awakes," and a man universally respected and esteemed. He died in 1895.

George Riesenberger was educated in the public schools of the Town of Union, whither his parents removed when he was eight years old. Reared in the florist's business, it was only natural that he should first adopt it as a vocation, and for some time he was actively associated with his father. Later he conducted with his brother William a floral establishment in New York City for about ten years. Then he engaged in cigar manufacturing in the Town of Union, and subsequently was cashier in the famous Eldorado and at the Guttenberg racetrack for about two years. For a time he also conducted a popular hotel and park resort at the Forty-second Street ferry in Weehawken.

GEORGE RIESENBERGER.

In August, 1895, Mr. Riesenberger became proprietor of his present hotel on the Hudson County Boulevard, corner of Towerhill, West New York. He has also been prominent in public affairs. In 1876 he became a Constable and Court Officer, and served in that capacity about five years. While in business in New York he was also, for about five years, Sergeant of Police in the Town of Union, resigning on account of other pressing interests. He has frequently served on juries, including the Grand Jury, and organized in the Town of Union the first Court of Foresters in North Hudson. This was Court Palisade, No. 7,646. He is a member of Court Stevens, Foresters of America, of Hoboken, and of the Einigkeit Singing Society, and for several years was an active member of the Union Hill Fire Department. He is also a member of the Palisade Fishing Club of the Town of Union, of which he was President for ten years. Mr. Riesenberger is a public spirited citizen and deeply interested in all movements affecting his town and county. He comes from a distinguished family, his father being noted as a man of unusual mental attainments, and his youngest brother, Adam, having been a professor in Stevens Institute, Hoboken, for over seventeen years.

Mr. Riesenberger married Emma Hoffman, daughter of Charles Frederick Hoffman, and of their seven children four are living, namely: Nicholas, William, Minnie, and Carrie.

EDWIN A. WESTERVELT, D.D.S., is descended in the ninth generation from Lubbert Lubbertsen (Von Westervelt), who emigrated to America from Meppel in the Province of Drenthe, Holland, with his wife and children, on the ship "Hope," in April, 1662. For a sketch of him see page 99.

Edwin A. Westervelt, one of his descendants, is the son of James J. and Mary E. Westervelt, and was born in New York City on the 19th of June, 1870. He was educated in the public schools of New York and Jersey City, at the New York University, and at the New York College of Dentistry, graduating from the latter institution. He is actively and successfully engaged in the practice of his profession in Jersey City, having an office at 54 Brinkerhoff Street. He is a member of the University Club and holds a high place in the esteem of the community.

DAVID PROVOOST VAN DEVENTER, Jr., is of Holland lineage, being descended in a direct line from Pieter Peters (1), a prominent and well-to-do resident of the City of Deventer in Holland. His son, Jan Petersen (2), who was baptized at Deventer, Holland, January 7, 1628, married there (1) Maria ———— and (2) Engletie Theunis. He emigrated to America in 1662. The register of the Dutch West India ship "Hope," which landed him at New Amsterdam in April of that year, discloses the fact that he was a tailor by trade, and had with him a wife and three children. He first settled in Brooklyn, but soon removed to New Utrecht, where he located permanently and acquired wealth and social importance. He joined the Dutch church, in which he was an active member, and was elected Scheppen of New Utrecht in 1673. He bought considerable land afterward, paying for one farm 6,000 gelders. His issue of the third generation were Pieter, James, Henry, Cornelius, Richard, and Femmetie.

Pieter Jansen Van Deventer (3) emigrated with his father and settled at New Utrecht, where he married, March 22, 1686, Maria Christina Van Doren, of New Utrecht. He joined the Dutch church in 1667, was a Deacon in 1697, and from 1698 to 1709 resided in New York City. His issue of the fourth generation were Christiaen, Maria, and Abraham and Isaac (twins).

Isaac P. Van Deventer (4), baptized on Long Island, September 5, 1697, married Anna Willett, and had issue of the fifth generation Christopher Van Deventer and others.

Christopher Van Deventer (5) married Rachel Vreeland and had issue of the sixth generation, one of whom was Jacob Van Deventer (6), who married Louise Provoost and had issue of the seventh generation, one of whom was David P. Van Deventer (7)), who married Maria Louise Shea and had issue of the eighth generation David P. Van Deventer, Jr. (8), the subject of this sketch.

David Provoost Van Deventer, Jr., was born at Matawan, Monmouth County, N. J., November 1, 1866. He was educated at Phillips Academy, Andover, Mass., and was graduated from the New York Law School with the degree of LL.B. in 1897, being admitted to the New Jersey bar in June of that year. Since then he has been successfully engaged in the general practice of his profession in Jersey City. He is a member of Lodge No. 52, I. O. O. F., of Matawan.

PATRICK J. DOOLEY was born on the 14th of May, 1873, in Jersey City, where he still resides. He is of Irish descent. He received his education at St. Peter's College in Jersey City and St. Francis Xavier College in New York, graduating in 1892 from the latter institution with the degree of A.B.

Mr. Dooley took up the study of law and was admitted as an attorney at the November term of the New Jersey Supreme Court in 1896. He is actively and successfully engaged in the practice of his profession in Jersey City.

HENRY EMORY ROTHE, M.D., of Harrison, N. J., was born in the Tenth Ward of New York City, Christmas Day, December 25, 1840. His ancestors were of good German stock, and were largely identified with the law and estates.

Dr. Rothe was educated in the Collegiate College in New York City and in the College of Physicians and Surgeons, also of New York, receiving therefrom the degree of M.D. Since graduation he has been actively and successfully engaged in the practice of medicine and for a time as a druggist and chemist. He is now the Pennsylvania Railroad surgeon for Harrison, where he resides.

In the Civil War Dr. Rothe enlisted in Company B, First Regiment (Washington Greys), N. G. N. J., under Captain Cox. He was also for a time on the United States steamer "Mercedita," as Surgeon's Steward and Assistant, U. S. N. Afterward he enlisted in the Thirty-ninth Regiment, New Jersey Volunteers, and had charge of the brigade medical supplies of the First Brigade, Second Division, Ninth Army Corps, and served until the end of the war in the field hospital. In political as well as in professional life Dr. Rothe has achieved prominence. He has served as Treasurer and Assessor of Harrison, was the first Postmaster of the town, and was Deputy County Physician of Hudson County from 1879 to 1895. He is a Commissioner of Deeds and a Notary Public, has served as Deputy Coroner of Hudson County, and has been a delegate to numerous town, county, State, and Congressional conventions. He is a member and examiner of Hon. E. F. McDonald Council, Royal Arcanum, Surgeon of the

Boggs Association of Naval Veterans, and a member of Lincoln Post, No. 11, G. A. R., and the Union Veteran Union.

Dr. Rothe stands high as a physician and surgeon and as a citizen is universally respected. He has been especially prominent in military and political affairs, and in various important capacities has rendered valuable service to the community. He was married, October 23, 1867, to Sarah J. Boyd, and has four children.

WILLIAM WRAY is the son of Ezekiel B. Wray, who was born near the Giant's Causeway, in the North of Ireland, and who was of English descent. Ezekiel was the son of a Captain in the English Army. He came to America when eleven years of age and settled in Canada, whence he subsequently removed to Albany, N. Y. He was a baker, and upon coming to New York opened a grocery store. He married Mary Ann Forbes, also a native of Ireland.

William Wray was born in Albany, N. Y., July 12, 1829, and removed to New York City with his parents in 1831. He was educated in Public Schools Nos. 4 and 8, of New York City, and afterward, when but fifteen years of age, was apprenticed to the jewelry trade. On August 11, 1853, he entered the Nassau Bank of New York, with which he has ever since been associated, and where he has been the manager of the safe deposit vaults since August 5, 1882.

He settled in Closter, Bergen County, N. J., in 1872, and still resides there. While in New York City he was a member of the Volunteer Fire Department, joining Washington Hose Company November 12, 1850. He was married, May 12, 1857, to Amelia Norris, daughter of Daniel W. Norris, of New York City. They have had seven children: Amelia (deceased), Lottie E., Katherine E., William N., Jane Amelia, Walter G., and Warren N.

WILLIAM NORRIS WRAY, eldest son of William and Amelia (Norris) Wray, was born in New York City on the 11th of November, 1863, and soon afterward removed with the family to Blauveltville, Rockland County, N. Y., and subsequently to Closter, N. J. He was educated in the Closter public schools, and at the age of fifteen entered the Metropolitan National Bank, Broadway and Pine Street, New York. That institution failed in 1884, and he has since been connected with the Chemical National Bank of New York.

In November, 1893, Mr. Wray also engaged in the coal and lumber business in Closter with John R. Demarest, under the firm name of Demarest & Wray. He still carries on that business under the same firm name, his present partner being John J. Demarest, son of John R., who took his father's place in the firm in November, 1898. Mr. Wray was one of the organizers and for eighteen years has been a member of the Knickerbocker Base Ball Club of Closter, which he served for five years as Captain. He is also a charter member of the Knickerbocker Hook and Ladder Company of Closter, and has been for several years a member of the governing board of the Closter Fire Department. Since the organization of the Firemen's Relief Association in 1896 he has served that body as Treasurer. He is also a charter member of the Closter Club, and in politics is a Democrat.

Mr. Wray was married, October 21, 1890, to Sophie W. Tanner, daughter of Charles and Leah Ann Tanner, of Closter, N. J. They have two children: Kenneth and Helen.

THEODORE G. VOLGER was born in Bremen, Germany, February 26, 1867, his parents being Gustav G. Volger and Sophie Huneken. His family is an old and honored one. The church in Wettbergen, Hanover, Germany, was built by Magnus Volger in 1580 and is still in use and in charge of the Volger family. All of its pastors have borne the name of Volger, and it is to-day probably the only church in the Fatherland which has the distinction of remaining continuously in one family. The Volgers date back to 1310 (on record) and are one of the oldest families in Germany. Some of them are buried in the Market Church at Hanover, while their coat of arms and history are in the provincial museum there. Volger's Weg, one of the most prominent thoroughfares in Hanover, was so named after the family. Dietrich Volger, who died in 1337, was Mayor of the City of Hanover; Goedeke Volger, who died in 1420, was Senator of Hanover; and Otto Johann Heinrich Volger, who died in 1725, was also Mayor of Hanover. The Adjutant-General of ex-Queen Marie of Hanover is a Volger of the same family. Since coming to America the family name has frequently appeared as Folger. They emigrated from Hanover to England and thence to this country, being among the first settlers in the colonies. Charles James Folger, born in Massachusetts in 1818, who became Secretary of the Treasury in 1881, is a member of this family.

Theodore G. Volger was educated in the high schools at Detmold and Lemgo, Germany. Coming to this country, he was a clerk in the cotton export house of Hubbard, Price & Co., of New York, in 1886 and 1887, and in 1888 became a clerk for Ufferhardt & Co., of Charleston, S. C., with whom he remained until 1890. Since 1891 he has been a member of the firm of Mittag & Volger, manufacturers of typewriter supplies at Park Ridge, N. J., where he resides. The firm has offices in New York, Chicago, and Paris, and has built up an extensive and successful business. In 1889 this business was the smallest of its kind; to-day it is the largest in the world, and much of its growth is due to Mr. Volger's ability, enterprise, and untiring energy.

He has also been prominent in public affairs, having served as a Councilman of Park Ridge Borough in 1894, 1895, and 1896, and as Mayor of the borough in 1897 and 1898. In 1895 and 1896 he was Postmaster of Park Ridge. He is Vice-President of the Eureka Building and Loan Association, and in every capacity has displayed sound judgment, great native ability, and commendable enterprise. He married, in 1894, May Marjorie Smith, and they have three children.

WILLIAM SUMNER HUNGERFORD, of Arlington, was born in East Haddam, Conn., August 3, 1854. He is the son of William E. Hungerford and Ellen Frances Sumner, daughter of William and Anna (Washburn) Sumner and granddaughter of William Sumner; a grandson of Zachariah and Anna (Lord) Hungerford; and a great-grandson of Zachariah Hungerford, Sr., and Lydia Bigelow. He is of English descent on both sides. His first American ancestor, Thomas Hungerford, came from Wiltshire, England, in 1639, and settled in New England. Zachariah Hungerford, great-grandfather of the subject of this sketch, was a Captain in the Connecticut State Militia and served in the Revolutionary War.

Mr. Hungerford was educated in the public schools of East Haddam, at Williston Seminary in Easthampton, Mass., and at Yale College, graduating from the latter institution in 1875. He also studied mining engineering at the Royal Saxon School in Freiberg, Saxony. He began the active practice of his profession in the gold mines of Northern Georgia. Subsequently he was in the mines of the Lake Superior region in Michigan and afterward in those of Colorado and New Mexico. Finally he became Superintendent of mines for the Lowmoor Iron Company in Virginia. In 1889 Mr. Hungerford came to Jersey City, N. J., as manager of W. Ames & Company, manufacturers of bar iron, railroad spikes, bolts, nuts, etc., which position he still holds, being also a partner in the firm. In all of these capacities he has displayed great native ability and enterprise. He

WILLIAM S. HUNGERFORD.

is one of the ablest mining engineers in East Jersey, and in both business and professional matters has achieved eminent success.

In politics Mr. Hungerford is a stanch Republican. He has been a member of the Board of Council of Arlington, where he resides, and is prominent and influential in the community. He is a member of the Sons of the American Revolution, the American Institute of Mining Engineers, the American Association for the Advancement of Science, the University Club and First Congregational Church of Jersey City, and the Third Ward Republican Club of Kearny. His activity in professional, business, social, and political affairs has brought him into wide prominence, and attests his popularity and the confidence and esteem in which he is held.

Mr. Hungerford has been twice married, first to Cora C. Paxton, deceased, of Lexington, Va., and second to Mary C. Bininger, of Arlington, N. J.

ROBERT STOCKTON GREEN, of Jersey City, was born in Elizabeth, N. J., on the 16th of October, 1865. He comes from a family of professional men who have long been prominent in the State. Robert Stockton Green, his father, was born in Princeton, March 25, 1831, and died in Elizabeth, May 7, 1895. He was graduated from Princeton College in 1850, read law with his father, James S. Green, and was admitted to the bar as an attorney in November, 1853, and as a counselor in November, 1856. He began active practice in Mercer County, and in 1856 removed to Elizabeth, where he resided until his death. He was appointed Prosecutor of the Pleas in Union County by Governor Newell in 1857, was elected Surrogate in 1862, and was a member of the Common Council of Elizabeth from 1868 to 1873. In 1879 Governor Randolph appointed him to represent New Jersey at the Commercial Convention in Louisville. He was appointed the first Law Judge of Union County in 1868, was elected to Congress in 1885, and in 1886 was elected Governor of New Jersey. At the close of his term as Governor he was appointed Vice-Chancellor and served in that capacity until his death, being also at that time a Judge of the Court of Errors and Appeals. He was a member of the Constitutional Convention of 1874, and as a Democrat went as a delegate to various political conventions, including the National conventions at Baltimore and St. Louis. In January, 1884, he was admitted to the New York bar and became a member of the law firm of Brown, Hall & Vanderpoel, which subsequently became Vanderpoel, Green & Cuming. Judge Green was married, October 1, 1857, to Mary E., daughter of Richard Thomas Mulligan and Catherine Coleman, his wife, of Fort Edward, N. Y. They had four children: Catherine, Isabelle W., Caroline Seward, and Robert S.

James Sproat Green, father of Governor Green and grandfather of the subject of this sketch, was the son of Dr. Ashbel Green, and was born in Philadelphia, Pa., July 22, 1792. He was graduated from Dickinson College in 1811, was licensed as an attorney in 1817 and as a counselor in 1821, and in 1834 was called to the rank of sergeant-at-law. For many years he held an eminent position at the bar of New Jersey. He represented the old County of Somerset in the State Legislature for several terms from 1829, was Reporter of the Supreme Court from 1831 to 1836, served as United States Attorney by appointment of President Jackson until the election of Harrison in 1840, and was nominated by President Tyler as Secretary of the Treasury, but with others failed of confirmation in the opposition Senate. He was Professor of the Law Department of Princeton College from 1847 to 1855, a Trustee of that institution from 1828 until his death, and for many years served as Treasurer of the Theological Seminary at Princeton. He was one of the original Directors of the Delaware and Raritan Canal Company and was Treasurer of the Joint Railroad and Canal Companies. He died in November, 1862.

Robert S. Green, the subject of this sketch, was educated at the Columbia Grammar School in New York City, graduating therefrom in 1882. He was graduated from Princeton College with the degree of B.A. in 1886 and received the degree of M.A. in course in 1889. From 1886 to 1890 he read law with his father, being also his father's private secretary while the latter was Governor of New Jersey from 1887 to 1890. He studied law with J. R. & N. English, of Elizabeth, and was admitted to the bar as an attorney in June, 1891. Immediately afterward he became a student at law in the office of Seward, Guthrie & Morawetz, of New York City.

Mr. Green was admitted to the bar of New York in November, 1893, and remained with the firm of Seward, Guthrie & Morawetz until December 1, 1896, when he settled in Jersey City and formed a co-partnership with Albert C. Wall under the firm name of Wall & Green. In April, 1896, he was appointed by Governor Griggs a member of the State Board of Assessors for a term of four years.

CHARLES A. THOMSON, of Kearny, Hudson County, is the son of Charles R. Thomson and Elizabeth Epslan and was born in Arbotah, Forfarshire, Scotland, December 7, 1864. His parents were both natives of Scotland, where the subject of this sketch received his education.

Mr. Thomson came to this country in 1888, landing in New York City. He went thence to Passaic, N. J., and four months later removed to Newark, where he lived for several years. He then removed to Kearny, Hudson County, where he still resides, and where he is engaged in the machine business, manufacturing stonecutting and breadmaking machinery. In this line of industry he has developed great inventive genius and is the originator and patentee of a number of important machines and appliances. He learned his trade with his brother, who owns one of the largest machine shops in Edinboro, Scotland, and in following it as his life-work has achieved eminent success. He is very progressive, always trying to improve machinery, and gaining in this respect the reputation of making some of the greatest improvements in breadmaking machinery in existence.

In politics Mr. Thomson is a Republican. He belongs to the Plymouth Brethren Church, and for a number of years has taken an active interest in local affairs. He was married, April 26, 1894, to Margaret C. Girgan, of Glasgow, Scotland, daughter of John and Margaret (Carson) Girgan. They have two children: Charles and Margaret.

JOHN KELLER, M.A., Rector of Trinity Church, Arlington, is the son of Peter Ruth Keller and Eleanor Steen and a grandson of John and Elizabeth (Ruth) Keller and of Isaac and Eliza (Braddock) Steen. His paternal grandfather came from Munich, Bavaria, Germany, while his maternal grandparents were residents of Mt. Holly, N. J. The Braddock family emigrated to America with William Penn in 1682.

Rev. John Keller was born in Philadelphia, Pa., on the 14th of May, 1861, and received his preliminary education in the public schools and in the Central High School of that city. He also studied under private tutors in Philadelphia, and at the General Theological Seminary (Episcopal) at Chelsea Square, New York. He was graduated with the degree of B.A. in 1880, with the degree of M.A. in 1885, and in theology in 1886. In the latter year he was made a Deacon. He was ordained to the priesthood in 1887, having been appointed in 1886 to the charge of Trinity Church, Arlington, N. J. In the meantime, from 1884 to 1886, he had charge of the music and was organist at the Chapel of the General Theological Seminary in New York, and during the same period gave lectures and instruction in plain song. In 1888 he was appointed Bishop's Chaplain and Private Secretary. He was elected Secretary of the Convention of the Diocese of Newark in 1899 and Recording Secretary of the Associate Alumni of the General Theological Seminary of New York in 1896. He is still Rector of Trinity Church, Arlington, Bishop's Chaplain and Private Secretary, Secretary of the Convention of the Diocese of Newark, and Recording Secretary of the Associate Alumni of the General Theological Seminary.

Rev. Mr. Keller was appointed Captain and Chaplain of the First Regiment, National Guard of New Jersey, July 26, 1895, being commissioned immediately afterward, and is still on the regimental staff. He has written and delivered a number of special original lectures on the History and the Construction of the Organ; on Ecclesiastical Music and Its Origin; on the Origin and Meaning of Certain Military Customs, Decorations, and Ceremonies, and on other important themes, including a Quarter of a Century History of the Diocese of Newark. His work in the ministry has been peculiarly successful and stamps him as a man of great ability and energy. He is possessed of literary talents of a high order, a fact which is abundantly demonstrated by his lectures and writings. As Rector of Trinity Church, Arlington, he is universally esteemed, and as a citizen he enjoys the confidence and respect of the entire community. He is a member of the Newark Clericus, of the Catholic Club of New York, of the Associate Alumni of the General Theological Seminary of New York, of Triune Lodge, No. 159, F. and A. M., and of America Council, No. 1304, Royal Arcanum.

HENRY WARD, Pastor of the Reformed Church of Closter, was born in Guilderland, N. Y., April 4, 1839. He is the son of Henry A. Ward and Eva Jacobson and a grandson of Peter L. and Margarette (Ogsbury) Ward, and is of Holland descent on his mother's side and English on his father's.

Mr. Ward was educated at Union College, Schenectady, N. Y., which he left at the age of twenty-three to enter the Theological Seminary at New Brunswick, N. J., where he remained three years. Afterward he was settled over the Reformed Church at New Hackensack, Dutchess County, N. Y., for twenty years. He then removed to Closter and has since been the Pastor of the Reformed Church of that place. In the ministry Mr. Ward has gained a high reputation. He is an able speaker, a sound theologian, and honored by all who know him.

He married Caroline Davis and has four sons: William D., Henry P., Alfred W., and Herbert E.

JOHN POTTER STOCKTON was born in Philadelphia, Pa., February 2, 1852. John Potter Stockton, Sr., his father, was born in Princeton, N. J., August 2, 1826, and died January 22, 1900. He was graduated from Princeton College in 1843. He read law with Judge Richard S. Field, was admitted to the bar as an attorney in April, 1847, and as a counselor in 1850, and practiced his profession in New Jersey with marked success until 1857, being appointed in the meantime commissioner to revise the laws of the State, and making in this capacity a report which was adopted by the Legislature. In 1857 he was appointed by President Buchanan United States Minister to Rome and served in that capacity until 1861, when he returned and resumed the practice of law in Trenton. He was elected United States Senator for the term commencing March 4, 1865, but was unseated on account of the election by a plurality act wanting one of a majority. He was re-elected United States Senator for the six years beginning March 4, 1869, and served a full term, being one of the leaders on the Democratic side. He then resumed his practice in Trenton. He was appointed Attorney-General of the State, April 8, 1877, and filled that office with eminent ability for four terms of five years each, being reappointed in 1882, 1887, and 1893. At the close of his fourth term on April 5, 1897, he resumed the practice of law in Jersey City. In 1845 he married Sarah Marks, of Philadelphia, Pa. His father was Commodore Robert Field Stockton, of the United States Navy. Richard Stockton, "The Duke," father of Commodore Robert F. Stockton and great-grandfather of the subject of this sketch, was a signer of the Declaration of Independence and a distinguished citizen of Princeton. The family came originally from England, where they were quite celebrated, one of the members being Lord Mayor of London. No name in New Jersey is more distinguished or more conspicuous in the professional and military history of the colony and State. For generations it has figured prominently in important affairs and has always maintained a place of dignity and honor.

Although born in Philadelphia, John P. Stockton, the subject of this article, has spent most of his life in New Jersey. He received his preparatory education at the Charlier Institute in New York City. The early part of his life was devoted to the study of railroads in New Jersey, and for a long time he was connected with the Erie Railroad, the New Jersey Southern Railroad, and the New Jersey Central Railroad Company. In 1883 he took up the study of medicine. The medical profession, however, was not to his taste, and he finally abandoned it for that of the law. He was admitted to the New Jersey bar as an attorney in 1895 and as a counselor in 1899, and has successfully practiced his profession in Jersey City, where he resides. He has displayed legal qualifications of a high order. As a citizen as well as a lawyer and advocate he has gained an honorable reputation and is respected and esteemed by all who know him. He has also devoted considerable attention to literature, having written articles for several magazines and a number of books, of which one entitled "Zaphra" has gained for him a considerable reputation as an author.

SAMUEL A. J. NEELY, of Bayonne, is the son of John J. Neely and Jane E. Patterson, and was born in Emmettsburg, Md., May 21, 1845. His mother was also a native of that place, while his father was born at Gettysburg, Pa. They were married in Fredericksburg, Md., and in 1886 removed from Emmettsburg to Jersey City, N. J., and thence, in 1888, to Bayonne. Mr. Neely was educated in the public schools of Emmettsburg, Md., and afterward engaged in railroading, a business he has always followed. He has been associated with the S. S. L. Railroad Company, the Philadelphia and Reading Railroad, and the New Jersey Central Railroad Company, by whom he is now employed as a train dispatcher.

In public as well as in railroad matters Mr. Neely has become a prominent factor. He is a Democrat in politics, and has served four years as a member of the Board of Aldermen of Bayonne City and one term as a member of the Board of Chosen Freeholders of Hudson County. He is a member of the Fire Department of Bayonne, an active and enterprising citizen, and highly respected by all who know him.

He was married, February 17, 1872, to Ella J. Lewis, daughter of John J. and Mary Lewis, of Gilberton, Pa. They have five children: John, William, Arthur J., Samuel A. J., Jr., and Jennie.

FRANK STEVENS, of Jersey City, was born in Dutchess County, N. Y., August 19, 1851. When he was four years old his parents moved to Wisconsin, where his father had large interests in mills and lumber. After a number of years the family removed to Chicago, where he received his education in the city schools. A few years later they returned East and settled in New Jersey.

Mr. Stevens attended Oberlin College, where he remained through the preparatory and junior scientific years. He then began his business career in Cleveland, Ohio, whence he removed in 1870 to New Jersey, entering a flour and grain commission house in New York City. Subsequently he entered the employ of the shipbuilding establishment of the late Michell S. Allison in Jersey City. In 1874 he established himself in the real estate business on his own account in Montgomery Street, Jersey City, later removed to No. 55, that street, and during the twenty-six succeeding years built up a business second to none in his line in New Jersey. In January, 1893, he organized his extensive business into the Real Estate Trusts Company, associating himself with a number of specialists in finance and organization, and largely increased the possibilities of the business. Mr. Stevens is extensively interested in real estate and in numerous companies. He is President of the Real Estate Trusts Company, and was one of the organizers of and secured the valuable charter under which the New Jersey Title Guarantee and Trust Company operates and has attained such wonderful success. He is one of its Directors and Chairman of its Finance Committee. He is Treasurer of the Jersey City Board of Trade and the Registrar and Transfer Company, was President of the Paulus Hook Building and Loan Association of Jersey City, and is a member of the principal clubs in Jersey City and a director in many companies.

ARTHUR J. STEVER, of Hillsdale, was born in New York City on the 3d of January, 1853. He is the son of Erastus Stever and Catharine A. Van Loon and a grandson of Jeremiah Stever. His ancestors came to this country from Germany. Mr. Stever was educated in Brooklyn, N. Y., at the Brooklyn Collegiate and Polytechnic Institute. He left school at the age of eighteen and studied architecture in the office of Vaux & Withers, of New York. Since then he has been actively and successfully engaged in practice as an architect.

He has represented Hillsdale Township on the Board of Chosen Freeholders and is a member of the Westwood Reformed Church and President of the Hillsdale Manor Improvement Company. As a resident of Hillsdale he has taken an active part in town affairs, and is highly esteemed for those qualities which stamp the public spirited, progressive, and patriotic citizen. He married Dora L. Whitman, daughter of Hon. Jarvis Whitman and Dorothy A. Hopkins, and has three children: Arthur J., Ralph H., and Dora A.

GEORGE E. TOOKER, of Demarest, Bergen County, was born in Buffalo, N. Y., June 22, 1858. He is the son of William A. Tooker and Sarah J. Blackburn and a grandson of William A. Tooker, Sr. His ancestors came to this country from England and for years have been prominent in business and professional affairs.

Mr. Tooker was educated in Brooklyn, N. Y. He left school at the age of twelve and became a clerk in a tea store, where he remained one and a half years. He then entered a dry goods store and continued as a clerk for five years, when he engaged in the printing business. After working in that capacity for four years he entered a millinery house, remaining eleven years, when he associated himself with Henry Seibert & Brother, lithographers, 411 Pearl Street, New York, with whom he still continues. He has served as Commissioner of Appeals of Huntington Township and a three-year term as Town Committeeman, and in both business and public capacities has displayed marked ability, sound judgment, and great enterprise. He is a member of the Knights of Honor, the Masonic fraternity, the Knights of Pythias, the Uniformed Rank of the Knights of Pythias, and the Baptist Church of Demarest, where he resides. He is the second Chief of the Demarest Fire Department. Mr. Tooker married Mary Lowenhaupt and has one son, George.

HERMAN L. TIMKEN was born in Lilienthal, Hanover, Germany, April 2, 1830. His father served as a soldier in the English Army under Wellington and in the German Army under Blücher, and after serving seven years in the Hanoverian Army was advanced to the rank of First Sergeant.

In 1857 Mr. Timken came to America and located in New York City. He was a turner and carver by trade. In 1859 he engaged in the flour business in Hoboken under the firm name of Krone & Timken, which subsequently became Timken & Rohdenburg. Mr. Timken succeeded to the business in 1870 and finally, after several changes, retired, leaving his son, J. Henry Timken, and a Mr. Hamball in charge of the concern under the style of Timken & Hamball.

In public life Mr. Timken also achieved prominence. He served as Councilman for several years, and in 1883 was elected Mayor of Hoboken, which office he filled with great credit for three terms. In 1891 he was a candidate for the nomination for Sheriff, but withdrew from the contest. He also served on the Board of Tax Commissioners. He was one of the organizers and Captain of Company D, First Battalion, of the old Second Regiment, and one of the founders and the first Vice-President of the Second National Bank of Hoboken. He was also the first President of the American District Telegraph Company of Hoboken and the builder of Meyer's Hotel, which is now owned and conducted by his son, J. H. Timken. He was a member of the German and Hoboken Quartette Clubs, a Past Master of Hudson Lodge, No. 71, F. and A. M., a Director of the United States Schuetzen Park Association, and a member of the New York Produce Exchange. In every capacity he displayed ability, enterprise, and probity of character, and gained the confidence and respect of all who knew him. He was a man of great energy, thoroughly identified with the affairs of Hoboken, and liberally contributed to its welfare and advancement. In 1859 he married Miss Betty Kotzenberg.

WARD VARIAN, of Closter, is the son of William Varian and Susan Cornell and a grandson of Isaac Varian and Abram Cornell, and was born in New York City on the 6th of November, 1842. His ancestors were French. Mr. Varian was educated in the Westchester County schools, which he left at the age of eighteen to enlist in Company E, One Hundred and Sixty-fifth New York Volunteers. He served with distinction in the War of the Rebellion, and afterward engaged in farming in Westchester County, where he remained seventeen years. He then removed to Closter, Bergen County, N. J., and has since continued in agricultural pursuits, being one of the best farmers in that section.

Mr. Varian has achieved success as a farmer, and has also taken a prominent part in public affairs. He has served for some time on the Township Committee of Harrington Township. In every capacity he has gained the respect and confidence of all who know him. He married Catherine Ann Reed.

GEORGE M. ECKERT, of Arlington, was born in the Eighth Ward of New York City on the 8th of October, 1869. He is the son of David R. Eckert and Dellyetta McKellop and a grandson of Martin Eckert. The Eckerts came originally from Holland and first settled on Manhattan Island, whence they removed to the vicinity of Kingston, where Martin

GEORGE M. ECKERT.

Eckert still lives, his home being at Ulster Park. He has always followed agricultural pursuits. The family have been prominent and influential in both public and business affairs, and from the first have taken an active part in all worthy objects.

Mr. Eckert was educated in the public schools of New York City and at the New York College. Since leaving the latter institution he has been associated with the well known dry goods house of Lord & Taylor, of New York, rising to the position of assistant manager of the carpet department, which he now holds. In public affairs he has held for several years a prominent place, taking an active part in town affairs, and filling every position with acknowledged ability. He was elected a member of the

Board of Aldermen in the spring of 1899, and is a member and Assistant Foreman of Hook and Ladder Company No. 1, of the Kearny Volunteer Fire Department. He is a member of the Episcopal Church. He married Mary L. Crissy and has one daughter, Alice Eckert.

ROBERT M. MARSHALL was born in Newark, N. J., October 17, 1869. He is the son of Samuel J. Marshall and Margaret Malcolm and a grandson of William and Jennie (Jackson) Marshall and of Robert and Jenet Malcolm. His ancestors were Scotch. The family came to America in 1866 and settled in Newark, and in 1885 removed to East Newark, where Samuel J. Marshall established the plumbing, gas, and steam fitting business which is still carried on by his three sons, Robert M., William C., and Samuel J., Jr., under the firm name of Marshall Brothers.

Robert M. Marshall was educated in the public schools of Newark and East Newark, and has always been engaged in the plumbing and gas and steam fitting business with marked success. The business of Marshall Brothers has been located at 442 John Street, East Newark, for about fifteen years. Mr. Marshall is a member of the Knox Presbyterian Church, and in both business and public capacities has displayed great public spirit and an active interest in the affairs of the community. He married Kate L. Robson, by whom he has two children living: William R. and Samuel J.

WILLIAM C. MARSHALL, another son of Samuel J. and Margaret (Malcolm) Marshall and a brother of Robert M., was born in Newark, N. J., and received his education in that city and in East Newark. He is successfully engaged in the plumbing, gas fitting, and steam fitting business with his brothers under the firm name of Marshall Brothers at 442 John Street, East Newark. He is a member of the North Reformed Church of Newark and a public spirited, progressive, and respected citizen. He married Anna Moffat and has one daughter, Jessie M.

SAMUEL J. MARSHALL, JR., another son of Samuel J. and Margaret (Malcolm) Marshall and a brother of Robert M. and William C., was born in Newark, N. J., and received his education in that city and East Newark, where the family removed in 1885. He is engaged in the plumbing, gas fitting, and steam fitting business with his brothers under the firm name of Marshall Brothers, 442 John Street, East Newark, and from the first has displayed great business ability, sound judgment, and enterprise. He is a member of Company G, First Regiment, N. G. N. J., and also a member of the North Reformed Church of Newark.

WILLIAM CHARLES FARR was born at Gettenbach, near Frankfort-on-the-Main, Germany, March 13, 1844. He received a district school education in his native town and came to this country in 1861, arriving in Baltimore, Md., on the 3d of August. About four months later he left Baltimore, and on January 9, 1862, became a resident of Bayonne, Hudson County, N. J., which has ever since been his home.

Although Mr. Farr had received only a district school education in Gettenbach, it was largely through his own efforts, after his arrival in this country, that he completed his studies and gained a practical experience. He began life as a day laborer. Afterward he purchased a canal boat and spent several years as captain of that craft. He lost money in this venture, however, but with characteristic energy and perseverance engaged in contracting on a small scale, and by faithful attention to business soon built up a large and successful business. He is now one of the largest contractors in Bayonne, doing almost the entire work for all the factories at Constable Hook. He is not only financially independent, but a large owner of real estate and one of the city's prominent and respected residents.

In public life Mr. Farr has also achieved a high reputation. He served as School Trustee in 1878, 1879, and 1880, and as Councilman in 1882, 1883, 1884, 1885, 1886, 1887, and 1890, being President of the board for two years. He was Mayor of the City of Bayonne in 1891, 1892, 1893, and 1894. During his administration electric lighting was introduced and a pure water supply for the city was inaugurated. The fire alarm system was established, and the cost of all the city improvements was reduced to about one-half of that under the preceding administrations. He re-organized an inefficient police department and inaugurated many other improvements which have since resulted in so much benefit to the community. His administration was so acceptable to the people that he received both the Democratic and Republican nominations in 1893, as well as several citizens' nominations. In that year he had no opponent. While in the Council he was instrumental in exposing a $40,000 defalcation in the treasurer's department. Mr. Farr organized the Centerville Building and Loan Association and was its President during the last nine years. He has been a member, a Deacon, and a Trustee of St. Paul's German Lutheran Church of Bayonne since its organization, and is also a member of the Bayonne Board of Trade, which he served for a long time as Vice-President. He is a Director of the Charity Organization Society, a member of the Board of Directors of the German Lutheran Hospital of New York City and Vicinity, and for several years served as President of the board. He is also a member of the Good Government Club of Bayonne, a member of the Board of Trustees of the German Lutheran Home for the Aged of New York City and Vicinity, a member of the Board of Directors of the Hudson County Society for the Prevention of Cruelty to Animals, a member of the Bayonne Musical Society, an honorary member of several fire companies and other associations, and until recently was a Trustee and Treasurer of the German Lutheran Emigrant Mission of New York City. In all these capacities he has displayed marked ability, sound judgment, and unselfish devotion. He is a public spirited citizen, thoroughly identified with the affairs of his adopted city and State, and active in promoting every worthy object. During his entire life he has maintained the confidence and respect of all who know him.

Mr. Farr was married, May 31, 1863, to Mary Dorethea Schmidt, of Bayonne, daughter of Henry and Magdalena Schmidt. They have five children: Charles John Farr, a grocer at Stapleton, Staten Island, N. Y.; Frederick William Farr, who served as private secretary to his father while the latter was Mayor, and who is now a practicing lawyer in Bayonne under the firm name of Anderson & Farr; and Emma Elizabeth, Laura Elizabeth, and Sybella Margaretta. All of the children are accomplished and well educated.

CHARLES DEDERER THOMPSON, of Jersey City, was born in Newton, Sussex County, N. J., June 28, 1853, his parents being David and Susanna (Dederer) Thompson. He is descended in the sixth generation from Thomas Thompson, a Scotchman, who settled at Elizabethtown, N. J., in 1664. His grandparents, Stephen and Susanna (Harris) Thompson, lived on the old homestead in Morris County which was purchased in 1740. David Thompson, his father, was born at Mendham, Morris County, N. J., October 26, 1808, and was graduated from Princeton College in 1825. For four years thereafter he was a teacher in the academy at Mendham. He read law with Jacob W. Miller, of Morristown, and Judge Thomas C. Ryerson, of Newton, and was admitted to the New Jersey bar as an attorney in November, 1833, and as a counselor in November, 1836. In November, 1838, he was appointed Surrogate of Sussex County by Governor Pennington and filled that office for five years. He continued in the practice of his profession until shortly before his death, which occurred at Newton, N. J., November 8, 1888. He was elected a Director of the Sussex Bank in Newton in 1844, served that institution for many years as its Vice-President, and in 1865 was elected President, which position he held until his death. He married Susanna, daughter of Joseph and Susanna Dederer, and their children were Alexander, deceased; Juliana, deceased, wife of David R. Hull, of Newton; Susanna Dederer Thompson, of Newton; William Armstrong Thompson, a civil engineer; and Charles Dederer Thompson, the subject of this sketch.

Charles D. Thompson was graduated from Princeton College in 1874 and from the Columbia College Law School with the degree of LL.B., attending that institution when it was under the direction of the noted Dr. Timothy W. Dwight. He read law with his father in Newton and was admitted to the New Jersey bar as an attorney in June, 1877, and as a counselor in June, 1880. He practiced his profession at Newton from June, 1877, until January, 1886, when he removed to Jersey City and formed a partnership with Colonel Asa W. Dickinson under the firm name of Dickinson & Thompson. In April, 1892, John S. McMaster was admitted to the firm, which was changed to Dickinson, Thompson & McMaster and so continued until Mr. Dickinson's death in 1899.

Mr. Thompson is still actively and successfully engaged in the general practice of his profession in Jersey City. He was a member of the Town Council of Montclair, N. J., where he resided, in 1894 and 1895, and in the latter year became a member of the Montclair Board of Health. In this and other capacities he has displayed marked ability, sound judgment, and great public spirit. He is an able lawyer and has gained an honorable reputation at the bar.

JOB HILLIARD LIPPINCOTT was born at Vincenttown, Burlington County, N. J., November 12, 1842. He was the son of a prosperous farmer. He was graduated from Mount Holly Seminary in 1861, and remained there as a teacher until 1863, when he entered the Dane Law School of Harvard University, from which he was graduated in 1865. He was admitted to the New Jersey bar in 1867, and opened an office opposite the Court House in what was then Hudson City, now a part of Jersey City. He was President of the Board of Education from 1868 to 1871, when Jersey City, Hudson City, and the Town of Bergen were consolidated. In 1874 he was appointed counsel of the Board of Freeholders, which position he held until 1886, when President Cleveland appointed him United States Attorney for the District of New Jersey. A year later he resigned, Governor Green having appointed him Judge of the Hudson County courts to succeed Alexander T. McGill, who became Chancellor. In 1888 he was reappointed for a full term of five years. In January, 1893, just before his term expired, he resigned, and Governor Werts appointed him an Associate Justice of the Supreme Court, which position the latter had vacated to become Governor. He was re-appointed by Governor Voorhees in March, 1900.

Justice Lippincott's reputation was based mainly on his imprisonment of the Jersey City ballot-box stuffers in 1892. Following the election for Governor in 1889, an investigation was started in 1890 which resulted in the finding of at least 5,000 fraudulent ballots. Although the proof was of the most convincing kind, it was only by extraordinary energy that indictments were secured against sixty-seven election officers. Justice Lippincott died July 5, 1900, in Jersey City.

GARRET VON DREHLE, of Secaucus, is the son of Bernard and Mary Von Drehle, and was born in Hanover, Germany, August 26, 1838. There he received his education. He came to America in 1845, and is now successfully engaged in gardening and farming in Secaucus, Hudson County, having removed there from New York in 1868. He is independent in politics, deeply interested in educational matters, and a public spirited, enterprising citizen.

Mr. Von Drehle married Mary Peterson, a native of Germany, and has three children: Mary, who married Charles Born and has five children; George, who married Kate Bunder; and Helena, who married Herman Smith and has one child.

MICHAEL C. McCROSKERY, of Weehawken, was born in New York City on the 29th of May, 1827. He is the son of Michael McCroskery and Eliza Greenleaf and a grandson of James McCroskery and of Robert and Elizabeth Greenleaf. His father was born in Scotland and his mother in New Durham, Hudson County, N. J.

Mr. McCroskery is one of the oldest residents in the County of Hudson. He was educated in the public schools of New Durham, whither his parents removed when he was young. After leaving school he engaged in the meat business, which he followed successfully for thirty years. He is now connected with the Hackensack Water Company. In politics he is a Republican. He is a member of the Reformed Church, a public spirited and progressive citizen, and has always been active in the affairs of the community. He married Euphemia Jane Deas and has four children: James, Eliza, and Julia and Clara (twins).

FRANK STEWART RIX, of New Durham, is the eldest son of Cornelius Frank Rix, who was born in Royalton, Vt., in 1831, and of his wife, Anna Mary Kelley, who was born in Minisink, Orange County, N. Y., December 17, 1840. She was the daughter of Timothy W. and Frances A. (Bodle) Kelley. His parents were married October 31, 1857. He is the grandson of Ebenezer Rix, who died in 1870, and Rhoda Dewey, his wife. He is descended from Revolutionary stock, and on both sides inherits the sturdy characteristics of an honorable ancestry. His father was for many years connected with railroad transportation departments.

Frank S. Rix received a public school education in the high school of Warwick, N. Y., from which he was graduated in 1881. He then engaged in railroading, and so continued for about seven years, becoming train dispatcher on the New York, Ontario, and Western Railroad. In 1896 he engaged in the coal, wood, hay, and grain business in New Durham, which he still continues and where he resides. He is a member of the Hamilton Wheelmen, of Mystic Tie Lodge, No. 123, F. and A. M., of Cyrus Chapter, R. A. M., of York Commandery, K. T., and of the Mystic Shrine, and a governor of the Craftsman's Club of New York. He has been successful in business, and in every capacity has gained the respect and confidence of all who know him.

AUGUST JOHN FREDERICK SUCCOW, of Jersey City, was born in Stargerd, Prussia, April 15, 1847. His parents, John Frederick Samuel Succow and Caroline Lorenz, were natives and residents of that place and representatives of honored and respected families.

Mr. Succow was educated in the public and high schools of Stargerd, Prussia, and in 1872 came to this country, settling in New York City. In 1880 he removed to Jersey City, where he still resides. While in New York he was a clerk for about thirteen years, and upon coming to Jersey City engaged in the bakery business, in which he has since continued, achieving marked success and a high reputation. He served for four years as a private soldier in the Prussian and French war. He is a member of the Jersey City Board of Education, a member of Teutonia Lodge, No. 72, F. and A. M., and a public spirited, progressive, and enterprising citizen. In every capacity he has won the confidence and respect of the entire community. He married Eliza Schirm and has four children: Caroline, Frances, August, and Erna.

JOHN SPINDLER, of West Hoboken, is the son of Andrew and Elizabeth Spindler, and was born in Germany on the 13th of July, 1861. He received his education in the Fatherland and in 1880 came to America.

Mr. Spindler is engaged in the meat and provision business on Clinton Avenue, West Hoboken, and has built up a large and successful trade. He is a member of the Municipal Club, of the Royal Arcanum, of the Independent Order of Foresters, and of Americus Hook and Ladder Company. He married Rosa Victoria Wagner and has four children: John, Jr., Joseph, August, and Cora.

GEORGE ALBERT WILLIAMS, of Jersey City, was born in Everett, Pa., August 20, 1874, and is the son of Jacob B. and Martha (Johnson) Williams and a grandson of Samuel and Catharine (Barndollar) Williams and of Joseph Johnson, whose wife was a Miss Falk. His father's family is of Welsh extraction, while on his mother's side he is of English descent.

Mr. Williams was educated at Wesleyan University, Middletown, Conn., and at the Centenary Collegiate Institute, Hackensack, N. J. After leaving college he engaged in the electrical contracting business in Middletown, Conn., where he remained from 1895 to 1897. He then removed to Jersey City, where he has since been successfully engaged in the business of engineering and contracting for electrical work of all kinds. He is a member of the Psi Upsilon fraternity, a public spirited citizen, and respected by all who know him.

JAMES WILHELM, of Harrison, belongs to the old Wilhelm family which settled in West Hudson County, N. J., at a comparatively early day. He resides on the old homestead at Harrison, where he was born April 26,

1859. He is the son of Peter Wilhelm and Mary Hasson, natives respectively of France and Ireland. They came to the United States when young and were married in Harrison.

Mr. Wilhelm was educated in the public schools of Harrison and Newark, and afterward learned the trade of painting and decorating, which he has since followed with marked success. He is a Democrat in politics, and a member of Ethic Lodge, No. 115, Knights of Pythias, of Harrison, and of Branch No. 45 of the Workingmen's Sick and Death Benefit Association, also of Harrison. In every capacity he has displayed sound judgment, marked ability, and great enterprise.

He was married in Hoboken, June 27, 1888, to Minnie Gloor, daughter of Jacob and Elizabeth Gloor, of Elizabeth, N. J.

GEORGE ZIMMERMAN, of Carlstadt, Bergen County, was born in New York City on the 27th of January, 1857. He is the son of Peter Zimmerman and Catherine Gerlach, natives of Germany, who came to America when young, were married in New York, and removed in 1857 to Carlstadt, N. J. There the subject of this sketch received his preliminary education, which was supplemented by attending the high school of Brooklyn, N. Y. In 1873 his father purchased of Adam Ruttenger the property now known as Zimmerman's Hotel, then a farm house, and an old landmark of the locality. Here Mr. Zimmerman has demonstrated his capacity as a business man, both in the real estate and insurance business. In politics he is a Democrat. When twenty-one years of age he was elected to his first office. In 1879 he was made Clerk of the Township of Lodi. Subsequently certain irregularities were discovered in the books of the Township Collector; a change in the office was demanded by a popular uprising of the people, and he was elected Township Collector by an overwhelming majority. He was appointed by President Cleveland Postmaster in 1885, without opposition, and the able manner in which he conducted this office gave great satisfaction.

He was nominated for the Assembly in 1889 and elected by a large majority. He has twice filled the office of Assemblyman, holding that place when the noted Reform Ballot Act was passed, and during the many heated controversies he was always found true to the interests of his constituents. In 1898 he was again nominated for the Assembly, but was defeated. In 1897 he was elected Mayor of his borough.

Mr. Zimmerman has successfully filled the offices of Fire Commissioner, President of the Fire Department, and Chief of the department. He was the founder of the Carlstadt Mutual Loan and Building Association, a successful institution which largely owes its existence to his good judgment and persevering spirit. As a real estate man he has been very successful. He is a member of Wieland Lodge, No. 113, I. O. O. F., of the Concordia Dramatic and Singing Society, and of William Tell Council of Chosen Friends.

Mr. Zimmerman was married, October 12, 1880, to Louisa Egert, daughter of Andrew and Margaretta Egert, of New York City. They have six children: Adolph Edward, Peter, George, Jr., Florence, John W., and Curtis.

DAVID MATHER TALMAGE, of Westwood, was born in Amoy, China, February 4, 1852. He is the son of Rev. John Van Nest Talmage and Abbie F. Woodruff and a grandson of David T. Talmage, born at Piscataway, N.

J., April 21, 1783, and Catharine Van Nest, born at Somerville, N. J., March 27, 1787. He is a lineal descendant of Enos Talmage, who landed at Charlestown, Mass., in 1630, and finally settled at East Hampton, Long Island. His son, Enos Talmage, Jr., was born at Branford, Conn., and had a son, Daniel Talmage, whose son, Thomas Talmage, Sr., was born at Elizabethtown, N. J., in 1722, whose son, Thomas Talmage, Jr., the great-grandfather of David M. Talmage, was born at Basking Ridge, N. J., October 24, 1755. Mr. Talmage's father, Rev. John Van Nest Talmage, was the fourth son in a family of seven brothers and five sisters. Four of the brothers devoted themselves to the gospel ministry. Of these Rev. Thomas De Witt Talmage is most widely known. The father of Rev. David M. Talmage was graduated from the college and seminary at New Brunswick and became a noted missionary in the far East, going to Amoy, China, in 1847. His life has been written by Rev. John G. Fagg under the title of *Forty Years in South China*. He died at Bound Brook, N. J., in 1892.

Rev. David M. Talmage is the eldest of five children. His two sisters, Katharine Murray and Mary Elizabeth Talmage, have been missionaries of the Reformed Church at Amoy for more than twenty-five years. One brother, John S. Talmage, is a rice merchant in New Orleans. The other brother, George Edwin Talmage, is the pastor of the Second Reformed Church in Schenectady, N. Y.

Rev. David M. Talmage was graduated from Rutgers College, New Brunswick, in 1874, and from the Theological Seminary of the Reformed Church at New Brunswick in 1877. In the fall of the latter year he went out as a missionary of the Reformed Church to Amoy, China, and after three years' service there returned on account of ill health, arriving in New York in March, 1881. For two years he was settled over the Reformed Church at Bound Brook, N. J., and for three and a half years over the Reformed Church of Clarkstown, Rockland County, N. Y. In April, 1888, he became the settled pastor of the Reformed Church at Westwood, N. J., where he still remains. During his ministry Mr. Talmage has gained a high reputation. He is strong and fearless in his utterances and in every sense of the word a devout Christian, beloved by all who know him.

He was married, February 23, 1897, to Catharine Amanda, daughter of Gabriel Hill, and widow of the late John B. Kipp.

ELOF SWENSON, of Arlington, is the son of Sven Nelson Hasel and Christeena Hasalquist, and was born in Sweden on the 29th of March, 1857. His parents were born and married in that country, and there the subject of this sketch received a public school education.

After leaving school Mr. Swenson learned the carpenter's trade, which he has since followed. He came to the United States in 1879, landing in New York City. He then located in Brooklyn, N. Y., where he worked at the carpenter's trade. In 1893 he moved to Arlington, N. J., where he still resides. There he has built up a large business as a carpenter and builder, and is well known for his public spirit, energy, and enterprise. He is a member of Royal Templars of Temperance, a member of the Baptist Church, and a Republican in politics.

Mr. Swenson was married at Brooklyn, N. Y., in 1882, to Augusta Hult, daughter of Peter and Clara Hult, of Sweden. They have five children: Fannie, Harry, Alma, David, and Arthur.

GENEALOGICAL

JAMES F. MULLIGAN is the son of John J. Mulligan and Mary A. Carr, and was born March 2, 1871, in Harrison, N. J., where he still resides. His father came to the United States from Ireland when two years old, while his mother was a native of Newark, N. J., where they were married. Mr. Mulligan received his education in the public schools of Harrison and in the Christian Brothers Academy at Newark. Afterward he learned the carpenter's trade, and still later engaged in the coal business in Harrison, in which he continues with marked success.

Mr. Mulligan has served as Tax Assessor for Harrison, and is a member of the Knights of Columbus and of the Young Men's Association of Newark. In politics he is a Democrat. He is prominently identified with the affairs of his native town and county, and respected for those qualities which mark the successful man.

JAMES R. BOWEN.

JAMES R. BOWEN, a prominent member of the New Jersey and New York bars, was born in New York City on the 5th of December, 1863. He is the son of John Bowen and Elizabeth Lewis, natives of Ireland, who came to this country in 1856 and 1853, respectively. In 1867 they removed with their family to Jersey City, where the subject of this sketch received a public and high school education, graduating from the latter institution in 1881.

He read law with Edmund H. Brown, of New York, and was admitted to the bar of that State as an attorney and counselor in November, 1885. In June, 1886, he was admitted to the New Jersey bar. Mr. Bowen is actively and successfully engaged in the general practice of his profession in both States, having offices in New York and Jersey City. He has established a high reputation for legal ability, and holds a prominent place at the bar. As a citizen he is public spirited, enterprising, and deeply interested in the affairs of the community.

He was married on the 3d of October, 1894, to Miss Mary E. Keegan, of Jersey City, where they reside.

GEORGE H. SEAMAN, of Rivervale, is the son of Moses Seaman and Hannah Sarles, and was born in Connecticut on the 14th of April, 1852. The family originally came from England. Mr. Seaman was educated in the schools of Westchester County, N. Y., whither his family removed when he was young. He left school at the age of fifteen and engaged in the dairy business, Scotvanah, N. Y., where he remained three years. He then removed to Bergen County and for three years was successfully engaged in farming. At the end of that period he learned the carpenter's trade with Peter L. Conklin, of Hackensack, with whom he was associated for three years. Subsequently he worked at railroading for a few years, and then engaged in farming at Rivervale, Bergen County, which he still follows.

Mr. Seaman has served on the Board of Education and for some time has been Treasurer of the Township Committee. He attends the Reformed Church, and has always maintained an excellent reputation as a public spirited, progressive, and enterprising citizen. He married Margaret L. Demarest, a member of an old and respected Bergen-County family, and has three children: Lilie M., Edward, and David.

ADDISON L. DAY, of Arlington, was born in Springfield, Mass., and received a common school education. He studied civil engineering at Dartmouth College in New Hampshire, graduating therefrom with high honors. He was connected with different railroads in Missouri, Kansas, and other States until about 1878, when he entered the Hoyt Metal Company at St. Louis as its private secretary. Subsequently he became manager of the eastern branch of their business. He established his residence at Arlington, N. J., where he has become thoroughly identified with the young city as a social leader.

He is President of the Beethoven Orchestra and of Council No. 86 of the National League of Musicians of the United States. He has been a delegate to National conventions, has served as Worshipful Master of Triune Lodge, No. 159, A. F. and A. M., and is connected with other organizations.

ERNEST LUHMANN, of Secaucus, is the son of Christian and Elizabeth Luhmann and a brother of Conrad Luhmann, and was born in Germany on the 22d of October, 1864. He received his education in the Fatherland and finished his studies in New York City, whither he came in 1880, and where he remained about six years. In 1886 he settled in Secaucus, Hudson County, N. J., and has since been actively and successfully engaged in farming and gardening. He is a member of the German Schuetzen social organization of New York City, and a progressive and enterprising citizen.

Mr. Luhmann married Mary Peterson, who died leaving one son, Hermann Luhmann, born October 26, 1897.

CONRAD LUHMANN, of Secaucus, was born in Germany on the 16th of July, 1855. He is the son of Christian and Elizabeth Luhmann, both natives of that country. He received his education in the Fatherland and afterward came to America, settling first in New York City. Later he settled in Secaucus, Hudson County, and engaged in farming and gardening, a business he still follows. He markets his produce in New York City and has achieved success. He is a member of the Democratic Club of Secaucus, a public spirited and progressive citizen, and honored and respected by all who know him.

Mr. Luhmann married Annie Evermeyer, a native of Germany, and has five children: William, Lizzie, Annie, Conrad, Jr., and Fred.

JOSEPH H. WHELAN, son of William and Catherine (Maher) Whelan, was born in Jersey City, N. J., October 28, 1864. There he received his education. He has been active in politics for a number of years, and as a Democrat has become a trustworthy leader in party councils. He has served as Deputy Sheriff, as County Index Clerk, and in other important capacities. He is a member of the Robert Davis Association, and one of the best known men in Hudson County. Mr. Whelan married Mary Walpole and has one daughter, Mary.

CHARLES W. WETYEN, of Closter, is the son of John H. and Adeline (Brickwedel) Wetyen, and was born in New York City on the 26th of July, 1858. He is of German descent. He was educated in New York City and Bergen County. At the age of eighteen he left school and during the remainder of his residence in New York followed various occupations. Subsequently he located on his father's farm at Closter, Bergen County, N. J., where he has since resided, engaged in agricultural pursuits.

Mr. Wetyen has served efficiently as a member of the Board of Education of Harrington Township. He is a Director of the Harrington Building and Loan Association and a member of the Reformed Church. In every capacity he has displayed great public spirit and enterprise. He married Annie L. Schenck and has eight children: Adeline, Charles W., Jr., Florence A., John H., Frank R., Carrie W., Hattie, and Mildred.

WILLIAM C. RYAN was born July 14, 1874, in Bayonne, N. J., where he still resides, and where his parents, Matthew Ryan and Mary Myers, natives of Ireland, were married. They came to the United States when young. Mr. Ryan was educated in the Bayonne public schools and afterward engaged in general contracting, a business he has followed with marked success. He has had several large contracts, each of which he has executed with energy, ability, and satisfaction.

He is a Democrat in politics, a public spirited and progressive citizen, and a member of Bayonne Lodge, No. 187, Independent Order of Redmen, of Protection Engine Company of Bayonne, and of the Edward Smith Association. He was married, February 16, 1897, to Alice L. Ford, daughter of George and Margaret Ford, of Bayonne. They have one son, Matthew.

JAMES F. McNALLY was born January 22, 1862, at Fort Lee, N. J., where he still resides. He is the son of James McNally and Catharine Campbell, both of Irish descent. Mr. McNally was educated in Bergen County, and at the age of fourteen engaged in the express business, which he followed for a number of years. He then engaged in the livery business, in which he still continues. He is also an undertaker and funeral director, and is widely known for his energy, enterprise, and public spirit. He is one of the leading undertakers in the region of the Palisades.

In public life Mr. McNally is also prominent and active. He was Judge of Elections for Ridgefield Township for a number of terms and afterward was a candidate for Coroner. He is a member of the Foresters, and one of the most popular men in his section.

EDWARD GALLAGHER, of Guttenberg, was born in Jersey City on the 1st of February, 1861. He is the son of John Gallagher and Margaret Modigan, natives of Ireland. Mr. Gallagher was educated in the public schools of North Hudson County and then engaged in quarrying, a business he has ever since been identified with. For some time he has had charge of the county work.

He has served as a member of the Council of Guttenberg and as a Justice of the Peace. He is a member of the Royal Arcanum, of the Independent Order of Foresters, and of the Guttenberg Fire Department. He is a Democrat in politics. He married Jane Dolan and has two children: Evelyn and Agnes.

FRANKLIN D. HAASE was born July 8, 1869, in North Bergen, N. J., where he still resides. He is the son of Carsten Haase and Emily Hoyer, who came to this country from Hanover, Germany.

He was educated in the public schools of North Bergen, and until twenty-one years old followed agricultural pursuits. He then engaged in the hotel business, in which he still continues. He is a member of the Bowling Club of North Bergen and a well known citizen of that section. He married Miss Sophie Shortmeyer, and has one daughter, Florence.

CLAUS BASSE, of Weehawken, was born in Hanover, Germany, February 4, 1856, the son of Barthold Basse and Mary Schield. There he received his education. In 1873 he came to this country, and since April 23 of that year has lived in Weehawken, N. J., where he has become prominent as a hotel keeper and as a public spirited citizen. For more than a quarter of a century he has been actively identified with the town. His hotel on the corner of Willow Avenue and Nineteenth Street is one of the best known hostelries in North Hudson County.

Establishing himself in business shortly after his arrival in this country, he has, by perseverance and energy, won the respect of his fellow-citizens and the confidence and esteem of numerous acquaintances. He has been a prominent member of the Hudson County Republican Committee since 1888. In 1887 he was elected a Councilman of Weehawken and filled that position for four years, serving also during his term of office as Town Treasurer. His faithful conduct of these duties was able and efficient. In 1898 he was the Republican candidate in his district for member of Assembly, and, although defeated, received a handsome vote, running more than 4,000 ahead of the gubernatorial ticket, and reducing the usual Democratic majority by several hundred. These facts not only attest his popularity, but have a special significance when it is remembered that the nomination was wholly unsought by him. He is a progressive, patriotic citizen, and in social and fraternal affairs has long been a prominent factor. He is a Past Master and an active member of Palisade Lodge, No. 84, F. and A. M., and a member of the Hoboken Independent Schuetzen Corps and of the New York Schuetzen Corps. In 1890 Mr. Basse organized in Weehawken the Germania Verein No. 1, and under his presidency during the first two years that body prospered and grew rapidly, being now one of the strongest social organizations in North Hudson County and including in its membership every prominent German-American in the town. He has shown rare tact in managing successfully several social functions in Weehawken.

He married Hellene Kuneke, of Jersey City Heights, by whom he has six children: Charles, Lillie, Henry, Anna, Edward, and Bertha.

JOHN MOYLAN, of North Bergen, is the son of John and Mary (Colhana) Moylan and a grandson of John Moylan, Sr., and Thomas Colhana. He was born in County Limerick, Ireland, November 18, 1841. After receiving a public school education he engaged in the grocery and liquor trade in Limerick, continuing two and one-half years.

In 1862 he came to this country and settled in New York, where he successfully followed the liquor business until April, 1891, when he moved to North Bergen, Hudson County, N. J. Here, on Bergenline Avenue, near the Guttenberg racetrack, Mr. Moylan purchased and still conducts one of the most popular hotels in his section. He is a consistent Democrat, but has never been active in political affairs, preferring to devote his time and energies wholly to business. In the growth and prosperity of the town, however, and especially in the development of his immediate neighborhood, he has been useful and influential. He was active in the organization of the North Bergen Fire Department, of which he has continually been a leading member, and which he served as Treasurer for three years, declining a fourth term in 1899. He is a public spirited citizen, and respected for those qualities which mark the successful man.

Mr. Moylan was married, August 15, 1871, to Mary Adams, daughter of Michael Adams, of County Limerick, Ireland. Their only child, Mary Moylan, died in 1877.

PATRICK M. COLLIGAN, of New Durham, was born March 17, 1854, at New Berne, N. C. He is the son of Michael Colligan and Mary McMahon, both natives of Ireland.

Mr. Colligan received his education in the public schools of his native State and for a time was engaged in the hotel business in New Berne. Later he conducted a hotel in Jersey City for about four years. In 1881 he removed to New Durham, Hudson County, where he is still engaged in the hotel business, and where he has become the owner of considerable real estate. He is a School Trustee, and in both public and business affairs is well known and respected.

On January 23, 1889, Mr. Colligan married Margaret Sheedy, daughter of Thomas Sheedy. They reside in New Durham.

JOSEPH KATZENBERGER, of North Bergen, was born in Germany about fifty-five years ago. He came to America about 1874 and first settled in New York City, where he found employment as a brewer. In this capacity he was connected with several large breweries and gained much practical experience.

About 1885 he removed to Weehawken, N. J., and engaged in the brewing business. Later he moved to the Town of Union and for a time was connected with the Union Brewing Company. In the fall of 1895 he settled in North Bergen and became a partner in the Roland Brewing Company, with which he is still identified.

He served for a time in the German Army before coming to America. In politics he is a Democrat. He is a member of the Ancient Order of United Workmen. He married Madeline Müller, daughter of Frederick Müller, of Germany. They have one son, William, born in Germany, May 7, 1874.

AUGUST BEWIG, of the City of Hoboken, was engaged in the grocery and provision business there for several years, and is now the agent for the Excelsior Brewery. He has long resided in Hoboken, Hudson County, N. J., where he is an active member of the Democratic party. He has been President of the Board of Water Commissioners and more recently served as an Alderman for a period of eight years. He also acted as Chairman of the Council for three years. He was Captain of the Independent Schuetzens for five years and President of the Plattdeutscher Volks Fest of New York, recently the largest of its kind in the United States. Mr. Bewig was born in Germany, March 9, 1843, the son of Henry Bewig and Christina Klusmann. He was educated in the public schools of his native town and came to the United States when a youth.

THEODORE F. WOLLENHAUPT, of Arlington, was born at Hicksville, Long Island, N. Y., January 7, 1863. His father, Henry Wollenhaupt, was born in Casel, Germany, while his mother, Nancy Van Houten, was a native of Brooklyn. The former came to this country when a young man, and throughout his life displayed the sterling characteristics of the German race.

Mr. Wollenhaupt was educated in the public schools of Hicksville, Long Island, and afterward became proprietor of the Forest Hotel at Arlington, N. J., which he has conducted with marked success for more than sixteen years. He is one of the popular men of Hudson County. In politics he is a Democrat. He is a member of Arlington Hose Company No. 3, of the Knights of Honor, and of the Order of Foresters, and during the past seventeen years has served as a Deputy Sheriff. He is the owner of considerable real estate, and identified with anything having for its factor the benefiting of Arlington.

He married Magdalina Warth and has three children: Theodore, Nancy, and Tilley.

JOSEPH KENNEL, of Homestead, Hudson County, was born in Alsace-Lorraine, Germany, on the 10th of May, 1872. He is the son of John Kennel and Barbara Haas. His ancestors on both sides were Germans.

Mr. Kennel received his education in Germany and afterward came to this country. He took up his residence in Homestead, Hudson County, N. J., where he is engaged in the hotel business. He was one of the organizers of the Jefferson Democratic Club of Homestead and is a member of the Bowling Club of that place. He married Mary W. Garlot and has two children: Joseph Ray and Jennie K.

JOHN HEFLICH, of West Hoboken, Hudson County, was born in New York City on the 5th of April, 1853, and there received his early education. In 1866 he removed to Jersey City and soon afterward to Secaucus. Finally he became a permanent settler of West Hoboken, where he soon identified himself with the growth and development of the town. Engaging in the hotel business on the corner of Summit and Paterson Avenues, he soon established a reputation and came into prominence as a man of enterprise and public spirit. He constantly made improvements until the property now owned and occupied by him is one of the finest in the place. Recently he has erected what is known as Heflich Hall, one of the best equipped halls in Hudson County. His whole property occupies four full lots.

Mr. Heflich has always been an ardent and active Democrat and for many years an acknowledged leader of his party. He has been twice elected a member of the West Hoboken Council, has often been a delegate to party conventions, and is an important factor in the political affairs of both the Town of West Hoboken and the County of Hudson. He was for twelve years Major of the Seventh Battalion of the Schuetzenbund of New Jersey, and is a member of the Foresters of America and of the Knights and Ladies of Honor.

Mr. Heflich married Miss Catherine Harms, of Secaucus, Hudson County, by whom he has four sons and four daughters: Henry, Annie (Mrs. Valentine Woerner), George, Katie (Mrs. Henry Schoppman), John, Lena, Grover, and Lizzie.

CHARLES LACHMANN, of Weehawken, is the son of Jacob Lachmann and Louisa Fossert, both natives of Gilshausen, Germany. He was also born there, May 6, 1859, and there received a public school education.

In 1880 Mr. Lachmann came to the United States, settling first in New York City, and removing thence to New Jersey in 1882. He worked in a brewery for six years, and then engaged in the grocery business for himself in the Town of Union, Hudson County. He is now engaged in the hotel business in Weehawken. He has served as Commissioner of Appeals and as a member of the Board of Council of Weehawken, where he still resides. He is a member of the Schuetzens, of the Free Masons, of the Foresters, of the Knights and Ladies of Honor, of the Weehawken Fire Department, and other organizations. In these and other capacities he is prominent and active. He is a member of the German Lutheran Church.

Mr. Lachmann married Barbara R. Schillinger and has six children: Charles, Jr., William, Louis, Fred, Barbara, and Louisa.

GEORGE NIENABER, proprietor of one of the best known hotels in Weehawken, is a native of Hanover, Germany, as were also his parents, Louis Nienaber and Charlotte Woermann. He was born on the 26th of July, 1847, and there received a thorough public school education. In 1862 he came to the United States and settled in New York City. About 1878 he came to Weehawken, N. J., where he has since resided.

For many years Mr. Nienaber has conducted at 101 Bull's Ferry Road in Weehawken one of the most popular hotels in North Hudson County. His popularity is attested by the fact that he has a large and lucrative business. He is a Republican in politics and a veteran member of the Fifth Regiment, National Guard of New York City, in which he served fourteen years. Other prominent organizations have also claimed his companionship and attention. He is a member of the Hudson Maennerchor of New York and of the Eintracht Singing Society of Union Hill. His patriotism and public spirit, his unswerving integrity, his enterprise and sound judgment have made him highly respected and esteemed, while his activity and usefulness as a citizen have won for him the confidence of the community. His success is the result of his own efforts. Beginning in a modest way, he has steadily increased his business to its present proportions. He married Miss Elizabeth Hinck.

HENRY ENGELBRECHT, proprietor of the well known Sunnyside Hotel in Secaucus, Hudson County, was born in Brooklyn, N. Y., June 24, 1866. His father, Henry Engelbrecht, Sr., son of Henry, was born in Germany, and when about six years old came with his parents to America. The family settled in Secaucus, where the elder Henry engaged in trucking, but later they moved to Brooklyn, where he died. Henry Engelbrecht, Sr., father of Henry, the subject of this sketch, married Ruth Ann Ludlow, a native of the Town of Union and daughter of Matthew Ludlow, a native of that town and a descendant of one of its earliest families. In 1872 Mr. Engelbrecht removed with his wife and children to Secaucus and purchased the present Sunnyside Hotel on the Paterson Plank Road, which he conducted until his death, June 18, 1886. The hotel then passed into the hands of his eldest son, William Henry Engelbrecht, who carried it on until 1890, when the present proprietor, Henry Engelbrecht, assumed charge.

Henry Engelbrecht, last named, was educated in the Secaucus public schools, and since completing his studies has been engaged in the hotel business, and since 1890 has conducted the Sunnyside Hotel. This is the oldest hostelry on the island of Secaucus, and the only one that has remained in one family or under one name any great length of time.

Mr. Engelbrecht has been active and influential in town affairs and especially in the organization and development of the local fire department, being one of the first to promote the movement which resulted in the formation of an independent company, of which he was assistant foreman. When the Township of North Bergen officially recognized the company as a part of its fire department he continued in active service, and in 1892 was elected Chief and served two years. He is still one of the most prominent firemen in the town. He has also served as Constable two terms, and was a member of the Executive Committee of the Hudson County Democratic Committee three years. He is a member of the Junior Order United American Mechanics, of the Royal Society of Good Fellows, and of the Germania Schuetzen Bund.

February 25, 1892, he married Miss Theresa Rehm, of Secaucus, N. J., and they have two children: Henry, Jr., and Theresa.

CORNELIUS MacCOLLUM, proprietor of the MacCollum House at Homestead, N. J., since 1856, is known as a progressive and public spirited citizen. He has long been a prominent and influential member of the Democratic party, and has held many minor positions of trust. In every office held by him his faithful discharge of its duties has added to his popularity and confirmed the public confidence reposed in his integrity.

Mr. MacCollum was brought up on a farm, and passed through the usual experiences of a farmer's boy. He received his education in the public schools of New York City and Hudson County, N. J., having been born in West Hoboken, November 25, 1823. He is the son of Benjamin MacCollum and Hannah, daughter of Garret Van Vorst, and a grandson of Peter

MacCollum. On the paternal side he descends from ancestors who were of Scotch-Irish antecedents, and who came to the United States from the North of Ireland. His father, Benjamin MacCollum, was born in Belleville, N. J., in 1790, and died in 1847. He was a soldier in the War of 1812, serving in the Dragoons. He was engaged in business as a tanner. His children were Mary, Susan, Sarah Ann, Cornelius, Garret, and John. On his mother's side Mr. MacCollum descends from the old Dutch family of Van Vorst, the founder of which in America came from Holland to New York during the early colonial period. His grandfather, Garret Van Vorst, was a patriot soldier during the Revolution. He died near New Durham, N. J., in 1833.

Mr. MacCollum is a member of Hoboken Lodge, Free and Accepted Masons. By his wife, who was formerly Mrs. Everson, he has had eight children: Charles, George, William, Susan, Sarah, Emma, Louisa, and Ida.

CHRISTIAN C. ROTTMAN, son of Cort and Elizabeth (Wichman) Rottman, was born in Galena, Ill., May 28, 1847, and has resided in Hudson County since 1874 and in West Hoboken since 1880. His parents came from Germany in 1844, finding their way up the Mississippi River when that section of the country was almost an unbroken wilderness or at the most but sparsely settled. Cort Rottman and his brother-in-law, Nicholas Wichman, both contractors and builders, erected the first church edifice in St. Paul, Minn. The former followed the vocation of builder in Illinois until his death, at Galena, on the 7th of July, 1854, when the subject of this article was only seven years old.

Mr. Rottman was reared chiefly under the direction of his mother, a woman of great strength of character and energy. He was educated in the public schools of Galena and then learned the cooper's trade, which he followed successfully, alternating, however, with steamboating on the Mississippi. The experience he gained in these capacities developed a naturally strong and ready mind and has proved of value in both business and public affairs. In 1874 he moved to Union Hill, Hudson County, N. J., and six years later he removed to the adjoining Town of West Hoboken, where he built, in 1880, his present residence. He is Collector for the Rottman Brewing Company, composed of John F. Rottman and his sons, the former being his paternal uncle.

In politics Mr. Rottman is a consistent Democrat. He has long been active and influential in the councils of his party and is a member of the Board of Council of West Hoboken. He is a member of the Odd Fellows fraternity, of the Knights of Honor, and of several minor organizations.

Mr. Rottman was married, first, to Miss Caroline Kruhse, by whom he had one child, Anna, deceased. His present wife is Feronica Volkmann, and they have three children: John H., Anna, and Edward William, the former being in business for himself.

HENRY HAGEMANN, the popular hotel proprietor and Deputy Sheriff of North Bergen, N. J., is the son of Richard Hagemann and Louisa Miland, and was born in Westphalia, Prussia, Germany, June 6, 1842. He received a good public school education in the Fatherland, and in 1866 came to this country and settled in New York City. During the next fourteen years he was engaged in farming and gardening in Harlem, on Manhattan Island. He then removed to North Bergen, but soon returned to Harlem and again engaged in agricultural pursuits until June 1, 1886. Returning to North

Bergen, Hudson County, he followed farming and gardening with marked success for several years. In 1893 he built his present home on the Hudson County Boulevard, and two years later opened a hotel, which he has since enlarged and converted into one of the finest and most popular hostelries in his section.

Mr. Hagemann has achieved marked success. He is a man of character, energy, and perseverance, and stands high in the esteem and confidence of his friends. He is a Democrat in politics, and was a member of the police force of North Bergen for about five years. He has been Deputy Sheriff since the fall of 1887 and is now serving his fourth term, and since the autumn of 1896 has been a member of the North Bergen Fire Department, of which he was Assistant Chief one year.

Mr. Hagemann was married, May 11, 1873, to Miss Louisa Luhmann, daughter of Christian and Louisa Luhmann, of Westphalia, Prussia, who came to America in 1872. They have two children: John and Minnie, of whom the latter married Henry Watskie, of North Bergen.

JOHN HAGEMANN was born in New York City, February 10, 1874. He has served on the North Bergen police force, was assistant foreman of Overlook Engine Company in 1898, is Township Recorder of North Bergen, and has served as Deputy Sheriff since 1896. He is also a Commissioner of Deeds and a Justice of the Peace.

FREDERICK RIPPE is one of the best known citizens of the Town of Union, Hudson County, and enjoys the confidence of the community, as has been shown by his election and service for three terms as a Freeholder of Hudson County, N. J. He is in every sense of the word a self-made man, and a typical example of the German-American of sterling character and enterprising spirit who comes to the United States, carves out his own fortune, and becomes a substantial and public spirited citizen, in perfect accord with the genius of our democratic institutions, and himself actively participating in their maintenance.

Mr. Rippe was born in Germany, February 27, 1849, and is the son of Costan Rippe and Adelpeid Glade. His ancestors, on both sides, were established in Germany for centuries, and in the public schools of that country he received his education. In 1867 he came to America, obtaining employment in New York City. In 1872 he successfully engaged in the grocery business there. He subsequently established a hotel in New York City, of which he was the proprietor. He was successful in this venture, and, having acquired property in Union Hill, Hudson County, N. J., he established himself in the hotel business here. Since 1891 he has conducted the hotel near the Bermes Brewery.

In politics Mr. Rippe is a Democrat and an influential leader in the councils of his party. Besides holding membership in various political societies, he is Past Master of Hermann Lodge, No. 268, Free and Accepted Masons, of New York City, and a member of Gramercy Lodge, Ancient Order of United Workmen.

He was married, in this country, to Adelpeid Wilkens, and has three children: Charles Rippe, Arnold H. Rippe, and Martha Rippe.

LEONARD HEMBERGER, the well known hotel proprietor of North Bergen, Hudson County, is the son of Magnus and Madeline Hemberger, and was born in Germany on the 9th of August, 1858. He received a liberal education in the Fatherland, graduating from the Institute of Bruchsal. In 1875 he came to this country and settled in Hoboken, N. J., where he remained thirteen years. He then returned to Germany, and on coming to America again located on Union Hill, Hudson County, and engaged in business on the Guttenberg racetrack. He subsequently engaged in the hotel business in North Bergen, in which he has continued to the present time.

Mr. Hemberger has made himself popular in the section in which he is so well known, and through his ability, integrity, and enterprise has achieved a reputation. Energetic, progressive, and alive to the best interests of his town and county, he has been a liberal supporter of every worthy project, and in business has been very successful. He is a member of the Royal Arcanum, and as a citizen is respected and esteemed.

He married Miss Amelia Frank, by whom he has had five children: Ferdinand, Leonard, Emily, Gussie, and Madeline (deceased).

JOHN H. MEIERDIERCK, proprietor of the well known Rock Cellar Park and Brewery on the Hudson County Boulevard, opposite Guttenberg, is a native of Hanover, Germany, born October 27, 1849. His parents were John H. Meierdierck and Meta Wellpin, both of whom possessed those sterling traits of character which distinguish their race.

Having received a thorough public school education in the Fatherland, Mr. Meierdierck came to America, and for many years was successfully engaged in the sodawater business in New York City. Here he found the field which his talents and ambition were seeking—a field broad and open for the exercise of his abilities and well adapted for one of his energy and courage. He achieved success as a business man, gained a wide acquaintance and reputation, and through his industry, integrity, and enterprise built up an extensive trade.

In 1889 Mr. Meierdierck came to North Bergen, N. J., and established on the Hudson County Boulevard, opposite Guttenberg, his present Rock Cellar Brewery, to which he added, about 1894, the Rock Cellar Hotel and Park, which he has conducted with success, making the whole one of the popular establishments of the kind in North Hudson. The brewery has a capacity of about 25,000 barrels per year.

He is an ardent Democrat, a liberal supporter of all worthy movements, and actively interested in the welfare of his town and county. He is also a prominent member of the Royal Society of Good Fellows.

Mr. Meierdierck married Miss Metta Fesbok, and has three children living, viz.: John H., Jr., Minnie, and Tillie.

HENRY NUNGESSER, of Fairview in North Bergen, Hudson County, N. J., is the son of Henry Nungesser, Sr., and Christina Fredericks and a grandson of George Nungesser and Margaret Matzer, all natives of Darmstadt, Germany. Henry Nungesser, Sr., was born in Germany on the 11th of August, 1841, and came to America when a young man. He successfully conducted for a number of years a large butchering trade in New York City, and is now engaged in the same business in North Bergen, N. J. For a term he served as Road Commissioner of that town, causing several substantial improvements to be made. He is a member of the Odd Fellows and of other social and fraternal organizations. His wife, Christina, died November 7, 1896, aged fifty-one.

Henry Nungesser was born in New York City, May 27, 1868, but in 1870 moved with his parents to North Bergen, N. J., where he received his education, and where he has since resided. He began at an early age to earn his own living. His first business was as a wholesale and retail butcher. Subsequently he succeeded his father as proprietor of the popular hostelry which the latter had established at Fairview in North Bergen in 1870, and which he has since conducted with success. He has been active in the affairs of his town and county, wielding a wholesome influence in the councils of the Democratic party, and aiding in various ways to promote the general welfare. For two years he was Marshal of Fairview and for three

UNION STREET, HACKENSACK.

years he served as Foreman of the Fairview Fire Company. He is a member of the Independent Order of Foresters, belonging to the lodge in West New York. In 1861 he enlisted in the Civil War as a member of the Fifth New York Heavy Artillery.

Mr. Nungesser married Emma Daer, daughter of William and Mariah Daer, and has had two children: Lora, who died in infancy, and Pauline, born April 4, 1896.

GARRET D. VAN REIPEN was born in the old Bergen district of Jersey City, N. J., January 26, 1826, and was descended from Garret Van Reipen, one of the early Dutch settlers of Communipaw, who came to this country about 1654.

In 1856 Mr. Van Reipen was elected Mayor of Hudson City, now a part of Jersey City. At the outbreak of the Civil War he volunteered, was made a Lieutenant of Company A, Second Regiment, and was afterward promoted to a Captaincy for bravery in the field. When the Fourth Regiment, N. G. N. J., was organized he was made its Paymaster. In 1863 he was again made Mayor of Hudson City, and was re-elected biennially until 1871, when Bergen and Hudson City were consolidated with Jersey City. He was also one of the founders of the Hudson City Savings Bank, and was its Treasurer from 1866 until 1870, when he became President and Treasurer, which positions he held up to his death.

In 1863-4 Mr. Van Reipen was a member of the Legislature, and in 1874-5 he was a member of the Jersey City Board of Finance. He was President of the County Board for the Equalization of Taxes from its organization, in 1873, having been re-elected every year through all its other changes of membership. He was also a Director of the Hudson County National Bank for many years. He was a Democrat. He died August 1, 1899, and is survived by a widow and one daughter.

EUGENE HOLDEN GOLDBERG, M.D., was born in Newark, N. J., October 4, 1868. He is the son of Eugene S. Goldberg and Sarah Caroline Ward, daughter of Stephen Nye Ward, of Morris County, N. J. The Doctor's mother, Sarah Caroline Goldberg, was born at Madison, N. J., April 12, 1844, and died at Harrison, N. J., November 22, 1896. She was a kind, true, Christian friend and a charitable and loving mother.

Dr. Goldberg received his preliminary education at Afton, Morris County, and in the schools of Harrison and Kearny, Hudson County, and afterward pursued a college preparatory course at the Newark Military Academy in Newark, N. J. He was graduated with the degree of Doctor of Medicine from the College of Physicians and Surgeons, New York, in June, 1889, and subsequently served three months on the staff of Bellevue Hospital in that city. Later he was for one and one-half years resident physician and surgeon respectively at the City Hospital, Newark, and at the end of that period (October, 1891) engaged in the active practice of his profession at his present location, 18 Kearny Avenue, Kearny, Hudson County. He resides on the corner of Kearny and Bergen Avenues. He has acquired a large and successful practice and stands high in the esteem and confidence of the community.

In both public and professional life Dr. Goldberg has achieved an eminent reputation. He was First Lieutenant and Assistant Surgeon of the Third Battalion, N. G. N. J., of Orange, in 1892 and 1893, and was appointed Treasurer of the Town of Kearny in 1896 and 1897. In 1898 he was elected a member of the Kearny Board of Aldermen by the largest majority in the town's history. Dr. Goldberg is a Methodist in religion, and a member of the Masonic fraternity, the Knights of Pythias, the Independent Order of Odd Fellows, the Improved Order of Heptasophs, the Daughters of Liberty, the Royal Arcanum, the Junior Order United American Mechanics, the Foresters of America, and the Widows' and Orphans' Society of Medical Men of New Jersey. In every capacity he has displayed marked ability, great public spirit, and sound judgment.

On June 10, 1891, he was married to Miss Bessie Burtis, daughter of Barnet Burtis, of Kearny, N. J., by whom he has three children: Eleanore Hughson, born May 23, 1893; Burtis Eugene, born May 23, 1894; and Karolyn Christine, born May 13, 1898.

PHILIP EASTMAN BROCKWAY, of Arlington, was born in New York City on the 18th of March, 1866. He is the son of Daniel Phillips Brockway and Elizabeth Eastman and a grandson of Nathaniel and Kaziah Brockway and Rilus Eastman. His maternal grandmother was a Gipsom. He is of English descent on both sides. His grandfather was a carpenter and builder in Saratoga County, N. Y., and finally became a farmer. Rilus Eastman was a civil engineer by profession and a prominent man of affairs. His judgment was frequently sought and respected. He resided in Bleecker, Fulton County, N. Y., where he died.

Philip E. Brockway was educated in the public schools of Saratoga, N. Y., whither he removed with his parents when he was nine years old, and where he remained until 1889. He then came to Arlington, Hudson County, N. J., where he has since resided. Here he has been engaged in the real estate and insurance business, achieving marked success and gaining a high reputation. He is also a Commissioner of Deeds and a Notary Public. He is the sole representative of several noted insurance companies in Arlington and has built up a large general office business.

He is especially active in every movement pertaining to the affairs of Arlington, the Township of Kearny, and Hudson County. He is a Republican in politics, and has been influential in various important movements. He has served as Vice-President of the Kearny Building and Loan Association, of which Isaac L. Newbery is President. He is a member of and officially connected with the Royal Arcanum and is one of the charter members of the organization in Arlington. In every capacity he has displayed ability, sound judgment, and enterprise, and is highly respected and esteemed by the entire community. He is a public spirited citizen, active in promoting the general welfare, and has always maintained the confidence of all who know him.

Mr. Brockway married Amelia C. Anderson, of New York City, by whom he has three children: Phyllis, Alexander, and Crosby.

HENRY CRIPPEN NEER, M.D., of Park Ridge, was born at Summit, Schoharie County, N. Y., November 10, 1838. He is the son of Samuel Neer and Lucinda Morrison, a grandson of Charles and Catherine (Hydlie) Neer and of John and Sarah (Pindar) Morrison, and a great-grandson of Bernard and Hannah Neer and of George Morrison, whose wife was a Miss Coleman. The Neers, Hydlies, and Pindars were of German descent, while the Morrisons were of Scotch ancestry. George Morrison was the private secretary of Colonel Peter Livingston, of Livingston Manor, New York. Charles Neer served through the whole of the Revolutionary War, most of the time as a scout and sharpshooter and a part of the time in the regular Continental Army under Captains Davis, Husted, Jacot, and De Freest. He also served under Colonel H. K. Van Rensselaer. Samuel Neer was an Orderly Sergeant of a cavalry company in the War of 1812, peace being declared while his organization was on its way to the front.

Dr. Neer was educated in the public schools and at the New York Conference Seminary. He studied medicine in the office of Dr. David Neer, of Paterson, N. J., and while a young man taught public and singing schools to assist him in paying his expenses. In 1860 he was graduated from the Berkshire Medical Institute with the degree of M.D. Since November of that year he has been actively and successfully engaged in the practice of his profession, residing at Park Ridge, N. J., since the spring of 1865. Dr. Neer is one of the oldest and best known physicians in Bergen County, and during his entire life has maintained a high reputation for ability, probity, and integrity of character. He has been a member of the Reformed Protestant Church since 1870. He was a charter member of Friendship Lodge, No. 102, F. and A. M., and was its first Master, serving it in that capacity for about twelve years. As a citizen he is universally respected. He was married, June 16, 1861, to Louisa A. Terpenning.

DENNIS O'NEILL, of Hillsdale, is the son of Joseph O'Neill and Mary Byrnes, and was born in Ireland on the 9th of June, 1839. He was educated in his native country. He left school when he was eleven years old and for ten years worked for his father. At the end of that period, in 1860, he came to America and entered the employ of John A. Hopper, a well known farmer of Bergen County, where he remained two years. Afterward he was employed for thirty-three years by Garret S. Demarest. He now owns a farm of his own in Hillsdale, and is honored and respected by all who know him.

Mr. O'Neill has always taken a deep interest in local affairs, and as a citizen has been influential and serviceable in the community. He is public spirited, progressive, and enterprising, and one of the best known citizens in his section. He married Mary Ring and has eight children living—two sons and six daughters.

JAMES H. O'NEIL, of Jersey City, is the son of James O'Neil, and was born in New York City on the 18th of October, 1853. In 1855 he removed with his parents to Hoboken, Hudson County, where he attended public school. Later he attended public school in Jersey City and Hudson City (now a part of Jersey City), and was graduated from the schools in the latter place.

After leaving school he became a clerk in a New York hardware store. He resigned that position March 1, 1869, to accept a clerkship under his father, who was Surrogate of Hudson County. He was the only clerk employed in the Surrogate's office when his father died in 1870, and he was retained as clerk by Surrogate Robert McCague, Jr., until 1880, when he was appointed Chief Clerk by William McAvoy, who was Surrogate from 1880 until his death in 1886. Governor Abbett appointed Mr. O'Neil Surrogate to fill the unexpired term and he was elected to the office by public election in the same year. He was re-elected in 1891 and served until the expiration of his second term in 1896.

Mr. O'Neil discharged the duties of his office with unfailing fidelity and acknowledged ability, and gained a high reputation. He is one of the best known men in Hudson County, and has always taken an active part in public and political affairs. He is a Democrat in politics, a member of the Benevolent and Protective Order of Elks, of the Royal Arcanum, of the New Jersey and Berkeley Clubs, and of other social and political bodies. He was married, in 1887, to Miss Agnes Fitzgerald, of Brooklyn, N. Y.

DANIEL J. MURRAY, of Bayonne, was born in Hoboken, N. J., February 27, 1867. His parents, Martin and Ann Murray, were natives of Ireland. They came to this country when young.

Mr. Murray was educated in the Bayonne public schools and at Columbia College Law School in New York, graduating from the latter institution in the class of 1889, and being admitted to the New Jersey bar in the same year. Since then he has been actively engaged in the general practice of his profession in Bayonne. He has achieved success at the bar and enjoys a high reputation as an able lawyer and advocate.

In public life he has also gained distinction. He was Tax Assessor of Bayonne in 1891 and Assistant Collector of Revenue from 1893 to 1895. In politics he is a Democrat. He is a member of the Hudson County Democratic Committee, one of the members of the Executive Committee of that committee, and a member of the Knights of Columbus, of the Catholic Benevolent Legion, and of the Bayonne Democratic Club.

Mr. Murray was married, September 8, 1890, to Margaret Carberry, daughter of John and Mary Carberry, of South Amboy, N. J. They have three sons: John Martin, Daniel, and Edward.

PETER STILLWELL, of Bayonne, was born at White House, Hunterdon County, N. J., August 22, 1863. He is the son of George Stillwell and Catharine Schomp, a grandson of John V. Stillwell and Peter Schomp, a great-grandson of Nicholas Stillwell and Peter Schomp, Sr., and a great-great-grandson of Richard Stillwell and John Schomp, who was a son of Peter Schomp. Richard Stillwell was the son of Nicholas Stillwell, who was the son of Jeremiah Stillwell, who was the son of Nicholas Stillwell, who was the first of the name in this country, emigrating from Holland in 1638 and settling on Manhattan Island. In England Nicholas Stillwell's name was Nicholas Cooke. He was driven from the country by persecutions during the reign of Charles I. and went to Holland, whence he came to America. Richard Stillwell, the great-great-grandfather of the subject of this sketch, was a Captain in the Fourth Regiment, Hunterdon County, New Jersey State troops, during the Revolutionary War.

Peter Stillwell was graduated from Rutgers College with the degree of B. A. in 1886, and two years later was admitted to the bar of Colorado. In 1889 he was admitted to the New Jersey bar, and since then has practiced in Bayonne. He was a member of the Bayonne Board of Education for four years, serving two terms as President of the board. He is a member of the Royal Arcanum, a public spirited citizen, and honored and respected by all who know him.

He was married, May 9, 1894, to Henrietta A. Helmke, and has three children: William Howard, Bernardine Rose, and Catharine Louise.

GEORGE WARD, of Harrington Park, was born in New York City on the 15th of August, 1820. He was the son of Daniel Ward and Eleanor Outhouse and a grandson of William Ward and James Outhouse. His ancestors came to this country from Holland.

Mr. Ward was educated in Public School No. 11, in New York City, and at the age of fifteen he engaged in the trade of butcher, which he continued for several years. Afterward he entered a law office in New York, where he remained two and a half years. He then engaged in the grocery business, which he continued for some forty odd years. In 1866 he moved to his farm in the neighborhood of Closter, now known as Harrington Park, where he died October 28, 1900, in his eighty-first year. He was a member of the Methodist Church, an active and influential citizen, and respected by all who knew him.

He married Margaret Graf and had six children, of whom four are living, namely: George W., David A., Frank P., and Isabella E.

WALTER STANTON, of Hillsdale, was born in Columbus, R. I., November 14, 1858, his parents being Samuel B. Stanton and Lida Conrad and his grandparents William B. Stanton and Peter T. Conrad. His ancestors came to this country from England. Both of his grandfathers served in the Revolutionary War, the one on his father's side being a Major and the one on the Conrad side a Captain. On his mother's side he is a direct descendant of General George Clinton, Governor of the State of New York.

Mr. Stanton was educated at Phillips Academy at Andover, Mass. He left school at the age of eighteen and engaged in the brokerage business in Wall Street, New York, in which he has ever since continued. He is one of the best known brokers in the metropolis, and during his entire career has displayed great business ability, sound judgment, and a thorough grasp of financial affairs. He is a member of the Dutch Reformed Church at Park Ridge and a public spirited and enterprising citizen. He married Grace Von Cott and has one child, Susa C.

J. EMIL WALSCHEID was born in the Town of Union, at 309 Fulton Street, where he still resides. He was educated at Hoboken Academy, from which institution he was graduated. He passed the next two years learning the silk business, and afterward entered the academic department of the New York University, graduating from that institution in the class of 1894, with the degree of Ph.B. He entered the Law School of the same university and was graduated with honors, receiving the degree of LL.B.

Mr. Walscheid was admitted to the New Jersey bar at the November term of the year of his graduation. He had previously served his legal apprenticeship in the law offices of Page & Taft, counsel to the New York, New Haven and Hartford Railroad, and also with the firm of Randolph, Condict & Black. After his admission to the New Jersey bar he opened an office in Union Hill, where he has enjoyed a lucrative and rapidly growing practice. He is an ardent Democrat, President of the Third Ward Democratic Club, a member of the Executive Committee of the Democratic Central Organization, and a member of the Democratic Town General Committee. He also belongs to the Iroquois Democratic Club, the John J. Eagan Association, the Emil Groth Association, the Robert Davis Association, and the Protective and Improvement Association. He is an enthusiastic member of the All Bees Bowling Club.

ALOYSIUS McMAHON is the son of Thomas McMahon and Margaret Donovan, and was born July 24, 1877, in Jersey City, N. J., where he still resides. On both sides he is of Irish descent. He was educated in the public schools of Jersey City and at the New York Law School, graduating from the latter institution with the degree of LL.B. in 1898. In October of the same year he was admitted to the New Jersey bar as an attorney at law, and since then he has practiced his profession in Jersey City with marked success. He was admitted to the New York bar as an attorney and counselor and also practices in that State, being a member of the law firm of McCarthy & McMahon.

Mr. McMahon is a Democrat in politics and an active and influential member of the Third Ward Democratic Club of Jersey City. In his profession as well as in public affairs he has displayed ability and other qualities which mark the successful man.

HUGH SHARKEY, of Bayonne, was born in Ireland on the 15th of August, 1854, his parents being James Sharkey and Mary Ward. He was educated in the public schools of his native country. In 1880 he came to this country and settled in Bayonne, Hudson County, N. J. He has been associated with the Standard Oil Company since 1881 and now holds the position of foreman of their yards in Bayonne.

In politics Mr. Sharkey is an ardent and consistent Democrat, active in party affairs, and honored and respected by all who know him. For five years he served as a School Trustee. In 1899 he became a member of the Bayonne Common Council, and in that capacity has rendered efficient service to the community. He is a member of the Catholic Legion, of the Ancient Order of United Workmen, of St. Patrick's Alliance, and of the Democratic Club, all of Bayonne. He is married and has four children.

RICHARD MORRISON, of Arlington, is the son of James Morrison and Jane Coulter, and was born in Belfast, Ireland, on the 22d of February, 1855. He was educated in his native city.

In December, 1872, Mr. Morrison came to America alone and settled in Jersey City Heights, whence he removed to New York City in 1876. He remained there until 1885, when he removed to Arlington, Hudson County, where he still resides. For four years he was connected with the well known dry goods house of A. T. Stewart, of New York. Afterward he entered the employ of Silver & Son, shoe manufacturers, with whom he still remains, holding the position of bookkeeper and cashier.

Mr. Morrison is a Republican in politics and a prohibitionist in principle. He was a member of the Republican County Committee of Hudson County and at one time was nominated for Assemblyman by the Prohibition party. He received a most complimentary vote. He was President of the Fourth District Republican Club for a time and is now a member and Treasurer of the First Baptist Church of Arlington, a member of the Royal Arcanum, and a Director of the Kearny Building and Loan Association. In every capacity Mr. Morrison has displayed that degree of ability and sound judgment which mark the successful man. He is thoroughly identified with the affairs of the town and county, active in promoting every worthy object, and honored and respected by all who know him. He has six children: George A., James E., Robert C., William J. S., Edward G. M., and Margaret M.

JOHN W. ZISGEN, of Hoboken, was born in Trenton, N. J., October 20, 1875. He is the son of John B. Zisgen, of German descent, and of Mary A. Zisgen, his wife, of Irish descent. He was educated at St. John's Parochial School in Trenton, which he attended until fourteen years of age. He then spent a year in the Trenton public schools and a year and a half in Stewart's Business College of Trenton.

At the age of eighteen Mr. Zisgen entered upon the study of law with Hon. Garret D. W. Vroom, of Trenton, Reporter of the Supreme Court of New Jersey, with whom he remained until he was admitted to the bar in February, 1897. He then opened an office in Trenton and began the active practice of his profession. In March, 1898, he removed to Jersey City. In July, 1900, Mr. Zisgen entered into partnership with Joseph M. Noonan and opened offices in Hoboken, where he has since practiced law with marked success. He was a member of the Fourth New Jersey Volunteer Regiment in the Spanish-American War, and both at the bar and in public life has established an honorable reputation.

WILLIAM VAN HORN, of Ramsey, was born in Mahwah, N. J., September 27, 1865, his parents being William Van Horn and Anna Van Dien, both members of old and respected New Jersey families. He was educated in the Mahwah public schools and at Lattimer's Business College in Paterson. Afterward he engaged in the importing business in New York City and still later in the grocery trade. He is now engaged in the meat business at Ramsey, N. J., where he resides.

Mr. Van Horn is a Democrat in politics, a public spirited and enterprising citizen, and actively identified with the affairs of his town and county. He has served as Town Clerk of Hohokus Township, and is a member of Hohokus Lodge, No. 178, I. O. O. F., and of Ramsey Council, No. 245, Junior Order United American Mechanics. He is also a member of the Reformed Church.

GEORGE WASHINGTON SCHAEFER was born in New York City, February 9, 1842, where his maternal grandfather, Conrad Warmkessel, a truck gardener, died at the age of one hundred and eight, and where the

CENTRAL AVENUE HACKENSACK.

latter's wife, Elizabeth, died, aged one hundred and four, their residence being on the corner of Avenue A and First Street. His parents, Constantine and Elizabeth (Warmkessel) Schaefer, were natives of Germany, where his paternal grandmother died at the age of one hundred and three. Constantine Schaefer, Sr., his grandfather, was a government building inspector in Germany, and died suddenly, while on duty, aged seventy-nine. Constantine Schaefer, Jr., came to New York City before 1835, and was first a hotel keeper on Cedar Street and later a tailor. On March 13, 1868, he moved to Union Hill, N. J., where he was one of the first lotowners, in 1853. His wife died in New York in March, 1856.

Mr. Schaefer has in his possession the original coat of arms of the Schaefer family, which was presented to them by King Ludwig A. D. 1329, and which bears this inscription: *Wappe des Geschlechts Schaefer*. The crest still stands above the door of the old family seat in Hoeheime,

Germany. The Schaefers were shepherds and later wine growers, and always bore a conspicuous part in public life.

George W. Schaefer was educated in New York City. He left school and on September 1, 1857, enlisted for five years as a drummer boy in the regular army on Governor's Island. In the fall of that year he was detailed with a company that was sent to New York to quell the bread riot. Later he joined Company D, First Regiment Heavy Artillery, at Fortress Monroe, and in 1859 was present at John Brown's raid and also at the hanging of the latter, serving under Colonel Robert E. Lee, later of the Confederate Army. Mr. Schaefer served in Texas under General Twiggs, being there at the outbreak of the Katenas (Indian) war, and later went to Baton Rouge, where his regiment surrendered, January 12, 1861, to the government of Louisiana, after that State had seceded. Lieutenant Todd, a brother of President Lincoln's wife, was the ordnance officer.

Returning North to Fort Hamilton about January 23, 1861, Mr. Schaefer arrived at Fort McHenry, in Maryland, about February 10, and five days later was in Washington, D. C., where he was a member of Lincoln's body guard during the inaugural, camping in a house near Salmon P. Chase's residence on Capitol Hill. In April, 1861, he went to Fort Washington and drilled artillery volunteers. He was wounded in the head while there, and subsequently was sent to Fort Taylor, Key West, Fla., where he participated in the capture of the rebel steamer "Florida." Later he was at Hilton Head, Beaufort, S. C., and was in the battles of Secessionville on James's Island and Seabrook Landing on Lady's Island. He received two bullet wounds in the leg, and was honorably discharged on the battlefield September 1, 1862. Mr. Schaefer then served in the Ordnance Department at Washington until 1864 and afterward in the Quartermaster's and Transportation Departments, Army of the Potomac, under Captain J. G. C. Lee, Quartermaster-General, until the close of the war, resigning August 31, 1865.

He returned home and followed his trade as a machinist and engineer in New York City, being for four years in the civil engineer's department at the Brooklyn Navy Yard under Chief Engineer Norman L. Stratton. For four years he had charge of the conversion of a building into a coffee and spice mill on the corner of Duane and Hudson Streets, New York, for Clark & Huntington. Later he had charge of what is now the Star building on Broadway, corner of Park Place, for four years, and in 1881 he became Superintendent of the Hackensack (N. J.) Gas Company, which position he held two years. Since 1883 he has been the resident engineer of the re-organized Hackensack Water Company, being located at the water tower on the Bull's Ferry road in Weehawken.

Mr. Schaefer is a member of the Independent Order of Odd Fellows, the old U. A. M., and the Royal Society of Good Fellows, of which he is Past Grand Ruler of New Jersey. For seven years he has been Treasurer of the order. He was one of the organizers of the Grand Lodge of Good Fellows in November, 1894, and was elected its first Grand Ruler. He is also a member and Adjutant of Ellsworth Post, No. 14, G. A. R., Department of New Jersey, and has served it two terms as Commander. In politics he has always been a Republican.

He was married, July 20, 1867, to Susan Marie Louisa Ridgeway, daughter of Charles E. and Catherine Ridgeway, of the Town of Union, N. J. They have had ten children: Katherine (Mrs. George Limouze) and Elizabeth (Mrs. Alfred Steger), both of the Town of Union; George W., Jr. (deceased); Minnie Augusta (Mrs. Robert Shaw), of Jersey City; Julia (deceased); William Gibson (deceased); Alfred (deceased); Susan M. L.; George W., 2d (deceased); and Floyd Goff.

AUGUSTUS A. HARDENBERGH, member of Congress from Jersey City for three terms, was born in New Brunswick, N. J., May 18, 1830. He was descended from one of the famous families of New Jersey. His great-grandfather, Jacob R. Hardenbergh, D.D., was the founder of Rutgers College and its first President. His father, Cornelius L. Hardenbergh, LL.D., was a prominent lawyer of New Brunswick.

Augustus Hardenbergh entered Rutgers College in 1844, but an infliction of blindness upon his father compelled him to leave before his course was finished to assist in his father's law office. In 1851 the college conferred upon him the degree of Bachelor of Arts in recognition of the good work he had accomplished during his brief collegiate career. In 1846 he entered a mercantile house in New York, becoming a resident of Jersey City. In 1852 he became connected with the Hudson County National Bank, was appointed its Cashier in 1858, and in 1878 was elected President, a position he held until his death.

Mr. Hardenbergh early became interested in politics. He was elected to the State Legislature as a Democrat when only twenty-three years of age (1853). During the session of 1854 he acquired a favorable State reputation by securing the passage of the general banking act and by opposing the Camden and Amboy Railroad monopoly. In 1857 he was elected a member of the Jersey City Common Council, as Alderman, and was re-elected thereafter until 1863, serving a part of the time as President of that body and as Chairman of the War Committee. In 1868 he was appointed State Director of Railroads.

Having removed to his Bergen County home, he was elected a delegate from the Fourth Congressional District to the Democratic National Convention at Baltimore, which nominated Horace Greeley for President, and in the same year was chosen President of the Northern Railroad Company of New Jersey. In the fall of 1872 he removed to Jersey City and in 1876 was elected to the Forty-fourth Congress, to which he was re-elected in 1878. In 1880 he consented to accept a re-nomination to Congress to save his party from threatened defeat and was again elected by over 5,000 majority. During this period he succeeded in making Jersey City a port of entry. In 1883 he was appointed a member of the Board of Finance and Taxation and his services were marked by saving the credit of the city during the financial depression of that year. In 1884 he was appointed by Governor Abbett as a Trustee of the State Reform School. He served as a member of the Board of Finance until 1889, when the board went out of office. The unique place which Mr. Hardenbergh held in the affections of the community is shown by the following newspaper characterization at the time of his death:

"Mr. Hardenbergh was one of the most widely known men in this section of the country. He made a record in Congress that brought him into close and intimate relations with the chief men of New York and Pennsylvania. Of course every man of any account in New Jersey was his personal friend. He has been so active in Hudson County, in public and private ways, that his name was a household word from Bull's Ferry to Bergen Point, and his death comes to almost every man, woman, and child here with the sting almost of a personal bereavement. Without a single exception he was the most popular man in the county, and his individual strength has more than once helped to save his party from disaster in times of threatened peril.

"His chief characteristic was his sterling integrity. All of his life has been spent under the public eye. He has been commissioned by the people to the discharge of countless trusts. Never a man carried himself so straight as he. Suspicion did not dare to blow even a breath at him. And he had the personal confidence of every man as thoroughly as he had the confidence of the masses as an aggregate.

"If a little estate was to be administered, Gus Hardenbergh—as everybody felt at liberty to call him, so close was he to men everywhere—was chosen to administer it. If a dispute was to be decided he was often made the final arbiter.

"Add to the influence such a reputation gave him his other qualities of mind and disposition, and wonder ceases as to the reasons for his personal strength. An entertaining companion, a fluent and often eloquent talker, a thinker of great mental force, a friend whose purse and services were always at the command of those who needed them, and a man of fearless honesty—that was Mr. Hardenbergh as this community knew him."

Mr. Hardenbergh died October 5, 1889. He was an eloquent speaker, a man of the highest integrity, a public spirited and progressive citizen, and closely identified with every movement which had the advancement of the city at heart.

LEMUEL LOZIER, a prominent civil engineer and surveyor residing at Hackensack, N. J., is of the seventh generation in line of descent from François le Seuer, the French emigrant, concerning whom and his children and grandchildren see page 505.

François's great-grandson, John Lozier (4), was born near Hackensack, March 14, 1740, and died at Schraalenburgh, August 4, 1805. His wife, Mary Bourdette, a daughter of Stephen Bourdette, was born in 1744 and died June 7, 1828. Among their children of the fifth generation was Stephen Lozier, born in 1777, who settled at Old Bridge, now River Edge, just north of Hackensack. Afterward he removed to New York City. He married, in 1808, Sarah Van Buskirk, born November 29, 1779. He died about 1860 and his wife followed February 15, 1871. They had issue of the sixth generation John S., Jacob S., Catharine, Abraham, and others.

John S. Lozier (6) was born October 4, 1809, and died February 19, 1871. He married (1) Fanny Van Zaun (who was born February 18, 1812, and died December 14, 1852) and (2) Margaret Banta. His issue of the seventh generation were Stephen (died), Mary Sarah, Catharine, Henry, Frances, Frances Ann, John, Robert G., and Lemuel, the latter being the subject of this sketch.

Lemuel Lozier (7) was born at Cherry Hill, N. J., March 13, 1862, and after preparatory courses in the public school at New Bridge entered the Hackensack Academy, from which he was graduated. He then took up civil engineering and surveying, which he has followed with success, ranking now as one of the leading and most reliable surveyors of the county.

Page 605, sketch of Ruben M. Hart should read as follows:

RUBEN M. HART, of Hackensack, was born in Montreal, Canada. and was educated at Nicolet and Jesuit Colleges. He was graduated from McGill University, and read law in Canada with Judge Cornwallis Monk and Sir James Rose. He was admitted to the Montreal bar, but devoted himself more to literature than to the practice of his profession, and finally, in 1882, settled in Hackensack, N. J. He was admitted as an attorney in this State in June. 1889, and as a counselor in June, 1892.

In 1883 he married May D. Moses, daughter of John M. and Ellen (Brown) Moses, of Hackensack.

REUBEN M. HART, of Hackensack, was born in Montreal, Canada, and was educated at Nicolet and Jesuit Colleges. He graduated from McGill University, and read law in Canada with Judge Cornwallis Munn and Sir James Rose. He was admitted to the Montreal bar, and, finally, in 1882, settled in Hackensack, N. J. He was for seven years the official stenographer of the Second Judicial District of New Jersey. He was admitted as an attorney in this State in June, 1889, and as a counselor in June, 1892.

PETER L. CONKLIN, of Hackensack, was born in Franklin Township, Bergen County, N. J., on the 28th of October, 1825. He was the son of Louis Conklin and Ellen Voorhis, members of old and respected New Jersey families.

Mr. Conklin received his education in the public schools of Bergen County. Subsequently he learned the trade of carpenter, which he followed with marked success until he reached the age of fifty-seven, when he retired from active business. During the Civil War he was for nine months at the front as a member of and color-bearer in the Twenty-second Regiment, New Jersey Volunteers. He was a public spirited, progressive, and enterprising citizen, thoroughly identified with the affairs of his native county, and honored and respected by all who knew him. Mr. Conklin was a member of McPherson Post, G. A. R., of Hackensack. He married Euphemia Frederick. He was a member of the Calvary Baptist Church of Hackensack. He died October 21, 1900, and is survived by two daughters: Mrs. Cornelius Zabriskie and Fannie De Wolf Conklin.

RALPH D. EARLE, JR., is a descendant in the eighth generation from Edward Earle, an Englishman, who came from Maryland to Bergen, N. J., with his son, Edward Earle, Jr., in 1676, and purchased (April 24, of that year) of the executors of Nicholas Varlet the Island of Secaucus, now in Hudson County, comprising about 2,000 acres. The deed of the island was made out to Edward Earle, Jr., then a young man. They took possession of the island and settled on it. Edward Earle, Sr., died December 15, 1711, and was buried at Bergen. His son, Edward, Jr., of the second generation, married, February 13, 1688, Elsie, daughter of Enoch Michaels Vreeland and a granddaughter of the first American ancestor of the Vreeland family. Edward, Jr., became a man of importance in the affairs of Bergen. He was appointed Tax Commissioner for Bergen in 1693, and the following year was Commissioner of the Highways for the town. In 1695 he was elected to the House of Deputies of East New Jersey. His widow, Elsie, married, June 24, 1716, Hendrick Meyer, of Hackensack.

Morris Earle (5), a grandson of the above named Edward Earle, Jr., married in New York (1), February 8, 1755, Johanna Mountayne and (2), May 23, 1761, Abagail Leach. Morris had several children of the sixth generation, one of whom was Thomas Earle, born in New York in 1767, married Matilda Harrison. Thomas (6) lived and died in New York City, leaving, among other children of the sixth generation, Thomas Earle (7), born in New York, February 10, 1809. He married Euphemia Demarest and had issue six children of the eighth generation, one of whom was Ralph Earle, who married Margaret Acken, and had, among other children of the ninth generation, Ralph D. Earle, Jr., the subject of this sketch.

Ralph D. Earle, Jr., was born in Jersey City, March 21, 1865, and there obtained a thorough public and high school education. At an early age he exhibited unusual tastes for mathematics, which he developed with perseverance and success. Leaving school, he entered the office of his uncle, Frank H. Earle, of Jersey City, with whom he remained several years, studying civil engineering and surveying and mastering every branch of the profession. He soon became an expert, so skillful and rapid was he in the manipulation of figures. In the autumn of 1883 he accepted a position with Charles B. Brush, of Hoboken, one of the largest civil engineers in the country, and remained with him for about three years, gaining a valuable experience in general engineering and surveying. Resigning this, he associated himself with the different elevated railways in Brooklyn, where he made preliminary surveys for several lines. In 1887 he returned to his former position with Mr. Brush, with whom he continued until 1895, having charge of Mr. Brush's construction work in North Hudson County, which included the $250,000 contract for the outlet sewer to Union Hill, the construction of the North Hudson County Railway to the Guttenberg racetrack, the improvement of the Meeks and Cossitt estates, the preliminary surveys for the Hudson River Bridge, and practically every large and important improvement in the northern part of the County of Hudson.

In 1895 Mr. Earle engaged in business for himself as a general civil engineer and surveyor, opening an office at 154 Bergenline Avenue, corner of Lewis Street. Since then he has had charge of almost all of the important work executed or projected in North Hudson County, continuing on the same lines that he had previously followed. Among these enterprises may be mentioned the construction of the main latteral sewer on Union Hill, the laying of the first brick pavement in Hudson County, and the construction of the Weehawken loop, a driveway five miles in length, on the edge of the Palisades, overlooking the Hudson River, and which has been extended into Hoboken. This loop involves the construction of a viaduct over the railroad tracks and a large amount of other work. In all of these capacities Mr. Earle has achieved success. Since 1895 he has also been county surveyor of Hudson County. In politics he is an ardent Democrat. He is a member of the Democratic Central Organization and of the Executive Committee of the Hudson County Democratic Committee. He was a member of the Board of Education of the Town of Union from 1895 to 1898, and in the latter year served as President of the board. He is a prominent member of the Knights of Pythias, the Elks, and the Royal Arcanum.

Mr. Earle was married, April 5, 1887, to Florence B. Hurley, daughter of Charles H. Hurley, of Philadelphia, Pa. They have three children: Charles H., Ralph D., 3d., and Carroll.

HENRY TRAPHAGEN was born June 1, 1842, in Jersey City, N. J., where he still resides. He is the son of Henry Mackaners Traphagen, a wealthy and prominent citizen of that place, and of Sarah Conselyea, his wife. His grandfather, Henry Traphagen, Jr., was graduated from Rutgers College in 1791 and married a daughter of Cornelius Van Vorst. His great-grandfather, Henry Traphagen, Sr., was a Trustee of Queens (now Rutgers) College in 1782. The Traphagens are one of the oldest families in Jersey City, and for generations have been prominent in business and professional affairs.

Mr. Traphagen was educated at Rutgers College and Brown University,

Providence, R. I. He read law in the office of the late Hon. Isaac W. Scudder and was admitted to the New Jersey bar as an attorney in November, 1864, and as a counselor in November, 1867. Since 1864 he has been successfully engaged in the general practice of his profession in Jersey City.

He served as Mayor of Jersey City from May 1, 1874, to May 1, 1876, and as Corporation Attorney from November, 1876, to March, 1881. Prior to the consolidation of the three cities—Jersey City, Hudson City, and Bergen,—composing what is now Jersey City, he was counsel for the Board of Water Commissioners of Jersey City. He is a member of the Holland Society of New York and was for one year (1891-92) one of its Vice-Presidents. November 9, 1869, he married Annie Matilda Campbell, daughter of David Campbell, of New York City.

JOHN W. VAN BLARCOM.—Blarcom or Blerkum is the name of a community near the City of Rotterdam in Holland, from whence one Johannes (John) Van Blarcom emigrated about the middle of the seventeenth century and settled at Hoboken in Hudson County, N. J. He is said to have brought with him a large family of children. He certainly had three sons of the second generation: Peter Jansen Van Blarcom, Gysbert Jansen Van Blarcom, and John Jansen Van Blarcom.

Peter (2) married (1) Jacomina Cornelis and (2), in 1719, Antie Meyer (widow). Gysbert (2) married (1) Magdalena la Comba in 1706 and (2) Antie Christie. John (2) married, July 16, 1693, Meta Jans. These three all settled at Bergen, now Jersey City. Gysbert went to Hackensack in 1715, joined the church there, and bought lands. His brothers Peter and John soon followed him and bought lands west of the Saddle River as well as in the Aquackanonck (Passaic) patent. Peter bought 500 or 800 acres in the Pompton district of Bergen County. Among his children of the third generation were Sarah, Garret, Jacomina, and Willempie. Gysbert's children of the third generation were John, Mary, Anthony, William, Henry, Ellen, and Jacobus. John's children of the third generation were Neltie, Jane, Elizabeth, Rachel, and Isaac. This family, composed principally of descendants of Peter and Gysbert, are very numerous in Franklin, Saddle River, Ridgewood, and Hohokus Townships in Bergen County.

John Van Blarcom (3), a grandson of John (1), married, in 1725, Jannetie Lent, of Rockland County, N. Y., and settled near Paramus in New Jersey. From there in 1735 he removed to near Nanuet in Rockland County, N. Y., where he bought a farm. His issue were Peter, 1727; Elizabeth, 1731; Peter, 1734; and David, 1736. His son, Garret Van Blarcom, born October 10, 1786, married Maria Hopper, also born in 1786. He died in 1854 and she in 1846. Their children were Peter, born in 1805, died November 20, 1862, and John, born in 1808, died in 1880. Peter Van Blarcom had three sons and five daughters: Garret; Mary, of Addison, N. Y.; William, deceased; Daniel, of Suffern, N. Y.; Henrietta and Bridget (twins), deceased; Eliza, of Brooklyn, N. Y.; and Jane, of Pearl River, N. Y.

Garret Van Blarcom, son of Peter, was born in May, 1829, and became a blacksmith at Tappan, N. Y. He was twice married and has a son, the subject of this sketch.

John W. Van Blarcom, son of Garret Van Blarcom and Elizabeth Post (died in 1853), was born at Tappan, N. Y., in July, 1852, and early learned the blacksmith's trade, which he has ever since followed. He married Margaret Jane, daughter of Peter A. Demarest, by whom he has two sons:

Frank and Demarest Van Blarcom. He resides at Norwood, N. J., where he is active in politics. He has been a member of the Harrington Township Road Board and is now a member of the Town Committee of that township.

HENRY A. GAEDE, of Hoboken, was born in Hudson City, now Jersey City Heights, N. J., September 10, 1857, and was graduated from old Public School No. 2, of that place, in 1872. On leaving school he took up the study of civil engineering with Otto F. Wegener, then city surveyor of Hoboken, and remained with him until October, 1874, when he entered the law office of the late John C. Besson, of the same city, as a student. He was admitted to the bar of New Jersey in November, 1878, and since then has successfully practiced his profession in Hoboken, becoming one of the prominent members of the Hudson County bar, and making a specialty of the examination of titles to real estate. He is counsel for a number of large corporations, including the Hoboken Bank for Savings and the Industrial Mutual Building and Loan Association of Jersey City. He was also attorney for Hudson County in the condemnation proceedings for land taken for the County Boulevard. Mr. Gaede has built up a large practice, and is heavily interested in real estate.

WILSON L. HEATH, of Arlington, was born in Wilsonville, Conn., September 9, 1846. He is the son of George W. Heath, a native of Putnam, Conn., and of Frances Sessions, who was born in Tompson in that State. Mr. Heath received a public school education in Wilsonville, and at the age of seventeen went to New York City, where he entered the employ of H. B. Claflin & Company. He has been identified with this firm ever since, holding responsible positions and discharging his duties with acknowledged ability and satisfaction.

Mr. Heath is also engaged in the dry goods business in Arlington, N. J., becoming a member of the firm of Allen & Roth in 1884. This firm was changed to Heath & Norris in 1888. Mr. Norris died in 1889 and his widow assumed his interest in the firm. Mr. Heath is a public spirited citizen and respected by all who know him. He married Miss Mary E. Welsch and has four children: Helen M., George W., Charlotte, and Carrie.

ALFRED SMEDBERG, of Kearny, is the son of Sevin and Maria Smedberg, and was born in Sweden on the 29th of April, 1860. His parents were both natives of that country, where he received his education.

In 1885 Mr. Smedberg came to the United States, settling in Newark, N. J., whence he removed to Kearny, Hudson County, where he now resides. After leaving school he learned the trade of carpenter and builder, a business he has always followed, achieving marked success. He was for two years a soldier in the army of Sweden before coming to this country. He belongs to the Swedish Church of Kearny and is a Republican in politics. As a carpenter and builder he has gained a high reputation, having erected a number of important buildings in his vicinity.

Mr. Smedberg married Mary Carlson, of Sweden, and has five children: Hannah, Harry, Hilda, Arthur, and Ella.

WILLIAM NOE, of Union Hill, is the son of John Noe and Barbara Schmidt and was born in Baden, Germany, on the 2d of March, 1846. He received a public school education and learned the blacksmith's trade in the Fatherland, and in 1866 came to America with his sister, settling in Union Hill, Hudson County, where he has since resided. In 1871 he engaged in the blacksmithing business for himself and so continued until 1875, when he was employed in New York City. In 1881 he established his present blacksmith shop on Bergenline Avenue in the Town of West New York.

Mr. Noe is a Republican in politics, a member of the Republican Club of Union Hill, and a member of the Dutch Reformed Church. He has been a member of the Haraguri since 1868, and is the only charter member of the nine original founders of his lodge who is living. In this order he has filled all the chairs. He is also a member of the Royal Society of Good Fellows, and in every capacity has won the confidence and respect of all who know him. He is a public spirited citizen, deeply interested in local affairs, and a man of acknowledged ability and enterprise.

July 4, 1871, Mr. Noe married Mrs. Cedonia (Flutz) Flood. They have one daughter, Clara Viola.

WILLIAM MARSHALL SEÜFERT, of Englewood, was born in New York City on the 22d of May, 1873. His parents, George G. Seüfert and Margaret G. Sienken, were both natives of that city, where they were married. Mr. Seüfert received his education at New York University, taking a postgraduate course in law in the class of 1892. He was admitted to the bars of New York and New Jersey and is actively and successfully engaged in the practice of his profession in both New York City and Englewood.

Mr. Seüfert is a member of the Englewood Club, of the Bogota Boat Club, and of the Episcopal Church. He is an able lawyer, a public spirited citizen, and respected by all who know him. He married Anna Evelyn Pope, daughter of John and Lauretta Pope, of Brooklyn, N. Y., the ceremony being performed in Leonia, N. J., January 28, 1898.

ROBERT GAW, of Union Hill, is the son of Charles Gaw and Margaret McKee and a grandson of Robert Gaw, all natives of the North of Ireland. The family came to America in the early fifties, settling in New York.

Mr. Gaw was born at Union Hill, Hudson County, December 9, 1879. He attended the public schools, both in Union Hill and West Hoboken, and later Cooper Institute, New York, where he studied engineering and higher mathematics. He was first employed by John W. Rutherford, contracting engineer, and by John G. Payne, engineer to the Riparian Commission. He was with James Moylan for a number of years, and assisted J. J. Tallon on the main lateral sewer, and completed the Boulevard sewer, in West Hoboken, after Mr. Tallon died. He was also engineer on the Summit Avenue and other improvements, including the paving on Clinton Avenue, West Hoboken. He is a member of the Fire Department, the Royal Arcanum, and the Junior Order United American Mechanics. In politics he is a Democrat.

SAMUEL PHILLIPS RUSSELL, D.D.S., comes from an old New England family, and inherits through several generations of ancestors those principles of application which characterize the race, and which are still evident in their descendants in every section of the country. His family has been prominent in the professions, in military and official affairs, and in business life, many of them having held exalted stations of trust and responsibility. He was born in Springfield, Mass., August 16, 1870, and there received a thorough grammar and high school education. As a youth he displayed a strong inclination for a professional career.

After leaving school he entered the New York College of Dentistry, in New York City, and was graduated therefrom in 1890, receiving the degree of Doctor of Dental Surgery. He began active practice in New York, where he soon built up a large and lucrative business. Five years later, on the advice of his physician, he retired and took a rest. In 1895 he went West and South, where he spent a year in travel. Upon his return in the spring of 1896 he opened his present dental parlors at 97 Bergenline Avenue in the Town of Union, where he has acquired an extensive and successful practice.

Dr. Russell is prominent in social and fraternal circles, where he occupies a number of important offices. He is a member of Mystic Tie Lodge, No. 123, F. and A. M., of Cyrus Chapter, No. 32, R. A. M., of Pilgrim Commandery, No. 16, K. T., of Mecca Temple, A. A. O. Nobles of the Mystic Shrine, of Jackson Lodge, No. 150, I. O. O. F., of Golden Rule Encampment, No. 44, I. O. O. F., of Hamilton Conclave, No. 383, I. O. H., of Mohawk Tribe, No. 207, I. O. R. M., of Garfield Council, No. 56, Jr. O. U. A. M., of Trinity Chapter, No. 18, Order of the Eastern Star, of Court Unity, No. 75, F. of A., of Camp S. L. Reeves, No. 1, A. P. L., of the Masonic Life Association, of Palisade Lodge, No. 128, K. P., of North Hudson Tent, No. 10, Knights of the Maccabees, of West Shore Council, No. 1,097, Royal Arcanum, of Columbia Hose Company, No. 2, of the Union Hill Schuetzen Corps, of Company C, Twenty-second Regiment, N. G. N. Y., of the Zwiebelberger Bowling Club, of the Thirteen Club, and of the Mecca Wheelmen.

GUSTAVE D. MEISTER, of Bayonne, is the son of George Meister and Mary Slegmann, and was born in Germany on the 9th of August, 1856. His parents were also natives of that country. In 1864 they left the Fatherland and came with their family to the United States, settling in Newark, N. J., where the subject of this sketch received a public school education. Mr. Meister has been for some time engaged in the liquor business and is the proprietor of the well known Meister Casino at Bayonne. He is a member of the Robert Davis Association, of the Arion Singing Society of Newark, of Newark Lodge, No. 21, B. P. O. Elks, and of the Newark Turners. In politics he is a Democrat. He is a public spirited citizen, deeply interested in local affairs, and one of the best known men in his locality.

He was married, April 4, 1882, to Mary Kirnhofer, daughter of John and Annie Kirnhofer, of Michigan. They have four children: Bertha, Laura, Clark, and Annie.

CHRISTOPHER D. ROEHR, of Weehawken, is the son of Frederick E. Roehr and Emma Müller, and was born in Bremerhaven, Germany, November 8, 1862. His parents, grandparents, and their ancestors for many generations were sturdy, respected people of the Fatherland.

Mr. Roehr attended the German public or national schools until he reached the age of mature boyhood, when he went to sea, thus gratifying a strong desire for adventure and travel. He also took a course in a noted school of navigation. In 1878 he came with his parents to America, settled on Staten Island, New York, and for several years followed the sea, sailing between New York and Australia, the East Indies, China, Japan, and South American ports. The experience he gained in the merchant marine service,

GENEALOGICAL 611

and the opportunities for study and observation which these travels afforded, enabled him to grasp a broad and comprehensive knowledge of the world.

In 1886 Mr. Roehr retired from the sea, settled in Weehawken, N. J., and engaged in the liquor business, which he has since followed. For several years he has been a member of the Board of School Trustees of Weehawken. He is a member of the Masonic and Odd Fellows fraternities, of the Royal Society of Good Fellows, and of the German Lutheran Church, and is President of the North Hudson Cyclers. In politics he is a Democrat. He is actively interested in the public welfare and is a public spirited, patriotic, and enterprising citizen.

Mr. Roehr married Miss Emilie Reyer and has one son, William T., born in 1887.

BERNHARD ROGGE, of Weehawken, was born in North Germany, of an old and respected family, on the 4th of October, 1874, his parents being Diedrich Rogge and Emilie Baedecker. His father and mother were natives of the Fatherland, and possessed of sturdy characteristics.

While the subject of this article was yet a boy the family emigrated to America and settled in the Town of Union, N. J., where he received a public school education. Since leaving school Mr. Rogge has been engaged in the liquor business in Weehawken, Hudson County. His public spirit, patriotism, and interest in the welfare of the town and county have gained for him the confidence of all who know him.

Mr. Rogge is a consistent Democrat, and a member of the German Lutheran Church, of the Free and Accepted Masons, and of other social and fraternal organizations. He married Miss Molly Restmeyer and has three children: Molly, Bernhard, Jr., and Henry.

CHARLES J. BOTT, of the Town of Union, is the son of George and Anna (Hoffman) Bott, and was born in Würtemberg, Germany, June 26, 1859. He received his education in the public schools of the Fatherland, and there learned the trade of jeweler. In 1879 he came to this country and settled in New York City, where he first engaged in the liquor trade and subsequently in the jewelry business, gaining in each marked success and a high reputation.

In 1884 Mr. Bott moved to the Town of Union, N. J., and two years later opened his present hotel on the corner of Bergenline Avenue and Fourth Street. He has made this one of the popular centers of hospitality in North Hudson. Mr. Bott is a prominent member of Jefferson Lodge, No. 125, I. O. O. F., of the Royal Society of Good Fellows, of the Knights of Honor, of the Knights and Ladies of Honor, of the Independent Schuetzen Corps of Union Hill, of the Maennerchor of Guttenberg, and of several other organizations. He is a public spirited, progressive citizen, and popular among a wide circle of acquaintances.

Mr. Bott was married, in 1881, to Miss Mary Suttler, of the Town of Union, N. J. They have three children: Frank, William, and Mary.

GEORGE MICHEL has been a resident of the Town of Union, Hudson County, N. J., for over thirty-five years, coming there from Germany, where he was born. He was long engaged in the liquor business with marked success. He is one of the oldest and best known German citizens of East

Jersey, and in retirement is enjoying the fruits of an active and honorable career.

He married Miss Barbara Elizabeth Fielder, also a native of Germany, and has six children living, viz.: Annie (Mrs. George Arnold), Katherine (Mrs. Frederick Sapp), Dorothy (Mrs. Frederick Feisel), John Robert, George, Jr., and Frederick.

JOHN ROBERT MICHEL, eldest son of George and Barbara Elizabeth (Fielder) Michel, was born February 8, 1873, in the Town of Union, N. J., where he has always resided. He received his education in the public schools of that town and at Hasbrouck Institute in Jersey City, and then entered the drug store of William Falkner, Fifty-second Street and Eighth Avenue, New York, where he remained about three years. His experience in this capacity has served him well in subsequent business affairs. Having graduated from Hasbrouck Institute in June, 1894, he began active life with a good classical training, and as a drug clerk supplemented his studies by a practical knowledge of commercial matters. On resigning his position in the store he succeeded his father in the liquor business at 215 Palisade Avenue, corner of Humboldt Street, in the Town of Union, which he has since conducted.

During the past eight years Mr. Michel has taken an active part in local politics, being the organizer and standard bearer of the B. J. Michel Association of the Town of Union, and having served three years as a member of the Democratic Town General Committee. He is also a member of the Executive Committee of the New Democratic Club of Union Hill and of the Second Ward Democratic Club, which he helped to organize in 1896, and of which he has been the only Treasurer. He is a member, also, of the Charles Bauer Association and of Wahwequa Tribe, No. 183, Independent Order of Redmen. Mr. Michel is perhaps better known by the name of "Bob" Michel, or as "B. J." Michel, the name borne by the association of which he is a founder and the Treasurer.

He was married, June 9, 1896, to Lillie, daughter of Henry and Meta

JOHN R. MICHEL.

In sketch of John J. Daley, page 613, the ninth line should read "was for four years a Commissioner of Appeals," etc., instead of "several years a School Trustee," as printed. Mr. Daley has been for four years and is now a Councilman for Guttenberg. He has seven (instead of six) children—five daughters and two sons—all born in Guttenberg.

Fisher, of Jersey City Heights, N. J. They have one child, Lillie Barbara Michel.

JOHN REILLY, of Weehawken, is the son of John Reilly, Sr., and Mary Lynch, both natives of Ireland. He was born in that country August 5, 1849, and there received his education. When a young man he came to the United States and for over twenty years has been successfully engaged in the hotel business in Weehawken. He was a member of Weehawken Town Council for five years, has served as Chief of the Weehawken Fire Department, and in other capacities has rendered valuable service to the community.

Mr. Reilly is a member of the Independent Order of Foresters, of the Weehawken Fire Department, of the Ancient Order of Hibernians of Hudson County, and of the C. V. and L. In politics he is a Democrat. He married Margaret Morran and has three children: John R., Mary R., and Katie.

JOHN J. DALEY, of Guttenberg, N. J., is a native and life-long resident of that town, having been born there July 9, 1860. His parents, Martin Daley and Catherine O'Brien, came to Guttenberg from Ireland.

Mr. Daley attended the public schools of Guttenberg, and afterward engaged in the block-stone business, which he followed for several years with marked success. After disposing of this business he established himself in the liquor trade, in Guttenberg, in which he still continues. As a Democrat Mr. Daley has long been prominent and influential in politics. He was for several years a School Trustee, and has been especially active in the formation and development of the Guttenberg Fire Department, being an organizer of Companies 1 and 4, and an exempt member of Hook and Ladder Company No. 1. He is a member of the Foresters of America and of the Catholic Church. He married Miss Catherine Buckley and has a family of six children.

GEORGE J. GOEHRIG, of North Bergen, was born in Ulster County, N. Y., October 29, 1865. He is the son of Charles Goehrig and Rosa Salzmann and a grandson of Leonard and Rose Salzmann, all natives of Germany.

Mr. Goehrig received his education in the public schools of his native county, and afterward learned the trade of butcher. Coming to North Bergen, N. J., he entered with energy into the affairs of the township, and soon established a reputation for industry, thrift, and integrity. For some time he has been engaged in butchering and also in the hotel and liquor business on the Hudson County Boulevard. He has served as Chief of the North Bergen Fire Department, as a member of the North Bergen Board of Education, and as President of the North Hudson Liquor Dealers' Association. He is a member of the Merry Owl Association and a public spirited, enterprising citizen. Mr. Goehrig was married March 20, 1887, to Bartona Wade.

ERNST BEHR, a well known citizen of the Town of Union, Hudson County, was born in Northern Germany on the 29th of May, 1864. His parents, William and Hermina (Rehmer) Behr, were respected and esteemed for those sturdy qualities which distinguish the German race.

Mr. Behr was educated in the public or national schools of the Fatherland. He also served a short time in the German Army. In 1882 he came to the United States and settled in Brooklyn, N. Y., where he was engaged in the grocery business for two years. In 1884 he removed to New York City and established himself in the liquor business, which he successfully conducted until 1891, when he came to the Town of Union, Hudson County, N. J. Here he has since resided, being engaged in the liquor trade on the corner of Bergenline Avenue and Lewis Street.

Mr. Behr is an active member of the Democratic party, a patriotic citizen, and a liberal supporter of every worthy movement. He married Barbara Kobbeck.

SAMUEL DECKER, of East Newark, was born in Passaic County, N. J., on Christmas Day, December 25, 1850. He is the son of William Decker and Julia Ann Rhinesmith and a grandson of Gabriel Decker and Barney and Rebecca (Bugsby) Rhinesmith. His maternal grandfather was a member of one of the old families of Passaic County, where the Deckers also settled at an early date. Both were prominent in the community.

Mr. Decker was educated in his native county, principally at Macopin, and for fifteen years lived in Newark, Essex County. In 1884 he moved to East Newark, Hudson County, where he still resides. Early in life he learned the mason's trade, which he followed with marked success for eight years. At the end of that period (1882) he engaged in the chemical charcoal business, and in 1897 formed a stock company, of which he is now (1900) President. This company supplies charcoal for Newark and vicinity, and maintains the largest business in that line in Eastern New Jersey.

An ardent and consistent Republican, Mr. Decker has earnestly advocated Republican principles ever since he cast his first vote. He is a public spirited, progressive, and enterprising citizen, prominent in party and business affairs, active and influential in promoting every worthy object, and thoroughly identified with the growth and prosperity of the community. His success in business has been the result of his own energy and ability. He is a member of the Knights and Ladies of the Golden Star, of the Order of Heptasophs, and of other organizations.

SAMUEL DECKER.

Mr. Decker married Amanda E. Meeker, of Hackettstown, N. J., and has one son, Herbert T.

JOHN O'LEARY, of Guttenberg, is the son of Dennis O'Leary and Mary Hefferen, and was born in Philadelphia, Pa., on the 30th of October, 1866. He is of Irish descent. He was educated in the public schools of Philadelphia, and for some time was extensively engaged in business there as a stevedore and truckman. Finally he removed to North Bergen, Hudson County, where he has since been engaged in the hotel business. He married Matilda Fay.

MARK LYDON, the well known Democratic leader and hotel proprietor of Shadyside in North Bergen, Hudson County, was born in Ireland on April 1, 1866, the son of Martin Lydon and Ann Bracken. Having received his education in the public schools of his native country, he came to America, and on the 15th of March, 1889, landed in New York, where he followed his trade of stonecutting for a short time. He soon removed to Shadyside in North Bergen, N. J., where he found employment at papermaking, and where he has since resided. May 1, 1894, he engaged in the hotel and liquor business, which he still follows.

Applying himself to business affairs and to the advancement of the Democratic party, Mr. Lydon soon came into prominence as a leader and for several years has been a power in his party in that locality. His influence upon both local and county matters has given him a wide reputation. He is a man of public spirit and enterprise, and has always taken a prominent part in local projects. He is a member of Eclipse Fire Company No. 1, of North Bergen, of the Democratic Club, and of the Gustav Scholp and Robert Davis Associations.

Mr. Lydon was married, June 21, 1893, to Annie F., daughter of John Flannery, of Shadyside, North Bergen, and they have two children: John and Florence.

JOHN J. REILLY, of Bayonne, was born at Ulster Heights, Ulster County, N. Y., November 27, 1864. His parents, Michael Reilly and Mary Donovan, were natives of Ireland. They came to the United States when young and were married in Brooklyn, N. Y., whence they removed to Ulster County. In 1872 they came to Bayonne, N. J., where the subject of this sketch received a public school education.

After leaving school John J. Reilly engaged in the liquor business in Bayonne, in which he has since continued. He is a prominent and influential Democrat and for several years has been a leader in party affairs. He is a member of the Independent Order of Foresters, of Hook and Ladder Company No. 3, of Bayonne, and of St. Paul's Alliance Society.

Mr. Reilly was married, June 25, 1891, to Fannie Brothers, of Bayonne, Hudson County. They have four children: Mamie, Fannie, Agnes, and Michael Francis.

EDWARD HOOS, of Jersey City, was born in Germany, at Neuwied on the Rhine, August 31, 1850. He was educated at the public schools, and began his business career as a clerk in a general store. At the same time he acquired a thorough knowledge of upholstery. He came to America in 1870, and soon found employment with an upholstery firm in New York City. He started in business for himself in 1872, manufacturing parlor suits and lounges at 133 Pavonia Avenue, Jersey City. Subsequently he was associated with Mullins & Schulz, and afterward formed the firm of Lampe & Hoos, which was dissolved in a year. He then took the management of John Mullins's business, and was with him until 1877. He then once more launched out alone at 67 Newark Avenue, but shortly joined John Sheehan, and for nine months the firm was Hoos & Sheehan. Mr. Hoos bought out his partner and removed to the old Metropolitan Hall Building, at 71 and 73 Newark Avenue, where the firm of Hoos & Schulz was formed, and was continued successfully until July 1, 1897, when Mr. Hoos was elected Mayor, and retired from business.

He entered politics in 1885. He was a member of the Board of Freeholders for two years. In 1889 he was elected an Alderman, and in 1891 was appointed by Mayor Cleveland a Commissioner of Appeals, resigning when Mayor Wanser was elected. Subsequently he was appointed to the Board of Education by Mayor Wanser, and re-appointed for two years. In 1895 he was nominated for President of the Board of Aldermen, but was defeated by Reuben Simpson, and in the same year was elected to the Assembly and served creditably. In 1897 he was elected Mayor of Jersey City.

Mr. Hoos is a Thirty-second degree Mason, a Past Deputy Grand Master, and Representative of the Grand Lodge of the State of Arkansas. He belongs to the Knights of Honor, the Legion of Honor, the Knights of Pythias, and the Board of Trade.

WILLIAM CRANSTOUN, of Hoboken and Summit, is the son of William and Marion (Paterson) Cranstoun, natives of Scotland, who settled in Canada in 1832, moved to New York City, and thence removed to Princeton, N. J., in 1837. They removed to Bordentown, N. J., in 1842, and in February, 1843, came to Hoboken, where the mother died April 28, 1882, and the father December 6, 1885.

Mr. Cranstoun was born in Hoboken, September 1, 1843, and finished his education at the parochial school of the Scotch Presbyterian Church in Fourteenth Street, New York. He read law with J. Harvey Lyons (his brother-in-law) and Hon. Abel I. Smith, both of Hoboken, and was admitted to the bar of New Jersey in February, 1875. Since then he has resided in Summit, N. J., and has successfully practiced his profession in that place and in Hoboken. His business has been confined principally to office work and in chancery, and largely involves real estate.

CHARLES PINNELL, one of the oldest residents of North Bergen, Hudson County, has held the office of Chairman of the Township Committee longer than any other man in New Jersey, having served in that capacity for twenty-three years, or almost continually from 1871 to the spring of 1897, when he resigned. Born in Wottenunderedge, Gloucestershire, England, on the 17th of February, 1823, he is the son of Robert Pinnell and Elizabeth Fowler and a descendant on both sides of honored English ancestors. As a boy he displayed sterling intellectual and physical qualities.

He obtained his education in Minchinhampton, England. In 1848 he came to America and settled in New York City, but in the spring of 1849 removed to Jersey City, N. J., and thence in 1857 to Hudson City, now a part of Jersey City. There he resided eight years. In 1865 he moved to New Durham in North Bergen, Hudson County, where he still lives. His business was that of a manufacturer of walking canes and crutches, and until 1867, when he retired, he had, in Cortlandt Street, New York, one of the largest and most successful establishments of the kind in the United States. Since 1867 he has devoted himself almost exclusively to private affairs and to the official duties which have been pressed upon him by his townsmen, his only other business of importance being a coal yard at Homestead in North Bergen, which he conducted about three years.

He was a School Trustee of South New Durham for about fifteen years and served most of that period as District Clerk, and was instrumental in causing the erection of the first brick school house in the township. This was old No. 3 school, built in 1871, and since remodeled and enlarged. He was also Collector of Arrears for a time and Township Collector one year.

Mr. Pinnell's ability, executive capacity, and active interest in local affairs caused him in the spring of 1871 to be elected Chairman of the Township Committee of North Bergen, and from that time until the spring of 1897, when he resigned, he was the acknowledged leader in all public matters, being continuously a member and Chairman of that committee with the exception of the years 1872, 1873, 1882, and 1883. This service of twenty-three years as Chairman of the governing body of the township is the longest accredited to any one man in the State. It is noteworty for the great amount of clerical labor and unceasing attention to duty which Mr. Pinnell freely and effectively rendered. He was indefatigable in the preparation of statistical tables, in efforts to reduce taxation and expenses, and in every reform calculated to benefit the township and its inhabitants, and his reports and public papers, many of which are still in existence and valuable, are models. One of these documents—the rarest and most important from his hands—is as applicable to-day as it was in 1879, when it was addressed to the property holders and taxpayers of Hudson County. It was adopted at a joint meeting of the Boards of Council of the Towns of Union and Guttenberg and the Township Committees of North Bergen, West Hoboken, Weehawken, and Union, on March 25, 1879. This paper and others issued in 1889, 1891, and 1894 stamp Mr. Pinnell as one of the ablest local reformers of his time. He brought to the conduct of township affairs a broad, progressive public spirit, an accurate knowledge of public business, great sagacity and foresight, and rare comprehension of economical problems. While he encouraged important public improvements and supported every project designed to advance the general welfare, he was unceasing in his efforts to keep taxes and public expenditures within the limits of practical economy, leaving the people unburdened by the extravagance which often marks township governments.

Mr. Pinnell has also had charge of several important estates and business properties. He was the assignee in 1890 of John Gardner, a wealthy lumber dealer of Jersey City Heights and Hoboken, and in similar capacities has exhibited marked ability and unquestioned integrity. He was especially active and useful in the matter of the State of New Jersey v. The Weehawken Cemetery, in 1885, carrying it through to success.

September 14, 1847, Mr. Pinnell married Ann Parker, daughter of William and Ann Parker, of Pontypool, Monmouthshire, England. They have three children: Sarah Ann, Charles H., and Elizabeth Martha. Charles H. Pinnell is superintendent of the American Gold Watch Case Company, Astor Place, New York City.

INDEX

	PAGE.
Bergen County settlers	22–41
Bergen, Town of	19
Borough governments	10
Boroughs in Bergen County	11
Dutch West India Company	15
Early records	4
Early settlers in Hudson County	12
Erection of townships	9
First settlers	1, 16, 18, 19, 20, 41–48
Formation of Hudson and Bergen Counties	4
Hoboken Hacking	16
Hudson County settlers	12–22
Landowners and settlers	41
Massacre of Pavonia	17
Pauleson, Michael	16
Pauw, Michael	16
Pavonia	16
Township governments	7

	PAGE.		PAGE.
Ackerman, Aaron E	55	Bantz, John	477
Ackerman, John N	53	Bardsley, William	453
Allan, James	371	Barkerding, Adolph H	459
Allen Family	107	Barricklo, William Reed	532
Allen, James Kitchell	374	Basse, Claus	586
Allen, Uriah	363	Bate, John J	401
Allen, Robert	532	Behr, Ernst	613
Allison, William Outis	148	Benny, Allan	381
Anders, Arthur	477	Bentley, Peter, Sr	121
Anderson, John H	551	Bentley, Peter, 2d	123
Andes, Henry	357	Bentley, Peter, 3d	126
Anson, Edward M	485	Berdan, Cornelius W	195
Applegate, Ivins D	287	Berger, Edward William	349
Armbruster, William O	465	Berger, George A	508
Armstrong, Samuel	422	Berger, Julius	264
Asmus, Ernst G	333	Bergkamp, George Bernhardt	398
Auryansen, Abram I	119	Bergmann, Frederick J., Jr	439
		Berry Family	100
Babbitt, Robert Oscar	198	Bertholf Family	107
Baldwin, Aaron Stockholm	180	Besson, John Case	226
Banta, William Sickles	513	Besson, Samuel Austin	225
Banta, William Williams	235	Best, John	463

INDEX

	PAGE.
Bewig, August	588
Bickhard, Conrad	432
Birdsall, Walter Kissam	268
Black, Charles Clarke	300
Black, James Edward	476
Black, James H	217
Blackledge Family	126
Blair, John Albert	84
Blair, William	455
Blanch Family	127
Blawvelt, David D	68
Blawvelt, George W	258
Blawvelt, John D	458
Blohm, Charles H	501
Bobbink, Lambertus C	475
Bode, Martin W	384
Bogert, Albert Z	132
Bogert, Daniel G., Jr	285
Bogert, Isaac D	310
Bogert, John	60, 479
Bogert, John J	133
Bogert, Matthew J	57
Bogert, Sandford	480
Bogert, Seba M	502
Bonn, Hillric John	270
Bonn, John Hillric	269
Bonn, John Hillric, Jr.	271
Born, Albert	488
Bott, Charles J	611
Bouton, John C	500
Bowe, James J	356
Bowe, John E	468
Bowen, James R	583
Bradley, Louis Henry	512
Bradley, William Henry	512
Branagan, John B	382
Brandt, Peter	431
Brierley, James	393
Brinkerhoff, Andrew H	274
Brinkerhoff, Cornelius	105
Brinkerhoff, Henry H., Jr., M.D.	101
Brock, Peter Anthony	470
Brockway, Philip Eastman	595
Brower Family	130
Brown, Joel W	454
Browning, J. Hull	113
Bruce, George	334
Bryan, Daniel Drake	261

	PAGE.
Buckley, Charles Pitman	114
Bulger, Thomas F	346
Burroughs, Charles W	452
Byram, Thomas J	487
Cadmus, George	260
Cadmus, John J	552
Callahan, John T	461
Camp, George Kingsland	522
Campbell, Luther A	203
Campbell, O. G	487
Canfield, Burton Edmund	483
Canfield, George Daniel	482
Cannon, Charles Kinsey	321
Cannon, Michael J	406
Carbin, Edward F	475
Carbrey, Thomas A	441
Carlson, John	512
Carragan, George	410
Carroll, Thomas	441
Case, Edwin Raynor	251
Case, Menzies R	251
Cass, Alexander	187
Cass, Willard	188
Cassidy, William A	421
Chapman, Robert	197
Chappell, George H	501
Child, Joseph	120
Christie, Cornelius	106
Christie, Cornelius	295
Christie, Walter	111
Churchill, Romeo Thompson, D.V.S.	427
Clark, James	381
Clark, William Mortimer	515
Close, James	429
Clouse, Halloway Whitfield	348
Cole Family	157
Colligan, Patrick M	587
Collignon, George W	476
Collignon, Peter C	482
Collins, Gilbert	70
Collins, Henry F	353
Condict, Henry V	522
Conklin Family	157
Conklin, Peter L	605
Conkling, Cook	153
Conkling, Livingston	271
Conley, John	417
Conover, Harry Martin	222

INDEX

Name	PAGE
Conrad, Edgar K., M.D.	511
Converse, Charles Crozat, LL.B., LL.D.	459
Conway, John	377
Cooper Family	160
Copin, August A.	524
Copin, George Felix	457
Courtman, Walter F.	353
Cowles, Elijah Strong	320
Cranstoun, William	616
Cranwell, George W.	395
Crear, Charles Lyman	501
Crowell, Joseph Franklin	360
Cumming, Thomas H.	216
Cunliffe, George	449
Currie, Mungo J.	534
Daley, John J.	613
Daly, William D.	467
Danielson, William H.	282
Darling, Henry Isaac	241
Darling, John Sidney	308
Darling, Ord	311
Davis, David	340
Davis, Andrew J.	229
Day, Addison L.	584
De Baun, Abram	138
De Bow Family	160
De Clark Family	130
De Clyne, Charles	254
De Clyne, Emil	254
De Clyne, Gustave	254
De Groot Family	162
De Motte, Dwight Wheeler	558
De Ronde, Frank S.	551
De Voe, John	519
Decker, Samuel	614
Demarest, Abraham	511
Demarest, Abraham Garrison	110
Demarest, Calvin	267
Demarest, Daniel I.	495
Demarest, David	67
Demarest, David A.	93
Demarest, Elmer Wilson	64
Demarest, Garret I.	66
Demarest, Jacob J.	497
Demarest, John H. Z.	496
Demarest, Milton	289
Demarest, Milton G.	497
Demarest, Samuel D.	450

Name	PAGE
Dennis, Frank H.	350
Denzer, George Valentine	373
Denzer, Valentine	372
Diehm, Louis, Jr.	339
Dippel, John, Jr	388
Dixon, Robert Campbell, Jr.	136
Dobbs, Thomas Jefferson	340
Dockray, William John	485
Donnelly, James J.	516
Dooley, Patrick J.	565
Doremus, Cornelius	295
Drayton, Albert Irving	87
Dressel, Frederick H.	462
Du Bois, John H.	301
Duffy, Joseph Alexander, M.A.	534
Duffy, Thomas A.	421
Dupuy, John J.	490
Durie, Garret D.	509
Duryee, Abraham Wilson, A.M.	507
Dwyre, John	384
Earle, Edward	232
Earle, Frank Hasbrouck	549
Earle, Ralph D., Jr.	605
Earle, Samuel E.	233
Eckerson, Cornelius A.	545
Eckerson, Jacob B.	549
Eckert, George M.	575
Eckhardt, William	516
Edge, Isaac, Jr.	152
Edge, Nelson James Harrison	151
Edsall Family	163
Edwards, William D.	194
Egbert, James Chidester, D.D.	90
Elliott, Robert Wallace	557
Ely, Addison	365
Endres, William C.	536
Engel, John	150
Engelbrecht, Henry	590
Ensor, Fred J.	518
Enstice, John	277
Erwin, James Shrewsbury	108
Everson, Edward	129
Eypper, Charles	553
Eypper, William J	554
Fallon, John Joseph	363
Farr, Frederick William	330
Farr, William Charles	576

INDEX

	PAGE
Ferdon, Jesse W	184
Ferdon, Warren	473
Ferdon, William Scott	263
Fink, James D	448
Fisher, Alexander	151
Fisher, John G	228
Fisher, Michael	319
Fitzgerald, Bartholomew	447
Fitzpatrick, John M	355
Flierboom Family	164
Foerch, Emil Joseph	401
Ford, Francis W	557
Formon, Louis	218
Francois, Judson Camille	414
Frank, August	333
Frankenstein, George	561
Freiberger, Jacob	402
Freir, Samuel P	558
Frost, John	393
Gaede, Henry A	608
Gaddis, Percy Almy	516
Galbraith, Richard Edwin	158
Galbraith, William	158
Gale, George Bancroft, M.D	561
Gallagher, Edward	586
Gardenier, John Calvin	483
Garrabrant Family	164
Garretsen Family	246
Garretson Abram Quick	88
Gautier Family	166
Gavegan, James F	410
Gaw, Robert	609
Gilligan, John M	421
Gilson, Herbert Clark	541
Girsham, Andrew	448
Goehrig, George J	613
Goetschius Family	166
Goldberg, Eugene Holden, M.D	595
Goodman, Peter J	392
Green, Robert Stockton	569
Green, Walter J	561
Green, William	351
Greenin, Edmond L	554
Greenleaf, Abram D	451
Griffin, J. William	336
Gunset, Jacob	348
Haase, Franklin D	586
Hackett, William, Jr	552

	PAGE
Hagan, William	390
Hagemann, Henry	591
Hageman, John	592
Hamilton, Charles A	147
Hanlon, Joseph J	550
Hardenbergh, Augustus A	603
Haring, Albert Zabriskie	63
Haring, Andrew H	202
Haring, Rev. Garret A	61
Haring, Garret T	201
Haring, Henry G	201
Haring, John T	154
Haring, Richard B	161
Hart, Ruben M	605
Harvey, Cornelius Burnham	73
Hasel, Rev. Joseph John	227
Hauck, Peter	525
Hauenstein, Louis C., Jr	530
Hausser, Louis	555
Heath, Wilson L	608
Hecht, Max, M.D., Ph.G	219
Heck, John	538
Heck, John W	112
Heflich, John	589
Heins, Charles A	435
Hemberger, Leonard	592
Hendrick, Charles C., M.D	375
Hennessy, D. M	554
Henry, Thomas	436
Herring, William C	562
Herron, Joseph	558
Hess, Samuel	330
Hickey, James S	389
Hiler, Edward	553
Hoffman, Charles	519
Holdrum, Abram C	237
Holdrum, James Demarest	559
Holdrum, John H	483
Holdrum, Peter M	485
Hoos, Edward	615
Hopper, Isaac A	275
Hopper, Jacob H	71
Horstman, Frederick W	243
Howe, William T	355
Huber, William H	352
Hulshizer, James Edwin, Jr	434
Hungerford, William Sumner	567
Huyler, Albert V	86

INDEX

	PAGE.
Jackson, Francis Douglas	305
Johnson, Darius S	261
Johnson, Edmund E	286
Johnson, William Mindred	166
Jones, J. Wyman	456
Justin, Rev. John	199
Justin, John Clement, M.D	200
Karl, Henry	519
Katzenberger, Joseph	587
Kehoe, John	498
Keller, John, M.A	570
Kelley, John M	533
Kelly, James A	427
Kelly, Simon	353
Kennedy, John J	176
Kennel, Joseph	588
Kiesewetter, Louis	433
Kimmerly, Frank Henry	526
Kingsland, Edmund W	67
Kipp, James	96
Kipp, William De Graw	98
Klass, John F	542
Koch, Frank	527
Koester, Ernest	187
Knox, Eugene De Witt	449
Krebs, Clemens A	397
Kudlich, William Tell, M.D	535
Kühl, Henry, Sr	404
Kühl, Henry, Jr	405
Kuhn, John	536
Kunz, Jacob	535
La Fetra Daniel W	508
La Roche, William Tell, D.D.S	560
Lachmann, Charles	589
Lachmund, John H., Jr	543
Laffey, Walter E	522
Lane, John	144
Laroe Family	169
Lawless, Martin	306
Lawrence, David W	205
Lawrence, Robert Linn	119
Lawrence, William Sumner	475
Leake, Eugene Walter	544
Lee, John F	453
Leicht, William Keudel	343
Lemmermann, Henry	491
Leonard, Clement De R	316

	PAGE.
Letts, Alonzo Worden	326
Leuly, Albert	531
Lillis, James T	279
Limouze, George	470
Lindemann, John H	273
Lippincott, Job Hilliard	578
Lockwood, David L	536
Long, Charles Frederick	473
Lord, Robert F	215
Loveridge, Edgar H	503
Lowry, Stewart	310
Lozier, John B	505
Lozier, Lemuel	604
Luhmann, Conrad	585
Luhmann, Ernest	584
Luxton, Charles	323
Luxton, George John	324
Lydecker, Cornelius	145
Lydon, Mark	615
Mabie Family	171
MacCollum, Cornelius	590
Macdonald, John Henry	303
Magee, Eugene Van Artsdalen	234
Maguire, Peter F	544
Manners, Edwin, A.M	117
Marion, John Francis	220
Marion, William Clayborn	230
Marks, Maurice	539
Marshall, Robert J	576
Marshall, Samuel J., Jr	576
Marshall, William C	576
Matthews, John	528
Maulbeek, Sebastian	407
McAuley, John	446
McCarty, William E	419
McCroskery, Michael C	579
McCrea, David W	204
McCurnin, Joseph Aloysius	439
McDermott, Edward	245
McDermott, Frank P	301
McDonough, Francis M	490
McFadden, George Howard, M.D	539
McGee, Charles	383
McGee, Flavel	299
McGill, Alexander Taggart, A.M., LL.D.	55
McKenzie, William	529
McMahon, Aloysius	599
McMahon, John P	483

INDEX

	PAGE
McMahon, Thomas J	391
McNally, James F	586
McNamara, Thomas Charles, M.D	411
McQuillan, Charles	466
Meeks, Hamilton Victor	297
Meierdierck, John H	593
Meisch, Sebastian	543
Meister, Gustave D	610
Melville, Frank H	183
Menegaux, Louis Albert	317
Mercer, James Wright	190
Merseles Family	172
Meyer Family	168
Michel, George	611
Michel, John Robert	612
Miller, James W	472
Mittag, Frank O	531
Mittag, James S	531
Mondorf, Camillus	477
Moore, John W	550
Moore, Peter E	118
Morrison, Richard	600
Moylan, John	587
Moylan, Michael Francis	408
Mullaney, G. W	540
Müller, John M	408
Mulligan, James F	583
Mulvaney, John Joseph	404
Murray, Daniel J	597
Naugle, David	398
Necker, William	488
Neely, Samuel A. J	572
Neer, Henry Crippen, M.D	596
Neuscheler, Louis C	441
Nevin, John, M.D	443
Nevin, John Joseph	161
Newbery, Isaac L	189
Newkirk, James S	131
Nienaber, George	589
Noe, William	608
Northrop, James Prentice	304
Nungesser, Henry	593
O'Brien, Thomas	406
O'Brine, James	372
O'Callaghan, Edward A	443
O'Donnell, John	424
Oetjen, John	438

	PAGE
O'Leary, John	615
Olendorf, John	386
O'Neil, James H	597
O'Neill, Dennis	597
O'Neill, William Montague	467
Otis, John E	314
Outwater Family	169
Parmly, Duncan Dunbar	82
Parmly, Randolph	82
Parmly, Wheelock Hendee, D.D	79
Parry, Joseph Saunders	370
Parsell, Lewis B., M.D	556
Peack Family	174
Pearsall, James W	288
Pierce, Harvey C	396
Pilson, Joseph H	455
Pinnell, Charles	616
Poor, Frank B	217
Porter, Millard Fillmore	543
Post, John H	72
Post, Thomas J	276
Potts, J. Herbert	220
Powless Family	175
Prendergast, James F	384
Puster, Henry	170
Quackenbush Family	178
Ramsey, John Rathbone	146
Randall, Charles Wesley	146
Reed, Samuel Burrage	291
Rees, William R	517
Reid, Gabriel B	342
Reilly, John	613
Reilly, John J	615
Reinhardt, John	389
Rich, Augustus A	214
Richardson, Milton T	155
Riesenberger, George	563
Ringger, Jacob	402
Rippe, Frederick	592
Ritchie, Michael Ney	524
Rix, Frank Stewart	579
Roberson, Horace	520
Roche, John W	248
Roehr, Christopher D	610
Rogge, Bernhard	611
Romaine, Isaac	78

INDEX

	PAGE.		PAGE.
Romeyn, James A	139	Snow, William D	500
Rothe, Henry Emory, M.D	565	Snyder, George M	328
Rottman, Christian C	591	Soley, Charles R	491
Ruempler, Carl Henry	335	Sölfleisch, Henry W	432
Russell, Samuel Phillips, D.D.S	609	Speer Family	209
Rutan, Daniel	175	Speer, William Henry	542
Rutman, George H	375	Spindler, John	580
Ryan, William C	585	Springer, Moses E	164
Ryerson Family	179	St. John, David, M.D	346
		Stack, Joseph Francis Xavier, M.D	223
Sahner, Emil	528	Stack, Maurice J	250
Salter, William D	503	Stagg, Peter W	258
Sandford, Oscar	430	Stanton, Walter	598
Sargent, Edward	385	Staples, Markham E	128
Schaefer, George Washington	601	Stephens, James H	266
Schindler, Charles A., Sr	192	Stevens, Edwin Augustus	494
Schindler, Charles A., Jr	193	Stevens, Frank	572
Schleicher, Adolph	422	Stevens, George	211
Schmidt, William H	435	Stevens, James Alexander	494
Scholp, Gustav W	369	Stevens, John	492
Schultze, Charles	447	Stevens, John Cox	493
Schuyler Family	176	Stevens, Robert Livingston	494
Schwartz, Frederick A	469	Stever, Arthur J	573
Seaman, George H	584	Stewart, William Lewis	303
Seeley, John	328	Stillwell, Peter	598
Seery, Peter H	417	Stilson, Henry J	389
Seguine, Ezra K	360	Stockfish, Henry, Jr	445
Seitz, Arthur	283	Stockton, John Potter	571
Seitz, August	282	Storm, George Wilkinson	212
Seüfert, William Marshall	609	Storms, Henry	545
Seymour, Egbert	129	Striffler, Edward C	228
Shafer, John	513	Stuart, Benjamin Cumberland	520
Sharkey, Hugh	599	Stuhr, William Sebastian	280
Shuart, James	306	Stuke, Frank J	387
Sickles Family	179	Stumpp, Charles Otto	385
Silliman, Chauncey H	223	Succow, August John Frederick	580
Singer, Charles, Jr	358	Sullivan, Patrick	499
Sip, Jan Adrainse	180	Swenson, Elof	582
Slote Family	182	Swiss, George	540
Smedberg, Alfred	608	Symes, James Henry	336
Smith, Abel I	206	Syms, John George	331
Smith, Baker B	194		
Smith, Charles	463	Tallman, Abram	506
Smith, Edward	317	Tallman, William	507
Smith Family	182	Talmage, David Mather	581
Smith, James	234	Terhune Family	210
Smith, William	403	Thompson, Charles Dederer	577
Smith, William B	542	Thompson, William	255
Sneden Family	183	Thomson, Charles A	570

INDEX

	PAGE.		PAGE.
Thourot, Alphonse	366	Voorhis, William Willcox	276
Tilley, Rev. William James	115	Vredenburgh, James B	103
Tilt, Sheldon	548	Vreeland, Jesse Kimball	262
Timken, Herman L	574		
Toers Family	212	Wakelee, Edmund W	186
Toffey, John James	313	Waldons, Hugo Frank	419
Tolen, William	428	Walker, Herman	249
Tooker, George E	573	Wallace, James G	345
Traphagen, Henry	606	Wallis, Hamilton	253
		Wallwork, James	414
Ullmyer, Philip J	394	Walscheid, J. Emil	599
Usher, Thomas B	327	Walsh, Walter A	445
		Ward, George	598
Van Blarcom, John H	607	Ward, Henry	571
Van Buskirk, Jacob L	190	Waters, Robert	377
Van Bussum Family	208	Weismann, Adolph	438
Vandelinda Family	172	Weismann, Adolph William	436
Vanderbeck Family	240	Weismann, Ferdinand	437
Vanderbilt, Henry Hope	308	Westervelt, Charles H	562
Vanderhoff Family	212	Westervelt, Edwin A., D.D.S	564
Van Deventer, David Provoost	564	Westervelt Family	99
Van Dien Family	239	Westervelt, John J	250
Van Dusen Family	213	Westervelt, Samuel	100
Van Dyck, Vedder	198	Westervelt, Warner W	109
Van Gelder Family	237	Wetyen, Charles W	585
Van Giesen Family	242	Wheeler, George Wakeman	208
Van Horn Family	236	Whelan, Joseph H	585
Van Horn, William	600	White, Addison D	311
Van Houten Family	237	White Family	247
Van Orden Family	244	White, Henry Simmons	113
Van Reipen, Garret D	594	White, John	438
Van Riper, Frederick P	521	White, Wallace, M.D	369
Van Saun Family	242	Whiteside, William J	373
Van Sickle, William M	229	Whittles, Jeremiah Clare	342
Van Valen, James M	537	Wiedermann, Walter W	481
Van Valen, Ralph	479	Wiley, George Lourie	173
Van Voorst Family	244	Wilhelm, James	580
Van Wagenen Family	246	Wilhelm, John P	359
Van Winkle Family	246	Wilhelm, William Henry	325
Varian, Ward	574	Williams, George Albert	580
Veale, Richard	362	Williams, John B	367
Verilhac, Oscar	420	Williams, Joseph L	352
Vogt, Theodore J	416	Winton, Henry D	88
Volger, Theodore G	567	Wollenhaupt, Theodore F	588
Volk, Anthony Jacob	265	Wood, Lorenzo, Jr	430
Von Drehle, Garret	579	Wortendyke, Raymond P	91
Voorhees, John J	83	Wortendyke, Robert H	472
Voorhis, Charles E	84	Wortendyke, Rynier J	102
Voorhis, William H	232		

INDEX

	PAGE.		PAGE.
Wouters, Herman Hubert	425	Young, Edwin Berkley	134
Wragg, Joseph Elliott	319		
Wray, William	566	Zabriskie, Abraham Oothout	49
Wray, William Norris	566	Zabriskie, David Demarest	137
Wright, William	543	Zeller, John	284
Wyckoff, Charles W	347	Zimmerman, George	581
Wyrill, George	443	Zisgen, John W	600